SHRI SAI SATCHARITA
The Life and Teachings of Shirdi Sai Baba

GOVIND R. DABHOLKAR (HEMAD PANT)

Translated from the original Marathi by

INDIRA KHER, M.A., Ph.D.

'*Shri Sai Satcharita*' is the Bible of Sai devotees in every sense of the word. It is a verse composition, originally in Marathi, styled on the renowned *Eknathi Bhagvat*. The book runs into 53 chapters and contains 9,308 verses. Every chapter has a judicious mixture of philosophy, stories and anecdotes and Sai Baba's teachings. The book is essentially a *Pothi* or *Gatha*.

Its idea was conceived during Baba's life-time and it was with the blessings and express permission of Sai Baba that the work was begun by the author who was a frequent visitor to Shirdi. The book was first published in 1929.

The book has been rendered into English, chapter by chapter, verse by verse and line by line and the rendering is by any reckoning a magnificent achievement.

Govind R. Dabholkar (Hemad Pant)
(1856 - 1929)

SHRI SAI SATCHARITA

The Life and Teachings
of
Shirdi Sai Baba

GOVIND R. DABHOLKAR (HEMAD PANT)

Translated from the original Marathi by

INDIRA KHER, M.A., Ph.D.

STERLING PUBLISHERS PRIVATE LIMITED
A-59, Okhla Industrial Area, Phase-II, New Delhi-110020.
Tel: 26387070, 26386209; Fax: 91-11-26383788
e-mail: mail@sterlingpublishers.com
www.sterlingpublishers.com

SHRI SAI SATCHARITA
The Life and Teachings of Shirdi Sai Baba
© Indira Kher
ISBN 978 81 207 2211 8 (HB)
ISBN 978 81 207 2153 1 (PB)
First Edition July 1999
Reprint 2005, 2006, 2007, 2008, 2009, 2010, 2011, 2012, 2013

PRINTED IN INDIA

Printed and Published by Sterling Publishers Pvt. Ltd., New Delhi-110020.

Foreword

When Vishwas B. Kher, my esteemed friend and co-author of the book, *Sai Baba of Shirdi: A Unique Saint,* approached the former Chief Justice and Vice-President of India, Shri Hidayatullah, for a foreword to it, he wrote:

> 'I am overwhelmed by the request... I hope the readers of this biography will read it with devotion and belief and the respect due to it. They will cover themselves with Divine Grace. I commend it to them and thank the authors for the privilege of giving me a chance to pay this homage...'

If a former Chief Justice and Vice-President of India could consider it a privilege to write a foreword to a book on Sai Baba of Shirdi, can one imagine what my feelings are as I pen these words? I feel like an ant before an elephant, entirely unworthy to write a foreword to so precious a work as a translation of *Shri Sai Satcharita* into English. I feel entirely inadequate if honoured and crave the reader's indulgence for my impertinence.

Those who have read *Sai Baba of Shirdi* would have noticed that towards the end of the book we had provided a bibliography of literature we had referred to in the preparation of our work but it did not then occur to us to comment either on the nature of our sources or their importance. As the bibliography which is fairly extensive would show, there are several books on Sai Baba, not only in English, but also in Hindi, Gujarati and Marathi. Actually, as source books the most valuable certainly are those works in Marathi like Govind Raghunath Dabholkar's *Shri Sai Satcharita* which was serialized in *Sri Sai Leela* which first came out in 1923, five years after the Baba passed away.

As is well known, and as the translator of this work into English, Smt Indira Kher, has pointedly drawn attention to the fact in her Note, '*Shri Sai Satcharita* is the Bible of Sai devotees in every sense of the word.' As Smt Kher has further put it : 'In its veracity, sanctity, faith and devotion that it inspires, and the deep satisfaction and a sense of fulfilment that it brings to the devotee, it has no equal'.

No, it hasn't. That is for sure. And why? To quote Smt Kher again: 'Its sanctity derives from the fact that its idea was conceived during Baba's lifetime and with his blessings and express permission'. Note the words. The *Satcharita* is not something written as an afterthought or long after the subject had passed away into history. It was begun during the lifetime of Baba with his 'Blessings' and 'express permission' and by one who was witness to Baba's '*leela*'. It is as if St John or St Luke or St Matthew had written about Jesus during the period of his mission, with his express knowledge and permission. Christ's mission hardly lasted a couple of years and at a time when it could not have been easy to put anything down on paper. Besides, he was constantly on the move and it would have been a heroic task for anyone to record every word that he said and every deed that he performed. But this was no problem for Shri Dabholkar in the nineteenth and first decade of the twentieth century. True, Shri Dabholkar began his writing only during 1922-23 and it was completed six years later but there were people still around who could challenge his facts or vouchsafe for their accuracy. The fact that the Baba's devotees cherish the work and use it with great faith and devotion, often reading a chapter or more as part of their daily worship, testifies to its absolute veracity and accuracy. There is no need for any further evidence. In any event it is impossible to conceive that Shri Dabholkar would concoct stories to embellish his work. For one thing it would have been a grievous hurt to the memory of Baba; for another Baba did not need any embellishment of his life and work. He was beyond praise and blame.

That is why *Shri Sai Satcharita* is of special relevance and that is why it is read with such reverence. It is well to remember that it was originally written in verse form. That would partly explain why it took Shri Dabholkar so long to complete it. A work of art is not completed in a hurry. And Shri Dabholkar was a conscientious poet; no wonder the Baba called him his 'Hemadpant', after the famous and learned court poet of the thirteenth century Yadavas.

The one drawback of *Shri Sai Satcharita* is that it was written in Marathi, that millions of Baba devotees are unable to read it. As Smt Kher has acknowledged 'it is little wonder that one hears many a sigh, a groan, a regret from those who cannot read' the book in the original. What is astonishing is that no serious attempt had ever been made at a detailed, chapter-wise English translation so far.

But now at last it has been done; and if a non-Maharashtrian with scant knowledge of Marathi may say so, it has been done superbly. The book has been translated chapter by chapter, verse by verse and line by line and it is by any reckoning a magnificent achievement. Smt Kher is eminently qualified to render the translation for three specific reasons:

* She is, and long has been, an ardent devotee of the Baba and would not, in any circumstances, be unfaithful to the original text.
* As a Maharashtrian born and bred, her knowledge of Marathi, her mother tongue, is impeccable.
* So, for that matter, is her knowledge of English. In fact, she took her Doctorate in English literature!

Knowing the Khers as I do, I may also reveal that whenever Smt Kher was stumped for the right word or the right nuance of a word, she had no hesitation in consulting an appropriate Marathi-English dictionary. This is not assumed humility but the practised approach of an English teacher steeled in the discipline of translation.

For those unaware of *Shri Sai Satcharita* it is necessary to add that in the original it runs into 53 chapters and contains more than 9,000 verses. Every chapter has a judicious mixture of philosophy, stories and anecdotes along with Baba's teachings. Baba was never didactic in the sense of wishing to give a sermon for the sake of a sermon. He met his disciples and admirers and conversed with them but in all his talk there was that subtle element, that unstressed message, that went straight to the heart, precisely because it was unstressed.

I have read this translation with utmost joy. It is written in plain English and what is more it gives us a flavour of the original Marathi. That is its special appeal. Smt Kher has resisted the temptation to provide only the gist of the original in an effort to 'cleanse' the Indianness of the original. Had she done so, she would have destroyed its essential beauty, its unique feature. Reading the translation one has the feel of the rhythm and beauty of the Marathi text — and that, thank heavens, is how it should be.

I commend this work of devotion to all *Sai bhaktas* in the sure knowledge that it meets a long-felt need. Like Shri Dabholkar himself, Smt. Kher has taken a long time to complete this work. It does her credit. And it does Baba's countless devotees a great favour. May the blessings of the *sadguru* be on all those who read it and savour its richness. As Shri Dabholkar wrote, quoting Baba:

'If my *leelas* are recorded, then any sins committed through ignorance will be dissipated. And when these are listened to, with faith and devotion, the cares and troubles of worldly life will be forgotten.

"Waves of love and devotion will surge on the ocean of the listening process, diving again and again into which will bring gems of wisdom in your hands."

Those 'gems of wisdom' are here gathered and are available for the mere asking. May the reader be richer for them. And may the grace of Sai Baba envelop them in his loving embrace.

M.V. Kamath

Preface

'*Shri Sai Satcharita*' is the Bible of Sai devotees in every sense of the word. In its veracity, sanctity, faith and devotion that it inspires and the deep satisfaction, a sense of fulfilment that it brings to the devotee, it has no equal.

It is a verse composition, styled on saint Eknath's renowned *Eknathi Bhagwat* and contains the known facts about Shri Sai Baba's life at Shirdi, as also his teachings. Its veracity lies in the fact that not only was its author a frequent visitor to Shirdi during Sai Baba's lifetime and a witness to many of the incidents that he refers to in the book, but most of the stories and anecdotes recorded therein, have been confirmed by one or the other of the devotees, who were his contemporaries.

Its sanctity derives from the fact that its idea was conceived during Baba's lifetime and it was with his blessings and express permission that the work of keeping a record of the many incidents, facts, etc., was begun. The actual writing started in 1922-23 and the book was completed and published in 1929.

The feeling of satisfaction, of fulfilment while reading the book, has its source in the love and faith that Sai Baba's unique, saintly personality inspires, as also in his fascinating *leelas* that captivate the devotee's heart. His simple, yet spiritually enriched, way of life with its supreme detachment and renunciation, and his method of imparting spiritual instruction and guidance to the devotees through instances and experiences of their daily lives have an unfailing appeal. The appeal endures and will continue to do so, for Baba's spirit was not confined to the three and a half cubits of his physical body, but pervades the entire creation, even to this day.

Sai Baba's was the *Guru-marg*, which believes in the Oneness between God and the guru, the guru and the devotee, between the Creator and His creation. Guru being the incarnation of God, without his grace and guidance, the highest goal of human existence, which is God realization or self-realisation, can never be achieved. But once the devotee succeeds in winning the guru's grace, the guru takes his responsibility, not only for this birth, but for birth after birth, till the goal is reached. Of the different ways of God realisation, Sai Baba advocated to his devotees the easier path of 'Bhakti' or devotion to the guru. The guru's grace can be won by absolute faith in and total self-surrender to the guru, and by infinite patience, forbearance and courage. This was the only *guru dakshina* Baba himself expected from the devotee.

Baba was divine and yet so human! He was so far and yet so near! He believed in teaching by example rather than by precept and he never sermonized. He performed no miracles. Miracles happened as a natural consequence of his spiritual and yogic powers. Like any of us, he would bargain for a fair price when purchasing anything and only after fixing the proper price would he reward the seller by paying him a little extra. To the man who brought a ladder for him to climb, he at once paid his due, showing that no labour should be accepted free of charge. Even in his last moments he did not forget to give in charity to Laxmibai Shinde. In these and a thousand other ways he taught the householder his duties, guiding him to the path of righteousness. His tender love and deep concern for the devotees' welfare — both spiritual and material — his tearful farewell to Megha, his delightful use of humour to teach a valuable lesson or to nip in the bud a threatened quarrel between the devotees, his sending away the devotees and close associates to escape the meshes of *Maya*, as the end drew near, — these and the such-like traits bring him closer to us by revealing the human side of his personality. And yet, who can miss the divine qualities that raise him to the eminence of a godhead? The perpetual state of *samadhi*, the total detachment and non-possession, the Peace, Benevolence, Mercy, — these leave us in no doubt that Baba, who was such a mine of virtues, was none other than God Incarnate.

But what lends charm to the story of this saint of Shirdi is a certain element of mystery and symbolism. Practically nothing, for instance, is known about his guru or his early spiritual *sadhana* and, as to whether he was a Hindu or a Muslim, the devotees could never determine, in the face of contrary indications. Similarly, his giving *udi* to all who came to him, or his asking for *dakshina* in the form of money, his *dhuni*, the collecting of alms from five households, etc., were all symbolic and often misunderstood as their real significance was completely missed.

And it was the symbolism in Baba's actions that first attracted the attention of the author of *Shri Sai Satcharita*. Shri Dabholkar was intrigued when he heard Baba's command to the women of the village to sprinkle the freshly ground wheat flour on the banks of the stream at the village boundary, which, he later learnt to his amazement, was to rid the village of the menacing cholera epidemic. This incident inspired him to write *Shri Sai Satcharita*.

The author Shri Govind Raghunath Dabholkar (1859-1929) was himself a Sai devotee who, on seeing some of the miracles, felt such an awe and wonder at Baba's *leelas* that he felt a strong urge to write an account of them for the devotees and especially for posterity. Shri Dabholkar did not have much academic education. He was a servant of the Bombay Government and his last appointment was as a magistrate in the Bandra suburb of Bombay. But, a poet by heart and well-versed in '*Jnaneshvari*', '*Eknathi Bhagwat*', and the like, he was able to move the hearts of the devotees and confirm them in their faith through this poetic composition in Marathi. So imaginative is the presentation of facts, replete with poetic embellishment and philosophical wisdom, and, so evocative in expression that there is hardly a reader who is not captivated by the book. Baba may have foreseen the result, for, even before he had started writing the book, Baba once jokingly conferred on the author, the title 'Hemadpant' (after the learned court-poet and author of the Yadavas in the thirteenth century, called Hemadpant). And as one completes reading the book, the mind is filled with a silent elation and a feeling of fulfilment.

The book runs into 53 chapters, containing 9,308 verses. Every chapter has a judicious mixture of philosophy, stories and anecdotes, and Baba's teachings, which always emerged as the implicit moral of a story. The proportion of these elements varies from chapter to chapter, some chapters being more philosophical than others, depending on the story narrated.

However, the book is essentially a '*pothi*' (a religious text) and as in all *pothis*, one does not look in it for historical truth or a chronological order of events. Moreover, in the original Marathi version, one tends to get a little confused with regard to Baba's original utterances and the author's philosophical commentary, as these are not clearly indicated by the placing of the inverted commas.

But the devotees cherish the book, use it with great faith and devotion, reading a chapter or more as part of daily worship. It is also used for a continuous reading to be completed in one week, in three days and so on, as personal worship and also as part of celebrations and festivals in Shirdi.

Such being the revered place of this book in the hearts of Sai devotees, it is small wonder that one hears many a sigh, a groan, a regret from those who cannot read it, because it is in Marathi or Gujarati, and not in English. No systematic attempt has been made, so far, at a detailed, chapter-wise English translation.

Hence in view of the demand for such a book, especially from the South, this humble attempt at an English translation, chapter by chapter, verse by verse, line by line, with notes to help the reader understand the text better. The latest prose version of the book in Marathi, with a wealth of information, by Lt. Col. M. B. Nimbalkar, has been of invaluable help to the present translator.

Acknowledgements

I wish to thank sincerely Shri M.V. Kamath for the gracious 'Foreword' he has contributed to this book.

I also acknowledge gratefully the invaluable help I have received from Dr Marianne Warren, Toronto, who with a sense of commitment and with untiring effort, put the MS on the computer and sent us the floppy discs.

Last but not least, my thanks also go to Shri S. K. Ghai, Managing Director of Sterling Publishers, Pvt. Ltd., New Delhi, for undertaking the publication of the book for the benefit of Shirdi Sai Baba devotees all over the world.

Indira Kher

Contents

1

The Invocation of the Divine

MY OBEISANCE TO SHRI GANESH, TO SHRI SARASWATI, AND SHRI GURU MAHARAJ! TO THE FAMILY DEITY, TO SHRI SITA-RAMACHANDRA, MY MOST HUMBLE OBEISANCE! I BOW IN REVERENCE TO THE MOST VENERABLE GURU SHRI SAINATH!

1. For a smooth, unhindered completion of a work once begun, the wise and the learned sing, at the outset, the praises of the tutelar deities, and invoke their blessings.
2. By so praising the deities, by making an obeisance to them all, impediments are sought to be forestalled and the desired goals achieved.
3. Let us, therefore, bow, first to Ganapati, the benign figure of the elephant-god, with his twisted trunk; the Protector of the Meek[1], and the Lord and Master of the fourteen branches of learning.[2]
4. Fourteen worlds are contained in your belly and hence you are called 'Lambodara', while in your hand is the powerful, sharp-edged axe with which you strike down the obstacles in the way of your devotees.
5. O Lord of the Ganas (of Shiva), O elephant-faced God, I bow to you who assuage the pain caused by impediments. Pour your Grace into my utterances, I pray!
6. You are the succour of your devotees. Under your anklets come rolling all the obstacles. Just one glance from you is enough to drive away all want and poverty.

7. In the ocean of worldly life, you are the Ark; the Light of Knowledge you are, in the Darkness of Ignorance! You, O Lord, with your twin consorts, Riddhi and Siddhi (signifying Prosperity and Success), look upon me graciously, I beseech!

8. Hail to you, O Lord, who are the destroyer of the woods of impediments, and whose vehicle is the humble mouse. O son of Girija, O God of the benign countenance, to you I bow!

9. Here do I follow the customary practice of making an obeisance to the tutelar deities, that I may complete my work unhindered, and be blessed with good fortune.

10. And yet, is not this Sai Himself Gajanan, and Ganapati, who, axe in hand, will remove the obstacles to the narration of his story?

11. He is indeed Gajanan and Bhalchandra with the crescent moon on his forehead. And he boasts of a single tusk, and elephantine ears. He is the Terrible One of the broken tooth, the Annihilator of the jungle of obstacles.

12. Most Auspicious among the Auspicious, O long-bellied Lambodara, O Compassionate Ganaraya! You are none other than Sai Himself. May you lead me on to the Abode of Eternal Joy and Peace.

13. I now make an obeisance to goddess Saraswati, the daughter of Brahma! May she with her art and ingenuity alight upon my tongue, making it her vehicle, the swan.

14. Goddess Saraswati, draped in spotless white, with the tiny vermilion mark on her forehead, holds the Brahma-veena gracefully in her hand, as she rides her swan. O Saraswati, look upon me kindly!

15. Unless the Presiding Goddess of Speech, this Mother of the Universe is propitiated, can ever literature or art, verse or tale, sit gracefully upon one? And, without her Grace, can I venture to write this story of Sai?

16. This Mother of the Universe, from whose womb were born the Vedas, verily is she the river of all the glorious Learning! May she make one and all, drink at my hands, the nectar-sweet story of Sai's Life.

17. It is, as if Sai Himself, as Bhagavati, as goddess Saraswati, holds the Omkar-veena in hand and sings His own Life-story for the deliverance of His devotees!

18. My obeisance, now, is to Brahma, Vishnu and Mahesh, who symbolise Creation, Preservation and Destruction, of the Universe, respectively. They are the epitomes of *Sattva* (Harmony), *Rajas* (Motion) and *Tamas* (Inertia).

19. O Self-illumined Sainath, to us you are truly, Ganadheesh and Brahma, Vishnu and Mahesh.

20. You alone are our Sadguru, the boat to ferry us safely across the Ocean of Life. And we, your devotees, are as travellers aboard the ship and beseech you to guide us to the shore yonder.

21. But for the merit of some good deeds of our past births, how could we have been so compellingly drawn to your holy feet, which have proved to be our sole refuge?

22. I now, bow to my family deity, Narayana Adinath, who abides in the Sea of Milk³, and is the Redeemer of all, from sorrow, suffering and pain.

23. When Parashuram forced back the waters of the ocean and created a new land called '*Konkan*', in that land appeared Narayana.

24. Narayana dwells within and rules over the hearts of all the creatures, protecting them with loving kindness. It is from Him that I draw my inspiration.

25. My obeisance, next, is to that great sage and my original ancestor, whom Bhargava (Parshuram) brought to Konkan, from Bengal, for the successful completion of the great Yajna (ritualistic sacrifice).

26. Bharadwaj, the greatest among the sages, the founder of my ancestry, who belonged to the Shakala branch of the Rig Veda, and who was also the founder of all the Adya Gaud Brahmins, — to him I bow respectfully.

27. Next, I make my obeisance to the Brahmins, who are the Brahman Incarnate, the veritable gods on this earth. And then, I proceed to pay my respects to the greatest among the yogis, — Yajnyavalkya, Bhrigu, Parashar, Narada, and others.

28. Ved Vyasa (son of Parashar); Sanak, Sanandan, Sanatsujat, Sanatkumar (born of the mind of Brahma); Shuka; Shaunak, the composer of Sutra; Vishwamitra and Vashistha;-

29. Valmiki; Vamdev; Jaimini; Vaishampayan, and the nine munis, i.e. Yogindra[4], etc. I prostrate in obeisance at the feet of all these sages.

30. Let me now worship all the saints, like Nivritti, Jnaneshvar, Mukta, Sopan, Eknath, Swami Janardan, Tukaram, Kanhoba, Narahari and others.

31. For a mention of all the saints by their names, this book will hardly have the space. Therefore, I make obeisance to them all and pray for their blessings.

32. Then, I bow in respect to Sadashiva, my grandfather, who was a man of impressive piety, and who, finding this worldly, material life meaningless and empty, took his abode at Badrinath and Kedarnath, to the end of his days.

33. My father was a worshipper of Shiva and, having made Shiva his personal god, always wore rudraksha beads round his neck. Respectfully, I bow to him.

34. And then, how can I ever repay the debt of my mother, who spared no trouble, bringing me into this world and rearing me? Humbly, I fall at her feet in obeisance.

35. But she soon passed away, leaving me, a mere infant, behind. My paternal aunt, a pious soul, then looked after me, bringing me up most painstakingly. At her feet, I bow my head in great reverence.

36. The love and affection of my eldest brother for me, has no parallel. For me, he would have willingly given up his life. I cannot but be filled with gratitude as I bow at his feet.

37. As for you, O my listeners! I make my obeisance to you respectfully, as I pray for your undivided attention. Unless you are attentive, how can I be happy?

38. The greater the connoisseur a listener is, waiting eagerly for more and more, the greater is the enthusiasm and verve of the speaker, as he goes on narrating.

39. If you yourselves are inattentive, then wherefore this narration? Hence it is, that I prostrate before you and implore you to listen to this tale with good cheer.

40. Full well you know, that I have no profound knowledge of science and literature. Nor have I perused any scholarly works, or even listened to the sacred stories of saints, being narrated.

41. I am aware of my shortcomings, too! I am conscious of my unworthiness. It is only in obedience to the guru's command that I have ventured to attempt writing his 'Life'.

42. My own heart tells me that before you, I am but a piece of straw. And yet, I beseech you to be gracious and accept me with all my faults.

43. And now, let us remember our Sadguru and worship his feet with love and devotion. With body, speech and mind, let us surrender to him, who is the mainspring of all wisdom and inspiration.

44. Sweet dish is always reserved for the end of a meal. In the same way, the sweet adoration of the Guru marks the end of this Invocation of the Divine.

45. OM Shri Sadguru! My obeisance to you, the only Refuge of this animate and inanimate Creation! You, and you alone, O Compassionate One, sustain this entire Universe, eternally.

46. *Hiranyagarbha* or the golden egg of the Brahman, from which comes the earth, its seven islands[5] and nine continents, the seven heavens and the seven netherworlds, is itself, the well-known Brahmanda.

47. The Sadguru dwells far beyond the cosmic illusion, which creates this Brahmanda and which is known by the name '*maya*' or the 'unmanifest'.

48. In trying to describe the greatness of the Sadguru, the *Ved-shastras* become silent. Know that ingenuity or tricks of logic are of no avail here.

49. O Sadguru, you defy all comparison; for, to whichever object you are likened, you already pervade it, by virtue of natural attributes. Whatever object the eye falls upon, is but a form assumed by yourself.

50. Such you are O Sainath, a Sea of Kindness, Samarth Sadguru, who can be comprehended only by your own self, and are beyond everything, without a beginning or an end. To you, I bow!

51. My obeisance to you, O Greatest among the Gurus, who are in perpetual Bliss, ever-content, self-effulgent, home of all auspiciousness, the Soul Beautiful!

52. In singing your praises, in trying to describe you, if even the *Vedas* and the *Shrutis* have fallen silent, how then, will my (scant) knowledge be enough to comprehend you?

53. Hail to you, O Sadguru, O treasure-house of kindness and mercy! Glory be to you, who are Brahma-Vishnu-Mahesh, and Dattatreya, who wanders at will on the banks of Godavari! I bow to you in obeisance!

54. That which is the very essence of Brahma comes only from the Sadguru. With his grace alone, it can be realized. At his feet should be offered the '*Panch-pran*' (the five vital airs) in a spirit of absolute surrender.

55. Bow your head before him in reverence; with your hands, press his feet gently; let your eyes gaze into his face intently, and, the nose inhale the fragrance of the water that washes his feet.

56. Let the ears listen to the praises of Sai constantly, and keeping Sai's form before the mind's eye, meditate on Sai incessantly. The ties of worldly life will then fall off, automatically.

57. With devotion, offer at the Sadguru's feet your body, mind, worldly wealth, — everything, and dedicate your entire life in the service of the guru.

58. Only after laborious efforts do rare privileges of *guru-naam*, guru's holy company, his grace and the sweetened milk washed off his feet, *guru-mantra* and the opportunity to stay in guru's abode, come your way.

59. Great is the power of all these. For they urge the devotee onwards, even without his knowing it, pushing him to the very threshold of *Moksha*. This has been tried and tested by those of single-minded devotion.

60. Guru's company is the pure water of the Ganges which purifies others, washing away all their impurities. What can be more fickle than the human mind? But even this mind is fixed steadfastly, by the guru, at the feet of God.

61. The service we offer at the Sadguru's feet is our *Veda–Shastra–Purana.* Prostrating at his feet in obeisance is, to us, yoga, ritual sacrifices, penance and all such means of deliverance.

62. The sacred name of the Sadguru is our *Veda-Shastra*; '*Sai Samarth*' is our '*mantra*' or the sacred chant. It is also our only '*yantra*' and '*tantra*'.[6]

63. Sai takes his devotees to that supreme state in which, self-experience brings them the conviction that 'Brahman alone is real', and a constant awareness stays with them that 'this world is an illusion or maya'.

64. The 'highest bliss', 'the joy of Self-realization', 'the happiness of being One with the Brahman'—all this is a tangle of idle words. What we need is an abidingly blissful state of mind.

65. Once this state of mind is firmly rooted and remains constant, happiness, peace and contentment come to us. And this is the most perfect state one can attain in this life.

66. Sai is a mine of such blissful happiness. Like the ocean, he is complete and full in himself. His devotee is blessed with good fortune and will never want for this Supreme Bliss.

67. Shiva and Shakti (the Supreme Spirit and Divine Energy), Purush and Prakriti (the Supreme Soul and Nature), Pran and Gati (the vital airs and their motion), the lamp and its brilliance—all these are modifications of the Pure Brahman. They are really One, but are considered as different.

68. 'Brahman does not like to be alone', and 'desires to be many', so says the Shruti[7]. Though the company of the other is desired and liked, yet they all again become one.

69. In the state of Pure Brahman, there is neither Purush nor Prakriti. Where the sun shines perpetually, can there be night and day?

70. Sai Baba is, essentially, beyond all attributes; he is without attributes. But, for the benefit of his devotees, Sai has assumed a form with the purest of attributes. I surrender to him whole-heartedly.

71. Those who have sought refuge and protection from Sai Samarth, have escaped many a calamity. Thus, with this same selfish purpose, I bow my head at his feet.

72. Obeisance to loving Sai, who is really one, but assumes form and duality to experience the joy of his devotees' love and thus sports with them.

73. To that Compassionate One, who is the cosmic consciousness in all beings and is the seat of Supreme Knowledge; who manifests himself through all the animate and inanimate creations, I bow to him in reverence.

74. O Gururaya! O Bliss Incarnate! You are my ultimate destination. You alone, are my repose, for only You can relieve the pain and suffering of this afflicted one.

75. Now, at the end of this paean, and as evidence of the fact that God alone dwells in all living beings, I make obeisance to them all, imploring them to accept me graciously.

76. I bow to all living creatures. May it please that Sustainer of the Universe, who pervades it, through and through, and is completely one with it without any duality.

77. Here I end the adoration that customarily comes at the beginning and at the end of a work. It is also, for this book, the Invocation of the Divine and the Holy. I shall now narrate the main purpose of this book.

78. Ever since Sai, very kindly, conferred his grace on me I have been thinking only of him day and night. That itself will destroy the fear of worldly life.

79. No more for me the chanting of other mantras, nor yet, any other penance! I see only the pure, manifest form of Shri Sai, all the time.

80. Gazing into Sai's face, hunger, thirst — everything is forgotten. What worldly pleasure can stand comparison to it? The trials and tribulations of worldly life are forgotten altogether.

81. Looking into Baba's eyes, one forgets one's self. And, as the love wells up from within, the mind is immersed into inexpressible joy.

82. To me service at Sai's feet is everything; — karma and dharma, Shastras and Puranas, yoga and ritual sacrifice, and, the performance of prescribed religious ceremonies, pilgrimages, penance, — everything!

83. A constant, scrupulous adherence to the guru's word, when firmly rooted in the mind, and backed by an unswerving faith, will bring to the mind, abiding peace.

84. Such was the state of my mind, a result, no doubt, of my past karma, which fostered in me a growing fondness and attachment to Sai's feet, and I experienced its incomprehensible power. How can I ever describe that power?

85. It is the power from which springs devotion and a loving attachment to Sai, which brings renunciation while yet in the worldly life, along with a state of incessant joy.

86. Many are the forms of devotion, described variously by different schools of thought. Briefly, and as carefully as possible, I shall now describe their characteristics.

87. Ceaseless meditation on one's real Self is the main characteristic of devotion; so say the Self-realized Acharyas, who are proficient in *Veda-Shastras*.

88. To express one's devotion by performing *pooja*, is the way prescribed by Vyasa, the son of the sage Parashar, and is another form of devotion, called '*Archan-Bhakti*'.

89. Parijat, and other such fragrant flowers should be gathered from the garden, for the guru. Then the courtyard of the guru's house should be swept clean, and washed, first, by sprinkling water, followed by a cow-dung wash.

90. Thereafter, one should take a bath, followed by Sandhya or the prescribed daily prayers. A sandalwood paste should then be prepared f or the gods and for the guru, which is to be applied to them when they are given the ritualistic bath. Lights and incense should then be waved before them.

91. Thereafter, the consecrated food-offering should be made and arati performed, to conclude the ritual. All this, when performed with love and devotion, is known as '*Archan*'.

92. The pure awakened Supreme Spirit in the heart should be invoked in the idol, and then the pooja should be started.

93. After the ritual is over, the consciousness of the Supreme Spirit should be regained in your heart.

94. Now, understand the characteristic of another form of devotion which was advocated by Gargacharya. In this, the mind gets totally absorbed in singing the praises of God through *keertan*. So much so, that the mind becomes one with the joyous spirit of the *Hari-kirtan*.

95. To be constantly meditating on the Self, to be narrating or singing the sacred stories of the Lord, and conforming in one's conduct to the prescribed rules of the *Shastras*, are the characteristics of the form of devotion described by Shandilya muni.

96. Those who wish to advance, spiritually, will conduct themselves according to the rules prescribed by the *Vedas*, avoiding all that is either not advocated or prohibited by the *Vedas* and which is therefore, not in their interest.

97. When the mind becomes totally devoid of conceit, so that it is no longer the doer of action nor the enjoyer of the fruit of action, it is then that it surrenders everything to God.

98. Performing action or karma in this spirit leads effortlessly to freedom from all action. Karma can never be given up totally by anyone. But what can be given up, is the conceit of being the doer of action.

99. A thorn can be removed only by a thorn. So also can karma be ended only by karma. With the realization of the Self, karma will be overcome completely.

100. Cessation of desire for the fruit of action, is the secret of the renunciation of desire for the fruit of action. Performance of the routine and specially prescribed religious rites and rituals is called the 'law of pure conduct'.

101. To offer all karma at the feet of God; to forget, for a moment, everything, making your mind totally detached; — these, very different characteristics, mark the devotion described by Narad muni.

102. Such are the many characteristics, one stranger than the other. But, as for ourselves, let us cross the ocean of worldly life, safely and quite untouched by its turbulent waters, only by a constant remembrance of the story of our Guru's life.

103. I too, developed a fondness and passion for listening to the story of the Guru, and was deeply engrossed in this pursuit. So that, I thought, I should also write a book about these numerous stories of actual experience and doubtless veracity.

104. It so came to pass, that once, while in Shirdi, I had gone to the mosque for Baba's darshan, when I saw, to my utter amazement, Baba grinding wheat.

105. But let me first tell you (of your gains in listening to) this story. Listen at your ease. And then, listen to how the idea of writing Sai's 'Life' was conceived from the above incident.

106. Describing, again and again, the excellent qualities of One who is of sacred celebrity, and, discussing together, in company, his fascinating stories, purifies the mind and brings perspicuity to the intellect.

107. By singing his praises, by listening to his *leelas* and his stories, one can please God. Sorrows and sufferings caused to us by the threefold afflictions (refer to Chapter 9 Note 2) are also warded off.

108. Hence, those plagued by the threefold afflictions, as also, those impelled by a desire for self-upliftment, and those intent on Self-meditation, — all such people fall at the feet of saints and are enriched by elevating personal experience.

109. And now, listen attentively to this fascinating account (of the aforementioned incident), and you will be amazed by Baba's kindness and compassion.

110. One day, in the morning, after he had finished washing his face, cleaning his teeth, etc., Baba sat down at the grinding stone, to grind.

111. Scuttle-basket in hand, he went to the bag of wheat and began taking out, by the brimfuls, measure upon measure, of wheat into the basket.

112. He spread out another empty sack on the ground, placed the quern on it and knocked its wooden peg firmly into place, to prevent its becoming loose while grinding.

113. He then rolled up his sleeves, tucked in the folds of his kafni (long robe), and he squatted near the quern, with his legs spread out.

114. 'What is this crazy idea of grinding wheat?' I just thought to myself, puzzled as I was, 'To a poor penniless one, without attachment to material possessions, why should there be anxiety about worldly things?'

115. However, with head bent down, Baba had taken a firm hold of the quern-handle and went on rotating the quern-stone, with his own hands, as if he was crushing, most certainly not wheat, but all enmity and hatred to a powder.

116. Many a saint had I met before; but here was the only one grinding at the quern. What pleasure could grinding afford him? Only he can understand his strange ways!

117. People watched him in astonishment, but no one dared ask him what he was doing. As the news travelled through the village, men and women came running.

118. The women gasped for breath, as they ran. Four of them hastily rushed up the steps of the mosque and seizing hold of Baba's hand roughly, snatched the quern handle away from him.

119. Baba began quarrelling with them; but without heeding him they started grinding all at once. And as they did so, they sang Baba's praises and of his marvellous *leelas*.

120. Touched by their genuine affection, Baba's mock anger vanished, giving way to tenderness and love, as an indulgent, pleased smile stole over his face.

121. All the wheat was ground, measuring full eight pounds (four *seers*); the scuttle-basket was emptied. And then began thoughts and conjectures, racing wildly through the minds of the ladies.

122. 'Baba prepares no wheat-bread for himself; to subsist on alms is his actual practice. What then, will he do with all this flour?' So they argued in their minds.

123. 'Moreover, he has no wife, no children. Baba is all alone, without encumbrances of a home and a hearth, or of material belongings. What then, should he want all this flour for?'

124. One of them said, 'Oh! Baba is compassion itself! All this sport is only for us. Just see! He will now give away all this flour to us.

125. Presently, he will make four shares in it, one for each of us!' They began building castles in the air.

126. But only Baba can understand his own ways; none other can divine his ultimate purpose. And yet their greed urged them on to loot Baba.

127. When all the wheat was over, the flour was spread out; the quern was put away to rest against the wall. The women filled the scuttle-basket with the flour, all in readiness to be taken to their respective homes.

128. All this while, not a word escaped Baba's lips. But as they proceeded to divide the flour into four equal parts, listen to what Baba said.

129. 'Are you out of your senses? Where are you taking the flour? Does it belong to your father that you are carrying it away? Go at once, to the village boundary and throw all the flour at the side of the brook there!

130. Free-booters, all! How they came running to loot me! Was it some borrowed wheat that you now stake a claim to the flour?'

131. Fretting and fuming in their hearts, and greatly ashamed of their greediness, the women, in their discomfiture began whispering

amongst themselves. But, all the same, they at once set out for the village boundary, as commanded.

132. No one understood Baba's intention, at first, and the reason for his actions appeared to be beyond one's understanding. A patient waiting was ultimately rewarded by an understanding of his marvellous ways!

133. Later, I asked people why Baba did all this, and they said that in this way Baba banished the disease from the village, altogether.

134. It was not wheat, but the terrible cholera epidemic that he fed to the quern to be crushed. Afterwards, he got the coarsely ground flour to be thrown along the side of the brook at the village border.

135. When the flour was thus thrown away, the epidemic was on the wane from then onwards and the days of distress were over for the village. Such was Baba's skilful handling!

136. A cholera epidemic chanced to erupt in the village, and this was the mysterious remedy employed by Baba to counter it. The disease was eradicated and, once again, the village enjoyed peace.

137. This spectacle of Baba grinding at the quern, filled me with admiration and wonder. How does one connect this action to its cause and to its effect? How can a correspondence be found between all these?

138. What connection can there be between the wheat and the dreaded disease? It was far beyond one's imagination. I felt that I must write a book about this.

139. Love rose in my heart, like the surging waves on the Sea of Milk, even as I felt a strong urge to sing to my heart's content, of the charming story of Baba's life.

140. Here ends the invocation of gods and goddesses. Obeisance to the saints, and to the relatives, and, the ceaseless adoration of the Sadguru has come to a close, too! Hemad seeks refuge at the feet of Sainath.

141. In the next chapter, I shall explain, to the best of my ability, the purpose of this work, persons for whom it is meant, and its relation to the main subject. Listen to it, O Listeners, at ease.

142.   It will also be explained, later, who this Hemadpant is, who has composed this *'Sai Satcharit'*, so very beneficial, both, to the listeners and to the speaker himself.

Weal be to all! Here ends
'The Invocation of the Divine',
the first chapter of
'Shri Sai Samarth Satcharit',
as inspired by the saints and the virtuous
and composed by his devotee Hemadpant.

Notes

1.   Heramb.
2.   These 14 branches of learning are: 4 Vedas, 6 Vedangas, the (18) Puranas, (2) Mimansas, Nyaya and Dharma. 14 Bhuvans are: 7 Heavens: Bhuh, Bhuvah, Swaha, Maha, Jana, Tapaloka, and Satya or Brahma. 7 Netherworlds are: Atal, Vital, Satal, Rasatal, Talatal, Mahatal, Patal.
3.   This is *'Ksheerasagar'*, one of the seven oceans or great seas in Hindu mythology.
4.   The nine munis are: Kavi, Hari, Antariksha, Prabuddha, Pippalayan, Avirhotra, Drumil, Chamas and Karabhajan.
5.   The seven islands are: Jambu, Kush, Plaksha, Shalmali, Kraunch, Shak and Pushkar.
6.   *'Yantras'* are particular geometrical figures described in *tantra* which are a combination of a point, a line and a circle. They represent the deep-rooted archetypes of an individual. *Tantra*: Etymology of the word *'tantra'* shows that it embraces two ideas and two roots, *'tan'* which means expansion, and *'tra'* which means liberation. Expansion means expansion of consciousness and liberation of energy, from the material base at the root of the spine. So *tantra* is a system of techniques for expansion of consciousness and consequently a liberation of Shakti.
7.   This is a reference to *Brihadaranyaka Upanishad* (1-4-3) and *Taittireya Upanishad* (2-6).

2

The Purpose of the Book – Naming of the Author

MY OBEISANCE TO SHRI GANESH, TO SHRI SARASWATI, AND SHRI GURUMAHARAJ! TO THE FAMILY DEITY, TO SHRI SITA-RAMACHANDRA, MY MOST HUMBLE OBEISANCE! I BOW IN REVERENCE TO THE MOST VENERABLE GURU SHRI SAINATH!

1. Invocation of the Divine has ended in the preceding chapter; the family gods and the Sadguru have been propitiated. The seed has been sown of Sai's Life-story. Let us now deal with the purpose of writing this book.
2. Who needs most to read this work and the connection of the work to the subject of the book will now be stated briefly, which will also introduce the listeners without effort, to the book itself.
3. In the first chapter, we saw how Baba, to the great surprise of the villagers, used the device of grinding wheat, to destroy the epidemic of cholera.
4. As I heard of these marvellous *leelas* of Sai, my heart was flooded with joy and love, which has burst forth in the form of this poetic composition.
5. So I thought I should describe, to the best of my ability, the blessed deeds of Sai, which will be instructive to the devotees and will expiate their sins.
6. And therefore, I have undertaken to write this very sacred 'Life' of Sai by commencing the writing of these stories, which make for happiness in this life and in the life hereafter.

7. Life of a saint is a guide to the path of righteousness; it is neither *Nyaya* (epistemology), nor *Tarkashastra* (logic). Hence, to one worthy of a saint's grace, nothing would be strange or surprising.

8. And so, my prayer to my listeners is, 'Come, and share in this joy. For great is the good fortune of him who is always engaged in listening to these sacred stories in the company of the virtuous.

9. 'If I am not able to sketch the picture of a most intimate friend, a long-standing companion, whose company I have enjoyed, day and night, how then can I write the 'Life' of a saint?

10. 'I, who know not fully, even my own true heart or mind, how can I faultlessly describe the thoughts in a saint's mind?

11. 'In trying to determine the true nature of the Self, all the four *Vedas* fell silent. How will I know, for certain, your true nature, O Sai?'

12. First, one must become a saint oneself. Only then can the saints be understood fully. How then, can I describe the saints? And this, my own unworthiness, I already know full well.

13. One may measure the volume of water of the seven great seas; the wide expanse of the sky may even be covered; but never can the saints be comprehended by the human mind.

14. In my heart I know, that I am but an abject human being. But Baba's boundless power and glory creates in me an irrepressible desire to sing, which is uncontrollable.

15. Glory to you, O Sai, who are the repose of the poor and the meek! Unfathomable is your Love, which simply cannot be described. Be gracious to me, your humble servant.

16. I sincerely wish to write this account of your life. But I am afraid that I will be biting off more than I can chew. Save me from the world's ridicule, I pray.

17. And yet, why should I have any fear? For Jnaneshvar Maharaj himself said that those who write the lives of saints, endear themselves to God.

18. And, it is that same God, who has kindled the inspiration in my heart to write. Hence, dull-witted though I am, He knows best how to have His own work accomplished.

19. In whatever manner their devotees resolve to serve them, it is really the saints themselves who get the service done through the devotees. The inspiration flows from the saints; devotees are but the instrument.

20. In short, it is Sai, who is getting his own 'Life' narrated through an ignorant fool like me. This is the glory of this story, which commands our respect.

21. Sages and saints, or even God Himself, narrates His own story, by placing his hand of benediction on the head of him, whom he chooses (as an instrument).

22. As for instance, in the *Shake* year seventeen hundred, Mahipati was similarly inspired, so that sadhus and saints, had their lives written by him, and his services accepted.

23. Service was similarly accepted by them at the hands of Das Ganu in the *Shake* year eighteen hundred, by making him write the lives of later saints, which were purifying and ennobling for all.

24. Just as *Bhaktavijay* and *Sant Vijay*, *Bhakta-leelamrut* and *Sant-leelamrut* are the four compositions of Mahipati, Das Ganu has also written two others.

25. Of these latter, one is called *Bhakta-leelamrut*, and the other *Sant-kathamrut*, both of which deal with saints and devotees who have come to be known recently.

26. *Bhakta-leelamrut* contains the fascinating life of Shri Sai, described in three chapters, which the listeners can read for themselves.

27. Similarly, chapter fifty-seven of *Sant-kathamrut* relates a highly instructive, interesting tale as narrated by Sai to a devotee.

28. Moreover, '*Raghunath-Savitri Bhajanmala*' (authored by Raghunath and Savitri Tendulkar), written from the authors' personal experience in the form of '*padas*' and '*abhangas*', about the marvellous *leelas* of Sai, is a source of great peace and happiness to people.

29. Out of an overwhelming love for Baba, a child of his (i.e. Hari Sitaram Dikshit) has written a Preface to this same '*Bhajanmala*' which is as a shower of nectar to the ever-thirsty Chakora (his devotees) and of which the reader should partake respectfully.

30. Das Ganu's miscellaneous poems are also full of deep feeling and will gladden the hearts of readers as they read of Baba's *leelas* in them.

31. Amidas Bhavanidas Mehta, too, has narrated with great love and devotion, some miraculous tales of Baba, in Gujarati, specially for the Gujarati readers.

32. Besides all these, some eminent Sai devotees have published from Pune, a collection of Baba's stories, under the name '*Sai Prabha*'.

33. So that, when numerous such works are available, where is the need for this book? So the listeners may well question. Listen, now, to my reply.

34. Sai's 'Life' is a great ocean — boundless, infinite, a mine of precious gems; which I, a tiny Titwi (Lapwing) bird is endeavouring to empty. How can this ever come about?

35. Sai's life is thus unfathomable, which it is just impossible to recount fully and satisfactorily. One should therefore, be content to narrate as much of it as one can, and to the best of one's ability.

36. Innumerable are the extraordinary stories of Baba, which assuage the worldly sufferings of the afflicted, enthuse the listeners for more and more and steady the minds of his devotees.

37. The stories Baba narrated were varied — some, of worldly wisdom, some of common experience and those that explained his mysterious deeds.

38. As the innumerable *Vedic* tales of divine origin are well-known, so also were the numerous stories, captivating and pregnant with meaning, that Baba used to tell.

39. And, when listened to with undivided attention, hunger-thirst was forgotten; an inner contentment reigned supreme. So that, all other pleasures appeared as straw.

40. Some may strive to be one with the Brahman, some may work for proficiency in the eightfold path of *Yoga*[1]; yet others may seek the fullness of the bliss of *Samadhi*. Listening to these stories they will all get what they seek.

41. These tales liberate the listeners from the bondage to their *karma*, bringing enlightenment to their minds and bring happiness to all, without making any distinction.

42. Hence a wish arose in my mind to weave together a garland of these variegated tales, so worthy of a collection, so as to make an offering to Baba. This, I felt was the best form of worship.

43. Even a few words of these stories, falling on the ear casually, are enough to make the misfortunes of a creature, recede, at once. If then, the entire story is heard, with reverence and faith, a simple, trusting devotee will surely and easily cross the ocean of worldly life.

44. Making me his instrument of writing, Baba will hold my hand to fashion the letters. I am but the instrument moving mechanically, as Baba guides.

45. Watching Baba's *leelas* for years together, my mind kept toying with the idea fondly, that Baba's tales may be collected together for the benefit of the simple and loving devotees.

46. Those who have not had the actual *darshan* of Baba, to pacify their eyes, may at least gain some merit by listening to the stories of his greatness.

47. And should a truly fortunate one feel the urge to read these stories, he will at least have the experience of joy and inner satisfaction, on doing so.

48. Such was the thought that came to my mind, which I conveyed to Madhavrao (Deshpande). But I still had my doubts whether I would be able to write a book.

49. For, I had already crossed the sixty-year mark, and, at sixty, the wicked mind is more prone to create problems and obstacles. Moreover, feebleness of body might prevent a full-blooded effort. And all that would then remain would be an empty babble of words.

50. And yet, rather than waste the effort on something meaningless and empty, it would far better be employed in Sai's service. It would at least make for some spiritual advancement. Hence this *yajna* (effort).

51. The thought came to my mind, that I should write down an account of what I experienced, by day and by night, a constant contemplation on which, will bring peace and repose to my mind.

52. I wished to present to the listeners those utterances of Baba, which came repeatedly, and with a natural ease, were so firmly rooted in self-experience and brought satiety to the Self.

53. Many were the tales of wisdom that Baba narrated; many devotees he guided to the path of bhajans. If I were to make a complete collection of these, it would become Sai Baba's 'Gatha' (sacred poetic composition).

54. Whoever narrates these stories, and whosoever listens to them respectfully, will both enjoy a rare peace of mind and repose.

55. Listening to these tales, which came straight from Baba's mouth, the devotees will become oblivious of their physical sufferings and as they meditate upon them constantly, they will be liberated automatically from the ties of the worldly life.

56. The words that came out of Sai's mouth are as sweet as nectar. How can I describe their beauty and charm? Listening to them, the heart will be filled with supreme bliss.

57. And, when I find someone narrating these stories, without any pretensions to learning or virtue, I feel that even if I rolled in the dust at his feet, deliverance for me will be near at hand.

58. The most remarkable style of presentation of these stories, as also the ingenious use of every word and phrase, holds the audience enthralled, bringing joy to one and all.

59. As the ears thirst for the stories, and the eyes long for his *darshan*, so will the mind transcend consciousness, being absorbed in divine concentration.

60. My loving Guru is my mother. As his stories travel from person to person, by the word of mouth, let us treasure them up in our ears, with reverence.

61. Let us bring the self-same stories to the mind, again and again, and store up as many as we can, binding them together in the ties of love. The treasure can then be shared with each other, in profusion.

62. In all this, nothing is mine. The impulse is wholly from Sainath himself. Whatever he prompts me to say, I say, you see!

63. But then, to say that 'I speak' is again my ego. It is Sai who really holds the strings. And it is he who moves my tongue to speech. Who am I to say that 'I speak'?

64. Once the ego is surrendered at Baba's feet, boundless joy will ensue. As the ego is overcome, the whole life will be filled with happiness.

65. When this idea occurred to me, I did have the opportunity, but not the courage, to put it to Baba. Suddenly, I saw Madhavrao and I at once conveyed my thoughts to him.

66. No one else was around, at the time, and Madhavrao seized the opportunity and asked Baba –

67. 'Baba, this Annasaheb (Dabholkar) here, says that he wants to write your life-story, to the very best of his ability, if you will but permit it.

68. 'Do not say, I am but a beggar, begging alms from door to door, subsisting somehow on bread, with or without greens!'

69. 'Of such a one as me, why do you want to write a life-story? It will only excite ridicule!' For, you are a diamond which must be set in a socket.'

70. If only you will give permission and extend your help, the book will write itself, or rather, you will get it written by me, by removing all the obstacles in the way.

71. Blessings of saints are, in themselves, the auspicious beginning of a book, while without your grace no writing can progress smoothly.

72. Reading my thoughts, Sai Samarth was moved by compassion and said, "Your wish will be fulfilled". I, at once, placed my head on his feet.

73. Placing his hand of benediction on my head, he gave me *udi* as *prasad*. Such is this Sai, well-versed in all the systems of divine faith and the liberation of his devotees from all the worldly ties.

74. On hearing Madhavrao's prayer, Sai took pity on me and began instilling courage to calm my agitated, impatient mind.

75. Knowing the sincerity of my purpose, words indicative of his consent came from his mouth. "Make a collection of all the authentic stories, experiences, conversations and talks, etc.

76. "It is better to keep a record. He has my full support. He is but the instrument; I myself will write my own story.

77. "My own tale I shall narrate myself and thus I shall fulfil the wishes of my devotee (to write my life-story). He should subdue his ego and offer it at my feet.

78. "He who conducts himself in this manner, in life, will not only get from me full assistance in the writing of the book, but I shall toil for him in every way.

79. "When ego and conceit are totally resolved, leaving not even a trace behind, it is then that I will dwell in him, writing the book with my own hand.

80. "When listening, reflection or writing is begun with this thought firmly governing it, then that work will be accomplished by myself, while he (Dabholkar) will only be made my instrument.

81. "A record must, of course, be kept. Inside the house or outside, or wherever else you may be, think of me, again and again, and you will enjoy peace.

82. "Listening to my stories, narrating them to others in a *kirtan*, contemplating on them will propagate love and devotion for me, which will destroy ignorance, instantly.

83. "Wherever there is faith and devotion together, I remain enslaved forever. Have no doubt about this. But otherwise, I always remain unattainable.

84. "When heard with virtuousness and a good feeling, these stories will generate devotion in the listeners' minds; self-experience and bliss will then follow most naturally and a state of perpetual joy will thus be attained.

85. "The devotee will have Self-realization, which will bring in tune, both, his *Jeeva* (Atman) and *Shiva* (Brahman); he will comprehend the Incomprehensible, which is without attributes, and the Supreme Spirit shall reveal Itself.

86. "Such is the reward, the fruit of my stories. What else would one want? This is also the ultimate objective of the *Shrutis* (*Vedas*) and so, by attaining this the devotee will be enriched.

87. "Where contentiousness prevails, ignorance and *Maya* abound. There is no thought for Deliverance and the mind is continually engaged in malicious, misconceived speculation.

88. "Such a one is not worthy of Self-knowledge. He is engulfed by ignorance alone. He can enjoy happiness neither on earth nor in heaven. Everywhere, and at all times, he is unhappy.

89. "Not for us, an obstinate maintenance of our point of view, nor the refutation of another's point of view. Nor yet, the exposition of the two contrary viewpoints. Why all this futile, unnecessary effort?"

90. 'Exposition of the two contrary viewpoints' was a phrase that reminded me of the promise I had given to my listeners, earlier.

91. At the time when the first chapter came to a close, I had promised the listeners that I will first tell them all, the story of how the name 'Hemad' was given to me.

92. When this tale-within-a-tale is heard, its appropriateness or otherwise, can be determined and your curiosity will be satisfied. In fact, this is also prompted by Sai.

93. Thereafter, the main story of Sai's life will be pursued from the point, where it was left off. Hence the listeners should listen to this story attentively.

94. At the end of every chapter we hear of its being 'composed by devotee Hemadpant'. But who is this 'Pant'?

95. This question will naturally arise in the minds of the listeners. And, to satisfy this curiosity they should listen attentively as to how the name came to be given (to the author).

96. From birth to death, sixteen purificatory rites of the human body have been prescribed in the *Shastras*, among which, the naming ceremony is one that is well-known to all.

97. Listen carefully, O listeners, to a short tale about this, which will explain the naming (of the author) as 'Hemadpant', in its proper course.

98. Mischievous as the present writer was, by nature, he was loquacious, too, and reviling and ridiculing — quite untouched by any knowledge or wisdom.

99. He knew not the importance and greatness of a Sadguru; but was the very image of evil-mindedness, priding himself on his own wisdom and eager for argumentation.

100. And yet, so powerful was his line of destiny, that by sheer good fortune, (and despite his resistance), he had the *darshan* of Sai's lotus-feet.

101. Had it not been for his indebtedness from the preceding births, to the great devotees Kakasaheb Dikshit and Nanasaheb Chandorkar, could he ever have gone to Shirdi?

102. Kakasaheb kept on pressing me, and the visit to Shirdi was fixed. But on the very day of departure, the decision was suddenly reversed.

103. This writer had a very close friend, who, initiated by his guru, was a devoted '*guru-putra*'. While at Lonavala, with his family, he was caught up in a very strange situation.

104. At that place of such salubrious climate, his only son, who was strong, healthy and virtuous, caught high fever and fell ill seriously.

105. All human remedies were tried. Charms and chants and religious rites were tried, too. Even the guru was called and made to sit at his bedside. But in the end, he gave the slip to everyone.

106. At the critical juncture, the guru was made to sit near him to avert the calamity. But everything was in vain.

107. Strange indeed, is human life! Whose is the son? Whose, the wife? So many things happen just because of the *karma*. Destiny, the result of our past *karma*, is inevitable.

108. When I heard these sad tidings, my mind became dejected and agitated. Is this all the utility that a guru has, that he could not even save an only son?

109. Such overwhelming power of destiny and *karma* weakened my resolve for Sai's *darshan* and became an impediment to my visit to Shirdi.

110. Why go to Shirdi at all? Just see the condition of my friend! Is this all the profit of a guru's company? What can a guru do before destiny?

111. If what is destined is bound to happen, then where is the need for a guru? Thus the visit to Shirdi was put off.

112. Why leave your own place? Why run after a guru? Why this love of inviting trouble in an otherwise happy existence?

113. Let us endure whatever is pre-ordained — be it pleasurable or distressing. What is the use of going to a guru, if the pre-destined cannot be averted?

114. And, much as one may wish to the contrary, things, events will come about according to the merit or otherwise, that one has earned. Nothing can prevent the working of Destiny. And, it was this, that ultimately dragged me to Shirdi.

115. Nanasaheb Chandorkar, who was a sub-divisional officer, set out from Thane, on a tour of Bassein and was waiting for his train at the Dadar railway station.

116. There was an hour in between, for the Bassein train to arrive and he thought he should utilise this time for some useful purpose.

117. Even as he got this impulse, a train going only up to Bandra, came to the station, which he then boarded.

118. On his reaching Bandra, I received a message from him and went to see him accordingly. He, at once, opened up the topic about Shirdi.

119. 'So, when do you propose to leave for Sai *darshan*? And, why all this slackness about visiting Shirdi? Why such delay in departure? How is it that there is no firmness of resolve in the mind?'

120. Nana's eagerness made me feel quite ashamed of myself. Very frankly, I then told him about the wavering in my mind.

121. Upon this, Nana gave me, very earnestly and lovingly, a piece of sound advice. On hearing it, happily, my desire to visit Shirdi was revived, once again.

122. Only after extracting from me a promise that I would start immediately, did Nana go. I too, then resolved to leave at once and went home.

123. I then, finished my packing, made all the necessary arrangements and set out, on the same evening, to go to Shirdi.

124. Thinking that the evening Mail will halt at Dadar, I paid the fare up to Dadar and bought a ticket.

125. As I boarded the train, which was still at Bandra, a Muslim[2] swiftly entered my compartment, even as the train was slowly moving out of the station.

126. Like a fly in the very first mouthful, my buying a ticket up to Dadar seemed to augur ill for my journey, right at the start.

127. Seeing all my luggage, 'Whereto this journey?' he asked me. So I said, 'I will go to Dadar and catch a train to Manmad'.

128. He, at once, alerted me, 'Do not get off at Dadar. The Mail will not halt there. Go straight to Victoria Terminus.'

129. Had this warning not come in good time. I would not have been able to catch the train at Dadar. And then, I know not what absurd ideas would have assailed the already wavering mind.

130. But, on that day, I was to seize that lucky chance and go to Shirdi. Hence all these intervening incidents took a turn favourable to me, quite unexpectedly.

131. Next day, I arrived in Shirdi at nine or ten o'clock, in the morning. Bhausaheb Dikshit had already been waiting for me, there.

132. It was in the year 1910, that this incident took place. Sathe *wada* was then the only place for the visitors to stay.

133. As I alighted from the *tonga*, my heart was so full of eagerness for Baba's *darshan*, that I could hardly wait to fall at his feet! Waves of joy surged up in my heart!

134. At that moment, Tatyasaheb Nulkar, one of Sai's great and well-known devotees, had just returned from the mosque and said to me 'Make haste and take *darshan* quickly!

135. 'Baba, with his devotees, has already come to the corner of the *wada*. Come as you are, for a '*dhool-bhet*'[3], first! For, he will then set out for the Lendi[4].

136. 'Have a bath, afterwards, and when Baba returns, then go to the mosque and have *darshan* comfortably, once again.'

137. On hearing this, I rushed to the place where Baba was and as I prostrated in the dust at his feet, I could hardly contain my joy.

138. Nanasaheb had already told me about Baba. But personally, I saw so much more than that. With his *darshan*, I considered myself blessed; and the eyes had fulfilled their purpose.

139. Never before had I heard of or seen Baba's comely figure. Seeing it now, my eyes were calmed; hunger, thirst, everything was forgotten; all senses stood still.

140. The touch I experienced, of Sai's feet, the kind enquiries that he made after me, were moments of highest plenitude in my life.

141. My indebtedness will always and inviolably be to those to whom I owe this saintly association, which has gladdened each and every part of my body.

142. Only those who help spiritual progress are the true kith and kin. No other relatives can be like them. This is what I believe in my heart.

143. So great is their obligation that I know not how I can repay them. So I only lower my head on their feet with reverence and with folded hands.

144. I was blessed with Sai's *darshan*. All my doubts were resolved. To add to it, I had Sai's sacred company. And I experienced the highest joy.

145. Such is the marvel of *Sai-darshan*! His mere *darshan* is enough to bring about a total change in one's manner and conduct. Whatever of the past *karmas* has remained, will be wiped out and a loathing for sensual pleasures will gradually grow upon you.

146. Sai's kindly glance destroyed the sins accumulated over past births and gave rise to the hope that his holy feet will bring me eternal joy.

147. By great good fortune have I found Sai's feet, which are as the great Manas lake[5], which will transform me, a crow, into a swan. Sai is an *acharya* (a spiritual head), a great *yogi*, a *Paramahansa*[6], the most excellent among the saints.

148. Annihilator of all sins, sufferings and adversity that he is, Sai's *darshan* and his sacred company has purified me greatly.

149. This meeting with Sai Maharaj was the fruit of my accumulated merit over several past births. Once this Sai pervades your vision, the whole creation appears to you as filled with Sai.

150. On the very day that I arrived in Shirdi, an argument arose between me and Balasaheb Bhate as to why one needs a guru at all.

151. Why give' up one's independence and voluntarily embrace subjugation to another? Where there is competence in the performance of one's duty, what is the necessity of a guru?

152. Each one must ultimately strive for himself. And if he doesn't, what can the guru do? He, who only stretches his limbs indolently, without so much as lifting a finger, what can anybody give to such a one?

153. This was the simple point of view I put forward. My opponents held a point of view exactly opposed to mine. Obstinate adherence to their own point of view, on either side, balanced equally. And so the controversy raged.

155. The opposite side firmly held that, however proficient in *Vedas* a learned pandit may be, without the guru's grace his deliverance would be confined only to the books.

156. A fierce argument, as to what is greater — Destiny or Free Will, raged. When you lean so heavily on destiny, what can happen? said I.

157. My opponents argued that whatever is to befall cannot be resisted. What is destined, is just inevitable. The most conceited among the egotists have wearied.

158. Who can work against Fate? You do one thing; the result is something else! Leave all your cleverness aside! But my ego would not accept defeat readily.

159. I said, 'But how can you say all this? Human endeavour is Power. What help can Fate give to one who sits back lazily?

160. 'Only by one's own efforts can one uplift oneself, the *Smritis* have proclaimed. And it is impossible that by ignoring this one should cross the ocean of this life safely.

161. 'Here one has to work for one's own Salvation. Why then, run after a guru? How will it suffice just to have a guru, unless one is watchful of one's own interests?

162. 'What *siddhi*, what success can a guru give to the fool who has thrown away his discriminating (between right and wrong) intellect, the means for achieving his end and his own self-purification?'

163. This debate remained inconclusive; nothing fruitful resulted from it. If anything, I lost my peace of mind, in the bargain. That is all I gained!

164. Arguing in this manner, where neither side showed the least sign of exhaustion, three-quarters of an hour passed by. So that, at last an end was put to it.

165. Later on, when we, along with others, went to the mosque, just listen to what Baba asked Kakasaheb!

166. "What was going on in the *wada*?" he said, "What was all that dispute about? And, what was this 'Hemadpant' saying?" He looked pointedly at me, as he said this, last.

167. Now, between the *wada* and the mosque, there is considerable distance. How then, did Baba know about this incident? I was quite astonished in my mind!

168. All the same I was struck dumb by these piercing words and hung my head in shame, that I should have behaved with such impropriety in the very first meeting!

169. This name, 'Hemadpant', which Baba gave me was, I felt, the direct result of the morning's heated disputation and I made a mental note that it must have been that incident which reminded Baba of 'Hemad'.

170. The great Yadav kings of Devgiri were the same as the Jadhavs of Daulatabad, and the prosperity of their kingdom in the thirteenth century had much enhanced the glory of Maharashtra.

171. One of their kings, Mahadev by name, was a valorous and mighty sovereign[7]. Equally famous was his nephew for his valour and virtuous deeds.

172. This latter, 'Ramaraja' by name, was a crest-jewel in the crown of the Yadav dynasty. And Hemadri, a man of many parts and exemplary qualities, was a minister to them both.

173. Author of a treatise on '*Dharmashastra*', a most munificent benefactor of the Brahmins, Hemadri was the earliest composer to arrange systematically, a code of conduct, which was consistent with *Shrutis* and *Smritis*.

174. Hemadri also wrote a book called '*Chaturvarga-Chintamani*', which discusses in detail, in the four chapters on religious vows and observances, charity, pilgrimages and *Moksha* or Salvation. Such was his famous compostition.

175. 'Hemadripant' of the Sanskrit language becomes 'Hemadpant' in the Prakrit (Marathi) language. He became well-known in those days as a great statesman, proficient in state-craft.

176. But his line of descent (*gotra*)[8] was from 'Vatsa'; mine from 'Bharadwaj'. His lineage (*pravara*) had five exalted persons; mine had three. He was *Yajurvedi*, and I was *Rigvedi*. He was well-versed whereas I was an ignoramus.

177. He belonged to the '*madhyandin*' branch of *Yajurveda*; I, to the '*Shakala*' branch of *Rigveda*. He was learned in *Dharmashastra*; but I was wild, incongruous. He had learning and wisdom while I was an inept fool. Why then this undeserved title to me?

178. He was a seasoned politician, a shrewd statesman; I was dull-witted and of little understanding. He was famous for '*Rajya-Prashasti*', his poetic composition in Sanskrit, whereas I was incapable of even a simple verse.

179. An adept that he was in the art of writing, I was an ignorant fool. He was learned, being proficient in *Dharmashastra*. But my understanding was very limited.

180. '*Lekhankalpataru*' is his collection of many and variegated poems. And I, Baba's ignorant child, cannot even compose a simple verse!

181. This was the period when Gora Kumbhar, Chokha Mahar, Sawata Mali, Nivrittinath, Jnaneshvar, Namdev and other promoters of *Bhagvat dharma*[9] had come up on the horizon.

182. In the same royal court which was adorned by learned gems like Pandit Bopadev, Hemadpant took his seat and earned fame among the learned and the talented.

183. Thereafter, Muslim armies invaded the Deccan from the north, spreading themselves out everywhere. And that was the end of the rule of the Deccan rulers.

184. But this title, no doubt, a tribute to my cleverness, was not conferred on me without a purpose. These incisive words were aimed at my contentious nature, and to shatter my egotism.

185. Strutting around with my meagre knowledge, mine was but an empty babble. But Baba opened my eyes to my inadequacy of knowledge, by the timely collyrium of admonition.

186. However, as stated earlier, the name — so significant and so well-timed — which came from Sai's mouth, I accepted as an ornament.

187. All the same, I felt I should learn my lesson and not allow contentiousness, a most evil quality, ever to touch me, even for a moment, for it brings on untold harm.

188. This name must have been given to me, so that I may shed my conceit about my argumentative power and that I may remember, to my dying day, to be always humble.

189. Even Shri Ram, the son of King Dasharath, who was an incarnation of God, of Knowledge itself, and a saviour of the Universe on whom the sages meditate all the time, even he used to catch the feet of his guru Vashishta.

190. Shri Krishna was the comely form of the Brahman Itself; but even he had to take a guru and brave great hardships, carrying logs of wood in the house of his guru Sandipani.

191. Compared to them, who am I? Why then, argue and debate at all? There is no Knowledge without the guru, nor Deliverance. This enunciation of the *Shastras* was thus firmly fixed in my mind.

192. Contentiousness is not good; nor so is the desire to vie with others. If there is no implicit faith, and courage and patience, spiritual progress cannot be made in the least.

193.   In the days that followed, I myself experienced this. In this way, with love, with a good feeling and a pure heart I humbly accepted the name, as an honour.

194.   But now, let this story, which refutes the idea of 'my party and the other party', which ends all argument and counter-argument, and is equally instructive for all, be set aside.

195.   And so, I have now narrated the purpose of the book, for whom it is meant, its connection with the subject, and also, the naming of the author as 'Hemad'.

196.   But now, enough of the lengthening of this Chapter! Later on, Hemad will offer humbly at Sai's feet, other detailed stories in their proper order. Listen attentively, O Listeners!

197.   Sai alone is our prosperity; Sai is our total consciousness of Bliss. He alone is our lasting detachment from worldly afflictions. And even our ultimate Refuge is none but Shri Sai!

198.   Be all ears to Sai's Story! By his grace alone can the fear of worldly life be overcome and the wicked sinful desires of this *Kaliyuga*[10] can be totally destroyed.

Weal be to all! Here ends the second chapter of
"*Shri Sai Samarth Satcharit*", called
'*The Purpose of the Book - Naming of the Author*',
as inspired by the saints and the virtuous,
and composed by his devotee, Hemadpant.

Notes

1. The eight-fold path of Yoga or *Ashtang-yoga* includes the following graded steps: *Yama, Niyama, Asana, Pranayam, Pratyahar, Dhyan, Dharana* and *Samadhi*.
2. This 'Muslim' was Sai Baba who appeared in the garb of a Muslim.
3. *Dhool-bhet*: Repairing to a temple or paying homage to an idol straight from the road (whilst the dust is on the feet), as by a pilgrim, on arrival.
4. A stream on the outskirts of Shirdi village.
5. Manas Lake or Sarovar: The name of a celebrated lake in the Himalaya mountains, the circumference of which is 54 miles.
6. A perfect man among Vedantins, who has reached the state of '*Sahaj-Samadhi*'.
7. In an inscription at Pandharpur, dated 1192, King Mahadev is referred to as "Proudh Pratap Chakravarti".
8. The connection of *gotra* and *pravara* may be stated thus: *Gotra* is the latest ancestor of a person by whose name his family has been known for generations while *pravara* is constituted by the sages or in some cases the remotest ancestors alone. *Pravara* commonly comprises three *rishis* but in some cases there may be one, two or five *rishis* but never four.
9. All these are the renowned saints of medieval Maharashtra.
10. *Kaliyuga* is the fourth age of the world, the iron age or that of vice. It commenced, according to some, 300, according to others, 3101, according to others 1370 years before the Christian era. Its duration is through 432,000 years, at the expiration of which period, the world is to be destroyed.

3

The Purpose of the Book – Baba's Approbation of His Gatha

MY OBEISANCE TO SHRI GANESH, TO SHRI SARASWATI, AND SHRI GURUMAHARAJ! TO THE FAMILY DEITY, TO SHRI SITA-RAMACHANDRA, MY MOST HUMBLE OBEISANCE! I BOW IN REVERENCE TO THE MOST VENERABLE GURU SHRI SAINATH!

1. Now, to resume the connection with the foregoing story, Sai gave his full assurance to me, saying, "You have my full consent to write my 'Life'".

2. "You do your own part well; have not the least hesitation in your mind. Trust my words fully and make a firm resolve in the mind.

3. "If my *'leelas'* are recorded, then any sins committed through ignorance will be dissipated. And when these are listened to, with faith and devotion, the cares and troubles of worldly life will be forgotten.

4. "Waves of love and devotion will surge on the ocean of listening, diving again and again, into which, will bring gems of wisdom into your hands."

5. On hearing this, my mind was cleared of all doubts. I bowed at Sai's feet and began writing his 'Life', as I could recollect it.

6. As these words came from Baba's lips, I committed the fact firmly to my mind, that this writing of Baba's life was definitely going to take place. And, I will only be a laborer pressed into service.

7. See how incomprehensible is Hari's *leela*! None but He can understand it! *Shruti, Dharmashastras, Vedas* — all fell silent. No one could fathom it!

8. Do not be taken in by those proficient in scriptures, or those engrossed in the letter (and not the Spirit) of the *Vedas*; the highly intelligent *Pandits* or those engaged in unprofitable wrangling, to prove a point with examples, as *ghat* (the earthern vessel), *pata* (cloth), etc.[1]

9. Shri Hari (God) is the sport of his own devotees (i.e. he dances to their tune), hungering for the simple and the guileless (devotees), and enslaved, altogether, by love. But to the hypocrites, He remains unattainable, always.

10. "Only in this lies your welfare. For me too, it means fulfilment of my descent upon this earth. And you see, this is what I always repeat frequently and this has been my constant concern.

11. "Moreover, one thing I tell you, Shama (Madhavrao Deshpande), I grant all the wishes of him who chants my name with love and faith, which, in turn, enhances his devotion to me.

12. "So that, he who fondly sings my praises or narrates the story of my life will always see me standing in front of him and behind, and everywhere around him.

13. "All the devotees who are attached to me, heart and soul, will naturally be delighted, listening to these stories.

14. "Whoever sings my praises in a *kirtan*, to him I shall give total, perfect happiness, peace and contentment, always. This is my promise.

15. "He who gives himself up to me with single-minded devotion, and sings my praises with full faith, remembers me and contemplates on me, the deliverance of him is my promise.

16. "Where my name, devotion, a record of my *leelas*, my *pothi* and my contemplation is constantly present in the heart, how can sensual desires ever arise there?

17. "Even if my stories are merely listened to, all the diseases will be cured. And I shall pull out my devotee from the jaws of death.

18. "Listen to the stories with reverence; reflect upon them deeply. After reflection, contemplate on them. This will bring great satisfaction.

19. "The mind will transcend the consciousness of self and the differentiated consciousness will dissolve. And by a single-minded absolute faith the heart (*chitta*) will become a mass of divine energy.

20. "Repetition of the name "*Sai, Sai*" will burn down sins, resulting from the evil desires of *Kaliyug*. A mere prostration before me is enough to destroy the past sins of speech and hearing."

21. Although the work (of writing Sai's 'Life') was no mean task, with profound reverence I obeyed his command. With so generous a giver as Baba, why should I accept a lowly position?

22. He got some (devotees) to build temples; some others, he got deeply interested in doing *kirtans*. Some he sent on pilgrimages; but as for me, he bade me write.

23. Of them all, I am the lowliest. By virtue of which quality in me, this Sai, this Ocean of Kindness and Mercy, was so pleased with me, I fail to understand.

24. But this is the marvel of guru's grace! So that, where there is not a drop of water, even on such a dry stiff tree, flowers bloom and fruit grows abundantly, without any effort.

25. In the days to come, some will build ashrams; some, temples; others will construct a *ghat* on the the river-bank, too! But let us follow the beaten track and read Sai's life-story.

26. Some offer *pooja* with great reverence; some others gently press his feet. But my heart was eager to sing Baba's praises.

27. What could be attained by meditation in the *Krita* or *Satyayuga*[2], by performing sacrifices in the *Tretayuga*, by ritualistic *pooja* in the *Dwarparyuga*, can all be attained in this *Kaliyuga* by praising the name of God and by worshipping the guru.

28. My unworthinesss (for this work) is blatant, as I am 'Jack of all trades, master of none'! Why then should I have taken upon myself, such a massive and difficult task?

29. To sit back, without making an effort will make me guilty of the sin of disobedience. And if I were to obey his command, how can I prove myself equal to the task?

30. After all, who can describe accurately and adequately, the inward state of Samarth Sai? Only when he himself bestows grace, for the sake of his own devotees, and himself makes his devotee describe it, is this possible.

31. But I have left no room for anyone to say as to why am I aspiring to do that which is beyond the reach of words.

32. For, the moment I took pen in hand, Baba subdued my ego, the 'I' in me, and took upon himself the writing of his own life-story. Thus all the credit for writing it, is entirely his.

33. This is, after all, the writing of a saint's life. Who else, but a saint himself, can do it? To try to comprehend the incomprehensible qualities of Baba is like attempting to embrace the boundless sky above.

34. Profound and unfathomable is his greatness, while, to describe it, I have not the intellectual capacity. It is better that he should take this work in his own hands and redeem his promise.

35. Baba, though I am a Brahmin by birth, yet I am without the two eyes of the *Vedas* and *Puranas*. And even though this is a blemish on my high birth (as a Brahmin), you have brought glory to it.

36. *Shruti* and *Smriti* are the two eyes of a Brahmin. When one of these is absent, he is blind in one eye, and when both are absent, he is totally blind. I am as deficient, as lowly as the latter.

37. But when you are my 'blind man's staff', why should I be distressed? Leaning on it, I will walk behind you, on the beaten track.

38. Now, how to proceed further, I, a lowly creature know not. You yourself must guide my mind to get your own purpose accomplished.

39. He alone understands his own artful ways, whose inconceivable, mysterious power moves the dumb to speak as Brihaspati[3], and the lame to cross the great Meru mountain[4].

40. I am but a slave at your feet. Do not disappoint me. So long as there is breath in this body, do get your own purpose accomplished.

41. And now, O my listeners! you have understood the purpose of writing this book. It is Sai himself, who will get it written. Nay he will himself write it for the benefit of his devotees.

42. What music it produces, is no concern of the flute or the harmonium. The effort comes entirely from the performer. Why then, should I become miserable?

43. Is the nectar that the *Chandrakant* (or the moon-gem)[5] exudes, a creation of its own? No, indeed! It is the marvel of the moon, her creation, as she rises on the horizon.

44. Again, when there is a high tide at sea, are the surging waves a handiwork of the sea? It cannot produce them on its own, but has once again, to depend upon the moon-rise.

45. Just as a buoy, with a red light, is anchored in the sea, to steer the ships clear of rocks and whirlpools, thereby speeding up their onward movements.

46. So these stories of Sainath, the sweetness of which puts even the nectar in the shade, will make easy and safe, the crossing of the otherwise impassable ocean of worldly life.

47. Blessed are these stories of the saints, which, as they enter the heart through the ear, clear it of the bodily conceit, so that the question of the pairs of opposites does not remain, at all.

48. And as these stories are being stored in the heart, so are all the doubts and questions in the mind, gradually resolved, pure Knowledge gets stored abundantly and the false puffed up pride in the body, climbs down.

49. Narration of Baba's pure, divine qualities, listening to it lovingly, will destroy the sins of his devotees. It is the most easy way for spiritual progress.

50. What is pure Brahman, beyond Maya? By what means can this Maya be overcome? And how does one endear oneself to God, by keeping his behaviour in conformity with *Karma dharma*?

51. What is the ultimate, the highest well-being of a man? What is devotion, deliverance and total detachment? What is *Varnashrama*

dharma[6] and *Advait* or non-duality? These and other such subjects are very abstruse.

52. Those who are interested in them should indulge their great desire for proficiency by reading various books written by Jnaneshvar, Eknath and others.

53. Restraint and control over the mind and the senses in *Kritayuga*, ritual sacrifices in the *Tretayuga*, ritualistic worship and *pooja* in the *Dwarparyuga* and chanting the '*naam*', narrating the stories and singing the praises of God in *Kaliyuga*, these are the easy ways for attaining Salvation.

54. To all the four *Varnas*, i.e. Brahmins, etc., there is only one means for Salvation and that is, listening to the stories of the guru. Be it a woman, or a *Shudra*, or even a caste-less one, this is but one means for them all.

55. Only he, with a store of accumulated merit, will listen to these tales. Some may even be overcome by sleep. Them too, Shri Hari will wake up!

56. Pining for unceasing sensual pleasures, and becoming abject when these cannot be had — even to such, the elixir of saints' 'Lives' will bring total freedom from sensual pleasures.

57. *Yoga, yajna* (sacrifices), *dhyan and dharana* entail arduous efforts. No effort is needed to listen to these tales, except your attention.

58. Such is this Sai's story, pure and sacred! May the loving, noble listeners listen to it. And even their five great sins[7] will be burned down and destroyed.

59. By the bondage of this worldly life are we relentlessly bound, and in the folds of this bondage is our true Self enveloped. Listening to the tale will loosen up these encircling folds and the original, real Self will be revealed.

60. And so, may these stories be remembered till we die. May their study be always carried on; so that they bring peace and contentment to the beings burnt in the conflagration of worldly life and its sorrows.

61. Reading the stories, listening to them with faith and devotion, contemplation will come of itself, readily, of Sai, whose form will then appear before the eyes and will be fixed in the heart.

62. May the worship of Sadguru be accomplished in this way, and a detachment from the worldly life come about. May a fondness grow within, for the remembrance of the guru and the mind be purified.

63. With this same thought in mind Sainath must have blessed me. Putting me forward as a pretext, he has himself accomplished his purpose.

64. Udders are painfully distended to overflowing with milk, but the cow will not let the milk flow without her calf. This is her natural instinct. Such is also Sai's liking.

65. As I, a Chatak bird, wished for this, my Mother rained on me a Cloud of happiness to quench, not only my mild thirst (small wish), but also that of the other devotees, abundantly.

66. Oh! for the marvel of (a mother's) devotion and love! Only a mother can instinctively feel her child's pangs of hunger and thrust the nipple of her breast into his mouth, without his even opening it.

67. But who will understand her strain, her weariness? The child is not even aware of it. But for the mother, who will offer the breast to the child, unasked?

68. When a child is adorned with little trinkets, he has neither any pleasure nor interest in it. Only the mother knows what joy and admiration it excites. Such are also the doings of the Sadguru.

69. And who but a mother will yearn with tenderness and concern as to who will satisfy her infant's childish pleasures? Rare is such tender, heart-felt affection!

70. To be born to a good righteous mother is indeed, the gift of God, enjoyed only by the most fortunate. The child knows not the birth pangs she suffers to bring it into the world.

71. Let me now narrate to you another of Baba's sayings with the same significance. O you virtuous listeners, give your respectful attention to it!

72. My government service was completed in the year 1916 and a suitable pension was fixed for me. It was also time to go to Shirdi.

73. It was the *Gurupoornima* day; devotees had gathered for the guru's *pooja*. Suddenly, on his own inspiration, Anna Chinchanikar made a request to Baba, strongly recommending my case.

74. In his genuine concern for me, Anna beseeched Baba thus, 'Have compassion on him (i.e. me) Baba, for the sake of his growing family.

75. 'Do give him another job. Is this pension going to suffice? Please do something whereby his worry is warded off.'

76. Baba then said in reply, "O, some service he will get; but he should now engage in my service and he will get happiness in this life.

77. "His plates will always be full. Never will they be empty so long as he lives! If he always seeks my protection with full faith in me, his troubles will end.

78. "People who say, 'What does it matter if we do as we like', know that they have strayed away from the path. And all those who have abandoned virtuous demeanour, we must, first and foremost, avoid.

79. "Take the other direction, when they come from the front. Consider them to be frightful; do not let even their shadow touch you, even if it means bearing some pain.

80. "How can he, who is devoid of a code of conduct, without character, thoughtless, neglectful of prescribed observances and ordinances, and indiscriminating between right and wrong, how can such a one achieve his real welfare?

81. "Moreover, do not repulse or reject anyone contemptuously — be it then, a dog, a pig, or a common fly. For, without some special bond from the previous birth, no one comes to us.

82. "Henceforward he (i.e. Hemadpant) should serve me with devotion and the Almighty take pity on him. He will attain the inexhaustible treasure laid up in Heaven.

83. "How, then, should this *pooja* be performed? How to know for certain, who I am? For, my (Sai's) physical body is mortal, while only Brahman, which is immortal, is worthy of being worshipped.

84. "(So, listen!) I pervade the Universe on all the four sides, in the form of the eightfold (*Ashtadha*) *Prakriti*[3]. Bhagvan Shrikrishna has also said the same to Arjuna in the *Gita*.

85. "Whatever exists in this sentient and insentient Universe as a name, a form or a shape is only myself bedecked as the eightfold *Prakriti*. It is also a marvel of my own creation!

86. "The mystical symbol 'OM' is expressive of me, and I alone, am the subject of that expression! Many are the things in this manifested Universe. But even these are all filled with me.

87. "Thus, where there is nothing different from the Self, what can one desire? I alone, pervade all the places in all the ten quarters of the Universe.

88. "With this awareness of my all-pervasiveness, where the feeling of 'I' and 'mine' has dissolved, what (objects) can be desirable? For all is filled with the Whole.

89. "Desires arise in the intellect and have no connection with the *Atman* or self. Since I (Sai Maharaj) am the embodiment of the *Atman*, how can there be any stirrings of desires?

90. "Worldly desires are of various types. But once the significance of 'who I am' is understood, they melt away as the hailstones by the heat of the sun's rays.

91. "I am not the gross form with the mind, intellect and other sense organs, nor the gigantic universe. Nor am I the unmanifest *Brahmanda*. I am the Seer, ancient and without beginning.

92. "In this way, I, who transcend the *gunas* and the senses, am not attracted to the sensual pleasures. There is not a place without me. I am neither the doer nor the one who causes it to be done.

93. "Only where there is a realisation that the intellect, mind and other sense organs are but gross instruments of the physical body, true detachment will appear, unveiling real knowledge.

94. "Oblivion of the Self is itself the appearance of *Maya* (or illusion that the world is real). Realisation of the Pure Bliss within is to know me, the Essence of all being.

95 "To such a one then, as me, when all the workings of the mind, all affections are turned, that is the true service and true worship

to me. To experience the bliss of consciousness (i.e. Me), is to be in that pure state which is knowledge.

96. "This *Atman* is Brahman; pure consciousness and bliss are Brahman. But this universe is not real and hence creates illusions about itself. In truth, the Brahman is me.

97. "I am Vasudev; I am 'OM'; I am eternal, pure, enlightened and emancipated. Worshipping Me with faith and devotion will only lead to self-upliftment.

98. "Thus, knowing who I am, I should truly be worshipped. Moreover, surrender to me whole-heartedly and become one with me."

99. When the river gives herself up to the ocean, can she ever come back again (as river)? Can she retain her separate identity as a river, once she has embraced the vast ocean?

100. An oil-soaked cotton-wick, as she meets the flame from the lamp, herself acquires greater brilliance and burns brighter. Such is also our progression at the feet of the saints.

101. He, whose mind reflects upon nothing except on *Allah Malik*, the Fountain of Life; who is unruffled and calm; has no desires or expectations and looks upon all equally, how can he have an identity separate from the Supreme Being?

102. Where the four divine qualities of detachment and desirelessness, freedom from conceit, from the pairs of opposites and non-possession, reside, how can consicouness of Self (as separate from Brahman), prevail there?

103. In short, when all these eight divine qualities dwell in Shri Sai, where is the room for the ego? How can I have an existence or individual identity apart from him?

104. For, my individual consciousnesss is but a tiny particle of his consciousness, which fills the Universe. So that to surrender my ego at Sai's feet is my most complete service to him.

105. In *Shrimad Bhagvat*, Bhagvan Shri Krishna has affirmed that 'he who serves me, sings my praises and surrenders to me whole-heartedly, becomes one with me'.

106. Even a worm that contemplates intently on the large black bee, is, by virtue of it, transformed into one. And so also the disciple, who worships his own guru, with the same intensity, becomes like his guru.

107. And yet, the degree of separateness implied by the word 'like' is something a guru cannot bear, even for a moment, For, there is no guru without the disciple and the disciple is inseparable from the guru.

108. And so, I have defined him, whom I have been commanded to worship. And here, I just remember a story, which because of its appropriateness in this context, I shall now narrate.

109. A Rohila (Pathan), who was greatly attracted by Baba's divine qualities, once came to Shirdi. For many days he stayed in Shirdi, during which time there grew in his heart, great love and devotion for Baba.

110. Like a fleshy, full-fed he-buffalo in his physique, and in behaviour, quite unrestrained and self-willed, he would heed no one. With only a *kafni*, reaching down to his feet, to cover him, he came and stayed at the mosque.

111. By day and by night, in the mosque or in the Chavadi (village hall), very fervently he would recite at the top of his voice, the *Kalmas* (verses) from the *Koran*, whenever it pleased him to do so.

112. Sai Maharaj himself was Peace Incarnate; but the villagers were growing very weary. Even at midnight his clamour continued disturbing everybody's sleep.

113. By day they toiled in the fields or in the woods under the scorching heat of the sun. But even at night there was no peaceful slumber. It vexed the people in the extreme.

114. Maybe, Baba was not troubled; but as for the people, it was a great ordeal. For at night too, they could not sleep in peace and comfort. They were enraged with the Rohila.

115. Caught between the devil and the deep sea, how long could they suffer patiently? Day and night, the irritating, disquieting noise continued. It became a source of great worry for them.

116. Hot-tempered as the Rohila already was, to add to it, he was receiving great encouragement from Baba. He then became even more uncontrollable than before.

117. Swollen with pride, he became arrogant and began abusing people, using foul language to people. He turned upon them, reckless and unrestrained. And then the village too, turned against him.

118, Sai, the most compassionate Mother, protector of all who surrendered to him, all the people in the village now turned to him, supplicating in piteous tones.

119. But Baba took no notice. On the contrary, it was the villagers whom he upbraided, saying, "Do not harass the Rohila; he is very dear to me.

120. "It is the wife of this Rohila who is dissolute, and cannot stay with him. Hence this termagant, this shrew, is eager to give him a slip, and come to me.

121. "The wretched woman has no modesty and is without shame. Even if she is driven out, she forces her way into the house.

122. "The moment he stops his shouting is the opportunity for this shrew to enter. But as he resumes his clamorous recitations, she flees, leaving him pure of body, speech and mind, which is greatly conducive to my peace and happiness.

123. "Do not cross his path; let him shout full-throatedly. Without him, I cannot pass the night in peace. He brings me great pleasure.

124. "His shouting in this manner is greatly beneficial to me. Thus this Rohila is my benefactor and a source of great comfort to me.

125. "Let him cry out to his heart's content, for there lies my good. Or else, that wicked Rohili will cause me great pain.

126. "Himself when he gets tired, he will, on his own, keep quiet. So will your purpose be achieved and that shrew will not wrestle with me, either."

127. When Maharaj himself said this, there was no other alternative. Moreover, if Baba's mind was not in the least perturbed, what business was it of ours, to complain?

128. As it is, the Rohila had boundless enthusiasm . And now to add to it, this encouragement from Baba! No wonder he ventured, unrestrained, on his loud recitation till his throat was parched.

129. The people were all simply amazed! How forgiving was Baba! What would have normally brought on a splitting headache, engrossed him so deeply!

130. Oh, how horrifying was that shouting! It was a wonder his throat did not run dry! As for Baba, his insistence was only this, "Do not intimidate the Rohila!"

131. To look at, the Rohila was as a madcap, but what veneration he had for Baba! And how happily he recited the *Kalmas*, in strict conformity with his religion!

132. Who is bothered whether the voice be melodious or harsh? Each time the inspiration seized him he would break out into a chant of Allah.

133. With the natural gift of a rattling voice, the Rohila regularly and unceasingly, kept on proclaiming loudly, '*Allah-ho-Akbar*', and the *Kalmas*, with great pleasure.

134. Baba shrank from being defiled by those who had a loathing for God's name and hence he said, why drive away needlessly, this Rohila who is so fond of singing God's praises?

135. "Where my devotees are singing my praises, I am present there, wide awake all the time". Such is the utterance of God, to prove the truth of which, Baba gave this experience.

136. One who subsisted on alms — dry food with or without gravy, and sometimes went without food altogether, to such a Rohila, whence a wife? And therefore, how will she go to Baba?

137. Pauper that the Rohila was, even a paisa was precious to him. What then, of his marriage? And, of his wife? Moreover, Baba was a celibate since childhood! Obviously, the whole story was fictitious!

138. Let him (Rohila) then cry himself hoarse! Baba was so very happy with the *Kalmas* that, day and night, he listened to them, sleep being poison compared to them.

139. Where the superior wisdom of the *Kalmas*, and where the hollow complaints, petty grievances of the villagers! It was really to bring the villagers to their senses that Baba made all this pretence!

140. Such indeed, was his import. In this way, Baba clearly brought it to the perception of all that 'I like the company of the Rohila because he loves God's name'.

141. To one, who sees only the Divine Spirit in the perceiver, the object of perception and the act of perceiving, all are equal — a Brahmin or a Pathan, or anyone else.

142. And now, listen to the sweet words that came out of Baba's mouth, on an occasion when the midday *arati*[9] was just over and people were about to go home to their respective houses.

143. "Wherever you are, whatever you do, always remember this one thing well, that I come to know, all the time, and in detail, what you are doing.

144. "And I, about whom you have such an experience, am nearest to all, and dwell in everybody's heart. I travel everywhere and am the Lord and Master of all.

145. "I fill this entire creation of beings, both animate and inanimate, and yet remain. All this is the Divine Scheme, in which I am the principal manager of the strings.

146. "I am the Mother of this Universe and all the beings therein; I am also the point of equilibrium of the *Trigunas*[10], — I alone provoke all the senses and, the Creator, Sustainer and Destroyer of this Universe am I, too!

147. "He who turns his attention to me can have no difficulties, whatsoever. But he who forgets me will be ruthlessly whipped by *Maya*.

148. "This visible world is my own manifestation, be it a worm or an ant, a pauper or a king. This immeasurable creation of the movable and the immovable, is really Baba's very Self".

149. How interesting, how significant is this hint! Between God and the saints, there is no separateness, as their incarnation on this earth is purely for the uplift of both the animate and inanimate creations, equally.

150. And should one want to be absorbed totally, at the guru's feet, he should go on singing the praises of the guru, or perform a *kirtan* of the guru's story, or at least, listen to such a story, with a devout mind.

151. A seeker should so listen to it that the distinction between the listeners and what he is listening to, will dissolve and as he passes into a state of *Unmana*[11], he will experience the presence of God Almighty!

152. While fully engrossed in the day-to-day, worldly life, if perchance a saint's story comes to the ear, it, by its very nature, benefits the listener, without an effort on his part.

153. If then, it be heard with a devout heart, how great a merit will come to hand! Let the listeners think of this in their minds, for their own benefit.

154. By that means, a fondness and love for the guru's feet will be cultivated and gradually, a state of highest well-being will set in. No other discipline or religious observances will be necessary. The highest good of human life will thus be attained.

155. When the mind is thus disciplined, the longing for listening to the tales will grow and the bondage of the sensual pleasures will break away, of its own. A state of Supreme Joy will then be experienced.

156. Hearing Baba's sweet words, I resolved in my mind that from then onwards I would give up serving men and devote myself only to the service of the guru.

157. And yet, in my heart there was a restlessness, a longing. "Some job he will get", was what Baba had said in reply. Will I get a proof of it?

158. That Baba's word will be in vain, was something that usually did not happen. And so, maybe, I will once again be connected with serving men; but it will never bring me any real benefit.

159. Self-prompted as Anna's question was, yet it is not as though I did not desire it. And this desire of mine was not 'Prarabdha'[12].

160. Inwardly, I too, felt that I should get a job, as a means of supporting my family. And Sai tempted me, all the while, pointing his finger at the piece of jaggery as he administered a potion to me.

161. I drank the potion in the hope of the jaggery, and, by my good fortune, I was satiated. Quite unexpectedly, I got a job[13], and in my greedy desire for money, I accepted it.

162. But how much can one eat even of a sweet? A point must come when the jaggery also repels. And then it was, that the nectar of Baba's teaching tasted so truly excellent!

163. The employment was not of long duration, and went away the way it came. And Baba put me back in my place, much to my enjoyment of my true and lasting happiness.

164. This entire creation of animate and inanimate things is truly, a manifestation of God. But the Almighty is beyond this Universe, the highest, Supreme Being.

165. God is not separate from the world, but this Universe is distinct from God. From the time of its creation, the Universe is filled with animate and inanimate things, whose main base is God.

166. Know that there are eight places of God's worship, such as, the idol, the sacrificial altar and others[14]. But, of them all, guru is the greatest.

167. Himself the Supreme Brahman, even Shri Krishna caught the feet of guru Sandipani and has said, 'When the Sadguru is remembered, I (i.e. Narayan) am pleased.

168. 'A thousand times would I like that the Sadguru's praises be sung rather than mine.' Such is the excellence and profound significance of a Sadguru.

169. He who turns his back to guru-worship is truly a wretched sinner, who has to suffer the torture of journeys between births and deaths. He ruins every prospect of self-upliftment.

170. Again a birth, again death! Wandering between the two has been our lot. Therefore, let us listen to the guru's story and attain self-deliverance.

171. Stories which casually come from the saints' lips can open up the knots of ignorance and become our preservers in the greatest of calamities. Hence let us store them up in our hearts.

172. What trying times are ahead, we know not, nor what forces will be at work. For all this is *Allahmiya's* sport! And his loving devotees are but spectators in it.

173. Without possessing the power of wisdom, I still got an all-powerful guru like Sai Samarth. Should this be considered as due to my powerful destiny? No, indeed! This too, is a sport of his!

174. And now, I have stated the purpose of this book; I have also narrated the assurance I have received from him, in which context, Baba guided us about his true nature and how he should be worshipped.

175. In the next chapter, O listeners! you will hear as to how Shri Sai Samarth first appeared in Shirdi.

176. And, all of you, young and old, keep aside for a moment your worldly cares and listen, you artless, trusting ones, to this extraordinary story of Sai.

177. Although he was quite unruffled and unaffected, as an incarnation of God, this Sai enacted different roles, engaging himself in the worldly life as an ordinary man, subject to the influence of *Maya*.

178. He, whose holy feet can be meditated upon by the short *mantra*[15] 'Samarth Sai', and who moves the strings for the deliverance of his devotees from the worldly life, his stories are most purifying and sacred.

179. To sum up, most holy is this Life of Sai. He who reads it and he who listens to it, are both blessed, for their hearts will be purified.

180. When the stories are lovingly listened to, the worldly sorrows will be dispelled; Sai the Compassionate One, will be propitiated and Pure, Absolute Knowledge will appear.

181. Sloth; an inattentive, wandering mind; attachment to sense objects and indulgence of the senses — these are impediments to attentive listening. Push these obstacles away and the listening will give you pleasure.

182. We need no religious vows or their ritualistic conclusions. Nor are fasts or mortification of flesh necessary. Even pilgrimages and journeys undertaken on their account are not required. Listen to this life-story and that is enough!

183. But our love should be steadfast and genuine; we should have grasped the very essence of true devotion. Only then can we attain the highest goal of human existence, i.e. *Moksha* or salvation. Then the obstacle, posed by ignorance, will be destroyed.

184. We need not exert after other means; we shall listen to Sai's life-story, so that all *karma*[16], past and present, is exhausted without leaving a trace behind.

185. A miser, wherever he may happen to be, has before his mind's eye, day and night, his buried treasure. In the same way may Sai be present in our hearts.

Weal be to all! Here ends the third chapter of
"Shri Sai Samarth Satcharit", called
'The Purpose of the Book – Baba's Approbation',
as inspired by the saints and the virtuous,
and composed by his devotee, Hemadpant.

Notes

1. Sri Ramakrishna Paramahansa made a similar remark to Pratap Chandra Mazumdar: "You have had enough of lectures, arguments, quarrels, discussions and dissensions. Can such things interest you any more? Now gather your whole mind and direct it to God. Plunge deep into God." (see *'The Gospel of Sri Ramakrishna'* by M. Sri Ramakrishna Math, Madras. 1947. Ch. 23, p. 407.)

2. *Yuga* = an age. The four *yugas* are: *Krita* or *Satyayuga, Tretayuga, Dwaparyuga,* and *Kaliyuga. Satyayuga* is the first age of Universal purity and probity, the golden age, comprising 17,28,000 years. *Tretayuga* is the second, comprising 12,96,000 years. *Dwaparyuga* is the third, comprising 8,64,000 years and *Kaliyuga,* the fourth is the iron age or age of vice, the duration of which is through 4,32,000 years, at the expiration of which period the world is to be destroyed.

3. Brihaspati is the Guru or preceptor of the gods.

4. The sacred mountain Meru is in the centre of the seven continents, supposed to mean the high land of Tartary, immediately to the north of the Himalaya mountains.

5. *Chandrakant* is a fabulous gem supposed to be formed from the congelation of the rays of the moon and accordingly, to dissolve under the influence of her light.

6. *Varnashrama* is the system of four castes (*varnas*) (based on occupations) and four stages of life (called *ashramas*), for the first three castes (Brahmins, Kshatriyas and Vaisyas), namely, *Brahmacharya* (student's stage), *Grihastha* (householder's stage), *Vanaprastha* (forest-dweller's stage) and *Sanyas* (stage of a recluse), sanctioned by the Hindu religion.

7. The five heinous sins are: killing a Brahmin, drinking spirituous liquors, stealing gold, committing incest with one's mother or adultery with the wife of one's guru, and associating with a person guilty of any of the four.

8. See *Bhagvad-Gita*: 7:4-'Earth, water, fire, air, ether, mind and reason also, and egoism — these are the eightfold divisions of my nature" (*Bhagvad Gita, The Lord's Song* by Annie Besant). *Ashtadha Prakriti* is a radical form or predicament of being. Eight are reckoned; *viz.* Earth (*Prithvi*), water (*Udak*), fire (*Agni*), air (*Vayu*), ether (*Akash*), the affections or heart (*Mana*), the understanding or mind (*Buddhi*), the consciousness or sense of personal being (*Ahankar*). To the first five of these, termed the gross or solid elements are attached, as respectively related to them, the *Panchsookshmabhoote* (*gandha* or smell to earth, *rasa* or taste to water, *roopa* or sight to fire, *sparsha* or touch to air and *shabda* or speech to ether).

9. The ceremony of waving around an idol or guru, a platter containing burning lamps and accompanied by songs in praise of the deity or the guru.

10. *Trigunas* are the three qualities incidental to created being, *viz.*, *Sattva*, *Rajas* and *Tamas*.

11. *Unmana* means transcending the three states of consciousness and the knowledge thereof.

12. See note 16 below.

13. This was a special appointment in the Secretariat, for a period of six months, which Shri Dabholkar got, five years after his retirement.

14. The eight places or objects of God's worship are: idol, the sacrificial altar, fire, heart, sun, water, a Brahmin and Gurudev.

15. *Mantra* is a mystical word or sentence; a formula sacred to a deity.

16. *Kriyaman* means the actions of the present life with reference to merit and demerit, and the consequent pleasure and pain to be experienced in births yet to be. *Sanchit* is the stock acquired through the good and evil works of the present and all the past births. *Prarabdha* is that part of the stock which is to be worked out in the present life and is therefore referred to as 'Destiny'.

4

Descent of Sai Samarth in Shirdi

MY OBEISANCE TO SHRI GANESH, TO SHRI SARASWATI, AND SHRI GURUMAHARAJ! TO THE FAMILY DEITY, TO SHRI SITA-RAMACHANDRA, MY MOST HUMBLE OBEISANCE! I BOW IN REVERENCE TO THE MOST VENERABLE GURU SHRI SAINATH!

1. In the two chapters following the "Invocation of the Divine", the object of this book has been stated and for whom it is meant, and its relationship with the subject of the book has also been sufficiently explained.
2. Now, listen to the reason, why these saints have to descend on this earth; or, in other words, what is this difficult task that necessitates their incarnating in human form, on this earth?
3. O my revered listeners! I am but a speck of dust from your feet, and am not ashamed of entreating you for the favour of your attention.
4. Delightful indeed, is the life-story of a saint. And, in that, this is the nectar-sweet story of Sai's life! May his faithful devotees drink of it deeply and be filled with joy.
5. When the Brahmins disregard the rules of conduct laid down by the *Varnashram*[1], and the Shudras aspire to become the Brahmins; when the Acharyas (the religious heads) are shown disrespect, to the extent of trying to castigate them;
6. When no one follows the religious precepts, everyone regarding himself as learned and wise and each one trying to score over the other, but no one prepared to listen to anyone;

7. When there is a total disregard to what is proper or improper for use, in general, or as food, and also, a disregard to the code of conduct (prescribed by religion); so that the Brahmins themselves consume meat and spirituous liquors openly, in front of everyone;

8. And, under the cover of '*dharma*', secretly perpetuate oppression and tyranny, stoking the embers of hatred between religious sects; all of which exasperates the common folk;

9. When the Brahmins shirk the daily rituals of '*Sandhya-snana*'[2], the orthodox tire of performing ceremonies and rituals for the propitiation of gods, and the yogis neglect yogic practices of chanting the name, meditation and penance — then the time is ripe for the appearance of saints on earth.

10. When men look upon wealth, honour, wife and children as the only source of happiness and turn away from the spiritual path, then it is that the saints appear on this earth.

11. When people fail to attain the highest goal of human life due to laxity in observing *dharma*, then for the revival of *dharma* the saints incarnate in human form.

12. When people dissipate their energies in physical pleasures of the palate and sex, to the detriment of health, longevity and prosperity, and miss the chance of self-upliftment altogether, then the saints appear on the earth.

13. For preservation of *varnashramdharma*, and eradication of unrighteousness; for the protection of the poor, the meek and the suffering, is the incarnation of saints on earth.

14. Essentially, the saints themselves are emancipated souls, engaged in the uplift of the meek and the lowly, all the time. Their '*avatar*' (incarnation) is only for the benefit of others, for they have no selfish interests.

15. They lay down a firm foundation of renunciation around the shaky structure of worldly life to erect the temple of spirituality, thus redeeming the devotees effortlessly.

16. They accomplish their religious mission of the revival of *dharma*, thereby fulfilling their purpose, after which they give up their mortal coil.

17. '*Jeevatma*' (individual soul) is the Supreme Spirit or God Himself, who brings joy to the whole world. And God is the Guru himself, who confers happiness and weal.

18. He is also the abode of Transcendent Love; He is the constant, eternal and the undifferentiated Whole; He is beyond space, time and causality and is indivisible.

19. Speech in all its four stages, *viz. Para, Pashyanti, Madhyama* and *Vaikhari*[3], has failed to describe Him. Nor have the *Vedas*, with all their wisdom, been able to do so and have accepted defeat, under the cover of '*Neti, neti*' (Not this, not this).

20. The *Shat-Darshanas*[4] and the *Shat-Shastras*[5] are shamed into silence; the *Puranas*[6] and the *Kirtans*[7] too, are exhausted in their attempts at description. Ultimately, the only means that is left is to make obeisance, surrendering to Him with all your actions, speech and thought.

21. Listening to the Story of such a saint as Sai, which is filled with his marvellous *leelas* and sacred tales, may our ears be purified.

22. He is the moving impulse of all the sense organs, and has given me the inspiration to write this book. It is he on whose prompting this 'Life-story' has come so effortlessly, in an orderly manner.

23. He dwells in the hearts of all and moves at will in this Universe, within and without. Why then, should I worry, needlessly?

24. As one recollects his many excellent qualities one after the other, the mind stands still. How then, can words ever describe him? Absolute silence is the only way to describe.

25. The nose smells the fragrance of a flower; the skin experiences the hot and cold touch; the eyes feast on beauty; each brings pleasure to itself.

26. The tongue, no doubt, experiences the sweetness of sugar, but cannot convey the experience to others. In the same way, I know not how to describe the virtues of Sai.

27. Only when the Sadguru himself so wishes he will inspire his own chosen ones to describe most aptly, and in great detail, that which is otherwise beyond description.

28. These words are not superficial, a mere formality; but spring from the feelings from the heart, hence I crave your respectful attention.

29. As Gangapur and Narsimhawadi, as Audumbar and Bhillawadi[8], so is Shirdi a famous place of pilgrimage on the banks of the holy river Godavari.

30. Oh, for the sacred banks of the Godavari and her holy waters! Oh for the cool breezes that play on her surface! These dispel the darkness of ignorance from the worldly life indeed!

31. The greatness of the Godavari which is so well-known in the whole world is most impressive. Great saints, one more eminent than the other, came from there.

32. Many are the places of pilgrimage on the banks of this Gomati, which are described in the *Puranas*, the water from which not only washes away the sins but also liberates from the sorrows of this life, when drunk or bathed in.

33. The self-same Godavari, as she winds her way by Kopergaon, in the Kopergaon *taluka* (subdivision), in the Ahmednagar district, guides the pilgrim to Shirdi.

34. Crossing over to the opposite bank of Godavari, as the *tonga* enters Nimgaon, which is about six miles away from the river bank, Shirdi comes within sight, right in front.

35. Nivritti, Jnanadev, Muktabai, Namdev, Janabai, Gora, Gonai, Tukaram, Narhari, Narsibhai, Sajan - *kasai* [butcher], Sawata - *mali* [gardener].

36. These have been saints of yore; and saints there have been even in the recent past. These virtuous saints have regarded the world as one family and have been the refuge of the afflicted and the suffering.

37. The great saint Ramdas left the banks of the Godavari to appear on the banks of the river Krishna, for the salvation of the world.

38. In the same way, Shri Sai, this greatest among *yogis*, appeared near Godavari, by the great good fortune of Shirdi, and for the deliverance of the world.

39. 'Parees' [or the philosopher's stone], turns a piece of iron into gold by its touch and the analogy of the *Parees* is used to describe

the saints. But so remarkable are the ways of the saints that they transform their devotees completely, raising them to their own exalted state.

40. Transcending all distinctions, to see the Brahman reflected in the entire Universe, animate and inanimate, to regard the glory of this creation as the undivided glory of Brahman;

41. And in this way, when the true knowledge, the realization that the whole Universe is nothing but 'I am that I am', comes, who can then describe the glorious feeling of joy that it will bring? He [the seeker] will attain to a high state of purity and goodness.

42. When such oneness [of the Self with the Universe] is experienced, so that nothing is known which is other than the Self, then to whom can one be hostile? And of whom, afraid?

43. As Damaji at Mangalvedha, Samarth Ramdas at Sajjangad, Narsimhasaraswati at Wadi, so was Sainath the saint of Shirdi.

44. Extremely difficult to accomplish, to cross over, as this worldly life is, he who has conquered it, is adorned by Peace, who is the Treasure of Knowledge personified;

45. A retreat for the Vaishnavites, the most benevolent among the benevolent, Karna[9] incarnate in bestowing spiritual wisdom, such is this Sai, the quintessence of Truth.

46. Without attachment to the transient, absorbed totally in the Self, and intent on attaining the highest goal of human life — how can this state of his being be described?

47. The worldly state holds for Him no prosperity or poverty; nor does He rejoice or grieve for the pleasures of the other world. His inner being is crystal clear as a mirror; the speech, always a shower of nectar.

48. He, in whose eyes a king and pauper, the poor and the meek are all equal; who knows not respect or disrespect towards his own self, he is himself the all-pervading God.

49. He moved and conversed with the common folks and watched with them the dancing and gesticulating of the *Muralis*[10]; he nodded appreciatively as he listened to the songs and *ghazals*[11] And yet his *Samadhi*[12] was unperturbed.

50. Allah's name constantly on his lips, is the sign to recognize him; in the dark night of all beings he awoke to the Light and what was day to other beings was night for him. Inwardly, he was as tranquil as the sea.

51. To which ashram [Stage of life] he belonged was something beyond human speculation; for he followed no code of conduct laid down for the specific ashrams. Usually he does not leave his place and yet he knows everything that is happening anywhere.

52. Though outwardly he held a splendid *durbar* [royal court] regularly and related a thousand and one stories, yet inwardly he was committed to silence.

53. Leaning against the wall he would stand and would go on his rounds, morning and afternoon, to the Lendi or *Chavadi*, yet his state of Self-absorption was constant.

54. I know not in which birth, on what occasion, at what time and in what manner, I must have undertaken penance that Sai should have taken me under his wing thus.

55. Wicked from birth that I am, how can I ever claim this to be the fruit of my penance? Nay, it is Sai himself who loves the meek and the lowly and surely this is nothing but his grace.

56. Though born a *siddha*, his behaviour was that of a *sadhaka* or seeker. By nature unconceited and very humble, he strove to please all.

57. As Eknath to Paithan, Jnaneshvar to Alandi, so did Shri Sai bring glory to the soil of Shirdi.

58. Blessed are the stones and the blades of grass, in Shirdi which, without effort, kissed Baba's feet every day, and held the sacred dust from his feet on their head.

59. Shirdi itself is our Pandharpur; Shirdi, our Jagannathpuri, our Dwarka; Shirdi alone is our Gaya, Kashi-Vishweshwar; and even our Rameshwar is in Shirdi[13].

60. Shirdi alone is our Badrikedar, our Nasik-Tryambakeshwar, Ujjain, Mahakaleshwar and also Mahabaleshwar-Gokarna.

61. Sai's sacred company in Shirdi is our *Agam* (scriptures on which temple worship is mainly founded) and *Nigam (Dharmashastras)*.

That itself is the assuagement of the sufferings and pain of the worldly life and the easiest way to deliverance.

62. Samarth Sai's *darshan* is for us the *Yoga-sadhan* and conversing with him is the washing away of our sins.

63. Pressing his feet softly is as the sacred bath at the confluence of the three rivers — Ganga, Yamuna and Saraswati and partaking of the holy water off his feet means the eradication of all desires.

64. His command to us is as an aphorism of the *Vedas* or a Gospel Truth. And eating his *Udi* and *prasad* is sanctifying, in every sense of the word.

65. Sai alone is to us the Supreme Brahman; in him is our highest goal of human life. Sai himself is Shri Krishna, Shri Ram, and he is our eternal refuge.

66. Sai is beyond the pair of opposites (such as joy and sorrow, anger and love, etc.); he is never elated or depressed, but always absorbed in the Self; and forever, the Ultimate Reality.

67. But Shirdi was only the centre from which emanated Baba's influence very widely, to Punjab, to Calcutta, to Gujarat, to the Deccan, to Karnataka — to all over India.

68. Sai's *Samadhi* at Shirdi is the place for the gathering of all saints, where, as one makes one's way, the bondage of worldly life breaks down at every step.

69. A mere *darshan* of this *Samadhi* is truly a fulfilment of this human birth; how then, can I describe the great good fortune of those who have spent their entire lives in his service?

70. On the mosque and on the *wada* (*Samadhi Mandir*), rows of beautiful flags flutter, high up in the skies, as if beckoning the devotees with their hands.

71. Baba became renowned as *Mahant* or *Sadhu*, and his fame spread from village to village. Some prayed to him, taking vows with true faith; some gained peace of mind by his *darshan*, alone.

72. Whatever the thoughts in anybody's mind, be they pure or vile, their minds experienced peace and calm by his *darshan*. In their hearts people were simply amazed.

73. The same marvellous experience of the *darshan* of Vitthal-Rakhumai in Pandharpur, was given by Sai Baba to his devotees in Shirdi.

74. Should anyone think this is an exaggeration, let them hear the words of Gaulibua, a dedicated devotee of Vitthal, to remove their doubts.

75. He was a *Warkari*[14] from Pandharpur, who, out of his devotion to Baba, came to Shirdi once a year, as regularly as he went to Pandharpur.

76. With a donkey and, for companion, a disciple, Bua set out on the pilgrimage with the constant chant of 'Ram-Krishna-Hari' on his lips.

77. Ninety-five years of age, he spent the '*Chaturmas*'[15] on the banks of the Ganga and the remaining eight months at Pandharpur, which made it possible for him to meet Baba, once a year, during these journeys.

78. Gazing into Baba's face, he would become humble and exclaim, "This, truly, is Pandharinath incarnate, the Refuge of the friendless and destitute, the All-merciful One!

79. "Does one become a saint merely by wearing a *dhoti* with a silk border? No, indeed! Here, one has to wear out one's bones, turn one's blood into water, by one's own arduous efforts!

80. "How can one become God, for nothing! But truly he (Sai) and he alone is Pandharirao! With a firm belief that this world is illusory, perceive the divinity behind it."

81. When such are the words of a great devotee of God, who is dedicated to the worship of Pandharinath, then what experience can a base, lowly creature like me, have? Let the listeners experience this for themselves!

82. With his great fondness for chanting God's name, Baba repeated '*Allah Malik*', ceaselessly and would often make his devotees hold a *naam-saptah* (a week-long chanting of the Name), in front of him which would go on day and night, continuously.

83. Once, Das Ganu was commanded to start a *Naam-saptah*, and Das Ganu said, 'Yes, but Vitthal must appear to me'.

84. Laying his hand on his heart, Baba said peremptorily, "Yes, yes, Vitthal will appear in form, before you! Only, the devotee must have faith enough!

85. "Dankapuri (Dakore in Gujarat) of Dakurnath, or Pandharpur of Vitthalraya, or Dwarka of Ranchchod, — everything is in Shirdi itself. You do not have to seek it far.

86. "After all, is Vitthal going to appear from a secret place? Moved by the intense love of his devotees, he will incarnate in this very place, for you.

87. "By his devoted service to his old parents, Pundalik had won over the Lord of Lords, who stood resting on a single brick, just for the love and devotion of Pundalik."

88. And so, as the *saptah* came to an end, it is said that Das Ganu did have the *Vitthal-darshan*, in Shirdi itself! So much for the truth of Baba's words!

89. Once, Kakasaheb Dikshit was sitting in meditation after his early morning bath, as was his daily practice, when he had the *darshan* of Vitthal.

90. Later, when he went for Baba's *darshan*, see the wonder of what Baba said to him, "So, Vitthal Patil had come, isn't it? And you did meet him, I'm sure!

91. "But mind you, that Vitthal is very elusive! Hold on to him fast and fix him in place, forcibly. Or else, he will give you the slip, if you are inattentive, even for a moment."

92. But this was just the incident of the morning, while later in the day, as the sun came overhead at noon, see how there was yet another proof of the glorious vision of Vitthal.

93. Someone from another village came to Shirdi bringing with him quite a few pictures of Vithoba of Pandharpur, with the intention of selling them.

94. And Dikshit was simply amazed to find them the exact replicas of the Vitthal who had appeared to him during his meditation, that morning! Baba's words at once, came to his mind.

95. With great love Dikshit bought one of the pictures, paying the price to the seller and with great devotion installed it for *pooja*.

96. Listen now, to yet another fascinating story, which, once again, brings out Sai's reverence towards the worship of Vitthal.

97. One Bhagvantrao Kshirsagar, whose father was a great devotee of Vitthal, used to go to Pandharpur very often.

98. There was an idol of Vitthal for daily *pooja*, in his house. But after the father's death, *pooja*, food-offerings, everything stopped. Even the annual rites and ceremonies for the dead ancestors were forgotten.

99. Not a word was ever uttered about the annual visit to Pandharpur! When Bhagvantrao came to Shirdi, Baba remembered his father, saying, "He was my friend.

100. "And since he (Bhagvantrao) is the son of that friend, I have dragged him over to Shirdi. He makes no food-offerings to the gods any more. He keeps me hungry, too.

101. "Even Vitthal, he has kept without food. So have I brought him to Shirdi. I shall now remind him about everything and thus make him perform the daily *pooja*".

102. On one occasion, knowing how it was the specially opportune time of *Parvakaal*[16], Das Ganu wished to take a dip in the river at Prayag[17] and came to Baba for his permission.

103. Baba replied that there was no need to travel so far, for that. Shirdi itself is our Prayag. Let there be firm faith in your mind.

104. And indeed, what a marvel of marvels! Even as he placed his hand on Baba's feet, water trickled down from both his toes, the twin streams of the holy Ganges and Yamuna oozed out in a trickle!

105. At the sight of this miracle, Das Ganu was choked with emotion. How great was Baba's favour! It moved him to tears of joy and gratitude.

106. Love brimmed up in his heart and stirred him to poetic utterance, which found its satisfaction only after describing Baba's boundless power and incomprehensible *leelas,* in verse.

107. Charming is this Das Ganu's *pada*! And, to satisfy the listeners's eager desire to hear it, I give here, at this appropriate juncture, the sublime song, as promised earlier:

[*Pada*]

O Sadguru, boundless is your power, marvellous your *leelas*!
To ferry the dull and the ignorant across the Ocean of life, you
are for ever the ark.   (Refrain)
Veni Madhav you became and brought Prayag at your feet,
Only to make Ganga and Yamuna flow from your toes.   (1)
The Lotus-born (Brahma), the consort of Lakshmi (Vishnu),
and Shiva-Har (Shankar), the quintessence of the *Trigunas*,
You have yourself become, O Sai Samarth, as you walked on this
earth.   (2)
Wisdom of Brahma pours out of your words, sometimes;
Sometimes, you assume the terrible form of Shiva, to show '*Tamas*'.
                                                                  (3)
Like Shri Krishna, you indulge, sometimes, in childish pranks;
And at times, you are the fabled swan on the lake of your devotees'
hearts.   (4)
If a Muslim, sandalwood-paste was (like Hindus) dear to you,
But if a Hindu, how happily you stayed always in the mosque!
                                                                  (5)
To call you wealthy, — but you went your rounds, begging for
alms,
And should you be a fakir, your munificence has put even Kuber[18]
to shame!   (6)
If the mosque be your abode, there is always, fire
Burning in the *dhuni*, to provide *Udi* to the people.   (7)
From dawn gather the faithful to worship you,
Till the sun is at zenith, and the mid-day *arati* is performed. (8)
All around the devotees stand, as the divine attendants on God,
Holding the *chowrie-chamar*[19] to wave softly over your head. (9)
Cornets resound, clarions make melody, the bells clang aloud,
As the *chopdar*[20], impressive with his belt, stands at the door
proclaiming your glory.   (10)
On your resplendent seat, you are as Lord Vishnu, during *arati*,
But you are Shankar (destroyer of Cupid) as you sit before the
dhuni, in the evenings.   (11)

Such *leelas* of the Trinity, we experience — in you, day after day,
O Baba Sai.   (12)
Even so, my mind wanders idly;
To steady it, is all I pray to you, now.   (13)
Vilest among the vile, a great sinner that I am; seeking refuge at
your feet
I come; avert the threefold afflictions of Das Ganu, O *Gururaya*!
                                                                      (14)

108. People go to the Ganges to wash away their terrible sins; while
     Ganges herself takes refuge at the saints' feet to cleanse her own
     sins.

109. Leaving Sai's holy feet, we need not go on a pilgrimage to the
     Ganges or Godavari. It is enough to listen to this hymn to a
     saint, this fascinating story of Sai, with a devout heart.

110. Just as, by great good fortune, Gonai found Nama in the Bhima
     river, and Tamaal found Kabir in an oyster shell in the Bhagirathi,

111. So also, Shri Sainath first appeared for his devotees, in the Shirdi
     village, under a Neem tree, at the tender age of sixteen.

112. Even at his first appearance, he was a *Brahmajnani,* untouched,
     even in his dreams, by sensual desire. *Maya* he had abandoned,
     totally, and *Moksha* rolled at his feet.

113. In which country, which righteous family, or in which parental
     abode, Baba took birth, this no one knew.

114. None knew his antecedents — who was his father, or who, his
     mother? All were exhausted asking him questions, but were none
     the wiser for all that.

115. Abandoning mother and father, friends and relations, caste and
     descent — in fact, renouncing the whole worldly life, he appeared
     in Shirdi for the benefit of the people.

116. An old lady of Shirdi, Nana Chopdar's mother, would often talk
     about the marvel of Baba's ways and of his behaviour.

117. In the beginning, said she, this lad, fair and handsome, was first
     seen sitting calmly in deep meditation, under a Neem tree.

118. When they saw this comely youth, people were quite astonished
to see him performing such arduous penance, at that tender age.
So much so, that the scorching heat or bitter cold were, to him,
the same.

119. Such tender age! And oh, what severe austerity! The villagers
were simply amazed to see it. People from the neighbouring
villages thronged Shirdi to have the boy's *darshan*.

120. Company, he kept none, during the day. Nor was he afraid of
anything or anyone, by the night. 'Where could this lad have
come from?', was the one question that puzzled everyone's mind.

121. So comely was his face; so handsome the form! Looking at him,
love welled up in the heart. He never visited anyone, but remained
near the Neem tree, day and night.

122. Everyone was quite mystified. How extraordinary was this lad!
Such tender age; so sweet and youthful a countenance! And how
could he stay, out in the open, night and day?

123. Outwardly, but a young boy, yet in his demeanour, he surpassed
even the greatest among men, the very incarnation of perfect
Renunciation! They could not stop wondering.

124. A strange thing happened, one day! A few persons were possessed
by the spirit of the deity, Khandoba. In their frenzy, they started
puffing and gasping and panting, emitting loud deep sounds. So
people began to ask them questions.

125. 'To which fortunate parents does this boy belong? From where
and how has he come up to here? O Khandoba, at least you find
the answers for us', one of them said to the god.

126. And the god said 'Go, get a hoe, and strike at the spot that I show
you. Strike here, with your hoes and you will get your answers
about this lad.'

127. Then, in the same spot, near the enclosing wall of the village,
under the same Neem tree, they struck blow upon blow with their
hoes till they came upon some bricks.

128. The layer of bricks over, they found an underground cell with
four metal lamps burning in it, the entrance to which was closed
by a quern-stone.

129. The cell was paved with limestone and contained a wooden seat, a *Gomukhi*[21] with a beautiful rosary. Then the god said, 'For twelve years this boy undertook penance at this spot'.

130. All the people were wonderstruck at this and started plying the boy with probing questions. But the lad was full of playful mischief and told them a story, altogether different.

131. "This is my Guru's seat", said he, "and my most sacred legacy. Listen to me this once and preserve it as it is".

132. So said Baba, said the listeners who were present. But why is this, my tongue, moved to say that Baba was giving it a different turn?

133. I was amazed at myself. Why should I think in such terms about Baba? But now I have realized that this must have been his spontaneous sense of humour.

134. Baba dearly loved a joke. Maybe, the cell was his own dwelling. But what does one lose in saying that it is the guru's? How does its importance suffer?

135. And so on his orders, the cell was, once again, sealed as his guru's seat, by restoring the bricks to their former position.

136. The Neem tree was to Baba as great and as sacred as the *Ashwathha (Peepul)* or *Audumbar* tree. He loved that Neem tree dearly, and greatly revered it.

137. Mhalsapati and other old residents of Shirdi village bow to this place as the *samadhi* of Baba's guru.

138. It is common knowledge among the villagers that Baba sat near this *samadhi*, in meditation, observing total silence for a period of twelve years.

139. Sathesaheb, one of Baba's devotees, acquired the land all around it, along with the *samadhi* and the Neem tree and raised a building with four verandahs connected at the centre.

140. This building, this very *wada*, was originally the common residence of the pilgrims, forever crowded with comings and goings of visitors.

141. Sathe raised a bank around the neem tree and an upper floor running North-South. When the northern staircase was laid, he pointed out the cell.

142. Under the staircase, facing south, is a beautiful niche. In front of it, facing north, the devotees sit on the bank.

143. "On Thursdays and Fridays, he who washes the floor with cowdung, at sunset, and burns incense for a moment, Shri Hari will surely bless him".

144. Listeners may doubt in their minds, whether this is true, or an exaggeration. But these are the words from Sai's mouth, which I have heard with my own ears.

145. This is no statement of my own making. Have not the slightest doubt. Those who have personally heard this are still amongst us.

146. Later came *Dikshit-wada* which provided spacious accommodation. And in the forepart a stone building was also built, very shortly thereafter (by Shri Buti).

147. Dikshit was already well-known for his virtuous deeds and was the very embodiment of faith and devotion. The seeds of his spiritual progress were sown during his sojurn to England.

148. Here, the listeners may well ask, how, instead of the holy places of pilgrimage, like Mathura, Kashi or Dwarka, could England which was proscribed by the then Hindu custom, be the beginning of his spiritual journey?

149. And it is quite natural for the listeners to raise this doubt. But all my listeners will surely forgive me for a slight digression in answering it, which in fact they will appreciate.

150. Dikshit had already accumulated enough religious merit by his pilgrimages to the holy places of Kashi, Prayag, Badrikedar, Mathura, Vrindavan, Dwarkapur, etc.

151. Moreover, by his father's virtuousness, his own extraordinary good fortune, and a dessert of the accumulated merit of his past births, he had the *darshan* of Shri Sai.

152. The immediate cause for this *darshan* was his lameness, decreed as if by Fate. For, while in England, his foot slipped and resulted in an infirmity of the leg.

153. To all appearances a misfortune, it was really a most auspicious and rare event, which led to his association with Sai. It was indeed, the fruit of all his good deeds!

154. Dikshit happened to meet Chandorkar, from whom he came to know of Sai's fame. Chandorkar said, 'You just see the marvel of his *darshan*! Your lameness will disappear, immediately!'

155. But it was not so much the infirmity of the leg that Dikshit considered to be a deficiency. The real infirmity, he said, is of the mind, which he beseeched Sai to remove.

156. What is this human frame, but a bag of flesh, bones, blood and skin; a mere load-cart of all the transient, worldly affairs! It mattered little, even if the lameness remained in the leg!

157. It was in the year 1909, on the second day of November, that Dikshit, for the first time had Sai's sacred *darshan*.

158. In that same year, he then went again to Shirdi, in the month of December, to have Sai's *darshan*, once again, and this time, he really felt that he should stay there for a longer period.

159. At first, a thought came to his mind that he should sell some twenty-five of his company shares, to build a shed, with corrugated iron sheets for a roof, so that it would also be useful to the pilgrims.

160. But later on, he resolved in his mind to build a *wada*, instead. And, in the very next year, the foundation stone for it was laid, to mark the auspicious beginning of the building work.

161. The day was 9th December. Baba's consent was obtained, and taking it to be the auspicious sign, the work of laying the foundation stone was accomplished.

162. As luck would have it, Dikshit's brother, who would not have come, normally, even on invitation, happened to be there already, on that very day and at that most auspicious time.

163. Shri Dadasaheb Khaparde had come to Shirdi alone, much earlier, and was in some difficulty over getting Baba's permission to return home.

164. Both of them got Baba's permission — Khaparde, to go home, and Dikshit to lay the foundation stone of the building, on the 10th of December.

165. This day is significant for yet another reason. From this very day was started, with great love and devotion, Baba's *arati* before he retired for the night, at the *chavadi*.

166. Later in the year 1911, the auspicious occasion of *Ramnavami* was availed of, for the 'Griha-pravesh'[22], with all the rituals and ceremonials.

167. Later on still, Buti's *wada* was built, with lavish expenditure and Baba was laid to rest in it after his *mahasamadhi*. So that all the money was well-spent.

168. Now there were three *wadas*, in all, where earlier, there was none. But in those early days, it was Sathe's *wada* that was most useful to everyone.

169. This *Sathewada* is important for another reason, too. In the beginning, on the very spot, there was a beautiful flower-garden grown by Baba, with his own hands.

170. A short account of this garden will be given in the next chapter. Hemad, with his listeners, bows humbly at Sai's feet.

171. Vaman Tatya (the potter) would supply the earthern pitchers, and Sai Samarth would water the plants, thus raising a garden on the rocky barren soil. Later, Baba just disappeared, one day.

172. Afterwards, he met Chand Patil, near Aurangabad, and with that marriage party he returned to Shirdi.

173. Thereafter, he met Devidas; he met Janakidas, too! And so also Gangagir. This threesome then got together in Shirdi.

174. The incident of Baba's wrestling with Mohiuddin then took place, and afterwards, Baba came to stay at the mosque. He grew fond of Dengle, and gradually, other devotees gathered round him.

175. All theses stories will be narrated in the next chapter, which can then be listened to, attentively. Hemad now prostrates whole-heartedly before Sai, as he seeks refuge at his feet.

Weal be to all! Here ends the fourth chapter of
'*Sri Sai Samarth Satcharit*', called
'*Descent of Sai Samarth in Shirdi*',
as inspired by the saints and the virtuous,
and composed by his devotee, Hemadpant.

Notes

1. Refer Ch. 3, note 6.
2. *Sandhya*: Religious meditation, repetition of *mantras*, sipping of water, etc., to be performed by the first three *varnas* of Hindus, at particular periods in the day, especially at sunrise, noon and sunset.
3. *Para*: speech in the first stage, the first stirring of breath or air, which is symbolized by the mystic syllable '*Om*'; *Pashyanti*: speech in the second stage, which has its seat in the *Antahkarana* or the mind and is characterized by *Vivek* or discrimination; *Madhyama*: speech in the third stage of its progress, which has its seat in the trachea; *Vaikhari*: speech in the fourth stage of articulate utterance.

4.   The *Shat-Darshanas* are: *Sankhya, yoga, Nyaya, Vaisheshika, Mimamsa* and *Vedanta*.
5.   The six *darshanas* and the six *shastras* are, strictly speaking, the same; but when the word '*shastra*' is used loosely, in the sense of '*Vedanga*', it can refer to the following six: *Shiksha, Chhandas, Vyakaran, Nirukta, Jyotish* and *Kalpa*. It is not clear in what sense it is used by the Author here.
6.   The *Purana* or sacred or poetical work. There are eighteen. They comprise the whole body of Hindu mythology. Each should treat of five topics especially; the creation, the destruction and the renovation of worlds, the genealogy of gods and heroes, the reigns of the *Manus* and the transactions of their descendants. They are called: *Brahma, Padma, Vishnu, Shiva, Linga, Gauda, Narada, Bhagvat, Agni, Skanda, Bhavishya, Brahmavaivarta, Markandeya, Vaman, Varah, Matsya, Koorma* and *Vayu*.
7.   *Kirtan* is the singing of God's praises to the accompaniment of music.
8.   All the four places are places of pilgrimage, associated with Shri Dattatreya.
9.   Karna was half-brother to the Pandav princes, famed for munificence; hence used appellatively of a liberal man.
10. *Muralis* are females dedicated to the service of the god Khandoba.
11. *Ghazal* is a Persian lyric poem, amatory ode, drinking-song or religious hymn. It consists usually of not less than five, or more than fifteen couplets, all with the same rhyme.
12. States of absolute Superconsciousness. Also an edifice erected over the burial place of a *sanyasi*, as in verse 137.
13. All these are palces of pilgrimage for the Hindus.
14. *Warkari* is a follower of the 600 year-old *Warkari Panth*, which is essentially a '*Bhakti-marg*', emphasizing the worship of Vitthal. A special feature of this *panth* is the two annual pilgrimages or '*waris*' undertaken by its members, on foot, between Alandi and Pandharpur.
15. This is a period of four months, but understood specially of the four monsoon months.
16. *Parva* is a common term for particular periods of the year (equinoxes, solstices, etc.) on which occasions particular ceremonies are commanded, and high degrees of merit are ascribed to obedience; an opportune period.
17. A place of pilgrimage at the confluence of the Ganges and the Yamuna rivers.
18. Kuber is the name of the treasurer of the gods, the Indian Plutus, and hence, appellatively, a rich man.
19. The tail of *Bos grunniens*, used to whisk off flies.
20. *Chopdar* is the Mace-bearer.
21. A '*Gomukhi*' is a glove, shaped like a cow's mouth, by which the hand is covered in telling the beads of a rosary.
22. The ceremony of occupying a just-built house; consulting signs and aspects, etc.; feasting and merry-making. The word answers to House-warming.

5

Sai's Disappearance and Return to Shirdi

MY OBEISANCE TO SHRI GANESH, TO SHRI SARASWATI, AND SHRI GURUMAHARAJ! TO THE FAMILY DEITY, TO SHRI SITA-RAMACHANDRA, MY MOST HUMBLE OBEISANCE! I BOW IN REVERENCE TO THE MOST VENERABLE GURU SHRI SAINATH!

1. Now in continuation with the previous story, listen to this account of how Baba suddenly disappeared from Shirdi, only to reappear, once again, in the company of Chand Patil;

2. How Baba himself carried water to create a garden; as also, the meeting together of Gangagir and other saints; listen to these stories which are sanctifying.

3. Baba had, for a time, disappeared; but later, it was in the marriage-party of a Muslim gentleman, which came to Shirdi, that this jewel was discovered.

4. Devidas, however, had already come to stay in Shirdi, before that. Later on came Janakidas Gosavi too, to live in Shirdi.

5. How all this came about, I shall now relate in detail. Be attentive, O listeners, as you respectfully listen to this.

6. In Dhoopkheda, a village of the Aurangabad district, there was a Muslim, of great good fortune, by the name of Chand Patil.

7. While journeying to Aurangabad, he lost his mare and for two months she could not be traced. 'No hope now of finding her!'

8. So thought the Patil, completely dejected, and felt very sorry and distressed for the loss of his mare. Finally, he flung the saddle across his back and turned back to go the way he came.

9. Leaving Aurangabad behind, he travelled about nine miles. There was a mango tree on the way, under which he saw this gem among men.

10. A cap in his hand, body covered by a *kafni* (a mendicant's robe), and a baton under the armpit — even as he crushed some tobacco in the palm of his hand and filled the *chillim* (clay pipe), a wonderful thing happened.

11. As Chand Patil was passing that way, he heard the fakir calling out to him, saying, 'Oh, you! Come, come here! Smoke this *chillim*, then go! Come, rest here a while, under the shade!'

12. The fakir then asked, 'What is this saddle for?' And the Patil replied, 'I have lost my mare, Sir!' Upon this he said, 'Go, search along this rivulet'. And lo! The mare was found immediately!.

13. Chand Patil was astonished, and said to himself, 'Truly, I have met a sage! There is no limit to this miraculous deed! How can he be called an ordinary human being!'

14. He then returned with the mare, and came back to the same place, again. The fakir made him sit by himself. He picked up with his own hands a pair of tongs;

15. Then he thrust it in the soil, in that same place, and brought out a burning ember from within the soil. He then placed it on the *chillim* in his hand and picked up the baton.

16. For there was no water to wet the strip of cloth, covering the *chillim*. So he struck the ground with his baton and water began to flow out.

17. Dipping the strip of cloth in water, he then squeezed it out and then wound it round the *chillim*. He smoked the *chillim* himself and made the Patil smoke it, too. The Patil was quite dazed, seeing all this.

18. The Fakir was then pressed to sanctify his home, by the Patil, by paying him a visit. The Fakir, who had come to this earth only for such divine *leelas*, conferred the favour on him.

19. The next day he went into the village to stay with the Patil, and spent some time there. Later, he came back to Shirdi.

20. This Chand Patil was the headman of the village Dhoopkheda and his wife's nephew was engaged to be married to a bride from Shirdi.

21. This nephew of his wife had come of a marriageable age and had the good fortune of marrying a bride from Shirdi!

22. So, with the bullock-carts and horses, the marriage-party set out to come to Shirdi, in due course. And then, Baba, drawn by his affection for Chandbhai, joined the party, too!

23. The wedding over, the marriage-party returned from Shirdi. Only Baba remained behind. He stayed back and then stayed on, forever! That marked the rise in Shirdi's good fortune.

24. Indestructible and ancient that Sai is, he is neither Hindu nor Muslim. He has no caste, no descent, no family, no *gotra*. The state of self-realization was the core of his being.

25. And 'Sai, Sai' that people called him, is that his real name? No, indeed! Out of respect he was first addressed as 'Welcome, Sai!' and that is how he got his name!

26. It was on the day that Baba arrived with the marriage-party in Mhalsapati's yard near the Khandoba temple, that this happened.

27. In the beginning this yard was Bhagat Mhalsapati's. Later it belonged to Aminbhai. The marriage-party, as it arrived, got down in this same place, under the banyan tree.

28. The bullocks were all unyoked in the yard, in the Khandoba temple compound. And Baba, too, got down there, with the marriage-party, along with all the others.

29. As this youthful fakir alighted from the cart, it was Bhagat, who first saw him and received him with the words 'Welcome Sai'. From then onwards, that name became his proper name.

30. Thereafter, people began to call him 'Sai, Sai', and the name came to be used commonly by all.

31. He then smoked the *chillim*, there (in Mhalsapati's yard) and thereafter went to stay at the mosque. He quite enjoyed Devidas's company. Altogether he was happy in Shirdi.

32. Sometimes, he would sit in the *Chavadi*, sometimes, he would be in the company of Devidas, or sometimes he would sit in the

Maruti temple. He would thus be engaged fondly, wherever it pleased him.

33.   This Devidas was already in Shirdi, much earlier than the time Baba came there. Janakidas Gosavi of the Mahanubhavi sect[2] came to Shirdi, thereafter.

34.   With this Janakidas, Maharaj would sit talking; or Janakidas would go and sit wherever Maharaj might be.

35.   Both were very fond of each other's company and would have regular meetings. This — their association with each other — was a source of great pleasure to everyone.

36.   So also, one Gangagir, a householder and a very famous devotee of the Vaishanava sect[3], from Puntambe, used to visit Shirdi, frequently.

37.   In the beginning, Gangagir used to be quite astonished in his mind to see Sai carry water from the well, holding earthern pitchers in both his hands.

38.   But later, when he met Sai face to face, Bua said, very clearly and quite emphatically, 'Blessed is this Shirdi and very fortunate too, to have this jewel among men associated with her.

39.   'Today he carries pitchers of water on his own shoulders. But this is no ordinary figure! It is by the great accumulated merit of this soil that he has come to this place.'

40.   Similarly, one other well-known saint, by the name of Anandnath, had also predicted Baba's wonderful and divine *leelas*.

41.   This very famous Anandnath had set up a *math* (monastery) at the village Yeola, and in the company of some residents of Shirdi, he came to Shirdi.

42.   Anandnath was the disciple of the great saint of Akkalkot. When he actually saw Sai, he exclaimed, 'Oh, he is a diamond, a veritable diamond!

43.   'Maybe, today he lies neglected in a rubbish heap, yet he is undoubtedly a diamond and not a piece of flint!' And remember, these were the words of Anandnath, while Sai was yet of a tender age!

44. 'Remember well these words of mine! Later on, you will be reminded of them'. Prophesying thus, he then returned to Yeole.

45. Sai then, used to allow his hair to grow and would not have his head shaved, ever! His dress used to be like a wrestler, when this Sai was in his youth.

46. Whenever he went to Rahata he would always bring back with him saplings of marigold and jasmine and would plant them with his own hands in desolate places and would also water them regularly.

47. His devotee, Vaman Tatya would supply him every day with two unbaked earthern pitchers for that purpose. And Baba would water the plants with his own hands.

48. From the stone-vessel near the well, he would fill the pitchers and carry them on his shoulders and at sunset, he would keep the pitchers under the Neem tree.

49. The moment they were placed there, they would (of their own) crack on the spot. The next morning Tatya would bring him two new pitchers.

50. When fully and properly baked, a pitcher is always better and lasts longer. But Baba would require only unbaked ones. Thus the potter was able to sell the pitchers, without the labour of baking them in the furnace.

51. For three years this was his preoccupation; in that open space, he raised a garden and in that same place, that today, by lucky chance people are enjoying the convenience of a *wada*.

52. And, also in the same place, under the Neem tree, a devotee called '*Bhai*' has installed the '*Padukas*' of Swami Samarth of Akkalkot, for those devotees who wish to offer '*pooja*' to Swami Samarth.

53. Swami Samarth of Akkalkot was Bhai's chosen deity and with great devotion, Bhai used to worship his photograph, very regularly.

54. Once he felt that he should go to Akkalkot to have a *darshan* of Swami's *padukas*, and offer a sincere *pooja*, with all attendant rituals, to the *Padukas*.

55.   So he made all the necessary preparations to leave for Akkalkot from Bombay. And he was just about to leave on the very next day, when he had to abandon his resolve and instead, he found himself on the way to Shirdi.

56.   Even as he was all set to leave the next day, he had a dream on the previous night, in which Swami Samarth exhorted him, saying, 'At the moment my stay is in Shirdi, so you leave for Shirdi'.

57.   Such being the command, Bhai obeyed it with great reverence and left Bombay for Shirdi, where he stayed on for six months in great peace and happiness.

58.   Bhai, being steadfast in his faith, installed the *padukas* of Swami Samarth under the neem tree to commemorate the vision he had had in his dream.

59.   In the year 1912, in the month of *Shravan* (i.e. August-September), during the bright half of the moon, which was also the auspicious *Parva-kaal*, he installed the *padukas* under the Neem tree, very lovingly with *pooja, bhajan,* etc.

60.   On an auspicious day, the installation was performed at the hands of Dada Kelkar and under the direction of Upasani, with all the rites and rituals prescribed by the *Shastras.*

61.   The arrangement for the daily worship of the *padukas* was entrusted to a Brahmin, named Dikshit, while Sagun Nayak looked after the overall arrangements. Such is the tale of the *padukas.*

62.   This is how these saints, the true incarnations of God, who are without attachments and desires, appear on this earth for their selfless mission of uplifting the world.

63.   A few days later, a very astonishing incident took place, which when the listeners hear attentively, will surprise them, too!

64.   Mohiuddinbhai, a seller of betel leaf, areca-nut, tobacco, etc., and Baba had some dispute between them, which flared up resulting into a bout of wrestling, both fighting each other fiercely.

65.   Both were skilled wrestlers, but mere physical prowess cannot prevail against destiny. So that Mohiuddin became more powerful

and Baba, his strength being unequal to his opponent, was defeated.

66. From then onwards, Baba's mind was made up. He changed his entire dress; he started wearing the long *kafni*, a *langot*[4] and a piece of cloth tied around his head.

67. Of the gunny bag, he made his seat and the gunny bag served as a bedding too! He found contentment even in the rags that he wore.

68. "Poverty holds the highest sovereignty, — a thousand times greater than the grandeur of the nobleman. Allah befriends the poor", so would Sai say, always.

69. Gangagir also had been in the same position once. Fond as he was of wrestling, once, while he was engaged in that sport, he suddenly grew weary of it, wanting to renounce it.

70. As the opportune moment came, the words of a *siddha* came to his ears, 'This body should rather wear itself out, in sporting with God'.

71. These words of Grace fell on his ears even as he was engaged in wrestling. He renounced the world and took to the spiritual path.

72. His *math* is on an isle, situated between the twin streams of the river Godavari, near Puntambe and there are his disciples too, eager to serve him.

73. As time went by, Sainath would only answer the questions put to him and would never talk to anyone of his own accord.

74. During the day, he would be seated under the Neem tree, sometimes he would sit in the shade of a horizontal branch of the Babul tree, that grew by the stream, at the village boundary.

75. Sometimes, when it pleased him, Baba would wander of an afternoon in the vicinity of Nimgaon, a mile or so away from Shirdi.

76. The famous Trimbak Dengle was the Jahagirdar of Nimgaon, and Babasaheb was a descendant of his. Baba was very fond of this Babasaheb.

77. Whenever Baba took a round of Nimgaon, he would go to his house and would love to spend a day talking to him.

78. He had a younger brother, Nanasaheb by name, who had no son, due to which, he would always feel sad at heart.

79. The first wife had dim chances of getting one so he married a second time. But no one can escape the decree of fate. Mysterious are the ways of destiny!

80. Then Babasaheb sent him for Sai's *darshan*. And by his blessings a son was born to Nana.

81. Thereafter Sai's fame began to grow and a large number of people thronged Shirdi for Sai's *darshan*. The news reached Ahmednagar, which is a district place.

82. In Ahmednagar, Nana used to move much in the Government circles and was influential with the officials, amongst whom was also, Chidambar Keshav, who was the secretary to the District Collector.

83. Nana wrote to him a letter, saying that he should visit Shirdi with his wife, children and friends for the *darshan* of Sai Samarth. The visit, he said, was worthwhile.

84. In this way, many began to come to Shirdi, one after the other, as Baba's fame began to spread and the ranks of his followers swelled.

85. Though Baba needed no company, during the day he would be surrounded by his devotees. After sunset, however, he would sleep in the dilapidated mosque in Shirdi.

86. *Chillim*, tobacco and a tumbler, were constantly by his side; Baba wore a long, flowing *kafni*, covering his head with a piece of white cloth and always had with him his baton.

87. He would tie around his head that piece of clean, white cloth, taken behind the left ear and twisted firmly, like the matted hair of a Gosavi, to form a shapely head gear.

88. Covering himself with such clothes, he would sometimes go without a bath even for eight days at a stretch; barefoot he walked and used only a gunny bag for a seat.

89. That piece of sack-cloth was thus his seat always. The comfort of a cushion, he knew not, and found contentment in whatever he had.

90. That old, worn-out sack-cloth was his favourite seat, which was forever in that same place — day in and day out.

91. That was all there was for a seat, or as a covering. He wore a *kaupin*[5], and no other sheet or covering. To ward off cold, there was the *dhuni*, of course!

92. Facing the south with the left hand resting on the railing, Baba would sit on this sack-cloth, in the mosque, gazing into the *dhuni* in front of him.

93. He seemed to be offering into the *dhuni* oblations of the ego, along with all the desires and the various affections of the mind, — in fact, all the temptations of the worldly life, by various wiles and ways.

94. That raging fire in the *dhuni* he fed with logs of conceited knowledge and raised the banner of Allah by chanting '*Allah-Malik*', ceaselessly.

95. And just how spacious was that mosque? It was but the space included betwixt two cross-beams, in which he lived, sat, moved about, met everybody, and slept.

96. The mattress, the cushions — they have all come now, when the devotees have gathered around him. But in the beginning, the devotees could not go near him without fear.

97. From the year 1912, everything changed. It was from that year that the transformation of the mosque really began.

98. Where there were knee-deep pits and holes in the ground in the mosque, it was paved overnight with *Shahabadi* (hewn) stones, on the strength of the devotees' labour of love.

99. Before he came to stay at the mosque, Baba used to live in the *takiya* or the resting place for the fakirs. He spent a long time there, and was quite happy.

100. It was there, in the *takiya*, that he used to tie ghungaroo (jingling bells) round his ankles and danced gracefully to the beat of the tambourine. He would also sing melodiously.

101. In the early days, Sai Samarth was very fond of lighting up the lamps and would himself go and ask the shop-keepers for oil to light them.

102.   Tumbler in hand, he would himself ask for oil at the grocers'
       shops and fill it in the earthen lamps.

103.   He would then burn the lamps bright, in the temple and in the
       mosque. This went on continuously for some days.

104.   He was very fond of worshipping the lamps and would celebrate
       Diwali, the festival of lights. Strips of cloth he would twist to
       form wicks and burn lights in the mosque.

105.   As for the oil, he used to bring it free, every day. Once, all the
       grocers conspired against him, thinking, now enough of this daily
       wearisome nuisance!

106.   Later, when Baba came to ask for oil, as was his daily practice,
       and all of them refused, what an amazing thing happened!

107.   Without a word, Baba turned back and placed the dry wicks in
       the earthen lamps. The grocers were watching with amusement
       as to what he would do without oil.

108.   Baba picked up the tumbler from the parapet of the mosque. In
       it there was just a drop or two of oil, which was barely sufficient
       even to light an evening lamp.

109.   He then poured water in that oil and drank it all up, offering it in
       this way to God; he then took pure water,

110.   This he poured into the earthen lamps to wet the wicks and
       lighting them up, showed how the lamps could burn brightly.

111.   Seeing the water thus kindled into a flame, the grocers were
       astounded and said to themselves that it was not a good thing
       that they lied to Baba.

112.   Without a trace of oil, the lamps burned all night and everybody
       began to say that the grocers did not deserve Sai's grace.

113.   'Oh, what marvellous powers Baba has!' said the grocers and
       repeated that they had not only sinned by their falsehood, but
       needlessly enraged Baba.

114.   However, being beyond anger and hatred, all this was farthest
       from Baba's thoughts. He had no enemy and no friend; to him
       all creatures were equal.

115. And now let us continue with the tale where we left off, i.e. Mohiuddin triumphed over Baba in wrestling. Now listen carefully to the story that follows: -

116. In the fifth year after this wrestling incident, a fakir, Jawahar Ali by name, who was a resident of Ahmednagar, came to Rahata, along with his disciples.

117. Choosing an open space near the Veerbhadra temple, the fakir set up his camp there. But the fakir was really very fortunate.

118. Had he not been so, how could he have had such a famous and delightful disciple as Sai?

119. There were many people in the village, of whom quite a few were Marathas. Amongst them was one Bhagu Sadaphal, who became his attendant.

120. The fakir was very learned. The *Quran-e-sharif* was at the tips of his fingers. Many people — some selfish, some spiritual, and some pious and faithful — became his followers.

121. He began constructing an *Idgah* (a place for prayer). Some time went by; he was then accused of defiling the temple of Veerbhadra.

122. Then the construction work of the *Idgah* came to a halt and the fakir was driven out of the village. From there he came to Shirdi and stayed with Baba in the mosque.

123. The fakir was a sweet talker. The whole village adored him and people said that he had cast a spell on Baba too, and charmed him completely.

124. 'You be my disciple' said he to Baba, and Baba, with his playful disposition, assented. The fakir was delighted and took Baba out of Shirdi.

125. With an eminent disciple like Baba, Jawahar Ali became the guru. Then they both decided to go and live in Rahata.

126. The guru did not know his disciple's marvellous ways; but the disciple knew the guru's short-comings. But never did the disciple show disrespect, thereby observing the duties of a good disciple.

127. Whatever command came from the guru's mouth, whether proper or improper, was obeyed, no sooner it was given. And he even carried water in the guru's abode.

128. Thus the days passed in the service of the guru. But then it so
      happened that he would come to Shirdi only once in a while.
      When this happened, just listen to what followed.

129. This began happening repeatedly and, in fact, he now stayed at
      Rahata for the most part. The people started feeling that Sai was
      bewitched by the fakir and was almost lost to Shirdi.

130. Whereas people thought that it was by his yogic powers that
      Jawahar Ali had bound Sai to himself, Baba's plan was altogether
      different. It was his way of destroying the ego.

131. And yet, how could Sai have any ego or conceit? So the listeners
      will naturally reason. But then, such conduct was for the good of
      the people, which was also the mission of his life.

132. But the villagers of Shirdi were Baba's loving devotees and had
      great affection for him. Staying away from Baba in this way,
      appeared quite improper to them.

133. The villagers were greatly agitated in their minds to see Sai so
      much in the power of Jawahar Ali and were in serious thought as
      to how he could be won back.

134. As gold and its lustre, as lamp and its light, so was the inseparable
      state of this guru and disciple. And they both had this experience
      of Oneness.

135. A group of devotees from Shirdi then went to that *Idgah* at Rahata,
      making plans in their minds, how they would try very, very hard
      and would then return all together, bringing Baba back with them.

136. But Baba took a stand, quite to the contrary. "This fakir is very
      hot-tempered", he said, "Do not try to persuade him; for he will
      never let go of me.

137. "You now get out of here quickly for he will return from the village
      presently. So terrible is his wrath, that he will make a clean work
      of you all!

138. "His anger is very fierce and will turn him red in the face. Go, go,
      be gone instantly, and take the road straight to Shirdi."

139. 'What should be done next?' they thought, 'for Baba speaks
      contrary to all expectation.' Meanwhile, the fakir came back,
      quite unexpectedly, and began to ask them,

140. 'So, have you come for this lad? And what are you discussing? If your intention is to take him back with you, you might as well not take the trouble; it will be in vain.'

141. Though he said so quite emphatically at the outset, in the end even he yielded to the pressure of the villagers and said, 'Take me also with you. We will all take this boy with us to Shirdi.'

142. Thus the fakir came back with them, too! He could not bear to part from Baba and even Baba could not let him go. How was this possible, was something no one could understand.

143. Sai was Brahman incarnate, while Jawahar Ali was full of misconceptions. When put to test by Devidas in Shirdi, all these misconceptions exploded.

144. Devidas had a beautiful figure, lustrous eyes, and a handsome face. He was only ten or eleven years old when he first came to Shirdi.

145. Such was this Gosavi of tender years, with only a *langot* round his loins, who had, at that time, put up at the Maruti temple.

146. Appa Bhil and Mhalsapati frequently visited him. Kashiram and others provided him with food grains, fuel, etc. He gradually gained in importance.

147. Twelve years before Baba came with the marriage party, Devidas had already come to stay in Shirdi.

148. He taught Appa Bhil to write on a slate and made everyone recite *Vyankatesh Stotra*, which he had taught and which they knew by heart. He conducted these lessons regularly.

149. Devidas was highly enlightened. Tatyaba (Tatya Ganapat Patil-Kote) made him his guru and Kashinath and others became his chief disciples and followers.

150. The fakir was brought before Devidas, who engaged him in a religious debate. With his ascetic powers, Devidas totally vanquished the fakir, who was then driven away from Shirdi.

151. As he escaped from Shirdi, the fakir went and stayed at Vaijapur. Years later, he came to Shirdi and bowed humbly before Sainath.

152. All his misconceptions about himself being the guru and Sai, his disciple, were dispelled and by repentance he was purified. Baba also accepted him with respect, as before.

153. Such were Baba's inscrutable ways! The issue got resolved when the proper time came, but till then, Baba honoured the *guru-shishya* relationship.

154. If he considered himself a guru, it was entirely his responsibility; but as a disciple, Baba knew and performed his duty perfectly. This is the moral of this story, which Sainath himself put into practice.

155. There is no better state than that one should completely surrender to one's guru, or that one should totally accept the disciple as one's own. Without this relationship one cannot cross the ocean of worldly life.

156. This is the one lesson of this story. But rare indeed is the man who will be daring enough to firmly resolve to shed his ego and conquer the fortress of the ego-less state.

157. Here ingenious speculations of one's intellect are of no avail; he who wants to attain his highest good must conduct himself without conceit or ego.

158. He who has burned out the conceit in his physical body is the one who will find fulfilment in this human birth. And to attain salvation, he will then accept the discipleship of anyone.

159. Seeing that desireless state, in so young and comely a figure, all the people, both great and small, were struck with amazement and wonder.

160. The bodily functions of a realized soul work out according to his past *Karma*; but he is not burdened by the *Prarabdha Karma*[6], for he is no longer the doer of action.

161. Just as the sun cannot remain in darkness, so also the man of enlightenment cannot remain in a state of duality; for the entire Universe is in his own Self and he dwells in *Advait* (non-duality).

162. This conduct as guru and disciple has been narrated in detail, as described by Mhalsapati, the great devotee of Sainath.

163. But now, let this story be. The next one is even more profound and will be related in its proper sequence. Be attentive while you listen to it.

164. What was the condition of the mosque earlier, and with what toil it was paved; how no one knew, for certain, whether Sai was Hindu or Muslim.

165. Baba's yogic practices, such as *dhoti-poti* (cleaning of internal organs) and *Khandayoga* (severing and reassembling organs of the body, at will), and, how he took upon himself the karmic sufferings of the devotees, — all this will be narrated in a proper manner, without omissions, later on.

166. Hemad surrenders to Sai, in all humility. This narration of his story is his *prasad* or grace. By merely listening to this sacred story, all the sins will be destroyed.

Weal be to all! Here ends the fifth chapter of
"Shri Sai Samarth Satcharit", called
'*Reappearance of Shri Sai in Shirdi*',
as inspired by the saints and the virtuous
and composed by his devotee, Hemadpant.

Notes

1. The dictionary meaning of the word 'Sai' is, lord, god, husband (beloved), fakir. The saint-poet Kabir has used the word 'Sai' in his compositions in the sense of Lord or God. Gorakshanath in his work '*Goraksha Kimayagar*' used the word for Mahavishnu.

2. *Mahanubhav Panth*: The followers of this *Panth* believe in *Panch Krishnas*: a) Bhagvan Shrikrishna, as *avatar* of God not Lord Vishnu, b) Dattatreya Prabhu as *avatar* of God, c) Chakrapani alias Changdev Raul, d) Govinda Prabhu alias Gundam Raul, and e) Chakradhar Swami. The last of these, viz. Chakradhar Swami, born in Gujarat, made Marathwada his home and gave concrete shape to this *Panth*, which does not believe in *Advait* and *Mayavad* of Shankaracharya, but advocates *Bhaktimarg* or single-minded devotion to God. It does not set much store by vows and rituals. Though it has lay followers, it is primiarily a *sanyas*-oriented *Panth*. (*Prachin Maharashtracha Dharmic Itihas*: by R.M. Bhusari; Marathi Sahitya Parishad, Hyderabad, 1965, p. 135)

3. *Vaishnav sect*: believes in the worship of Lord Vishnu. It was popularised in Tamil Nadu by Alawar saints, in ancient times, by Ramanuj Acharya, the founder of the *Vishishtadvait*, in the 11th century. This is a *Bhaktimarg*. (Ibid., p. 108)

4. This is a piece of cloth, worn around the loins, covering the privities.

5. A cloth-covering, worn over the privities.

6. That part of the accumulated *Karma*, with which you are born.

6

The Story of the Festival of Shri Ram's Birth in Shirdi

MY OBEISANCE TO SHRI GANESH, TO SHRI SARASWATI, AND SHRI GURUMAHARAJ! TO THE FAMILY DEITY, TO SHRI SITA-RAMACHANDRA, MY MOST HUMBLE OBEISANCE! I BOW IN REVERENCE TO THE MOST VENERABLE GURU SHRI SAINATH!

1. Be it a striving after spiritual progress or after material prosperity, where Sadguru is the helmsman, he alone will steer the boat to the other shore.
2. When the word 'Sadguru' stirs the feelings of the heart, it is Sai who immediately comes before the mind. He, in fact, actually stands in front of you and places his hand of benediction on your heart!
3. When his hand of blessing with the *udi* from the *dhuni* falls on your head, the heart swells with self-rejoicing, the eyes overflow with tears of love.
4. Such is the marvel of the subtle touch of the guru's hand that it burns up that astral body[1] to ashes, by his merest touch, which even the funeral pyre[2] cannot consume.
5. It brings peace and stability even to those who get a headache or burst out into wild, meaningless babble, even at an accidental mention about gods and their divine tales.
6. As he places his lotus-hand on the head, the sins of so many past births which have reached a point of culmination, are all washed away, leaving Sai's loving devotees purified.

7.   As the eyes rest on that comely form, you are choked by the rapture; tears of joy spring to the eyes; in the heart arise the *Ashta-bhava*[3].

8.   The feeling that 'I am That' is awakened, giving the experience of the blissful joy within. Dissolving all duality, it celebrates the union with the Supreme One.

9.   Whatever sacred books, *Puranas*, one may read, one is reminded of the Sadguru at every step, so that it is only Sai, who appears as Ram or Krishna and makes us listen to his own story.

10. As you sit down to listen to the *Bhagwat*, Krishna appears as none other than Sai, right from tip to toe, who is singing the '*Uddhav-Geet*', for the benefit of his devotees.

11. Even in your casual conversations, you are suddenly reminded of one or the other of Sai's stories to illustrate a point properly.

12. You pull up a sheet of paper with the intention of writing, but cannot compose even a word. Yet when Sai himself, with his grace, inspires you to write, you know not how to stop the flow of words.

13. Whenever ego raises its head, he firmly presses it underneath his own hand. In addition, by pouring his grace into the devotee, he brings fulfilment to him.

14. When you surrender at the feet of Sai Samarth in act, speech and thought, then *dharma, artha, kama* and *Moksha* (the four ends of human life) come into the hands automatically.

15. The four paths of *Karma* (action) *Jnana* (Knowledge), *Yoga* and *Bhakti* (devotion) are for the attainment of God. Though they proceed in four different directions, they all lead you to God-realisation.

16. The path of Devotion (*Bhakti*) is like the way through a forest of the prickly Babul[4] trees, full of pits and holes and difficult to cross. Though it is a narrow pathway, for only one person, it directly takes you near God.

17. The easiest way to traverse it is to take every step carefully to avoid the thorns. Only then will you reach your eternal abode without fear. This is what Guru, the Mother, warns you clearly.

18. When the rich, fertile soil of the mind is sprinkled with the water of devotion, renunciation sprouts; knowledge blossoms; *kaivalya* comes to fruition; and the rapture thereof, bursts forth. Avoiding of birth and death is then a certainty.

19. The primal Supreme soul is by itself perfect. He is also the threefold nature of *Sat, Chit* and *Anand* (Being, Consciousness and Bliss). Due to natural properties disguising the Spirit, it is awakened and manifests Itself for instructing devotees.

20. As the Brahman became manifest through its three said attributes, *maya* (illusion) became active, too, and manifested her properties, by stirring up *Sattva* (Righteous, Harmony), *Rajas* (Activity/Motion) and *Tamas* (Inertia/Darkness).

21. Really, it is clay, moulded to a particular shape, that is called a pot. But when it breaks, the name, form and identity, everything leaves it.

22. This whole world is created out of *Maya*. They are both thus related to each other as cause and effect. In fact, it is *Maya* who has assumed a form and has appeared as this manifest world.

23. If the state of this *Maya*, prior to the creation of the world, is considered, she had not manifested herself but was absorbed in the Supreme and gathered together in the Unmanifest.

24. Manifest or Unmanifest, *Maya* has always been a part of the Supreme Being. Hence this *Maya* is the Supreme Being and quite inseparable from It.

25. From *Tamoguna* (Inertia) *Maya* created the material objects, lifeless and motionless. This was her first act of creation.

26. Then as the *Rajoguna* (Motion), combined with the Life force of the Supreme Being, it opened up a whole world of consciousness (a variety of moving creatures), by virtue of the aspects of both.

27. The *Sattvaguna* (Righteousness) of this *Maya* then created the intellect, which, when permeated with the Divine Bliss, brought the sport of Creation to completion.

28. Thus *Maya* is susceptible to great modifications. So long as she is not stirred into action and does not create the above-mentioned things, the *Trigunas* remain unmanifest.

29. *Maya* is not manifest until she becomes active in her three *gunas*. Know, that as long as she herself remains passive, she can remain unmanifest.

30. *Maya* is the creation of the Supreme Being, while this world is the creation of *Maya*. 'All the visible world is Brahman' means that all these three (i.e. the Supreme Being, *Maya* and the world) are one.

31. Those in whose mind there is a keen desire to know how this unity can be experienced should see the *Vedas*.

32. A study of *Vedas, Shruti* and *Smriti* will give the power of discrimination (between real and unreal), which will give the experience that the guru's word is itself the *Vedanta*. This will, in turn, be conducive to the highest Bliss.

33. Shri Sai's devotees have always known that he gave an assurance to the effect that in the homes of his devotees there will be no want for food and clothing.

34. 'I consider it to be my promise, to look after the sustenance and protection of those who worship me single-mindedly and serve me with reverence in their hearts'.

35. This is the affirmation in the *Bhagvad Gita* which, Sai says, should be taken as the Truth. There will be no want of food and clothing; do not strive after these.

36. Seek honour in the court of God; beseech His Grace, alone; strive to attain only His blessings and do not hanker after worldly honours.

37. Why should just a nod of their heads by the people in appreciation turn your head? Rather, it should be your chosen deity whose heart should melt in compassion and burst out into beads of perspiration!

38. And may you love to strive after such an objective! May all the senses be seized by a devotional passion and the sensual desires be so transformed as to sprout into devotional worship, instead! Oh, how wonderful it would then be!

39. May such worship be forever, leaving no relish for anything else. May the mind be absorbed in my name, and all else be totally forgotten.

40. The mind will then become detached — from the physical body, household concerns and wealth and will be in divine Bliss. It will attain equanimity and serenity, ultimately finding fulfilment.

41. A contented mind is the surest mark of being in saintly companay. How can a restless mind that flits from one object to another be deemed to be one with the Supreme?

42. Hence, O listeners! give all attention as you listen to this narration with loving devotion. And may your mind turn to devotion while listening to this Life-story of Sai.

43. As the story progresses further, it will bring contentment; the restive mind will become restful; all agitation will be quietened, and peace and happiness will reign.

44. But now, let us continue with the story narrated previously, — about the renovation of the mosque and about the birth of Shri Ram.

45. There was a devotee called Gopal Gund, who had great devotion for Baba and who spent his time in the ceaseless chanting of Baba's name.

46. He had no issue. But later on, with Sai's blessing, a son was born to him. This made him very happy.

47. Gopal Gund felt that a fair (*yatra*) or celebration should be held every year at the Shirdi village, which will bring joy to everyone.

48. Tatya Kote, Dada Kote, Madhavrao and other prominent people in the village, liked the idea and began making preparations for it.

49. But the celebrations of such annual festivals was subject to a regulation according to which, the permission of the District Collector was necessary.

50. But when attempts were made to obtain it, the *Kulkarni* (the Revenue Officer) of the village maliciously opposed it, thus creating obstacles in the way.

51. As a result of the objections raised by the Kulkarni, the District Collector passed an order that the fair should not be held at Shirdi.

52. But it was Baba's wish too, that this fair should be held in Shirdi and he had given his consent with his blessings, for it.

53. The villagers pursued the matter with determination and tried their utmost, with the result that the order was reversed by the authorities, in deference to the wishes of all.

54. From then onwards, with Baba's consent, it was decided to hold the fair on *Ramanavami* day. Tatya Kote supervised all the arrangements. Multitudes now gather every year, for this fair.

55. On the day of *Ramanavami, pooja* and *bhajan*-singing took place amidst drum beats and sweet music made by musical instruments. Pilgrims from all directions flocked to Shirdi for the festivities.

56. Every year, two new flags used to be taken out in a procession ceremoniously, to be tied to the spire of the mosque and later to be fixed there.

57. Of these, one was Nimonkar's, the other Damuanna's. Both these, taken in a grand procession, would be fluttering high up at the tip of the spire.

58. Now listen to the interesting account of how the idea of celebrating *Ramanamavi* originated from the celebration of the *Urus* which is the honour that Shirdi gives to the Deity.

59. In the year 1911, Ramanavami was first celebrated and the idea had originated from the *Urus*. It continues to be celebrated, uninterrupted, to this day.

60. The idea was first conceived by the well-known *kirtankar* Krishna Jageshwar Bhishma[5], who felt that the birth of Shri Rama should be celebrated, for it would be beneficial to all.

61. Till then only the *Urus* and the fair were being held on a large scale, every year. But out of it there arose (the idea of) the wonderful celebration of the birth of Rama that year.

62. Once, as Bhishma sat in the *wada*, at his leisure, Kaka Mahajani was getting ready to go to the mosque with all the articles of *pooja*.

63. With the purpose of Sai's *darshan* in mind, and also to enjoy the festivities of the *Urus*, Kaka would always be present in Shirdi a day earlier for the celebrations.

64. Finding the time to be opportune, Bhishma then asked Kaka, 'To my mind has come a really good idea. But will you help me in carrying it out?

65. '*Urus* is held here every year. It is also the day of the birth of Ram and therefore affords us an opportunity to celebrate the occasion, without any extra efffort'.

66. Kaka liked the idea and said, 'Take Baba's permission. All depends on his word. Thereafter, of course, there will be no delay in the matter.'

67. But there still remained the question of arranging for the *kirtan*, for that would be necessary for such a celebration. Where could one find a Haridas to perform the *kirtan*, in a village? The difficulty remained!

68. Bhishma then said, 'I will be the *Kirtankar* and you accompany me on the harmonium, Radhakrishnabai will prepare the *Sunthawada*⁶ as *prasad*, for the occasion.

69. 'Come then, let us go to Baba. Any delay in an auspicious piece of work always creates problems. A good work, accomplished speedily, ensures success, right away!

70. 'Come, let us go and ask his permission for performing the *kirtan*'. So saying, they both then went to the mosque.

71. As Kaka began performing the *pooja*, it was Baba who first asked the question, "So, what was going on in the *wada*?" But it did not occur to Kaka to ask the relevant question.

72. At once, Baba put the same question, differently, to Bhishma. "So Bua, what do you say?" he asked Bhishma.

73. It was then that Kaka suddenly remembered and told him what they wished to do. Baba approved of their idea and the celebration was decided upon.

74. Next day in the morning, as soon as they saw Baba going to the Lendi, they tied up a cradle in the *sabha-mandap*, amidst the ceremonial preparations for the performance of the *kirtan*.

75. At the appropriate time, an audience gathered together for the kirtan. Baba returned (from the Lendi); Bhishma got up to begin; Kaka took his seat in front of the harmonium. And suddenly, Kaka was sent for, by Baba.

76. 'Baba has called you' the message came. Kaka was terrified on hearing these words. Why should his mind have any misgivings, he could not understand, but hoped that nothing would mar the spirit of the *kirtan*.

77. On hearing Baba's message, Kaka trembled in his shoes, with fright. 'Why should Baba be so agitated in his mind? Will the *kirtan* proceed without a hurdle or not?' he worried.

78. In his nervous anxiety, he faltered at every step as he climbed the steps of the mosque with slow, heavy footsteps.

79. Baba then asked him, why the cradle was tied there. And when it was briefly explained to him about the *kirtan* and the plans for the celebration, Baba was delighted.

80. Then from a niche in the wall nearby, he took out a beautiful garland and put it round Kaka's neck, giving him another one for Bhishma.

81. Baba's question about the cradle had caused great anxiety. But on seeing Kaka thus honoured with a garland, everyone was relieved.

82. Bhishma was really a versatile man, well-versed in religious lore. Naturally, his *kirtan* was full of spirit and beauty and enthralled the audience.

83. Baba's face had a pleased expression, too! As he had given his consent, so he now got the celebrations performed by the devotees, along with *bhajan* and *kirtan*.

84. In the hour of Ram's birth, particles of *gulal* (a red powder) got into Baba's eyes (as it was being freely showered during the ceremony), and then, it was as if Baba had become Narsimha incarnate[7], and not the infant Rama in the palace of Kausalya!

85. But '*gulal*' was just a pretext. His furious expression was really a manifestation of his fervour at the birth of Shri Ram who would destroy the demoniac forces of the ego and other evil propensities of man.

86. All of a sudden his anger flared up and he appeared to be Narasimha himself, in his rage! A volley of curses and abuses ensued, coming in a torrent.

87. Radhakrishnabai was greatly agitated, fearing in her mind that the cradle would now fall to pieces. How to keep it whole was the problem that confronted her.

88. She kept on urging and pressing that the cradle be taken down quickly. So Kaka moved forward to untie it.

89. This irritated Baba greatly. He became quite fierce and snappish and rushed forward aggressively, as if to attack Kaka. The untying of the cradle was stayed. Slowly, Baba also calmed down.

90. Later that afternoon, permission was sought to take it down, when Baba said in great surprise, "How can you take the cradle down just yet? There is still need for it!"

91. 'What could be this need?' I thought, 'for Sai's words are never in vain!' And then I realized that all the ceremonies were not yet complete.

92. The ceremonies had been performed for that particular day, but until the next day dawned and the *'Gopalkaala'*[8] was over, the festival could not be deemed to be over.

93. In this way, *kirtan*, *Gopalkaala*, etc., were performed the next day. And then Baba gave permission to take down the cradle.

94. Next year, Bhishma was not available. So Balabua Satarkar was approached for performing the *kirtan*. But he had to go to *Kavathe*[9] and was not available, too.

95. So Kaka Mahajani brought another *kirtankar* by the name Balabua Bhajani, known widely as the 'modern Tukaram'. The ceremonies were performed at his hands.

96. Even if he had not been available, Kaka would have himself stood up for the *kirtan*, for he knew by heart the *Katha* for *Ramanavami*, composed by Das Ganu.

97. In the third year, Balabua Satarkar himself came to Shirdi at the appropriate time. Now listen carefully how this came about.

98. Having heard of Sai Baba's fame, a desire for his *darshan* arose in his mind. But he wanted some company, on the way. And how to get that, was his worry.

99. Balabua was himself a Haridas and originally came from Satara, but was, at this time, staying at Parel, Bombay.

100. In the Satara district, there is a shrine called *Birhad Siddha-Kavathe* and Bua received an annual allowance for performing there, on the occasion of *Ramanavami*.

101. Bua was really concerned with two annual festivals there, viz. *Ashadhi Ekadashi* (in July-August) and *Ramanavami* in *Chaitra* (in March-April).

102. According to a Charter of the Moghul Emperor (Akbar), a sum of rupees one hundred and twenty-four had been sanctioned for the expenses and was accordingly allotted for the expenses of the deity as per the original scheme of the (Sangli) *Sansthan*.

103. And so, for these two festivals, Bua received an allowance of thirty rupees. But that year cholera broke out at Kavathe and the villagers faced a problem.

104. Hence *Ramanavami* could not be celebrated. Bua received letters from the village, saying that he should come next year, as the whole village was deserted.

105. In short, that year he lost the chance of serving Rama and receiving his allowance. But this was his opportunity to go to Shirdi. So he met Dikshit in this connection.

106. He thought that since Dikshit was such a great devotee of Baba, if he takes it in his mind, then his wish to go to Shirdi will be fulfilled, and thus both his purposes — of self-interest and spiritual benefit — will be served.

107. So he said to Dikshit, 'This year I have missed my annual allowance. So I felt that I should take Baba's *darshan*, and also perform *kirtan* at Shirdi.'

108. Bhausaheb (Dikshit) then replied, 'About the allowance, there is no guarantee. To give it or not, is entirely in Baba's hands. And as for the *kirtan*, his permission will be needed for that, too!'

109. Even as they were talking thus, Kaka Mahajani came there, quite unexpectedly, and he gave *udi* and *prasad* from Shirdi to everybody, which was considered as a good omen.

110. Mahajani had just come from Shirdi at that time and had come to say that all was well at Shirdi. Soon he went back to his house.

111. So Dikshit then, very lovingly said to Bua that he would seek Baba's permission and if given, he would definitely let him know.

112. And that when the letter came Bua should come to Shirdi, without worrying about the travelling expenses. For that, one should not trouble oneself and entertain any doubts in one's mind.

113. Later on, Dikshit went to Shirdi; Baba also gave his consent. Balabua then came to Shirdi and had Baba's *darshan* to his heart's content.

114. Sai Baba also, very lovingly had the *kirtan* performed in front of him with all the ceremonies and festivities of *Ramanavami* at the hands of Balabua.

115. Balabua, on his part, was very pleased that his objective was fulfilled, and so was Sai. Everybody was thus satisfied.

116. Bua was remunerated handsomely. A hundred and fifty rupees was paid to him by Baba's command. Bua's joy knew no bounds.

117. For Baba had given him for that one festival, an amount which he would have received after five years at Kavathe. Why then should Balabua not rejoice and be grateful to Baba?

118. However, later on when Das Ganu had once come to Shirdi, the annual festival was entrusted to him thereafter, with Baba's permission.

119. From then till now, the birth celebrations of Ram take place with pomp and pageantry, food being plentifully served to one and all, — even to the lowliest of the low and to their great joy and satisfaction.

120. On the occasion, at the portals of the *Samadhi Mandir* and amidst the resounding of the musical instruments rises the chant of Sai's name to fill the skies and suffuse them with waves of joy.

121. As with the holding of the fair or *Urus*, so was Gopal Gund also inspired with the idea of renovating and beautifying the dilapidated mosque.

122. Devotee Gopal Gund decided that even the mosque should be properly renovated and that too, at his own hands. So he got the stones ready.

123. But it appears that Gund was not to play a part in the renovation work. And later, as per Baba's wishes, a good opportunity came for accomplishing this piece of work.

124. It now seems that Baba wanted this to be done by Nanasaheb Chandorkar, and wished that Kakasaheb Dikshit should then get the floor paved.

125. And so it came to pass, a little later. At first, they tried in vain to get his permission, until they were exhausted. Mhalsapati was then asked to mediate. Only then did Baba give his consent.

126. However, when the flooring of the mosque was paved overnight, then from the very next day Baba started using a cushioned seat.

127. In the year 1911, a portico (*sabha-mandap*) was built. But oh, what a Herculean effort it involved! What toil and bother! Besides, it made them all tremble with fear!

128. However, that piece of work was also completed with arduous effort by the devotees, in the same way, under the same circumstances, in one night.

129. With great effort, the devotees would ram the columns at night; the next morning Baba would start pulling them out. Seizing an opportunity, the devotees would fix them again. Thus would the effort exhaust them all!

130. All would gird their loins, turning night into day, and toil away to fulfil the one great desire of their hearts!

131. Originally, it was an open space with a tiny yard in it, which Dikshit thought would be suitable for building a portico.

132. No matter how much money it required, but they bought iron columns and angle-brackets and seeing that, Baba had gone to the *Chavadi* for the night, they accomplished their task.

133.   Working at it all night, the devotees would thus ram the columns with great effort. No sooner Baba returned from the *Chavadi* in the morning then he would begin pulling them out.

134.   Then on one occasion Baba lost his temper. Holding Tatya by his neck with one hand, with the other he tried to tug at the column in an attempt to pull it out.

135.   Shaking the column vigorously, he loosened it. Then he took out Tatya's turban, and lighting it up with a match-stick, threw it into a pit, in great fury.

136.   At that time his eyes appeared to be like balls of fire. Who dared look him in the face at that time? They all lost their nerve!

137.   At once he then put his hand in the pocket and took out a one rupee coin, which he threw into the pit, too, as if to mark the auspicious moment.

138.   Curses, abuses came down in a shower. Tatya was terrified, at heart. A very tricky situation had arisen. But how did this happen?

139.   People were all stunned! Why such an ominous portent today? How can Tatya Patil be rescued from this calamity? they wondered.

140.   Bhagoji Shinde made bold and cautiously moved forward, only to fall an easy prey to Baba's wrath. He, too, was belaboured by Baba, to his heart's content.

141.   Even Madhavrao got caught and was rewarded with Baba's favour in the form of a few bricks hurled at him. Whoever else tried to mediate similarly received Baba's Grace (i.e. bricks).

142.   Even as people were still wondering as to 'who will dare to go in front of Baba? How can Tatya be freed?' Baba's anger slowly began to cool down and finally, he calmed down completely.

143.   A cloth merchant was sent for, at once, and a turban with a gold border was ordered. Baba himself got it tied round Tatya's head, as if to bestow upon him a mark of honour from a Rajah.

144.   But people were still puzzled as to the cause of this sudden anger, of the attack on Tatya, with all the abusing and reviling.

145.   For what reason did he flare up, so? And in a moment how did he appear so pleased and happy? The reason behind all this could not be understood at all, by anyone.

146. Sometimes he would be so calm and composed and would converse lovingly, sometimes, in a flash, and without apparent reason, his mind would be in great agitation.

147. Such then are the tales of Baba. As you are narrating one, another comes to mind, bewildering the narrator's mind as to which he should narrate and which, keep back. Moreover, it is not really correct to be partial in the selection.

148. Nor can I bring myself to be partial. Whichever tale is appropriate for the occasion will find its way to the reader to satisfy his desire to listen to these tales.

149. And now, listen, in the next chapter to the stories of the past, heard from the mouths of old people, which I shall narrate according to my capacity, — whether Sai baba was Hindu or Muslim.

150. How the money taken under the pretext of *dakshina* was used by him for the renovation of old temples; how he mortified his flesh through *dhoti-poti* and *Khandayoga*;

151. How he toiled for the welfare of others and warded off the difficulties of his devotees; — all this will become clear in the next chapter and will satisfy the listeners.

Weal be to all! Here ends the sixth chapter of
"Shri Sai Samarth Satcharit", called
'*The Story of the Festival of Shri Rama's Birth*,
as inspired by the saints and the virtuous,
and composed by his devotee, Hemadpant.

Notes

1. Astral body is the ethereal body; the subtle vehicle of the *Jeevatma* or sentient soul and the causative principle and archetype of the gross and material frame. It consists of the heart or seat of feeling, the judgement or discriminating faculty, the ten senses or faculties of perception and action and the five vital airs.
2. The word '*Pralaya*' used in the text has two meanings. Literally, it refers to the general destruction at the close of a Kalpa, i.e. period of 432,000,000 years. It also means death, dissolution, loss, annihilation, etc. Here the second meaning appears more apt.
3. The eight forms of *Sattvik* changes (spiritual modifications or ecstasies) that shake the body and mind are: motionlessness, perspiration, horripilation, indistinctness of speech, tremor, paleness, tears and loss of consciousness.
4. Gum-Arabic tree, *Acacia Araabica*.
5. A Vedic scholar, *kirtankar* and author of '*Shri Sadguru Sainath Sagunopasana*'.
6. A preparation of ginger, molasses, sugar, etc., distributed to the audience upon the conclusion of a *katha*, *kirtan*, etc.
7. God Vishnu in his fourth *Avatar* or descent as the man-lion, to destroy Hiranyakashipu, a demon prince. Hence the term *Narasimha-avatar* means to be furiously angry.
8. The feasting and the merriment which concludes the festival of *Gokul-ashtami* in honour of Krishna.
9. He had an annual grant for performing *kirtan* at Birhad *Siddha-Kavathe* in Satara district.

7

What was Sai Baba?

MY OBEISANCE TO SHRI GANESH, TO SHRI SARASWATI, AND SHRI GURUMAHARAJ! TO THE FAMILY DEITY, TO SHRI SITA-RAMACHANDRA, MY MOST HUMBLE OBEISANCE! I BOW IN REVERENCE TO THE MOST VENERABLE GURU SHRI SAINATH!

1. Now let us recall to our minds the connection of the previous story: how Baba was fond of renovating the old temples;

2. How he would exert himself for the benefit of others, how he would protect his devotees, taking upon himself their sorrows and sufferings and wearing away his body in their cause;

3. How he practised *khandayoga, dhoti-poti* along with *Samadhi* — sometimes severing from his body, hands, legs and the head, sometimes joining them together, as before.

4. If considered a Hindu, he looked like a Muslim; and if a Muslim, he exhibited all the qualities of a good Hindu. Who, even with all his proficiency and learning, can describe such an extraordinary *Avatar*?

5. No one could trace in the least, whether he was a Hindu or Muslim, for his conduct towards both these was always the same.

6. *Ramanavami* is really a Hindu festival; but he himself got it celebrated. He would have the cradle tied in the *sabhamandap*, and have the *Katha-Kirtan* performed.

7. In the square in front, would the cradle be put up and he would have the *Ram-kirtan* performed. On the same night he would also give permission to the Muslims to take out the 'Sandal'[1] procession.

8. Collecting together as many Muslims as possible, the '*Sandal*' procession would be taken out ceremoniously. Thus he got both the festivals celebrated equally well and with great joy.

9. As the *Ramanavami* festival came round, he would be greatly interested in arranging wrestling events and would be delighted in giving away horses, *todas*[2] and turbans as prizes.

10. When the festival of *Gokul-ashtami* came, he would get *Gopal-kala*[3] performed. Similarly, when '*Id*' came, the Muslims were not prohibited from doing their *Namaz*.

11. Once, as the festival of Muharram approached, some Muslims came to the mosque proposing that a *Taja* (Taboot)[4] be made and taken in procession through the village.

12. On being permitted to do so, the *Taja* was got ready and kept for four days. On the fifth day it was taken down without his feeling any pleasure or pain.

13. If a Muslim, his ears were pierced; but if a Hindu, his circumcision[5] proved it to be otherwise. Neither a Hindu nor a Muslim — such was this Sai, the very incarnation of sanctity.

14. If he is called a Hindu, he always lived in the mosque, and if he is called a Muslim, the fire burns day and night in the mosque.

15. In the mosque there was grinding in a quern; in the mosque too, resounded the bells, the conch, and so also in that mosque there was the offering of rice in the holy fire; what kind of a Muslim was this?

16. In the mosque the *bhajan* went on all the time; and the distribution of food to the people also went on in that mosque. Again, the Hindus worshipped his feet, offered oblations to him in the mosque! How can he be a Muslim?

17. If a Muslim, how was he worshipped by the best among Brahmins, and the *Agnihotri* prostrated before him giving up their pride in their *sovale*[6]?

18. So the people wondered in their minds. Those who came to find out for themselves, behaved in the same manner, too! And after having his *darshan*, fell silent!

19. Indeed, he who seeks refuge in *Hari* (God), forever, how can he be called a Hindu or a Muslim? He may even be a *shudra*, or the lowest among the *shudras*, or even without a caste; his caste is not at all the criterion or standard for judging him.

20. He who has no bodily conceit and treats all the *varnas* among the Hindus, or Muslims as equals, does not differentiate between the castes.

21. Eating in the company of the fakirs, he would eat meat, or if occasion required it, would also eat fish. But even there, should a dog put his mouth to the food, he did not turn away in disgust.

22. A peasant always stores up in large bundles the crop of the current year, so that, if there be a shortage of grain next year, it could be used to make up for the deficiency.

23. Similarly, Baba always had in store a bag of wheat. For grinding, there was a quern in the mosque and there was also a scuttle basket for sifting corn. Nothing was wanting for carrying on the business of life.

24. In the portico there was a beautiful and proper *Tulsi-Brindavan*[7]. In the same place there was also a wooden chariot engraved with auspicious signs.

25. Some merit must have been accumulated by us in the previous births, that we have met such a saint, a God Incarnate. Hold him firmly in the casket of your heart so that you will not lose him, till you die.

26. It must be by some good fortune, earned in the past births that we are thus drawn to his feet, which have brought us peace of mind and freedom from worldly cares.

27. However great the prosperity and happinesss I may enjoy, in days to come, this happiness in the company of Shri Sai Samarth, with which I am blessed, will never come back again.

28. Self-rejoicing, Self-absorbed as Sai is, how can I describe his marvellous ways adequately? Whoever remains absorbed at his feet, is confirmed in his faith by Sai.

29. Ascetics with a *sanyasin*'s staff and the deer-skin; those residing at holy places of pilgrimage, like Hardwar; religious mendicants;

sanyasins; those that have renounced the world; the *Udasis*[8], and many such came to Baba.

30. Baba would talk and laugh and move freely with all. The words *'Allah Malik'* were constantly on his lips. He disliked arguments and unprofitable wranglings. His staff (i.e. the baton) was always kept near at hand.

31. By disposition an ascetic, he was tranquil and had conquered the senses and the mind. From his speech flowed perfect *Vedanta*. Till the end, nobody could gauge Baba's true nature.

32. Be he a king or a beggar, they received equal treatment in all matters. For both a rich man and a pauper, the measure was the same.

33. Somebody's deeds, good or bad, or his innermost secrets were all known to him and he used to astonish the devotees by giving a sign or an indication of them.

34. He was the reservoir of Knowledge and Wisdom under the guise of feigned ignorance. To exert himself for honour and recognition in the world was too irksome for him. Such was the disposition of Sai.

35. Though his physical frame was human, his deeds matched those of the gods, in being unexcelled. It was people's faith that he was God Incarnate, in Shirdi!

36. Oh! for the miracles of Baba! How much can I, a lowly person, describe them! Innumerable were the renovations that Baba got done to the idols and the temples of gods.

37. In Shirdi, the condition of Shani, Ganpati, Shankar-Parvati, Gramdevi (village-deity) and Maruti temples was also improved at the hands of Tatya Patil.

38. The money that Baba accepted from people under the guise of *dakshina*, was, in part, given away for charitable works and, in part, just given away to people.

39. To some, thirty rupees, to some others ten or fifteen or fifty rupees, as and to whom it pleased him, were daily distributed with great enthusiasm.

40. All this money came from charity. Those who received it also believed it to be so and even Baba wished that it should be expended for a good cause.

41. And thus, many became healthy and robust by his mere *darshan*, some changed their wicked ways and became good; many were cured of their leprosy and so many enjoyed weal.

42. Without the medicated collyrium or a herbal remedy, so many sightless regained their sight and the lame regained power in their legs, just by falling at his feet.

43. Limitless was Baba's power and greatness which no one could fathom. People from all the four directions started coming to Shirdi in multitudes, for his *darshan*.

44. He would always be sitting at the same place near the *dhuni*, absorbed in meditation after his morning ablutions, sometimes after a bath or sometimes without having one.

45. A nice white turban on the head, he would wear a clean *dhoti* round his waist and would don a long shirt. Such was his dress in the beginning.

46. He used to administer indigenous medicines in the village. By observing the symptoms he gave medicine and had a good deal of success so that he became a famous *Hakim*[9].

47. Once a devotee had red, inflamed eyes which appeared as red balls due to the swelling. Both the eyeballs were blood-shot. No doctor was locally available in Shirdi.

48. The simple, trusting devotee showed his eyes to Baba. At once Baba got some *Bibba* seed crushed and made into balls[10].

49. For such an ailment some will apply *Surma*[11]; some may put cotton soaked in cow's milk, or some others may use the cooling camphor tablets or collyrium.

50. But Baba's remedy was most unusual. He picked up the balls, one at a time, with his own hands and rammed them into each of the eyes, bandaging finally, with a piece of cloth.

51. The next day the bandage was removed from the eyes and water was poured over them in a continuous stream. The swelling had subsided completely and the eyeballs had become clear and normal.

52. Such a delicate organ like the eye! But even the *Bibba* seeds caused no burning or pain. In fact they cured the eye ailment absolutely! Many are such experiences!

53. Baba knew *'dhoti-poti'* (a *Hathayoga* practice). Without anybody's knowledge, he would go to some secluded spot, take a bath and then bring out his intestines (through the mouth), which he would then wash and hang them up to dry.

54. Equidistant as the well from the mosque, was a banyan tree and beyond this tree was another well. To this latter, he used to go every two days.

55. In the scorching heat, at high noon, seeing that no one was around, he would himself draw water from the well and wash his mouth, face, etc.

56. And so, on one such occasion, when he was sitting down to his bath, he hurriedly brought out his intestines and began washing them at that place.

57. When a goat is killed, its intestines are turned inside out, washed clean, and put, fold upon fold, to dry.

58. Similarly, he took out his intestines, and turning them inside out, cleaned them carefully. He then spread them out on the guava tree, to the consternation of the people around.

59. Even now, there are people alive in Shirdi, who have seen Baba in this condition with their own eyes, who say that he was a unique saint.

60. Sometimes he would practise *Khandyoga*, separating hands, legs, etc., from the trunk. And these parts of his body could be seen fallen off at different places in the mosque.

61. And when the people, in large numbers, came running to see the shocking spectacle of his body thus severed into parts, what they always saw was Baba, whole and in one piece.

62. Once a spectator was terrified on seeing such a scene and thought that some wicked person must have killed Baba and committed such an atrocity.

63. In the four corners of the mosque, parts of the body could be seen scattered at different places. It was the midnight hour and not a soul was around. He became greatly worried.

64. If he were to go and tell anyone, he would himself get implicated. This was his difficulty. So he went and sat outside.

65. But that it could be some yogic practice of Sai, he did not even dream. The sight of the mutilated body struck terror in his heart.

66. He wanted very much to inform somebody of what he had seen, but the fear that, being the first informer, he would himself be accused of the crime, —

67. Prevented him from telling anyone. Doubts and fears crowded his mind. So once again, at dawn, he went to see and was quite astonished.

68. What he had seen earlier had vanished completely, and Baba sat in his usual place, hale and hearty. He began to wonder whether this was a dream.

69. These yogic practices of *dhoti-poti*, etc., were being practised by Baba, since childhood. But nobody could comprehend the extent of his yogic powers and the mysterious behaviour consequent upon it.

70. Never did he touch even a farthing of anybody. His fame (as a physician) rested only on his success in effecting a cure. He nursed the poor and the weak back to health and became renowned as a *Hakim* in that district.

71. But this *Hakim* lived only for the benefit of others. About his own profit, he was most disinterested. And to achieve the good of others, he would bear intolerable pain and suffering.

72. In this context, I shall now narrate an extraordinary incident for the benefit of the listeners, which will bring out Baba's compassion and all-pervasiveness.

73. In the year 1910, on the *Dhanteras* day, on the eve of *Diwali* (the Festival of Lights), Baba was sitting near the *dhuni*, putting logs of wood to the fire, in a casual manner.

74. The fire in the *dhuni* was raging, and there sat Baba, his hand thrust in the fire, but quite oblivious and unconcerned about it. The hand was naturally, scorched quite severely.

75. Madhav, his attendant, noticed it at once. Madhavrao Deshpande, who was nearby, noticed it, too, and ran instantly.

76. He squatted at the back and putting his hands tightly round Baba's waist, pulled him back, exclaiming,

77. 'Alas! Baba, what have you done!' As he said so, Baba at once came back to the waking state (from super-consciousnmess) and said, "Oh, Shama, you know, a child slipped from its mother's arms suddenly, and fell into the smith's forge!

78. "Hearing her husband call out to her, the smith's wife began to blow the bellows vigorously, out of fear, while holding the child in her armpit all the while.

79. "While doing so, quite inadvertently, she forgot the child in her armpit for a moment. The restless, over-active child slipped from there. But Shama, no sooner did she fall than I picked her up.

80. "And as I was picking her up, this is what happened! Let the hand be scorched, but at least the child's life is saved!"

81. 'How should the hand be now treated, and by whom?' wondered Madhavrao. He decided to write a letter to Chandorkar.

82. So he wrote a detailed letter and Chandorkar came to Shirdi at once, bringing with him Paramanand, a well-known doctor.

83. Equipped with a variety of medicines to soothe the burning pain and accompanied by Paramanand, Nanasaheb came and stood before Baba.

84. Making obeisance to Baba, he made the customary enquiries after his well-being and then disclosed the purpose of his visit, requesting him to show his injured hand.

85. Already, from the day the hand was burned, Bhagoji Shinde was massaging it with *ghee* (clarified butter) and, after covering it with a leaf, was bandaging it tightly, every day.

86. To take the bandages out to have a look at the hand, and show it to Paramanand also, so that proper medication could begin and Baba could get relief -

87. Such was the good intention in Nana's mind, with which he entreated Baba in various ways; even Paramanand made many attempts to induce Baba to take off the bandages so that he could see for himself the condition of the hand.

88. But Baba kept on postponing from day to day, and saying all the while that "Allah is our *Vaidya*". So that he never gave him his hand to see and had no regrets about it.

89. The medicines that Paramanand had brought with him never saw the light of day in Shirdi. But it was destined that he should experience the joy of Sai's *darshan*, on account of it.

90. Bhagoji alone had the privilege of serving him thus, every day. And so, Bhagoji alone would massage his hand. As a result, the hand healed in the course of time. All were relieved and happy.

91. Though the hand healed in this way, one knows not what insatiety it could be, that made Baba go through the process of bandaging, massaging and so on, every day, as the usual time for it approached in the morning.

92. Even without any pain or injury, it was unnecessarily tended with great care regularly, being given a massage of *ghee*, where no wound or injury remained. And this continued to the end.

93. Himself a *Siddha*, Sai did not need this service from Bhagoji. But out of his intense desire for the welfare of his devotees, he got Bhagoji to render it regularly.

94. As a result of the great sins of his past births, Bhagoji was afflicted with leprosy. But great indeed was his good fortune that he had the privilege of Sai's company.

95. As Baba set out on his daily round to the Lendi, Bhagoji would be his umbrella-bearer. His body was full of bleeding sores, yet he was the foremost among the attendants.

96. Every day in the morning, as Baba sat comfortably leaning against the pillar near the *dhuni*, Bhagya would present himself for his service.

97. Removing the bandages from the hands and the legs, he would then massage the muscles of those limbs and would rub some *ghee* into them. Such was the service Bhagya rendered.

98. A great sinner from previous births, with a body festered with bleeding leprosy, severely afflicted that Bhagya was, he was yet a great devotee of Baba.

99. The fingers and the toes had fallen off due to leprosy; the whole body with its stink was repulsive, — such were the grave misfortunes of him, whose great good fortune was the great happiness of serving Baba.

100. Oh, how much can I describe to the listeners of the marvellous *leelas* of Baba! Once the epidemic of plague broke out in the village. Just listen to the miracle that took place then!

101. Dadasaheb Khaparde had a very young son who was at Shirdi, with his mother, enjoying the great happiness of Baba's company.

102. The boy was very small. Moreover, he was burning with a high fever, which seemed to break the mother's heart. She grew very restless.

103. As her home was at Amaravati, she thought she should go back thither. So, finding a suitable opportunity in the evening, she came to take Baba's permission.

104. During his evening round, as Baba came near the *wada*, the lady came and clasped his feet, relating to him what had happened.

105. As it is, women are nervous by nature, and then, the child's shivering would not stop. Moreover, there was the fear of the dreaded plague. She kept on harping on what had happened.

106. Gently Baba said, "The sky is overcast, but it will rain, bringing forth the harvest and the clouds will all melt away.

107. "Why be afraid?" So saying, he lifted his *kafni* up to the waist and showed the inflamed buboes to everyone.

108. The size of a hen's egg, four inflamed buboes could be seen spread in four directions. "See, I have to take upon myself all your sufferings", said Baba.

109. Seeing this extraordinary divine act, people were amazed. Oh, how these saints take upon themselves the innumerable sufferings of their devotees!

110. They have a heart softer than wax itself, — as if it were a lump of butter! Their love for the devotees is truly selfless, for the devotees alone are their kith and kin!

111. Once it so happened that Nanasaheb left Nandurbar to go to Pandharpur.

112. Nana was most fortunate, indeed! His devotion and service to Baba seemed to have borne fruit, and he attained *Vaikunth*, the abode of Lord Vishnu, on this earth itself! For he was appointed *Mamlatdar* to Pandharpur.

113. On receiving the order at Nandurbar, he was required to leave as early as possible. So he immediately made preparations to leave, with a keen desire to have Baba's *darshan*.

114. He decided to go to Shirdi with his entire family, for Shirdi was to him Pandharpur itself and he first wanted to make obeisance to Baba.

115. However, no letter was sent to anyone at Shirdi, nor had any message or news preceded his arrival. Packing all his luggage he hurriedly boarded the train.

116. No one in Shirdi could have known that Nana had started from Nandurbar in this (hurried) manner. But Sai, whose eyes were everywhere, knew everything.

117. Nana had started speedily and may have just reached the border of Nimgaon, when a miracle took place in Shirdi. Listen to it!

118. Baba was in the mosque, talking to Mhalsapati, Appa Shinde, Kashiram and some other devotees.

119. Suddenly he said, "Come, let all the four of us sing *bhajan* together. The portals of the temple at Pandharpur have opened. Let us go on singing our *bhajan* merrily!"

120. Sai, who knew everything — past, present and future — had known about Nana's arrival and when Nana had reached the stream at the village border, Baba suddenly showed great enthusiasm for singing the *bhajan*:

> To Pandharpur, I go, I go,
> There alone, do I stay,
> There alone, do I stay, I stay,
> In that abode of my Lord!

121. Baba was singing the *bhajan* himself and the devotees sitting around repeated the refrain. All were overcome by the feeling of love and devotion to Vithoba of Pandhari. And then Nana arrived, quite suddenly!

122. He, with his family, bowed at Baba's feet, saying, 'Maharaj, please be with us as we proceed to Pandharpur, and remain there at your leisure.'

123. But the request was hardly necessary! The people then told him about Baba's enthusiasm to go to Pandharpur and the *bhajan* that it inspired.

124. In his heart, Nana was wonderstruck. Baba's *leela* had astonished him absolutely! He was choked with emotion as he placed his head on Baba's feet.

125. After receiving *udi* and *prasad* with Baba's blessings, Chandorkar took Baba's leave to go to Pandharpur.

126. And now, if I go on narrating all these stories, the book will become too expansive. Hence I shall now end this subject of Baba's *leelas* for relieving the suffering of others.

127. So let us now conclude this chapter, for there is no end to Baba's stories. In the next chapter, I shall narrate some miscellaneous stories for my own benefit.

128. Oh, for this self-conceit of mine, which, try as I may, I am not able to overcome! And yet, who is this 'I', I know not, for certain! Really it is Sai himself, who will narrate his own Story.

129. He will explain the importance of this human birth and describe his routine of collecting alms, the single-minded devotion of Bayjabai, as also about his manner of having his meals.

130. Listen also, to how Baba used to sleep in the mosque with Mhalsapati and with Tatya Kote Patil.

131. Hemadpant submits totally to Sai and regards himself but a slipper on the feet of Sai-devotees. To him, Sai's word is the only Truth, the only Standard. Thus, the narration of Sai's Story has come so far.

Weal be to all! Here ends the seventh chapter of
"Shri Sai Samarth Satcharit", called
'Narration of Various Tales',
as inspired by the saints and the virtuous,
and composed by his devotee, Hemadpant.

Notes

1. *'Sandal'* means levigated and powdered sandalwood. This is placed in a metal vessel of
    a certain form and size and incense is burnt before it and an *agarbatti* lighted. It is then
    taken in procession through the Shirdi village up to the mosque and then palm
    impressions of levigated sandalwood are put at that place. This custom was first started
    in Shirdi by Baba's well-known devotee, Amir Shakkar.
2. A ring of gold or silver for the wrist or ankle.
3. See Ch. 6, note No. 8.
4. *Taja and Taboot*: *Taja* means the elegy sung by Muhammadans during the Muharram.
    But as the footnote in the original indicates, the word is used here for *'Taboot'*, which
    means bier, especially that of Hussain and Hassan, carried about in Muharram by the
    Muhammadans.
5. This statement of Dabholkar's does not seem to have been based on facts. In this
    connection, a reference to the Gujarati translation of Das Ganu's *'Shri Sainath Stavan
    Manjiri'*, by the late Swami Shri Sai-Sharananand', is interesting and informative. In
    the footnote to verse 67 in this translation, Swamiji says, "...As per this translator's own
    knowledge and observation, Baba's ears were pierced and he had not undergone
    circumcision. If any *prasad* was brought at a time other than the afternoon *Naivedya*
    and if Bade Baba or any other Muslims were present, Baba would order the first sura of
    the Koran to be recited and would himself join in it. But in the absence of any Muslims,
    this practice was not followed."
6. The word *'sovale'* is used in the original text. Among Brahmins, pure, holy, clean, i.e. in
    the state contra-distinguished from *'ovale'*; that has by ablution or other purificatory
    ceremony, attained qualification for the highest and most sacred rites of religion, and
    whom the touch of persons or things in the *'ovala'* would disqualify. The word is used
    also for clothes, culinary vessels, food and things in general, which, by washing or other
    act or rite of purification are rendered fit, and of certain things (such as silken or woollen
    cloths) which are inherently and unvaryingly fit for the touch or use of the *'sovala'*
    person.'
7. This is a square erection (an altar) in front of a Hindu home, in which is planted a Tulsi
    or the holy Basil plant or *Ocymum sanctum*.
8. An order of Gosavis, said to be one of the eighteen sub-sects of the *Nath Sampradaya*.
9. A physician. The word is used particularly of a Muhammadan physician practising
    Unani system of medicine.
10. *Semecarpus anacardium* or the marking nut.
11. Sulphuret of antimony.

Importance of Human birth – Partaking Food collected by Alms – Bayajabai's Devotion – Sleeping with Tatya and Mhalsapati

MY OBEISANCE TO SHRI GANESH, TO SHRI SARASWATI, AND SHRI GURUMAHARAJ! TO THE FAMILY DEITY, TO SHRI SITA-RAMACHANDRA, MY MOST HUMBLE OBEISANCE! I BOW IN REVERENCE TO THE MOST VENERABLE GURU SHRI SAINATH!

1. In the last chapter it has been narrated how no one could say if Sai was a Hindu or a Muslim; how great was the good fortune of Shirdi that Baba made it his own home;

2. How, initially, Baba came as a young lad and had later become a 'mad fakir' to the people; how he made a beautiful garden out of a place which was originally rough and barren;

3. How, after a time, on that same spot came up a *wada;* also how Baba excelled in the bold yogic practices of *dhoti-poti* and *khand-yoga.*

4. And Protector of the Devotees that he was, how Baba wore out his body, taking their suffering upon himself. How can I describe all these adequately.

5. Now listen further, to the great significance of being born a human, to the description of Baba's practice of collecting alms and of

Bayajabai's selfless service to the saints as also, of Baba's astonishing way of taking meals.

6. How the three of them, i.e. Tatya, Baba and Mhalsapati, used to sleep in the mosque and how Sai Samarth used to go to the house of Khushalchand at Rahata.

7. The day dawns and sets in the evening. Years are devoured thus. Half the lifetime passes in slumber and even the remaining half brings no peace and happiness.

8. Childhood is spent absorbed in play; the youth, in amorous pursuit of the youthful maiden, and old age, in the weariness brought on by debility and disease — and forever plagued by maladies.

9. To come into this world only to fatten the body, to keep on breathing and live up to a ripe old age — is this the fulfilment of this human birth?

10. Attainment of the Supreme is really the highest achievement of human life. Or else, what is so wanting in the existence of dogs, pigs and other animals?

11. The dogs also fill their bellies and go on procreating to their heart's content. Then what is the great significance of a human birth, when both, a dog and a human being, are in the same position?

12. If nurture of the physical body and copulation alone are the means of fulfilment of the ultimate goal of human existence, then this human birth is meaningless, indeed!

13. If the life be spent only in the fourfold activity of eating, and drinking[1], sleep, etc., then what is the difference between dogs and humans? Think for yourselves and judge.

14. If this alone is the fulfilment of the human body, then what is the deficiency in the existence of bees and plants? The bellows too, breathe in and out, and even dogs nourish and fatten their bodies!

15. But a human being is emancipated; he is fearless and he is free and he is everlasting. To have this awareness itself is the fulfilment of this birth.

16. From where do I come? Who am I? Why have I a human birth? He who knows the principle of all this is a proficient man. Without this knowledge everything is futile.

17. Just as the flame of the *Nandadeep*[2] appears to be the same from the beginning to the end but undergoes change from moment to moment, so also is the state of the body.

18. Childhood, youth and old age — these are states apparent to all people, but they come and go most naturally without anyone ever realizing it.

19. The state of the flame that we see this moment ends in that same instant and appears to be the same, though constantly changing; similarly, what this body is this moment, it will not be the same the next moment.

20. This body is the outlet for excreta, dirt, phlegm, pus, saliva. Such are the ill-boding qualities it bears.

21. This human body is the habitation of worms and insects, is a storehouse of various diseases, is mortal and transient.

22. It is a cart loaded with flesh, blood and muscle, a frame of skin and bone, a stinking pit of excrement and urine, an encumbering appendage of the soul, indeed!

23. This body, with its skin, flesh, blood, muscle, fat, marrow, bones, air (as one of the humors of the body) and certain loathsome parts like the genitals and the anus — is but short-lived.

24. But unpropitious, destructible and transient as this human body is, yet it is the only instrument of attaining God, the home of all sanctity.

25. Pursued as we are, all the time, by birth and death, the horror of its very idea dogs our footsteps. And yet when life departs, it leaves all of a sudden.

26. Who keeps count of how many come and how many go, by day and by night? Some are even born with the longevity of the sage Markandeya[3]. But even they cannot escape death.

27. While in such a transient human body, the time spent in listening to the stories of the saints — by remembering whom, merit is acquired — is the time well spent. The rest of the time is wasted.

28. When such awareness comes with a certainty, it is in itself the advantage of being born a human. But without personal experience, nobody is convinced of the truth of this.

29. And yet, one has to undertake a deep study even to get this experience. Hence he who desires lasting happiness should endeavour to attain this glory.

30. Wife, son, prosperity, wealth, in fact the kingdom of this boundless earth, a man may attain by God's grace. And yet his heart is insatiated.

31. But with lasting happiness and peace as the objective before the mind, when God is worshipped by seeing Him in every living being, it will lead to attainment of salvation or *moksha*.

32. By putting together the skin, flesh, blood and bones, this human frame is made up, which is a great obstacle in the spiritual path. Hence give up all attachment to it.

33. Treat it only as your servant. Do not exalt it unduly. Do not pamper it all the time and allow it to pave the way to Hell.

34. Give it food and clothing enough for subsistence, as also nurture, for the time being. So that it may be made use of for your spiritual upliftment and the final liberation from birth and death.

35. Subject to calamities of birth, death, etc., about to be destroyed any moment, — such is this perpetually unhappy human existence! Of what use is its momentary happiness?

36. As the lightning which disappears in a flash, or the ripples that momentarily appear on the ocean, such are the short-lived pleasures of the body. Give some thought to this.

37. Knowing full well that the body, house, wife and children, and the people around him are all destructible, and having borne the biers of the parents on his shoulder to the grave, a man yet does not awaken to the truth.

38. He still continues the same way as those who have already departed before him, thus making the rounds of the birth-death cycle; but does not stop a moment to think as to the means by which these could be restrained.

39. In attending, all the time, to the well-being and prosperity of the family, life passes away swiftly, but Time is diligent in counting the years as they pass and will never forget its duty.

40. And when the last moment comes, he will not pause even for a moment, but will, like a fisherman, pull the net tightly, and then, in that moment of death, the human being will toss about in helpless agony, like a fish caught in the net.

41. It is by a plenitude of great good fortune, and by accumulating scores of meritorious deeds that this human body is acquired. Hence make the most of this opportunity you have.

42. Even with the gigantic efforts of a *Bhagirath*[4], this human body cannot be attained. Only by destiny it comes in our hands quite unexpectedly. Do not throw it away in the dust in vain.

43. One who postpones anything to the next birth is a fool to believe that though in this birth this human body slips out of his hands, he will definitely get it back in the next.

44. So many sinners mingle with the male semen and appear at the entrance to the womb to get a human body, according to their *karma*.

45. Many, even more vile, as a result of their *karma*, move from the lower order of mobile creatures to be born as immobile beings.

46. In accordance with the knowledge attained and the *karma* performed, one is ordained to get a particular body. This is acknowledged by the *Shrutis*, also.

47. For *Shruti*, the compassionate Mother says, 'According to one's knowledge, one is born'. As is the store of knowledge, so is also the birth that a being gets.

48. Incomprehensible are the ways of God. It is impossible to understand them fully. Blessed is that human being who can attain even a fraction of knowledge about them.

49. By greatest good fortune one gets human birth and by great accumulated merit is one born a Brahmin. But God's Grace alone brings one to Sai's feet. Rare indeed, is the perfect gain to have all three!

50. Varied are the species of created beings; but that of the human beings is the highest among them. For it is only possible for the humans to think, 'Who has created us? From where do we come?' and the like.

51. Other species do not understand anything. They are born and one day they die, without any understanding of the past, present or future, or of the existence of the Supreme Being.

52. So God was happy to create the human being, thinking that man will use his discretion and wisdom, will embrace renunciation and detachment, and will worship Him.

53. Since there is none other in this Creation who is endowed with the means as that of the human body, to attain salvation, He thought, man will use that body for *sadhana* and will attain the immortality of Narayan Himself.

54. A magician is himself very clever. He never performs his tricks before an audience that is ignorant. He anticipates an audience that will appreciate the secret of his deftness.

55. Similarly, after having created innumerable birds, animals, trees, worms and insects, the Lord of this creation was left with a feeling of great astonishment and regret thinking that all His achievement was meaningless.

56. Oh, such a boundless expanse of this universe (totality of all worlds including all the galaxies), with the sun, the moon, the countless stars! And yet — no one has the least thought or admiration for this marvellous achievement of the Creator!

57. 'Not a creature knows for certain, what is my purpose as the Lord of the Universe in creating this sport!

58. 'Until, therefore, a creature is created with so sharp an intellect as to understand and admire the incomparable glory of my work, all this achievement of mine is in vain!'

59. So, the Almighty created a being in human form. He thought, 'With the power of his discriminating intellect, man will know me.

60. 'He will be amazed with the knowledge of my inconceivable grandeur, as also my unexcelled prowess and will realize that the entire universe is but a sport of my *Maya*.

61. 'Only he will be able to acquire Knowledge, reflect and meditate upon me and be filled with awe and wonder. And that will bring my sport to completion.

62. 'The happiness of the spectators is in itself the fullness of my sport. Seeing my perfect control over the world, man will feel fulfilled.'

63. To perform pleasurable *karmas* or to earn wealth is not the purpose of nurturing the body; the fulfilment of human life lies in acquiring the Supreme Knowledge, till breath leaves the body.

64. Realization of non-duality (between *Jeevatma* and *Paramatma*) is this Supreme Knowledge. It is what the Upanishads call '*Brahma-jnana*'. And the worship and service to the Lord is also the same. This is what is implied in saying 'Bhagvan of the devotees'

65. He who has gained this knowledge of non-duality (that the Guru and the Brahman are not separable), and worships in this spirit, will find it easy to overcome *Maya*.

66. Those men of faith, who have attained knowledge and renunciation are alone fit to enjoy self-absorption. Know, that such devotees are truly fortunate.

67. To regard oneself as fulfilled and perfect, without having removed the ignorance arising out of an awareness of the true Self, creates a strange impediment.

68. Knowledge and ignorance are both states of mind that give rise to illusions and errors. As one thorn is pulled out by another thorn, so remove the one with the other.

69. Dispel ignorance by knowledge. However, the highest purpose of human existence is to go beyond knowledge and ignorance and merge in the Pure Self.

70. Unless the oil of sensual attachments is burnt out completely, the darkness of ignorance is reduced to ashes, and the wick of 'me' and 'mine' (i.e. the ego) is burnt to cinders, Knowledge will not shine forth in all its radiance.

71. Know, that all actions pertaining to the human body, whether evitable or inevitable, are performed with a conscious determination or plan.

72. If one has no other work to do, one should quietly enjoy comfort and prosperity or take *Ram-naam*. It will bring freedom from cares and from desires.

73. The bodily organs, mind and intellect are all limitations to which the *Atman* is subject. Due to these, though himself without a beginning and a non-enjoyer, the *Atman* brings upon himself the suffering, resulting from *karma*.

74. Thus, though a non-enjoyer by nature, the suffering of the *Atman* is due to his limitations. And for this *Nyaya-shastra* has given proof by making use of *Anvaya-Vyatirek*[5].

75. Know this to be the one vital principle and leave the necessary *karma* or action, as also the various processes of the mind, to the intellect. As for yourself, act as a non-doer of action.

76. Conduct yourself according to the dictates of your own *dharma*[6]. Always contemplate on the *Atman* (Self), distinguishing him from the *Anatman* (non-Self). This is the ultimate goal of human life, which lies in the contentment that comes from Self-absorption.

77. There is no other means of obtaining the four objectives of human life (*viz. Artha, Dharma, Kama* and *Moksha*), except the human body. And the man who devotes himself to the study of how this can be done will attain the status of Shri Narayan Himself.

78. Hence, while this body is not yet fallen, endeavour to know your true Self. Do not waste even a moment of this human birth.

79. The salt water of the ocean undergoes a transformation in the clouds to become sweet water. Happiness follows similarly when one is absorbed at the guru's feet.

80. No one except the guru knows how this human body can be truly liberated and it is only when the guru takes them in hand that the dull and ignorant beings are uplifted.

81. *Mantra*, places of pilgrimage, God, Brahmins, practitioners of astrology and astronomy, Vaidyas, and lastly, the seventh one, that is, Gururaj — all these are effective only according to one's faith in them.

82. In the same proportion as the degree of faith is reposed in any of these, will the measure of success be achieved.

83. Saints turn a worldly man into a spiritual seeker and such a seeker into a man emancipated. And to do this, they become manifest from their unmanifested state, all for the benefit of others.

84. That which cannot be accomplished by lectures or *Puranas*, is easily accomplished by merely observing the behaviour of the saints. Their movements, their conduct are wordless instruction.

85. Rare indeed is a man who practises forgiveness, calm, detachment, compassion for all beings, benevolence, self-restraint and humility.

86. What cannot be learnt by reading a book is easily learnt by observing a person in action. The light that the numerous constellations of stars cannot give is given by the sun alone.

87. So it is with these benevolent saints! All their natural actions liberate the living beings from worldly bondage, bringing them great happiness.

88. Sai Maharaj was one of these great saints, with boundless spiritual wealth and grandeur. Always Self-absorbed, his conduct was yet like a fakir.

89. He always looked upon all equally, had no attachment to 'me' and 'mine', and was compassionate towards all beings, as he saw the Supreme Being in all creatures.

90. Pleasure brought him no elation; sorrow, no grief; the wealthy and the pauper were to him the same. How can this wonderful state of mind be commonplace!

91. He who could make a wealthy man of a pauper by merely lifting an eyebrow, would however go himself from door to door, a *jholi*[7] in hand.

92. Blessed indeed are those at whose door Baba appeared to collect alms and, spreading out his palms, called out, "O my daughter, bring me a quarter from your *bhakari* (bread made from *jowar*, etc.)."

93. Picking up a tumbler in one hand and in the other hand the *jholi*, he would himself go from door to door to a few fixed households every day.

94. Vegetables, curried or dry, milk, buttermilk — all these food items were poured into that one tumbler by the people. O, what an extraordinary way of collecting food!

95. And, to receive the cooked rice or *bhakari*, he would spread out the *jholi*. But the liquid dishes, whatever they might be, were all poured together into that one tumbler.

96. And, from where should the relish from each separate dish arise? When the palate knew not the indulgence of enjoying tastes and flavours, how can such a desire arise in the mind, at all?

97. Whatever fell into the *jholi* fortuitously, he would be content to eat. Whether it was tasty or tasteless, it mattered not — as if the tongue was devoid of all taste!

98. Every day, in the morning, he would collect alms in the village, with which he would satisfy his hunger and be content.

99. And the alms — were they even collected regularly? No, indeed! Only when he felt so inclined would he go for them! With the result, sometimes he would go into the village for the alms as many as twelve times in one day!

100. The food so collected would then be put into a wide-mouthed earthern jar in the mosque, from which crows and dogs freely partook of the food.

101. The lady who swept the mosque and the courtyard also took home some ten or twelve *bhakaris* from it. And no one prohibited her from doing so!

102. He would not even dream of shooing away cats and dogs — how will he ever refuse food to the poor and weak? Blessed, blessed was his life!

103. In the beginning, he became well-known to the people as the 'mad fakir'. What greatness could they expect in one who filled his belly by begging for morsels!

104. But the fakir was generous, friendly and without any expectations; volatile outwardly, inwardly he was steadfast and tranquil. His ways were beyond all comprehension!

105. But even in that mean petty village, there were some who were very kind by nature. They considered him to be a *sadhu*.

106. Tatya Kote's mother, Bayjabai, used to carry a basket on her head with *bhakaris* and take them to the forest, at noon.

107. Mile after mile she would wander in the forest in search of the fakir, trampling over the thick shrubs and bushes, and would trace this mad fakir, falling at his feet when she found him.

108. How great was her kindness and nobility! Going into the woods and forests, she used to feed Baba a simple meal of dry or curried vegetables and *bhakari*, in the afternoon.

109. And to the end of his days, Baba also did not forget this devoted service of hers. Remembering it full well, he saw to her son's welfare.

110. Both Bayjabai and her husband truly had a firm faith in the fakir. In fact, the fakir was to them both the Lord Almighty, Himself! After all, it is only to the faithful that God really belongs.

111. The fakir used to be in deep meditation. Bayjabai would set out a leaf, serve food from the basket on it, and with some effort would feed him.

112. Baba always said, "Fakiri[8] is the true kingship. For fakiri is everlasting, but see how transient riches are!"

113. Later, Baba abandoned the forest and came to stay in the village. He began to take food in the mosque, thereby saving mother (Bayjabai) all that arduous effort.

114. From then onwards, this regular practice (of taking food for Baba) was kept up by the couple, and after them, by Tatya.

115. Blessed, blessed are the saints in whose hearts dwells Vasudev (God), for ever! Blessed are those devotees too, who, by rare good fortune, are enriched in their saintly company!

116. Tatya was very lucky indeed! Mhalsapati also must have accumulated great past merit! For they both enjoyed the privilege of Baba's company, equally.

117. Tatya and Mhalsapati both slept in the mosque itself. The love that Baba had equally for both was just indescribable.

118. Their heads used to be in three directions — east, west and north, while their feet would touch each other's at the centre.

119. Thus spreading out their sheets, they would keep on talking, of all manner of things. And if one of them appeared to be dozing off, another would waken him.

120. If Tatya started snoring, Baba would suddenly get up and, turning him upside down, would press his head down.

121. Taking Mhalsapati with him, both would clasp Tatya closely, squeeze him tight, press his legs and would also rub his back vigorously.

122. In this way, for full fourteen years, Tatya slept in the mosque with Baba. Oh, how wonderful were those days! They were etched in their memory permanently.

123. Leaving the parents at home, Tatya, out of his fondness for Baba, used to sleep in the mosque. With what measure can that love be measured? Who can assess the value of that Grace?

124. Then his father died; the responsibility of the household fell on Tatya. He became the head of the family and himself became a husband. Then he started sleeping in his own house.

125. Only when there is such steadfast faith will there be Sai's marvellous experiences, even without being asked for. And to the devotee, it is a miracle.

126. Similarly, there was a very well-known gentleman of Rahata called Khushalchand, who was a wealthy *Nagarshet*[9] of the village.

127. Just as the well-known devotee Ganapat Kote Patil was a great favourite with Baba, so also was Khushalchand's uncle very dear to him.

128. Though of the Marwari community, he had great fondness for Baba and they used to meet frequently, to the great pleasure of both.

129. After some time, as God willed it, the senior Shetji passed away. But Baba did not forget the friendship. In fact, his loving concern for the family redoubled.

130. Later on too, Baba's affection for Khushalchand grew steadily and so long as he lived, he watched over his welfare, day and night.

131. Taking with him his loving companions, Baba would go to Rahata, a mile and a half away from Shirdi; sometimes in a bullock-cart, sometimes in a *tonga*.

132. At the village boundary, he would be received by the villagers amid a clash of musical instruments like drums, *shehnai*, etc. With loving devotion they would then bow at his feet.

133. Lovingly, Baba would then be taken into the village with ceremony, to the delight of everyone.

134. Khushalchand would then take Baba to his own house and making him comfortable in his seat, would offer him some refreshment.

135. Both would then recall old times, which made them very happy. Who can describe their joy?

136. When the joyful meeting, light refreshment of fruits, etc., were over, Baba would return to Shirdi with his companions, filled with rejoicing in the Self.

137. Rahata village was situated on one side; on the other was Nimgoan. Between these two stood Shirdi.

138. From this central point of Shirdi, although Baba never physically went beyond these two villages, during his lifetime, yet he knew everything that happened anywhere.

139. To no other place did he ever go, nor had he seen a train; but the arrival-departure and the time-table of the trains he knew perfectly.

140. To catch the train in good time, the devotees would make great preparations. But when they went to take his permission, Baba would merely say, "Why have you become so impatient?"

141. 'But Baba, if I don't make haste now, I will miss my train to Bombay and my job will be in jeopardy, for my boss will surely sack me.'

142. "There is no other master here! Go, have a piece of *bhakari*. Have your meal at noon and then go!"

143. And who had the intrepidity to defy these words? Young and old, wise and discerning — they all had experienced their truth!

144. Whoever obeyed his order, never missed his train; but he who disobeyed him readily experienced difficulty.

145. Innumerable are such experiences, one after the other, and each a new and unique one, which I shall narrate briefly.

146. Hemad now seeks refuge at Sai's feet. In the next chapter, the same narration of how the devotees had to take Baba's permission to return home, will be made.

147. How, he who had the permission would go and he who did not have it would stay back; but he who disobeyed, would come to harm, will be described in the next chapter.

148. Similarly, Baba's adopting the '*madhukari*'[10] practice and why Baba chose to eat food collected as alms; how he absolved himself from sins such as '*Panchasoona*', etc., will be explained later.

149. Hence, with great insistence, I pray to my listeners, from moment to moment, that they should listen to this Story of Sai, for their own benefit.

Weal be to all! Here ends the eighth chapter of
"*Shri Sai Samarth Satcharit*", called
'*Importance of Human Birth, – Partaking Food collected by
Alms – Bayajabai's Devotion – Sleeping with Tatya and Mhalsapati*'[11],
as inspired by the saints and the virtuous,
and composed by his devotee, Hemadpant.

Notes

1. The other two activities as mentioned later in Ch. 14, v. 19, are copulation and fear.
2. A light kept night and day before an idol.
3. One of the eight *Chiranjivis*, son of the sage Mrukandu, was destined to be short-lived, but at the time of his death, by means of *Shiva-Upasana* (worship), he earned a life of fourteen *kalpas*. Therefore appellatively used for 'long life'.
4. The name of a king, who is fabled to have brought the river Bhagirathi or Ganges on earth from heaven. Hence, any prodigious and marvellous effort.
5. *Anvay* is the law of positiveness, or being of one thing under the being of some other things, as in the example, 'wherever there is smoke there is fire'. *Vyatirek* is the law of negation, or the necessary non-being of one thing under the non-being of some other things, as in the example, 'Where there is no fire there is no smoke'.
6. *Dharma* - religion; duty. A comprehensive Sanskrit term embracing the concepts of law, justice, duty and virtue rolled into one.
7. A piece of cloth gathered up at the corners, to collect alms by the mendicants.
8. Detachment or freedom from worldly encumbrances and cares.
9. The leader of the local business community.
10. The word has its origin in the business of a bee, collecting honey from flower to flower; so, begging from door to door.
11. The title for this chapter in the original text being a duplication of that of the fourth chapter, a devotee has suggested this title, which refers to the subjects dealt with here, and has been incorporated in the new edition of '*Shri Sai Satcharit*', brought out by the Shirdi Sansthan.

9

Consequences of Disobeying Baba – Baba's Alms collection and Panchsoona and other sins – Stories of the Devotee Tarkhad

MY OBEISANCE TO SHRI GANESH, TO SHRI SARASWATI, AND SHRI GURUMAHARAJ! TO THE FAMILY DEITY, TO SHRI SITA-RAMACHANDRA, MY MOST HUMBLE OBEISANCE! I BOW IN REVERENCE TO THE MOST VENERABLE GURU SHRI SAINATH!

1. Now, to continue from the stories in the previous chapter, (I shall describe) how devotees suffered, if they returned to their respective places, without Baba permitting them to do so;

2. Similarly, about Baba's practice of collecting alms, which he followed till the end of his life, to avert *Panchsoona*[1] and other such sins, only for the benefit of his devotees;

3. And also, how Sai pervades this whole Universe, — right from Brahma to all the inanimate objects; that Sai himself, by his Grace, impresses upon us that God dwells in all beings.

4. Hence, O my listeners, I entreat your full attention while listening. For when these sacred stories are heard with reverence, you will attain your weal.

5. There is one special characteristic of the pilgrimage to Shirdi. If a pilgrim returns home without taking Baba's permission, he invites only trouble for himself.

6. But once such permission is granted, then he cannot stay even a moment longer in Shirdi. Should he persist, sure enough, he would bring trouble upon himself. All have experienced this already!

7. Those who disobeyed Baba's orders had to face a great many difficulties on the way. Many were robbed by thieves, an experience which they remembered all their lives.

8. Those who started out on an empty stomach[2], in a hurry, despite being told to have their meal before leaving, not only missed the train, but were wearied out by hunger and exasperation, as many devotees have seen for themselves.

9. Patil Tatya Kote once wanted to go to Kopergaon, for the weekly market and so came to the mosque.

10. The *tonga* was kept waiting outside; he had Baba's *darshan* and, as if to take Baba's permission, he, in fact, only bowed at Baba's feet to take his leave.

11. Time and again would the devotees avoid or put off (taking his permission). But Baba knew the good times and the bad. Seeing Tatya's impatience to go, he said, "Just wait a moment!

12. "Let the marketing be; it can be done later! But do not go outside the village." Yet, on seeing Tatya's great insistence, he added, "Do take Shama with you".

13. 'O where is the need for Shama!' thought Tatya to himself and disregarding Baba's words he went and sat in the *tonga* to go to the market.

14. Of the two horses of the *tonga*, one was swift-footed and had cost three hundred rupees. As they approached Saool Vihir (a village 3 km from Shirdi), the horse began to gallop ever so fast, becoming wild and wayward.

15. The horse, that had never known the whip and was accustomed to making his way to the market in no time, tripped and fell, giving a sudden violent jolt to the *tonga* and spraining Tatya's loins sorely, as a result.

16. Alas! what marketing and shopping! Tatya at once remembered Sai, his Mother! 'Had I but heeded Sai's words, this mishap could

have been averted', he thought, regretfully, 'Now what has happened, has happened, nothing can be done'.

17. On another occasion, a similar thing happened! This time Tatya was all set to go to a place called Kolhar. Horses were harnessed to the *tonga*, and as he came, all ready, to ask for permission, he just bowed at Baba's feet.

18. 'I will be back in no time', he said, and although he had not obtained Baba's clear consent, Tatya set out. But now just listen to what happened.

19. Already the *tonga* was small and light-weight; in that the horses ran unbridled and wild, and would not stop even at the cavities and pits. Tatya's life stood in imminent peril!

20. But Sai's Grace saved him. The *tonga* banged into a Babul tree and it was as well that it broke down there. For it averted further disaster.

21. Similarly, once a highly-placed English gentleman from Bombay came for Baba's *darshan*, with some definite purpose in mind.

22. He carried a recommendation from Chandorkar in a letter, which had been addressed to Madhavrao. He asked for a tent to stay and was quite comfortable in it.

23. Everyone knew well, how impossible it was for anyone to climb up the steps of that mosque and take Baba's *darshan* to his heart's content, against Baba's wishes.

24. Three times did the gentleman make an attempt to climb the mosque, but it was all fruitless! The visitor was greatly disheartened!

25. In his innermost heart he had wished to go up to the mosque, make obeisance to Baba on bended knees, kiss his hands, and sit for a while.

26. Such indeed, was his wish; but Baba would not allow him to come up and sit near him, at that time, in the mosque.

27. Baba wanted him to be in the *sabhamandap* below — to sit there and take *darshan* from that place itself, if he so desired. But he definitely did not want him to come up.

28. So he got up to go and came to the courtyard to take leave, before returning home. "But you can go tomorrow", Baba said to him, "Why all this hurry?"

29. People around were also trying to persuade him, entreating him in many ways not to go, and telling him how those who went without taking permission, regretted it greatly.

30. But nobody can prevail against the pre-destined! He was not convinced and set out without permission, only to face troubles and tribulations on the way.

31. Initially, the *tonga* ran smoothly enough. But afterwards, the horses went off the track. And hardly had they gone past Saool Vihir, when all of a sudden, a bicycle crossed their path.

32. The gentleman was sitting at the back, while in the front the horses ran amuck startled by the sudden interruption. The gentleman was knocked off his balance and fell flat across the road.

33. With enormous effort the *tonga* was stopped. The man had gone sliding down, but was then lifted up and seated in the *tonga*. And then the *tonga* proceeded on its journey.

34. Alas! Shirdi remained on one side; Bombay on the other! Instead, it was to a hospital in Kopergaon that the *tonga* drove to.

35. Tormented by remorse, suffering as an expiation of the sin of disobeying Baba, the gentleman had to spend some days in that hospital.

36. People had innumerable such experiences. As a result they began to have doubts and apprehensions on such occasions, and started obeying Baba's orders. No one dared to disobey.

37. Sometimes the wheel[3] came off the carriage; at other times, the horses were tired out. Trains were missed, people starved, and so many were left moaning and fretting with frustration!

38. But those who obeyed his command always caught the train — sometimes even running out of its schedule, and had a pleasant comfortable journey, which they remembered all their lives!

39. Should anyone have a doubt as to why Baba preferred the practice of collecting alms and followed it, for years together, listen now to this explanation.

40. Actually, if one considers Baba's lifestyle and conduct, as a whole, one will realize that collecting of alms was most befitting. For by so doing, he gave an opportunity to people to perform the duty of a householder, all for their own good, which brought them great satisfaction.

41. It is the devotee, steadfast in his faith, and who surrenders everything — body, speech, mind and wealth — at his feet, who is very dear to Sai.

42. In *Grihasthashram* (i.e. the householder's or the second of the four stages or *ashramas*), whatever food is cooked in the house, is first to be offered by the householder to the sacred fire, in the name of the *sanyasin* and the *Brahmachari*.

43. If however, the householder partakes of the food without first making such an offering, then he has to perform the *Chandrayana* ritual[4], for the purification of his speech, mind and action, according to the *Shastras*.

44. *Sanyasins* and *Brahmacharis* are forbidden to cook food. If they start doing it, they too will most certainly be saddled with this *Chandrayana* ritual.

45. Hence the *Shastras* have entrusted the responsibility of feeding them to the householders. *Sanyasins* never take up any occupation to satisfy their hunger.

46. Baba was not a householder; nor was he in the *Vanaprastha* stage, but he was a celibate who had renounced the world from childhood. For such a one then, subsisting on collected alms was most fitting.

47. He who regards the whole universe as his home, knows for certain that he is himself Vasudeva and Vishwambhar (all-pervading), that he is the everlasting Brahman,

48. Only such a member of the world-family has the true, perfect right to the food collected by alms. As for all others, just look at the vulgar display and the mockery they have made of this practice!

49. First, a man should give up the desire for a son (for children and family); then the desire for wealth; and also, for fame (for honour in the world). He who is free from these threefold desires can alone think of subsisting on alms.

50. Or else the verses of Tukoba Maharaj, where he says, 'It is a disgraceful existence to resort to the begging bowl', will become meaningless and futile.

51. The young and the old, the great and the small, all knew too well what a great *siddha* Sai Samarth was. It is we, who are always bound by our worldly hopes and desires and are not steadfast in our devotion to his holy feet.

52. The five great sacrificial offerings[5] without which a householder was forbidden (by *Shastras*) to take his meal, Sai himself got performed every day in Shirdi, thereby sanctifying the food prepared.

53. Every day he would go to five houses (for alms) to remind the householders of their duty to offer food first to a guest. Fortunate indeed were those who learnt this lesson, sitting in their own homes.

54. After making the five great sacrificial offerings, those who partake of the remaining food will have their five great sins (*Panchsoona*) which are so difficult to understand and committed quite unknowingly, destroyed altogether.

55. Among the people, these *Panchsoona* are known as the five great sins of *Kandani, Choolli, Peshani, Udkumbhi* and *Marjani.*

56. When the stone-mortar is fed with food grain which is then pounded with the pestle to remove the chaff and bran from it, tiny little creatures are killed unknowingly.

57. But until it goes through this entire process the grain will not get cooked. Hence this is the very first sin of the *Panchsoona* and is called *Kandani.*

58. When wood is kindled in the fireplace to cook the food, there too living beings are destroyed quite unknowingly. This is the second sin, called *Choolli.*

59. Taking a quern or a hand-mill, when the grain is ground into flour, once again innumerable little beings are crushed, unawares. This sin is called *Peshani*.

60. When in a pitcher water is taken out from a well, or a tank, or a lake, or when men and women wash their clothes, again, numerous creatures die.

61. In order to clean the pitchers, when they are scrubbed or washed by hand (with mud or ash), living beings are unintentionally killed. This is the fourth sin called *Udkumbhi*.

62. Similarly, when bathing with hot or cold water, or sprinkling the cow-dung water for cleaning the floor, the great destruction of life that takes place is called *Marjani*.

63. To free himself from five great sins, a householder has to make the five great sacrificial offerings. Once these sins are warded off thus, the householders will attain self-purification.

64. It is by the power of self-purification that pure, sacred knowledge is attained and after such knowledge, these fortunate ones attain salvation which is ever-lasting.

65. However, in describing Sai's practice in collecting alms, the book has become expansive! But now, listen to a true story in this connection and then we shall end this chapter.

66. Whatever you send for Baba, and with whosoever you send it, provided it is sent with sincere, heart-felt love, Baba will ask for it, without fail, even if the bearer of that small offering forgets!

67. Be it then a simple offering of *bhakari* and vegetable, or be it a sweetmeat like a *pedha* (made from milk and sugar), so long as it was offered with loving devotion, it did not matter! And oh, how Sai's heart overflowed with love when he met with such unswerving faith!

68. This is the story of one such loving devotee, listening to which you will be filled with joy. If any devotee failed to carry out a responsibility undertaken by him, Sai himself guided him to the path of his duty.

69. And so gentle and sweet was his manner of instruction that at the proper time he would awaken the devotee to his duty. Blessed are

those fortunate ones who have themselves experienced this! Their happiness is beyond all description.

70. One of Sai's great devotees was, by name, Ramchandra, his father Atmaram, and his surname Tarkhad, who had taken refuge in Sai, the Abode of Peace.

71. But he was always called Babasaheb Tarkhad. And it is about him that we shall narrate a story, there being no better reason for this narration.

72. Oh, how delightful it was to listen to Tarkhad, when, his heart overflowing with Sai's love, he would begin to describe his own experiences!

73. And when he narrated, one after the other, with gestures and expressions of deep feeling, the novel experiences that he had had at every step, O, what a grand devotion it revealed!

74. Incomparable as his love was, Babasaheb had installed a drawing of Sai in a beautiful sandalwood shrine at home for the purpose of worship, every morning, noon and evening.

75. Tarkhad was very fortunate in having also a son who was equally devoted to Sai. So much so, that without offering *naivedya* (food-offering) to Sai, he would never touch food himself.

76. Every morning, after taking his bath, he used to offer *pooja* to Baba's picture, with all his heart and soul and body, which ritual he ended with offering *naivedya*.

77. Even as he continued this regular practice untiringly, all his efforts bore fruit in the excellent, most unique experience that he had.

78. His mother, who was a great devotee of Sai, was eager to go to Shirdi and the father felt that the son should be with her in the journey.

79. She wished to go to Shirdi, take Shri Sai's *darshan*, spend a few days there and serve Sai, in person.

80. Although such was the father's wish, the son did not really want to go. For he was worried as to who would regularly perform the *pooja* in the house in his absence.

81. The father was a Prarthana Samajist (who did not believe in ritualistic idol-worship). 'Would it then be proper to trouble him with *pooja?*' was the son's doubt.

82. And yet, knowing his secret wish, the son was ready to go. And just listen to what he, very lovingly, entreated his father.

83. 'Unless I am promised that nobody in the house will take food without first offering *naivedya* to Sai, I certainly cannot go.'

84. The father was already aware of the son's vow. 'Go, I will offer the *naivedya* regularly, you may rest assured', he said.

85. 'Without first offering *naivedya* to Sai, none of us will take food. Trust my word and have no doubts. Go with an easy mind'.

86. On getting such an assurance the boy went to Shirdi. As the next day dawned, Tarkhad himself performed the *pooja*.

87. On that day, right at the beginning of the *pooja* ritual, Babasaheb Tarkhad prostrated before Sai's picture and prayed,

88. 'Baba, let my service (of performing *pooja*) to you be the same as that of my son. Let it not be a mechanical exercise at my hands, but let true love spring in my heart while performing it.'

89. Early morning before the sunrise, which is the most perfect time for worship, Tarkhad would begin the *pooja* with this prayer, every day and offer *naivedya* at the end.

90. This he continued without a break and offered a piece of sugar-candy by way of *naivedya*, until one day there was a lapse in this daily routine.

91. His mind preoccupied with business matters, one day, Tarkhad did not remember the *naivedya*. Everybody had their meal without making the food offering to Sai.

92. Tarkhad was the chief officer, in charge of a well-known textile mill, and had to go out every morning for his work.

93. Later in the afternoon when he returned, he was served at mealtime the *prasad* of sugar-candy, offered to Sai in the morning.

94. Such was the daily routine, when one day he forgot to offer sugar-candy as *naivedya* and consequently had no *prasad* at lunch.

95. It was the cook who used to serve the remaining sugar-candy on his plate every day when he sat down to his meal, that itself serving as purification of the food.

96. But on that day, for some reason, he was in a hurry while performing the *pooja* and the offering of *naivedya* was forgotten. So the *prasad* too, was not served, as every day.

97. At once, Tarkhad got up from the meal, full of remorse, and prostrating before Sai's picture, said with tearful eyes,

98. 'Baba, what is this *Maya* of yours! How did you stupefy my mind so? Really, it was just a mechanical exercise that you made me perform! But now, please grant me your forgiveness, first!

99. 'It is no mere bewilderment of mind, but a great sin that I have committed and am filled with remorse. Oh, it is my fault, entirely my fault, shameless as I am! Be compassionate to me, O Maharaj!'

100. He prostrated at Baba's feet in the picture and with a heart overcome with regret and repentance, said, 'O Compassionate Maharaj, have mercy on me!'

101. So saying, he wrote a letter to the son, in a helpless, wretched state of mind, saying, 'Entreat Baba's forgiveness; say that a great sin has been committed at my hands!

102. 'Pray for his mercy on one who has totally surrendered to him. With these words, invoke his compassion and pray for an assurance of forgiveness and grace, on behalf of this humble servant.'

103. While this was happening at Bandra, at about 200 miles away in Shirdi, the news reached instantly. Listen to what Baba said there.

104. Here is the actual proof of Sai Maharaj's knowledge of past, present and future, that knew no barriers of space and time.

105. Although the boy was at Shirdi, all this while, listen O listeners, carefully to what happened when he went to pay obeisance to Baba, on that same day and at the same time!

106. As the boy came very eagerly, with his mother and bowed at Baba's feet, he was quite astonished to hear what Sai said to his mother.

107. "What could I do, O mother? Today, as every day, I went to Bandra. But there was no rice, no gruel, nothing to eat or drink. And hungry, I had to return!

108. "Just see the '*rinanubandha*' (the ties of the past births); though the door was closed, I entered at my own sweet will. Who is to prevent me?

109. "The master was not at home. My intestines were groaning with hunger. But in that same instant, at the height of noon, I turned back without a morsel!"

110. On hearing these words, the son at once guessed that most probably his father forgot and missed making the food-offering!

111. He pleaded with Baba, 'Let me go home!' But Baba would hear none of it! Instead, he made him offer *pooja* there itself.

112. The same day the son sent a detailed letter from Shirdi, on reading which the father's heart simply melted!

113. The letter from Bandra reached Shirdi, too! The son was amazed. His eyes too, filled with tears, which freely flowed down the cheek.

114. Just see this wonderful sport of Sai! How will love not well up in the heart? Can there be such a heart of stone that will not melt by this?

115. It was the loving mother of this same boy, who was blessed by Sai Baba, while she was once at Shirdi. And now, listen to this marvellous tale!

116. She was in the dining hall; food was served and everybody was about to begin, when suddenly, at that hour of the noon, a hungry dog came to the door, where the lady sat.

117. The lady at once gave a quarter of the *bhakari* from her plate to the dog. But, at the same moment, there also came a hungry pig, smeared all over with mud (whom too she fed the *bhakari*).

118. It all happened so naturally, that the lady soon forgot all about it. But in the afternoon, Baba himself brought up the subject.

119. In the afternoon, after lunch, when the lady came to the mosque as usual and sat down at some distance, Baba said to her affectionately,

120. "Mother, you fed me today and with all that food my stomach is full, almost to the throat. I was suffering acutely from hunger but you appeased me by giving me food.

121. "This is what you should always do. For truly, this alone will stand you in good stead. It can never be, that sitting here, in the mosque, I would speak an untruth.

122. "Always have such compassion. First feed those who are hungry, then eat yourself. Preserve this truth carefully in your heart."

123. The lady could not understand what Sai Samarth was saying. What could he mean? For, his words are never without significance!

124. So she said, 'How is it possible that I have given you food? I myself depend on others and eat whatever I get, after paying a price for it'.

125. "After eating the *bhakari*, given to me so lovingly, I am satiated most truly, — nay I am still belching[6] with that satiation!

126. "When you sat down to lunch, you suddenly saw that a hungry dog with an empty stomach, who came to the door. Know that I am one with him.

127. "And so also the pig that you saw suffering from pangs of hunger, and smeared all over with mud, — I am one with him, too!"

128. As she heard Baba's words, the lady was quite astonished in her mind. So many dogs, pigs, cats roam around. Is Baba one with them all?

129. "Sometimes I am a dog and sometimes a pig; sometimes I am a cow, sometimes a cat, and sometimes an ant , a fly, an aquatic creature — in such various forms do I move about in this world.

130. "Know, that I like only him who sees me in all the living beings. So give up the sense of differentiation. This is the way to worship me."

131. These were not just words; they were the purest nectar; listening to them the lady was choked with emotion. A lump rose in her throat and her eyes filled with tears of joy.

132. There is another sweet tale about this lady's loving devotion, which is also a mark of Sai's oneness with his devotees.

133. Once Purandare (another devotee) set out for Shirdi with his wife and children. This lady (i.e. Mrs Tarkhad), very lovingly, sent with him some brinjals for Baba.

134. She requested Purandare's wife to prepare '*bharit*' (i.e. dressing the roasted brinjal with seasoning) for Baba with one brinjal and with the other, to slice and fry it crisply with seasoning, etc., called '*kachrya*', and serve a liberal helping thereof to Baba.

135. 'All right', she said as she took the brinjals. On reaching Shirdi, she took '*bharit*' to serve Baba at lunchtime, after the *arati*.

136. As usual, she offered *naivedya* and went away, leaving the plate of food for Baba. After collecting together everybody's *naivedya*, Baba then sat down to the meal.

137. When he tasted the '*bharit*' everyone thought that he found it delicious, so that he then felt like having fried brinjal slices. For he said, "Bring them just now!"

138. A message went to Radhakrishnabai at once that Baba wished to have fried brinjal slices and was waiting for them to begin his lunch; and they were at a loss what to do.

139. This was really not the season for brinjals; then how can a dish be prepared? A frantic search began for Purandare's wife because of the '*bharit*' she had served.

140. For it was in the plate that she had brought, that '*bharit*' was served. So, maybe, in her baggage there are some more brinjals, they thought.

141. And hence, when she was asked, the mystery behind the sudden desire for fried brinjal slices was solved and everyone understood why Baba had such a great love for them!

142. The lady explained that she had made '*bharit*' out of one brinjal and served it in the afternoon, and had thought she would fry the slices of the other one later, which she had already sliced for the purpose.

143. Later on, when everyone came to know, by and by, this story of the brinjals, right from its beginning, they were all amazed to see Sai's all-pervasiveness.

144. On another occasion, in the month of December, in the year 1915, this same lady (Mrs Tarkhad) sent a *pedha* (a sweetmeat made with milk and sugar) for Baba, with great affection.

145. Balaram (Mankar) had passed away and his son was to go to Shirdi for performing the obsequies and came to Tarkhad to tell him.

146. He came to Tarkhad to say that he was going to Shirdi. So Tarkhad's wife wanted to send with him, something for Baba.

147. As she searched in the house, there was nothing to send but just one *pedha* and that too, had been already offered as *naivedya*. But the boy was in a hurry to leave.

148. Moreover, that boy was in mourning; the one *pedha* in the house was also used already as *naivedya*; but she sent the same with him to offer to Sai,

149. Saying, 'There is nothing else. So now, take this *pedha* and offer it with love. Sai will eat it with relish.'

150. Govindji (Balaram Mankar's son) took the *pedha* with him. But when he went for Baba's *darshan*, it was forgotten at his lodging. Baba was patient with him.

151. Later, in the afternoon, the boy came again in Sai's court. But as before he forgot again and came to the mosque empty-handed.

152. Baba tried asking him, "What have you brought for me?" And when he replied, 'Nothing', then He reminded him gently,

153. "Has no one given you anything for me?" 'No', he said. Then Sai Samarth asked him directly,

154. "My boy, did not mother very lovingly send with you some sweets for me, when you left home?" It was only then that he remembered!

155. And, Oh! he felt ever so ashamed of himself! How could he have forgotten it! His head hung in shame, he prayed for forgiveness and touching Baba's feet, he set out at once!

156. Running, he went to the lodging, brought the *pedha* and offered it to Sai. The moment it came in the hand, Baba at once put it in his mouth and gratified the mother's feelings.

157. It is thus that this Sai, the great *Mahatma*, glorifies love and devotion by giving each devotee the experience according to his faith.

158. Another significance that emerges from these stories is, that one should always see God in all living creatures. This is also recognized by all the *Shastras*. And this is the demonstrated conclusion here, too.

159. Now, in listening to the next chapter, you will come to know how Baba lived; where, at which place, he slept, etc. Listen to it attentively.

160. Hemadpant surrenders at Sai's feet. The listeners should reflect, with reverence, on the stories narrated, contemplate on them, for it will be beneficial to them.

Weal be to all! Here ends the ninth chapter of
"Shri Sai Samarth Satcharit", called
'*Consequences of Disobeying Baba - Baba's Alms
Collection and Panchsoona and other Sins -
Stories of the Devotee Tarkhad*'[7],
as inspired by the saints and the virtuous,
and composed by his devotee, Hemadpant.

Notes

1. The destruction of life in the five operations of pounding, grinding, lighting the fire, filling water and sweeping which result in the five great sins.

2. Once, the families of Tatyasaheb Noolkar and Bhausaheb Dikshit were to set out from Shirdi. Maharaj said to them, 'Go tomorrow morning and go after having meal at Kopergaon'. Accordingly, they made preparations and also sent word to the eating-house at Kopergaon to keep food ready. But when they reached Kopergaon the food was not ready and as it was time for the arrival of the train, they went to the station without having food. But they reached the station only to find the train running late by an hour and a half. So they sent the *tongawallah* (who was Brahmin) into the town to get food from that eating house and they all had food at the station. Ten minutes after the meal was over, the train came.

    On the other hand, Raghuvir Bhaskar Purandare, who had once gone with his family for Baba's *darshan*, asked Baba's permission to go to Nasik on their return journey at his mother's insistence. Maharaj said, 'Go, stay for two days and then proceed.' So all of them went to Nasik. But on that same day, his younger brother ran a very high temperature. Everyone was frightened and felt they should proceed to Bombay at once. Their priest also said the same. But Purandare said, 'Maharaj has asked us to stay for two days. So unless two days are over I shall not move from here.' Helpless, they all stayed on. Next day the brother's fever came down on its own and on the third day, they all reached Bombay safely.

3. This was the experience of the present writer, himself (i.e. Dabholkar). In the beginning, he once left Shirdi for the railway station, with his wife and children, by the bullock cart, in a great hurry, and totally disregarded Baba's command to have a meal before leaving. The bullock cart was driven full speed to catch the train in time, when suddenly the left wheel of the cart flew off into the gutter. It was a great good fortune that the cart did not break down nor was anyone injured. But by the time the wheel was fixed again and the cart was on it way to the station, the train had already gone. They had then to stop at a common eating place for meals and could only board the next train to Bombay.

4. *Chandrayana* is a vow, a form of penance, according to which only fifteen mouthfuls are to be eaten on the full-moon day, while in the dark phase of the moon one mouthful is to be reduced daily till on the *Amavasya* day food is to be totally abstained from. But in the bright half, one mouthful of food is to be increased, reaching a total number of fifteen on the full-moon.

5. The five great sacrifices or sacrificial offerings are: *Brahmayajna* — reading of *Vedas* and *Puranas; Devayajna* — offering of food in the sacred fire to gods; *Pitruyajna* — offering of food in the sacred fire to the forefathers; *Bhutayajna* — keeping aside by way of offering a tiny portion of food to all living beings, before starting a meal; and *Manushyayajna* — serving food to a guest or guests.

6. In the olden days, when a guest was invited to a meal the host would feed him to the point of satiety, of which belching was an indication.

7. In the original, this chapter has no title. The above title has been suggested by a devotee and has been incorporated into the later editions of the book.

10

The Mahima of Shri Sai Samarth

MY OBEISANCE TO SHRI GANESH, TO SHRI SARASWATI, AND SHRI GURUMAHARAJ! TO THE FAMILY DEITY, TO SHRI SITA-RAMACHANDRA, MY MOST HUMBLE OBEISANCE! I BOW IN REVERENCE TO THE MOST VENERABLE GURU SHRI SAINATH!

1. He, who is engaged in the welfare of all the people; but is himself, for ever, one with the Brahman, remember him ceaselessly, with a loving heart.

2. He, whose mere remembrance is enough to free us from the entanglement of birth and death, is the best among all the means (of redemption), a means which does not cost even a farthing.

3. And, with the least effort, most easily and naturally, comes to hand, the fruit, which is not trivial, by any means. Hence, while the bodily organs are yet strong and healthy, every passing moment should be fully utilized (for achieving the goal).

4. All other gods are illusory, unreal; the guru alone is the God Eternal. Once you repose your faith in him, he will help you overcome even the pre-destined.

5. Where there is pure, sincere service of the guru there is a total extirpation of worldly life. No hair-splitting discussions of *Nyaya*, Mimamsa, etc.,[1] or any other strenuous intellectual effort is required.

6. When the Sadguru captains the ship the faithful devotees overcome all the threefold afflictions[2] — the *adhibhoot, adhyatmic* and *adhidaivic*.

7. To cross over this ocean of worldly affairs, you need to trust the Helmsman. The same trust is to be reposed in your guru to cross the ocean of life.

8. Seeing the devotee's faith and devotion, he (the guru) gives the Supreme Knowledge, made as easy of comprehension, as if it rested in the palm of your hand, and enables you to attain with natural ease *Moksha* which is characterized by pure Bliss.

9. Let us now sing the praises of him (Sadguru), by whose *darshan* alone, all the confusion of the mind (caused by the illusions of duality between the mind and the soul) is cleared, all the sensual desires cease and *Sanchit* and *Kriyaman*[3] are slowly destroyed.

10. In the eighth chapter the purpose of human birth has been related. In the ninth, we have heard about the inconceivable mystery behind Baba's vow of collecting alms.

11. Bayajabai's *bhakari*-vegetable at noon, Baba's concern for Khushalchand's well-being, his sleeping in the company of Tatya, Mhalsapati, etc., has also been described, which has delighted the listeners.

12. And now, O listeners! Listen attentively to the following part of Baba's story — how he lived, where he slept, in what an incomprehensible manner he moved about.

13. How praiseworthy was Baba's life! To both, Hindus and Muslims, he was a mother; a trusted refuge — to a tiger and a goat alike, where both moved about in an atmosphere of fearlessness and mutual affection.

14. So much for the business of living! Now listen respectfully, O listeners, to how Sai lived; where, at which place he slept, and so on.

15. A wooden plank, four times an arm's length, wide as an outstretched palm (the measure of the thumb and the little finger, extended) would be suspended from the rafter, like a swing, fastened at both ends by pieces of rags.

16. On such a plank Baba used to sleep. Earthen oil-lamps burned at the head and foot of his bed. No one ever understood when he climbed up or down from it.

17. He would either sit up there, with head bent, or would be sleeping on it. But when he climbed up or got down from it, nobody ever saw him doing so.

18. The plank was secured by strips of rags — but how did it balance Baba's weight? Well, when all the *Mahasiddhis* reside in you, is not the plank only for name's sake?

19. Where even the tiniest particle pricks the eye, a man who has attained the *siddhi* of *Anima* (ability to reduce oneself to an atom) can hide quite comfortably in it. Hence Baba's power to move with ease in the form of a fly or a worm or an ant.

20. He who has *Anima* as his slave, will he take long, transforming himself into a fly? And he who can stay suspended in mid-air, of what consequence is a wooden plank to such a one?

21. The *Ashtasiddhis*[4] like *Anima, Mahima, Laghima,* etc., and the *Navanidhis*[5] stood by his side with folded hands. The plank was to him but an instrumental cause!

22. Worms and ants, pigs and dogs, birds and even human beings, all great and small, kings or paupers — he looked upon them all, equally.

23. Apparently, he resided in Shirdi; possessed nothing else except a physical frame measuring three and a half cubits in length; yet Sai Maharaj, the Storehouse of Virtue, dwells in the hearts of all.

24. Inwardly, detached and ascetical; yet outwardly, there was a strong urge to guide people on the right path; totally desireless from within, forever there was a genuine attachment to the devotees, from without.

25. There was no expectation of the fruit of action, whatsoever, in the innermost heart, but the desire for the welfare of the devotees that appeared outwardly, was genuine. An Abode of Eternal Peace within, he yet exhibited anger, occasionally.

26. One with God, always, at times he showed ghoulish tendencies, outwardly. Firmly committed to non-duality, within, he was yet involved in the complexities in the world.

27. Sometimes he treated people with great affection; sometimes he charged at them, stone in hand. There was a volley of curses and

abuses, on occasions, as there was an embrace of blissful joy on other occasions.

28. But in truth he was calm and self-restrained; detached and patient, forever in deep meditation; one with the Self and totally absorbed in It; pleased and gracious to his devotees.

29. Always Self-engrossed, sitting still in one *asana* (posture), without the botheration of going or coming here and there; with his baton as the treasured staff of a *sannyasin*, — his was indeed a quiet peaceful existence, free from worldly cares!

30. Without the least desire for wealth or fame, and alms collection as the sole means of subsistence, he passed his days in this yogic state of withdrawal of all the senses (from the attraction of sensual pleasures)[6].

31. He dressed exactly like a *yati sannyasin*[7], with his baton serving as a *sannyasin*'s staff, in his hand. On his lips were the words "*Allah Malik*", repeatedly, and for the devotees, his love and affection flowed constantly.

32. Such was the physical manifestation of Sai who had appeared in a human form. Only by our accumulated past merit has this treasure come so unexpectedly, to our hands.

33. Those who thought of him as just another human being were indeed, dull-witted and unfortunate. Strange is their destiny! For, how will they enjoy this rare good fortune?

34. Sai is a mine of Self-knowledge; filled with pure joy is Sai's person. Cling to him for protection instantly, to be able to cross over the ocean of worldly life, safely.

35. The most constant, undifferentiated Supreme Spirit, which is personified in Baba, is boundless and infinite and fills this entire Universe from Brahma right down to a tiny shrub.

36. The time span of the *Kaliyuga* is four lakh thirty two thousand years. After about five thousand years had elapsed, Baba incarnated on this earth.

37. Listeners may raise a doubt here, that without knowing Baba's birth date, on what grounds could this period be fixed? So, listen attentively, now.

38. With a firm determination to remain a resident of the holy Shirdi village, to the end of his life, Baba spent sixty years there, like a *Kshetrasannyasin*[8].

39. In the beginning, Baba had appeared at Shirdi at the age of sixteen and had stayed on, at that time, for three years.

40. Then, he slipped away from Shirdi only to be rediscovered in the distant Nizam kingdom. Thereafter he returned with the marriage party and remained in Shirdi for ever.

41. He was then twenty years old, and for the next sixty years he constantly remained in Shirdi, as everyone knows.

42. Baba left his mortal coil on the *Vijayadashami* day in the month of *Ashwin*, in the year *shake* eighteen hundred and forty (i.e. October, 15 1918).

43. Thus Baba's life-span was eighty years and his birth date can thus be roughly determined to be *shake* seventeen hundred and sixty (i.e. 1838).

44. Can one ever determine for certain, the life-span of great saints, who have conquered death itself? It is a task most difficult to accomplish!

45. These great *Mahatmas* always abide in their own place without birth or death even, as the sun never rises or sets, but is constant and steady in its place.

46. In the year 1681, Ramdas took *samadhi*. Hardly had two centuries gone by, when this unique personality appeared.

47. *Bharatbhoomi* (India) was invaded by the Muslims; the Hindu kings were vanquished. The path of devotional worship slowly disappeared and people began abandoning the *dharma* (path of righteousness).

48. It was then that Ramdas took birth. With the help of Shivaji Maharaj he protected the kingdom, the Brahmins and the sacred cow from the Muslims.

49. Hardly had two centuries elapsed after this, when once again, disorder set in and there was a divide between the Hindus and the Muslims, which Baba tried to bridge.

50. When Ram and Rahim are one, without even the least difference between them, then why should their followers insist on their separateness? And why should they fall out with each other?

51. Oh! what foolish children you are! Let the ties of friendship bring Hindus and Muslims together; let generous, benevolent thoughts take a firm root in your minds. Only then will you reach the Shore Beyond!

52. Disputations, arguments are not profitable nor do we want to compete with each other. Let us always be mindful of our own good and Shri Hari (God) will protect us.

53. Yoga, ritualistic sacrifices (*yajna*), penance and Knowledge — these are the means of attaining God. But with all these, if God does not dwell in the heart, in vain is the life, the devotion of such a man.

54. 'Even when someone harms you, you should not retaliate; but do him a good turn, instead, whenever possible.' This was the essence of Baba's teaching.

55. For one's material as well as spiritual welfare, this advice is most beneficial. This straight-forward course can be followed by all — high and low, women and *Shudras.*

56. Just as the grandeur of a dream-kingdom disappears on waking up, so will the illusory quality of this worldly life, said Baba.

57. He, whose philosophy of worldly life regarded the pleasures and pains as false, had dispelled their dream-like quality by Self-absorption and attained Emancipation.

58. Seeing the devotee's attachment to the material world, his heart was moved with compassionate concern. And he was anxious, day and night, as to how the devotee would overcome this attachment to the physical body.

59 An attitude of mind that 'I am Brahman', a disposition of blissful happiness, personified, and a lasting state of desirelessness — in such a one, detachment and renunciation had taken refuge.

60. *Veena* (the stringed musical instrument) and cymbals in hand, to wander from door to door, with a pitiful countenance and an outstretched hand — this was something that he had never known.

61. There are many such gurus, who get hold of people to make disciples of them, whispering forcibly into their ears, some *mantra* and cheating them for the sake of money.

62. They teach '*dharma*' to the disciples, while themselves following the path of '*adharma*', all the while. How can they take the disciple safely across the worldly life and help him to avoid the birth-death cycle?

63. But here was this unique personality of Sai, in whose mind there was no thought, no desire for publicising his righteousnesss or to win the public acclaim for it.

64. Such was this wonderful personality (of Sai) that in him there was no place for ego. On the other hand, there was always an inclination to love his devotees deeply.

65. Among the gurus, there are two types: *Niyat* (ordained by God) and *Aniyat* (not so ordained). Let me explain to the listeners the specific functions of each.

66. To encourage the growth and the ripening of the virtuous qualities so as to purify the heart and to guide the disciple to the path of Salvation — such alone is the gift of an *Aniyat* guru.

67. But the association with a *Niyat* guru results in removing all duality and in an awakening of a feeling of 'Oneness', thereby proving the truth of the Vedic aphorism, 'You are That' (i.e. Brahman) (*Sama Veda*), through actual experience.

68. These (*Niyat*) gurus pervade this Universe in an unmanifest state and incarnate for the benefit of their devotees. And once their life's mission is over, they give up their mortal coil.

69. It is to this second category that Sai belongs. How can I describe his *leelas* adequately? As he guides my mind, so will this narration take shape.

70. There are many gurus for material sciences and arts. But only he who gives you Self-Knowledge is the Sadguru. He alone, who shows you the shore beyond, is all-powerful. Inconceivable is his greatness, indeed!

71. Whoever went to have his *darshan* would be told the whole secret of his past, future and present, without his asking for it.

72. He who saw the Brahman or God Himself in all the living creatures; who looked equally upon friend and foe, made not the slightest distinction between them.

73. He expected nothing from anyone, but treated them all alike and showered blessings even on those who were ungrateful. Fortune or misfortune, did not disturb his equilibrium; nor was he ever touched by doubts or misgivings.

74. While in the mortal body, he had no attachment to material objects, like the physical body, house, etc. Thus, only outwardly in the physical body, but inwardly he was totally detached from it. To such a one salvation comes in this life, itself!

75. Blessed are the people of Shirdi, to whom Sai himself symbolized God-worship; who incessantly remembered Sai, while eating and drinking or sleeping.

76. Blessed, blessed is their devotion and love that makes them sing his praises all the time — while at work in the barn or the courtyard, grinding at the quern or pounding the grain or churning buttermilk.

77. Sitting at leisure, or while at meals, or even while sleeping, it was Baba's name constantly on their lips. And, but for Baba, and Baba alone, they worshipped no other god!

78. Oh, how wonderful was the love these ladies cherished for Baba! How very sweet their loving devotion! It is only such pure love, and not erudite learning, that inspires such delightful poetic compositions!

79. No doubt, the language is simple; the expression direct, without a touch of learning. But the poetry that shines forth through the words will earn a nod of appreciation even from the learned!

80. Real poetry is an expression of sincere, genuine love and the listeners can feel it in the words of these ladies!

81. If Sai Baba so wishes, maybe, I will be able to have a whole collection of these verses to make into a complete chapter, which will satisfy the listeners' desire to hear them.

82. Formless as God is, He appeared in Shirdi in the form of Sai. But to know Him, the ego, all passions and desires, must first

disappear. For it is only by love and devotion that He can be known.

83. Or, maybe, it was the collective merit of the devotees that came to fruition, and, reaching the point of saturation, sprouted into a shoot at the appropriate moment, in the form of Sai, which, in the course of time, bore fruit in his manifestation in Shirdi.

84. The Indescribable found expression; the One without a birth was most truly born; the Formless assumed a form, when love and compassion was poured into the mould of a human being (i.e. Sai).

85. Success and Wealth, Renunciation and Wisdom, Power and Munificence — such were the six most excellent qualities that adorned this form.

86. Extraordinary was Baba's restraint! Himself without any possessions and in an unmanifest state, he yet took on a physical body for bestowing grace on his devotees.

87. Oh, how kind he was! He won the love and trust of his devotees. But as to his real nature, perhaps, even God Himself could not have understood him fully!

88. Such were his (wise and powerful) words that even the Goddess of Speech would not have ventured to utter and they would have shamed their listeners into humility. These were the words that Sai spoke for the benefit of the devotees.

89. And these words — which, rather than translate them, it is better to remain silent — have yet, perforce to be narrated, since it would not be proper to neglect one's duty.

90. Full of compassion for his devotees, Baba said, with utmost humility, "A slave of slaves that I am, I am indebted to you and have set out to have your *darshan*.

91. "It is indeed, by your great kindness that I have met you. I am but a worm in your faeces[9], by virtue of which position, I am most blessed in this Universe."

92. Oh, what modesty Baba had! What fondness for being humble! And what a perfect state of egolessness, too! Such was also his courteousness!

93. Baba's above words have been cited as being genuinely true. Should anyone think that I am being disrespectful, I can only beg their forgiveness!

94. If my speech is defiled thereby, and if you are to be absolved from the sin of listening to it, let us chant *Sai-naam* repeatedly, which will clear the blemishes of all.

95. Sai's Grace is the fruit of our penance of several births. It brings us a joy as boundless as that of a thirsty traveller, who finds a '*paan-poyi*'[10].

96. Although it appeared to all, as if the palate relished the different tastes and flavours, he was not even conscious of it, for the tongue knew no relish for the food it tasted.

97. When there were no sensual desires at all, how could he enjoy the pleasures thereof? And when such pleasures had not the power to rouse the sense organs, could he get entangled in them, ever?

98. The eyes saw whatever objects came in front of them; but he was not conscious of what they saw. For here again, there was no desire to take notice of anything.

99. The *langot* (symbolizing celibacy) with which he was born, as the myth goes of Shri Hanuman, it is said was seen by none, except his mother and Shri Ram. Who then, could stand comparison to his Brahmacharya (celibacy)?

100. And, if even the mother had never seen the genitals, what to say of others? Such was also the strict celibacy of Baba, the perfection of which was most unique!

101. He always wore the *langot* round the loins. Except for micturition, the private parts were as redundant as the ball of flesh near the throat of a he-goat — an organ just for the sake of an organ!

102. This was the position so far as Baba's physical body was concerned. Though the bodily organs performed their normal functions, there was not the least desire or even an awareness of a desire for sensual pleasures.

103. To all appearances, the three *gunas* — *Sattva*, *Rajas* and *Tamas* were present in the bodily organs; he even appeared to be the

doer of action. But in reality, he was without any attachment to the body and beyond the *Trigunas.*

104. Totally detached, Pure Knowledge Incarnate, and Self-rejoicing that Baba was, passions, like anger or lust, took repose at his feet. He was always desireless, totally satiated.

105. Such was his perfect state of Emancipation, that for him, even the sense objects became Brahma. Beyond sin and merit, it was the ultimate resting place for all.

106. He had no ego, nor did he ever dream of making a distinction between people. And when Nanavalli asked him to get up from his seat, he at once moved aside, making room for him.

107. He had nothing to gain in this world, nor was anything left in the other world to be gained. Such was this saint who had appeared on this earth only to bestow grace on the people.

108. These most compassionate saints incarnate on the earth for no other purpose than to bestow grace on others. They are kindness itself in the cause of others.

109. Their heart is as soft as butter, say some. But whereas the butter melts only on being heated, the hearts of the saints melt on seeing others scorched by suffering.

110. He, who clothed himself with a *kafni,* patched in a hundred places; whose seat and bedding was made up of coarse sack-cloth; and whose heart was free of all passion — of what value is a silver throne to him?

111. Such a throne would, if anything, be only an obstacle to him. Yet if the devotees were to slide it underneath from behind, he would not try to resist, in deference to their feelings of love and devotion.

112. On the placid lake that was Shirdi, bloomed a beautiful lotus in the form of Baba. The faithful inhaled its fragrance joyously; but mud and slime fell to the lot of unlucky, unbelieving frogs, who continued to wallow in the mud.

113. Baba prescribed no *Yogasanas,* no *Pranayama,* no violent suppression of the sense organs, nor *mantra, tantra* or *yantra pooja.* And he did not ever whisper *mantra* in the ears of his devotees.

114. Outwardly, he seemed to follow the ways and customs of the people, but inwardly he was totally different. And so watchful, so correct in his worldly dealings was he, that no one could have matched his skill there!

115. For the benefit of the devotees, the saints incarnate; for the devotees alone, are all their feelings, their emotions, their worldly dealings. Remember this!

116. Sai Maharaj is the Abode of Peace, a dwelling of Pure, Blissful Joy! I prostrate before him in obeisance, with a heart pure and unconceited.

117. The place to which Maharaj came walking, of his own free will, is a holy place of great merit. Without tremendous merit from the past, such a treasure is hard to come by.

118. 'A pure, robust seed will bring forth juicy, delectable fruit', so goes the well-known adage, which has been tested by the people of Shirdi.

119. Baba is neither Hindu nor Muslim, and he is beyond *Ashrama* and *Varna*. But he can eradicate and totally destroy the afflictions of this worldly life.

120. Unbounded, unending as the sky above, Baba's life is beyond all comprehension. Who but he, and he alone, can comprehend it fully?

121. The function of the mind is to think, to reflect, without which it will not rest even for a moment. Offer it sensual pleasures and it will dwell on them; offer the Guru as its object, and it will reflect on him.

122. Hence, concentrating all your senses in the ears, when you heard about the importance and greatness of the guru, it was itself an effortless remembrance of the guru; it was a *kirtan*, a *bhajan* of Sai that occurred naturally and easily.

123. *Panchagnisadhan*[11], *Yajna* (ritual sacrifice), *Mantra*, *Tantra*, *Ashtanga-yoga* — these are the ways of worship possible only to the twice-born.[12] Of what use are they to the others?

124. But the stories of the saints are not like that. They guide all the people to the path of virtue; they destroy the fear and sufferings

of worldly life and bring the realization of how salvation can be attained.

125. By listening to them and relflecting upon them; by a concentrated study and contemplation of these saints' stories, not only the twice-born, but even the *Shudras* and women are purified.

126. There cannot be a man in whom love is altogether absent. In some, it is for one thing; in others, it is for another. The object of love varies with different people.

127. For some, the object of love is their children; for others, it may be wealth, honour, riches — the body, the house, fame and glory; and for some, it is the acquisition of knowledge.

128. When all the love one feels for an object is concentrated and boiled down to its essence and poured into the mould of the feet of God, it is that which then appears in the form of devotion (to God).

129. Hence surrender your Being at the feet of Sai, offering up to him all the material objects of worldly life. He will then bless you. This is an easy way to get his blessings.

130. Such are the means, small and easy, by which people can reap the highest benefit. Why then all this disinterest, this indifference?

131. The listeners will naturally have a doubt in their minds, that if so much gain lies in such effortless and easy means, why are people in general so indifferent as to neglect it?

132. There is only one reason for this. Such a desire will not arise without God's Grace. But when God is pleased to bestow His Grace, the fondness, the desire to listen will arise at once.

133. So, seek refuge in Sai and Narayana will bless you. The desire and longing to listen (to these stories) will arise and you will have found an easy way to spiritual progress.

134. Keep the saintly company of the Sadguru; disentangle yourself from the meshes of this worldly life. It is in this that your fulfilment lies. Of this, have no doubt whatsoever, in your mind.

135. Give up all your ingenious arguments. Instead, repeat 'Sai', 'Sai', constantly, and see how smoothly you sail to the shore beyond! Let there be no doubts about this.

136. These are not my words; they are words of Sai, with a profound significance. Do not consider them vain; do not even try to evaluate them (for they are priceless!).

137. Bad company is always detrimental; it is the home of excessive sorrow and suffering and will lead you astray without your knowledge. It drives all happiness away.

138. Who else but Sainath or the Sadguru can remove the evil resulting from such bad company?

139. Preserve carefully, O devotees, these words of such compassionate concern that fell from the mouth of the guru. They will ward off the evil influence of bad company.

140. As this created universe attracts the eye, the heart, always captivated by beauty, is lost in admiration. But when the same eye is turned inwards, it gets engrossed in the company of the saints.

141. So great is the importance of this *Satsang* (the company of the holy) that it completely destroys the ego. Hence no other means is as effective as *Satsang*.

142. Always keep the company of saintly men; the company of all others is always defective. Only the holy company is free from blemish, for in all its aspects it is pure.

143. *Satsang* will free you from bodily attachment. So immense is its power that once you devote yourself to it, you are at once liberated from the bondage of worldly life.

144. If you are fortunate enough to have *Satsang*, perfect spiritual instruction will come to you effortlessly, and in that instant, the attraction for bad company will disappear. Instead the mind will get totally absorbed therein (i.e. *Satsang*).

145. For initiation into the spiritual path, detachment from the sensual pleasures is the only way. And unless there is a strong urge for the company of the holy, the true Self is never discovered.

146. After joy comes sorrow, and only after suffering will there be happiness. But man always welcomes happiness and turns away from pain.

147. Whether welcomed or abhorred, what will be, will be. And saintly company alone can take us beyond pleasure and pain.

148. *Satsang* destroys ego; *Satsang* breaks the birth-death cycle; *Satsang* helps reach God by severing the bonds of this material world, instantly.

149. To attain an excellent spiritual state, holy company is the most perfect means of purification. If you surrender to the saints whole-heartedly, you attain lasting Peace.

150. Saints incarnate on this earth to turn towards God, the minds of those who never utter His Name, or make an obeisance to Him; have no faith nor devotion and never praise Him.

151. Ganga-Bhagirathi, Godavari, Krishna, Venya, Kaveri, Narmada, (although pure and holy in themselves), also wish for the touch of the lotus feet of the *sadhus* and await their visit to bathe in their waters.

152. Though these rivers wash away the sins of the world, their own sins can never be washed away without the touch of the holy *sadhus'* feet.

153. It is our great good fortune of several births that we have discovered the holy feet of Sai Maharaj. The cycle of birth and death has thus been stayed; the fear of worldly life is totally destroyed.

154. And now, my virtuous listeners! Let us reflect on what we have heard, while we rest ourselves awhile. Further narration will follow thereafter.

155. Hemad surrenders at Sai's feet. I am but a sandal of his foot and will go on narrating his stories, for it will only enhance my pleasure.

156. Oh, what a comely figure was Sai's! He would stand on the edge of the mosque, distributing *Udi* to the devotees, one by one, with the sole purpose of their welfare, at heart.

157. He who knew how illusory this worldly life is, and was constantly engaged in blissful Self-absorption, with a mind like a flower in full bloom, before him I prostrate in obeisance.

158. He who gives *Brahmajnana* or Supreme Knowledge, by applying the collyrium of Knowledge into the eye, to that great Sai, I bow in obeisance.

159. The next chapter is even better than this, which, as it enters your heart through the ears, will purify it and cleanse it of all its impurities.

Weal be to all! Here ends the tenth chapter of
"Shri Sai Samarth Satcharit", called
'The Mahima of Shri Sai Samarth'
as inspired by the saints and the virtuous,
and composed by his devotee, Hemadpant.

NOTES

1. Refer Ch. 4, note 4.
2. The three-fold afflications are: *adhibhoot*, i.e. physical, such as earthquakes, storms, etc.; *adhyatmic*, or psychical or corporeal, such as sorrow, sickness etc.; and *adhidaivic*, i.e. from gods or devils or fate, such as injury from lightning, pestilence, etc.
3. Refer Ch. 3, note 16.
4. There are twenty-three *siddhis* in all, which have been graded into three classes: Great, Medium and Small. The great *siddhis* are eight in number and are very difficult to accquire. Only he who is established in the Self, who has lost all consciousness of his body and of the sense of 'I' and 'mine', such a one can acquire them. They are: *Anima* — the reduction of one's form to an atom, assuming the subtle and invisible state; *Mahima or garima* — to make the body weighty or heavy; *Laghima* — to make the body excessively light and beyond what is natural; *Prapti* — to acquire objects of sense pertaining to the respective organs; *Praakaashya* — to see and know invisible things in the other worlds; *Ishitaa* — to stimulate bodies and creatures, to have control over natural forces; *Vashitaa* — to have supremacy over the senses; *Yatkaamastadavasyati* — literally, the power to obtain joys in the three worlds effortlessly, by mere willing. However, this power leads to the state of the highest bliss through ending of all desires.
5. The nine treasures of the god Kuber or Plutus, viz. *Padma*, *Mahapadma*, *Shankh*, *Makar*, *Kachchap*, *Mukund*, *Nand*, *Neel* and *Kharva*.
6. Compare with *Bhagvad-Gita*, Ch. 2, v. 58:
    'The tortoise can draw in his limbs; the Seer can draw in his senses. He is called "illumined".
7. A wandering ascetic.
8. A *sannyasin* who stays at a holy place of pilgrimage and vows not to leave it till he dies.
9. Swami Sai-Sharan-Anand has interpreted verse 91 differently. According to him the word '*paya*' in the original Marathi version is not to be literally construed to mean the 'foot', but its deeper meaning is indicated by the Sanskrit word '*payu*' or anus, which is the seat of the Ego of the astral body and its deity is Death. The Vedic doctrine is that the spontaneous consciousness of 'I AM' is *Atman* or *Paramatman*. The *Bhagvad Gita* supports this doctrine and it is observed in verse 61 of Ch. 18 thereof that God resides in the hearts of all beings. So the true meaning of this verse is, 'This worm of consciousness which resides in your body with faeces, which causes your actions, is myself. I am the controller of your inner being. As a result of your coming to me, you have become one with me through your *Bhakti* or devotion and I consider myself blessed by the *darshan* of God residing in your heart.'
10. The shed or stand erected for the purpose of supplying water to the travellers.
11. Performance of a particular austere devotion — sitting in the midst of four fires kindled severally to the north, south, east, west and under the sun through his day's course.
12. The term 'twice-born' refers to the first three *Varnas* of the Hindus, viz. *Brahmins*, *Kshatriyas* and *Vaishyas*, who are called in common parlance '*Savarnas*'. A *Savarna* is said to be twice-born after he undergoes the thread ceremony at the age of 8 or so, when *Gayatri mantra* is whispered into his ears.

11

A Narration of Sai's Greatness

MY OBEISANCE TO SHRI GANESH, TO SHRI SARASWATI, AND SHRI GURUMAHARAJ! TO THE FAMILY DEITY, TO SHRI SITA-RAMACHANDRA, MY MOST HUMBLE OBEISANCE! I BOW IN REVERENCE TO THE MOST VENERABLE GURU SHRI SAINATH!

1. To continue from the previous tale, Baba slept on a narrow wooden plank, from which his descending or ascending had never been seen by anyone and which only revealed his incomprehensible ways.

2. A Hindu or a Muslim, to him both were equal. And so, we have surveyed, so far, the life of Baba who was the deity of Shirdi.

3. And now, we begin this eleventh chapter, which, adorned as it is with sweet tales of the guru, should, I feel, be offered with unswerving devotion, at Sai's feet.

4. By doing so, we will be contemplating on Baba's manifest form, which will be as meritorious as the eleven readings of the *Rudra*[1], and will give us a proof of Baba's power over the five elements, thereby revealing Baba's greatness.

5. Now let me narrate how Indra, Agni, Varun[2], etc., obeyed Baba's command. Be attentive, O listeners!

6. A personification of the highest renunciation, Sai's manifest form is the repose of his faithful devotees. Let us bring him to mind with love and affection.

7. We offer him as a seat our unswerving faith in our guru's Word. And with the 'Sankalpa'[3] to renounce all desires, we begin our worship.

8. Greater even than all the most sacred places of *pooja* — i.e. idol, sacrificial altar[4], fire, light, sun, water and the Brahmin — is Gururaj. Hence let us worship him with steadfast devotion.

9. Once you surrender at his feet with single-minded devotion, not only the guru, but God Himself will be moved. Such is the marvel of guru-worship, which the guru-devotees should experience for themselves.

10. Only so long as a guru-worshipper is keenly aware of his physical self does he need a guru in a human form. But for one who has gone beyond his physical self, a formless guru suffices. Such is the proclamation of the *Shastras*.

11. Devotion cannot arise without a physical form to meditate upon, and in the absence of such loving devotion the unbloomed flower of the mind does not open up.

12. And unless it blossoms, the bud, by herself, can give out no fragrance, no honey. Nor will the buzzing bee hover around it, even for a moment.

13. That which is with attributes *(saguna)*, also has a form; without attributes *(nirguna)* is the formless One. But they both do not differ from each other. With or without form, they are both one and the same.

14. *Ghee* (clarified butter), when frozen is *ghee* solidified. But when melted, it is still called *ghee*. That with form and that without it, in harmony with each other fill the universe.

15. To be able to gaze at it till the eyes are satiated; to be able to lower the head at its feet, from where Knowledge flows freely and directly, it is there that the heart grows fond.

16. He with whom one can converse lovingly, whom one can worship, with all the elaborate rituals, he has to be in a manifest form.

17. Truly, it is so much easier to comprehend a manifest Form rather than the unmanifest, the Formless One. And when love and devotion for the manifest is once rooted firmly in the mind, comprehension of the Formless One follows automatically.

18. In innumerable ways did Baba try to bring to the devotees a comprehension of the Formless One. According to the spiritual

authority of each, he would make them sit apart or deny *darshan* for long periods.

19. He would send one away from Shirdi, while another would be confined in solitude in Shirdi itself. Yet another would be restricted to the *Wada* and made to read the *Pothi* (sacred text) regularly, as prescribed by himself.

20. The purpose of the whole exercise was that after such a deep study is pursued over the years, the longing for Baba's Presence in an unmanifest form would intensify and his Presence would be felt all the time — sitting, sleeping or eating.

21. Mortal as this body is, it is going to die some day or other. Hence the devotees should not grieve for it but concentrate their minds on Him who is without beginning or end, i.e. God.

22. This Creation, spread out before us in its rich variety, is all an illusory manifestation of the Unmanifest. It has taken shape out of the Unmanifest and it is to the Unmanifest that it will return.

23. The whole of it (Creation), right from the Brahma down to the smallest bush[5], taken either as individual components of the whole, or as the aggregate of all the component parts, merges with the Unmanifest, from which it came into being.

24. Hence no one ever dies. How can it be true, then, of Baba? Shri Sai is eternally pure, Wisdom Incarnate, Perfect and Immortal.

25. Some may call him a devotee of God; some may call him a great Vaishnav (devotee of Shri Vishnu); but to us, he appears as God Incarnate!

26. As the Ganga wends her way to merge with the vast ocean, she brings a soothing coolness to those oppressed by the sun's heat, along her way; gives life to the trees on her banks and quenches the thirst of all.

27. Such is also the case with the incarnation of saints on this earth. They appear and depart. But by the manner in which they conduct themselves, they purify the world.

28. Forgiving to the utmost, remarkably unruffled and calm, guileless and forbearing by nature, and incomparable in their perfect contentment — such a one was Baba.

29. Though he appears to be in a human form, he is formless, tranquil, unruffled. He is self-contained and liberated inwardly, even as he moves about in this world.

30. Though Godhead Himself, even Shri Krishna says that 'the saints are my heart and soul; saints are my living image; the loving, compassionate saints are none other than myself.

31. 'And yet, even to call them my 'image' would not be correct. For they are a constant, unchanging image of mine. And it is for their sake that I carry the burden (of the responsibility) of my devotees.

32. 'I bow too, at the feet of him, who surrenders himself whole-heartedly to the saints.' Thus has Shri Krishna himself proclaimed the greatness of the saints to Uddhava.

33. Most perfect among those with a Form and among those without it, the most excellent attribute of those with attributes and possessing the highest virtue among the virtuous, and king among them all;

34. Satiated in all his desires, he who is fulfilled, is always content with what is ordained; constantly Self-absorbed and beyond joys and sorrows;

35. Who is the splendour of Blissful Joy — who can describe the glory of such a one? He is Brahma Incarnate and therefore always beyond any description.

36. It is this power, which defies all description, that has appeared in a visible form on this earth. He is indeed that same Truth, Knowledge and Joy, personified; it is the full awareness of Knowledge.

37. He whose heart is one with the Brahman, who is liberated from worldly life and is exempt from the mundane, worldly concerns; he always enjoys a state of Oneness with the Brahman and is an image of unalloyed Happiness.

38. Listeners have always heard the *Shruti* proclaim that 'Pure Joy is God Himself'; the readers too have read it in the sacred texts. But the faithful actually experience it in Shirdi.

39. Strange indeed is this worldly life, characterized by *dharma, adharma,* etc., about which, only those who have not realized their true Self, find it necessary to bother and take care of.

40. But is of no concern to the realized souls, for they take refuge only in their real Self. They are for ever free and full of joy, who are the very image of pure Knowledge.

41. Baba was himself the refuge, the support for all. Wherefore then, a seat to support him? And that too, the seat of a silver throne? But Baba was indulgent and cared for the devotees' feelings.

42. There was his old, old seat — a piece of sack-cloth, on which the devotees would very lovingly put a cushioned seat for him to sit on.

43. And would also place a cushion against the wall at the back, that he used to lean on. Honouring the feelings of the devotees, Baba too complied with their wishes.

44. Though he appeared to be stationed in Shirdi, Baba moved everywhere quite freely. This was the experience that Sai always gave to his devotees.

45. Unruffled, detached as he was, Baba would accept from his devotees the various rituals of *pooja* — from each according to his faith, and in deference to his feelings.

46. Thus, some waved the *Chowri* (to whisk away the flies), as some fanned him gently with a fan; some others offered worship by playing musical instruments like kettle-drums, clarinets, etc.

47. Some washed his hands and feet, some applied fragrant perfumes and sandalwood paste; some made a special food offering followed by the ceremonious betel-leaf (*paan*), made with thirteen ingredients.

48. There were still others who applied sandalwood paste, drawing two lines with two fingers, as on a *Shivalinga*, while some mixed the fragrant musk with it before applying.

49. Once and only once, Dr Pandit, who was a friend of Tatyasaheb Noolkar came to Shirdi to have Sai Baba's *darshan*.

50. The moment he put his foot into Shirdi, he at once went to the mosque and making obeisance to Baba, sat down there for a moment to rest.

51. Baba then said to him, "Go, go to Dadabhat's, go this way!" So saying, he pointed the way with his finger, packing him off, thus!

52. Pandit went to Dada's house and was received by him with courtesy. Dada then, was all set to leave for the mosque to perform Baba's *pooja* and asked Pandit whether he would like to accompany him.

53. Pandit agreed and went with Dada. Dada then performed the *pooja*. Till then, no one had dared to apply the round sandal paste marks on Baba's forehead.

54. Whoever the devotee and for whatever reason he might come, Baba would not allow him to apply sandalwood paste on the forehead. Only Mhalsapati would smear it on the throat; the rest applied it to the feet.

55. But Pandit was naive, simple and devout. He grabbed the small dish of sandalwood paste from Dada's hands and holding Shri Sai's head with one hand, drew a neat '*Tripundra*'[6] on his forehead, with the other.

56. On seeing Pandit's daring, Dada felt some trepidation at heart. 'O what daring, indeed! And wouldn't Baba flare up by it!' (he thought).

57. But although the most improbable had actually taken place, Baba said not a word! Rather, he looked quite pleased! He showed not a trace of anger.

58. The incident was allowed to pass. But in Dada's mind rankled an uneasiness, a disquiet. And on the same evening he asked Baba about it.

59. 'When we try to put ever so tiny a mark of sandal paste on your forehead, you do not even allow us to touch it. What is this that happened this morning?

60. 'For our sandal paste mark there is so much distaste and disinterest; and for that Pandit's '*tripundra*', so much love? What a very strange behaviour! There is no consistency in it.'

61. With a smile playing on his face Baba then uttered these sweet words very lovingly to Dada. Listen to them carefully.

62. "Dada, remember, his guru is a Brahmin, and I, a Muslim. Yet, regarding me to be the same as his own guru, he offered me *guru-pooja*.

63. "Not once did the doubt arise in his mind that 'I am a Brahmin, pure and holy and he, an impure Muslim. How can I worship him?'

64. "And that is how he deceived me, leaving me no other option. Far from my denying him, it was he who won me over completely."

65. Dada heard this explanation, but treated it lightly, as a joke. And it was not until he returned home that its true significance dawned on Dada.

66. Dada was deeply offended by the inconsistency in Baba's behaviour. But it was while talking the incident over with Pandit, that he realized at once, how consistent Baba had been in his behaviour.

67. Raghunath of Dhopeshwar (1821-1910) was a *Siddha*, who was well-known as 'Kaka Puranik', at whose feet Pandit was devotedly attached as a disciple, from an association of past births.

68. He called out to Kaka, his guru, and the experience that followed confirmed him in his faith. As is the steadfastness of faith, so is also the power of devotion.

69. However, these *pooja* rituals were allowed only when it pleased Baba. Otherwise Baba would throw away the *pooja* offerings, exhibiting the wrath and temper of Narsimha himself.

70. And while in this terrible form, who had the courage to stand near him? Seeing him so incensed, each and everyone ran for the fear of his life.

71. Suddenly flying into a rage, he would sometimes take out his anger on the devotees. At other times, softer even than wax, he would be the very image of Tranquillity and Forgiveness.

72. Sometimes he appeared as ferocious as the Fire of Universal Destruction and kept the devotees as on the sharp edge of a sword. But sometimes he was cheerful and even softer than butter.

73. Outwardly, he may tremble with rage; rotate his eyeballs vigorously; but at heart, there flowed a spring of compassion, as in a mother for her child.

74. In the very next moment, he regained his usual calm and composure and called out loudly to the devotees to come to him, saying, "Even if I seem to be angry with someone, my heart knows no anger.

75. "Should a mother push her child away with a kick, or the ocean send the river back, only then is it possible that I will repulse you or harm you in any way.

76. "I am absolutely in the power of my devotees and stand by their side. For ever I am hungering after their love and readily answer their call in distress."

77. Even while narrating this part of the story, another, most appropriate tale comes to my mind which I shall narrate. Listen to it attentively, O listeners!

78. Siddique Phalake, a Muslim resident of Kalyan, once came to Shirdi, having just returned from the pilgrimage to Mecca-Medina.

79. The old Haji put up in the northward-facing *Chavadi*. For the first nine months, Baba did not favour him with any notice and seemed displeased.

80. Time was not yet ripe, and all his wearisome trips to the mosque were wasted. He tried in different ways, but Baba would not even look at him.

81. The doors of the mosque were open to all; nobody had to manoeuvre a secret entry. But Phalake had no permission to come up the steps of the mosque.

82. Phalake grew very sad at heart. 'How strange is this Fate, that I cannot even put my foot in that mosque! I wonder what terrible sin I could have committed!

83. 'By what means can I win his grace?' This was the only thought that tormented Phalake's heart, like a disease, day and night.

84. Suddenly, someone said to him, 'Do not despair; seek Madhavrao's help and your wish will be fulfilled.

85. 'If you neglect to take the *darshan* of Nandi[7] first, how do you expect Shankar to be pleased?' To Phalake, this appeared to be a better course to follow.

86. *Prima facie*, this may appear to be an exaggeration to the listeners. But such indeed had been the experience of the devotees when they went to Shirdi for Baba's *darshan*.

87. Those who wished to have a quiet, undisturbed conversation with Baba, would always take Madhavrao with them, initially.

88. He would then introduce the topic in soft sweet tones as to who had come, from where and for what purpose. On this introduction, Samarth would then be induced to converse.

89. Hearing all this, Haji importuned Madhavrao, saying, 'Please remove this restless agitation of my mind, once for all, and help me attain the unattainable'.

90. Under such urging upon his consideration, Madhavrao resolved firmly, that whether the task be easy or difficult, he would give it a try.

91. He went to the mosque and ventured to bring up the topic slowly, cautiously, 'Baba, that old man is so sad, so distressed! Oh, why don't you oblige him?

92. 'That Haji has been to Mecca-Medina and has now come to Shirdi for your *darshan*. How can you not feel compassion for him? Oh, do please allow him to come to the mosque!

93. 'Countless people come, take *darshan* in the mosque, returning instantaneously. Why then is he singled out to waste away in languor?

94. 'Do be kind and compassionate towards him, at last, and let him come to the mosque. Then he will also be able to say to you what he wishes and go away immediately.'

95. "Shama, you are as a new-born infant, as yet! Unless Allah favours him, what can I do?

96. "Can anyone step up to this mosque without being Allahmiya's debtor? Inscrutable are the ways of this Fakir here. Over Him, I have no control.

97. "All the same, go and ask him clearly whether he will carefully walk up the narrrow path, which goes straight, beyond the well Baravi."

98. When asked, the Haji said, 'However difficult it may be, I shall carefully tread on the path. But give me personal audience, O Sai; let me sit at your feet.'

99. On hearing this reply from Shama, Baba said, "Ask him further, 'will you give me forty thousand rupees in four instalments?'"

100. To Madhavrao, who conveyed this message, the Haji said, 'Is this any question to be asked! Oh, will I not give even forty lakhs when asked? What then, of thousands!'

101. When Baba heard this, he said further, "We intend to kill a goat in the mosque today. Ask him which part of the meat he wants.

102. "Does he want the meat-covered bones, or is his heart set on having the sex organs? Go, ask that old fellow what it is that he definitely wants."

103. Madhavrao conveyed Baba's message fully to the Haji. And the Haji said categorically, 'I want none of it.

104. 'If he wishes to give me something, then I have only one wish — that even if I can get a morsel from that earthen vessel of food, I shall be blessed.'

105. Madhavrao duly conveyed Haji's reply. But as he heard it, Baba at once flew into a rage.

106. Himself, he picked up the earthen vessel of food and pitchers of water and flung them out of the door. Fiercely biting his own hands, he came and stood next to the Haji.

107. Catching his *kafni* with both his hands, he lifted it up in front of the Haji and said, "Who do you think you are that you boast vainly in my presence?

108. "You are flaunting the wisdom of your old age! Is this how you read your *Quran* — that a pilgrimage to Mecca has made you so proud and haughty? But you do not know me yet!"

109. He reviled him thus, hurled at him unutterable abuses! The Haji was absolutely stunned! Baba then went back.

110. On entering the courtyard of the mosque, he saw some farm-women selling mangoes. He bought all their baskets of fruit and sent them to the Haji.

111. At once he turned back and once again, went to that Phalake and taking out fifty-five rupees from his pocket, counted them, one by one, on the Haji's hand.

112. The affection between them grew thereafter. The Haji was invited for a meal — as if both had forgotten all that had passed before! And the Haji was absorbed in the experience of pure joy.

113. Later, the Haji left Shirdi, but returned once again, and became more and more attached to Baba. And even afterwards, Baba continued to give him money, from time to time.

114. Once I saw Sai Samarth praying to Indra, the god of thunder, who rules over the clouds, and I was struck with amazement.

115. It was a most terrifying moment. The entire sky was overcast and dark. Birds and animals were stricken with fear. There was a fierce gale, accompanied by heavy showers.

116. It was late evening; the sun had already set. Suddenly there was a whirlwind and as the wind roared there was a great commotion everywhere.

117. To add to it, the clouds thundered overhead; the lightning cracked, the squally wind continued to roar and there followed a heavy downpour of rain.

118. The clouds rained cats and dogs; pit-pat came the hailstones, thick and fast; the villagers were full of apprehensions; the cattle bellowed helplessly.

119. Under the eaves of the mosque the beggars thronged together for shelter. The cattle with their calves huddled there, too! The mosque was over-crowded.

120. There was water, and nothing but water, everywhere, and in each quarter! The grass was forcefully borne away on the torrent of water, and the crop in the barn, all cut and ready, was soaked through and through. Among the people chaos and bewilderment reigned supreme.

121. The villagers panicked and huddled into the *Sabha-mandap*; some took shelter under the eaves of the mosque. They had all come in supplication to Baba.

122. Jogai, Jakhai, Mariai, Shani, Shankar, Ambabai, Maruti, Khandoba, Mhalsapati — all these gods and goddesses were in Shirdi, in some place or the other.

123. But in times of trouble, none was of help to the villagers. It was Sai alone — their living God, who came running to their rescue in the hour of need.

124. And he needed no animal sacrifice — of a goat or a cock; nor any offering of money. Sincere love and faith was all that he hungered after and then, all their troubles would be destroyed.

125. When he saw how terrified the people were, Maharaj's heart was deeply moved by compassion. Leaving his seat he came forward and stood on the edge of the raised front portion of the mosque.

126. The sky thundered; the lightning flashed and cracked. And in the midst of all this stood Sai Maharaj, raising his voice to the highest pitch and straining every nerve, as he roared.

127. Dearer than their own life are the devotees, the sadhus and saints, to the gods and it is according to their wishes that the gods act. For them, the gods even appear on the earth.

128. When the devotees implore their help, gods have to take up the cudgels on their behalf and rush to their rescue, recalling their great devotion.

129. Roar followed upon a terrifying roar and the sound seemed to fill the sky above. The mosque itself seemed to shake, to tremble as the sound deafened the ears of all.

130. The high-pitched voice resounded, like a mountain-echo, through mosques and temples. At once, the Cloud restrained its thunder; the pouring rain checked itself.

131. Baba's mighty voice shook the entire *Sabha-mandap*. Perplexed and motionless, the devotees stood still, wherever they happened to be.

132. Truly, how inscrutable are Baba's ways! The rain abated; the wind receded at once; the haziness of the fog melted away.

133. Gradually, the rain tapered off; the squally wind subsided; clusters of stars appeared as the veil of darkness lifted from the sky, at that time.

134. Later, the rain ceased altogether. The fierce wind was becalmed; the moon appeared in the sky. Everybody was happy and at peace.

135. Lord Indra seemed to have taken pity! Moreover, a saint's word had to be honoured. Thus the clouds dispersed in every direction and calm reigned after the storm.

136. The rain ceased, altogether; a gentle breeze began to blow; the rumblings in the sky subsided completely and the birds and animals took heart.

137. The cattle wandered off, with their calves, from the shelter they had found under the eaves of houses and roamed around freely and fearlessly. The birds flew high into the sky.

138. Being witness earlier to the terrifying spectacle, people now thanked Baba profusely and went back to their respective homes. The cattle, now reassured, scattered here and there.

139. Such is this Sai, Kindness incarnate! Great is his love for his devotees, and as tender as a mother's love for her child! How can I ever describe it adequately?

140. Equally great was his power over fire. Listen attentively, O Listeners! to a brief story in this connection. It will illustrate Baba's unique power and control over the elements.

141. Once, the fire in the *dhuni* suddenly flared up at midday. At such a time, who had the courage to stand near it? The flames soared up in a tumultuous surge.

142. The fire raged wildly as tongues of flame leapt up, touching the wooden planks of the ceiling. The mosque, it seemed, would be reduced to ashes in no time in this conflagration.

143. Yet Baba was unruffled and calm. Utterly amazed, the people in their worry and anxiety exclaimed, 'Oh, how perfectly calm and composed Baba is!'

144. Someone cried, 'Hurry up! Bring some water!' Another said, 'But who will pour it? If you try to do so, the baton will come down heavily on you. Who will dare to come forward?'

145. Their minds were all agitated and impatient. But none had the courage to ask. Then Baba himself stirred restlessly and put his hand to the baton.

146. Looking at the blazing fire he took the baton in hand and struck blow upon blow, saying, "Move, move back! Go!"

147. He struck hard at the column, which stood at about an arm's length from the *dhuni*, and staring at the flame kept on saying, "Calm, calm down!"

148. With every stroke the flame began to cower, losing its fierceness. Gradually the *dhuni* became calm. People too lost their fear.

149. Such is this Sai, the greatest among the saints, an Incarnation of God Himself, who will place his hand of benediction on your head as you place it on his feet in total surrender.

150. He who will read this chapter regularly with faith and devotion, will enjoy peace of mind and be free from all trouble.

151. What more can I say? Purify your heart, be regular in religious observances and worship Sai whole-heartedly and you will attain the Eternal Brahman (i.e. God).

152. All your desires — even the most uncommon ones — will be fulfilled and you will become completely free from all desires in the end. You will thus attain to a state of '*Sayujya-mukti*'[8], which is difficult to attain. Everlasting peace and contentment will fill your heart.

153. Hence the devotees who wish to enjoy a never-ending awareness of spiritual bliss, should read this chapter with reverence, again and again.

154. Such repeated readings of the stories will purify the mind and turn it towards the attainment of spiritual welfare; all that is undesirable and evil will be warded off and that which is desirable and good will be attained. Everyone can experience Baba's wonderful power (by such readings).

155. Hemadpant surrenders to Sai. The next chapter is very sacred and describes the greatness of *guru-shishya* relationship and how a *guru-putra* had his guru Gholap's *darshan*.

156. 'However sore the trial, a devotee should never abandon his own *guru-dev.*' This is the truth of which Sai gave an actual experience to his devotees and confirmed them in their faith in their own guru.

157. All the devotees who surrendered to him were given the marvellous experience of seeing their own guru in Sai's place as they took his *darshan.* Some in one way, others in another, but each was confirmed in his faith and devotion to his own personal guru.

Weal be to all! Here ends the eleventh chapter of
"*Shri Sai Samarth Satcharit*", called
'*A Narration of Sai's Greatness*',
as inspired by the saints and the virtuous,
and composed by his devotee, Hemadpant.

Notes

1. This is a chapter called '*Rudradhyaya*' in Yajurveda, which contains the famous *mantra* of Lord Shiva.
2. The gods of rain, fire and water, respectively.
3. '*Sankalpa*' means a solemn and formal enunciation of purpose as preparatory to entrance upon any religious rite or work.
4. This is a levelled, squared, and somewhat raised piece of ground as prepared for a sacrifice.
5. The words used in the original Marathi version are '*vyashti*' and '*samashti*', which have been explained thus: '*Vyashti*' is the state of an individual in the species; of a species in the genus; of a genus in the class or order. '*Samashti*' is the state of the species as the comprehension of its individuals; of the genus as the comprehension of its species; of the class or order as the comprehension of its genera. '*Vyasti*' is the state of an ingredient, — a tree, a fruit, a drop, a soldier, a citizen; and '*Samashti*' is the state of the compound, — the forest, the cluster, the ocean, the army, the city.
6. Three horizontal lines drawn on the forehead with ashes by the Smart (worshipper of Shiva) sect. Vaishnavas (worshippers of Vishnu) draw three vertical lines of *Gopichandan*.
7. Nandi, the bull, is the vehicle of Lord Shiva, whose stone image is always installed in front of a Shiva temple.
8. The fourth of the four states into which *mukti* (liberation) is distinguished. These are: '*Salokya*' (residence in the heaven of a particular deity worshipped as the Supreme); '*Samipya*' (proximity or nearness to the deity); '*Sarupya*' (assimilation in the form of the deity); and '*Sayujya*' (absorption into the essence of Brahman).

12

Shri Saint Gholap - Ramdarshan

MY OBEISANCE TO SHRI GANESH, TO SHRI SARASWATI, AND SHRI GURUMAHARAJ! TO THE FAMILY DEITY, TO SHRI SITA-RAMACHANDRA, MY MOST HUMBLE OBEISANCE! I BOW IN REVERENCE TO THE MOST VENERABLE GURU SHRI SAINATH!

1. Glory be to you, O Sadguru Sainath. I bow my head at your feet in obeisance. Unperturbed by passions, and forever Self-absorbed that you are, have mercy on him (i.e. me), who has taken refuge at your feet.

2. Truth, Knowledge and Joy Incarnate, a store of blissful happiness, you are the source of comfort and pleasure to the suffering (humanity) who are scorched by the worldly sorrows. Your teaching of non-duality removes the illusion of duality from the minds of even the most slow-witted of people.

3. Most fortunate indeed are those who have not only described you as all-pervading, and as expansive as the sky above, but have actually experienced these qualities.

4. To protect the *sadhus* and to destroy the wicked — this is the purpose of the incarnation of God on this earth. But stranger still is the case with these saints.

5. To them the *sadhu* and the wicked are both equal. Their heart knows not to differentiate between them as one being great and the other, mean. Both are the same to them.

6. In fact, the saints are, in a sense, greater than gods themselves. For, moved by compassion and love for the meek and the poor, they first set the unrighteous on the path of righteousness.

7. To the ocean of worldly life, they are as the sage Agasti[1]; to the darkness of ignorance they are as the sun. It is thus, in them, that God dwells, in fact, they are not different from God at all.

8. My Sai is one amongst these, and has appeared on this earth for the welfare of his devotees. He is Jnandev incarnate, fixed in the grandeur and light of *Kaivalya* (Oneness of God).

9. With great compassion and love for all the living creatures, he was yet totally without any attachment to all else. But though he had affection for one and detachment for the others, he looked upon all, equally and without hostility.

10. Without enmity or friendship, treating rich and poor alike — such was this Sai, the great Mahatma. And now listen to his greatness and glory.

11. Saints expend freely of their accumulated merit in the cause of their devotees, to whom they are drawn by their loving devotion. And no obstacle, neither the hill nor the dale, is too great for them to overcome when they rush to the rescue of their devotees.

12. There are people who, in their ignorance, know not what spirituality is. They are caught up in their attachment to their wife, sons, wealth. Leave out these poor, ignorant creatures.

13. Even God is merciful, loving and tender to these ignorant, guileless beings. But those who turn their backs to God and move away from Him burn in their own conceit.

14. A saint will be moved to compassion and will take the ignorant under his wings so that faith may spring in them at once. But vain is the arrogant pride of learning.

15. The foolish, who consider themselves learned, are puffed up with empty pride and deride the path of devotion. But not for us the company of these fools!

16. We want neither the revolt against the *Varnas* nor yet an undue, exaggerated pride in them. We should not turn rigid adherents of *Varnashram-dharma* nor be the pretentious, learned *Pandits* who deny the very authority of the Vedas.

17. Those who have mastered the *Vedas* and the *Vedangas* and are thereby intoxicated with pride in their learning, it is they who come in the way of devotion and have no hope of being saved.

18. An ignorant man will overcome the fear of worldly life on the strength of his faith. But no one can ever solve the puzzles of these learned Pandits.

19. By reposing faith in the saints, the ignorance of the ignorant will be dispelled and the learned who pride themselves on their own learning, will be spared numerous doubts and surmises, giving rise to good thoughts and feelings in their hearts.

20. And now, just listen to what a strange thing once came to pass, out of sheer good fortune! A rigid ritualist was thus destined to enjoy the rare good fortune of meeting Sai.

21. His avowed purpose of the visit was quite different from what Fate willed it to be. As a result, he gained by his visit to Shirdi where he had *darshan* of his own guru.

22. You must listen, O listeners, to that most interesting tale which brings out the greatness of the guru and he gives an actual experience of his love to the guru-devotees.

23. Once, a rigid ritualistic Agnihotri Brahmin, Mulay by name, came from Nasik, the holy place of pilgrimage, to Shirdi, by virtue of his accumulated past merit.

24. Without a store of such merit, no one could stay in Shirdi, even for a moment. However firm one's resolve to stay might be, all machinations failed before Baba's wish.

25. One may well say, 'I will go and stay there as long as I wish'; but it is not in his hands to do so, for he is totally in the power of another.

26. Many who had firmly resolved and were absolutely certain of succeeding, gave up the effort, ultimately, in helplessness. Sai is a deity with his own indomitable will before whom the conceit of others falls off altogether.

27. Till such time as it is destined, Baba will not remember us, nor even will his praises fall on our ears. Where, then, is the question of our being inspired to take his *darshan*?

28. Many had cherished the fond wish to go for the *darshan* of Sai Samarth. Finally, Sai attained *Nirvana*, but such an opportunity never came their way.

29. There were others who kept on postponing the visit from time to time and their propensity for delaying itself came in the way of their visit. Ultimately, they never made it to Shirdi and Baba too, passed away.

30. Postponing it from morrow to morrow, in the end, they missed the opportunity to meet him in person and regretted it forever. Thus they lost the chance of having his *darshan* altogether.

31. It is the unfulfilled wish of all such people that will be satisfied by listening respectfully and with faith, to these stories; although it can be but a poor substitute.

32. But then, even those who, by their good fortune, did go; and were satiated by his *darshan*, by his touch — were they able to stay in Shirdi to their heart's desire? Well, it is Baba who must permit!

33. By his own efforts alone, none could go; nor could one stay on, however keen his desire. One could stay only as Baba commanded and return, the moment he said, "Go back".

34. Kaka Mahajani once travelled from Bombay to Shirdi, intending to stay there for a week and then come back.

35. Preparations for the birth celebrations of Lord Krishna would begin in advance. The Chavadi would be decorated beautifully; a cradle would be tied in front of Baba's seat, amidst great rejoicing.

36. Kaka had arrived at Shirdi a little early, intending to participate in the festivities of the joyous *Gokulashtami* celebrations, in person.

37. But, right at the beginning, as he went for *darshan*, Baba said, "So when do you return home?" On hearing this, Kaka was taken aback!

38. 'Why this question the moment I met him?' wondered Kaka. In fact, he was very keen on staying in Shirdi for eight days.

39. But as Baba put the question, he himself prompted the expected answer to Kaka. The answer that Kaka gave was thus the most appropriate one.

40. 'Whenever Baba gives me the command, I shall return home', he said. And even as these words came from Kaka's mouth, "Do go back tomorrow", Baba said.

41. Obeying the command with great reverence, he made obeisance to Baba and left on that same day, although it was the very special occasion of the *Gokulashtami* festival.

42. But later, when he reached home and went to his place of work, he saw that his employer was anxiously waiting for his return.

43. The *munim* (managing clerk) had suddenly taken ill and the employer was in urgent need of Kaka's help. In fact, he had already dispatched a letter to Shirdi, calling Kaka back, at once.

44. And when the postman came enquiring after him, Kaka had already left Shirdi. The letter was then sent back and Kaka received it on reaching home.

45. Running contrary to this is the short tale about how the devotees do not understand their own welfare, whereas Sai knows it clearly. Just listen to it!

46. Once, a renowned lawyer of Nasik, Bhausaheb Dhumal by name, and one of Baba's loving devotees, came to Shirdi, just to have Baba's *darshan*.

47. He had intended to take darshan quickly, make obeisance at Baba's feet and on getting Baba's blessings and *udi*, to return at once.

48. On his return journey, Dhumal had to get down at Niphad where he had to attend a court case.

49. Though such had been his plan, Baba knew what was right for him and what was not. So when he asked leave to return, Baba refused it to him.

50. Moreover, Baba detained him for a week, refusing permission, in no uncertain terms. And the hearing of the court case was also delayed, the matter being adjourned thrice.

51. Dhumal was made to stay a few days over a week; while on the dates set for the hearing, the judge too, would become unwell.

52. Never before had the judge suffered such unbearable colic as he did on those days! With the result, the hearing was inevitably

adjourned. As for Dhumal, his time was put to the best possible use.

53. For Dhumal, it was the privilege of Sai's company; for his client, a relief from anxiety and worry; everything came about so easily and effortlessly by just reposing full trust in Sai.

54. Later, at the right time, Dhumal was granted leave to go and his work was accomplished satisfactorily. Such is the inscrutable *leela* of Sai.

55. The court case went on for four months, the matter passing through the hands of four different judges. But in the end, Dhumal succeeded in getting an acquittal for his client.

56. Now listen to this incident, when Sai once, took up the side of Mrs Nimonkar, wife of his most excellent devotee, Nanasaheb Nimonkar.

57. A *'vatandar'*[2] of the village Nimon, the government had also vested in his hands the powers of an honorary magistrate. He was therefore, very influential.

58. Eldest among Madhavrao's cousins, he was very advanced in age and very highly respected. His wife was also a devout lady and Sai was the tutelar deity to them both.

59. Leaving their *'vatani'* village, they had both come to stay in Shirdi and pledging their trust in Sai, they spent their days in contentment.

60. Long before sunrise would they be up and would finish their early morning bath, *pooja*, etc. They would then come with unfailing regularity to the *Chavadi* to perform the *arati* at daybreak.

61. Thereafter, Nana used to stay with Baba till sunset, busy in his service as he recited to himself his daily *'stotras'*.

62. He would accompany Baba on his daily round to the Lendi, bringing him back to the mosque at the end. Very lovingly he served Baba, in whatever way he could.

63. The lady would also serve Baba during the day with loving devotion, doing everything in her power, to be of use.

64. Only for having a bath, cooking the meals or sleeping at night, would she repair to her lodgings.

65. The rest of the time was spent by this devout couple, in Baba's company, morning, noon and evening.

66. If the dedicated service of these two were to be narrated in detail, this book will far exceed its limit. Hence, I shall now narrate only what is relevant in the present context.

67. The lady wanted to go to Belapur where her son was slightly unwell. So, after conferring with her husband, she made preparations to go thither.

68. Later, she consulted Baba too, as was the usual practice and when he gave his consent she conveyed it to her husband.

69. Everything was thus fixed for her visit to Belapur. But Nana then said that she must return the very next day.

70. Of course, Nana had his reasons for so saying. And so, he said to her, 'Go, but return immediately'. His wife was rather sad at heart on hearing this.

71. The next day was the new moon of '*Pola*'³, which she wanted to spend there. Nay, it was her ardent wish. But Nana would not agree.

72. Moreover, it was the new moon and inauspicious for travel. The lady was greatly worried as to how the problem could be resolved.

73. Unless she went to Belapur her mind would not be at rest. Yet, she did not want to hurt her husband's feelings. How then, could she disobey his word?

74. All the same, she made preparations for the journey and as she was about to set out she came to make obeisance to Baba when he was going to the Lendi.

75. Whenever people are going on a journey, they bow in obeisance to the gods for a safe journey. This same custom was followed in Shirdi, too.

76. And since Sai was their god in Shirdi, whatever may be their hurry and urgency, people always bowed at his feet before leaving.

77. Accordingly, the lady bowed at Baba's feet, as Baba stood for a moment in front of the *Sathe-wada*.

78. All, young and old, including Nanasaheb Nimonkar, who had come there for *darshan*, made obeisance to Baba.

79. In front of all these people and especially in the presence of Nana, Baba spoke to the lady, words which were most befitting the occasion.

80. As she lowered her head on his feet and asked for permission to leave, "Go, go quickly", he said "and let your mind be at rest.

81. "And having gone so far, all the way, stay on for 3-4 days happily at Belapur, meet everyone there and then return to Shirdi".

82. Baba's words, coming quite unexpectedly, brought great relief and satisfaction to the lady. Nimonkar also took the hint. Both were thus satisfied.

83. In short, we may make plans, but we know not what has gone before or is to follow after. Only the saints know what is good or bad for us; for there is nothing that they do not know.

84. Past, present and future, is to them as clear as a myrobalan in the palm of their hand. It follows then that when devotees act in obedience to their command, they enjoy happiness and peace.

85. And now, I shall proceed with the narration of the main story, to continue what has already been told as to how Sai was gracious to Mulay and gave him the *darshan* of his own guru.

86. Mulay had really come to meet Shrimant Bapusaheb Butti, in Shirdi, wanting to return immediately thereafter.

87. Although such had been his plan, Baba had another purpose for his visit. Listen carefully now, to that miracle, to that secret purpose.

88. Mulay met Shrimant (Butti) as he had intended. Thereafter Butti and some others got up to go to the mosque, seeing which, Mulay also, felt a desire to join them. So he set out with them.

89. Now Mulay had not only studied the six *Shastras* deeply, but was also proficient in Astrology and well-versed in Chiromancy or Palmistry. He was absolutely delighted on having Baba's *darshan*.

90. The loving devotees made sincere offerings to Baba, of a profusion of fruit and sweetmeats like *pedhas, barfi,* coconuts, etc.

91. Moreover, there came to the door, the farm women to sell guavas, bananas, sugar-cane, etc. When Baba so wished, he would buy these things spending money from his own pocket.

92. He would spend his money to buy baskets of mangoes or call for large quantities of bananas and distribute them to the devotees to his heart's content.

93. Picking up the mangoes, one by one, in his hand, he would press and rub the fruit betwen his palms to soften it. And then he would pass it on to the devotees to suck the juice.

94. Thus softened, the mango had just to be put to the lips and all the juice could be sucked at once as if from a dish filled with mango juice. The skin and the stone could then be thrown away.

95. Most remarkable was his way with the bananas! The devotees were given the sweet fleshy part of the fruit while Baba would eat only the skin. O how marvellous were Baba's ways!

96. And this fruit would be distributed to all his devotees by Baba, with his own hands; while as for himself, only once in a while would he taste just one out of it all.

97. According to his usual practice, Baba had bought baskets full of bananas on that day and was distributing them at the time.

98. Shastribua (i.e. Mulay) was, however, quite astonished when he saw Baba's feet and had a great desire to read the lines, signs of good fortune, etc., on his feet.

99. Kakasaheb Dikshit was nearby at the time. He picked up four bananas and placed them in Baba's hands.

100. Somebody urged Baba, 'Baba, this is Mulay Shastri who resides in the holy city of Nasik and by his great good fortune has come here to bow at your feet. Do give him that fruit as *prasad*!'

101. Entreaties or otherwise, unless Baba himself wished it, he would never give anything to anyone! So what could they do?

102. Moreover, Mulay too, did not want the bananas; he wanted Baba's hand to read the lines, and he stretched out his own for it. Baba paid no attention, but continued to distribute the *prasad* to all.

103. Mulay pleaded with Baba, 'Not the fruit, but give me your hand. I can read the lines and the signs on it'. But Baba just would not give him his hand.

104. Still, Mulay kept on forging his way ahead, stretching out his hand for Baba's, for palm-reading. Baba continued to take no notice, as if he was totally unaware of any such happening!

105. And in fact, he just placed those four bananas on Mulay's outstretched hand and asked him to sit down. But, to give his hand in Mulay's, he just refused.

106. He, whose body had been worn out in the service of God, all his life, what had he to do with Palmistry? Sai, the Father and Mother to his good devotees, was fulfilled in all his desires.

107. Observing Baba's detached state, his utter disinterest in Palmistry, Shastribua then restrained himself and gave up the attempt as hopeless.

108. For a while, he sat in silence and then returned to the *wada* with the others. He then took a bath, clad the *'sovala'*[4] and began his daily ritual of *Agnihotra*[5].

109. Baba, here, set out, as usual, to go to the Lendi and said, "Let us take with us today, an ochre chalk. We will wear ochre-coloured robes today".

110. Everyone was surprised and wondered what Baba was going to do with an ochre chalk, why he should suddenly think of this ochre chalk on that particular day.

111. Such cryptic style was characteristic of Baba. What could one make of it? But carefully stored in our ears, when one pondered over it, many interpretations could be found for it.

112. Moreover, the words of a saint are never without meaning, but are full of profound significance. Who can weigh their importance adequately?

113. Careful thought first, and then the utterance — such is the usual practice of these saints. And their utterances too, are really translated into conduct directly afterwards.

114. As per this established truth, words of the saints are never without meaning and when carefully examined reveal deep significance.

115. Baba then returned from the Lendi. At once the kettledrums, horns, etc., began to resound. Bapusaheb Jog quickly suggested to Mulay;

116. 'It is time for the *arati*. Are you coming to the mosque?' But Shastribua, with his rigid adherence to the rules of *sovala*, felt all the awkwardness of his own situation.

117. So he replied, 'I will take *darshan* later in the afternoon'. Jog then began to make preparations for the *arati*.

118. Baba had already come back and was sitting on his seat, talking to people. The people offered their *pooja* and now, everything was ready for the *arati* to start.

119. Suddenly Baba said, "Go, bring *dakshina*, from that Brahmin who has just arrived". At once, Bapusaheb Butti himself set out to ask for *dakshina*.

120. Mulay had just finished his bath and having donned the *sovala*, was sitting in an *asan* (yogic posture), with a calm and steady mind.

121. As he heard Baba's message, doubt at once assailed his mind, 'Why should I give *dakshina*? I am a pure, *Agnihotri Brahmin*.

122. 'Baba may be a great saint, but I am not beholden to him in any way! Why does he ask me for *dakshina*?' His mind was divided.

123. '(On the other hand), a saint like Sai is asking for *dakshina*, a millionaire brings me the message'. Mulay had doubts in his mind, yet he took some *dakshina* with him.

124. There was one more doubt. How could he go to the mosque, leaving incomplete the ritual he had already begun? But, he could not bring himself to say 'no' to Baba.

125. A doubting mind has no firmness of resolve, for his mind always wavers. It never decides one way or the other. His state was like a *Trishanku*[6].

126. But then, he made up his mind to go, entered the *Sabhamandap* and stood at a distance.

127. 'I am *sovala*, but the mosque is *ovala*. How can I go near Baba?' So thinking, he showered flowers on Baba, from the palms overclosing each other. But all this took place only from a distance.

128. And lo! Before his very eyes a miracle took place! Baba became invisible on his seat; instead he saw there his own revered guru, Gholap!

129. Everyone else saw only Sai Samarth, as usual, but for Mulay's eyes, it was Gholapnath, who had already taken *samadhi*, long ago. Mulay was astonished beyond words.

130. Although the guru had, in fact, taken *samadhi*, Mulay was amazed when he saw him in person, in front of him. Fresh doubts arose in his mind.

131. To think that all this was a dream, he was certainly not asleep. And yet, if awake, how could his guru be sitting before him in person? How was his mind so confused, so flustered? For a moment he was left speechless!

132. To make sure, he pinched himself, saying, this cannot be all false. Why should I have needless doubts and suspicions? I am here, not alone, but with all these others, too!

133. Mulay was really, a Gholap-devotee. And though he had doubts about Baba earlier, later on he became Baba's devotee, with a pure unblemished mind.

134. Himself a high-caste Brahmin, who had acquired proficiency in *Vedas* and *Vedangas*, the *darshan* of guru Gholap in the mosque had left him wonderstruck!

135. He then went up the steps, bowed at the feet of his own guru and stood, at a loss for words, with folded hands.

136. As he saw his Gholapswami in ochre robes, in the ochre '*chhati*' of the sannyasin, Mulay rushed forward at once and embraced his feet.

137. The pride in his high *varna* fell off in an instant, the eyes were purified with the collyrium of Knowledge as he met his guru, the Light Eternal, and his soul was enriched with that Treasure of Knowledge.

138. The proclivity to doubts and suspicions melted away; love for Baba gushed out; with half-closed eyes he stood gazing at Baba's feet.

139. It was the accumulated merit of several births that had come to fruition, when he had Sai's *darshan*, and as he bathed in the sacred water, that was Sai's feet, he felt that good fortune had smiled upon him.

140. Everybody wondered what had happened all of a sudden, that after throwing flowers at Baba from a distance, how was he, now actually lowering his head on Baba's feet!

141. All the others were singing Baba's *arati*; but Mulay proclaimed in loud tones, Gholap's name and sang his *arati* at the top of his voice as he got more and more absorbed in the love of his guru.

142. The pride in the special purity and sacredness of his '*sovala*' evaporated; the rigidity about touching and not-touching softened. Instead, he prostrated himself before Baba in obeisance, as his eyes closed in blissful joy.

143. But as he got up and opened his eyes, Gholapswami had disappeared and in his place he saw Sai Samarth, asking for *dakshina*.

144. He saw Baba, the Joy Incarnate with his marvellous Power. The mind stood still in awe and wonder, he forgot his earlier attitude towards Baba.

145. Having seen Sai's wonderful *leela*, he forgot hunger, thirst, everything! Mulay was in ecstasy to have his own guru's *darshan*.

146. His mind was satiated. He prostrated before Baba and tears of joy welled up as he bowed his head at Baba's feet.

147. He offered whatever *dakshina* he had brought. Once again, he lowered his head on Baba's feet and his eyes filled up with tears of love, the hair on his body stood on end with rapturous delight.

148. A lump rose in the throat and the *ashta-bhavas* choked his heart as he said, 'Not only are all my doubts resolved, but I have also met my guru'.

149. All present there, including Mulay himself, were overcome by powerful emotions of love and awe at Baba's unique *leelas*. It was only then, after the actual experience, that they understood the significance of the ochre chalk!

150. It was the same Sai Maharaj, Mulay too, was the same person. How then, did the transformation come about at that particular time, was what they wondered at. But who can comprehend Baba's mysterious ways? Inscrutable indeed, are his *leelas*!

151. Equally wonderful was the experience of the mamlatdar, who was keenly desirous of *Sai-darshan* and set out for Shirdi, taking with him a doctor friend.

152. The doctor, a Brahmin, was a righteous man and a great devotee of Shri Ram. He was a scrupulous follower of the discipline of rites, rituals, vows, etc., as prescribed by the *Shastras*.

153. Sai Baba was a Muslim; whereas his tutelary deity was Shri Ram. Hence he had already warned his friend that he would not bow before Baba in obeisance.

154. 'I cannot bring myself to make obeisance at the feet of a Muslim and therefore I have had reservations about going to Shirdi, right from the beginning'.

155. 'No one will press you to touch his feet. Nobody will be obdurate on this point. Do not entertain any such ideas and make up your mind firmly to go.

156. 'Never will Baba say "Make obeisance to me"'. When the *mamlatdar* gave this firm assurance, the doctor had the inclination to go.

157. In deference to his friend's words he made up his mind firmly, pushing aside all his doubts and set out to have Baba's *darshan*.

158. And, the wonder of wonders! When he arrived in Shirdi and went to the mosque for *darshan*, it was he himself, who first prostrated before Baba! His friend stared in amazement.

159. So he asked him, 'How did you forget your own firm resolve? And how did you prostrate before a Muslim? And that too, in my presence?'

160. It was then that the doctor narrated to him the marvel of his experience! 'It was Shri Ram, He of the dark blue complexion, whom I saw and I at once bowed to that pure, beautiful, comely figure!

161. 'See, it is he who is sitting on the seat; He it is, who is speaking to all.' But even as he spoke these words, in an instant, he began to see Sai's figure in the place of Shri Ram.

162. At this, the doctor was all astonished! 'How can I call this a dream? How can he be a Muslim? No, indeed! He is a yogi, an Incarnation of God!'

163. The great saint Chokhamela was a *Mahar*[7], by caste; Rohidas was a cobbler; Sajan was a butcher, who killed animals for a livelihood. But who ever thinks of the caste of these saints?

164. The saints incarnate in this world, leaving their formless, attributeless state, only for the benefit of the world, to free the devotees from the cycle of births and deaths.

165. And this Sai is the veritable *Kalpa-druma*, the wish-fulfilling tree! This moment he is Sai, in the next moment he becomes Ram! Truly, he has destroyed the illusion of my self-conceit, by making me bow my head in obeisance!

166. On the very next day, he took a vow that he would not put his foot into the mosque unless Baba blesses him with his grace. And to this end, he undertook a fast in Shirdi.

167. Three days passed by. As the fourth day dawned, listen attentively to what happened.

168. A friend of his, who had settled down in Khandesh, suddenly arrived in Shirdi for Sai's *darshan*.

169. Meeting him after nine long years, his joy knew no bounds. At once, the doctor too followed his friend to the mosque!

170. He immediately made obeisance when he went. So Baba said, "So doctor, did anyone come to call you? Then tell me first, why have you come?"

171. As he heard this pointed question, the doctor's heart was overcome with emotion. He remembered his own resolve and was filled with sadness and regret.

172. But on that same day, in the hour of midnight, Baba's Grace descended on him, as he tasted the sweetness of blissful happiness in his sleep.

173. Later, the doctor returned to his own village, but continued to experience that state of Perfect Bliss for the next fifteen days. His faith and devotion towards Sai grew steadily thereafter.

174. Innumerable are such experiences of Sai which are, one more marvellous than the other, and will only enhance the glory of this book. But I restrain myself from narrating them all for fear of lengthening the book.

175. My listeners must have been amazed on reading the main story of Mulay that came in the beginning. But they must know its essence, the moral of the story.

176. 'Whoever may be one's guru, one must repose one's full and firm trust in him. It should not be placed anywhere else.' This is the real significace of the story, which should be firmly fixed in our minds.

177. There seems no other purpose than this in this marvellous *leela* of Baba. Whatever else others may draw from it, this is the true significance here.

178. Far greater may be the fame of other gurus; our guru may have none of it. But full faith must be reposed only in our own guru. This is the moral of the story.

179. Whichever sacred texts or *Puranas* you search, in essence they are full of the same significance. But faith does not come easily, unless one gets a direct proof of it, as in this particular experience.

180. Without a steadfast faith, those who parade themselves as 'Self-realized souls', suffer all through their lives, as we see clearly, time and again.

181. They are neither here nor there, are perpetually wrapped up in cares and worries, without having a moment's peace or rest. And yet, they boast of being emancipated!

182. Now, the next chapter will be even more absorbing than this one. Sai's *darshan*, taken over and over again, will bring the experience of joy, unbounded.

183. I will narrate how his devotee Bhimaji Patil was cured of tuberculosis and how Baba confirmed his faith in Chandorkar, through a vision.

184. Such is the immense power of the mere *darshan* of Sai, which frees us from all our sins, and gives us, in abundant measure, highest pleasures of this world as well as those of the life hereafter.

185. Just a merest glance of the great Yogis can wash away the sins of the atheists, then what of the believers? Their sins are destroyed most easily.

186. He, who has fixed his mind in the Brahman, has directly experienced Revelation, such a *mahatma*, by the power of his merest glance, will enable one to overcome the most unsurmountable of sins.

187. Such are Baba's incomprehensible *leelas*! Baba has love for you. Hence all of you, learned or ignorant, listen to his story with a pure heart.

188. Where there is a tender, loving devotion, where there is a fond attachment to Baba, there alone is the manifestation of a true yearning of love. There alone is to be seen a real joy in listening to his story.

189. Hemad bows at Sai's feet, which alone are a sure and true refuge of the faithful. To their power, there is no limit. They are strong enough to destroy the fear of worldly life.

Weal be to all! Here ends the twelfth chapter of
"*Shri Sai Samarth Satcharit*", called
'*Shri Sant Gholap – Ramdarshan*',
as inspired by the saints and the virtuous,
and composed by his devotee, Hemadpant.

Notes

1. *Agasti*, a sage and the Regent of the star Canopus, who once swallowed up the ocean, taking it in the palm of his hand.
2. A holder of a '*vatan*' or an hereditary estate, office, right or due.
3. A festive day for cattle — the day of the New Moon of *Shravan* or *Bhadrapad* month. Bullocks are exempted from labour, variously decorated and paraded about in worship.
4. Refer Ch. 7, note 6.
5. Maintenance of a perpetual and sacred fire.
6. A famous king of the Solar ancestry. Sage Vishwamitra sent him to heaven, but he could not gain an entry there, and so remained suspended between the heaven and the earth.
7. An individual of a scheduled caste, formerly employed mostly as village gate-keepers, watchmen, messengers, guides, porters, etc.

13

The Cure of Bhimaji's Tuberculosis

MY OBEISANCE TO SHRI GANESH, TO SHRI SARASWATI, AND SHRI GURUMAHARAJ! TO THE FAMILY DEITY, TO SHRI SITA-RAMACHANDRA, MY MOST HUMBLE OBEISANCE! I BOW IN REVERENCE TO THE MOST VENERABLE GURU SHRI SAINATH!

1. In expression, very brief and aphoristic, but in the gravity of their meaning, most profound; wide and comprehensive in their application, and yet, equally compressed —

2. Such were Baba's words, which were very deep in significance and substance; and so perfectly well-balanced and precious — they were never meaningless or in vain!

3. Follow your goal, consistent with what has gone before and what is to follow; act in compliance with what has been ordained. For ever be content and never leave place for worry or anxiety.

4. "Look! Even though I have become a fakir, freeing myself from all care, without the encumbrances of a house and a family and am sitting in one place, calm and still, abandoning all the cares and vexations of life,

5. "Still this irrestrainable *Maya* harasses me, time and again. I may well forget her, but she never forgets me, but clings fast to me, all the time!

6. "She is the *Adimaya* of Shri Hari, who has distracted even Brahma and other gods! What then, is the case of a weak fakir like me, before her?

7. "But when Hari Himself is pleased, only then will she be destroyed. Without ceaseless Hari-*bhajan*, there is no release from this *Maya*."

8. Such was the great importance of *Maya* that Baba explained to his devotees. And to ward off her influence, he advised God's service through constant singing of His praises.

9. 'Saints are my living image'. So said Shri Krishna Himself in the *Bhagvat*. Who does not know these words pronounced so clearly to Uddhava by Hari?

10. Hence, listen with humility to the profound Truth that Sai Samarth the Compassionate One, uttered for the welfare of his devotees.

11. "Only those virtuous souls, whose sins had all been obviated, worshipped me and recognised my mark.

12. "If only you will utter 'Sai, Sai' all the time, I will with my grace present you even the seven seas (i.e. protect you even beyond the seven seas). Trust these words of mine and you will achieve your welfare, most certainly.

13. "I do not need either all the elaborate articles of *pooja* or the sixteen[1], even eightfold ceremonies or rites of *pooja*. Where there is boundless faith, I abide there."

14. So Baba had said, time and time again, out of his love for his devotees. Now we can find comfort only in remembering his affectionate words.

15. And just see, what a marvellous thing was done by this Sai, the Compassionate Friend, the Protector of all who seek refuge, clearly espousing the cause of his devotees!

16. Without allowing the mind to be diverted, with full concentration, listen to the whole of this new story and you will find fulfilment.

17. Where the shower of nectarine words from Sai's mouth is itself the fountain of strength and satisfaction, who, with his own welfare in mind, will tire of the effort to come to Shirdi?

18. In the last chapter, the story of an *Agnihotri Brahmin* was narrated, where he was given *darshan* of his own guru, who had already taken *samadhi*, thereby bringing him great joy.

19. Now this chapter is even sweeter than the last. A devotee, enfeebled by tuberculosis, was restored to good health by breaking off his evil habit, in a dream.

20. And so, listen, O faithful ones, with full concentration, to this marvellous Life of Sainath, which destroys all sin.

21. This 'Life' is as purifying, as sanctifying, as the water of the Ganges, which helps attain liberation in this world as in the next. Blessed, blessed are the ears of those who listen to it!

22. We may compare it with the '*Amrit*' (or the drink of the Immortals), but can it be sweeter than this? And if '*Amrit*' protects life, this 'Life' protects us from future births altogether.

23. Living beings think they are all powerful. But he who thinks he can do what pleases him, should listen to this story.

24. If the living being were truly free, why should sorrow and suffering alone be his lot, when he toils for happiness, day and night? But such indeed, is the power of his Fate.

25. Though always quick to avoid suffering, here, there, everywhere — yet it follows him promptly.

26. In trying to ward it off, it embraces him more closely; in shaking it off, it clings faster than ever! In vain does the creature struggle! In vain is the arduous effort, day in and day out!.

27. Had the creature been really free, he would have sought nothing but happiness and would not have touched anything with even a suspicion of sorrow or suffering.

28. Because of his free will he would never have committed a sin, but would have accumulated merit in abundance, to ensure greater happiness for himself.

29. But a creature is not free. He is pursued by a chain of *karma*. And strange are the workings of this *karma*, which pulls the strings in the life of a living being.

30. With the result, though we may set our sights on virtue, we are drawn compellingly towards sin. While looking for good, virtuous deeds, the body always comes in contact with evil deeds.

31. But now, listen my listeners, to the story of Bhimaji Patil of Narayangaon, which is in the Junnar *taluka* of Pune district. In sweetness, the tale is a veritable overflow of *Amrit*.

32. Bhimaji was well-to-do and hospitable to the visitors, especially in the matter of serving food. Never touched by sadness, his countenance always had a glow of happiness.

33. But inexplicable are the ways of Destiny, which brings us gains and losses for which we cannot account. Sufferings resulting from our *karma* come to our lot, and disease afflicts us that we do not seem to deserve.

34. In the year 1909, misfortune dogged Bhimaji, when he had an attack of pulmonary consumption and began to run a temperature.

35. Then started fits of unbearable coughing; the fever began to rise sharply and waxed stronger, day after day. Bhimaji was dismayed.

36. There would be froth at the mouth, all the time and mouthfuls of brackish spittles of blood. The stomach would have a nauseating sensation and the restless tossing of the body would not cease.

37. The patient was bed-ridden; his body became emaciated and began to shrivel up, though remedies were tried to the utmost. He was greatly troubled in his mind.

38. He did not relish any food or drink, nor was even gruel or any other regimen tolerated. All this made him feel restless and quite lost. The suffering of the body was beyond all endurance.

39. Propitiation of gods, exorcising — everything was tried; the doctors, the *vaidyas*, they had given up all effort. Patil too, had given up all hopes of survival and felt quite puzzled in his mind.

40. He was distressed; his days seemed numbered. Day by day the exhaustion grew. Many days passed in this manner.

41. He propitiated the family deity, but to no avail. It did not restore him to good health. He now grew weary of consulting astrologers and exorcisers.

42. Some said, 'What physical malady is this! O, what Fate is this to bring on such suffering! Human remedies all seem futile!'

43. Doctors were tried. *Hakims* were summoned. But in treating him, they all came to their wits' end. No one could do anything. All their efforts failed.

44. Patil became weary and despondent, saying to himself, 'O God, what have I done? Why has everything failed? What terrible sin could I have committed to deserve such suffering?'

45. And yet, how strange are God's ways! He is not remembered, even for a moment by one who is enjoying happiness. Inscrutable is His *leela*!

46. When He Himself, so wishes, he sends a chain of calamities of various kinds thereby making man remember Him and cry out in anguish, 'Help me, O Narayana!'

47. And when God heard Patil's anguished cry for help, He was at once, moved by compassion! And Bhimaji suddenly thought that he should write a letter to Nana (Chandorkar).

48. 'Nana will surely do something that others will not be able to do.' Such was the great confidence that Patil felt.

49. And that was indeed a good omen for him; that was the beginning of the cure of his disease! Later, he wrote a detailed letter to Nana.

50. To have remembered Nanasaheb at that moment was nothing but Sainath's prompting. It was the cause of the removal of his disease. The ways of the saints are most wonderful.

51. Even in the rotation of the wheel of Fortune there seems to be a Divine Plan. Hence no one should imagine it to be otherwise and boast vainly.

52. To all the good actions and bad, it is God who holds the strings. It is He who preserves and He who destroys. He alone is the Doer.

53. Patil wrote to Chandorkar, 'I am tired of taking medicines. I am really fed up of this life, itself! The world, to me, seems so cheerless and dreary!

54. 'Doctors have given up hope, concluding that the disease is incurable. *Vaidyas* and *Hakims* too, are at a loss for a remedy. And as for me, my hopes are sunk to their lowest.

55. 'And so, I have to make only one last humble request! It is the one strong desire of my heart — to be able to meet you, with the utmost certainty.'

56. On reading the letter Chandorkar's heart was filled with sadness. For Bhimaji Patil, he knew, was a good man and his heart was deeply touched with compassion.

57. 'In reply to your letter', he wrote, 'I suggest only one remedy. Hold fast to Sai Baba's feet! This is the only ultimate remedy. For he alone is our Father, our Mother!

58. 'He is the only Compassionate Mother to all, who will come running at our call for help, will pick us up with a mother's affection and will understand her child's need.

59. 'When even a dreaded disease like leprosy is cured by his mere *darshan*, what of tuberculosis? Have not the slightest doubt. Go, and catch Sai's feet tightly!

60. 'Whatever anyone asks him for, he always gives it to him. This is his Promise, to which he is bound. Hence I say, hurry up and take Sai's *darshan*.

61. 'What is the greatest among all the fears, but the fear of death? Go and clasp Sai's feet firmly. For he alone will make you fearless.'

62. So unbearable was Patil's agony, so precariously balanced his life, that he became very impatient, thinking, 'When will I meet Sainath? When will I achieve my purpose?'

63. Great was Patil's restlessness. 'Pack everything, at once', he said, 'Prepare to leave early, tomorrow. Let us be on our way to Shirdi, quickly.'

64. Having made this firm resolve, Patil took leave of everybody and set out for Shirdi to have *darshan* of Sai Maharaj.

65. Taking his relatives with him, Bhimaji started at once, with a heart full of anxious anticipation as to how he would reach Shirdi as quickly as possible.

66. Patil's cart came to the square near the mosque and thence to its front door. Four people bore Bhimaji on their hands and brought him up.

67. Nanasaheb was accompanying him and Madhavrao, because of whom it was easy for everyone to meet Baba, had already come there, too!

68. On seeing Patil, Baba said, "Shama, how many more thieves are you going to burden me with? What, is this right on your part?"

69. Bhimaji lowered his head on Sai's feet and said, 'Sainath, have mercy on me, this friendless destitute! Protect me, O Dinanath!'

70. Sainath was moved by pity on seeing Patil's suffering. In that moment, Patil felt assured in his mind, and his suffering was allayed.

71. On seeing Bhimaji's great distress, Sai Samarth, the Ocean of Compassion, was deeply touched and said, with a smile on his countenance,

72. "Rest assured, give up all anxiety. The thoughtful and the reflective do not bemoan. The moment you put your foot in Shirdi, your suffering has ended.

73. "You may be up to your neck in the sea of obstacles, you may have sunk deep into the great pit of sorrow and suffering, but know, that he who once climbs the steps of this mosque will enjoy the greatest happiness.

74. "The Fakir of this place is very kind; He will eradicate your disease and pain. He who has compassion for all, will look after you very lovingly.

75. "Hence you rest assured. Stay in the house of Bhimabai. Go now, and in a day or two you will get relief."

76. Just as one, who has no hope of survival, suddenly, by a stroke of luck, gets a shower of nectar and instantly gets a new lease of life, such was the satisfaction that Patil felt.

77. As he heard the words coming from Sai's mouth, Patil experienced a deep satisfaction as that of one on his death-bed receiving a draught of nectar or one parched with thirst, a drink of water.

78. The mouthfuls of spittle of blood that rose to the mouth every five minutes, subsided when Baba sat with him for one hour.

79. Baba did not examine the patient, did not ask about the causes that gave rise to the disease. His Glance of Grace alone, was enough to destroy the very roots of the disease, in an instant.

80. Enough is his glance of kindness, and even a withered log would sprout into leaf, and the flowers would bloom before it is Spring; and the trees would be heavy with luscious fruit.

81. What is disease or health? Unless one's merit or sins cease to be, or unless one works out one's *karma*, no other remedy will work.

82. Only by working it out will the *karma* cease to be. This one thing is most certain, birth after birth. Unless we work out our *karma*, no other means will liberate us.

83. Yet, if by one's extraordinary good fortune, one has the *darshan* of a saint, it is able to remove the affliction and the afflicted one will then bear the painful malady, easily and without pain.

84. Disease brings severe pain and suffering; the saint, with his compassionate glance, removes disease without causing any suffering.

85. It is Baba's word that is the authority. That alone is the most infallible remedy. Malaria was once cured, similarly, when a black dog was fed on rice and curds.

86. These shorter tales may be looked upon as a digression from the main story, but when heard in their gist, their appropriateness will be evident. Moreover, is it not Sai himself, who brings them to my mind?

87. "I will myself narrate my own story", Sai has said, and it is he who has reminded me of these stories, at this juncture.

88. A very devout tailor, Bala Ganapat by name, once came to the mosque and stood in front of Sai, entreating him with a piteous face.

89. 'What is such a great sin that I have committed? Why does this malarial fever not leave me? Baba, numerous are the remedies that I have tried, but this fever does not leave my body.

90. 'O, what shall I do now? I have tried herbal remedies, decoctions, everything! At least you tell me a remedy whereby this fever will go!'

91. Baba's heart melted, and in reply, he suggested a novel remedy for malaria. Just listen to it!

92. "Feed a black dog, near the temple of the goddess Laxmi, with a few mouthfuls of rice and curd and you will be cured, instantly!"

93. With some trepidity, Bala then went home to look for the food. Luckily, he saw some rice under a cover. Curd too, was found nearby.

94. Bala thought, it is good that curd and rice are found. But will there be a black dog, near the Temple, at the right time?

95. Baseless was Bala's worry! For, no sooner did he reach the place indicated than he saw a black dog approaching him, wagging his tail.

96. Bala was simply delighted to find everything happening according to Baba's indications. He then fed the curd and rice to the dog and afterwards narrated to Baba everything that had happened.

97. In short, whatever one may say about this incident, the fact is that, from that moment, the malarial fever left Bala and he got relief.

98. Similarly, Bapusaheb Butti once had severe diarrhoea and repeated bouts of vomiting due to a chill in the stomach.

99. The cupboard was full of medicines of all sorts. But not one of them was effective. Bapusaheb was frightened in his heart and began to worry.

100. Repeated motions and bouts of vomiting left Bapusaheb exhausted and weak. He had not the energy even to go for Baba's *darshan*, as was his daily practice.

101. News reached Baba's ears. He sent for Butti and made him sit in front of himself, "Mind you!" he said, "From now on, you will not go for evacuation of bowels!

102. "And remember, even the vomiting must cease". Facing him, he waved his forefinger and once again, repeated the same words to him.

103. In short, such was the awe produced by those words, that in fright, both the afflictions took to their heels, at once! Butti, however, experienced great relief.

104. Once before, too, Butti had suffered similarly from loose motions and vomiting, when there had been an outbreak of cholera at

Shirdi. His throat parched with thirst, the stomach had a constant sick, queasy feeling.

105. Near at hand was Doctor Pillay, who tried all remedies. And when nothing worked, in the end he went to Baba.

106. Humbly, he related everything to Baba and then Pillay asked Baba, 'Should he be given coffee? Or, is water preferable?'

107. And Baba said to him, "Give him milk! And almonds, pistachio, walnuts to eat! Give him '*taran*'[2] to drink.

108. "That will quench his thirst and his suffering will cease, instantly". The point is, when this '*taran*' was given to him to drink, his complaint disappeared, altogether!

109. Oh, that the words 'Eat walnuts, pistachio, almonds' should bring relief to a victim of cholera! The seat of faith was really Baba's words. There was no room for any doubts there.

110. Once a *Swami*[3] from Alandi came to Shirdi, wishing to have the *darshan* of Sai Samarth. He arrived at Baba's abode (i.e. the mosque).

111. He was suffering from an affliction of the ear, which had brought on restlessness and a loss of sleep. He had an operation performed, but it was not of the slightest use.

112. There were unbearable, shooting pains and no remedy worked. So he decided to leave Alandi and came to Baba for blessings.

113. The *Swami* bowed at Sai's feet, received *udi prasad* and then asked for blessings, praying that Baba's grace should always be with him.

114. Madhavrao Deshpande entreated on his behalf, to Baba, to have mercy on his afflicted ear. "Allah will make everything all right", Maharaj assured him.

115. On receiving this blessing, *Swami* returned to Pune. After eight days, a letter was received from him that the shooting pains had stopped immediately.

116. Swelling however, was still there and another operation was recommended, 'for which purpose I came to Bombay, once again.

117. 'I went to that same doctor. I wonder if Baba found himself in a strait. But as the doctor examined my ear, he could not locate the swelling.

118. 'And so the doctor said there was no need for an operation.' The *Swami* was relieved of his greatest anxiety. Everybody was amazed at Baba's *leela*.

119. A similar story comes to my mind, in this context. I shall narrate that to the listeners and then I will end this chapter.

120. Just eight days before the work of paving the floor of the *Sabhamandap* commenced, Mahajani suffered from a severe attack of cholera.

121. He began to pass many loose motions. But in his innermost heart, his entire dependence was on Baba and so, he would not take any treatment or medicine, though he was wearied out by the illness completely.

122. Mahajani knew what a great seer Baba was. Hence he did not tell him of his great discomfort.

123. He went on bearing the pain and suffering in the full faith that when Baba wishes it, he will, on his own, remove the affliction.

124. His only strong desire, all along, was that even though he was prepared to undergo all the suffering, there should not be a break in his daily *pooja* and *arati*.

125. And when the motions — so many of them and so frequent — went beyond the limit, just in order that he did not miss his daily service of performing Baba's *arati*, what he would do was;

126. He would keep at his side a copper vessel, filled with water, in the mosque, at a place where it would be easily accessible even in the dark.

127. Himself he would sit near Baba, pressing his feet and would be present for the *arati*, without fail, as was his daily practice.

128. If there was griping or pain in the stomach, the water vessel was always at hand. He would find an unfrequented spot, relieve himself and return.

129. And now, when Tatya asked for permission to start paving the floor, Baba gave it to him. And listen, what he said to him.

130. "We are now going to the Lendi. But when we return from there, then, at that moment, start the work of paving".

131. Later, Baba came back and went and sat on his usual seat. Kaka also came at the right time and began to press his feet.

132. *Tongas* arrived from Kopergaon. Devotees from Bombay reached there too! Laden with *pooja* articles, the devotees climbed up and made obeisance to Baba.

133. Along with all the others came the Patil from Andheri, bringing with him flowers, consecrated rice, and other *pooja* articles and sat down waiting for his turn.

134. Suddenly, down in the large, open court below, where the chariot used to be kept, exactly at that spot fell the first stroke of the hoe. The work on the floor had begun.

135. No sooner did he hear the sound than Baba cried out aloud in a strange voice, assuming, at once, the fierceness of Narsimha, with wild, glaring eyes.

136. "Who strikes his hoe there? I shall break his back!" So saying, he got up, immediately and picked up his baton, striking terror into the hearts of all present.

137. The worker dropped his hoe and ran for his life. They all took to their heels. Kaka too, was startled, when suddenly Baba took hold of his hand.

138. "Where are you going?" he said,, "Come, sit down". Meanwhile, Tatya and Laxmi came. Baba hurled abuses freely at them to his heart's content.

139. Abuses were showered even on those who stood outside the yard. Suddenly Baba pulled up a bag of roasted peanuts which was lying there.

140. The bag must have fallen from the hands of someone, among those in the mosque who, stricken by panic, ran helter-skelter, when Baba was in a fit of rage.

141. The nuts must have measured a full seer. Taking them out by the fistfuls, he would rub them in his palms and clean them by blowing off the skins.

142. He would then make Mahajani eat the cleaned nuts, even as the abusing continued on one side, and rubbing the skins off the nuts, on the other.

143. "Eat them up", he kept on urging as he placed the nuts on Mahajani's hand; a few, he occasionally put in his own mouth, too! In this way the entire bag was emptied.

144. As the peanuts were finished, "Bring water; I am thirsty", he said. Kaka filled up the spouted drinking vessel with water and brought it to him. He drank from it and also asked Kaka to drink.

145. And as Kaka drank the water, he said to him, "Go now, your motions have stopped! But where, O where, have those Brahmins gone? Go and bring them here".

146. Later, people came in; the mosque became full, as before. Once again, the work of paving began. But Kaka was cured of his cholera.

147. But oh! what a medicine for loose motions! The real medicine is the Word of the Saint. He who takes it as 'prasad', needs no other medicine.

148. A gentleman from Harada city was afflicted with colic and had been suffering for fourteen years. He had tried all remedies, to no avail.

149. His name was Dattopant. News had travelled to him, by word of mouth, that in Shirdi there is a great saint called Sai, whose *darshan* alone, removes all afflictions.

150. On hearing such fame, he went to Shirdi and bowed his head at Sai's feet, beseeching his mercy.

151. 'Baba, full fourteen years have passed, this colic has pursued me relentlessly. Enough, O enough! I have now reached the limit of my patience. Nor do I have the strength to take any more suffering!

152. 'Never have I betrayed or harmed anyone; nor have I ever shown disrespect to my mother and father. I do not remember my *karma* from a previous birth, due to which I have to endure so much suffering!'

153. It is only the loving, compassionate glance of the saints, their blessings and *prasad* that remove all afflictions. Nothing more is then needed.

154. And such was also Dattopant's experience! As Baba's hand rested on his head, and he received *vibhuti* and blessings, his mind was relieved and comforted.

155. Maharaj then made him stay for a few days. Gradually the colic, the pain subsided completely.

156. Such indeed, are the *mahatmas*! How can I describe their greatness, their power, adequately? Well-disposed towards all the creatures, benevolence is their constant nature.

157. Even as I sing these praises, I recollect other stories — one more wonderful than the other. But now, let us pick up the threads of the main narrative and continue Bhimaji's tale.

158. And so, Baba sent for the *udi*, of which he gave a little to Bhimaji, smearing a little on his forehead. He then placed his hand of benediction on Bhimaji's head.

159. Bhimaji was then commanded to return to his lodgings. Patil took a few steps and then walked up to the cart. He felt quite energetic.

160. He went to the place suggested by Baba (i.e. Bhimabai's house). Though the place was closed and narrow, Baba had suggested it. Therein lay its importance.

161. Being recently levelled with clay, the floor was wet. But he obeyed Baba's command and made arrangements to stay there, itself.

162. Of course, a drier place would have been available in the village, for Bhimaji knew many people. But, the place, mention of which came from Baba's mouth, could not be changed for any other.

163. So he spread out two sacks in that place, over which he spread out his bedding, and putting his mind at rest, he lay down on it.

164. The same night, it so happened that Bhimaji had a dream, in which appeared a teacher of his childhood, who started beating him.

165. Cane in hand, he began beating hard, almost breaking his back, so as to make him learn by heart, some *Prakrit* verses. To his student, he caused great pain and trouble, thereby.

166. The listeners must be very curious to know what these verses were. Hence I cite below what I have heard, in detail, and word for word.

> "She, to whom, stepping into any other house (except her own) is like stepping on a snake's head;
> The words from whose mouth are as hard to obtain, as wealth from a miser's hands;
> To whom, her husband's company is the highest happiness, though there be no wealth in the house;
> And, who acts calmly, with her husband's approval;
> Only she is the true 'sati'[4] amongst men."

167. But, for what fault was this the punishment, it was difficult to understand. And yet, the teacher would not let go of the cane. He was seized by a fit of obstinacy.

168. Immediately after, he had another dream; it was still stranger than the first. Some gentleman came and sat on his chest, pressing it down heavily.

169. Picking up a stone-roller, he literally made a grinding stone of his chest. In his extreme agony, life itself seemed to leap to his mouth, as if he was already on his way to heaven.

170. The dream ended and he fell asleep, which brought him some comfort. The sun came up on the horizon and the Patil awoke.

171. He felt refreshed, as never before! The feeling of being unwell had vanished altogether. Who remembered to check for the tell-tale signs of the grinding stone and the roller, or of the cane?

172. People regard dreams as illusory; but sometimes our experience is to the contrary. In that same auspicious moment, the disease was destroyed and Patil's suffering came to an end.

173. Patil was very pleased in his heart and felt it to be his regeneration. He then slowly set out to have Baba's *darshan*.

174. As he looked upon Baba's moon-like countenance, the ocean of joy in Patil's heart surged higher and higher. His own face glowed with happiness, the eyes closed in a sweet, pleasant drowsiness.

175. Flood-gates were opened to tears of love, as he placed his forehead on Baba's feet. The ultimate outcome of the punishments of caning and pressing the chest till the heart seemed to burst, was clearly a happy one.

176. 'It is impossible that a lowly creature like me should ever be able to repay the great kindness shown to me. Hence I only lower my head on your feet.

177. 'This is the only way in which I can, in some measure, repay the debt. There is none other. Baba Sai, your wonderful ways are simply incomprehensible!'

178. Patil then stayed there for a month, singing Baba's praises and returned home later, with a deep sense of fulfilment, remembering Nana's kindness with gratitude.

179. Filled with devotion, faith and a heart-felt happiness, the Patil, who was ever so grateful to Sai for his kindness, came to Shirdi quite frequently.

180. And what does Sainath want but the two hands and a head, steadfast faith and single-minded devotion! It is enough for him that the devotee feels sincere gratitude.

181. When a person is in trouble, he promises a *pooja* to Satyanarayana and performs it with its complete ritual, once he is free from trouble.

182. Similarly, from then onwards, the Patil began to observe the vow of Satya Sai on every Thursday, with a purifying bath and other observances laid down for it.

183. People read the story of Satyanarayana on such an occasion. Instead, Patil would, very lovingly, read *Saicharitra* from Das Ganu's '*Arvachin Bhaktaleelamruta*'.

184. In the forty-five chapters of that book Das Ganu has narrated the lives of many great devotees. And amongst these, the three chapters on Sainath form the *Satya-Sai katha*.

185. Best amongst all the observances, are the three chapters which Patil used to read. And as a result of it, he enjoyed boundless happiness and peace of mind.

186. Patil would invite all his relatives, brothers and friends, and would observe this *Satya Sai Vrata* (vow), regularly, with a joyful heart.

187. The *naivedya* too, was prepared, observing the same proportions of ingredients as for the *Satyanarayana naivedya*[5]; and the celebration would also be the same, except that here it was Sai being propitiated; there it is Shri Vishnu. Nothing else was wanting.

188. Patil thus set the trend and it became a custom in the village. One after the other, people began observing *Satya Sai Vrata*.

189. Such is the kindness of saints! When Fortune smiles on the devotee, their mere *darshan* removes his worldly sufferings; nay, even Death is made to turn back.

190. Now the next story will describe the anxiety of one, for having children and incidentally, the oneness between all saints will appear to us as a miracle.

191. A wealthy resident of Nanded, belonging to the Parsi community, received Baba's blessings and a son was born to him.

192. Oneness between Maulisaheb of Nanded, a saint, and Baba was shown. Full of joy, the Parsi then went back to his place.

193. The story is very touching. Listen to it with a calm mind, O listeners! And you will then realise Sai's all-pervasiveness, as also his great affection.

194. Hemadpant surrenders to Sai, absolutely! And bows to the saints and to his listeners. To this narration in the next chapter, give a respectful ear!

Weal be to all! Here ends the thirteenth chapter of
"*Shri Sai Samarth Satcharit*", called
'*The Cure of Bhimaji's Tuberculosis*',
as inspired by the saints and the virtuous,
and composed by his devotee, Hemadpant.

Notes

1. The sixteen ceremonies or rites of *pooja* are: 1) *Awahan* (invocation of a divinity to occupy an image or idol); 2) *Asan* (offering a seat to the deity); 3) *Padya* (water for washing the feet); 4) *Arghya* (an oblation to gods of rice, *Durva* grass and flowers with water, or of water only); 5) *Achaman* (sipping water before or after religious ceremonies or meals, from the palm of the hand); 6) *Snana* (giving bath to the deity); 7) *Vastra* (offering clothes); 8) *Yagnopavita* (sacrificial thread worn by Brahmins; 9) *Gandha* (sandalwood paste); 10) *Pushpa* (flowers); 11) *Dhoop* (frankincense); 12) *Deep* (lamp or light); 13) *Naivedya* (food-offering); 14) *Dakshina* (money offering); 15) *Pradakshina* (circumambulation of an idol by way of reverence); 16) *Mantrapushpa* (double handful of flowers accompanied by the recitation of a mantra, thrown on the idol's head, as at conclusion of worship, etc.

2. '*Taran*' is water in which split pulse, rice-bits, etc., have been boiled.

3. His name was Padmanabhendra Swami.

4. A chaste and virtuous wife.

5. For *Satyanaryana naivedya*, all ingredients like ghee, sugar, semolina are taken in equal proportion, that proportion being one and a quarter measure of each, to prepare the sweet.

14

Ratanji's Meeting with Sai

MY OBEISANCE TO SHRI GANESH, TO SHRI SARASWATI, AND SHRI GURUMAHARAJ! TO THE FAMILY DEITY, TO SHRI SITA-RAMACHANDRA, MY MOST HUMBLE OBEISANCE! I BOW IN REVERENCE TO THE MOST VENERABLE GURU SHRI SAINATH!

1. Glory to you, O Sainath, greatest among the saints! Hail to you, O most Compassionate One, laden with virtue and excellences, and of a constant, unchanging nature! O Supreme Spirit, O Boundless, Faultless One, glory to you!

2. Out of compassion for your devotees and mindful of things which are inconceivable to them, you appear to the devotees under different guises, to help them overcome obstacles.

3. Baba was also a divine incarnation, who appeared to uplift the lowly and meek, and to destroy the vicious, uncontrollable demons or evil desires in the devotees.

4. All those who came for his *darshan* with a pure mind drank deeply of blissful Self-realization; their hearts overflowed with joy and they swayed to the rapture of love and devotion.

5. On the feet of Sai Samarth, the most Virtuous One, I, a lowly, poor, meek creature prostrate humbly in obeisance.

6. I now continue from the previous story, where I had narrated how a devotee suffering from malaria, was cured, when the black dog ate curds and rice;

7. How a dangerous disease, cholera disappeared by his raising the index finger, by giving '*taran*' to drink and roasted peanuts to eat;

8. Similarly, how the colic of one, ear-ache of another and severe tuberculosis of yet another were destroyed merely by Sai's *darshan*.

9. How by Sai's grace Bhimaji enjoyed peace and happiness and how he surrendered, with gratitude, to Sai, ever afterwards.

10. Equally novel is the present incident and as unique a miracle as the earlier ones. Knowing too well, how eagerly interested the listeners are, I shall now narrate it.

11. If the listeners are not attentive, how will the narrator be inspired? How will the narration excel? How will it be infused with life and spirit?

12. And then, what can the narrator do? For he is totally in the power of his audience. They are his main support, through whose response the narration gains in spirit and beauty.

13. The 'Life' of a saint that this is, it is naturally fascinating, from within and without. For, his way of life — his food habits, movements, behaviour — everything is charming and even his casual utterances are full of sweetness.

14. Indeed, this is not a mere Life-story, but it is the life-supporting Water of Self-rejoicing, which the All-merciful Sai Maharaj has showered lovingly on his devotees as a means of remembering him.

15. Speaking about how one should conduct oneself worthily in this worldly life, he actually showed them the path of renunciation. Such, truly, are these stories of saints which deal with both worldly and spiritual life.

16. Their purpose must be that one should be happy in the worldly life and yet be always alert and wakeful about one's spiritual welfare, so that the purpose of this human birth is fulfilled.

17. It is only on the strength of the greatest merit, accumulated in the past births, that a being gets this human frame, quite unexpectedly. To add to it, when he also attains spiritual progress, it is a rare good fortune.

18. But he who will not make the best of this opportunity, makes of himself a senseless burden to this earth. How is his joy in living any different from that of an animal?

19. Such a man is truly an animal without a tail and horns, who knows nothing else but eating, sleeping, fear and copulation.

20. Oh, how great is the significance of human birth! It is only through this that devotion and worship of God and the attainment of the four *Muktis*[1] is possible. Through it alone, will come Self-realization.

21. Like a streak of lightning in the clouds is this worldly life — fleeting and transitory. Even a moment of happiness is rare to the people here, who are devoured by the fear of the serpent of Death.

22. Father and mother, brother and sister, wife, son, daughter or uncle — they all come together, momentarily, as floating logs of wood in the mainstream of a river.

23. One moment they seem to come together, but are thrown apart in the next moment, by the surging waves. And once the parting comes, never again will the setting be the same as before.

24. He who has not achieved his spiritual welfare in this world, has made his mother suffer the birthpangs in vain. And unless he surrenders himself at the feet of the saints, his life is a total waste.

25. The moment a creature is born, he begins his journey towards Death. So he who believes that death will not come today, or wait until tomorrow or the day after, is only deluding himself.

26. Let not the thought of Death be away from your mind. After all, this physical body is but as fodder for Death. Such is the characteristic of worldly life. Hence be alert!

27. He who enters into worldly transactions with discrimination and wisdom, will make spiritual progress, effortlessly. Therefore, in worldly matters there should be no slackness or indolence; regarding the fourfold objectives of human life there should be no disinterest or unconcern.

28. Those who listen to Sai's story with love, will attain the most excellent thing in life; their devotion to Sai will grow and the great treasure of happiness will be theirs.

29. Those who love Sai deeply, will be reminded of Sai's lotus-feet at every step, by this collection of stories.

30. This story is an expression in words of what is inexpressible; an experience through the senses, of what is beyond the senses. And

hence, however deeply you may drink of these nectar-sweet stories, there is no satiety.

31. Inconceivable are the *leelas* of these saints; indescribable is their greatness! Who has the power to describe them adequately in words?

32. And as these tales fall on the ears, all the while, Sai will also come, always, before the eyes. He will thus remain in the mind, in thoughts and meditation, and in memory day and night.

33. Waking and in dreams; sitting, sleeping or eating, he will appear to you and will always be with you, wherever you may come or go — in the crowds or in the forest.

34. When he has thus become the object of deep contemplation, your mind will enter into the state of '*Unmani*'[2]. And when this happens every day, your mind will merge with the Universal Consciousness.

35. But now, let us begin the story referred to at the end of the last chapter. Listen to it with respect, O Listeners!

36. Faith and devotion are like a feast of '*Sheera-puri*' (a sweet dish). The more you eat it, the more you want! And even when you eat it to your full capacity, yet there can never be complete satiety!

37. So now, O Listeners! if you listen attentively to this second story, you will be convinced of the great significance of a saint's *darshan*.

38. Outwardly, Baba seemed to do nothing. He did not even leave his seat to go anywhere. But sitting in one place, he knew everything and gave proof of it to all the people.

39. '*Brahman*' or '*Sat*', which is in our bodies, is also present equally in the entire Universe. Always remember this and consecrate your body in God's service.

40. Know that he who has surrendered to Brahman, will see only Oneness in all. And he who believes in duality will be caught in the chain of births and deaths.

41. The intellect that firmly establishes duality is, truly, ignorance itself. The mind is purified by coming into contact with the guru. Because of him comes the attainment of the state of Self-realization.

42. Release from such ignorance is in itself the realization of the Oneness of all things. How can there be a state of complete Oneness if there is even a trace of duality in the mind?

43. From Brahma, etc., right down to the immovable things in this Universe, whatever exhibits a different property from the Brahman, appears as non-Brahman to the indiscriminating mind, although it is really Brahman from every angle.

44. That which is, by its very nature, the most profound knowledge of every sort; has no place for duties of worldly life; has wiped off all traces of Name or Form — that indeed, is the Brahman, without appendages or parts.

45. Because of its natural tendency to consider itself as different from Brahman, and from the blunders arising out of ignorance, tempation, etc., the mind which is distracted by the illusion of duality, becomes calm and peaceful as it attains the knowledge of this Oneness.

46. He who does not feel that 'I am different, people are different'; who sees this whole world as one, filled with the one and the same spirit, he finds nothing that is separate from himself.

47. To regard Name, Form, doing of actions as obstacles; to give up altogether, any idea of duality, is itself to become Brahman.

48. 'I alone, am; there is not a place where I am not; I pervade all the ten directions. Nothing exists apart from me.'

49. Hold fast to this one idea; thrust aside *Maya* that deludes. Bearing in mind that 'there is nothing that is separate from me', concentrate your thoughts on the Self.

50. Listeners might naturally ask how this duality arises at all! Brahman is the object of Knowledge, while the Being is one who tries to get this Knowledge. By what means, then, can this feeling of duality be removed?

51. Even the slightest trace of duality in the mind will destroy this complete Oneness and at once give rise to a sense of differentiation which becomes the cause of births and deaths.

52. When the darkness of ignorance is dispelled. the whole Creation seems to dissolve and the vision is filled with Oneness

of the Self with everything else. The illusion of duality disappears, at once.

53. When pure water is mixed with pure water, it all becomes one. What it was before and what it has become now appears as inseparable, without a trace of difference.

54. Logs of wood differ in their shapes. But as fire they are indistinguishable. They lose their separateness, their shapes merging into one mass, as fire.

55. Similarly, the knowledge of the oneness of the *Atman* needs no other proof. The *Atman* dwells in all living creatures, but is always without a form.

56. False, conflicting notions cause delusions in the mind, all the time, and hence the mind is always agitated by experiencing the sufferings of birth-death, etc.

57. He who has overcome the obstacles of Name, Form, etc., and has attained to a state of God-realization, is a *Siddha*, unharmed by *Maya* and always Self-absorbed.

58. Shri Sai is such a state personified. Blessed, blessed are those who were fortunate to have his *darshan*.

59. The moon seems to be in the water, but is really outside. So are also the saints who appear to be surrounded by the devotees, but are inwardly detached.

60. For ever in the midst of devotees, they have attachment nowhere. Their minds are absorbed in the Self; nothing else appears before their vision.

61. Such are the great *sadhus* and saints, through whose words God himself speaks. For them nothing is unattainable; nothing unknown.

62. There are innumerable gurus and *shishyas* in this world, who give and take spiritual instruction. But rare indeed, is the guru who gives actual experience along with knowledge.

63. But enough now, of this prelude! Let us proceed with the main story, whereby my listeners, who are full of eager anticipation, may be enriched by what they hear.

64. At Nanded city, in the Nizam's kingdom, there lived a Parsi merchant, who was very religious and well-loved among the people. His name was Ratanji[3].

65. He had abundant wealth and extensive property — carriages, horses, farms and woodlands. His doors were always open to all, from where no one ever went back spurned.

66. Though outwardly, he was immersed in this way, in the Ocean of joy, day and night, inwardly his mind was hemmed in, all the time, by the alligator of great worry.

67. It is the Divine Law that no one can enjoy pure, unalloyed happiness. To some, it may be one thing; to others, it is another. Each one has some sorrow or longing.

68. One may say, 'I alone am great in all my prosperity and opulence', and, puffed up with empty pride, may begin to walk on the wrong path.

69. But it seems quite clear that, lest an evil eye be cast on the faultless, perfect one, God Himself leaves him with a slight blemish, just as a mother smears a little lamp-black with her finger on her child's cheek to protect him from an evil eye.

70. Opulence of wealth, of gold that Ratanji enjoyed, made him generous with food to everyone who came to him. He would help alleviate the sufferings of the meek and the poor. He always appeared to be cheerful.

71. Thus, from the point of view of the world, Shetji was happy. But this joy of wealth is always of little use to him who has no son.

72. One after the other, he had no less than twelve daughters. How then, will he enjoy even a moment's pleasure? How will his mind be ever at peace?

73. *Hari-kirtan* without loving devotion to God; song without rhythm or musical notes; a Brahmin without the sacrifical thread — where, O where is the beauty in all this?

74. Proficient in all arts, but without the discriminating knowledge; of good, exemplary conduct, but without kindness and compassion for the living beings — where indeed, is the grace in such a one?

75. Forehead bearing *Gopichandan* marks and the neck adorned by *Tulsi* necklaces, but if the tongue derides and mocks the saints, wherein lies the virtue, the sanctity?

76. Pilgrimages without repentance; ornaments without the necklace; a household without a son, — from where will they derive their beauty or joy?

77. 'Will Narayan bless me with at least one son?' Such was his musing every day. His mind would not be rid of the worry.

78. Due to this Shetji was sad. He did not relish food or drink. Day and night, he felt dejected, his mind being always full of worry.

79. 'O God, remove this one blemish on my happiness and make me free of the stigma. Give me but one son to continue my family line. Save me, O Prabhuraya, from this disgrace!'

80. He had great faith in Das Ganu and it was to him that Shetji related his heart's secret desire. Das Ganu said, 'Go to Shirdi and the ardent wish of your heart will be fulfilled.

81. 'Take Baba's *darshan*, make obeisance at his feet and tell him, in detail, your secret wish. He will bless you.

82. 'Go, you will prosper. For, Baba's ways are inconceivable! Surrender to him whole-heartedly and you will be happy.'

83. The idea appealed to Ratanji and he made a firm resolve to go. Accordingly, after a few days had passed, Ratanji arrived at Shirdi.

84. He went to the mosque for *darshan* and prostrated himself at Sai's feet. Love welled up in his heart as he looked at Maharaj, a mine of highest virtue.

85. He opened up the basket of flowers and taking out a flower-garland, put it round Baba's neck, very lovingly. Then he offered at his feet, a profusion of choice fruit.

86. With great reverence, Ratanji then sat down near Baba, in all humility. And now, listen to his prayer to Baba.

87. 'When people are in great trouble, they come to Baba's feet and he protects them immediately. This is what I have heard.

88. 'Hence have I come all the way here, to see you with an ardent wish, which I shall respectfully relate at your feet. Please do not turn me away, O Maharaj!'

89. Baba then said to him, "And so, after all these days, you have come to me today! But then, give me first, whatever *dakshina* you wish to give. Only then will you get your satisfaction."

90. Whenever anyone came to take *darshan* and began worshipping his feet, he would first ask him for *dakshina* — be he a Hindu, Muslim or a Parsi.

91. And, was it just a modest sum — a rupee or two or an aggregate of five? Not at all! He would ask for a hundred, a thousand, a lakh, and even a crore, if it pleased him!

92. Offered once, he would say, 'Bring more.' If told that the money was over, he would say, "Do go and borrow it". And when it could not be borrowed from anywhere, only then would he stop asking for it.

93. And he would say to the devotee, "Do not worry in the least! I will give you pots of money. Sit quietly with me and give up worrying!

94. "In this world, everybody has someone or the other. But we have nobody here. Only Allah is for us, here.

95. "What I want is, one who will love me dearer than his own life. And to such a one, I repay a hundredfold of what he gives me!"

96. He may well be a millionaire, but even he was ordered by Maharaj to borrow some *dakshina* and that, from a poor man's house.

97. Whether a rich man or a beggar, poor, weak and moneyless, Sai never differentiated between them, as one being less important and the other, more.

98. Thus, whoever he might be, he would obey Baba's command respectfully and, shedding off all his conceit, would go to the houses of poor people to beg for money, for Baba's sake.

99. In short, under the pretext of asking for *dakshina*, Baba was really teaching his devotees a lesson in humility.

100. A doubt may arise in anybody's mind, why does a *sadhu* want wealth? But when carefully thought over, the doubt will be resolved quite easily.

101. If Sai is one fully satiated in all his desires, where is the need to ask for *dakshina*? And how can he be called desireless who asks his devotees for money?

102. He to whom a diamond and flint-stone, a copper coin or a gold one, both measure equal in value, why does he spread out his hands for money?

103. He who goes for alms only to sustain himself, and has taken a vow of austerity and renunciation, to such a detached, desireless soul, why this expectation of *dakshina*?

104. He, upon whom the '*Ashtasiddhis*'[4] wait, with folded hands, and at whose command the '*Navanidhis*'[5] are readily laid open — to such a one, why this state of wretchedness for money?

105. Having abandoned the pleasures of worldly life with contempt, and turned away from heavenly bliss, equally, with scornful indifference, why should such detached *sadhus*, who know where their good lies, require money at all?

106. Those saints, *sadhus*, righteous souls, who have reached perfection, and whose life is dedicated to the welfare of their devotees, why should they require wealth?

107. Why should the *sadhus* require *dakshina*? Their minds should be really free of all desires. They become fakirs, but cannot withstand temptations and are in pursuit of money, all the time!

108. For the first *darshan*, he accepts *dakshina*, for the second *darshan*, he again asks for *dakshina*; and at the time of leave-taking, he once again says, "Bring *dakshina*". Why this *dakshina* at every step?

109. In the ritual worship, water is first given for devotional sipping from the palm of the hand, after a meal; water is then offered for washing hands and mouth; then perfume is applied to the hand and betel leaf *paan* is offered. After all this is over, *dakshina* is given in the end.

110. But the order followed by Baba was most unusual. As the sandalwood paste was being applied or as he was being adorned with consecrated rice, etc., he would expect *dakshina* to be offered to him, at once.

111. Even as the prayer of adoration at the beginning of the *pooja*, commenced, he would first ask for *dakshina* and the *dakshina* had to be offered to that Self-existing Brahman[6] at that very moment, which should normally come at the end of the *pooja*.

112. Yet this doubt can be resolved without making any great effort. If you pay attention for a moment, you will be quite satisfied.

113. The object of accumulating wealth is to be able to spend it in charity. But instead, it gets expended mostly, for petty sensual pleasures.

114. Wealth facilitates *Dharma*[7]; from *Dharma* comes the Knowledge of the Supreme Being. Money thus takes us on the spiritual path, which brings peace and happiness to the mind.

115. Initally, for a very long time, Baba did not accept anything, but would collect only the burnt match-sticks and fill his pocket with them.

116. Whether a devotee or otherwise, he asked for nothing from anyone. If someone placed a copper coin before him, of one pice or half a pice, he used to buy tobacco or oil with it.

117. He was very fond of tobacco and used to smoke a *bidi*[8] or a clay-pipe, filled with it. Limitless was the service rendered by this clay-pipe, for it hardly ever remained unkindled.

118. Later, someone thought how he could go for a saint's *darshan* empty-handed (i.e. without *dakshina*)? And so he took some *dakshina* with him.

119. If a '*didaki*'[9] was given to Baba, he would put it in his pocket. But if anyone placed a coin of two pice, he would return it to the giver, all intact. For a long time such was his practice.

120. Later, after some time, Baba's fame spread. Devotees flocked to Shirdi in large numbers and Baba's *pooja* began to take place with all the rites and rituals.

121. Now, the worshippers knew, on the authority of the *Shastras*, that no *pooja* can conclude without an offering of gold, flowers and *dakshina*.

122. While sprinkling sacred water at the coronation of a king or while worshipping his feet, the worshippers bring offerings and presents. In the same way, for the *guru-pooja, dakshina* is to be offered.

123. Those who offer *dakshina* attain to a high state (i.e. heaven); those who offer gold attain the highest Knowledge (i.e. *Moksha*); those who give gold become pure of heart. So say the *Vedas.*

124. By applying sandalwood paste comes sanctity and purity; by offering consecrated rice, one gets longevity; flowers and betel-leaf *paan* bring wealth and prosperity. Similarly, offering gold and *dakshina* gives the fruit of opulence.

125. Just as sandal-paste, consecrated rice, flowers and *paan* are important in the *pooja* ingredients, so also are *dakshina* and the gold and flowers which give the fruit of increasing wealth.

126. *Dakshina* is necessary for the ritualistic worship of a deity. And so it is also, at the concluding ritual of a vow and an offering or a present of gold is required.

127. All the worldly transactions proceed on the basis of hard cash, and to live up to their reputation and honour, people spend liberally on such occasions.

128. If *dakshina* becomes acceptable for the *pooja* of a deity by the recitation of a *mantra* like 'Hiranyagarbh garbhastha', then why should it not be so for a saint's *pooja?*

129. While going for a saint's *darshan,* different people go with different ideas, each according to his knowledge. And about this any unanimity is rare.

130. Some go with faith and devotion; some, to test the saint's powers, while some others feel that if he can read what is in their minds, only then is he a saint!

131. Some pray for a long life; some, for elephants, gold, wealth, property. Again, some ask for sons, grandchildren, etc., and some, for undiminishing, constant power.

132. But Baba's ways were most astonishing! Those who came only to mock, to ridicule, they stayed to worship his feet, their evil minds being destroyed altogether.

133. Had they not been fortunate enough to have even this much, they would at least repent at heart, and their faith being confirmed by direct experience, would overcome their ego.

134. And yet, these were all common, ordinary people, very much involved in the worldly life. And Baba wished them to become pure of heart by giving *dakshina*[10].

135. The *Shruti* 'Yagnen, danen, tapasa' explains in clear words that those who are anxious for Self-knowledge will find its secret in the giving of *dakshina*, as one of the means of attaining it.

136. The devotee, whether a seeker of the material or of the spiritual end, has to give *dakshina* to his guru for the fulfilment of his desire and in his own interest.

137. Even Brahmadev told his three children — God, Demon and Man — the same, when they asked his advice, on the completion of their period of celibacy.

138. He instructed them in the monosyllable 'da' and impressed it on their minds by asking what each understood by it. Truly, the *leelas* of guru and *shishya* are marvellous!

139. 'Practice restraint', God interpreted; 'Be merciful', the Demon understood; 'Give in charity', so thought Man. 'Well done! Fine!' said Brahmadev.

140. Gods are none other than men, differing from them only in their disposition. Men endowed with excellent qualities, but unsubdued senses — they are called gods.

141. Even the demons dwell only among men and are those who are vicious, cruel and prone to violence. As for men themselves, they are tormented by uncontrollable avarice. These are the three types among men.

142. Hence, to pull the greed-engulfed man out of the abyss of avarice, Sainath, the ocean of Kindness, takes his devotees out by the hand, wishing for their welfare.

143. The eleventh 'Anuvac' (i.e. section) of the *Taittiriyopanishad* describes many types of gifts. Listen to each one of them.

144. To begin with, whatever is to be given should always be given with faith. For, if given without faith, it bears no fruit. Out of fear

for the king's command, for the dictates of the *Shastras*, or, at least out of shame, something should be given.

145. Even at ceremonial occasions like weddings, etc., some gift is to be given, to fulfil obligations of friendship. Such are the dictates of social custom.

146. So Baba too, asked of his devotees the same, as indicated by the letter '*da*' and for their own good. 'Be compassionate, give generously and subdue your senses. And you will experience great happiness.'

147. Gururaya was making use of this short, monosyllabic *mantra* for his devotees to destroy their three-fold faults of unsubdued senses, etc.

148. Lust, anger and greed are not conducive to Self-upliftment and they are very difficult to conquer. Hence was this easy way recommended.

149. As in the *Shruti*, so also in the *Smriti*, has this means been approved. But I give it below, so that the listeners may be able to follow it properly:

> The gateway of this Hell, leading to the ruin of the Soul is threefold — lust, anger and greed. Therefore these three, one should abandon.
>
> *Shrimad Bhagvad Gita*, Ch. 16, v 21.[11]

150. Know that lust, wrath and avarice are the three gates to Hell, which lead to Self-destruction. Hence, they should be scrupulously abandoned.

151. Most Merciful Sai Samarth asked for *dakshina* only for the good of his devotees. He was educating them in renunciation.

152. Of what great value was that *dakshina* to him? And of what significance was his spirituality, who would not instantly lay down his life for the guru's Word?

153. Indeed, of what use was *dakshina* to Baba but for the spiritual welfare of his devotees? For his subsistence, for his life, he did not depend on their dakshina!

154. He collected alms for sustenance. Hence there could be no selfish thought behind collecting *dakshina*. His only object was that by giving *dakshina* his devotees should become pure of heart.

155. According to Vedic saying, mentioned above, the *guru-pooja* cannot be complete unless an offering of *dakshina* is first made.

156. But now, enough of this treatise on *dakshina*! The significance is amply clear that *dakshina* was not asked for out of greed or selfishness, but only for the benefit of devotees, themselves.

157. So let us now proceed with the detailed narration of the story. Listen to Sai's wonderful *leela* on Ratanji's offering him *dakshina*.

158. Listeners should be gracious enough to listen attentively to this marvellous story and see for themselves Sai's all-pervasive, remarkable nature!

159. While he asked Shetji (Ratanji) for *dakshina*, Sai narrated to him an incident of the past. But Shetji could not remember it and hence was quite puzzled.

160. "I know that you have already given me three rupees and fourteen annas. Now give me the remaining money which you have brought with you, as *dakshina*".

161. Since this was Baba's first *darshan*, Shetji was quite astonished to hear Baba's words and tried hard to recollect.

162. 'Never have I come to Shirdi before; nor have I sent anything with anyone', (he thought). 'Such being the case, what Sai Maharaj is saying, is really a puzzle to me!'

163. Never, never had such a thing happened, at all! It made Ratanji feel most embarrassed. He gave *dakshina*, bowed at Sai's feet, but the riddle still remained unsolved.

164. However, the subject was left at that. Ratanji then narrated the purpose of his visit, prostrated once again, at Baba's feet and sat down with folded hands.

165. At heart, Shetji felt completely satisfied and said, 'Baba, it was, indeed, well that by my good fortune I had your *darshan* today.

166. 'I am a luckless one, and without much knowledge. I know nothing about *pooja*, *yajna*, etc. By my good fortune, I had today,

the *darshan* of one who knows past, present and future and is
wise.

167. 'You know my anxiety only too well. Remove it, O Gracious One!
Do not push this faithful devotee away from your feet, O All-
merciful One!'

168. Sainath was moved by pity and said, "Do not worry, needlessly!
Your misfortune is on the wane from hence".

169. He then gave *udi-prasad* in his hand, placed the hand of
benediction on his head and blessed Shetji with the words, "Allah
will fulfil your heart's desire".

170. Ratanji then took permission and returned to Nanded. There he
related to Ganu Das, in detail and in its proper sequence, all that
had happened.

171. 'I had a proper *darshan* and was delighted. I also had his assurance,
along with the *prasad* and his blessings.

172. 'Everything took place in a most satisfying manner. But there
was only one thing that I did not follow. Of what Maharaj said to
me, I did not understand at all!

173. "Three rupees fourteen annas you have given me, I know". What
is this that Baba said? Please explain to me all this, clearly.

174. 'What rupees and what annas? How could I have given anything
to him before? This was my first visit to Shirdi. O, I do not
understand the significance of this, in the least!

175. 'At least I am not able to resolve this. To me, it appears as a great
mystery, a puzzle I cannot solve. Can you, at least, solve it for
me?'

176. This was indeed, a mystery! Das Ganu began to ponder what its
significance could be! But he could not make up his mind.

177. After some deep thinking, he suddenly remembered. And, the
figure of a Muslim saint called Maulisaheb[12], suddenly came before
his mind.

178. Born in the Muslim community, his way of life was like that of a
saint. He worked as a porter, living a life that Fate had ordained
for him.

179. But a detailed account of his life here, will only lead to a digression from the main story. Everyone in Nanded knows the life-story of Maulisaheb.

180. So, when it was decided to go to Shirdi, Maulisaheb had casually, and of his own will, come to Shetji's house.

181. Both had boundless affection for each other. And Maulisaheb was offered flower-garlands, fruit, etc., with proper rituals.

182. On the occasion, Shetji was suddenly inspired to serve a light meal to Mauli. And Ganu Das was, at once, reminded of the expense incurred for it.

183. The list of expenditure was called for, every single pice was counted. It was all then added up and the total tallied perfectly.

184. It came to exactly three rupees and fourteen annas — neither more nor less! But that Baba should acknowledge the receipt of it only amazed everyone! It revealed Baba's many-faceted personality.

185. Sai Maharaj is a treasure of knowledge. Sitting inside the mosque, he knew the past, present and future, in whichever part of the world it might occur.

186. Unless there was oneness between all living beings, could Sai Samarth have experienced this or told others?

187. Nanded is miles away from Shirdi, both being divided from each other by considerable distance. Moreover, both the saints were also unknown to each other. How should Sai receive this telegraphic message then?

188. Any thought of separateness, that 'I am Sai Maharaj, while Maulisaheb is somebody quite different', was not present between the two of them.

189. Maulisaheb's *Atman* was the same as that of all the others. Yet, blessed indeed, is he who will understand this secret of oneness between all.

190. Though outwardly inhabiting two separate bodies, inwardly, both were one at heart. In fact, to use the words 'they both' is in itself not proper at all. For they were never separate.

191. In knowledge, in spirit, in their very aims and objectives, they were one. Both were of the same Essence, of the same disposition.

192. No doubt, great distance separated Shirdi from Nanded. But their hearts, their lifeforce, their bodies were as one. And hence this telegraphic message to each other was possible.

193. Oh, how astounding are these *sadhus* and saints, who are as wireless telegraphic machines! Whatever happens in the Universe and wherever it may happen, they know all about it.

194. Later, after a suitable passage of time, God rewarded Ratanji. His wife became pregnant. The tree of hope sprouted into leaf.

195. On the auspicious moment, his wife delivered. The blessing came true. To the great joy of Ratanji, a son was born to him.

196. As after years of drought, there should be a sudden downpour of rain, such was Shetji's joy and satisfaction at the birth of a son.

197. Thereafter as time went by, the family tree began to spread out and blossom, being happily laden with sons and daughters. Ratanji was now fully satisfied.

198. But even thereafter, he continued to go for *Sai-darshan*. With Sai's blessings, all his desires were fulfilled and Ratanji was filled with joy.

199. In Spring, the mango tree is heavy with fruit, but not all the fruit will ripen. Of the twelve sons, only four have survived and today, they live happily.

200. And, even-tempered that he was, Ratanji too, accepted willingly and without the slightest regret, what had been ordained by Fate.

201. And now, for the significance of the next story! This whole Creation, animate and inanimate, is pervaded by Sai. Anyone may just sit still, anywhere, and experience it for himself;

202. How Guruvar was pleased with the faith and devotion of a poor, humble man from Thane, whose surname was Cholkar;

203. How this man took a vow before Sai, whom he had never seen before, and how his wishes were fulfilled, and he was given personal, direct experiences!

204. What is a *bhajan* without love, or reciting a sacred text without understanding its meaning? And where, O where is God without faith? Is it not all an effort in vain?

205. A forehead without the auspicious *kumkum* mark, knowledge without actual experience, are all futile. These are not words of book-learning. Experience their truth for yourselves and then judge.

206. Why this book about Sai's *leelas*, you may ask. Its purpose, I do not know. It is Sai who got it written through me and he alone, knows its purpose.

207. Moreover, to write such a book requires a man of spiritual authority. And I am but a servant of Sai, who keeps these records by his command. I am only a slave of his command.

208. My listeners are as the thirsty Chatak birds while Sai Samarth is the bliss-filled rain cloud who showers rain through these stories to quench their thirst.

209. May this body roll over and over in the dust at the feet of that Power, which moves my speech and whose Life I narrate.

210. It is he who prompts my speech; it is he who narrates his own story. May this fickle mind of mine become steady and steadfast at his feet.

211. May this *bhajan* be not only physical, not only verbal, but also mental and bring me everlasting joy, for I am just a meek and humble messenger of Sai.

212. The Narrator and the Cause of the narration is, no doubt, Sai himself. And yet, is the listener separate from him? No, for he is not remote from Sai.

213. To all appearances, this is just a Life-story; but in reality, it is all Sai's sport. He has himself become the loving Sport-maker and has started this powerful play.

214. Sai Baba's Life is inscrutable! He has made me his instrument and has given amazing experiences to the devotees. Thereby he satisfies his own innumerable devotees.

215. This is no mere Life-story; it is a store of happiness. The sweet nectar of Salvation, which can be enjoyed only by the most fortunate one who has faith and devotion.

216. I have toiled hard to write this book for the peace and happiness of the devotees and we, the devotees may always remember the greatness and the marvel of the Guru's Grace.

217. When related with loving devotion, this story will enhance the pleasure of the listeners in listening to it. When read over and over again, and the moral lesson of the stories is translated into practice, it will increase devotion and love.

218. When listened to, day and night, it will snap the bondage of *Maya* and temptations; the consciousness of the *triputis* will disappear and the listeners will enjoy happiness.

219. Holding fast to Sai's feet, Hemad surrenders to him whole-heartedly and remains prostrated at his feet, for ever, without leaving them even for a moment.

Weal be to all! Here ends the fourteenth chapter of
"Shri Sai Samarth Satcharit", called
'*Ratanji's Meeting with Sai*',
as inspired by the saints and the virtuous,
and composed by his devotee, Hemadpant.

Notes

1. Refer Ch. 11, note 8.
2. Refer Ch. 3, note 12.
3. His full name was Ratanji Shapoorji Wadia, mill contractor.
4. Refer Ch. 10, note 4.
5. Refer ch. 10, note 5.
6. The *mantra* to be recited when offering *dakshina* is "*Om tat sat Brahmarpanamastu*".
7. The Universal moral law governing both the sacred and secular aspects of human life is known as '*Dharma*'.
8. Tobacco rolled up in a leaf, or a roll of a tobacco-leaf to be smoked as a cigar.
9. Three-quarters of a pice.
10. Once Baba said cryptically, "I give people what they want in the hope that they will begin to want what I want to give them!"
11. '*The Bhagvad Gita*', by S. Radhakrishnan, p. 340. (George Allen & Unwin Ltd., London, 1949).
12. He belonged to a Momin family of Nanded. Short-statured but strong in constitution, and fair of complexion, he beamed with lustre and presented a very attractive appearance. He was either moving about nude or only with a loin cloth. Sometimes he put on full dress with a turban. His age was about 82. He died in 1916. (*Shri Sant Sangh Pustakmala*, Part 4, p. 114. Compiled by Krishna Jagannath Thally, 1927)

15

The Story of Cholkar's vow of Sugar-candy

MY OBEISANCE TO SHRI GANESH, TO SHRI SARASWATI, AND SHRI GURUMAHARAJ! TO THE FAMILY DEITY, TO SHRI SITA-RAMACHANDRA, MY MOST HUMBLE OBEISANCE! I BOW IN REVERENCE TO THE MOST VENERABLE GURU SHRI SAINATH!

1. Only those whose innumerable meritorious deeds have come to fruition can have Sai's *darshan*; are not affected by the threefold afflictions and can successfully attain by the means, the spiritual end.

2. Be kind, O listeners! Meditate for a moment on your guru and then listen respectfully to the story by giving me your full attention.

3. Please do not say with disdain, 'Oh, don't we know you full well! Why all this futile effort, then?' Forgive me, for you are comparable only to the ocean.

4. The ocean which, though full to the brim, will not send the river back and contains within itself a thousand streams of water that the cloud pours.

5. And such are you, too, my good listeners! I wish to bathe in your waters. Do not turn me away with scorn, for it is not good to abandon the meek and the poor.

6. Be it the pure waters of the Ganges or the turbid flow of the village streamlet, they both find a place equally, in the vast expanse of the ocean, without causing any turbulence at their confluence.

7. Hence, O my listeners, your eager interest in listening to the stories of saints, will be automatically satisfied, if you take kindly to my effort.

8. When this nectar-sweet story is heard respectfully, and with faith and forbearance, the listeners will experience a loving devotion and will find fulfilment.

9. Devotees will attain effortlessly, the most excellent thing (i.e. God), the listeners will experience devotion as well as Deliverance; the simple, faithful souls will enjoy peace and happiness and all will find their Ultimate Refuge.

10. As they listen to the stories that came from the guru's mouth, the fear of worldly life will be removed and the listeners' hearts will be gladdened when they experience Oneness with their true Self.

11. In this chapter there will be a narration of how the loving devotees pray to Sai and how Sai favours them with his *darshan*. Listen to it carefully!

12. A cat might have come out, having just suckled her little ones. But even if she goes back at that instant, the kittens will start running all over her to suckle at her teats, lovingly, once again.

13. The mother growls wearily, and, for a moment the kittens appear subdued. But it is enough for them to see her relax, and there they begin again, going round and round in circles, to suck at her teats.

14. But as they suck, devouring the milk in large gulps, so lovingly, the milk begins to trickle from the mother's teats and, forgetting her earlier growl and weariness, the mother too, stretches herself out, affectionately, on the ground.

15. All the weariness is gone; instead, love surges up in her breast as she embraces her young ones, holding them tightly with her four feet and licks them instinctively, again and again. It is indeed, unique, this celebration of a mother's love!

16. The deeper the sharp nails of the kittens are dug and bruise her teats, the faster flows the love through the many streams of milk that gush out.

17. Just as the deep love and devotion of the little ones produces more and more milk in the mother's teats, so also will your single-minded love and attachment to Sai's feet stir Sai's heart to deep compassion.

18. Once the people of Thane had organized, near Kaupineshwar Mandir, a programme of *Hari-bhaktiparayan*[1], Das Ganu's *kirtan*, which was a pleasure to hear.

19. When persuaded by prominent citizens, Das Ganu used to agree graciously to perform *kirtan*, without expecting a pice and without undue obstinacy.

20. Not a pice was expected to be paid for the *kirtan*. Bare-bodied except for the plain *dhoti* round the waist, and without a '*pagdi*' (headgear) on his head, he used to perform. Yet the large crowds that gathered were difficult to control.

21. Incidentally, the story behind such unusual dress is sure to amuse when heard carefully. Listen to it at ease and see Baba's amazing ways, for yourself.

22. Once, Das Ganu was to perform *kirtan* at Shirdi and came out donning an '*angarakha*' (a long, outer frock-like garment for men), an '*uparna*' (a small piece of cloth) on his shoulders and a turban on his head.

23. Quite pleased with himself, he went to make obeisance to Baba, as was the custom, when Baba was heard remarking, "Bravo! You are indeed, decked out like a bridegroom!

24. "But, so adorned, where do you proceed?" asked Baba. Das Ganu then replied that he was going to perform *kirtan*.

25. Baba further said, "Why this '*angarakha*'? Why this '*uparna*', this turban? What for, all this effort? These things are not for us!

26. "Take them off before me, right now! Why carry their burden on your body?" Obeying Baba's command immediately, he took them off and placed them at Baba's feet.

27. From then onwards to this day, while performing *kirtan*, Das Ganu is always seen with a bare, healthy-looking body, '*chiplis*'[2] in hand and a garland round the neck.

28. Although this style is unconventional, it has a solid, pure foundation. It is the style of the famed Naradmuni, who is the most learned among the learned.

29. This tradition originated from Narad and it is from here that the long line of Haridas (*kirtankars*) has started. They are not burdened with the outward trappings of dress; their sights are set on the inner purity of heart.

30. Too familiar is the figure of Narad, with only the lower half of the body covered, the hands playing on the *Veena* and *chiplis*, while on the lips, a loud proclamation of *Harinaam*, constantly.

31. By the grace of Sai Samarth, Das Ganu himself composed *kathas* of saints and narrated them in his *kirtans*, which he performed free of charge. Through these he became renowned.

32. Das Ganu thus generated great enthusiasm for Sai-devotion among the people, fostering love and devotion for Sai, the Ocean of Self-rejoicing.

33. No less a contribution has been made by Chandorkar, the most eminent among the Sai devotees, for it is he who is really responsible for spreading Sai-worship.

34. It was solely due to Chandorkar that Das Ganu first came here (to Bombay) and started performing bhajans and *kirtans* of Sai in various places.

35. Maharaj was already well-known in Pune, Sholapur and Nagar districts, but amongst the people of Konkan, it was these two who spread Sai-devotion.

36. Thus amongst the people of the Bombay presidency, Sai worship started by the efforts of these two persons. The All-merciful Sai Maharaj appeared in Bombay through these two people.

37. In the Shri Kaupineshwar Mandir, on that day in the midst of the loud proclamations of Sai's Grace in the *kirtan* and of the *Harinaam*, Cholkar experienced a sudden, strong urge.

38. Many had come for the *Hari-kirtan*, each one appreciating it for a different reason. Some liked Bua's proficiency in the *Shastras*; some admired his expressive gestures and gesticulations.

39. Admiration of some was reserved for Bua's singing. 'Excellent! Oh, how wonderful is Bua's singing. How totally absorbed he becomes, taking *Vitthal-naam*! And how he dances enraptured narrating the *katha*!'

40. Some were more interested in the prelude to the main *katha*, while others loved to hear the main story. Some liked to watch the imitations and mimicry that the Haridas resorted to in the course of his narration, while some others were fond of listening to parables and fables (that came in the latter half).

41. Whether the Bua is an erudite Sanskrit scholar or ignorant of it; whether he can unfold levels of meaning from line to line or is an adept only at explaining the philosophical statements that come in the latter half of the *kirtan* — it makes little difference. For, the ways of the listeners remain the same.

42. Of these types, there are many listeners. But it is hard to find that class of listeners in whom faith and devotion to God or saints grows steadily as they listen.

43. And what indeed, is the fruit of that listening, where *katha* after *katha* is being listened to, indiscriminately, while there accumulates layer upon layer of ignorance? In vain is such listening without discrimination!

44. Can it be called soap when it does not remove the dirt? Can it be called discriminate listening which does not remove ignorance?

45. Simple, trusting soul that Cholkar was, love for Sai surged up in his heart as he said to himself, 'O Compassionate Baba, please look after this meek, helpless creature.'

46. Cholkar was a probationer, poor and moneyless, who was unable to shoulder the burden of providing for the family and put the entire responsibility on Baba for obtaining the means of livelihood through the government job.

47. People keenly desiring something, take a vow that if their wishes are fulfilled they would serve to the Brahmins whatever food they desired, and to their heart's content.

48. The rich promise to feed a thousand people or to offer a hundred cows, if their heart's wishes are fulfilled.

49. But moneyless that Cholkar was, when he took a vow, remembering Sai's feet, in all humility he said,

50. 'Baba, mine is a poor household, my entire dependence being on getting a job. But to become permanent in my job, this examination must be passed.

51. 'With great diligence and hard work have I prepared for the examination, all my reliance being on passing it. Or else I will lose my job as a probationer, too!

52. 'If by your Grace I pass this examination, I will humbly present myself at your feet and distribute sugar-candy in your name. This is my most firm resolve!'

53. Such was the vow he took. Later, to his great joy, his wish was fulfilled. But the fulfillment of his promise was delayed. So, to atone for it, he gave up eating sugar.

54. He knew that he would require money on the journey. Moreover, how could he go to Baba empty-handed? So he kept on postponing the visit from morrow to morrow, in painful waiting.

55. It may be easier to cross Naneghat[3], the dangerous cliff of the Sahyadri range; but it is far more difficult for a householder to cross the threshold of his house.

56. So long as the promise made at Shirdi remained unfulfilled, any dish with sugar in it remained excluded for Cholkar, who continued to drink even his tea without sugar.

57. After some days had passed in this manner, the time came for Cholkar to go to Shirdi. So he went there, fulfilled the vow that he had taken and was very happy.

58. As he took Sai's *darshan*, Cholkar prostrated before him and bowing at Baba's feet, was filled with satisfaction and joy.

59. With a heart so purified, he then distributed sugar, offered coconut to Baba and said, 'Today, all my heart's desires have borne fruit.'

60. *Sai-darshan* made him happy, his conversation with Sai gladdened his heart. Since he was Jog's guest, he naturally had to go with Jog to his house.

61. When Jog got up to go, his guest got up, too! Baba then said to Jog, "Serve him cups full of tea, well sweetened with sugar!"

62. Cholkar was astonished to hear these significant words referring to his secret. His eyes filled with tears of joy as he placed his head on Sai's feet.

63. Jog was filled with a fond admiration for Baba; and as for Cholkar — he felt it twice as much! He alone knew the reason for it, as in his innermost heart he recognized the sign.

64. Baba had never touched tea in his life. Then why, all of a sudden, should he think of it at that particular moment? It was, of course, to reaffirm Cholkar's faith and to impress on his heart the mark of devotion.

65. Suddenly, Baba gave an even clearer signal that he knew everything, by saying, "Cholkar, your promised sugar-candy has reached me! And so, your vow (of giving up sugar) is fulfilled, too!

66. "Your agitated mind when you took the vow, your atonement for the inordinate delay in fulfilling it — all, all have I known, though you wanted to keep it a secret.

67. "Wherever you all may be, when you spread your hand before me in supplication, with faith and devotion, there I stand behind you, day and night, as steadfast as your faith and devotion is.

68. "I may be here in my physical body, and you may be far away, beyond the seven seas. Yet, whatever you do there, I know it here, instantly.

69. "You may go anywhere in this world, and there I go with you. My abode is your heart; I dwell within you.

70. "I, who thus abide in your heart, it is me that you should always worship. Even in the hearts of all the living creatures, it is I alone, who dwell.

71. "Hence, whoever you may come across, in the house or outside of it, or on the way, they are all my manifestations; I pervade them all.

72. "An insect, an ant, creatures living in water or moving in the sky, or animals on the land — a dog or a pig, I pervade them all, most truly and always.

73. "Hence, do not consider yourself as separate from me. Great is the good fortune of him, who will know me as not being different from himself".

74. Trivial as these words may appear to be, they are great in significance. How great must be Baba's fondness for this Cholkar that he gave him the treasure of devotion!

75. What there was in his mind, was thus revealed to him by Baba, through direct, actual experience. O, how skilful are the ways of the saints!

76. Baba's words were priceless, and as they entered deep down into the devotee's heart they became the sap of life to the orchard of devotion and love; to devotion they are as a mast is to the ship.

77. The cloud compassionately rains water to quench the thirst of the *Chataka*, but in the process the whole earth is cooled by the raindrops. Such is also the case here.

78. Cholkar, poor soul! Was he not a total stranger, unknown, unheard of? And, for that matter, even Das Ganu's *kirtan* was only an instrumental cause that created an urge in Cholkar's heart to take a vow, which ultimately resulted in his receiving Baba's Grace!

79. And because of this followed the miracle, revealing the mind of the saints! Baba, who was always keen on instructing the devotees, created such occasions for it.

80. Here, Cholkar was but an instrument. As usual, it was Baba's inconceivable *leela* to instruct his devotees, which never ceases to amaze us!

81. Let us now narrate another incident that reveals Baba's dexterity, after which we shall end this chapter. It is about how someone asked a question and how Baba answered it.

82. Once, as Baba was sitting in his usual seat in the mosque, a devotee who sat in front of him, heard a lizard chirp.

83. As the chirping of a lizard or its falling on any part of one's body is considered to be a bad omen of the events to come, the devotee, quite casually and out of curiosity, asked Baba a question.

84. 'Baba, why does that lizard on the back wall keep chirping? What could be in her mind? I hope it is not anything unpropitious or unlucky.'

85. Baba said to him, "The lizard is overcome with joy that her sister is coming here to meet her from Aurangabad".

86. What, after all, is a creature like the lizard! And then, to talk of her mother, father or brother and sister? How is she involved in these worldly, human relationships?

87. So the devotee thought to himself that Baba must have said something by way of a witty reply and he sat quietly for a moment.

88. Suddenly, a man on horseback came from Aurangabad to take Baba's *darshan*. Baba was then having a bath.

89. As the man had to travel further and the horse could not have gone on without his daily feed of grain, he set out towards the market to buy some gram.

90. The devotee, who had questioned Baba earlier about the lizard, was staring in astonishment at the just-arrived trader from Aurangabad, when the latter suddenly pulled out the horse's mouth-bag from under his arm and shook it vigorously to clear the rubbish.

91. As he dashed it on the ground, turning it inside out, there dropped out from it, a lizard that slid swiftly across, in great trepidation, in front of their own eyes!

92. Baba then said to his questioner, "Now, keep a careful eye on her! This indeed, is the sister of that lizard. Just watch this marvel!"

93. As she set out from there, the lizard made straight towards her elder sister, who was already chirping incessantly. Aiming in the direction of that sound, she set out, strutting and stalking.

94. After so many days the two sisters were meeting. They hugged and embraced and kissed each other on the mouth. It was a unique celebration of love!

95. Circling around each other, gyrating round and round with joy, they whirled in all directions, as it pleased them — vertical, horizontal, oblique!

96. Where Aurangabad, where Shirdi! How strange, the whole incident! How should this rider suddenly appear as from nowhere? And that a lizard should also be with him? O, how strange!

97. Maybe, the lizard was in Aurangabad and had entered into the horse's mouth-bag. But how did the question-answer take place at that most opportune moment? Its perfect timing was a real marvel!

98. Oh! That the lizard should start chirping, prompting the devotee to ask that question! And how Baba should have explained its significance, which received confirmation immediately through the actual experience!

99. It was an incident, unparalleled! Humour is loved universally and the saints make use of this incomparable device to enhance the welfare of the devotees.

100. Just consider! Had this inquisitive devotee not been there, or had no one put the question to Baba, how would Sai's greatness have been revealed? And who would ever have understood the meaning?

101. Many a lizard have we all heard, so often, making these sounds. But who has bothered to find out the meaning of the sounds or even about why they chirp?

102. In short, mysterious and inscrutable are the strings that control the great sport of this Universe. Who can imagine them? They leave everyone puzzled!

103. People say, quite to the contrary, that if these lizards are heard chirping, it is inauspicious. The evil can however be averted if you repeat the name '*Krishna, Krishna*'.

104. Be it as it may! But it is, for sure, an excellent device of Baba's to confirm the faith of his devotees, in himself. It was not just a miracle!

105. He who reads this chapter with reverence, or makes repeated readings of it regularly, will be freed from all obstacles by Gururaya.

106. He who lowers his head on Sai's feet with single-minded devotion, will truly find in him, his one and only Refuge and Protector, the Doer of all action and the Destroyer of all evil.

107. Make no mistake, have no doubt about this! For such indeed, is this Sainath! And I narrate the secret significance of my own experience, only for the benefit of the devotees.

108. In this entire world, only I am; there is nothing else other than me. And not only in this, but in all the three worlds, I and I alone, exist.

109. Where such non-duality is inspired, there not a trace of fear remains. For such a one, everything is filled with the Universal Consciousness, which is the unconceited, egoless state.

110. Hemadpant surrenders to Sai, absolutely, and does not part from his feet even for a moment. For that is the only way to cross the ocean of worldly life, safely. Now listen to the interesting narration that follows.

111. In the next chapter, Sai, the greatest among the Gurus, will create an incident of great significance as to how people ask for *Brahma-Jnana*, as if it is as easy and quick as the snapping of a thumb and a finger.

112. A greedy man will ask Sai for *Brahma-Jnana* and Maharaj will give it to him, out of the man's own pocket.

113. When the listeners hear this story, they will perceive Baba's marvellous ways to show how, unless one is totally free from avarice, the attainment of the Brahman is, beyond a doubt, impossible.

114. But no one ever thinks as to who has that spiritual authority. How it is attainable and to whom, will be explained by Maharaj.

115. I am but a slave of his slaves and hope, in earnest supplication, that you will hear with enthusiasm this glorious Sport of Sai's Love.

116. Your heart will be filled with joy and you will have the satisfaction of understanding. Hence, O listeners, give your attention and you will know the greatness of the Saints.

Weal be to all! Here ends the fifteenth chapter of
"*Shri Sai Samarth Satcharit*", called
'*The Story of Cholkar's Vow of Sugar-candy*',
as inspired by the saints and the virtuous,
and composed by his devotee, Hemadpant.

Notes

1. A title which means 'devoted to Hari-worship'.
2. A pair of wooden sticks with metal discs at the two ends and a handle for clapping
    them as an accompaniment to the singing during *kirtan* or *arati*.
3. In the Murbad *taluka* of Thane district, there is this difficult pass in the Sahyadri range
    of mountains, through which people from the coastal strip of Konkan cross over to the
    middle country and vice versa.

16

A Narration About Brahma-Jnana (1)

MY OBEISANCE TO SHRI GANESH, TO SHRI SARASWATI, AND SHRI GURUMAHARAJ! TO THE FAMILY DEITY, TO SHRI SITA-RAMACHANDRA, MY MOST HUMBLE OBEISANCE! I BOW IN REVERENCE TO THE MOST VENERABLE GURU SHRI SAINATH!

1. The King of kings, Lord Paramount, enthroned on the throne of Peace; Master of the Empire of the Blissful Self and our one and only Refuge, Shri Gururaj — to him let us make obeisance.

2. On his either side are being waved gently, the two *'chowries'* (feather-brushes) of steadfast devotion and *'Sahaj-Sthiti'* (*Sahaj-Samadhi*); and fanning him with great reverence are *'Swanubhuti'* (direct intuitive perception of the divine) and instant experience.

3. Self-absorption is the royal parasol over his head; peaceful, benign feelings are the staff in the hands of his royal staff-bearers. The *'Shadripus'*[1] and *Maya*, temptations, etc., will not endure here, even for a moment.

4. Oh, for the splendour of his royal court! Four (*Vedas*), six (*Darshanas*), eighteen (*Puranas*) are the royal minstrels that sing his praises. The radiance of Pure Knowledge forms the brilliant awning overhead and Inner Bliss, dense and thick, suffuses the atmosphere.

5. Detachment, devotion, Pure Knowledge; listening, reflection, contemplation, incessant concentration on the Self and actual

Perception of God, — these are his eight ministers of State, engaged in his service.

6. He whose throat is adorned by the divine gems — Peace and Self-restraint — whose melodious speech transports the nectar from the Ocean of *Vedanta*;

7. At the sight of whose hand, raised high, to strike with the lustrous, sharp-edged sword of Knowledge, the tree of worldly life, which trembles with fear;

8. Glory be to such a one as you, O Pure Immortal *Yogiraya*, who are beyond the *gunas* and have assumed this human form only for the benefit of others and for the upliftment of the meek and the poor.

9. In the last chapter, the story was narrated of how, for confirming the devotee in his faith, Baba brought about the fulfilment of his vow and gave him the mark that he knew his secret.

10. The Sadguru is for ever satiated in all his desires. How can a devotee then, satisfy his desires? In fact, it is the guru who satisfies the devotee's wish of serving the guru, thereby making him free of all desires.

11. A flower, a leaf, when offered with true devotion, will be lovingly accepted by him. The same, when offered with pride and conceit, he will spurn, turning his head away, at once.

12. He who is the Ocean of Truth, Knowledge and Joy, of what importance are to him these details of ritualistic worship? But, when offered with faith and devotion, he accepts them gladly.

13. Under the cover of not knowing anything, he, in reality, removes ignorance and gives us knowledge. Without transgressing the limits set by the *Shastras*, he imparts instruction to his devotees in a pleasant manner.

14. When he is served faithfully, the worshipper experiences oneness with the Brahman. Abandon all other means and serve the guru in utmost humility.

15. Slightest negligence in that service or even a suspicion of over-smartness in it, will only harm the Seeker. What is needed here is steadfast faith in the guru.

16. Moreover, what does a devotee do by his own efforts? Nay, it is the Sadguru who facilitates whatever he does. For the devotee does not know his own difficulties and it is the guru who helps him overcome them, though he does not know it.

17. There is no other benefactor in all the three worlds, than the guru, himself. Let us then surrender whole-heartedly to him, who is the greatest, everlasting Refuge of the Supplicants.

18. If the guru were to be compared to the *Chintamani*[2], that divine gem will grant you only what you wish for; whereas, to the astonishment of the devotee, the guru will grant him the most inconceivable of things!

19. If compared to the *Kalpataru*, that Wishing-Tree of Indra's heaven satisfies only what the devotee desires, but Gururaya gives to him the most unimaginable state of '*Nirvikalpa*' or Superconsciousness.

20. '*Kamadhenu*', the wish-fulfilling Cow, instantly gives whatever is wished for, but far greater than her is the Guru, the Divine Cow. Who else but he can be adorned with the title, 'The giver of the Inconceivable'?

21. And now I have only one request to make to the listeners — to listen attentively to the story which I said at the end of the last chapter that I would narrate — the story about the man who came to Baba desiring to know the Brahman.

22. Listen now, to the *summum bonum* of life; as to how Baba satisfied the man who came to him with a fond wish to get *Brahma-jnana* and how Baba instructed him and also his own devotees.

23. Saints are always free from desires, being completely satiated, already. But the devotees are full of desires, which always remain unfulfilled.

24. Some ask for a son, some for an everlasting kingdom. Some wish to have faith and devotion; but only rarely will one ask for liberation from the worldly life.

25. One such devotee of simple faith, but who was always engrossed in accumulating wealth, once had a strong urge to take Baba's *darshan*, as he had heard of Baba's great renown.

26. At home he had everything in abundance — wealth, children, a host of servants. Yet he wished to have Baba's *darshan* as Baba was the very image of Munificence.

27. 'Baba', he thought, 'is a great *Brahma-Jnani*, the brightest gem among the *sadhus* and saints. Let me place my head on his feet, for his ways are just inscrutable!

28. I want for nothing, so let me ask for *Brahma-Jnana*[3]. If I can get even this, very easily, I shall be blessed, indeed!'

29. His friend then said to him, 'It is not easy to know the Brahman. And to a greedy person like you, it is most difficult that it should reveal itself.

30. 'You who know no other source of happiness except wealth, wife and children, and the like — Brahman, to you, is an aberration. How will it bring you any peace or happiness?

31. 'When the bodily organs become feeble, the world does not care for you. It is then that the idle mind whiles away its time, spinning away the yarn of the Brahman.

32. 'Of such a kind is your curiosity about the Brahman. Miserly that you are, and reluctant to part with even a pice, you will not find anyone who will satisfy your wish.'

33. However, with such a desire in his heart, the Seeker of Brahman set out to go to Shirdi, having engaged a *tonga* for the return journey, too! And thus he arrived at Sai's feet.

34. He took Sai's *darshan* and made an obeisance at his feet. And now listen, O listeners, to the sweet words that Sai addressed to him.

35. For, this *Kalpataru* of Sai's tales, when watered by the water of attentive listening, will take a firm root and as the listener's reverence grows, so will it bring forth an abundance of fruit.

36. It will become succulent in each and every part, will blossom into fragrant flowers, will bow down with the weight of delicious fruit and the desire of the Enjoyers will be satisfied.

37. So he said, 'Baba, please show me the Brahman! With this sole desire in my heart have I come. People say that Shirdi Baba shows Brahman without any delay.

38. 'Hence I have come all this long way and after my journey I am very tired. But if I can now attain that Brahman I will have accomplished the object of all my efforts.'

39. Baba said, "Do not worry, I will show you the Brahman promptly, at once! There is no question of credit dealings here. But oh, it is people like you who ask for Brahman, who are rare!

40. "People do ask for an abundance of wealth and prosperity, or for the cure of disease, removal of difficulties, or for fame, honour, power and authority. It is happiness that they always ask for.

41. "People come running to Shirdi, only to ask for material pleasures and worship me, a mere fakir, for it. But no one asks for the Brahman!

42. "Of these (pleasure-loving) people, I have an abundance. It is people like you, who are in dearth. And I crave for such seekers after the Brahman, meeting whom is a *'Parvakal'*[4] for me.

43. "By the fear of this Brahman the Sun and the Moon move in their set orbits, rising and setting regularly and the sunlight and the moonlight appear at their appointed time;

44. "So also the seasons, summer and spring and winter - come and go in their proper order; and Indra and other gods, the guardians of the people appointed to the eight directions[5], look after their subjects — all this takes place due to this Brahman.

45. "Hence before the physical body is cast off, a wise man attains the highest objective of life, i.e. Brahman. Or else, the continuous cycle of birth and death pursues him relentlessly.

46. "If the body falls, without having known this Brahman, the bondage of worldly life will follow and rebirth will become inevitable.

47. "I shall show you not only the Brahman but the entire coil or the essence that is Brahman, which is enveloping you from tip to toe and which I shall unwind and separate."

48. Oh! how nectar-sweet was that speech, a mine of the highest, the most incomparable Bliss, which had the power to uplift, even those who wavered in their doubts!

49. By the power of Baba's words, those engaged day and night in the pursuit of transient fleeting pleasures will also be guided firmly to the path prescribed by the *Shastras*.

50. If *Chitamani* (Ganesh) is pleased all the material pleasures are attained; if Mahendra is pleased the wealth of Heaven is gained.

51. But more remarkable than these is the Guru. For there is no benefactor like the guru who will reveal the hard-to-attain Brahman to his devotee, when he is pleased.

52. By listening to that sweet tale all the cares and sorrows of worldly life will be forgotten. Baba also knew too well, how to instruct the seekers of Brahman.

53. So he then made him sit down, engaging his attention elsewhere, for a moment, and making him feel as if he had forgotten all about his question.

54. And then, what Baba did was, he called one boy to him, saying, "Go, go quickly to Nandu[6], and give him the message, —

55. 'Baba urgently needs to borrow five rupees, so give quickly the money for the occasion, to be returned shortly'".

56. The boy went to Nandu's house, but there was a lock on his door. So he at once came back and told Baba so.

57. Baba said, "Go back, again. Go to the grocer, Bala. Maybe he is at home and give him the same message. Bring back the money, quickly. Go!"

58. But even this trip was wasted. For even Bala was not at home! The boy narrated to Baba all that had happened.

59. Baba sent him in great haste, on the same errand, to one or two other places. The boy grew quite weary of these unprofitable trips, but was not able to bring back even a pice.

60. Baba knew full well that neither Nandu nor Bala, nor any of the others would be at home. For Maharaj had intuitive knowledge about everything.

61. Himself a living, conversing Brahman, will Baba ever be short for a mere five rupees? But it was all a sport for the benefit of that Seeker of Brahman.

62. When a sweet dish or *seera* is prepared in honour of a guest who comes home, the feast is enjoyed by all the others, too!

63. Similarly, this *Brahma-bhokta*[7] was but a pretext put forward by Maharaj to instruct his devotees, for the benefit of all.

64. In that Seeker's pocket there was a bundle of notes worth more than two hundred and fifty rupees. And Sainath knew it.

65. And did not that Seeker of Brhaman know it? Did he not have eyes to see it? But the perplexity of his own doubts and hesitation restrained him, though the bundles of notes lay in his pocket.

66. Here he comes to ask for Revelation, but has not the heart to loan a mere five rupees to Sai, and that too, just for a short while!

67. Sai Maharaj, well he knew, was true to his word and the amount to be lent, just for a little while was small, too! But the moment he was inclined to lend the money, doubts at once assailed his mind.

68. After all, what was a mere five rupees to him! But even that, he could not bring himself to part with! Indeed, he was Avarice personified, who could not accommodate Sai for such a small amount!

69. Had it been any simple, trusting soul, who had genuine affection for Sai, he would not have been able to bear the spectacle of borrowing and lending, taking place before his very eyes!

70. He, who was thirsting after the *Brahma-jnana* so much, could not he have understood the question? I do not think so, at all! But he was totally engulfed by his greed for wealth.

71. And then, he could at least have kept quiet after all this! But no! He was in a mighty hurry to go back and said with impatience, 'O Baba Sai, show me the Brahman quickly!'

72. Baba then said, "And have I not made every effort, so far, to show you the Brahman from the place where you are? Have you understood absolutely nothing?"

73. For the sake of the Brahman one has to surrender the five vital airs, the five organs of Knowledge[8], the five organs of Action[9], ego, intellect and mind.

74. The path of *Brahma-jnana* is very difficult; it is not easily attainable by one and all. It reveals itself suddenly to the fortunate one when his fortune is in ascendancy.

75. He who is detached and is unaffected by the glory even of the *Brahmapada* itself, such a one alone has the authority to gain *Brahmavidya*. For he is totally detached from all else.

76. Whoever it is who gives the *Brahma-jnana* and in however complete a form, will he ever succeed if the seeker does not have even a trace of renunciation?

77. Those with the highest spiritual authority attain *Brahma-jnana* easily and without any difficulty. But those whose authority is mediocre always have to proceed slowly, according to the religious tradition (laid down by the *Shastras*).

78. For one it is as swift as the flight of a bird; for the other, it is a slow step-by-step climb on the ladder of religious tradition. But for him without any spiritual authority at all, to attempt to know the Brahman is altogether a fruitless task.

79. That there is no higher, no excellent means of attaining the Brahman without a discriminating knowledge of the real and the unreal, is no doubt, a very true aphorism of the *Vedanta*. But is such a discriminating knowledge in the power of everyone?

80. With deep study and arduous efforts, and when the physical frame is worn down to a skeleton, only then does it dawn slowly in the light of the Guru's Grace.

81. When *Brahmadeva* becomes egoistic and thinks that 'I am the Supreme God; I am the Controller', and he forgets his true Self, it is then that the Universe is created.

82. But when the knowledge comes that 'I am myself, the Brahman', then the Knower becomes one with his real Self and in that moment the illusion about the reality of this Universe is dispelled. So proclaims the *Shruti*.

83. Once the Self-awakening comes, bringing with it the feeling of oneness with the all-pervading Brahman, this Universe becomes the sacrificial offering to the Fire-god, i.e. Brahman. The Creation is thus reduced to ashes.

84. Such is also the condition of the living creatures. When their misconceptions are removed, their delusions about the rope, the sun-beams and the oyster-shell are at once dispelled.

85. Ignorance of its being an oyster-shell creates the illusion of silver. But a true knowledge of the nature of silver, at once, brings the realization that it is only an oyster-shell. In that moment, the illusion of silver disappears altogether and the oyster-shell is perceived clearly and definitely, for what it is.

86. It is symptomatic of reciprocal ignorance. Burnish the lamp of knowledge by scouring and scrubbing the impurities of ignorance, so that all the illusions are destroyed.

87. Had there been no bondage of birth and death, why would there be this determined pursuit of *Moksha*? What would our concern be, then, with the *Vedanta*? And wherefor this discourse on *Brahma-jnana*, at all?

88. But he who firmly believes and is determined that 'I am in bondage and want to be liberated', only he has the authority to be a seeker here — neither the totally ignorant nor the complete *Jnani*.

89. When there is no bondage, how can there be liberation? This is the real truth. Bondage and liberation arise from the association with the *trigunas*. Such is the experience of all.

90. But in the absence of any duality, who binds and who liberates? Here nobody is in bondage and nobody is liberated, once the feeling of duality disappears through non-duality.

91. Are the phenomena of day and night a creation of the sun? It is all a matter of the delusion of the eye, for the Sun is aloof from it.

92. When the joys of heaven and the sorrows of hell are experienced with the ego that 'I am the doer', 'I am the enjoyer', the intentness and attachment to desires increases.

93. The Self is constant, ancient and indestructible. It is without the changes of birth, death, etc. The letter '*Omkar*' is its symbol. It is continual, without a beginning and an end.

94. He who regards this body itself as the Self and feels that he is separate, the Creation is separate; such a one will never get Self-

knowledge that comes from Self-experience, however hard he may toil for it.

95. Conquer speech and all other senses; make a firm resolve of the mind; then extinguish the involuntary activity of that mind and hold fast to the intellect.

96. Intellect which gives knowledge and is in the form of Light; it is here that the mind should be concentrated. For, the group of all the sense organs, including the mind, are controlled by the intellect.

97. The initial source of an earthen pot is the clay. So is intellect to the sense organs. In the same sense it is their constant state. Such is the pervasiveness of the intellect.

98. By virtue of its all-pervasive nature, the intellect fills all the senses, like the mind, etc. Hence, merge this intellect into the all-pervading Divine Consciousness and that Divine Principle into the Self.

99. When a sum-total is made in this way, the true nature of the Self is revealed, with a certainty. And then, the silver of the oyster-shell, the mirage in the sand, the serpent in the rope become only optical illusions.

100. It is this Self, complete, not with any distinguishing quality, without birth and death, that we must realize, to attain our lasting good. So say the sages.

101. All effects have a cause; but the soul is self-existent and without a cause. It is ancient, but from the beginning It is new and beyond past, present and future. By Its very nature, It is beyond the reach of the intellect.

102. Inviolable as the sky, beyond birth and death, Self-sustained and pure, Its support is 'Om Pranava'.

103. The Infinite Brahman is to be known; the Brahman which becomes finite, is to be attained. Its symbol 'Om' is to be meditated upon and to be worshipped, always.

104. 'Omkar' in the form of Pranava or Brahman is the essence of all the Vedas, and the ascertainment of its meaning is the real contemplation of the Mahavakyas[10] of the Vedas.

105. That which the *Vedas* themselves have established and which the Seekers achieve with the greatest effort and by observing celibacy, that is called the highest state of '*Om*'.

106. However, extremely difficult as it is to ascend to that state, it becomes easy to attain for him who studies hard, once he receives his guru's grace.

107. Beginning with the most gross among the physical organs, when an untiring Seeker, in his arduous study, reaches that most subtle discriminating intellect, he attains to that state.

108. Such is this letter '*Om*', to be pronounced through the speech, which is the sum-total of all forms of penance, the mere utterance of which brings out its essential meaning and a constant repetition of which will result in a Vision or manifestation of God.

109. Blessed is that steadfast devotee of the Sadguru, who will know that all-pervading Spirit, which is unaffected by the changes of growth and decay.

110. How can they, who are for ever afflicted by the threefold afflictions of *Adhyatma*, *Adhibhoot* and *Adhidaiva*, ever enjoy such good fortune? Such glory is only for the saints!

111. Out of ignorance arises the birth-death cycle and the only means to be liberated from it is the realization of oneness between the Brahman and the Self. This can be achieved through the saints.

112. When the mind is free from all thoughts of sense objects, and by repeating the Vedic aphorism, 'I am Brahman', the intellect tends to think the same;

113. Convinced by the truth of the words of the Guru and the *Shastras*, when the tendency to do *karma*, mentally and physically, ceases altogther, it is then that the Self is fully realized.

114. Only then is Knowledge attained fully and clearly. Salvation comes from the material means of sensual pleasure. The meshes of ignorance, etc., in the heart are disentangled and the Seeker enters the Unmanifest to become one with It.

115. More subtle than the sublest atom in the ray of light, so small and subtle is the *Atman*. Such is the definite idea of the *Atman*.

116. *Atman* is larger even than the *Brahmanda*, which is the largest among the large. But all this is only a relative standard. *Atman* is really beyond all measurement.

117. In subtlety, it is the subtlest among the subtle; in largeness, it is the largest among the large. Hence name or form are merely discriminative appellations, while the *Atman* is perfect and without appellations.

118. The *Atman* has no birth, no death; nor has it any causal origin. It is unborn, constant, indestructible and ancient. It is difficult to know it clearly, effortlessly.

119. '*Omkar*', the symbol of Brahman, is Its fundamental nature, which, it has been difficult even for the Vedas or *Shastras* to understand. Will it be then easy to know it, for one and all?

120. In trying to understand it, the *Vedas* were exhausted, the ascetics repaired to the woods; the *Upanishads* gave up in despair, as none could ascertain it.

121. To realize the true nature of the *Atman*, it is necessary to have an *Acharya*, who has realized the non-duality between God and the *Atman*. When even those skilled in reasoning gain no entry here, what to say of the others?

122. There is no place for logicians here, for they will be caught up in the whirlpool created by their own chaotic mind. Except the *Veda-shastras* and the guru, no one else has the steadiness of mind needed for Self-realization.

123. The innumerable stars of one's own intellectual speculations and theories cannot help one avoid the eighty-four *lakh* cycles of birth and death. It is enough to have that one moon, — the guru and the *Shastras* — and even the last traces of darkness (of ignorance) are then cleared away.

124. He who holds fast to his Sadguru will achieve with little effort what others fail to achieve with hard, painful effort. For he will receive the light of Knowledge or *Brahma-jnana*.

125. Where ignorance is removed without effort and blissful Self-Knowledge comes to stay, and the state of Self-absorption emerges, it is indeed the state for which *Moksha* is just another name.

126. This, and this alone, is the most desirable, the highest goal of human existence. It is for this that the *Brahmayogis*, who strive to be one with the Brahman, and the Seekers, who are constantly Self-absorbed, made great efforts.

127. He who turns away from the Self is caught up in the tumult of sensual desires. But once he is firmly concentrated in his true Self, his sensual desires become weak.

128. For one who has turned away from his Self, the sensual pleasures are near at hand. But the moment he turns inwards to his true Self, the sensual desires turn away from him.

129. He, who desires nothing but *Moksha* and has no other desires in his mind, has no temptations either in this world or in the next, - he alone is deserving of *Moksha* or Salvation.

130. Know this clearly, that he, who lacks even in one of these qualities, is not a true Seeker. He only pretends to be a Seeker as a man, blind in one eye, pretends to see.[11]

131. Unless the ego completely falls off, unless greed is totally eradicated, and the mind is detached and free of desires, *Brahma-jnana* will not be firmly imprinted.

132. Identification of the Self with the body is itself a delusion. Attachment to anything is a bondage. Give up these promptings of sensual desires and their memory, and you will attain the Brahman.

133. Brahman, in its attributeless state, is difficult to realize. Hence wise men know the inportance of Brahman in its manifest, finite form and consider its worship to be their *dharma*.

134. *Vedantins* know this truth that the *Atman* dwells in all creatures secretly, mysteriously. But where is there undisputed proof of it that can be intuitively experienced by everyone?

135. First, the heart must be purified; over and above that, the intellect has to be subtle, sharp as the point of the Kush-grass. Only then will this *Atman*, in its thrice-purified state and in its kindness, reveal Itself, all on Its own.

136. The *Atman* is constant, unaffected by changes (such as birth, death, growth, etc.). The Self-realized never grieves and he alone

is truly courageous and wise and is, for ever, liberated from worldly life.

137. The skill, the fluency of a '*pravachan*', or the power of grasping the significance of books is of no avail. Even an intimate knowledge of *Vedas* and *Shrutis* will not explain anything.

138. The *Atman* is constant and free from changes of form or nature; the body is transitory and subject to continual changes. Knowing this, he who works for his own good is aware, all the time, of what is proper or improper in his actions.

139. The Self-realized is always fearless and knows that he alone is and that nothing else exists apart from himself. When duality is thus wiped out, totally, destruction of all sorrow results, most certainly.

140. Although it is difficult to know the *Atman*, which cannot be known by listening to '*pravachans*'; though mere intellect is of no use in trying to understand It, yet It can be easily realized when proper means are pursued.

141. He who is always without desires, except for the one desire for Self-knowledge, such a one, when he constantly beseeches the *Atman*, he alone will gain this highest gain.

142. The *Atman* will bestow its grace on him, who bears in mind the non-duality between the Self and God all the time, saying to himself, 'I am He', as he listens to *Katha, kirtan*, etc., and meditates upon it.

143. He who has never refrained from sinful behaviour and has attachment; who is always unquiet and unmeditative, cannot attain this even by Knowledge.

144. He who acts according to what the *Shruti* and *Smriti* commend, and eschews what is forbidden; whose mind is always concentrated in meditation, such a one has the *Atman* in his power.

145. He who is free from sinful behaviour, and surrenders himself humbly at the feet of the Guru, whose desire for the fruit of action has ceased, only such a one can attain the *Atman*.

146. Without becoming free from sensual desires, without desiring anything else but the *Atman*, and without a cessation of all the

natural propensities and affections of the mind, it is very difficult to know the *Atman*.

147. Seeing the austerity and penance of the Seeker, the *Atman* Itself will be roused to pity and only then will It manifest Its true nature. But this is not easy at all, unless one has a guru.

148. Hence, to know the Self or *Atman*, a Seeker should listen to sacred texts, contemplate on them, bearing in mind, constantly, the principle of non-duality. Only then will Self-knowledge come easily.

149. This worldly life is filled with ignorance and its widely spread manifestation also originates from ignorance. Know well, that without Knowledge, *Moksha* or Salvation has no place, at all.

150. To experience the truth of the *Shastras*, reasoning power and ingenuity of mind are necessary. But Knowledge comes only after the illusion of worldly life is destroyed, without which it is impossible.

151. He alone is a great soul, who moves in the world realizing that every living being, a saint or a sinner, is God Himself. For he alone sees the non-duality between God and His creatures.

152. The experience of oneness between God and the Self is the end of all knowledge. Once Self-knowledge comes, all ignorance will disappear.

153. When the Self is realized fully, nothing more remains to be known. Due to his actual, personal experience, everything is known to the Seeker, as a thing in the palm of his hand.

154. He enjoys the fruit of this *Brahma-jnana* in his complete liberation from the worldly life; in an immediate experience of Bliss and an abundance of *Moksha*.

155. It is only to enable the intellect to comprehend its all-pervasiveness that the *Atman* is described as 'subtler even than the subtle and larger even than the large'.

156. In itself the *Atman* is neither subtle nor large; the distinction of comparative size is here imaginary. This *Atman* fully pervades the whole creation, from *Brahmadev* to the tiniest shrub.

157. Indescribable as this *Atman* is, and though It is in Itself infinite, It is limited by putting It into speech, so that the intellect may be able to grasp it.

158. The true essence of the *Atman* will never be grasped on the strength of a powerful intellect. Its attainment comes from the grace of *sadhus*, saints and the Sadguru, which is the fruit of devoted service to them.

159. Is there any dearth of ready, detailed descriptions of the Brahman in the sacred books and *pothis*? But so long as the Sadguru does not bestow his grace, however hard one may try, one can never attain the Brahman, to the end of this world.

160. In the absence of the daily religious rituals and observances, when the mind is not purified by their influence, the Brahman can never be known and experienced.

161. It is a truth thrice-proclaimed that only the Brahman is constant; all else is transient. All that meets the eye is without constancy.

162. Rare is the speaker who can describe the Brahman. Rare also is the listener who is pure of heart. But rarer still it is, to get the Sadguru who is loving and Self-experienced.

163. Is Brahman a thing to be got for the asking? Great *yogis* inhabiting secluded mountains and caverns, caught up in self-imposed austerities and disciplines and engrossed in deep meditation;

164. Even they have not been able to perceive the Brahman without the guru's grace; then how can It be attained by a person like you, who are a personification of Greed itself?

165. He, who has a never-ending attachment to wealth, can never, even to the end of the world, attain *Brahma-jnana*. Know this to be a certainty.

166. While listening to the spiritual discourse, when the mind yet meditates on sensual pleasures and reflects incessantly on matters of worldly life, then the self-realization that comes, is also of the same kind.

167. Impure negative emotions (like anger, envy, etc.), ascription of the false (*vikshep*) and veiling of the true (*avaran*) are the three sources of error for the mind. Actions performed without an

expectation of fruit remove the impure, negative tendencies; worship and devotion cleanse the mind of false delusions.

168. Proper actions and worship, performed in this way, bring maturity to the doer's mind. When negative tendencies and delusions are thus eradicated, all that remains is the veiling of the Truth.

169. And this veil, which is the root of all evil, is destroyed once Knowledge appears, as darkness is destroyed by the rising of the sun.

170. It is this Brahman — which, those proficient in the *Vedanta* have described as being characterized by Truth, Knowledge, Infinity — which illumines the *Jnani*, who becomes Self-absorbed.

171. The traveller, walking alone through a jungle, in the darkness of the night which is only partially illumined by the dim moonlight, is startled, mistaking the stump of a tree for a robber and hides himself, in great fear.

172. 'I walk alone', he muses, 'and am carrying money, too! He, like a way-side robber, is lying in wait for me. What is there to think, now? There is no guarantee even of this life!'

173. But suddenly, as a lamp approaches in the distance, and the reality of the supposed robber is revealed, his fear disappears and he realizes that the robber was only an illusion.

174. So, I have narrated to the listeners all the obstacles in the way of realizing the Brahman. In the next chapter, the nature of the highest Bliss will be revealed to one who seeks such Bliss.

175. Hemad rolls at Sai's feet and talks wildly, whatever comes to his lips. May the simple, faithful ones listen to whatever pleases Sai to make me utter.

Weal be to all! Here ends the sixteenth chapter of
"*Shri Sai Samarth Satcharit*", called
'*A Narration about Brahma-jnana (1)*',
as inspired by the saints and the virtuous,
and composed by his devotee, Hemadpant.

Notes

1.   The six enemies of the soul are: lust, anger, covetousness, delusion, pride and envy.
2.   A gem of Heaven supposed to yield to its possessor everything wanted.
3.   A similar incident has been narrated by Mouni Sadhu, an English disciple of Shri Raman Maharshi, in his book *Samadhi* (p. 99) and runs as follows:

'One beautiful summer evening, eleven years ago (i.e. 1950), when I was sitting at the feet of my Master (Shri Raman Maharshi), a gentleman entered the hall in which the Maharshi lived, sitting on his couch and giving his *Darshan* (or personal appearance), as the Hindus say. The man was a leading engineer from a large Western firm, which, I believe, delivered locomotives and other machinery to Madras. Hearing about the powers of Bhagavan, as well as being slightly acquainted with the so-called 'Self-realisation' movement in the U.S.A. founded by one of the minor Indian yogis, he bluntly, but with due reverence and sincerity, asked the Master Maharshi to give him Self-realisation, before the evening, if possible, as he had very important business in Madras, and had to return there, leaving the Ashram before sunset.'

The author comments on this incident: 'Men are liable to expect some thundering words from Teachers which will immediately transform them, and turn them into angels, despite the fact that they are still full of relativity in their lower desires and egoistic ways of life. This can never happen.

'Do not let us be like this otherwise quite decent man, but who was deeply merged in basic ignorance of the character, technique and true aims of a spiritual search and attainment.' (Mouni Sadhu, *Samadhi*, George Allen & Unwin Ltd., London, 1962, p. 99.)

4.   A holy day or festival.
5.   These eight *Lokpals* are: Indra, Agni, Yama, Nairuti, Varun, Vayu, Kuber and Eeshan.
6.   A Marwari shopkeeper in Shirdi.
7.   The enjoyer or experiencer of Brahman.
8.   These are the organs of touch, sight, taste, smell and hearing.
9.   These are: hand, foot, larynx or voice, generation and feculent excretion.
10. *Mahavakyas* are the four great aphoristic dicta which reveal the Supreme Truth. They are: *Prajnanam Brahma* (*Rig Veda*), i.e. literally Brahma is Pure Consciousness; *Tat Twam Asi* (*Sama Veda*), i.e. You are That Brahman; *Aham Brahmasmi* (*Yajur Veda*), i.e. to experience the state that I am not the body or the mind but the *Sakshi* which is Brahman; and *Ayam Atma Brahma*, i.e. *Atman* who is the *Sakshi* or Witness of your mind is the Brahman.
11. In another context Swami Sai Sharan Anand suggests that the deeper meaning of 'blind in one eye' is that the vision of life with only one eye, either that of '*nirguna*' or of '*saguna*', is incomplete. In the full state of *Brahmavastha* there is neither *dvaita* nor *advaita*.

17

A Narration about
Brahma-Jnana (Concluded)

MY OBEISANCE TO SHRI GANESH, TO SHRI SARASWATI, AND SHRI GURUMAHARAJ! TO THE FAMILY DEITY, TO SHRI SITA-RAMACHANDRA, MY MOST HUMBLE OBEISANCE! I BOW IN REVERENCE TO THE MOST VENERABLE GURU SHRI SAINATH!

1. It has been promised in the last chapter that in this chapter will follow a narration of the characteristics of the '*Shreya*'[1] and the '*Preya*'[2]. So now listen to it carefully.
2. Just as light and darkness appear, in their properties, to be mutually connected closely and yet are altogether different from each other, so are *Shreya* and *Preya*.
3. He, whose mind runs after *Preya*, is doomed to a fall by his own selfishness. *Shreya* is discriminating; *Preya* is indiscriminating.
4. The object of *Shreya* is pure knowledge; of the *Preya*, it is pure ignorance. The wise are never tempted by *Preya*; the ignorant do not like *Shreya*.
5. So long as there is hankering after gold and lust, the senses are attached to sensual pleasures and discriminating knowledge and renunciation have not been attained, till then there is a fondness for *Preya*.
6. The mixing of *Shreya* and *Preya* is like mixing milk with water. And from this mixture, as the swans of the Manas lake will only drink the pure milk, separating it from water,

7. So also will those of firm resolution, high intelligence; of discriminating knowledge and good fortune, be attached to *Shreya* and always averse to *Preya*.

8. But just consider those dull-witted people! In the interest of the material well-being, they seek sensual pleasures, animals, sons, wealth, fame and honour etc., and thus attain only the *Preya*.

9. Whether it is *Shreya* or *Preya*, even when both are comprehended for what they are, man, with an independent mind, has to choose for himself, between the two.

10. But, when faced with both, it is difficult to choose. And as the sense objects tend to triumph over dull wit, it is *Preya* that embraces him firmly.

11. The highest achievement of human life, however, lies in pushing *Preya* aside and welcoming *Shreya* — like the swan that separates the milk from the water.

12. Although *Preya* and *Shreya* are both within the power of man, a dull-witted, indiscriminating man is powerless to discriminate between the two.

13. First of all, it must be definitely understood in what one's *Shreya* lies. Only then can one devise means to completely overcome the obstacles in the way of its achievement.

14. It is here that man is confronted with the necessity of a powerful, determined human effort. Therefore, making a firm resolve of the mind, one must carry on the struggle for the achievement of *Shreya*.

15. Inconceivable are the turnings of the wheel of worldly life! It rotates ceaselessly, day and night, bringing upon man the intense suffering of the threefold afflictions, which cannot be averted.

16. He is harassed while undergoing such excessive suffering and begins to look around for easy, comfortable means of overcoming them.

17. Unbearable as this rotation of the wheel of worldly life becomes, he begins to look for answers to questions such as 'How can this rotating wheel be arrested? Is there any means to bring this about?'

18. If, by one's great good fortune, such thoughts arise in the mind, it is the beginning of human endeavour to achieve the highest good in this life (i.e. *Shreya*) and then, for his own personal benefit, such a man will pursue the proper means for his own goal.

19. This ignorance or *Maya*, which has no beginning, is as deceptive and futile as the illusion of silver in the oyster-shell or of water in the mirage. This great impediment of false, erroneous ascription must be removed.

20. It rains hail-stones of gold, but only in the dream. And one may collect them aplenty and with great effort, so that they will be useful when needed. But as one wakes up, everything is gone.

21. To desire sensual pleasures, already enjoyed or otherwise; to hope, to long for them or to wish for them — these are always the impediments. Therefore, eradicate them, first.

22. That which cannot be seen even in the bright light of the sun, where the intellect cannot penetrate and therefore turns back; where *Vedas* and *Shrutis* cannot even gain a foothold; it is that which the guru points out with his own hand.

23. Lust and anger are both affections of the mind which impede the attainment of knowledge and interrupt listening, reflection and *Samadhi*, in a trice.

24. Is it possible that camphor and the flame will ever push each other aside, when they come into contact? No sooner than the twain meet, the camphor becomes one with the flame.

25. He who constantly rolls in sinful deeds, which are prohibited by the *Shruti* and *Smriti* and knows not the right deeds from the wrong, what good will he achieve, though he may be a *Jnani*?

26. Similarly, he who is never at peace; whose heart is restless and whose mind is agitated by the fickleness of the sense organs, such a one can never be perfect in knowledge.

27. He who has a contented heart, who is a true righteous *guru–putra* and whose Self-absorption is firm and steady, he alone is endowed with knowledge.

28. Whether pursuing worldly life or the path of Salvation, if one has to reach one's eternal abode, one must become the master of

the chariot of this physical body. What can he achieve who is merely clever of speech?

29. Here there is no place for mere eloquence. Study is its essence. Let your body be the chariot in which you sit calm and steady.

30. Of this chariot (your body), let your intellect be the charioteer. And as for yourself, you sit in this chariot as the Master, with a mind calm and composed.

31. Then guide the charioteer so as to overcome the various traditional ways of enjoying sensual pleasures, which are difficult to conquer. And let the reins of your mind control the wild, wilful horses of the ten sense organs.

32. Though the horses will tend to run amuck, the reins will keep them in place. Entrust the reins in the hands of the charioteer and sit back, relaxed.

33. Only if the charioteer is skilled and efficient will the horses move vigorously and properly. But if the charioteer (intellect) himself is under the control of the reins (the mind), then the horses become feeble and powerless.

34. Only he will attain Salvation whose discriminating intellect, with a complete control over the mind and a total concentration of the Self, is at the helm. All the others get exhausted on the way.

35. He whose mind is always uncontrolled will never experience contentment and will not reach that state nor will he escape the cycle of worldly life.

36. And this highest, most excellent state appears, all on its own, resolving any doubts or questions in the mind as to where it really is to be found.

37. Here logic, reiteration to clarify, hearsay, statements or assertions and discussions will not help. Difficulties are removed only by God's grace. Debates and disputations are all in vain.

38. All the ingenuity of logical reasoning is of no avail, here. The most knowledgeable of the logicians are non-plussed and confounded. Simple, unquestioning faith alone, succeeds. Such is the marvel!

39. Different is the path that leads to the highest knowledge; different also is that intellect; and so is the learned one in the *Shastras*, who imparts this excellent knowledge. Remember this!

40. This priceless human body is being frittered away. Evanescent as the noon-shadow is this hankering after wealth. It is difficult to overcome God's illusory *Maya*. Know this and fall at the feet of the saints.

41. Saints are the Ark in the Ocean of worldly life. Be a traveller on it. For, who but they have the power to ferry you across safely?

42. He who can combine in himself the two qualities of discrimination and renunciation, will not find it difficult to cross the ocean of worldly life, dull and stupid as a stone though he may be.

43. The glory of the Lord is vested in the six excellences, of which the first and the foremost is the quality of Renunciation. No one except those of rare good fortune can hope for a share in it.

44. Without performing the *Karma* ordained by the *Shastras*, the purification of the heart will not come about, and know this, that if the heart is not purified, Knowledge will not be attained.

45. Hence remember that the root cause of all attainment of Knowledge is *Karma* itself. By performing the rituals of daily worship (such as *pooja, upasana,* etc.) and the religious rites on special occasions (such as the annual rites and rituals for the dead) is the only way of washing away the impurities of the heart.

46. In the heart so purified are born discrimination and renunciation and the various means like *Shama, Dama,* etc.,[3] for attaining *Brahma-jnana* are then attained. Thus while still in this body one experiences the state of the extinction of body-consciousness.

47. He who gives up the desire for the fruit of his actions, and the volition or resolve; who surrenders to the guru by concentrating his mind on him, will enjoy the full protection of the Sadguru.

48. He whose attachment to the outward worldly activities has ceased, such a single-mindedly devout devotee will attain wisdom (through Self-knowledge). No other device will work, there.

49. But even after attaining such Self-knowledge, if he behaves unrighteously, he will neither be on the earth below nor in the heaven above, but will remain suspended midway, like '*Trishanku*'[4].

50. It is the ignorance of man that draws him towards worldly life. Attainment of Self-knowledge gives emancipation from mundane life, — he is in the world, but not of it.

51. The Self-realized one is always without ego; for him there is no merit or sin, propitiousness or unpropitiousness. To such a one, then, of what importance is the gain or loss in worldly life?

52. Where the egoistic conceit of the physical body has melted away, renunciation comes to stay instantly. Know this for certain, that this is that state of Oneness with the Absolute.

53. Friends and foes belong to *Pravritti* or the active, worldly life. But *Nivritti* or the contemplative life is peculiar. When one sees the 'I' pervading everywhere and everything, what, then, of friendship or enmity?

54. Before this highest Bliss, the severest of the bodily sufferings is but nothing. And when such perfect happiness is found, who will shed a tear for the worldly, transient pleasures?

55. And such an excellent mountain of courage will not be moved by a fraction, even when mountainous worldly sorrows and sufferings come hurtling down on him.

56. God gives renunciation only to him with whom He is pleased; empowers him with the discriminating judgment and takes him safely across the ocean of worldly life.

57. He whose purpose of Self-realization is as clear as the reflection of a face in a mirror, will find a place either on this earth or in the '*Brahmaloka*' above — there can be no third place for him.

58. When gods are propitiated by performing sacrifices, one attains the '*Pitruloka*'[5] and enjoys the fruits of his *karma*, but does not get Self-knowledge.

59. Self-knowledge that one gets in the *Gandharvaloka, Mahaloka, Janaloka, Tapaloka* and *Satyaloka*[6] is very unclear and vague. Hence those who long for Self-realization desire a long life on this earth.

60. For here the heart is purified; the intellect becomes as clean and pure as a mirror and reflects the pure, sacred form of the true Self.

61. The knowledge of the Self can also be gained in the second region of *Brahmaloka*. But it calls for arduous effort, which is very painful.

62. Like a snake, *Maya* coils herself round and presses and squeezes the intestines within as she holds the body in a tight embrace from without. Who has the power to escape her?

63. "There you sit, watching with total unconcern, when in your own pocket you have fifty times the money I had asked for! Just take it out, now! There, in your own pocket lies the Brahma!"

64. As Baba said this, the gentlemen put his hand in his pocket and pulled out a wad of notes from it, counting out twenty-five notes of Rs.10/-.

65. He felt ashamed of himself, in the heart of his hearts, awed by this intuitive knowledge of Maharaj. Eager for his blessingss, he at once placed his head on Baba's feet.

66. Then Baba said to him at that time, "Wind up your bundle of *Brahma-jnana*! Until your greed is utterly destroyed you will never find Brahman!

67. "He, whose mind is totally engrossed with sons, animals, accumulation of wealth, etc., how will he get *Brahma-jnana* unless the impediment of wealth is removed?

68. "The temptation of wealth is very difficult to overcome; it is like a dark, deep river-bed of sorrow and suffering, which is full of whirlpools (of avarice) and infested with crocodiles of arrogance and envy, so difficult to battle with. Only he who is free from desire, will survive.

69. "Brahma is, for ever, at war with greed, which latter, leaves no time for concentration or meditation. Then how can there be detachment or liberation? An avaricious man is always negligent of prescribed rites and duties.

70. "Greed knows no peace, nor contentment, nor yet, freedom from care. Once greed is entrenched in the mind it sets at nought all the means of spiritual progress.

71. "He, who is always engaged in sinful activity, which is regarded as improper and therefore condemned by the *Shrutis*, such a one has no peace of mind.

72. "This is called a 'confused or bewildered mind'. Always engaged in sinful activity, rolling, for ever, in the mire of sensual desires, he is unmindful of his own good.

73. "He may well gain the wealth of Supreme Knowledge; but if he has no detachment for the fruit of his action, all his efforts for Self-realization are in vain; he does not have real Self-knowledge.

74. "When anyone asks for anything, the saints first see his spiritual authority and give to each only that which he deserves.

75. "He who is consumed by self-conceit, day and night, and dwells only on sense objects, the guru's instruction is wasted on him and he loses out on both the worldly life and the spiritual life.

76. "He who tries to enter the spiritual path, without his heart being first purified, only parades his knowledge. It is, in truth, a fruitless effort.

77. "Hence speak only that which will appeal; eat only so much as can be digested. Or else, it will result in indigestion. Everyone knows this.

78. "My treasury is full; I will give to whoever comes and whatever he wants, but first I see the capacity of the taker and give only as much as he can cope with.

79. "If you listen to this with attention you will achieve your spiritual weal. Sitting in this sacred mosque, I never speak an untruth."

80. With a heart full of faith, if you dive into the river of nectar that flows from the utterances of a saint, you will be purified both inwardly and outwardly, as all the impurities are thereby washed away.

81. Such is the greatness of Sainath; there is no limit to describing it. How can I compare to anything, the Incomparable One? He can be won over only by pure love.

82. Mother of all that he is, he is the repose of the afflicted and of those wearied out by sorrow and pain; he is the *Kalpataru* to those

who take refuge in him, providing cool shade and protection to the meek and the helpless.

83. One may renounce the world and, in the interest of one's own spiritual progress, retire to the solitary hills and dales in silent meditation.

84. Many are such saints, who only achieve their own selfish ends or their own spiritual end. But, of what use are they to others?

85. But Sai Baba was not a '*mahant*'[7] of that type. Without relations and friends, without kith and kin, a home or wife, sons and family, he yet remained in the world.

86. Collecting from door to door the food placed on his palm at five households; living under a tree all the twenty-four hours, with his scant worldly possessions spread around, he was teaching the people how to conduct themselves in life.

87. Rare indeed, are such magnanimous saints in this world, who have attained Self-realization and yet wear themselves out for the spiritual welfare of others.

88. Blessed is that country, blessed the family; blessed are those pure-hearted parents and blessed the sacred womb that gave birth to this precious gem!

89. Without any effort, this Philosopher's stone came in their hands, but many mistook it for an ordinary stone and threw it away. For a long time, no one in Shirdi recognized the true worth of this great Divinity.

90. He was like a priceless gem, lying in a dung-heap, which is discovered by children, who kick and throw it about, trampling over it, as if it is a stone.

91. So in this way that fond seeker of Brahman felt gratified on receiving Baba's blessings. We all go the same way — when the path is difficult, we just abandon it!

92. So long as there is enjoyment of sense experiences such as the sound of words, sensations of touch, inhaling of fragrance, seeing the external aspect of things, it is not possible to restrain the senses.

93. And unless the senses are restrained, the natural detachment from sensual pleasures, the realization of the true Self or Knowledge about its nature is also impossible.

94. One must first become free from all desires and then, surrender single-mindedly to the Sadguru. Only he who has such steadfast faith and devotion is deserving of Self-knowledge.

95. When the five sense organs, like the ear, etc., give up their attachment to their respective sense objects; when the mind, on its own, ceases its activity of making resolves, entertaining doubts, etc.;

96. And, in such a totally detached mind, when the intellect also ceases its activity of making resolves, then that is truly the highest, most excellent state or *Moksha* and that itself is the attainment of that Unvariable Brahman.

97. He also, and none other, will get Self-knowledge and will be truly a blessed one, whose intellect has ceased to resolve about anything and who has become Self-aware.

98. Having once turned away from the sense objects, the sense organs will turn to the *Atman* and only then will blissful joy be experienced — everything else becoming devoid of happiness.

99. The self is most subtle and difficult to perceive. Being covered by the passions and affections of the senses, it is most difficult to comprehend. Knowledge of that Self is the means to the Supreme Bliss.

100. He who is detached from everything in this world and the next, right to the desire for the most exalted position of *Brahmadev*, he alone is installed on the *Brahmapada*; he alone should be considered as liberated.

101. Slowly, the mind must be turned back from the sense objects and fixed on the real Self, so as to gain Self-knowledge.

102. Only the wise can enjoy detachment from the fruit of *karma*, in this world and the next, and freedom from the pairs of opposites, like joy and sorrow. This is the true path of Self-knowledge.

103. Who can really be happy in the scalding waters of the ocean of worldly life, which gets heated over the flames of the '*Vadavanal*'[8]

of the three worldly afflictions, *viz. Adhidaivik, Adhyatmic* and *Adhibhautik?*

104. To be completely free from all these, be blessed by Sai's grace. Read, listen to and reflect on his Life, with reverence.

105. If this '*Shri Sainath Charitra*' is heard by the listeners in the company of wife, sons, friends and relatives, they will achieve all the good that they desire in this world and the next. Strange indeed, is Baba's *leela!*

106. Only those listeners, faithful and devoted, who are fortunate, will listen to these stories. And as one listens with a tender heart, tranquillity itself becomes tranquil!

107. In the flowing waters of the spring of these stories, the salt of *karma*, good and bad, gets dissolved and by listening to them, comes before the eyes, the comely figure of Sai.

108. Listening to Sai's story destroys all sins; by listening to his story the listener is ready to fight and vanquish Death itself, and the listeners effortlessly have the experience of the highest happiness.

109. Listening to this tale purifies the heart; such listening releases the listener from the birth-death cycle and enables him to attain the highest state of *Brahmapada*, merely by offering all his *karma* to Brahman, without a desire for its fruit.

110. In this way, this desire to serve Sai will render the devotee desire-less, for ever. And Shri Sai Ram will give repose to his devotees, always.

111. O Listeners! read at least a part of this book daily, or listen to it; study it sincerely, reflect, and contemplate on it, ceaselessly!

112. Baba seemed to be repeating to his devotees the same famous *Taittiriya Shruti-siddhanta*, which says that 'Perfect happiness itself is Brahman. This I know for certain.' (*Taittiriya Upanishad,* III, 6)

113. "Do not worry in the least; always be full of joy; never, never worry to the end of your life". This is what Baba said, all the time.

114.   And so, the aim of this chapter is to ascertain the nature of Brahman so that it will be as a boat to cross the ocean of worldly life for those who surrender to Shri Sai.

115.   Baba used to follow the words of *Shastras* which say, 'Render good advice to others, again and again; always be kind and benevolent towards others', and Baba acted too, accordingly.

116.   'Is it consistent? Or, is it inconsistent?' All these are personal differences of opinion. But this book aims at what will please and benefit the common people.

117.   Such indeed, is the purpose here. Baba knew the cause and effect of things. And know this, that whatever was in Baba's mind would come to pass.

118.   Stories coming out of the guru's mouth should be listened to, and his inscrutable *leelas* experienced. And as many of them as can be remembered, should be collected together and narrated to others.

119.   When the marvellous tale of Sai's life is heard with reverence, the sorrow and sufferings of the narrator and the listeners are destroyed, bringing their days of mis-fortune to an end.

120.   Can there be one so unfortunate as not to be dazed by Baba's wonderful *leelas* or be becalmed by his mere *darshan* and surrender humbly at his lotus-feet?

121.   Pure and sacred are the tales of this Sai — to be listened to with a generous heart. When such a happy opportunity (to listen to them) comes, who will let go of it for nothing?

122.   Wife, sons, friends are as whirlpools in the ocean of worldly life, which is infested with crocodiles of passions such as lust, anger, etc. Its waters are, for ever, rising due to the big Timingal fish (various diseases) and are whipped to a fury by the tumultuous hopes and desires.

123.   Once in a while, one is seized by a fit of vexation and sadness and is caught up in the pairs of opposites that give rise to doubt. But still, one cannot bring oneself to snap all ties with them.

124.   You must remind yourself that you are yourself the pure Brahman, held captive by your association with the physical body — like

the parrot that holds fast to the perch in the cage, with his feet and suspends himself, head downwards.

125. You are deluded by temptations and *Maya*, due to which you have forgotten your real, lasting good. You must become alert by your own effort and turn to your real Self.

126. Delusions add to bewilderment. Know that illusions such as bodily conceit, the feeling of 'me' and 'mine' are all deceptive as a mirage, and therefore become detached and ego-less.

127. Consider carefully as to why you should get entangled in the meshes of 'I' and 'you'; free your feet from the bondage, O parrot! You can then soar high up in the sky!

128. Liberation implies bondage. Only where there is bondage, can there be freedom. Steer clear of both these states and abide in your true, pure Self.

129. But all such knowledge is relative. Joy and sorrow really come from ignorance. Rid yourself of this and acquire true intuitional experience. And *Brahma-jnana* will be near at hand.

130. So long as you have the feeling of 'yours' and 'mine', you are not really mindful of your real good. Give it up, fling away the avaricious attachment to the body and turn to your true Self.

131. If Kuber, in all his wealth, begins to go collecting alms, is it not a misfortune, an adversity born of ignorance?

132. Always listen to the sacred *Shastras*; obey with faith, the guru's word and be ever watchful to achieve the ultimate goal.

133. By observing this code of conduct, people will find the path of Self-upliftment. Thereby innumerable creatures will be liberated easily.

134. He who has an earnest longing, by day and by night, as to when the moment of release from the bondage of worldly life will come, will quickly snap that bondage.

135. Availing of whatever solitude that is possible, knowing firmly that this worldly life is futile, be engaged all the while, in study and contemplation of the Self.

136. Unless the devotee humbly prostrates, in total surrender, with a heart full of faith and devotion, the guru will not give him the store of knowledge.

137. Serve the guru whole-heartedly, surrendering to him your all; get him to explain matters of bondage and liberation; ask him questions about Knowledge and Ignorance, so that you receive the best fruit from the guru.

138. No one except the guru can explain who is *Atman* and who is *Paramatman*. And the guru too, will not impart even a particle of knowledge unless his disciple surrenders to him totally.

139. When anyone else, other than the guru, gives knowledge, it will not bring release from the worldly life; it will not bring Salvation and will never get firmly imprinted on the mind.

140. Hence there is no knowledge without the guru and all the wise and learned people know this. Only the guru has the power to give the experience of the oneness between the *Atman* and the Brahman.

141. Show no unconcern, no disregard there; give up all conceit and ego; prostrate yourself on the ground, always, and humbly lower your head on the guru's feet.

142. With a firm and resolute mind, say the words, 'I am the humblest of all your servants and am fulfilled by reposing faith in you and you alone'.

143. And then just see his marvel! Guru, the Ocean of Compassionate Love will be stirred to pity and he will hold you aloft, catching you up upon his bed of ripples.

144. On the head will he place his hand of Protection, destroying all calamities and sorrows and burning down piles of sins, he will smear *Udi* on your forehead.

145. Thus exposition of the nature of Brahman to that Seeker was but a pretext under which Baba explained, in detail, to his devotees, the mark of oneness between *Jeeva* and *Shiva*.

146. Now, when Maharaj had such incomparable knowledge and profound wisdom, why did he give so much importance to jesting and joking? Why so much fondness for humour?

147. Such a doubt arising in the mind is quite natural. But when carefully considered, it will be clear that there is only one satisfactory reason for it.

148. When we are talking to little children and are amused by their childish prattle, can there be any serious, adult talk?

149. And is it because we love them any the less? So also are humorous jokes and jesting a special skill used to impart instruction.

150. Can a child understand what disease it is suffering from? So when it refuses adamantly to drink the potion of bitter drug or medicinal herbs, the mother has perforce to make it drink —

151. Sometimes by coaxing and cajoling; sometimes by glaring angrily; sometimes by resorting to the cane and sometimes even by a loving embrace!

152. But as the children grow older, even when you feel like petting and caressing them, you have to consider the sharpness or dullness of their intellect. The same is true of Knowledge.

153. The sharper the intellect, the quicker is the grasp; and it does not take even a moment to take in instruction. But with a dull intellect, it is a different matter altogether and calls for great effort.

154. Samarth Sai is a store of Knowledge. According to the intellectual capacity of each devotee, he first ascertains the purity and worth of the vessel before pouring in the wealth of Knowledge.

155. He has complete intuitive knowledge and knows about everyone, beforehand. Whatever is the appropriate means for each devotee, so he prescribes the discipline.

156. According to the spiritual authority of each, Baba considers their worthiness or unworthiness first, before taking on their responsibility.

157. Similarly, old as we may appear in years, but before Sai, the *Siddha*, truly, we are smaller even than a child, and so are always eager for jokes and laughter.

158. Baba was a store of humour. He satisfies the devotees by granting each one, in abundant measure, what he is fond of.

159. Intelligent and dull-witted, all will experience blissful joy on reading this chapter; all will want to hear more as they listen to

this and by contemplating on it they will have the satisfaction of experiencing Bliss.

160. Repeated readings of it will bring knowledge of the spiritual path. Constant contemplation of it will bring great happiness and everlasting, unhampered joy. Such is Baba's inscrutable *leela*!

161. He who has been fortunate enough to have this experience, in however small a measure, is sure to be attached to Sai with all his heart and speech and action. Inconceivable indeed, is Sai's *leela*!

162. Hemad surrenders at Sai's feet. Imparting knowledge through humour and laughter is one of the ways of uplifting the devotees. The seeker of *Brahma-jnana* was just an excuse.

163. The next chapter is sweeter still! The listeners will be satisfied. The secret wish of my heart will be bared and satisfied.

164. Listen carefully to the detailed narration of how I will go to Madhavrao (Deshpande) and give him Baba's message, after which I will receive Baba's grace.

Weal be to all! Here ends the seventeenth chapter of
"*Shri Sai Samarth Satcharit*", called
'*A Narration about Brahma-jnana (concluded)*',
as inspired by the saints and the virtuous,
and composed by his devotee, Hemadpant.

Notes

1. *Shreya* is pursuit of the spiritual.
2. *Preya* is pursuit of the material.
3. The six '*sadhan*' or acquisitions necessary for *Samadhi* are: (i) *Shama* — mental restraint, (ii) *Dama* — control of the body and senses, (iii) *Titiksha* — forebearance, bearing heat and cold, happiness and misery and all pairs of apposites, (iv) *Uparati* — withdrawal; abstaining from sense objects, (v) *Shraddha* — faith in one's guru and Vedanta, and (vi) *Samadhan* — concentration of the mind on scriptural or other elevating truths.
4. Refer Ch. 12, note 6.
5. The region or heaven inhabited by the *manes* or deified progenitors of mankind.
6. Refer Ch. 1, note 2.
7. A religious superior; the chief or head of an order of *Gosavis, Byragis,* etc.
8. A fabulous submarine fire.

18

I Receive Baba's Grace (1)

MY OBEISANCE TO SHRI GANESH, TO SHRI SARASWATI, AND SHRI GURUMAHARAJ! TO THE FAMILY DEITY, TO SHRI SITA-RAMACHANDRA, MY MOST HUMBLE OBEISANCE! I BOW IN REVERENCE TO THE MOST VENERABLE GURU SHRI SAINATH!

1. Hail to You, my Everlasting, most Excellent Sadguru! Glory be to You, O Sadguru, who are Parabrahma Incarnate, and who rule over *Maya*, the illusion of this world.

2. Victory to you, who are without a beginning and an end; who are beyond the pairs of opposites and are devoid of passion! You and you alone, can bring the realization of the true Self.

3. If a doll made of salt, dives into the waters of the ocean to bathe, would she come out? This can never happen! So it is with you.

4. You point out with your finger so effortlessly, to your devotees, That about which the *Vedas* and the *Shrutis* engage in debate, day and night, and that is the Incomprehensible Parabrahma.

5. Should it ever, by any chance, come to pass that one be caught up in your close embrace, then there is no place for petty considerations such as 'mine' and 'somebody else's'.

6. In the last chapter, the mysterious tangle of the Brahman was disentangled and clarified, and it was narrated how the greed of the seeker after *Brahma-jnana* was the impediment in his way, through a tale, most purifying.

7. Now listen attentively, O listeners, to the story of how I received Baba's Grace. It will reveal Baba's way of guiding his devotees.

8. This too, is a sweet tale. Which I shall now narrate, just as it came to pass. And the listeners should listen to it at their ease and for their own benefit.

9. When the listeners are eager, the narrator is eager, too, and is enthused as the hearts of both exude love, filling them with joy.

10. Without disturbing or unsettling the mind in the slightest degree, Baba, through his instruction, guides each devotee to the true path, according to his level of understanding.

11. Many are of the view that one should not tell others what the guru has told one. Or else the guru's words become fruitless.

12. But this is only imaginary and much ado about nothing, and hence, meaningless. In fact, not only such direct, personally given spiritual instruction, but also that given in a dream, should be conveyed to all, as it is good, beneficial knowledge.

13. If this be considered as being without proof or authority, then such proof is to be found in the wise Kaushik rishi, who narrated to all what was revealed to him as an initiation, in his dream, in the form of the '*Shri Ram-raksha stotra*'.

14. The guru is like a charged monsoon cloud that happily rains eternal Bliss on one and all. And is such Bliss something to be stowed away and hoarded? No, indeed! It is to be enjoyed to the heart's content and shared with others.

15. Gently lifting his chin, the mother lovingly makes the child drink the medicinal potion, all for his own good health. Just such was Baba's skill in imparting instruction.

16. His was not a mysterious or secret path. And now listen attentively as to how and in what way he fulfilled the wishes of his devotees, quite unexpectedly.

17. Blessed, blessed is the company of the Sadguru. Who can describe its importance adequately? As his utterances are recollected, one after the other, the enthusiasm too, grows in describing them.

18. When God is worshipped with devoted love; when the guru is served and worshipped with steadfast faith, then one can attain from the guru the knowledge that he can impart. All other means of attaining such knowledge are futile.

19. Ascription of the false (*vikshep*), and veiling of the true (*avaran*) make the path of worldly life dim and confused. And it is the guru's word that is the ray of iight to guide on the path without any impediments.

20. Guru is God Incarnate; he is Brahma, Vishnu, Maheshwar; in fact, the God Almighty, the Supreme Brahman is none other than *Gururaya*.

21. Guru is the Mother; guru, the Father. When gods are angry, the guru protects and preserves. But when the guru is angry, there is no one to protect. Always bear this in mind!

22. Guru is the guide in worldly life, — a guide in pilgrimages and vows, in renunciation, *dharma* and *adharma* and detachment. He is the expounder of the *Vedas* and *Shrutis*.

23. Awakening the eye of intellect, the saints reveal the celebration of the true Self. Extremely compassionate and tender that they are, they also satisfy men's desires and longings born out of devotion.

24. Then the desire for sensual pleasures subsides and one begins to talk, even in sleep, about Knowledge; and the twin fruit of discriminating knowledge and renunciation comes to hand by the grace of the saints.

25. The saints are like a *Kalpadrum* to their devotees. If one remains in their saintly company, serves them with loving devotion, they will prevent all laborious effort.

26. Therefore, always be attached to the saints; listen to their tales and worship their feet so that all the sins are washed away.

27. When Lord Ray was the governor of Bombay Presidency, and an enquiry had been instituted into the administration of Mr Crawford (the Municipal Commissioner), a well-known gentleman of the time became devoted to Baba.

28. Having suffered a great loss in business, he felt a weariness and disgust for the world and, realizing the futility of this worldly life, which is riddled with the threefold afflictions, he set out with a '*lota*'[1].

29. Greatly agitated in mind, he felt like going on a long journey to enjoy solitude. This was the plan that he firmly resolved upon.

30. When great calamities befall a man, then, in his utter misery, he remembers God and begins to call out to Him frantically, all the time, pursuing Him with great perseverance.

31. But so long as sinful deeds continue unabated, God's name does not rise to the lips. However, once it does, then seeing his love and devotion, God brings about his meeting with a saint.

32. The same was the case with that devotee. Seeing how exhausted he was by the worldly life, his friends gave him a piece of sound advice. Listen to it.

33. 'Why not go to Shirdi for Samarth Sainath's *darshan*? Do go there and pray to that most compassionate saint!

34. 'Even a moment spent in the saint's company steadies and calms an agitated mind, fixes it at once at the feet of *Hari*. And after that, it is difficult to turn it back from thence.

35. 'From countries far and wide, people flock there; roll in the dust at Sai's feet; obey the word of Maharaj and have all their wishes fulfilled by serving him.

36. 'Such is his fame! Everyone, young and old, knows him. If he takes compassion on you, you will be free from pain and suffering.

37. 'Nowadays, Shirdi has become a sacred place, with a continuous flow of pilgrims, day and night. You too, can experience for yourself, how beneficial the *darshan* of a saint is.'

38. As a sudden downpour from the cloud to a man impoverished by drought or, a feast of sweetmeats laid before a starving, ravenously hungry man —

39. So were these words of his friends to the ears of that devotee. He now wanted to experience it for himself and so he set out to go to Shirdi.

40. He arrived at the village, took *darshan* and prostrated himself at Sai's feet. His eyes were becalmed and he was filled with satisfaction.

41. As he looked upon the Perfect Brahman, — the Eternal, Self-illumined, Unblemished Form of Sai, his mind was overcome with joy.

42. And he felt that it was indeed due to the merit of his past births that he was able to meet Shri Sai, whose *darshan* had brought him peace and freedom from anxiety.

43. The surname of the devotee was Sathe. A man of great determination, he started a regular reading of '*Guru Charitra*', with great perseverance.

44. On the same night that he completed his reading in one week, Baba appeared to him in a dream and, *pothi* in hand, began explaining its meaning to Sathe.

45. Sitting calmly on his own seat, he made Sathe sit in front of him and, taking up the '*Guru Charitra*' *pothi* in hand, was all ready to begin the exposition.

46. Baba was reading the book, expounding its meaning like a *Puranik*[2] and Sathe, like a listener, listened calmly and respectfully to the *guru-katha*.

47. 'What is this reversal of roles?' thought Sathe. Greatly surprised, he was overcome with love.

48. 'That you, O Compassionate One, should awaken those who, resting their head on the dark pillow of ignorance, incline towards sensual desires and snore away!

49. 'And it was in just such a state, O Merciful One, that you awakened me with a pat, to feed me the nectar of '*Guru Charitra*'.

50. And even as he was having this vision, Sathe woke up. He narrated in great detail all that happened, to Kakasaheb Dikshit;

51. And said, 'I cannot understand the significance of this. Only Baba has the power to know it. I do not know what is really in his mind. Kaka, do please ask him about it.

52. 'Should I begin another reading or is it enough, what I have already done? Please ask Baba what he wishes me to do. Only then will my mind be at rest.'

53. Seizing an opportunity, Kaka then narrated to Baba Sathe's dream. 'Baba, what did you want to tell Sathe through this dream?

54. 'Should another week-long reading be started or should it be stopped from now onwards? Please explain the significance of the Vision, yourself! And show him the way clearly.

55. 'This is my only request to you. Sathe is a great devotee, simple and honest. Have mercy on him and satisfy his wish.'

56. Baba then commanded, "Let there be one more reading. By reading this sacred story of the guru, devotees become pure.

57. "By reading this *pothi*, you will achieve your own good, God will be pleased and you will become free from the bondage of worldly life."

58. While Baba was saying this, I was pressing his feet. I was quite astonished to hear these words and a thought sprang up in my mind,

59. 'Strange indeed, are Baba's ways! Sathe's small effort bore fruit in seven days, whereas I have spent years together!

60. 'Sathe has done only one reading of *'Guru Charitra'* for seven days. But is there no consideration for one who has been reading it for the last forty years?

61. 'One enjoys the fruit of his effort in seven days. Another spends seven fruitless years. I have been waiting intently like a Chatak bird as to when this Cloud of Compassion will rain mercy on me.

62. 'When will that day come when this greatest among the saints will satisfy my fond wish? Will he ever give me spiritual instruction?'

63. Just see the marvel of Satguru Sai, the ever Merciful One to his devotees! No sooner did the thought arise in my mind than he knew it.

64. It is out of such ignorance (as mine) that crores and crores of desires — both good and bad — arise instantly in the mind and Baba knows them all.

65. Everyone knows surely, that our mind (being its own enemy) conjures up evils which even our worst enemy will not harbour.

And although no one else may know these, Maharaj knows them at once!

66. But that most gracious Mother overlooks all that is detestable, and encourages and motivates at the opportune moment, the good and the generous impulses.

67. And so, reading my thoughts at once, Baba said to me, "Get up, go to that Shamya (Madhavrao Deshpande) and bring fifteen rupees from him.

68. "Sit with him for a while, talk to each other about things. Then come back soon bringing with you the *dakshina* that he gives."

69. Sainath felt compassion for me and under the pretext of *dakshina*, said, "Go at once and ask Shama for the money on my behalf."

70. Once such a command came, who had the temerity to sit in front of him? It would only amount to disobedience! So taking his leave, I got up.

71. Then I set out, at once. Shamrao also came out. He had just had a bath and stood there as he wore his *dhoti*.

72. He had just finished his bath and having donned clean, washed clothes, he was arranging the folds of his *dhoti*, with the murmur of *naam* on his lips.

73. He said, 'Hello! how come you are here at this hour? You seem to have come from the mosque! But why does this restlessness appear on your face? And how is it that you have come alone today?

74. 'Come, come! Sit down. I have just bathed and have come out pleating my *dhoti*. I will just finish my daily *pooja* and return the same instant.

75. 'Even as you prepare a *paan* for yourself I will finish the *pooja* in no time. Then we can talk in peace and satisfaction.'

76. So saying, Madhavrao went in. Then I casually picked up the sacred *Nath Bhagvat pothi* which was on the window-sill.

77. I opened the book at random and the page at which I began reading, unexpectedly, turned out to be the same portion which I had left incomplete in the morning.

78. I was quite amazed! The reading that I had neglected in the morning, Baba made me complete, thereby disciplining me properly.

79. Discipline, here, means regular reading of the book selected. And when it is not completed at ease, never to move from the place leaving that regular worship incomplete.

80. Now there is another minor story about this *Nath Bhagvat*, which I recollect in this context, which cannot be left out. Let the listeners listen to it attentively.

81. It is this *Nath Bhagvat*, which is full of the nectar of Guru-devotion and worthy of Sai's favour, which Kakasaheb Dikshit used to read regularly.

82. The seed which Shri Vishnu sowed for the uplift of the world, in the soil, i.e. Brahmadev, came to fruition in the standing corn in the cornfield, i.e. Narad;

83. From which cornfield, Vyasmuni harvested and stored up the ears of corn, endowed with the ten excellent attributes, which ears of corn were then treaded and thrashed by Shukdev in the open barn, i.e. King Parikshit;

84. Which Shridharswami then sifted and winnowed in the scuttle-basket; which was then measured and evaluated by Janardanswami and from which Eknath Maharaj prepared a feast of numerous delicious sweets —

85. It is this very same *Bhagvat Puran*, the eleventh chapter of which is a veritable mine of blissful, loving devotion. And of this work, which is like Vrindavan, the sporting ground of Lord Krishna, and consisting of thirty-two parts or chapters[3] — of this work Dikshit used to do a daily reading.

86. During the day, he used to read this aloud accompanied by an exposition. At night, he used to read *Bhavarth Ramayan*. This latter work also became to Dikshit a standard work of true Knowledge, only by the guru's command.

87. *Nath Bhagvat* is thus the very essence of the nectar of loving devotion. It is almost like a second *avatar* of Jnaneshvari and

Nath Maharaj's great obligation on Maharashtra, in a concrete form.

88. After the early morning bath, Sai's regular *pooja* and the worship of other gods and goddesses, after the lights were waved, the *naivedya* offered to the god,

89. Dikshit would share with his listeners, the *prasad* of milk with light refreshments, and would begin reading the *pothi*, very respectfully.

90. Who can describe the sweetness of that book which led Tukaram, that great devotee of God, to undertake a thousand readings of it, in the solitude of the Bhandara hills?

91. Oh! What a divinely inspired book! And, what a steadfast, faithful devotee, Dikshit! It was hence that Sai Samarth had commanded him to read it for the spiritual benefit of the people.

92. There is no need to retire to the forest. God Himself appears in this *Uddhav-geet* (11th chapter of the *Bhagvat*). And those who read it with faith, attain God readily.

93. The *Mahabharat* describes the dialogue between Krishna and Arjun; but this dialogue between Krishna and Uddhav is even more beautiful. And it is this message that has been described in this *Bhagvat* by Eknath Maharaj in his language of divine love.

94. Thus the most merciful Sai Samarth would make his devotees read regularly, in Shirdi, this divine work, along with *Jnaneshvari* or Jnanadev's '*Bhavarth-Deepika*'.

95. Baba had told Sakharam Hari Jog to read it, which he used to do in the *Sathe-wada*, to the great benefit of the devotees.

96. Every day, Baba made so many of the devotees listen to it, with a sincere wish for their spiritual progress.

97. Unfathomable was Baba's skill in instructing his devotees. This he did in various ways. Whether they were near or far away, Baba was always with them, dwelling in their hearts.

98. Though he himself sat in the same mosque, he would delegate work to each and imparting his own strength to them, would get that work done through them.

99. To Bapusaheb Jog, he would ask to read the *pothi* in the *wada*, which Jog read every day regularly and an audience gathered there to hear it!

100. And Jog too, would go to Baba daily in the afternoon, after the meal, and after making his obeisance and receiving *udi* from him, would ask his leave to read the *pothi*.

101. Sometimes he would read *Jnaneshvari*; sometimes he would start a reading of *Nath Bhagvat* with commentary, with great pleasure.

102. After granting permission to Jog to read the *pothi*, Baba would immediately send many devotees who came for his *darshan*, to listen to it.

103. Sometimes Baba used to narrate brief stories and even as the listener tried to store them in his ears, he would say, "Get up; go to the *wada* for the *pothi*".

104. As the trusting devotee went to listen to the *pothi*, the story in the *pothi* would turn out to be such as would only confirm what he had heard from Baba, earlier, and its significance would be understood better and more fully.

105. To his great amazement, *Jnaneshvari* of *Jnaneshvar* or the verses of Eknath only reiterated the story that Baba had narrated.

106. Even when there was no specific instruction to read a particular portion from a particular *pothi*, Jog would unmistakably read what had a direct relevance to the tale Baba had narrated earlier.

107. These were mainly the two books which Jog read every day, both containing the essence of *Bhagvat dharma*, viz. *Bhagvad Gita* and *Bhagvat*.

108. *Jnaneshvari* is a commentary on the *Bhagvad Gita* and is also called 'Bhavarth Deepika', whereas the eleventh chapter of the *Bhagvat* is the very basis of Eknath's exposition of spiritual matters.

109. And so, in keeping with this tradition of the *Bhagvat dharma*, I too, used to read it every day. But on that day there was a break in my daily routine.

110. I had read half of one story and as everybody was setting out for the mosque, leaving aside the reading of the *pothi*, I also rushed there with them.

111. I wished to listen to Baba's stories, but Baba had something else in mind. That I should abandon the reading of *Bhagvat* halfway, and resort to other things, did not please Baba.

112. And it was for this reason, I feel, that he made me read the remainder of my daily reading of *Bhagvat*. Such are Baba's marvellous ways! Recollecting them, the heart is overcome with love!

113. The story about *Nath Bhagvat* ends here, and so does the anecdote connected with it. Madhavrao had finished his *pooja* and he now came out, and I said, —

114. 'Baba has sent you a message and so I have come to give it - "Bring from Shama Rs.15/- as *dakshina*".

115. 'I was pressing his feet. Suddenly he remembered you, "Go to Shama", he said, "and come back with the *dakshina*.

116. "Sit with him; talk to him for a while. After you have talked to each other, then you come back"'.

117. When Madhavrao heard this, he was very much surprised. 'Instead of the rupees, give him my respectful salutations as my *dakshina*', he said.

118. 'All right, I have taken with me your fifteen salutations. And that is over! But now, come soon and talk to me', I said to him.

119. 'Tell me now, what stories you will, and gratify the longing of my ears. Let us dive deep into the holy, purifying Ganga of Baba's glorious tales to wash away all our sins.'

120. Madhavrao then said, 'Wait! Just rest awhile! You know too well, how unique are the *leelas* of this God!

121. 'Take this and help yourself to the betel leaf — lime, betel-nut[4], kath, all the ingredients are in this box. I will just put on my cap and come. I won't be a moment!

122. 'Inscrutable are Sai Baba's *leelas*! Oh, how many can I tell you! And have we not seen enough already, since we came to Shirdi?

123. 'I am but an uneducated rustic. You are all city-dwellers. To you, what can I say of his incomprehensible *leelas*?'

124. So saying, he went inside, offered flowers to the gods, put on his cap and returned at once. He then sat talking to me.

125. 'Oh! His *leelas* are simply inconceivable! Who will ever understand his skilful ways? There is no end to his sport. It is he who plays the game and yet, is never in it!

126. 'You are all ardent seekers of Knowledge, one more learned than the other. What do we, the ignorant villagers, understand of Baba's inconceivable life?

127. 'Instead of telling his story himself, why does he send you to us? He alone knows his own ways, which are not human, but divine.

128. 'In this context, I am also reminded of a nice story. Let us then talk of something so as to make the best use of our time.

129. 'I will now tell you of an incident that took place here, before my very eyes. It shows that whatever be your resolve, Baba will see to its proper fulfilment.

130. 'Sometimes Baba also tries a man to the utmost; puts his devotion and love to a severe test. Only then will he give him spiritual instruction.'

131. The moment the words 'spiritual instruction' fell on my ears, I was at once reminded of the incident of Sathe's *Guru Charitra*; it was like a flash of lightning in my mind.

132. Could it be that this idea of sending me to Shama was just meant to steady my mind which was so agitated when I was in the mosque? Strange are Baba's ways!

133. However, I suppressed this thought that came to my mind. For, the eagerness to hear the story had doubled and I wanted to satisfy it quickly!

134. Then, as stories about Baba's *leelas* gradually began, bringing out his compassion for the devotees, they gladdened the heart.

135. He then related one more story. There was a lady, he said, with the surname Deshmukh, who suddenly felt that she should spend time in the holy company of saints.

136.   Having heard of Sai Baba's fame, the lady came to Shirdi, with a keen desire to have Baba's *darshan,* along with some people from Sangamner.

137.   This lady was the mother of Khashaba Deshmukh and her name was Radhabai. With unswerving faith in Sai, she took his *darshan.*

138.   She had a most satisfying *darshan*; so that the exhaustion of the journey was all gone and a loving devotion for Baba grew in her heart. But then she remembered the purpose of her visit.

139.   In her mind there was a keen desire to make Sai Samarth her guru, so that she could receive from him proper spiritual instruction which would make for her spiritual progress.

140.   The lady was advanced in age, but great was her faith and reliance on Baba. In order to obtain spiritual instruction from Baba, she made a firm resolve in her mind,

141.   That, 'Until Baba gives me independently some '*kaan-mantra*'[5] and thus makes me worthy of his grace, I shall not go anywhere else from Shirdi.

142.   'And the *mantra* should only come from Sai's mouth; for, taken from elsewhere it will not be sacred. May Shri Sai, the holiest and greatest among the saints, make me worthy of his Grace.'

143.   Making such a firm determination in her mind, the lady gave up all food and drink, and sat holding pertinaciously to her resolution.

144.   Already of an advanced age, with not a morsel of food in her stomach, she refused to take even a sip of water. Such was her faith and firm reliance on Baba's *mantra.*

145.   For three days, the old lady continued her fast, day and night, vowing to remain without food or water till the day that Baba would give her the *mantra.*

146.   Of what use was coming to or going from Shirdi, without taking the *mantra*? So she continued to adhere strictly to her vow, at the very place where she had been staying, determined to carry her vow to its ultimate conclusion, come what may!

147.   For three days, she undertook the penance giving up food and drink, at the end of which she was sad and exhausted and became dejected in spirit.

148. Madhavrao was worried. What was happening was not good. How could the disaster be averted? For the old lady was not daunted by the prospect of death.

149. So he then went to the mosque and seated himself before Baba. As usual, Baba enquired about the general well-being, with genuine concern.

150. "So Shama, what is the news? Is everything all right? That oilman, Narayan, has gone astray and is troubling me greatly."

151. Seeing the old lady's resolve, Shama was already feeling very sad. So he at once asked Baba, 'Really, what should be done now?

152. 'And what is this mystery of yours, O God? No one can understand your sport! It is you who bring men, one by one, to this village and ask us for their news!

153. 'That Radhabai Deshmukh, very old that she is, she has remained for three days without food and water and is fasting in order to win your grace.

154. 'The old lady is extremely obstinate; but her faith in you is unshakeable. And you — you do not even look at her! Why do you make her so unhappy?

155. 'As it is, she is all shrivelled up like a dry stick; she is obstinate, cross-grained and difficult. And it is obvious that without food, her life itself will be snuffed out.

156. 'And then it will be said, the old lady went to take his *darshan* with a keen desire to take spiritual instruction from him. But Sai Baba had no compassion and left her to die.

157. 'Baba, let not people talk in this manner. Why do you not favour her by giving her advice beneficial to her? Do ward off such an accusation!

158. 'She is left with no strength to struggle; and in great agony the old lady will die, bringing you into discredit.

159. 'The observance of her vow is fraught with great difficulties and we are greatly worried. If by ill luck, the old lady dies, it will be most improper.

160. 'The lady adamantly threatens to give up her life, if you do not favour her with your grace. Really, I see no hope for her! Do tell her something, yourself!'

161. Here we reach the limit of this chapter. The listeners' desire to know what happened next, will be satisfied in the next chapter, which is full of loving devotion.

162. The advice and instruction that Baba then gave so lovingly to that old lady, will remove all ignorance when carefully listened to.

163. Hemad surrenders at Sai's feet and prostrates before his audience, entreating them to be attentive in listening, so as to be able to cross the ocean of worldly life, effortlessly.

Weal be to all! Here ends the eighteenth chapter of
"*Shri Sai Samarth Satcharit*", called
'*I Receive Baba's Grace (1)*',
as inspired by the saints and the virtuous,
and composed by his devotee, Hemadpant.

Notes

1. A metal waterpot or drinking vessel.
2. A Brahmin well-read in the *Puranas*, who is a public expounder of them.
3. Though it is stated that there are 32 chapters in all in *Eknathi Bhagvat*, actually there are only 31 chapters therein.
4. Extract of *Mimosa Catechu* tree, used as an ingredient in preparing *paan*.
5. A *mantra* whispered by the guru in the disciple's ear for reasons of secrecy.

19

I Receive Baba's Grace (Concluded)

*MY OBEISANCE TO SHRI GANESH, TO SHRI SARASWATI, AND SHRI
GURUMAHARAJ! TO THE FAMILY DEITY, TO SHRI SITA-RAMACHANDRA,
MY MOST HUMBLE OBEISANCE! I BOW IN REVERENCE TO THE MOST
VENERABLE GURU SHRI SAINATH!*

1. More subtle than the subtlest, larger even than the largest is this
   Sai; from Brahmadev right down to a small shrub — in the entire
   Creation is this Sai.
2. And a desire arose in the mind to see with the naked eye, such a
   Parabrahman by endowing It with a form, a shape, a colour.
3. Hence the Sun-worshippers kindle with great devotion the wicks
   in the lamps to wave *arati* before him. Or, the devotees of the god
   Ganesh make his image out of jaggery, offering jaggery also as
   naivedya.
4. And some people offer to the ocean an oblation, holding its water
   in the palm of their hands. This appears, on the face of it, to be
   quite improper.
5. But highly powerful as the Sun and the ocean are, they are generous
   enough to see only the faith of the devotees. Where is the question
   of what is proper and what is improper, when their only purpose
   is to glorify the devotion of the devotees?
6. Though as a common rule, like-minded people with similar
   interests befriend each other, yet the conjunction of the body and
   the spirit is one great, inevitable exception to the rule.
7. Widely different though they are in nature, from each other, the
   friendship between the two is most extraordinary. So much so

that one cannot rest without the other; they cannot remain apart from each other, even for a moment.'

8. And yet, this body is destructible while the soul is without change and indestructible. But boundless is their love for each other. Hence these repeated revolutions of this wheel of worldly life.

9. *Atman* is a great power; but more subtle and unmanifest than It is the Ether. It is the *Prakriti* or the Unmanifest. The same is also called *Maya*.

10. Subtler, however, than all these is the *Purush*, where all sense-organs repose. This is the ultimate destination of all and this is the Pure Brahman.

11. Such is this *Atman* that appears to be bonded to the worldly life by *Maya* and one's *karma*, although in Itself, It is unchangeable, unblemished and pure as a crystal.

12. Red, black or yellow, a crystal will just reflect the colour in front of it. But in itself it is different from any of these colours, being pure and unchanging.

13. The mirage over the distant plain appears as water; the oyster-shell appears as scintillating silver and the sight of the coiled rope creates the illusion of a coiled serpent, needlessly.

14. Just as the ascription of a snake to a rope is, in fact, a baseless semblance, similarly, to the liberated *Atman* the ego that "I am the body" creates an illusory bondage.

15. The *Atman* has attributes different from the body, sense organs, mind and the vital airs. It is Self-illumined Pure Consciousness, without form and without change.

16. So long as there is conceit about the body, the intellect, the mind and the vital airs, there will also be actions or doings, and the experience of pleasure and pain. For a consciousness of these is inevitable.

17. The seed of the Banyan tree is ever so tiny, but stores up in its womb the power and strength of a huge Banyan tree. And the trees store up innumerable such seeds with the potential to produce crores of trees.

18. Thus each seed carries within itself a tree — a phenomenon which will continue to the end of this world! And the same is in fact happening in this world, too! Look at it attentively.

19. Consistence, fearlessness, emancipation, independence and the attainment of God — this is the fulfilment of life and life's ultimate goal.

20. There is no liberation without knowledge and without renunciation knowledge cannot be gained. But so long as this worldly life does not appear transient to the mind, the thought of renunciation does not arise.

21. For when one begins to consider the worldly life as transient, the illusory Creation around us confronts one and the traveller is utterly bewildered, not knowing which way to proceed.

22. Such is the illusion that is this Universe. It is *Maya* or the deceptive sport of the Almighty or the Infinite Consciousness. It is as a scene in a dream arising from the worldly life. And for such a delusion, why all the needless effort?

23. On waking up from a dream, the dream fades away. Hence he who abides in his true Self will not think of the material goals of worldly life.

24. Unless the knowledge based on experience, of the oneness of the *Atman* with everything, is gained and unless the true nature of the *Atman* is understood, there is no other way to wake up to the realization that the bondage of sorrow, temptation, etc. must be snapped.

25. Although Baba advocated, day and night, the greatness of Knowledge above everything else, yet he generally advised the devotees to follow the path of devotion.

26. He would stress the importance of the path of Knowledge by comparing it to a 'Ramphal'[1]; the path of devotion, he said, was like savouring a 'Sitaphal'[2], which is easily accessible and yet sweet and delicious.

27. Devotion is the 'Sitaphal', bright and clear; Knowledge is a perfectly ripened 'Ramphal', each more juicy and delectable than the other and deliciously fragrant.

28. When plucked before time and ripened artificially, the pulp at the core of the Ramphal gives a flavour, too strong for enjoyment. Only he who has the patience for the fruit to ripen on the tree itself, will savour its real sweetness.

29. When the Ramphal ripens fully upon the tree, right up to its stalk, its sweetness is exceeding. Fallen to the ground, its aroma is too strong, but when allowed to ripen on the tree, it is very sweet.

30. He alone, who lets it ripen perfectly upon the tree, can savour its sweetness. But the Sitaphal needs no such effort. Though not endowed with equal excellences, it is most valuable.

31. Ramphal has the danger of falling to the ground, nor is a *Jnani* free from the danger of a fall unless he has a perfect command over the *siddhis*. Even a slight negligence in the matter on his part will not do.

32. Hence Sai, the Compassionate One, explained to his devotees (the importance of) devotion and reciting the *naam*.

33. Higher than Knowledge is meditation, said Bhagavan Shri krishna to Arjun. Sai also prescribed it to the devotees as a means of snapping the ties of worldly life.

34. But now, I shall narrate to my listeners the story in this connection, which has remained incomplete in the previous chapter. So listen to it.

35. Old in years, grown feeble in physical strength, an old lady obstinately stuck to her resolve by beginning a fast unto death in order to get a *mantra* from Sai.

36. Seeing her condition, Madhavrao was scared and went to Baba to mediate. This is the link with the story narrated so far.

37. The lamp, i.e. *Sri Sai Satcharit*, has been kindled to indicate Sai's thoughts so that its light may guide the faithful devotees to find their way.

38. According to Baba's command, Madhavrao had begun telling me an interesting story, which I shall now narrate further.

39. He said, 'Seeing the determination of the old lady', Baba conferred favour on her and brought about a change in her thinking. And the story took a novel turn!

40. Later, Baba called out to her affectionately and said, 'Mother, why do you sit so adamantly observing a fast? Why do you think of giving up your life thus?'

41. He always addressed a grown-up lady, whoever she may be, as 'Mother' and an elderly gentleman as 'Kaka', 'Bapu' or 'Bhai'. Such was his charming form of address.

42. Affectionate as the heart was, his words too were melodious. For Sai was the Protector of the meek and compassionate towards the afflicted and the suffering.

43. And so, he called out to her, made her sit in front of him and passed on lovingly to her the secret key to his greatness.

44. And now, drink deeply of the water of the blissful Self-rejoicing, which Baba, the Cloud of Knowledge rained to quench the thirst of the Chakor birds, i.e. his devotees, to mitigate the sorrow and suffering of their worldly existence.

45. He said, 'Mother, tell me truly! Why do you inflict so much suffering on yourself? I am but a fakir, who goes round collecting morsels of food. Be kind to me!

46. Really, I am your son and you, my mother. Now listen to me. I will tell you a wonderful story which will give you great happiness.

47. You see, my guru was a great saint, an Ocean of Compassion. And I went on serving him till I was exhausted, but he would not whisper the *mantra* in my ear.

48. I too, had a strong desire never to give up his refuge and to receive from his own mouth a *mantra* even if it meant a prolonged effort.

49. Initially, he tricked me, asking me for only two pice. Those I gave him at once and prayed and entreated for the letter of the *mantra*.

50. My guru was fully satiated in all his desires. What did he want the two pice for? And how can I call him free from desires, who asks the disciple for money?

51. But let not such a doubt assail your mind. He did not desire money in the worldly sense. This was not his idea. What had he to do with gold or money?

52. Faith and Forbearance — these were the two pice — and nothing else! And when I immediately gave them to him, Guru, my Mother, was pleased with me.

53. Courage, O Mother, is really the same as this forbearance and patience. Never cast it away. Whenever faced with a difficult situation, it will take you across safely.

54. This forbearance is the essence of manliness in a man that overcomes sin, suffering and adversity; averts disaster ingenuously and drives away all fear.

55. Forbearance or patience alone, succeeds; it scuttles calamities away in all directions. The thorns of thoughtless indiscretion prick no one here.

56. Forbearance is a mine of Virtue; the queen of the noble, virtuous thought. Unswerving faith is its own sister, both being to each other, dearer than life itself.

57. Without forbearance, the plight of a man is pitiful. Be he a learned Pandit or a virtuous man, without it his life is futile.

58. Himself, the guru may be very powerful, but from the disciple he expects only a penetrating insight, unwavering faith in the guru and the strength of a courageous forbearance.

59. Just as a stone and a gem, both get cleansed when rubbed against the levigating slab, but a stone yet remains just a stone while a gem becomes a scintillating gem.

60. Both go through the same process of polishing up, but can a stone ever acquire the scintillating quality of a gem? Can it ever be transformed into a brilliant piece of diamond? The stone will, at best, become glossy and smooth, due to its natural properties.

61. And so, for twelve years I remained at the guru's feet. He reared me as a child till I grew up. There was no dearth of food or clothes and his heart abounded with love for me.

62. He was the very image of devotion and love and had a genuine affection for the disciple. Rare indeed, is a guru like mine. I just cannot describe the happiness I enjoyed in his company.

63. Oh, how can I describe that love! As I looked at his face, my eyes would be absorbed in meditation, giving us both an experience of bliss. To look at anything else, I just did not know.

64. Day and night, I lovingly gazed into his face. I knew no hunger, no thirst. Without the guru the mind would grow restless.

65. Except him, I could meditate on nothing else; except him, I had no other objective. He alone, was my constant goal. Truly, the skill of the guru is simply marvellous!

66. And my guru also expected only this; he desired nothing more than this. He never treated me with indifference or unconcern, but always protected me in my troubles.

67. Sometimes I was allowed to remain at his feet; sometimes, beyond the shores of the sea. But never did I lose the joy of his company. He was looking after me very kindly.

68. As the mother-tortoise feeds her little ones on her loving glance, so was the way of my guru, who looked after the child with loving glances.

69. Mother, accept it as the truth what I tell you, sitting in the mosque. If the guru never whispered the *mantra* even in my ears, how can I whisper it in yours?

70. Love in the mother's gaze is enough to bring happiness and contentment to the little tortoises. Mother, why do you make yourself so miserable? I really know no other instruction.

71. The mother tortoise is on this bank of the river and her little ones are in the desert, on the other. They are nurtured and reared only on glances. So I say, why persist in the futile efforts for a *mantra*?

72. You now go and eat some food; do not put your life in danger. Only just have steadfast faith in me and spiritual progress will come to hand.

73. You look up to me with single-minded devotion. And I will look after you, similarly. My guru never taught me anything else."

74. It is not necessary to know the elaborate means of Knowledge[3], nor is proficiency in the six *shastras*[4] needed. There should be a steadfast faith that guru alone is the Protector and the Destroyer.

75. Hence is the great significance of the guru. He is the very image of Brahma, Hari (Vishnu) and Har (Shiva). Blessed is he in all the three worlds, who realizes this important position of the guru.

76. In this way, when the old lady was instructed, and advised, the story was deeply impressed upon her mind. Placing her head on Maharaj's feet, she then ended her vow.

77. Listening to this story from the beginning and realizing its total relevance to my situation, my heart was filled with wonder and joy at the appropriateness of the tale.

78. Seeing Baba's *leela*, my throat was choked with joy; I was overcome by a profusion of love. The excellent lesson was deeply imprinted on my mind.

79. On seeing me thus choked by emotion Madhavrao said to me, "Why are you so overcome with emotion, Annasaheb? How is it, you have suddenly become silent?

80. "Innumerable are such stories of Baba. How many can I tell you, really!" As Madhavrao was saying this, the sound of the bell was heard.

81. Daily, before the afternoon meal, devotees would go and sit in the mosque and perform an elaborate ritualistic *pooja*, by washing Baba's hands and feet with water, by applying sandalwood paste, showering on him the consecrated rice, etc.

82. Thereafter, Bapusaheb Jog performed the '*Pancharati*'[5] with loving devotion, while the devotees sang *aratis*.

83. It was indicative of that *arati* that the big bell had begun clanging loudly. Heart's desire being fully satisfied, we too, picked our way to the mosque.

84. This *arati* was performed at noon by the men and women together, with the ladies occupying the mosque above, and the gentlemen the open *sabha-mandap*, below.

85. And then, with great joy, they would sing the *aratis* at the top of their voices, to the accompaniment of the drum-beat and other festive musical instruments.

86. When we reached the door of the *sabha-mandap*, the *arati* was loudly in progress; the steps were totally surrounded by all the men who had crowded together, leaving no room for anyone to go up.

87. I had intended to remain below until the *arati* was over and once it was over, then to go to Baba along with the other people.

88. But even as I said so to myself, Madhavrao who had climbed the step, held my hand and pulled me up too, taking me straight near Baba.

89. Baba sat on his own usual seat, smoking a chillim, leisurely. In front of him stood Jog, waving the '*Pancharati*', and tinkling the bell held in his left hand.

90. And in the joyous spirit of that *arati*, Madhavrao seated himself in front of Baba, to his right and made me sit also, facing Baba.

91. Then Baba, the Gem among the Saints, the Peace Incarnate, said in a sweet voice, 'Bring here what *dakshina* Shamrao has given for me.'

92. 'Baba, Shamrao himself is here and has given salutations instead of *dakshina*. These, he says, are in themselves fifteen rupees, which should be offered to Baba.'

93. 'All right. But did you talk to each other? Did you converse? Tell me now, in detail, what you talked about.

94. 'Let the tale of the salutations be! But did you talk to him? About what? And how? Tell me everything.'

95. Eager as I was to tell the story, the *arati* was being sung very loudly. But I could hardly contain the great joy within and it flowed out from my lips, unrestrained.

96. Baba who sat leaning against the cushion, now leaned forward to listen. I also put my face forward as I began to narrate.

97. 'Baba, all that we talked about there, delighted my heart. But among them, that one story about the old lady was really marvellous.

98. 'As Shamrao told me that story, I could see your inconceivable ways! It was as if you most certainly conferred your grace on me, under the pretext of that story.'

99. Baba then said most eagerly, 'Tell me, tell me that whole story. Let us see what is so wonderful about it and how through it I conferred grace on you!'

100. The story had just been heard and was fresh in my mind. Moreover, it had made a deep impression on me. I now narrated it to Baba without faltering. Baba seemed pleased as he listened to it.

101. Thus I narrated all that happened. Baba also listened very attentively. At once, he said to me, 'Keep this carefully in mind.'

102. Again he asked enthusiastically, 'How sweet is the story you have just heard! But is it impressed on your mind? Have you really found it meaningful?'

103. 'Baba, after listening to this story, I felt at peace with myself. The doubts, the distress in my mind have disappeared and I have found a definite path.'

104. 'Are not our ways unique!' said Baba. 'Remember this one thing. It will be very useful to you.

105. 'Knowledge of the *Atman* based on one's experience, is gained by meditating on it single-mindedly and such meditating itself is the act of propitiating it. It alone brings self-satisfaction.

106. 'Becoming first, free from all desires, the Almighty dwelling in all creatures should then be brought to the mind. The meditation will then be satisfactory and the objective of life will be achieved.

107. 'Know that that which is Knowledge incarnate, or Supreme Pure Consciousness or Blissful Joy — that is my true nature. So meditate on it regularly.

108. 'If this is not possible, then meditate on my manifest Form. Bring to the mind, by day and by night, my figure from head to foot, with all its attributes.

109. 'Meditating on me in this way, your mind will gradually concentrate so closely that the distinction between meditation, meditator and the object of meditation (the *Triputi*) will cease to exist for you.

110. 'In this way, when this *triputi* disappears, the meditator will experience the Pure Supreme Consciousness. This is the be-all and end-all of all meditation, for you will become one with Brahman.

111. 'The mother-tortoise is on this bank of the river; her young ones are on the other, without milk and warmth of affection. It is merely the loving glances of the mother that nourish and fatten the offspring.

112. 'The young ones are always intent on the mother; they need do nothing else. They require no milk, no grass, no food. To gaze at the mother is in itself their sole nourishment.

113. 'The tender glance of the mother is as a shower of nectar, which brings to the offspring the nourishment of Self-rejoicing. Same is the experience of oneness between the guru and his disciple.'

114. No sooner had these words come from Sai's mouth than the loud singing of the *arati* also ceased, with everyone proclaiming loudly, 'Glory to Shri Satchidananda Sadguru.'

115. The waving of lights and other ritualistic details of the *arati* were over, too! And as Jog offered lump-sugar, Baba put out the palm of his hand to receive it.

116. On that hand, Jog very lovingly put a handful of sugar with an obeisance, as was his daily practice.

117. The whole of that lump-sugar Baba then emptied on my hand and said, 'If you bear this well in mind, your condition will be as this sugar-candy.

118. 'As this sugar-candy is sweet, similarly the wishes of your heart will be fulfilled and you will be blessed with good fortune. All your innermost longings will be satisfied.'

119. I then made obeisance to Baba, praying for his grace, and said, 'This, your benediction alone, is enough for me! Please bear with me!'

120. Baba said, 'Listen to the story, contemplate on it and meditate upon it repeatedly. When thus remembered, and contemplated upon, greatest joy will manifest itself.

121. 'In this way, that which you heard with your ears, if you store in your heart, you will have opened up for yourself a mine of your own weal and all your sins will be washed away.

122. 'When there is a fierce wind blowing, the waves of the sea rise in lofty waves that dash against the shore instantly breaking up into innumerable bubbles that appear as froth.

123. 'Waves, bubbles, froth and eddies — all these are different forms of the same water. They are optical illusions and disappear when the winds subside.

124. 'Can it be said that these various forms had existed and are destroyed? Knowing them to be the work of *Maya*, their existing or being destroyed should also be treated as such.

125. 'Such are also all the dealings of the Universe. The wise and discriminating have no admiration for them. They have no attachment to the transient, but attain the permanent.

126. 'The importance of meditation is greater than that of Knowledge. But for that, the right knowledge about the object of meditation is needed. Thus, without a complete understanding of the Brahman, proper meditation is not possible.

127. 'Proper knowledge of the *Atman* based on experience is, therefore, the basis of meditation. It is also the *karma* or act of propitiating the true Self. But how can you bring to the mind or meditate upon that which is without any special qualities?

128. 'He eludes us. Therefore the innermost Self is God Himself and He who is God is also the Guru. There is not the slightest difference between these three.

129. 'When repeated contemplation becomes perfect and the difference between meditation and the meditator disappears, then the mind becomes calm and steady, like the lamp on a windless night. This is *Samadhi*.

130. 'Free from all desires, and knowing that He dwells in all living beings, that 'nothing exists in the world but I', when a state of

fearlessness comes, it is then that the real Self appears in the meditation.

131. 'Then the ties of *karma*, born out of ignorance begin to snap, one by one; the restraints of laws about what should and what should not be done are shed and the joy of complete liberation is experienced.

132. 'First, all the six *shastras* should be searched for answers to the questions, 'Does the *Atman* exist or not?', 'Is He one and the same, or does he differ from one living being to another?' 'Is he the Doer or non-doer of action?'

133. 'To experience the oneness of the Self in all beings is the utmost limit of all Knowledge. Emancipation and Bliss are really born from such knowledge.

134. 'To describe an elephant to a blind man, even if you bring a skilled orator like Brihaspati, his oratory will not bring to his mind the form of the elephant. What is beyond description cannot be conjured by speech.

135. 'Can the tongue of a speaker and the ears of the listeners bring back the missing sight? Eyes alone are needed to see the form of the elephant.

136. 'Without the eyes how can the blind man have the experience of seeing an elephant? Similarly, only when the guru gives the Divine Eye, will the treasure of Knowledge come to hand.

137. 'Sai Baba is himself a storehouse of perfect, complete Knowledge, based on experience. And to know his nature truly and completely is in itself the act to propitiate and meditate upon him. This is his true *darshan*.

138. 'To obtain a total release from the bondage of ignorance, desire and *karma*, there is absolutely no other device. Have this firmly fixed in your mind.

139. 'Sai is not merely yours or ours, he really dwells in all the beings. As the sun belongs to the whole world, so also does he.'

140. Now listen to his words spoken from time to time; though general, they are priceless. If you always keep them in mind, they will be fruitful and beneficial to you.

141. 'Without a bond or tie of the previous birth, nobody goes anywhere. Therefore, whether a man or a beast or a bird, do not shoo it away contemptuously.

142. 'Treat with due respect whoever may come to you. Give water to the thirsty, food to the hungry, clothes to the unclothed and shelter to the destitute. It will please God.

143. 'When someone wants money and you hesitate to give it, do not give, but do not bark at him like a dog.

144. 'Others may rebuke you in a hundred and one ways, but you yourself should never use bitter hurting words in reply. You will experience unbounded happinesss, if you bear with them patiently.

145. 'The world may go topsy-turvy, but we should not falter. Sticking to our ground firmly, we should calmly watch the sport of this world.

146. 'Break and demolish completely the wall between the self and this. Then we shall have a wide pathway to go to and fro, without fear.

147. 'The attitude of 'you' and 'me' is this wall between the guru and his disciple. If it is not pulled down, the state of oneness between them is difficult to breach.

148. 'There is no other protector except 'Allah the Master; Allah the Master'. Unique are his doings, priceless and inconceivable!

149. 'Only that will come to pass which He wants to happen; He will Himself show His way. The time will come, without a moment's delay, when our cherished wishes will be fulfilled.

150. 'By the bond of past births we have been fortunate enough to meet. Let us embrace each other with a heart-felt love and experience its joy and contentment.

151. 'Who is immortal here? He who has made spiritual advancement has found fulfilment. Otherwise the creatures live so long as they continue to breathe.'

152. As these gracious words fell on my ears, my eager heart was comforted. Thirsty that I was, I found water and was filled with happiness.

153. One may have unparalleled intelligence and even unswerving faith. But to enjoy the protection of a guru like Sai, a tremendous good fortune alone is needed.

154. When the essence of this is considered, what Bhagvan Shri krishna said in the *Bhagvad Gita* is absolutely true, when he said, 'In whatsoever way men approach Me, even so do I render to them' (*Bhagvad Gita, Ch.4, v.11*). The whole burden is on one's *karma*.

155. As your *karma*, as is the knowledge you acquire, as is your *sadhana*, so is your gain. This is the covert purpose of this chapter. This is the nectar-sweet lesson here.

156. 'To those men who worship Me alone, thinking of no other, of those ever harmonious, I shall supply all their needs and protect their possessions from loss.' This, the vital significance of the *Bhagvad Gita* applies here, too!.

157. On listening to these sweet words of advice, the statement from the *Smritis* comes to mind, 'By sacrifice shalt thou honour the gods and the gods will then love thee.' (*Bhagvad Gita, Ch.3, v.11*)

158. You start doing the press-ups (arduous efforts)[6], giving up all worry about the milk (fruit of your effort). For here I stand, right behind you, ready with a '*wati*'[7] of milk.

159. But if you were to say that I do the hard exercise and you empty glass upon glass of milk till satiated — well, such a thing I know not! One should always be quick and alert in doing his own work.

160. Know that he who considers this pledge of Baba as the truth and acts accordingly, will have found a mine of happinesss on earth and in heaven.

161. Now, once again, I request the listeners that they concentrate their minds for a moment and listen to a tale of my own experience, which shows how Baba strengthens one's good resolves.

162. Listen to how Maharaj encourages good deeds made into a regular practice by the devotees and confers his grace, even without being asked for it.

163. The devotee should, however, surrender to him single-mindedly and then see the marvel of devotion. He can thus experience Baba's wonderful ways, which are forever, new.

164. As one wakes up from sleep, early in the morning, if a benign thought arises in the mind, the same should be followed up resolutely.

165. These thoughts, when nourished, will make for great happiness; the intellect will also bloom, giving pleasure to the mind.

166. This is an utterance of a saint and I thought, let me experience its truth for myself. To my surprise, the actual experience brought great peace to my mind.

167. A holy place like Shirdi and an auspicious day like Thursday! I suddenly felt that I should start a ceaseless chanting of *Ram-naam*.

168. On Wednesday night, as I lay on my bed, I kept my mind engaged in contemplation of Shri Ram, keeping it going in my heart, till I fell asleep.

169. As I woke up in the morning, *Ram-naam* came to my mind and with the arising of such a good thought, I felt my tongue had truly served its purpose.

170. With determination, I steadied my mind and after the morning ablutions, set out for the morning *darshan* of Sai, taking with me whatever flowers I could get.

171. Leaving Dikshit's *wada* behind, as I came out from Butti-*wada*, I heard Aurangabadkar singing a melodious, beautiful *pada*[8].

172. If I were to express it in the form of an *ovi*[9], the appropriateness and sweetness of the original *pada* will be lost and the listeners will be disappointed.

173. Hence I shall quote the original in its entirety, letter for letter, which will delight the listeners to know the message of the original, in its purity:

> I am blessed O my Brother! with the collyrium of Guru's Grace;
>
> Now, I trust none other than Rama! (Refrain)
>
> Rama is within, and Rama is without,

> Even in the dream, I see only Sita-Rama (1)
> Sleeping or waking, there is but Rama;
> Wherever I look, I see only the Ever-satiated One (2)
> Eknath (the disciple) of Janardan
> (Swami) enjoys the purest, most holy experience,
> Of seeing Rama, all the time, wherever he looks! (3)

174. The mind had already resolved to make it a rule to concentrate on *Ram-naam*. And no sooner had I put my resolve into practice than it received confirmation from this *pada*.

175. As a result, a realization came to the mind that, maybe, the compassionate Sai Samarth is sprinkling the water of this *pada* on the sapling of my resolution.

176. *Tamburi*[10] in hand, Aurangabadkar stood in the open courtyard, in front of Sai and sang at a high pitch when I heard these sweet notes.

177. Aurangabadkar was Baba's devotee and, like me, attached to Baba. When he knew so many other *padas* by heart, why was he inspired to sing only this *pada* at this time?

178. No one knew of the secret resolve in my mind, why should he sing this particular *pada* then? As Baba pulls the strings so will the inspiration come to the mind.

179. We are all just puppets and Mother Sai, the string-puller. Without uttering a word, he unmistakably gave in my hands the best form of worship.

180. It was as though my innermost thoughts were reflected in Baba's mind! In this way, he gave me direct, definite experience.

181. Oh, how great is the significance of the Name that the saints and the religious teachers describe! What more can a lowly person like me say in its praise? It is only through the Name that Self-realization comes.

182. The two letters '*Rama*', chanted even in the reverse order, uplifted that *Koli*[11] and wayside robber, so that Valya became the sage Valmiki and acquired the *siddhi* whereby his utterances came true.

183. Chanting the name in reverse order as '*Mara*', '*Mara*', his tongue was blessed by Rama and even before Rama was born, he wrote Rama's life story.

184. *Ram-naam* purifies the sinners; *Ram-naam* brings great good fortune; *Ram-naam* is bhajan undivided; *Ram-naam* is the means to attain Brahman.

185. By chanting *Ram-naam* repeatedly comes liberation from the birth-death cycle. By just repeating *Ram-naam*, there is immeasurable gain.

186. Where *Ram-naam* is proclaimed loudly, there revolves Shri Vishnu's disc, Sudarshan, to destroy innumerable obstacles. Such is this *naam*, the Protector of the Meek and the Poor.

187. To instruct his devotees, Sai needed no particular place or time. All instruction came from him, while walking or sitting, with natural ease and clarity.

188. Listen attentively, O listeners, to an interesting story in this connection. It will bring out Sai's kindness and all-pervasiveness.

189. Once, a great devotee, while talking about somebody, was drawn into entertaining uncharitable thoughts and busied himself with censuring and criticizing.

190. The good qualities of that person were left out; criticism began to flow out of the mouth, full-force. The main topic of conversation was ruined, as reviling and criticism boiled over.

191. If there is some valid reason, if somebody's conduct is reproachable, he should rather be pitied and given corrective advice directly, to his face.

192. 'Never criticize or censure anyone' is something everyone knows. But when this tendency is not curbed, it cannot be contained in the heart.

193. It then rises to the throat and from the throat to the tip of the tongue; from thence, slowly to the lips from where it flows out happily.

194. In all the three worlds, there is no greater benefactor than the critic. He confers the highest benefit on him whom he criticizes.

195. Some remove the impurities or dirt by using 'ritha'[12]; some, by soap and other such means; some, by clean, pure water. But the critics remove it by their tongues.

196. They put up with their own mental degradation for benefitting others. Truly indescribable is their great obligation. The critics are undoubtedly, deserving of the highest praise.

197. They warn at every step; under the guise of criticism, they let us know our faults and thus avert numerous disasters of the future. Oh, how can I praise their generosity enough?

198. I prostrate myself in obeisance before the gathering of critics whose greatness has been described in so many ways by the *sadhus* and saints.

199. The listeners were disgusted to see all this. The critic then set out towards the stream for morning ablutions. People were already going to the mosque for Baba's *darshan*.

200. Baba had complete intuitive knowledge of everything and would give timely advice to his devotees. Now listen to the incident that he brought about, later on.

201. Baba enquired about that devotee (the critic) when he was going to the Lendibag with his devotees. They told him that he had gone to the stream for morning ablutions.

202. After completing the routine observances, Baba returned; the devotee (the critic) also turned his steps homewards from the stream.

203. With folded hands, I now entreat the listeners to listen to what happened at the time the two parties met each other.

204. In that same place, near a compound-fence, a village sow was feasting to her heart's content, on the excrement, smacking her lips. Baba pointed out that sow with his hand.

205. 'See how that tongue relishes crushing and mashing the excrement of the public, to gratify her inordinate desire of venting out her anger on her kith and kin.

206. 'He who fritters away this precious human birth which has come to him as a result of great past merit and is thus bent on self-

destruction, to such a one, what happinesss or peace can this Shirdi give?'

207. Baba went on speaking in this manner and the devotee (the critic) was stung to the quick. He remembered all that had happened in the morning. The words smote his heart!

208. Thus Baba instructed his devotees in different ways according to the occasion. When the significance of his precious words is carefully stored in the heart, can spiritual advancement be far behind?

209. The adage which says, 'If God's Grace is upon me, I shall get everything, sitting where I am and without lifting a finger', is true, no doubt; but only for food and clothing.

210. He who applies it to spiritual matters, will find himself cheated out of spiritual gain altogether. 'As he sows, so he reaps'. These are Baba's priceless words.

211. The more one listens to Baba's words, the more they make one sway in blissful joy and if the soil is soft with faith and devotion, the roots will go deep.

212. 'I am present everywhere — in water, on land, or even in a dry twig; among men and in wilderness; in foreign lands and in my own. I pervade even the radiant sky. I am not confined to any one country.

213. 'To dispel the misconception of those who regard my presence as confined to 3 1/2 cubits of this human frame, I have incarnated on this earth.

214. 'Those who worship me, day and night, single-mindedly and without any expectations, they overcome the duality and become one with me.

215. 'Sweetness may depart from the jaggery, the sea from its waves and the eye from its sparkle; but never will my simple, faithful devotee be without me.

216. 'He who most certainly wants to escape the cycle of birth and death, should make conscious efforts to be righteous by following the *shastras* and should always keep his mind calm and peaceful.

217. 'He should avoid speaking words which will sting and hurt and not strike anyone on the vital spot. But should always engage himself in pure, virtuous deeds, keeping his mind, all the time, firmly on his duty.

218. 'Offer your mind and intellect to me, remembering me all the time. Such a one will not care what befalls his body or when. Surely, he is without fear.

219. 'He who looks up to me single-mindedly, narrates and listens to my Self-purifying tales and is devoted to none other but me, his mind will become one with God.'

220. He kept on telling everyone, 'Take my name; surrender to me.' But to know who he was, he exhorted the devotees to listen to and contemplate on his stories.

221. To one, he advised *naam-smaran* (chanting the name) of Bhagvan; to another, listening to the stories of Bhagvan; to yet another, offering *pooja* at Bhagvan's feet — prescribing different rules and observances to people with spiritual authority.

222. Someone was asked to read *Adhyatma Ramayan*; another a reading of *Jnaneshwari*, with all its attendant rites. Yet another was asked to read *Hari Varada* while someone else was instructed to read *Guru Charitra*.

223. One was made to sit at his own feet while another was sent to the Khandoba temple. Someone else was forcibly but with great loving concern made to read *Vishnu Sahasranamavali* (thousand names of Shri Vishnu).

224. Someone was instructed to read *Ram-Vijaya*; someone else was explained the importance of meditation and *naam*. Yet another was told to experience with faith the natural sweetness of *Chandogya Upanishad* and *Geeta-Rahasya*.

225. To some, this; to others, that — there was no limit to his various ways of initiation. Some were instructed personally and directly; others received it in a Vision. The novelty of his ways was unique!

226. Devotees of every caste and creed came running to him for his *darshan*. He would even appear in the dream of one addicted to liquor.

227. Sitting on his chest, he would press him down with his hands and feet, until he promised, with his hands on his ears, that he would never touch liquor again, and released him only after he took the oath to give it up, totally.

228. Just as astrologers draw pictures of Hari (Vishnu) and Hara (Shiva) on the wall for marriage in the house, similarly Baba would write the *mantra 'Gurur Brahma'*, etc., for a devotee, by going in his dream.

229. If someone practised *yogasanas* or other practices of *Hathayoga*, on the sly, Baba would know it intuitively and would let him know it without a mistake, through piercing words.

230. Getting hold of a stranger, he would send the message, 'Can you not stay content with what you have? Have patience!'

231. To someone, he would personally tell in a peremptory manner, 'We are a stern and unrelenting class. We will try warning once or twice, failing which, we will resort to harsh measures.

232. 'He who pays no heed to our words, him we will cut in two and throw away, even if it be our own child!'[13]

233. Sai Baba was endowed with all the excellences and was a generous-hearted Mahatma. How can I, a petty, lowly creature describe his mysterious deeds? To some, he gave Knowledge and renunciation; to others, good thoughts and devotion.

234. Some, he disciplined into unblemished and commendable conduct in worldly life. I will just narrate to the audience, a pungent anecdote as an example.

235. Once, at high noon, one wonders what came into Baba's mind, but he came near Radhakrishnabai's house, quite unexpectedly.

236. There were some people with him, to whom he said, 'Bring, bring a ladder just now!' One of them immediately went to bring the ladder which he placed there.

237. Baba then placed it against the house and himself climbed on it to the roof. No one knew what plan he had in mind.

238. The ladder was, at that time, placed against the house of Vaman Gondkar. Shri Sai quickly climbed the ladder going on to the roof.

239. From there he went on to the roof of Radhakrishnabai's house which was next to Gondkar's. That roof also, he crossed over quickly. No one could understand this mystery.

240. But at that time, Radhakrishnabai was suffering from a severe attack of ague and was feeling very restless.

241. Baba could walk only if two people, on either side of him, supported him. When he was himself so feeble, from where did this strength come?

242. At once, he came down the slope of the roof on the other side, to its edge and got the same ladder shifted there, which he then used to climb down.

243. As his feet touched the ground, he remembered to pay Rs.2/- to the owner of that ladder, very promptly, without a moment's delay.

244. All the labour that he could boast of was that he put up the ladder at two places! And for that, why did Baba pay him so generously?

245. People were naturally curious and said, 'Ask Baba why he gave so much money to that owner of the ladder!'

246. Then one of them took courage and asked. Baba replied, 'Never take even the least labour from anybody, free.

247. 'Take work from others, but understand their effort. And make it a rule never to take anybody's toil free.'

248. Who knows the real intention as to why Baba did this? It is something that he alone knows. The mind of the saints is mysterious and incomprehensible.

249. Our only reliance is on the words we hear from his mouth and if we resolve to act according to them, life in the world becomes smooth and free from trouble.

250. And so, the next chapter is even sweeter than this. An innocent child of a maid-servant will solve the puzzle from the *Shrutis*.

251. Ganu Das was a divinely inspired Haridas, who resolved upon rendering into Marathi the Sanskrit Upsanishad called '*Ishavasya*', for the benefit of the common man.

252.   By Sai's grace, he wrote the book, but some profound significance
       of some lines eluded him, which left a doubt in his mind. How
       did Baba resolve it?

253.   Sitting in Shirdi, Baba said, 'When you return to Vile Parle, Kaka's
       (Dikshit) maid will resolve your doubt.'

254.   And so, in this chapter, Saraswati, the goddess of Speech will,
       like a black bee, fly humming and circling around the lotus of
       Ishavasya Upanisad, to enjoy the fragrance of which, the ingenious
       listeners should employ all their art and skill.

255.   So, this will be narrated in the next chapter. The whole and sole
       Doer of action is Sai, the Compassionate One. Listen to it, O
       listeners, at the proper time. It will be beneficial.

256.   Pant Hemad surrenders to Sai and bows humbly at the feet of the
       Almighty and also to the living creatures. May the listeners favour
       this sweet narration about Sai, with their attention.

Weal be to all! Here ends the nineteenth chapter of
"Shri Sai Samarth Satcharit", called
'I Receive Baba's Grace'(2),'
as inspired by the saints and the virtuous,
and composed by his devotee Hemadpant.

Notes

1. The fruit called Bullock's Heart or *Annona reticulata*.
2. The Custard Apple or *Annona squamosa*.
3. Refer Chapter 17, note 3.
4. Refer Chapter 4, notes 4 & 5.
5. A dish or platter fitted to receive five lamps to be waved around an idol, etc.
6. An indigenous exercise called '*Dand*', in which muscles of the limbs and trunk are exercised.
7. A saucer-form vessel of metal.
8. A variety of metrical composition used in hymns or anthems.
9. A *prakrit* verse. A light air sung by women while grinding or lulling infants, etc.
10. A small Turkish guitar with four wires.
11. A tribe with sub-castes whose men are engaged in fishing, agriculture, fighting or predatory activities.
12. Fruit of the soap-nut tree.
13. Prof, G.G. Narke of Poona Engineering College, who was a well-known devotee of Sai Baba, states in his testimony, 'When the devotee failed to improve himself, in spite of repeated warning and fell into evil ways, he let them suffer. His justice was severe. "You have to sever your child from the umbilical cord when it falls athwart the womb." ' (*Devotees' Experiences of Shri Sai Baba, Part I*, by B.N. Narsimha Swami, p. 39.)

20

The Essence of Isha–Upanishad Revealed

MY OBEISANCE TO SHRI GANESH, TO SHRI SARASWATI, AND SHRI GURUMAHARAJ! TO THE FAMILY DEITY, AND TO SHRI SITA-RAMACHANDRA MY MOST HUMBLE OBEISANCE! I BOW IN REVERENCE TO THE MOST VENERABLE GURU SHRI SAINATH!

1. My obeisance to you, O Sadguru! you are the Manas lake[1], producing pearls of gracious words and at whose feet the swans, i.e. your steadfast devotees, find an asylum.
2. Generous-hearted that you are, you feed these protected ones on the pearls of your Grace and establish them in their true Self, thereby liberating them from the birth-death cycle.
3. How wonderful is this Sai! He is the very abode of the *Siddhas*, who have attained *moksha*. His mere *darshan* mitigates the suffering and weariness of worldly life, the delusions about which are destroyed in being continually in his company, for those who are always with him.
4. Basically, Sai is without a form; but in the cause of the devotees, he has taken on a form, and accepting the challenge of that great actress *Maya*, he too, like a seasoned actor, has played his part to perfection.
5. Such is this Sai, whom we shall now bring to the mind. Let us go to Shirdi for a moment and observe carefully, what happens there after the midday *arati*.
6. After the arati at noon, Maharaj would come to the edge of the parapet in the mosque and very kindly he would distribute *udi* to the devotees.

7. And the loving devotees would also embrace his feet, at once, and standing there, would gaze into his face while they were being showered with the *udi*.

8. Baba would also pour *udi* into their palms, by the handful, putting a little on their foreheads with his thumb. Such was the irrepressible love in his heart, for the devotees.

9. 'Go Bhau, go and have your meal! Anna, go and enjoy a delectable meal! Go, go everyone of you to your own homes.' So he would say to them all.

10. Although it is no longer possible to experience it, such happy time of the past, associated with particular places and particular times in Shirdi, can yet be conjured when it is brought to the mind with concentration.

11. Let us then, concentrate the mind thus, and gaze at Baba's form, from the toes right up to his face and prostrating before him with loving devotion, let us continue with our narrative.

12. At the end of the last chapter, the listeners had been told that Baba had unfolded the significance of a *Shruti* at the hands of a maid-servant.

13. Ganu Das had started writing '*Ishavasya Bhavarthbodhini*', but as some doubts arose in his mind while writing it, he brought them at the feet of his Sadguru in Shirdi.

14. The words that Baba uttered on this occasion — 'when you go back, the maid-servant in Kaka's house will resolve your doubts'—

15. These words form the context of the present narrative. From here we continue the story. Let the listeners listen carefully so that what they hear will be faultlessly clear.

16. To explain in verse form, word for word, the significance of the Upanishad '*Ishavasya*', for those who do not know Sanskrit —

17. This was the keen desire in Ganu Das' mind when he started rendering it as '*Ishavasya Bhavarthbodhini*' into the easily understandable Marathi.

18. This *Upanishad* is full of profound, abstruse significance. He did translate it word for word, but Ganu Das was not satisfied or happy in his mind until its profound significance was grasped.

19. The essence of the four Vedas is the real treasure of the *Upanishads* and without God's grace, it is most difficult to attain.

20. If one were to say that I am proficient in learning and with my own efforts I will try to understand the *Upanishads* and give an adequate exposition of the same, —

21. Then such a thing is just not possible — even to the end of the world. Without the guru's grace, obstacles come in the way and the mysterious essence still remains unfathomed. Every step on the way is riddled with difficulties.

22. But he who surrenders whole-heartedly to the guru, will face no difficulties in the least. And the profound significance opens up before him, on its own.

23. Such is this Science of Self-knowledge, a weapon though it is to destroy the birth-death cycle. Only those who are free from egoism and emancipated from the bondage of worldly life have the authority to give an exposition of it.

24. And when we rely on such people, then in a moment the true meaning dawns on us; the mental impediments are removed and the obscure meaning becomes revealed.

25. While translating 'Ishavasya' into Prakrit, Das Ganu was in the same position. But when Sainath bestowed grace on him, the difficulties in his work disappeared.

26. His knowledge of Sanskrit was inadequate; but bowing reverently at the feet of Acharya Vidyaranya[2] and Shri Sai Baba, he began writing his verses.

27. Das Ganu's speech was like a stream of milk and Baba's Grace was the sugar added to it. May the listeners savour, for a moment, that continuous flow of sweetness.

28. But this was just by way of an introduction to the 'Bhavarthbodhini'. To know its vital significance, the listeners should see the original. The purpose of my story here is however, quite different. Listen to it, now!

29. Just see how Maharaj resolved the difficulty of abstruse passages from the book which his devotee was reading, without himself uttering a word!

30. And this is the real purpose of this story, which is all that I wished to narrate to the listeners in brief and in its essence. So listen attentively!

31. Ganu Das wrote his commentary in verse form which was acclaimed by the learned pandits. His heart's desire was fulfilled. But one doubt still remained.

32. He put it before the pandits. A great debate followed, but still, no one could resolve it satisfactorily.

33. Meanwhile, Das Ganu happened to go to Shirdi for some work and quite effortlessly, his doubt got resolved.

34. He went to take Sai's *darshan*; he prostrated in obeisance, placing his head on Baba's feet, which made him feel pleased and happy.

35. A gracious look from the saints; sweet words from the saints' mouth, their smiling countenance — these alone bring great good fortune to the devotees.

36. The mere *darshan* of the saints washes away all the sins. Then who can describe the great merit accumulated by those who are always in their company?

37. 'And so Ganu, from whence this sudden appearance?', said Baba, 'Are things well with you? Are you content and happy at heart?'

38. And Ganu Das replied, 'When I enjoy the protection of your Grace, why should I be sad at heart? No, indeed! I am very happy.

39. 'But you yourself know everything, too, and ask these questions only as a matter of convention! In my mind, I am aware also, as to why you are asking about my welfare.

40. 'You yourself make me start something and when the work begins to take shape, suddenly you put such an obstacle in the way that, try as one may, nobody can remove it!'

41. And thus the dialogue continued while Ganu Das was pressing Baba's feet, when he gently asked Baba the question about *'Ishavasya Bhavarthbodhini'*.

42. 'Baba, as I sit down to write *'Ishavasya Bhavarthbodhini'*, my pen falters as doubts and misgivings assail my mind. Baba, please explain them to me!'

43.   He then narrated to Baba, in detail, what had happened, putting
      before him also, the doubt that defied solution.

44.   And then Ganu Das entreated Sainath, 'Baba, all my efforts in
      writing this book are being wasted. You know full well this story
      of my *Ishavasya!*'

45.   'Unless this doubt is cleared, the deeper significance of the book
      cannot be grasped.' Maharaj then blessed him, saying 'Be Happy!

46.   'And pray, what is so difficult in all this? As you return to the
      place from where you came, that maid-servant of Kaka's will most
      surely resolve your doubt!'

47.   Kaka, here, refers to Bhausaheb Dikshit, who was one of Baba's
      loving devotees, engaged, all the time, in serving his guru, with
      his body, speech and mind.

48.   This Haribhau lived in the suburb called Ville Parle, which is
      situated at a short distance from the famous Bombay city.

49.   His real name, as given to him by his parents, was Hari and though
      people called him Bhausaheb, Baba had given him altogether a
      different name.

50.   Kaka Mahajani, he called 'Bade Kaka' and Nanasaheb Nimonkar
      was 'Old man Kaka'. And Bhausaheb, he named 'the lame Kaka'
      and sometimes also as 'Bambya Kaka'.

51.   Father and mother give one name to the child; in the horoscope,
      it is another. Sometimes a person is also addressed by a nick-
      name. Varied are the customs that prevail.

52.   When Maharaj gave such various names to people, from time to
      time, these same names became prevalent and the devotees too,
      accepted them lovingly and felt honoured, as if they were titles of
      special merit.

53.   Sometimes 'Bhikshu' (one who solicits alms), sometimes 'Kaka',
      such was the stamp that Baba had put on Dikshit and it was by
      this name 'Kaka' that Dikshit came to be commonly known among
      the people of Shirdi.

54.   Ganu Das was quite surprised, and everyone else was puzzled.
      What! Kaka's maid-servant, of all people! And how was she going
      to solve the puzzle?

55. After all, a maid is a maid! What education can she have? What can be so great about her learning or wisdom? It was all most extraordinary!

56. Oh, where the profound learning required for the exposition of the *Shrutis*, and where, the intellectual capacity of a maid-servant! 'Maharaj must be joking,' said all the people.

57. Everyone thought that Maharaj must be really joking. But to Ganu Das, even this jesting remark was full of significance.

58. To the people, who heard these words of Sai, they appeared, outwardly, to be uttered light-heartedly. Not so to Das Ganu, who felt they were the truth.

59. And although people thought that Sai had said it jokingly, yet, as usual, they became eager to watch his *leela*, arising out of these words.

60. Whether the words were spoken in jest or not, they were never pronounced in vain. For every word that Baba spoke was a mine of deep significance.

61. What Baba uttered were not merely words, but were the *'Brahma-likhit'* [3], not a word of which was in vain and would come true at the proper time.

62. This was Das Ganu's firm faith, whatever else it might mean to others. And as your faith — wherever you might repose it — so is the fruit that you will get.

63. As is the faith, so is the fruit; as is the faith, so is its power; the more loving is the heart, the purer is the knowledge, too.

64. Most eminent among the *Jnanis* that he was, Sai's words will never be futile and it was his Promise that he would fulfil the wishes of his devotees.

65. Guru's words are never in vain. Listen to this story with all your heart and the sorrows of worldly life will vanish and you will be on the spiritual path.

66. Ganu Das returned to Parle and to the house of Kakasaheb Dikshit, with an eagerness to see how Kaka's maid would serve the purpose.

67. Next day, at dawn, while Ganu Das was still in bed, enjoying the sweet early morning snooze, a wonderful thing happened.

68. A small Kunabi girl (a peasant girl of the Kunabi caste) was heard singing in a melodious voice, the sweet notes of which smote Das Ganu's heart.

69. On hearing that song with its deep melodious strains and with the beauty of its composition, his heart was captivated as he listened to it with utmost attention.

70. He got up with a start as his attention was caught by the meaning of the song. He kept on listening with concentration, and it brought him great happiness.

71. 'Whose child is she,' he asked, 'who is singing so solemnly, so tunefully? But she has indeed solved the great puzzle of Ishavasya!

72. And so, this is the maid-servant! Let me see her, through whose rustic, unrefined tongue I have realized the significance of the *Shruti.*'

73. As he came out to see, it was really a Kunabi girl who was scrubbing the vessels in Kaka's '*mori*'[4].

74. On enquiry, he found out that there was a servant called 'Namya' at Dikshit's house and this girl was his sister.

75. So this was that maid-servant at Kaka's house! But his doubts were indeed removed by her song. What can the saints not do! Even a he-buffalo was made to recite the *Vedas* (by Jnaneshwar).

76. Such was the girl's singing. Das Ganu was fully satisfied. And everyone realized the great significance of what Baba had said, even jestingly!

77. Some say that Das Ganu was performing *pooja* in the worship room in Kaka's house when he heard this song.

78. Be it as it may! The sum and substance of it is only one — to see how Maharaj taught his devotees under various pretexts.

79. 'Stay where you are and just ask me! Why do you needlessly roam the woods and the wilds searching for answers? I will satisfy your desire (for knowledge). Have this much faith in me.

80. 'My presence fills everyone; there is no place where I am not. And, for the devotion of my devotees, I appear to them anyhow, anywhere.'

81. So that eight-year old girl, with a torn rag for the tuck of a *sari*, was singing all the same, of the grandeur of an orange coloured *sari*, in her melodious song.

82. Oh, how splendid was that gold-threaded *sari*. How exquisite its border! And with a marvellous '*padar*'⁵ to it, too! She was totally engrossed in the description, as she sang.

83. She had not enough to eat, nor sufficient to cover herself. Yet she was filled with joy at the splendour of the orange *sari* that was somebody else's.

84. Seeing her gay, blithe spirit amidst her abject poverty, Das Ganu was moved by pity and said to Moreshwar (Pradhan):

85. 'Just look at her barely covered body! Do please, give her a *sari*! God will be pleased and you will have earned some merit.'

86. Compassionate as Moreshwar himself was, Das Ganu's request only urged him on further. He bought a beautiful *sari* and happily presented it to the child.

87. To her, who was only used to eating dry coarse grains, it was like a feast of sweetmeats. Such was her joy on seeing that *sari*.

88. The next day she wore that *sari* and merrily went around and around, wildly gambolling and dancing, in a '*Fugadi*'⁶ to express her joy. She was in love with the *sari* and looked grander than all the other girls by wearing it.

89. But the very next day, she put away the *sari* in her bundle of special clothes and wrapped the same old torn rag round herself, but without appearing to be dispirited in any way.

90. Though she did not wear the *sari* and had stored it away, yet to Das Ganu, it appeared as though her earlier poverty had disappeared with his new vision.

91. Although she had left the new *sari* at home and had come wearing a torn one, yet there was no sadness in her heart for the want of a new *sari* was no longer there.

92. Wearing torn rags out of helplessness and doing the same when one can afford better — this is called wearing your poverty with dignity. Happiness or sorrow are only a matter of feeling.

93. This was Das Ganu's puzzle which when solved in this way, led to the answer to his doubts in 'Ishavasya' and its significance became clear .

94. When this entire Creation is overspread with the presence of God, then who can think of a place without Him?

95. 'That is perfect. This is perfect. Perfect comes from perfect. Take perfect from perfect, the remainder is perfect.'[7]

96. In the poverty of that child was a divine element; the torn *sari* also had that element; the giver, the act of giving and the gift — everything is pervaded by that one God.

97. Rid yourself totally of the feeling 'I, mine', and always act without ego. Enjoy what he gives you in a spirit of renunciation or dedication. Do not covet anybody's wealth or possessions.

98. Such were Baba's powerful utterances the truth of which was experienced by many. Without leaving Shirdi all his life, he yet appeared to his devotees anywhere and everywhere — amidst crowds or in secluded woods and jungles.

99. He appeared at will, to some at Machchindergad; to others at any of the cities, Kolhapur, Solapur or Rameshwar.

100. To some, he appeared in his usual, familiar person; to others, he gave *darshan* in the day or at night; waking or in a dream, thus satisfying their desire.

101. Innumerable are such experiences! Oh, how many can one describe? Though Baba resided in Shirdi, he travelled anywhere, without anybody's knowledge.

102. Now, just consider this! Who was this girl and related to whom? She was but a poor servant girl. And the song about the orange *sari* came so naturally from her lips!

103. That a doubt should be put before Baba and that this maid should resolve it! And that she too, should be present at Kaka's place! Is this whole arrangement not a work of *Maya*?

104. First of all how did Baba know that this maid would be there? And how is it that at a future date she would be singing a song to explain the significance of the *Shruti*?

105. But that it happened so, is certain. Ganu Das was surprised. But his doubt was resolved and the meaning of '*Ishavasya*' became clear to him.

106. In their minds, the listeners might wonder, why all these plans and arrangements? Why did Baba not resolve the doubt himself, there and then?

107. Could he not have done it there itself? But then the great significance of that incident would not have been understood. How God dwelt even in that poor little maid-servant, was what Baba demonstrated.

108. To describe the nature of the Self accurately is the ultimate goal of all the *Upanishads*. This is the essence of the discipline for *Moksha* and this is the exposition, too, of the real significance of the *Bhagvad Gita*.

109. Living beings may differ from each other, but their *Atman* is one. This Self is the non-doer of action and a non-enjoyer; it cannot be impure, is beyond sin or merit and is free from the observance of duty or *karma*.

110. As long as there is a feeling of separateness that 'I am a high-caste Brahmin; others belong to castes lower than mine', so long is it necessary to perform *karma*.

111. That 'I am formless, omnipresent, the One and Only, as none other than me exists, and that I pervade all' — this is the true knowledge of the Self.

112. This *Jeevatma*, who is one with Brahman, has moved away from It. That he should again become one with It, as before, is the definite goal.

113. This is the dictum of all — *Shruti, Smriti* and *Vedanta*. This is the ultimate objective, that that which has moved away should become One with the Brahman.

114. So long as the mind does not reach the state, where it recognizes that God dwells in the hearts of all beings alike, so long as

Shri Krishna (Rishikesh), the Spirit of all the creatures cannot light the torch of true knowledge.

115. When the mind is purified by observing the rites and rituals prescribed by the *Shastras*, then gradually the knowledge of non-duality will come and *Siddha* or perfect, absolute knowledge, which negates sorrow, suffering, temptations, etc., will reveal itself.

116. God Almighty, whose Presence fills all the three worlds and all the living and non-living things in them; He who is Himself unchanging and non-doer, pure and the greatest among all, He is the formless, eternal Truth.

117. I Myself, am the God Almighty, who fills this entire Creation of forms and names, inside and outside. It is Me and Me alone, and without any special attributes, who pervades everything.

118. That which is, in reality, without a form, appears to have a form because of *Maya*. This worldly life exists only for him who is filled with desires; to one who is detached and free from desires, it is empty and futile.

119. Hence one should have this one conviction, beyond any doubt, that this Creation, made up of the five elements and of the living and non-living creatures, is insignificant, while God alone is One without a second.

120. Even if this discriminating Knowledge about the world is not acceptable to the mind, at least, give up the greedy pursuit of wealth, gold, etc.

121. And if even this is not possible, then know, that you are capable only of doing *karma* and continue doing it to the end of your life — even if it means a hundred years!

122. And that *karma* also has to be appropriate to your *varna, ashram*, as prescribed by the *Shastras*, like *Agnihotra*, with all its proper rites and rituals, till the mind becomes unblemished and pure.

123. This is one way of Self-purification (i.e. *Karma yoga*); the other is to renounce the worldly life (i.e. *Jnana yoga*). If neither of these ways is followed, all that remains to be done is to go through pleasure and pain, in life, as ordained by fate.

124. Sadguru, who knows the spiritual authority of each, will not give the highest knowledge (of the Self) and the knowledge of the *Upanishads* to all. For, unless the principle of non-differentiation is fully imbibed in the mind, the message of the *Upanishads* remains only so many words.

125. And yet, such literal, verbal knowledge also has to be acquired, because the seekers of knowledge ask for it, first. Hence Baba sent him back, saying that the maid-servant will explain.

126. If Baba were to explain it himself, then all that happened would not have taken place and the lesson that 'He alone is, and nothing else exists' would not have come home (to him).

127. Who else is Kaka's maid-servant but me? That 'I am her' is the sign that Baba gave and explained the significance of 'Ishavasya', through actual, personal experience.

128. In the absence of even the smallest degree of Divine Grace and the special favour of the *Sadguru*, it is the instruction of a *Siddha* that is necessary for a man to get to Self-knowledge.

129. Listen carefully only to those *Shastras* which will speak of Self-knowledge and speak only of the fact that 'I pervade everything, there is nothing anywhere except me.'

130. Thus when the true nature of the Self is explained, only he who concentrates and meditates on the oneness between Me and the Self, will propitiate the Atman.

131. Thus when all discussion and concentration is upon the *Atman*, when such unswerving and constant union with the Self is achieved, then God is near at hand.

132. As for the stories in the following chapter, the story of Vinayak Thakur, etc., will be narrated. May the listeners listen to them with respect, so that they will be attracted to spiritual subjects.

133. These stories are also as sweet and listening to them will satisfy the longing of the listeners for the *darshan* of the great and the saintly, the fond wish of the devotees will also be satisfied.

134. As darkness is dispelled when the sun rises, so will this nectar-sweet story dispel *Maya*.

135.   Inconceivable are the *leelas* of Sai. Who but himself, can describe
       them adequately? I am but his instrument. It is he, who will
       make me speak.

Weal be to all! Here ends the twentieth chapter of
"Shri Sai Samarth Satcharit", called
'Ishavasya Bhavarthbodhanam',
as inspired by the saints and the virtuous,
·and composed by his devotee, Hemadpant.

Notes

1.   Refer Ch. 2, note 5.
2.   Shri Vidyaranya Swami (1295-1386 A.D.) is said to have been the head of the Shringeri
     Math, from 1380 to 1386, established by Shri Adi Shankaracharya himself. The
     'Panchadashi' of Vidyaranya Swami is an Advaita Vedanta classic of great celebrity.
     Many other Sanskrit works are also ascribed to him.
3.   The destiny of each creature as written on its forehead by Brahma.
4.   A small enclosure for washing vessels.
5.   That ornamental end of a sari which covers and falls back from the shoulder.
6.   A kind of wild gambol or dance. Two or more, holding hands, fling themselves about,
     keeping time to their movements by puffing with their mouths.
7.   *The Ten Principal Upanishads: put into English*, by Shree Purohit Swami and W.B. Yeats;
     Faber and Faber Ltd., London. 1937. p. 15.
     Swami Prabhavananda puts it thus in *The Upanishads* (Shri Ramakrishna Math; Madras,
     1983):

                    'Filled full with Brahman are the things we see,
                    Filled full with Brahman are the things we see not,
                    From out of Brahman floweth all that is;
                    From Brahman all — yet is he still the same.'

21

Bestowal of Grace

MY OBEISANCE TO SHRI GANESH, TO SHRI SARASWATI, AND SHRI GURUMAHARAJ! TO THE FAMILY DEITY, TO SHRI SITA-RAMACHANDRA, MY MOST HUMBLE OBEISANCE! I BOW IN REVERENCE TO THE MOST VENERABLE GURU SHRI SAINATH!

1. Now listen with concentration to how Thakur and others had the *darshan* of the great saint (i.e. Sai Baba), as has already been mentioned at the end of the last chapter.

2. In vain are the words of that speaker, which, when they fall on the ears of his listeners, do not make them sway with joy or make the hair on their bodies stand on end with a deep emotion.

3. The narration, listening to which the listeners are not delighted, or their throats are not choked with emotion and tears of joy do not trickle from their eyes — that narration has truly gone waste.

4. Baba's speech was captivating; his style of instructing was most remarkable. I bow my head humbly at his feet, whose *leelas* were marvellous and novel, at every step.

5. Unless Fortune smiles, one does not meet *sadhus* and saints. And even when such a one is close at hand, to the great sinner he is not visible.

6. And to testify to the truth of this, one does not have to seek far into the country or into another land. Why, I will narrate my very own experience to the listeners!

7. There was a *siddha*, well-known by the name Pir Maulana in the Bandra town (now a suburb of Bombay city). For his holy *darshan* the Hindus, the Parsis and the wise and learned of even other religions came to him.

8. I was a magistrate in that suburb at the time. He had a devotee called Yunus, who served him devotedly. And this Yunus pursued me, day and night, to go for his *darshan.*

9. Thousands of people flocked there, then why should I go there too? Just out of respect for his feelings, why should I allow myself to be persuaded and thus lose my reputation?

10. Some such considerations would always come to my mind and I never went for his *darshan* — as if I was afraid of my own shadow. Or perhaps, it was my ill-luck that came in the way of taking his *darshan!*

11. Many years passed thus. Thereafter I was transferred from there. But later on, when the appropriate time came, a lasting association with Shirdi came to be established.

12. In short, in the company of saints, the unfortunate gain no entry, while it is easy for those who enjoy God's grace. Otherwise, such an opportunity is very difficult to come by.

13. And now, my listeners, listen to an interesting tale about this, and see how these saints have associations and secret arrangements with each other, from time immemorial.

14. At the proper time and as the occasion demands, they incarnate at the place of their choice, to accomplish their purpose. But they are not different from each other.

15. Though their place, time and purpose may differ, each saint knows the mind of the other completely. At heart, they are all one.

16. Just as an emperor of the whole earth has his officers posted at various camps, in different regions of his kingdom and thus brings prosperity to it,.

17. Similarly, this Emperor of the Joyful Self appears in different places and steers the ship of his empire smoothly by guiding its course secretly.

18. Once there was a gentleman, with the advantage of English education and adorned with a B.A. degree, who gradually rose to be a renowned officer.

19. Later on, he became a *mamlatdar* and, rising higher and higher, became a Deputy Collector. By his good fortune, he was blessed with Sai Baba's company.

20. The high office of a *mamlatdar*, though outwardly attractive, is like a hill that appears beautiful from a distance, but is surrounded by the *kajri*[1] plants, on a closer view. In prestige, however, it is still great.

21. Gone are those happy days of yore when there was a great fondness for enjoying this authority and among the people too, there was respect for the officers, thus making everybody happy.

22. But who can describe the toil and suffering that it entails now? Those days are over when this was a comfortable job. Now, there is an abundance only of responsibilities; as for money, it may be a-plenty, but so is the drudgery that goes with it.

23. Even when one works rigorously and sincerely today, there is no longer that respect which the *mamlatdar* once commanded and the grandeur that went with the office, which equalled that of a Deputy Collector.

24. Moreover, even to get this post of power and authority, who could hope to succeed without spending money in plenty and without an arduous and continuous study?

25. He had to pass his B.A. first. Then he would become an accounts clerk in the Revenue Department on a monthly pay of Rs.30. Such would be his slow progress.

26. At the proper time, he would then go eastwards across the Ghats, to be trained in measuring of land and would be required to stay among the land surveyors, so that he could pass the departmental examination.

27. Later, when a vacancy arose by the demise of an officer, it would become useful to him.

28. But now, enough of this long-winding tale! Why should one just go on babbling? So, listen to the story of how one such person met Sai.

29.   There is a village near Belgaum called Vadgaon, where a contingent of surveyors came on a visit and camped.

30.   In that village, there was a saintly man[2]. He therefore went for his *darshan*, placed his head on his feet and received his blessings with *prasad*.

31.   At that time the saint had in his hand a book called '*Vichar-sagar*'[3] by Nischaldas, which he was then reading.

32.   After a while, as he got up to take leave, listen to what that *sadhu* said to him very joyfully —

33.   'So, you may go, now. But have a look at this book. Remember, that by so doing, your wishes will be fulfilled.

34.   'And later, when you proceed northwards for your work, on your way you will, by your good fortune, have the *darshan* of a great saint.

35.   'He will guide you on your course ahead and bring stability and peace of mind. He will himself then instruct you and imprint his teachings on your mind.'

36.   His work there was then over and he was transferred to Junnar (in Poona district) and for going there it became imperative to cross over the Naneghat[4], which is known for its great height and the consequent peril in crossing it.

37.   The way there is hazardous and it can be climbed only by riding a he-buffalo. That being the sole means of transport, a he-buffalo was procured from nearby, to ride upon.

38.   Maybe, one day in the future he would rise to be a high official and have horses, cars, etc. But on the present occasion he had to make do, as best as he could, with the he-buffalo that was present there.

39.   It was impossible to climb the ghat on foot and but for the he-buffalo, there was no other vehicle. Such was that wonderful Naneghat. And such indeed, the unique means of transport!

40.   He then made up his mind, got the he-buffalo to be saddled, with stuffed cushions on its back and, with great difficulty, he mounted it.

41. Mount he did; but the climb was steep and, to add to it, he had the most extraordinary vehicle in that he-buffalo! What with the jolts and jerks and violent oscillations! His back was sprained most painfully.

42. At last, the journey ended. The business at Junnar was completed satisfactorily. Then came his transfer order and he moved out of the place.

43. He was transferred to Kalyan, where he met Chandorkar. When he heard from him the fame of Sainath, he too felt like having his *darshan.*

44. An opportunity for it presented itself the very next day. Chandorkar was all ready to leave for Shirdi and said to him, 'Come, let us make this trip to Shirdi together.

45. 'We will both have his *darshan*, make obeisance to him and after spending a day or two there, will return to Kalyan.'

46. But on that very day, the hearing of a court case had been fixed in the Thane Civil Court. And so, he had to abandon the idea of accompanying Chandorkar.

47. In vain did Nanasaheb urge him to come, saying 'Baba is all-powerful and will satisfy your desire for his *darshan*. Of what consequence is that court case!'

48. But he could not be convinced, for he was afraid of missing the hearing. After all, who can escape the fruitless, toilsome journeys written by Fate on the forehead?

49. Nanasaheb Chandorkar narrated earlier experiences, of how all obstacles were removed when one had a strong urge in his heart for Baba's *darshan.*

50. But he could not bring himself to believe his words. How could he help his own nature? He said, 'Let me first see this court case through to its end and get rid of this nagging worry.'

51. So he went to Thane and Chandorkar set out for Shirdi. He took Baba's *darshan* and started on his way back. Meanwhile an amazing thing had happened at Thane.

52. Though he was present for the hearing, the matter got adjourned to a future date. But now, Chandorkar had gone, too. In his heart he felt quite abashed.

53. 'Oh, how much better it would have been, if only I had believed him! Chandorkar would have taken me with him and my purpose of taking *darshan* would have been accomplished, quite at my ease, in Shirdi.

54. 'Now, not only does this court matter remain unfinished, but I have also lost the chance of the *sadhu*'s company.' But he at once decided to go to Shirdi.

55. 'Maybe', he thought, 'if I go to Shirdi and am lucky enough to meet Nana, he will himself commit me to the protection of Sainath, which will make me happy.

56. 'In Shirdi I know no one. I am altogether new to the place. It will be just right if I meet Nana, although the chances are dim.'

57. So thinking, he boarded the train and reached Shirdi the next day. Of course, Nana was not there.

58. The day he set out for Shirdi, Nana too, had started on his return journey. He was dejected and felt quite disheartened in his mind.

59. However, he met there another good friend, who helped him have Sai's *darshan* and his heart's desire was satisfied.

60. On having Baba's *darshan*, Thakur was drawn to his feet. He prostrated, in obeisance, before Sai. Overcome with emotion, the hair on his body stood on end and tears of love and joy brimmed over from his eyes.

61. Then, as he stood still for a moment before him, listen carefully to what Baba, who is omniscient, said to him with a smile on his face.

62. 'What the Kannad Appa told you was like climbing the ghat mounted on a he-buffalo. But it is not so easy to tread on this path. Here it is inevitable that one wears out one's body in hard toil.'

63. As these significant words fell on his ears, Thakur's heart overflowed with greater joy. These words actually experienced, only confirmed the truth of what that other saint had said earlier.

64. With both his hands folded, he then placed his head on Sai's feet and said, 'Maharaj, have mercy on me, this friendless one, and take me under your wing.

65. 'You and you alone, are my saint. Only today have I understood fully the message of the book by Nischaldas and have thus experienced the highest pleasure.

66. 'Oh, where that Vadgaon and where Shirdi! And what a pair indeed, of the saint and the saintly! How concise but clear, the language and what skill in instructing!!

67. 'One said, 'Read the book. Later you will meet a great saint, who will truly guide you to your path of duty in future.'

68. 'Luckily, I met that great saint, too! And he gave me the mark that he was that same saint. As advised by one, I read the book. And now, I must act according to the advice of the other.'

69. Sainath said to him, "What Appa told you was perfectly right! But when you put all that into practice, only then will your wishes be fulfilled."

70. At Vadgaon, *'Vichar-sagar'* of Nischaldas was recommended for the benefit of the devotee. After some time and when the book had been read carefully, it was explained in Shirdi as to how it could be put into practice.

71. The book should be listened to carefully, first; then the same should be contemplated upon. It should be perused from the beginning to the end and read repeatedly in this manner. That is how it is meditated upon all the time.

72. And merely reading it is not the end of the matter. It must come into practice. Or else, it will be like pouring water over a vessel turned upside down.

73. In vain indeed, is all that reading, which does not give knowledge based on self-experience. Without the grace of the guru, who has himself obtained *Brahma-jnana*, such bookish knowledge is unproductive.

74. A short tale, in this context, will reveal the true importance of devotion and the great need for human effort. May the listener listen carefully, in his own interest.

75. Once, a resident of Poona, Anantrao Patankar by name, felt a strong urge for Sai's *darshan* and came to Shirdi at once.

76. He had listened to *Vedanta*; had also read the original Sanskrit *Upanishads*, along with the commentaries. But it had not brought him peace of mind; the restlessness would.not leave him.

77. But after taking the *darshan* of Sai Samarth, Patankar felt at peace. He made obeisance at Baba's feet and offered *pooja* with all the rites and rituals.

78. With folded hands, Anantrao then sat in front of Baba and in a tone of supplication, very lovingly asked him,

79. 'Many great books have I seen; and I have carefully studied the *Ved-Vedangas* and the *Upanishads*. I have also listened to the excellent *Shastras* and *Puranas*. And yet, how is my mind so wearied, so tired?

80. 'So that now I am beginning to feel that whatever I have read is all wasted. The illiterate faithful ones appear to me to be better than myself.

81. 'In vain indeed, has beeen my reading of books; in vain, the deep study of the *Shastras*! Futile is all the bookish knowledge, so long as this mind is not at peace!

82. 'Oh, how hollow is the proficiency in the *Shastras*! And wherefore the chanting of the Mahavakyas[5], either, if they do not bring peace to the mind? And Oh, what hope is there of attaining *Brahma-jnana*?

83. 'Travelling by word of mouth, the news reached me that *Sai-darshan* removes all the worries, all the anxieties and that amidst light-hearted, humorous talk, Sai effortlessly guides you to the right path.

84. 'Therefore, O Maharaj, who are the very treasure-house of devout austerity, I have humbly come at your feet. Do bless me with the benediction that my mind will become calm and steady.'

85. Maharaj then narrated a humorous allegorical tale, which brought satisfaction to Anantrao that the knowledge he had acquired so far, had been worthwhile.

86. I shall now narrate that tale, which is concise, but with profound significance. Listen attentively to it. Humorous no doubt, but it is most instructive. Who will disregard such a story?

87. Baba then replied, "There once came a merchant, when a horse standing in front of him happened to drop nine nodules of dung.

88. "Quick to seize his own advantage, the merchant at once spread his *uparna* (a small piece of cloth on the shoulder) to catch them and as he tied them all up securely in it, his mind became steady and concentrated."

89. What is this that Sai Samarth said? What could be its significance? Why did that merchant collect all those nodules of dung? The meaning of all this is not clear at all!

90. Pondering over it, Anantrao came back and narrated that conversation, in detail, to Dada Kelkar.

91. 'Who', he asked, 'is this merchant? And what is the occasion for mentioning the horse dung? Moreover, why only nine nodules? Please explain this all to me.

92. 'Dada, what is this riddle? I am too slow-witted to resolve it. Tell me simply and clearly, so that Baba's purpose will be understood.'

93. And Dada said, 'Such are Baba's utterances that even I do not understand them. But by his own inspiration, I will tell you what I have understood.

94. 'God's grace is this horse. And the nine lumps of the dung are the nine different types of devotion. Without devotion God cannot be attained. By knowledge alone, He cannot be reached.

95. 'Know, that the ninefold path of devotion is as follows. The first is *Shravan* (hearing the attributes, excellences or wondrous achievements of, as read or recited); the second *Keertan* (reciting); the third *Smaran* (calling to mind and meditating upon the names and perfections of); fourth, *Paadsevan* (washing, kneading, etc., of the feet of); fifth, *Archana* (outward worship or common service and presenting *naivedya*); sixth, *Vandan* (adoration); seventh, *Daasya* (service, in general); eighth, *Sakhya* (cultivating fellowship) and ninth, *Atmanivedan* (consecration of one's self unto).

96. 'If even one out of these is practised with implicit trust in the heart, Shri Hari, who hungers after nothing else (but devotion), will appear to the devotee in his own abode.

97. 'Chanting the Name, penance, religious vows and observances, Yoga-sadhana, a study of *Vedas* and *Upanishads*, or even the exposition of spiritual knowledge in profusion — all these are futile when devoid of devotion.

98. 'It is not the proficiency in *Veda-Shastras*, nor the world-wide fame as a *Jnani*, nor yet a fondness for a dry, loveless devotion that is required. What is needed is a devotion full of love.

99. 'Consider yourself to be the merchant and then try to understand the implications of this transaction, which is, that once the banner of the ninefold path of devotion flies high, God, the Lord of Knowledge, is pleased.

100. 'The horse dropped nine nodules of dung, which the merchant eagerly ran forward to catch. Similarly, if you hold fast to the ninefold path of devotion, your mind will repose in peace.

101. 'And that alone will steady the mind, make it solemn and serious and will create goodwill towards all. In its absence, wavering and unsteadiness are inevitable. So says Guruvarya, affectionately.'

102. The next day, as Anantrao went to worship Sai's feet, he was asked, "What! have you securely tied up the dung nodules in your *uparna?*"

103. And Anantrao prayed 'If your grace is with this poor, meek creature, they can be easily tied up, after all, what is so great about them?'

104. Baba then blessed him and assured him that all would be well with him. Anantrao's heart was gladdened by hearing these words and he enjoyed peace and happiness.

105. And now, O listeners! Listen to one more short tale attentively and you will realize Baba's power of intuitive knowledge, as also his way of guiding devotees on the path of righteousness.

106. Once a lawyer came to Shirdi and went at once to the mosque. He took Sainath's *darshan* and bowed at his feet.

107. He then offered the *dakshina* that he carried with him and, at once, sat down on one side. He suddenly got interested in listening to Baba's conversation with others that was going on there.

108. Baba turned his face towards him and uttered something referring to him. The words stung him to the quick, causing remorse in his heart.

109. "Oh! how insincere people are! They will bow at the feet, even offer *dakshina*, and yet curse you all the time in their heart! How strange, indeed!"

110. On hearing this, the lawyer kept quiet, but in his heart he had understood full well. He knew that Baba's words were just. The lesson went home, all right!

111. Later, when he returned to the *wada*, he said to Dikshit that 'piercing as Baba's words had been, all that he said was absolutely right!

112. 'The volley of accusations that Baba fired at me, the moment I entered, was really only a warning given to me that I should give no place in my mind to reviling, abusive talk about others.

113. 'Our *Munsiff* (civil judge), who was suffering from ill health, came here on leave, to rest and improve his health.

114. 'While in the lawyer's common-room, the topic about the *Munsiff* came up, during conversation. Discussions, arguments followed, though it was none of their business.

115. 'Can these physical ailments be cured, in the absence of proper medication, merely by going after Sai? Does this sort of behaviour become a man, who has risen to be a *Munsiff*?

116. 'While such reviling and criticising of the Munsiff was going on and even Sai was not spared derision, I was also a party to it, in however small a measure it may be. And it was the impropriety of this that Baba demonstrated.

117. 'It was not a volley of censorous remarks, but his grace to teach me that futile debates and discussions, scornful, critical revilings and such wicked thoughts about anyone, should be given up altogether.

118. 'It was yet one more proof that though a hundred miles away, Sai knew everybody's mind. He was truly omniscient.

119. 'One other thing was resolved, too. Hills and mountains may stand between, but nothing is hidden from Sai's sight. Even the most secret matter lies bared before him.'

120. And so, from then onwards, the lawyer firmly resolved never to indulge in censure or criticism, or to entertain any wicked thoughts about anyone.

121. Whatever we do and wherever we may be, nothing escapes Sai's knowledge. About this, he was convinced and his propensity towards wicked deeds vanished gradually.

122. The urge for good, righteous deeds arose in his mind and the faith took a firm root in his heart that Sai is with you, in front of you and behind. Who is so powerful as to deceive him?

123. And when we consider carefully, although this story has a direct connection to that lawyer, in every sense and in every way, it is equally instructive for all.

124. And I pray sincerely that like that lawyer, the narrator here, all his listeners and Sai's other devotees should also nurture the same faith and the same conviction.

125. When Sai, the Cloud of Compassion, showers his grace, we will all be satiated. In this there is hardly any wonder. All who are thirsty will be satiated.

126. Unfathomable is Sai's greatness; limitless are his great tales. Sai's life-story has no bounds. For he is Parabrahma Incarnate.

127. Now, in the next chapter, listen carefully, O faithful devotees, to a story which will satisfy your wishes and bring steadiness and peace to your minds.

128. Sai Samarth knew beforehand what calamities were to befall his devotees and he would avert them in the midst of jesting and joking and playful laughter.

129. Devotee Hemad surrenders to Sai. This story is now complete. The story that follows is about averting the calamities of the devotees.

130. Knowing the future calamities of the devotees beforehand, how Sai, the Ocean of Kindness, averted them by giving a timely warning.

Weal be to all! Here ends the twenty-first chapter of
"*Shri Sai Samarth Satcharit*," called
'*Bestowal of Grace*',
as inspired by the saints and the virtuous,
and composed by his devotee, Hemadpant.

Notes

1. A tree, *strychnos nux vomia*.
2. The famous Kannada saint, Appa Maharaj.
3. A work in Hindi, written in 1849, on *Advait Philosophy*.
4. A ghat connecting Murbad (Thane district) to Junnar, by which people in Konkan used to cross over to Junnar (Poona district) in the past.
5. Refer Ch. 16. note no. 10.

22

Averting Accidental Deaths

MY OBEISANCE TO SHRI GANESH, TO SHRI SARASWATI, AND SHRI GURUMAHARAJ! TO THE FAMILY DEITY, TO SHRI SITA-RAMACHANDRA MY MOST HUMBLE OBEISANCE! I BOW IN REVERENCE TO THE MOST VENERABLE GURU SHRI SAINATH!

1. Glory to You, O Sadguru, of Full and Perfect Joy, an Incarnation of Knowledge itself, who are most sacred. Hail to you, O Most Perfect One, the Destroyer of the fear of worldly life and of the evil propensities of this *Kaliyuga*.

2. You are the Ocean of Joy, on the surface of which rise the ripples of various feelings and thoughts. And you and you alone, out of kindness to your devotees, restrain them.

3. What appears to be a snake in the semi-darkness, automatically becomes a rope in the light. You alone are the creator of both, the semi-darkness and bright light.

4. You first give rise to fear by creating the illusion in the shape of a snake. And in the end, it is you who dispels that fear.

5. First, when there was total darkness, with neither a snake nor a rope; and therefore no room for an illusion, that darkness without a form or a shape, was also filled with your presence.

6. Later, when a form appeared in that state of formlessness, and that too, in a dim light, the illusion of a snake appeared. This illusion was also your own creation.

7. This feeling of seeing things one moment and their disappearance, the next, is really the result of your joyful nature, which is without any change or modification and which no one has been able to fathom.

8. When, trying to understand you, the *Shrutis* became silent and the Sheshnaag[1], praising you with all his mouths, could not understand your real nature. Then how can I understand it?

9. Baba, nothing now interests the mind except the revelation of your Divine Form and I feel like meditating upon it, bringing it, all the time, before the eyes.

10. Pure, Perfect Knowledge Incarnate that you are, in order to enjoy the highest happiness, we have no other way, except to fall at your feet.

11. Oh, what a manner of sitting you always have! Numerous devotees, as they come for your *darshan*, place their heads on your feet and are overcome with an inner joy and love.

12. And that foot of yours — Oh, how does one describe it? One may say that like the connection between the moon and the branch of a tree, the devotees also satisfy their strong desire for your *darshan* by holding tightly to the big toe of your foot.

13. Once the fifteenth day of Krishna *paksha* (the dark phase of the moon), the dark night of *Amavasya* (New moon) is over, everyone is naturally eager to see the moon.

14. As soon as the night of Krishna *paksha* is over, each and everyone looks towards the West, gazing intently at the sky, in the hope of seeing the moon rise.

15. Similarly, you satisfy the intense desire of your devotees for *darshan*, at your own feet, when you sit resting your right foot on your left knee.

16. In the space between the forefinger and the middle finger of the left hand (which resemble the two forked branches of a tree), which tightly clasp the big toe, near that big toe of the right foot shines brightly, the toe-nail, which resembles the shining crescent of the second day of the waxing moon.

17. Great is the eagerness for seeing the moon. But the tiny crescent is not easily spotted in the sky. A knowledgeable man will then say, fix your eyes on the sky from between the forked branches of a tree,

18. And then you will have the *darshan* of the moon from between the branches, right in front of you. Even though the line of the moon is so thin it is seen clearly from there.

19. Blessed is this big toe with its great significance! Baba himself became Venimadhav (Shri Krishna) and satisfied Das Ganu's wish by making the sacred Ganga and Yamuna flow from that big toe.

20. When Das Ganu asked leave of Baba to bathe at the sacred Prayag, "Know that this big toe of mine is itself Prayag so bathe here only" —

21. Said Baba and as Das Ganu bowed at his feet, Ganga-Yamuna both appeared at once there, at his feet.

22. And the beautiful *pada* composed by Das Ganu on that occasion, though it has already been heard by the ever-eager listeners,

23. Which has already been given in Das Ganu's own words in the fourth chapter of *Shri Sai Satcharit*, if the listeners were to read it again, they will once again experience the same wonder, as on first hearing it.

24. Hence, in accordance with the reasoning of the moon-and-branch connection, Baba showed an easy way of *darshan* by holding his big toe between the forefinger and the middle finger.

25. Thereby he seems to suggest: 'Give up your ego and bow your head before all the living beings, meditating on my big toe. This is an easy way of devotion.'

26. Now, to go back to the previous tale! The narration of his bestowal of grace on the devotees, has ended. But now, listen attentively to the wonderful story that follows.

27. Shirdi became a holy place of pilgrimage, highly sanctified by Baba's presence. Day and night, a steady stream of pilgrims flowed. Many seekers in search of spiritual merit flocked there.

28. Sai Baba, the veritable boon-granting *Kalpavriksha* (wish-fulfilling tree), whose Presence filled all the ten directions, directly or indirectly, actually incarnated in Shirdi.

29. Penniless and wealthy, he treated them all alike and by showing his inconceivable *leela*, he ensured the welfare of his devotees.

30. Oh, what boundless love he had in his heart, and the *Brahmajnana* was just natural to him! It was his firm conviction that the spirit in all beings is one and the same. Blessed is he, who was fortunate enough to have a personal experience of Baba.

31. Sometimes, to hold a resolute silence would itself be his discourse on the Brahman; sometimes this Cloud of Universal Consciousness and Joy, would be surrounded by his throng of devotees.

32. Sometimes, his utterances would be pregnant with profound meaning; sometimes he would talk jestingly in a light, humorous vein. Sometimes he would leave aside his usual cryptic speech and feign anger.

33. Sometimes, implied and suggestive; sometimes to be known by discrimination and sometimes open and determined — such were his different ways of giving instructions to different people.

34. Beyond the power of the mind, intellect and speech was the behaviour of Sai Samarth. And his actions were simply beyond one's imagination, difficult to comprehend and quite unexpected.

35. Long as one may gaze into his face, one's desire knew no satiety; conversing with him, a longing grew for more and more; listening to his words, left behind a craving for it to continue. And the joy it brought could hardly be contained in the heart.

36. One may be able to count the lines of the streaming rain or constrain the wind with utmost effort to a bundle. But where is the measurer who can count Sai's miracles?

37. But now, listen at your ease, to the next story of Sai's great concern about protecting the devotees; as also, of how he warded off difficult situations.

38. How, knowing the alarming danger to the devotees, he would instil courage into them and averting their calamity, always watchful for their welfare that he was, he would confirm their faith in him.

39. A tale, in this context, will entertain you, O eager listeners! It will enhance your pleasure in Sai's company and will give rise to faith in the hearts of the simple and guileless.

40. May they be the meek, the lowly, the poor; but their fondness for Sai's stories will increase. And if they chant Sai's name all the time, Sai will surely take them safely to the shore beyond.

41. Kakasaheb Mirikar was a resident of Ahmednagar city, pleased with whose service the government had conferred on him the title 'Sardar'.

42. Equally duty-conscious was his son, Balasaheb, who was Mamlatdar of Kopergaon, and while on tour to Chithali, he once came to Shirdi for Baba's *darshan*.

43. As he went to the mosque and sat down after bowing his head at Baba's feet, conversation started, Baba asking him after the welfare of everybody.

44. Many people were present there at the time. And so also was Madhavrao, quite close by. O my most attentive listeners, savour the sweetness of this nectar-sweet tale, now!

45. It is really Baba's marvel, how he would forewarn his devotees of the calamities to befall them, along with a plan to avert the danger and thus protect them.

46. Now just see the question that Baba, quite unexpectedly, asked Mirikar at that time, "Do you really know that Dwarakamayee (name of his mosque) of ours?"

47. Balasaheb was totally at a loss to understand the question. So Baba continued, "Now see, Dwarakamayee is none other than this very mosque.

48. "This is our own, our very own, Dwarakamayee. When you sit on her lap, she gives you full protection, as to a child. And there then remains no cause for worry, at all!

49. "So very kind is this *mashidmayee*, a mother unto the simple, faithful ones! Whoever may be caught up and in however grave a danger, she will protect him, there and then!

50. "He who once sits on her lap, has overcome all his difficulties. He, who rests under her shade, has really mounted a seat of peace and comfort.

51. "This, this is that Dwaraka, that Dwaravati!" Baba then gave him *Udi*, placing his hand of Protection on his head, as Mirikar set out to go.

52. And, Baba suddenly felt like asking Mirikar, the question, "Do you know that long *Bawa* (snake) and also his wonder?"

53. Curling the palm of the left hand, he held its elbow with the right hand and moving that curled palm up and down (like the snake head), he said, "So terrible he is!

54. "But what harm can he do us? We are the children of Dwarakamayee. No one can comprehend her power! Let us just wait and watch her marvel in silence!

55. "When Dwarakamayee is our Protector, how can the long *Bawa* kill? How much can be the power of the killer before that of this Saviour?"

56. Why should Baba come out with this explanation at that particular moment? And what was its connection to Mirikar? Everyone was most curious to know.

57. But no one had the courage to ask Baba. And so, placing his head on Baba's feet and muttering something about getting late to reach Chithali, Mirikar came down the steps of the mosque.

58. Hardly had he and Madhavrao, who was with him, reached the door of the *Sabha-mandap* then Baba called out to Madhavrao, saying, "Come back for just a moment!"

59. He then said, "Shama, you too, get ready and go with him. Go, make a trip to Chithali! It will be enjoyable!"

60. At once Shama came down, went to Mirikar and said, 'I have to come with you in your tonga, to Chithali.

61. 'I will just go home and get ready. I will join you in no time. Baba says that I should go with you to Chithali.'

62. Mirikar said to him, 'But what will you do, coming all the way to Chithali? It is unnecessary trouble for you!'

63. Madhavrao turned back and told Baba what had taken place. Baba said "All right! what do we lose?

64. "In the *mantra*, place of pilgrimage, Brahmin, God, astrologer, *vaidya* or guru, as is your faith, so will be the fruit that you get.

65. "We should always wish for the best interest of others and give proper advice. Whatever is in their destiny, so will it happen, most certainly!"

66. Suddenly Mirikar had a doubt! Baba's words must be respected. So he quietly signalled to Madhavrao, saying, 'Come with me to Chithali!'

67. But now Madhavrao said, 'Wait! I will come, but let me take Baba's permission again! As soon as he says 'Yes', I will come at once. I will come back, just now!

68. 'I was coming but you sent me back. Baba said, all right! What have we to lose? And he made me sit quietly.

69. 'Now, I will consult him again. The moment he says 'yes', I will come back quickly. Whatever he says, I will do. For I am but his obedient servant.'

70. He then went back to Baba and said, 'Mirikar wants me to come. He is taking me to Chithali with him and wants your permission.'

71. With a smile, Sai said, "All right! If he is taking you, you go! *Mashidmayee* is her name, will she ever go back on her Promise?

72. "A mother is, after all, a mother, full of love and tenderly merciful towards her child! But when the children themselves are untrusting, how can she look after them?"

73. Madhavrao then made obeisance and set out. He came to sit in the tonga in which Mirikar was already seated.

74. Both of them went to Chithali. On enquiry, they found out that the District officials who were to come, had not come. So, they sat back leisurely.

75. Arrangements had been made for them to stay at the Maruti temple. So both of them retired there, at once.

76. It was past ten o'clock, at night. They both spread out their cotton carpets, bedding, pillows, etc., and under the light of the lamp, sat talking.

77. A newspaper was lying there, which Mirikar opened and began reading. His attention was totally engrossed in reading some special news item, when a most curious thing happened!

78. At that fateful moment, a snake sat there all coiled up. How. or from where he had crept in, eluding the notice of everyone, no one knew.

79. A loose end of the *uparna* lay on Mirikar's waist and on that soft seat he rested, quiet and fearless.

80. As he was gliding up slowly, the newspaper made a sibilant sound. But nobody connected the sound with the suspicion of a snake.

81. So horrifying was the occasion, yet Mirikar was absolutely absorbed in the newspaper. It was the peon, in whose mind the wild suspicion first came.

82. From where does this sound come? And what could produce it? So saying, as he lifted up the lamp a little, he saw the long *Bawa*.

83. He panicked, as he saw it and cried out softly, 'Snake, snake!' Mirikar, on hearing this, lost his nerve and began to tremble all over.

84. Shamrao was dumbfounded, too, as he said 'Baba, what is this you have done! From where have you sent this unwanted peril? Now, you yourself must avert it.'

85. However, seeing the grave danger of the situation, each one picked up whatever came to hand and ran forward noiselessly.

86. But even as they moved, they saw the snake slowly gliding down Mirikar's waist. To them, it appeared to be no snake, but a calamity personified that seemed to be climbing down.

87. The eclipse cleared, in no time! As the snake came down, the cudgels in raised hands came crashing down heavily on the reptile, cutting it into pieces.

88. Seeing the danger averted in this way, Mirikar was overcome with emotion; love for Sai Samarth overflowed his heart.

89. The tremors of pain subsided and tears of love flowed freely from the eyes. Oh, what a terrible calamity was averted! And how did Baba know it?

90. The great danger was overcome, indeed! And what a timely warning Baba gave! He sent Shama for my assistance, making him sit in the tonga, in spite of my saying 'no'.

91. Truly, his heart simply overflows with compassion! And what intuitive knowledge he has! Knowing the bad times ahead, he gave the proper advice.

92. He revealed the great power of his *darshan* and the importance of the mosque was impressed upon their minds. Through his *leela* he revealed his love for the devotees, most effortlessly.

93. Listen now to what Nana Dengale, a great astrologer with Shrimant Butti, once said to Butti.

94. 'Today is the most inauspicious day for you, for, there is great danger to you. But have courage in your heart and be very alert.'

95. When Dengale said this, Bapusaheb became very restless in his mind and kept on worrying. The day seemed ever so long!

96. Later, at the usual time, Bapusaheb, Nana, and all the others set out for the mosque and sat down with Baba.

97. At once Baba asked Butti, "What, what does this Nana say? Is he all set to kill you? But we need not be afraid!

98. "Let us see how he kills you! Tell him without any fear, that he may kill you, if he can!" Just see the miracle that followed after this conversation.

99. In the evening, when Bapusaheb had gone to the privy for toilette, a snake had crept in there at that time.

100. Seeing that terrible obstruction, Bapusaheb came out, at once. His servant, Lahanu, thought that he would kill the snake with a stone.

101. But as he was about to pick up a stone, Bapusaheb restrained him, saying, 'Go get a stick, instead. Hurry, in such matters, is not good.'

102. And even as the servant went for the stick, the snake began to climb on the wall, but lost his balance and suddenly fell down, gliding out of the hole.

103. From there, then, he went away. Thus there now remained no reason to kill him. Butti remembered Baba's words and marvelled at Baba's way of averting the danger, both to himself and the snake.

104. He, who has been fortunate enough to see with his own eyes, the glorious pageant of Sai's association with his devotees, will never be able to forget it.

105. By giving many such experiences, he attracted the hearts of devotees. Space will not be enough if all these experiences were to be described. Such descriptions have no end.

106. And now, listen to another such incident, which actually happened in the Chawadi at about one o'clock at night, and right in front of Baba.

107. In Kopargaon taluka, there is a place called Korale, which was a village of '*vatan*'[2] of one Amir Shakkar, who had great devotion for Sai Baba.

108. Born a butcher, his occupation was that of a middleman and he was quite well known in Bandra. He was afflicted with a serious disease, which left him severely debilitated.

109. When afflictions come, God is remembered, at once! Giving up all the toil and botheration attendant upon his business, winding up all his transactions, he raced down to Shirdi.

110. Kunti, the mother of the five Pandavas, though she suffered numerous hardships, when she lived in concealment and in the forest, she yet prayed to God for more difficulties.

111. O God Almighty! she said, give happiness to those who ask for it. But to me, give always a succession of hardships. Let me not forget to take your name.

112. That is my only request. If you will give, give me only this, so that your name will become a lasting ornament to my throat.

113. O listeners, and this narrator too, let us ask of Sai, this and this alone, that 'Let us never forget your Name and give us refuge at your feet.'

114. And so, Amir made obeisance and kissed Baba's hand with its attendant ritual. He described in detail his malady and prayed for liberation from pain and suffering.

115. He asked Baba for a remedy for rheumatism that had afflicted him. Baba replied, 'Go, and sit quietly in the *Chawadi*.'

116. The *Chawadi*, where Baba went from the mosque every alternate night, was to be the dwelling for Amir.

117. Amir, who was tormented by rheumatic pains, could happily have stayed anywhere else in the village. He would even have gone back to Korale — any other place would have suited him fine!

118. As for this *Chawadi*, it was ancient (literally from the time of Malik Amber, Dewan of Ahmednagar, from 1597) and was quite worn out and decayed, from above and from below. Chameleons, lizards, scorpions and snakes lived here, freely.

119. Moreover, there lived lepers in that place and so did dogs, feasting on the leavings and fragments of food. Amir felt very sad. But before Baba, no arguments prevailed.

120. The rear portions of this *Chawadi* were filled with debris; there were numerous pot-holes, some knee-deep. His misery was worse than a dog's wretchedness. Truly, it was as a fruitless journey of life!

121. Rain leaking from above; dampness and moisture in the ground below! Unlevelled, the place was full of ups and downs and hollows. To add to everything, the wind and the cold played havoc. In his mind, Amir was greatly worried.

122. The joints of his body had become stiff with all this exposure to wind and rain, which left behind a constant dampness in the place. The only medicine was Baba's word.

123. To him, Baba had said firmly, "There may be rain, there may be dampness. There may be ups and downs and big hollows! But think nothing of them!"

124. There may have been doubts (about the suitability of the place), but he considered Sai's company as its greatest blessing, and Sai's words his only medicine. So he stayed happily.

125. For full nine months, Amir Shakkar stayed on in that *Chawadi*, having spread out his bed in the middle of the room, right in front of you, as you climbed up the steps of the *Chawadi*.

126. Rheumatism had taken a firm root in his body and, at least outwardly, the remedy seemed just the opposite of what it should

be. But the faith within was staunch and unwavering, due to which everything turned out to be all right.

127. Amir had been ordered to stay there for nine months. Going to the mosque for *darshan* was forbidden, too!

128. But that *Chawadi* was a place allotted to him, where he used to get Baba's *darshan*, automatically, without an effort.

129. And that *darshan* too, he had daily, morning and evening. On every alternate day, twice in the day, he could watch the festive ceremony at the *Chawadi*, to his heart's content.

130. When Baba went to collect alms every morning, his route went past the *Chawadi*. So, while coming and going, his *darshan* was easily available to him, without his even having to leave his place.

131. Similarly, everyday in the evening, Baba would come before the *Chawadi* and would stand engrossed in saluting all the directions by shaking his head and the index finger.

132. From there, he would then go back to the corner of the *Samadhi mandir* and from thence, he would return to the mosque, accompanied by his devotees.

133. He would go to the *Chawadi* every alternate night, where only a nominal partition of a door of wooden planks stood between the two of them. And both were very fond of talking.

134. *Pooja, arati,* etc., took place there itself, after which the devotees went home. Thereafter both of them would talk to each other, leisurely.

135. Confinement though it was, outwardly, the enjoyment of a very close association with Sai, was a gain, which is hard to get, without a good fortune.

136. And yet Amir was bored. To stay confined in that one place all the time, was to him an imprisonment. He felt that he wanted to go away to some other place.

137. So fond of his freedom, how could he like such dependence? Oh, enough of this confinement, rose a strong urge in Amir's mind.

138. Without Baba's permission, he set out, abandoning his appointed place. He went to Kopergaon and stayed in a *dharmashala*[3].

139. And now, see the marvel that took place! A fakir[4], on the threshold of death, was dying of thirst and entreated for a draught of water to drink.

140. Moved by compassion, Amir went to give him some water. The moment he drank it, the body of that fakir fell to the ground, lifeless, there and then.

141. He was dead. No one was around. Moreover, it was night. Amir's mind grew confused and agitated.

142. In the morning, there will be an inquest and people will be arrested in connection with this sudden death. Government will hold an inquiry.

143. Even if the truth were told, who will at once believe it to be so? The judgement will depend on witnesses and evidence. Such is the procedure of law.

144. I myself gave him water and the fakir, all of a sudden, lost his life. If I were to tell this truth, I myself will be caught quite easily.

145. Seeing my direct involvement in this, they will catch me, first. Later on, when the real cause of death is determined, I will be acquitted.

146. But the interim period, before it is determined, will become unbearable with suffering. So thinking, he decided at once to go back the same way he came.

147. So thinking, Amir set out from there, in that very night. On the way, he was uneasy in his mind that anyone might see him and so, kept looking back every few steps that he took forward.

148. How he would make it to the *Chawadi*, for till then, his mind would not be at rest. With much misgiving in his mind Amir proceeded towards Shirdi.

149. Said he to himself, 'Baba, what is this you have done! What sin of mine is visiting upon me? Oh, it is my own *karma* that I am paying for. This I now know full well.

150. 'To seek happiness, I left the *Chawadi*. Hence you have punished me. But now, please relieve my pain and suffering and take me to Shirdi safely.'

151. Amir packed up in no time and leaving that corpse there in that *dharmashala*, at night, set out in that same night.

152. With 'Baba, Baba', on his lips all the time, entreating his forgiveness, when he reached the *Chawadi* at last, his mind was at rest.

153. Thus Amir learnt his lesson. From then onwards, he made a firm resolve and abandoning wicked, evil ways, began to follow the path of righteousness!

154. His faith cured him and he became free from rheumatic pain. Now just listen to what took place, later on.

155. The *Chawadi* was divided into only three parts. The south-east quarter was Baba's seat, walled on all the four sides by wooden planks. Baba used to sleep there.

156. The whole night, lamps were kept burning. For he always slept in the light of the lamps. On the outer side, in the darkness, sat fakirs, bairagis and beggars.

157. Amir was treated as one among them. There used to be other people around, who would also be lying down in that same place. Of these, there were many.

158. There, behind Baba's seat, where all the stores and miscellaneous things were kept, Baba's most detached and faithful devotee, Abdul, was, in person, ever ready to render service.

159. On one occasion, at around midnight, Baba suddenly called out to Abdul, saying 'Just see, a ghost stands at my bedside!'

160. Call upon call, he gave to Abdul, who came there at once with a light in hand. Baba said to him, loudly, 'But it was here, just now!'

161. Abdul said, 'I have looked everywhere, but I can find nothing here.' Baba said, 'Look carefully everywhere, keeping your eyes wide open.'

162. Abdul looked, again and again. Baba began striking the ground with his baton. All the people sleeping outside, woke up to see what had happened.

163. Amir Shakkar woke up, too, saying, 'Oh, what is this wild shouting, this vehemence today? And why these repeated strokes of the baton, at this unearthly hour of the night?

164. Seeing this Baba's *leela*, Amir at once understood in his mind that a snake must have entered somewhere and Baba had come to know of it.

165. He had much experience of Baba's ways; he knew Baba's nature and his manner of talking. So he understood everything.

166. When danger stalked close to the devotees, Baba would say it stood at his own side. Amir knew this language. So, in his own mind he at once drew the inference.

167. Suddenly, at his own bedside, he saw something wriggling. 'Abdul, bring, bring that lamp here, first!' Amir cried out.

168. As soon as the lamp was brought, he saw the huge expanse of the coiled snake, who, dazed by the light, was moving his head up and down.

169. The snake was laid to rest there itself (by those assembled). They thanked Baba profusely, saying, 'What a very strange way of alerting the devotees, indeed!'

170. What ghost and what light! It was only an ingenious device to warn his devotees, of the imminent danger and to protect them from it.

171. There are innumerable such instances about snakes in Baba's life-story, which can be narrated. And they have been briefly narrated here only to avoid expanding the book.

172. 'Snakes, scorpions, they are all Narayan (God)' says the saint Tukaram. 'But they should all be bowed to from far.' These are also his words.

173. Moreover, he also calls them 'unrighteous' and hence, he says, they should be dealt with, with one's slippers. This means that one does not really know with any certainty how they should be treated.

174. The truth of the matter here is, as is one's nature and one's destiny, so is his *karma* or action.

175. Baba, however, had only one answer to this question. All living beings, he said, are equal and therefore, non-violence towards all, is the one common rule.

176. Whether it be a scorpion or a snake, God dwells in all alike. And so, when He does not will it so, can they harm anyone?

177. This whole universe is controlled by God. Nothing here is independent of His will. Such was Baba's knowledge, based on experience. But still, our baseless, offensive conceit will not leave us.

178. A scorpion that has fallen in a tank, rolls and tosses in his struggle to come out, but sinks, nevertheless, to the bottom of the tank. Seeing this, one claps gleefully, saying, 'You also torment others, similarly.'

179. At the sound of the claps, another comes running to that tank and seeing the drowning scorpion, sinking and rising, repeatedly, is moved by compassion.

180. Going near him, he then catches the scorpion firmly between his thumb and the forefinger and the scorpion, true to his nature, springs back in retaliation and stings his little finger.

181. Of what use is all our knowledge here? We are altogether in the power of another. God is the giver of disposition and whatever He wills, will happen.

182. Varied are the experiences of various people. I will also narrate my own experience, here. Baba's words must be respected by keeping implicit trust in him. For it is only through such firm faith that his greatness and glory can be experienced.

183. Kakasaheb Dikshit used to read *Nath Bhagvat* during the day and similarly, every night he used to read, without fail, *Bhavarth Ramayan* (of Eknath Maharaj).

184. He may forget to offer flowers to God; may even forget to bathe; may forget all other rules and disciplines; but it was impossible that he would ever forget the appointed time for reading.

185. Both these books are by Eknath and contain the essence of spirituality. It was truly the mark of Samarth Sai's grace bestowed on Dikshit.

186. In these unparalleled, absorbing books, there burns the ethereal three-fold flame of Self-knowledge, Renunciation and a code of righteous behaviour, for ever.

187. The fortunate one, to whose lips comes the glass of this nectar-sweet spiritual instruction, will have at once, overcome the three-fold afflictions and *Moksha* will come rolling at his feet.

188. Dikshit was to get a listener for his reading and, by Sai's grace, I had this opportunity to listen to *Bhagvat*. It was a great boon to me.

189. I started going, day and night, to listen to those sacred stories. By my good fortune, it was the beginning of a series of listening sessions, which sanctified my ears.

190. And so, on one such night, while these highly purifying tales were being read out, a strange, though minor incident took place. Listen, O listeners to this tale!

191. What can I do? While narrating one story, another suddenly comes to my mind in the middle of it. And, knowing how worthy it is of being heard, how can I disregard it?

192. An interesting story from the Ramayan was in progress. Although Hanumant had, on his own, recognized the true mark of Shri Ram that his mother had told him about, he wanted to put his Swami's power to test and ended up by bringing upon himself a great calamity.

193. A merest brush of the air from the feathers on Ram's arrow sent him spinning round and round in the sky, until, in extreme agony, he began to gasp for breath. His father Vayu (wind), then came upon the scene.

194. Taking his advice, Hanumant then surrendered to Shri Ram. While this part of the story was being narrated, just see what a strange thing happened.

195. The listeners' attention was fully engrossed in listening to the story, when a scorpion, a disaster personified, appeared on the scene, one knows not how.

196. What interest he found in the story, one wonders! But, without the least awareness on my part, he jumped onto my shoulder, hiding there securely and savouring the sweetness of the tale.

197. Even here, I experienced Baba's protection, for I had not noticed anything. But he who is attentive to the *Hari-katha*, will be protected by Hari Himself.

198. Casually, my eyes turned in that direction, only to find a terrible scorpion, sitting happily on my *uparna* that rested on my right shoulder.

199. No wriggling, no movement, he sat quietly like an attentive listener, who is carefully listening to the story from his own seat.

200. Even if he had moved his tail ever so slightly, with a natural instinct, he would have given me no peace, causing me great anxiety.

201. Story of Rama was becoming more and more interesting; the narrator, the listeners were all completely absorbed in it, when everything would have been completely spoiled by such a dangerous, wicked creature.

202. But such is the power of *Ram-katha* that dangers and calamities become powerless before it, forgetting their natural tendencies and become appeased.

203. It was Rama's grace that I thought of throwing away softly that dangerous creature and not to trust his capricious nature, till the situation got out of hand.

204. So, very carefully, I caught hold of the two sides of the *uparna* that I was wearing, rolling up the scorpion securely within and taking it to the garden, spread it out.

205. By nature, a scorpion is terrible and may, at times, behave according to his natural instinct. Such was my fear. And yet, very firm and resolute was Baba's command. So I dared not kill it.

206. Here the listeners may naturally ask, is not a scorpion treacherous and therefore deserves to be killed? If he stings, is it going to bring any pleasure? One wonders why it should not be killed!

207. Snakes, scorpions and other venomous creatures will never be neglected by anyone. Why will Baba ask them to be let off?

208. This doubt raised by the listeners is a very real one. I myself, had the same doubt. But listen to Baba's words on one other such occasion in the past.

209. It was a question far more difficult than this. Once, in Shirdi, in Kaka's *wada*, a terrible snake was discovered near the window on the upper storey.

210. He had entered the room from the hole below the window-frame. His eyes were dazed by the light of the lamp, as he sat coiled up there.

211. Although he was dazed by the lamp-light, he was bewildered by the human presence. The noise and confusion startled him and for a moment, he lay very still.

212. He would move neither forward nor backward, but only moved his head up and down. Then there started a great hustle and bustle, each one thinking of the best way to kill him.

213. Some picked up batons; some, sticks and hurried at once. The place where he sat was narrow and awkward and their minds were exercised greatly.

214. Had he made but one swift movement to glide down the wall, he would have landed himself straight into the roll of my bedding. And that would have been my greatest peril.

215. Moreover, if the blows aimed at the most vital spot in his body were missed, he would have, for ever, nursed a deep hatred and caused untold harm. As the lamps were brought closer to inspect his hiding place properly, the snake seized the opportunity to escape.

216. The time had not yet come for him to die. And our luck was also great. Although the moment was fatal, Baba protected us.

217. Swiftly, he glided away the way he had entered, thereby making himself and us, free from fear, to our mutual relief.

218. Muktaram then, got up, saying, 'Poor creature! It is well that he escaped. If he had not slipped away from that hole, he would have lost his life.'

219. Muktaram's compassionate attitude made me feel very sad at heart. What is the use of compassion towards the wicked? How can the world go on like this?

220. Muktaram comes here only once in a while, whereas we sit here, morning and evening. My bedding was just near that window and hence I did not like Muktaram's remarks.

221. He put forth his argument at the beginning; I argued from the opposite point of view, replying to his argument. The debate raged; the final result remained inconclusive.

222. One said the snake should be killed. It should not be delayed even by a moment. The other said, Why hate an innocent creature?

223. One side rejected Muktaram's argument, indignantly. One side advocated my views. The debate gathered momentum. But there was no end to it, in sight.

224. Muktaram then went down. I changed my place, plugged that hole and spread out my bedding to sleep.

225. Drowsiness crept over the eyes; people too, went away to sleep. I began to yawn and the discussion came to an end, on its own.

226. The night over, we finished our morning ablutions. Baba also returned from the Lendi and people gathered in the mosque.

227. As usual, I came to the mosque at the usual time. Muktaram and others came too, and took their own places.

228. Somebody was crushing the tobacco in the palm of his hand; somebody else was filling Baba's clay-pipe; some were pressing his hands and feet. In this way, they were serving Baba in some way or the other.

229. Baba knew everbody's thoughts. He then asked in a low voice, 'What was that controversy going on in the *wada* last night?'

230. I then told Baba what had happened, in that same order and asked whether one should kill or not kill the snake under these cirumstances.

231. Baba had only one thing to say, whether it is a snake or a scorpion, God dwells in all of them. So love them all.

232. God is the controller of this world and every one acts according to His command. Even if it be a snake or a scorpion, he will not act contrary to His command.

233. Hence have love and compassion for all the creatures. Give up rashness and have patience and forbearance. God is the Protector of all.

234. In this way, how many of the innumerable stories of Sai Baba can be narrated? Hence the listeners must take the essence from them all.

235. The next chapter is even more interesting, as it will bring out the rare combination of devotion and staunch faith, when his great devotee Dikshit, had to face a difficult situation as he got ready to kill a goat, in deference to Baba's command.

Weal be to all! Here ends the twenty-second chapter of
"Shri Sai Samarth Satcharit," called
'*Averting Accidental Death*' (of devotees)
as inspired by the saints and the virtuous,
and composed by his devotee Hemadpant.

Notes

1. Sheshnaag is the king of the serpent-race, as a large thousand-headed snake, at once the couch and canopy of Vishnu and the upholder of the world which rests on one of its heads.
2. Refer to Ch. 12, note 2.
3. A building erected for the accommodation of travellers.
4. Was it Baba in the garb of a fakir?

23

Leelas of the Guru and His Devotees

MY OBEISANCE TO SHRI GANESH, TO SHRI SARASWATI, AND SHRI GURUMAHARAJ! TO THE FAMILY DEITY, TO SHRI SITA-RAMACHANDRA, MY MOST HUMBLE OBEISANCE! I BOW IN REVERENCE TO THE MOST VENERABLE GURU SHRI SAINATH!

1. This *Jeevatma* is, in fact, beyond the *trigunas* but being bewitched by *Maya*, he forgets his true divine nature of Truth, Consciousness and Bliss and identifies himself with the body.

2. Then, with the ego of his body, he begins to believe that 'I am the doer; I am the enjoyer', and is vexed by a series of calamities, which he does not know how to escape.

3. A loving devotion at the guru's feet is the only way to overcome these obstacles. This most artful Sai, who is himself *Shrirang* (Shri Krishna), draws his devotees into his joyous sport.

4. We may regard him as an '*avatar*', because he has all those characteristics. As for himself, he has always said, 'I am a slave in Allah's service.'

5. Although an '*avatar*' himself, he followed the conventional code of conduct, completely, and advocated a scrupulous adherence to the rules laid down by the *Varnas* and *Ashramas*.

6. He never competed with anyone, in any way, nor did he encourage others to do so. Such humility alone, became one, who saw the all-pervasive God in this whole creation.

7. He never scorned anyone, nor did he consider anyone contemptible. For he saw in all creatures the presence of Narayana, the Cloud of Consciousness.

8. He never claimed 'I am God'; but 'I am his poor slave, a *Yade Hakka*¹'. He constantly chanted '*Allah Malik*'².

9. Of any saint, the criteria to understand his spiritual authority are not his caste, his food habits, his conduct. For it is something that lies beyond all these considerations.

10. It is by God's grace that these benevolent saints incarnate on this earth to uplift the dull-witted creatures.

11. Only if there is accumulated merit from previous births will there arise a fondness to listen to the stories of saints, which bring peace and happiness to the mind.

12. Once a great student of *Yoga*³ arrived at the mosque, bringing Chandorkar with him.

13. He had studied the *Yogashastra* of the great sage Patanjali, very thoroughly. But if his experiences were considered, they were very strange. And, try as he may, he could not enter the state of *samadhi*, even for a moment.

14. 'If Sai Maharaj, this greatest of the yogis, will bestow grace on me, my doubts will be resolved, and I will be able to enter into *samadhi*, most certainly'.

15. With this purpose in mind, he came for Sai's *darshan*, only to find him sitting eating *bhakri* (*Jowar* bread) with an onion.

16. When he saw Baba holding a piece of stale bread and a dry onion to his mouth, a serious doubt assailed his mind, as to how such a person could ever remove his doubts.

17. Even as this doubt arose in his mind, Sai Maharaj knew it with his intuitive knowledge and said, 'Nana, only they should eat an onion who can digest it!

18. 'He who has the power to digest it, should eat the onion, without a fear in the world!' Hearing this, the yogi felt quite abashed in his mind and surrendered to Baba with a pure heart.

19. Later on, that student of yoga came and sat near Baba, with an unblemished mind, as Baba came to sit on his usual seat.

20. Cautiously, he then asked his doubt which was answered satisfactorily by Baba. Then he went back happily having received *Udi* and blessings from Baba.

21. There are many such stories, which when heard with faith, will remove the physical and mental obstacles, like sorrow, temptations, etc.

22. However small the pool of water and however offensive its stench, a pig will undoubtedly look upon it as a source of greatest pleasure.

23. There is one similarity between the *Jeevatma* and a parrot. They are both imprisoned — one in a body the other in a cage. Though he has lost his freedom, the parrot prefers his confinement.

24. Like a well-frog, not knowing the pleasure of freedom, the parrot too, finds all his happinesss in that cage. A *Jeevatma*, full of desires, is like that.

25. Oh, how wonderful is my cage! And how enjoyable my little flutterings to and from its golden rod! Even if I suspend myself from it, head downwards, no fear of losing my foothold!

26. But once outside the cage, I will lose all these pleasures. No more the pomegranate-pips, no more the delicious chillies! Truly it will be forfeiting all one's pleasures at one's own hands!

27. And yet, as the opportune time comes, the parrot experiences that wonderful moment which, with an affectionate pat on his back, opens his eyes with the collyrium of knowledge, to the joy of freedom.

28. The pat awakens his inherent consciousness of freedom and the bird escapes. His eyes are now fully opened and flapping his wings joyfully, he flies freely in the sky. Who can then restrain him?

29. The whole wide world stands beckoning him. He can now feast to his heart's content, in the orchards of pomegranates and guavas. The vast expanse of the sky is now open before him, to fly about, in his new-found freedom, which he enjoys to the utmost.

30. Such is also the state of this *Jeevatma*. When he enjoys God's grace and finds a guru, he experiences not only the release from bondage, but also the great joy of freedom.

31. And now, O faithful listeners, will you all listen for a moment, with full attention, to a fascinating tale of pure love?

32. In the last chapter, you saw the marvel of how Baba sent Mirikar on his journey to Chithali, telling Shama to accompany him;

33. Knowing the future, Sai gave a timely warning to Mirikar, alerting him about the danger from the *long Bawa* or the snake.

34. How he not only warned him, but also provided the means of overcoming a calamity. In fact, he forced them on him despite his refusal and thus protected Mirikar from danger.

35. Quick and eager as Baba always was, to ensure the welfare of his devotees, he averted the calamity about to befall Balasaheb Mirikar, giving him thus, a strange experience.

36. But stranger still was the experience of Shama. When he was suddenly bitten by a snake and was in grave danger to his life, Baba saved him.

37. That too, is yet another of Baba's *leelas*! Let me narrate it first, to the listeners. A snake had actually bitten Shama, but just see what remedy Baba used for it!

38. It was about seven o'clock when a snake suddenly bit the little finger of his hand, the poison causing intense burning in that part of the hand.

39. The pain was so unbearable that life itself seemed to have reached its end. Madhavrao's mind was clouded with worry and fear.

40. His whole body turned red; friends and relatives gathered around, urging him to come to the Viroba temple[4], since his life was in such grave danger.

41. Nimonkar (Madhavrao's uncle) then came forward and said, 'Take *udi*, first; then go'. Madhavrao rushed to the mosque. But lo! what did Baba do?

42. Baba's ways are truly astonishing! For as his eyes met Shama's, he began abusing and cursing and would not allow him to come up the steps.

43. "Do not climb up, O Bhaturdya! (a term of anger and contempt for a Brahmin). If you dare climb up, just beware! Get out, at once! Climb down and be gone!" he roared.

44. It was astonishing to see Baba so angry. Most unexpectedly, he began breathing fire and fury. Madhavrao was stunned! He wondered why Baba was uttering such harsh words.

45. On seeing all this, Madhavrao panicked within. He could think of nothing and sat down, dazed and dejected.

46. When Baba himself thus became angry, Madhavrao's heart sank. He felt that when Baba had rejected him, all hope of a cure was lost.

47. And who would not be frightened? Seeing him provoked to such terrible wrath, listening to the shower of abuses and curses, the whole situation appeared terrifying.

48. This mosque is as my maternal home and I, Sai's own child! This being so, why is the Mother so exceedingly angry with her child, today?

49. To whom but the mother should the complaint be taken, when a snake has bitten? And when she herself kicks him away, will not the child make a pitiful face?

50. As a child to the mother, so was Madhavrao to Baba. When such had been the relationship, day and night, why such a sorry state, only today?

51. When the child is kicked away by the mother herself, who will then protect him? At that moment, Madhavrao had given up all hope of survival.

52. After a while, when Baba had calmed down, Madhavrao took up courage, went up to him and sat down.

53. Baba then said, "Do not lose courage and have no worry, whatsoever, in your mind. All will be well; give up worrying. The Fakir is compassionate and will protect you.

54. "Go home and sit quietly. Do not go out of the house. Be brave and do not worry! Keep trust in me."

55. Then, when he had hardly reached home, Baba sent Tatya Kote to enquire after him and with a message.

56. "Tell him not to sleep. He should keep walking about in the house itself. He may eat whatever he wants. But let him be careful only of this one thing."

57. That night, Baba said also to Kakasaheb Dikshit, that he (Madhavrao) might feel drowsy that night, but should not be allowed to sleep.

58. And thus, taking this precaution, his pain and suffering passed away. True, a little burning sensation still lingered, due to the poison, in that little finger.

59. Later, even that disappeared. Oh, how that terrible moment was overcome! Such indeed is the compassion of this Sai, whose heart is stirred by kindness and love for his devotee.

60. "Do not climb up, O Bhaturdya!" was the verbal chastisement from Baba. But was it aimed at Madhavrao?

61. No, indeed! The piercing words were not aimed at Madhavrao, at all! It was a sharp command to the poison of the snake that had bitten.

62. "If you dare climb up, just beware!" was the stern command from Sai's mouth, which at once arrested on the spot, the onward flow of the poison.

63. And as if this was not enough, Sai's brief *mantra* "Get out, at once! Climb down and be gone!" made the poison come down, immediately.

64. Without using any other means, like the conventional *mantrik* or *Panchakshari*[5], this Sai, the Espouser of his devotees' cause, averted their calamities in various ways.

65. He did not chant any *mantra*, nor did he empower rice and water with charms, nor yet did he sprinkle any water. How then, did the poison become ineffective?

66. What, is this not a miracle? Merely by the words from a saint's mouth, Madhavrao was relieved of his agonizing pain. Truly, there is no limit to Sai's grace!

67. And now, my listeners! Listen attentively to a detailed narration of the interesting, marvellous tale, that was mentioned in the last chapter.

68. This story is more wonderful than the one narrated in the last chapter. It will now be narrated to the listeners, how Sai used to show his *leela*!

69. When these fascinating tales are listened to, the guru's words will be deeply impressed on the mind and the feeling of being a doer of good or bad deeds, or that of being a non-doer, will all vanish. The faith in the guru will grow stronger.

70. The easiest of all easy ways is to remember Sai in your heart. This is the only refuge and the only way to destroy *Maya*.

71. Great is the fear of this worldly life, a turbulence that arises out of *Maya*. But by listening to these stories, *Maya* will be shattered and the highest happiness attained.

72. Once an epidemic of cholera broke out in Shirdi. The villagers were terrified at heart and decided unanimously on having the drums beaten by the public crier to halt all communication with the outsiders.

73. So great was this fear of cholera that the villagers had taken a dread of the disease. They would have nothing to do with any outsiders, while the epidemic lasted. All trade and communication came to a standstill.

74. So long as this epidemic of cholera continued in the village, no one was to kill a goat or allow a cart from outside to cross the village boundary. Everyone was expected to follow the rule strictly.

75. Baba, however, did not approve of this blind faith of the villagers in God. In his opinion, these false notions only went to prove the ignorance of the villagers.

76. So that, while on the one hand, the villagers laid down rules and regulations, Baba, on the other hand, would set them at nought. Listen carefully as to how he did it.

77. The villagers sincerely obeyed this resolution of the Grampanchayat. For, if anyone violated the rule even a little, he would be released only on paying a fine.

78. Baba had no fear of the fine; he was, for ever, fearless. The mind having ceased to exist in devotion to God, he was always invincible in the most adverse of cirmumstances.

79. Once a cart filled with firewood, from another village, crossed the village boundary, creating a difficult situation. Differences and disagreements arose between the people.

80. The villagers were fully aware that firewood was scarce in the village. But it was equally improper to violate the rule. It made them feel quite dejected.

81. So they turned upon the poor cartman and tried to send the cart back. News reached Baba. At once, he arrived on the spot.

82. He went and stood before the cart, seeing which, the cartman's courage rose high. The resistance of the villagers broke down and the cart pushed its way, crossing the village boundary.

83. Baba then made him drive the cart from there straight to the door of the *Sabhamandap* and empty it inside. Not a word passed out of the mouth of anyone.

84. Be it summer, winter, autumn or spring or monsoon, Baba kept the *dhuni* burning in the mosque, twenty-four hours.

85. Strange indeed, was Baba's resolve! Like the *'agnihotra'*[6] of an *'Agnihotri'*, Baba's sacred *dhuni* was burning day and night.

86. Only for this *dhuni* would he buy bundles of faggots, piling them up in a heap against the wall of the *mandap*.

87. Taking advantage of the weekly market day, Baba would carefully store up the firewood. But even on that, the neighbours would cast their greedy eyes. Rare indeed, is he, who is slow to see his own advantage.

88. 'Baba, there is not a faggot for the hearth and without firewood, the home fire will not burn today!' So would they make false pretences. Thus even they would get a share in the wood.

89. Selfish people are, by their very nature, wicked! The *Sabhamandap* had no door, which gave them their opportunity. Needy and deceitful, both benefitted equally.

90. Baba was exceedingly generous. How can his greatness be described? Outwardly, he looked stern; but he was very soft and tender within.

91. Unfathomable is his greatness. Only when Speech gives up its conceit and bows at his feet in humility, can it have the power to describe it.

92. Keeping in mind all the time, that God Almighty fills this whole Universe and still remains, he had no enmity towards anyone.

93. God pervades this entire Creation, the ten directions, in front and behind; hence malignant attitude towards anyone made him very sad.

94. Although absolutely detached within, he himself behaved like a householder, for instructing his followers and guiding them on the path of righteousness.

95. And oh, what humility this great mahatma had! Listening to its description, you will be simply amazed! Moreover, it will bring out his love for his devotees and the fulfilment of the purpose of his incarnation.

96. Incomparable was his boundless compassion. And he was always fond of taking to himself the smaller or lowlier place. Crores of stories can be related to bear this out.

97. Never did he undertake fasts; nor did he practise the arduous *Hathyoga* practices. He had no hankering after food to pamper his palate, but always took food in moderation.

98. Going to a few fixed households, he would ask for bhakri — either dry or dressed. These and these alms alone, were his usual '*madhukari*'[7], for he never indulged the palate.

99. Never having indulged the palate, he had no hankering after sweetmeats. Whether he received alms or not, and of however indifferent quality they might be, he was content with what he got.

100. In this manner he sustained life and protected the body, only because it is the one means of obtaining Knowledge and Salvation. But he never identified himself with it.

101. Why would he, who was adorned by an inner Peace, need necklaces round his neck? Nor did he need to smear on his body, sandalwood paste or *udi*. Shri Sai was himself the Perfect Brahman.

102. This story, in which the one feeling of loving devotion predominates, is very sacred and instructive. Those who listen to it with full attention, will find their awareness of the worldly life slowly disappearing.

103. And as the faith of the listeners strengthens, Sai's rich treasures will open up to them, even more. But this gain is not for the wicked and the vexatious. A loving, trusting devotee alone will enjoy it.

104. Now, if the listeners listen with concentration to the story that follows, their hearts will be overcome with love and their eyes will shed tears of joy.

105. Most ingenious were Baba's ways, indeed! How wonderful were his plans and their objectives! His staunch devotees knew from their repeated experience, the essence of all these.

106. Listening to Sai's story is like drinking sweet nectar! Concentrate your minds on the guru with reverence, and listen to the story that follows.

107. This tale is a unique feast, which is not to be savoured in a hurry. For each and every dish needs to be tasted with relish, to enjoy its novelty to the heart's content.

108. But now, enough of the tale of that cart! Far more strange than that is the story of the he-goat, which will amaze the listeners and fill the guru-devotees with joy.

109. Once a most remarkable incident took place in Shirdi. Somebody brought a he-goat who was on the verge of death and had grown extremely feeble. People at once gathered round to see him.

110. Mother Sai always looked after him, who had no master, no protector. All the afflicted, the suffering, the rejected, found refuge in the mosque.

111. Bade Baba[8] was there, near at hand, at the time. So Baba said to him, "Offer him in sacrifice; kill him with just one stroke!"

112. Great was the importance that this Bade Baba enjoyed. His place was always at Baba's right hand side. Baba would smoke a *chillim* only after Bade Baba had first smoked it!

113. And so far as Sai Baba was concerned, not a leaf would flutter without Bade Baba. Unless Bade Baba had eaten, Baba would not take his food.

114. Once, it so happened, that on the festive occasion of *Diwali* (the Festival of Lights), when all the sweets, etc., were served on the

plates and the diners had taken their respective places, Bade Baba just walked away in a huff, offended.

115. Unless Bade Baba was present, Sai Baba would not touch his food and when Sai Baba himself did not touch it, how would the others do so?

116. And so, everybody sat there, waiting. They searched for Bade Baba and brought him back. Only when he thus joined them did Baba eat.

117. And now, leaving the present narrative aside, I am tempted to give some information to the listeners about this as a digression.

118. Bade Baba was Baba's guest and at meal times, he would sit waiting in the *Sabhamandap* below, straining his ears for Baba to call him.

119. Two rows of diners would sit on either side with Baba seated in the middle. Bade Baba's place was reserved on Baba's left hand.

120. When all the food offerings were served on the plates, the plates were placed in two rows. As the meal time approached, and the diners took their respective places,

121. Baba himself, called out, very respectfully, in a loud voice. And as soon as he called out, 'Bade Miyan!' Bade Baba would quickly come up the steps, making obeisance.

122. What respect did he deserve, who turned away from food, in a huff and for no reason at all? Why so much honour to him, who thus insulted food?

123. But even this was just a way of instructing people, by first practising it himself. He thus demonstrated how improper it was to take food without calling your guest to participate.

124. This rule for the householders (laid down by the *Shastras*), to avert future calamities, was never violated by Baba. He himself, followed it scrupulously.

125. By thus honouring the guest, all the desires are fulfilled. By so doing, all that is evil is warded off. But if it is neglected, harm is sure to follow. Hence the venerable always offer *pooja* to their guest.

126. When the guest remains without food, it portends the loss of animals, sons, wealth, stocks of food-grains, etc. Thus a guest remaining on an empty stomach is an invitation to trouble.

127. Every day, Sai Baba used to give Rs.50 to Bade Baba, by way of *dakshina* and would himself walk a hundred steps with him, to see him off.

128. And this was the Bade Baba from whose lips quickly came the excuse, when he was first asked to kill the he-goat, 'But how to kill him without any reason?'

129. Madhavrao was present there, too! So Baba commanded him, "Shama, at least you go now and get a knife to kill this goat! Go quickly!"

130. A fearless devotee that Madhavrao was, he went to Radhakrishnabai and brought a knife which he then placed before Baba.

131. Although bringing that knife was, for Madhavrao, a very painful effort, Baba would not have liked to see him come back without it.

132. Meanwhile, news reached Radhakrishna's ears and, moved by compassion, she at once called back for the knife.

133. Once again, Madhavrao set out to fetch another knife, but then he stayed away this time, sitting in the *wada*, lest the killing took place at his hands.

134. To test Kaka's mind, Baba then commanded him, "Go, you get a knife to cut that goat. Do relieve him of his suffering and pain".

135. Full well did Baba know that Kaka was as pure, tested gold; but people would never be satisfied, unless he was tested in the burning furnace.

136. Without applying the test of rubbing it against the steel file or making a hole, to find out whether the gold was pure or alloyed, one of discerning or enquiring mind will not trust anybody's word.

137. Even a diamond has to bear the blows of a hammer before it acquires its own lustre. For, not without paying the price of suffering the hammer blows, shall the glory of a Godhead be easily attained.

138. True, Kaka was precious as a talisman round the neck; but how were others to be convinced? Even a diamond is tied with a thread and tested in the fire by the connoisseur of gems to determine its worth.

139. Never will the resolves be fulfilled, of one who doubts the words of a saint; they will, at best, be only an unsubstantial fruitless babble of words and will bring him no spiritual progress, even in the least degree.

140. But he who reveres the deeply significant words of a guru will succeed in securing his worldly advantage as also his spiritual advancement, but he who finds fault and malice there, will only ensure his own fall.

141. Ever ready to serve the guru, he bows before only the guru's command, leaving all consideration of the propriety or impropriety of the act on the guru's head.

142. He is a slave to the guru's command and has no independent judgement of his own. Always eager to obey the guru's word, he will not consider the good or bad of it.

143. Mind absorbed in chanting *Sai-naam*, eyes fixed on the holy feet of Sai Samarth and the mind intent on meditating on Sai, his whole body is offered at the service of Sai.

144. Even if a brief moment were to elapse between the guru's utterance of a command and his execution of it, that little delay too, is unbearable to him. Most extraordinary is this acting (on the command of the guru).

145. Dikshit was pure, unalloyed essence of goodness; in courage and determination, a *Maha-Meru*[9], whom the doubt as to how to kill that living goat, did not even touch.

146. That an innocent he-goat will die, his soul will be in an agony of pain; that his own pure, good reputation will be tainted as he will be committing a great sin, thereby —

147. Such a thought never crossed his mind at all. Disobeying the command was, to him, the greatest sin and obeying it, at once and in every possible way, was the greatest merit.

148. He, to whom the guru's command was the only standard of truth, was strangely excited and tremulous as his naturally tender heart was thus induced to take the goat's life.

149. Then he went to *Sathe-wada* and brought the weapon as per Baba's command. He got himself all ready to kill that he-goat, without any faltering.

150. Total obedience to the guru's command inspired great courage. He took up the weapon and steeled his heart.

151. Born in a Brahmin family, pure and sacred; with a vow of non-violence observed since the day he was born — and oh, what a situation for such a one, to be in! How will his hand be raised for such a deed?

152. Undaunted, where obedience to the guru's command is concerned, he made up his mind, once for all. And yet, the heart pounded furiously within; perspiration flowed profusely.

153. He had never known a harsh word, in speech, thought or action, and that he should have to strike with a weapon! It was truly, an occurrence of rare misfortune!

154. Those who disregard the guru's word are, most certainly, destined to lose all the merit accumulated over the past births.

155. Absolute obedience of the guru's command is the most precious among all ornaments. It is the one sure mark of a good disciple whereas violation of that command is the greatest of all sins.

156. Guru's command should be obeyed without a moment's delay. And he who doubts and hesitates is truly, a wretched one — in fact, he is a beast without a tail, in the form of a man.

157. There is no need to look for an auspicious moment here, no question of good and bad, of instant or deferred action. He who obeys is wise and discerning; he who delays is unfortunate.

158. Tucking in the end of his *dhoti*, with one hand and gathering up the weapon with the other, he rolled up his sleeves, as he approached the spot where the goat was.

159. The villagers were quite astonished — 'What is this extraordinary deed! Where has the tenderness of Kaka's heart disappeared?

160. 'A Muslim and a non-vegetarian like Fakir Baba, but whereas even he would not lift a weapon on a poor, tormented goat, Kaka here is all ready to do it!'

161. Those who are extraordinary among men, they are harder than a *vajra* (thunderbolt), but softer than a flower, at heart.

162. Then, clutching the knife tightly in hand, which was raised high to strike, he said, 'So Baba, must I now strike him? Tell me, just this once!'

163. The weapon that is meant for the protection of the meek and the afflicted, is it also to be used to kill an innocent goat? But on the other hand, he was sold, heart and soul, to the service of the guru. Hence this little hesitation!

164. And yet, as he was trying to get the killing over, as quickly as possible, suddenly his heart was moved to pity, the hand holding the knife, faltered, came back and would not move forward, again!

165. "Hmm! Kill it now! What are you waiting for?" As this final and ultimate order came, Kaka turned a half-circle, in a bid to strike hard.

166. He lifted his hand, holding the knife; for the goat, the fatal moment had arrived; but God, his Protector, rushed to his rescue, in the nick of time!

167. Certain that Dikshit would now strike, Mother Sai thought that if he waited a moment longer, it would be a disaster and said quickly, "Oh, but let it be! Let it be!

168. "No, no, Kaka! Turn back! Oh, how heartless you are! A Brahmin, and still you want to kill? Is there no consideration in your heart?"

169. No sooner he heard this, Kaka at once dropped the knife. Old and young, all were astonished. The goat had received a gift of life and guru-devotion had reached its culmination!

170. Listen carefully now, to what Kaka then said, as he dropped the knife, 'Baba, your nectar-like words are as *dharma-shastra* to us.

171. 'We do not know any *dharma* other than that. And we are not ashamed or disgraced. Obedience to the guru's Word is of the very essence; it is, to us, the *Ved-shastra*.

172.   'In obeying the guru's command lies the true discipleship of a
       disciple. This alone is our adornment, while disobedience to it,
       in any sense, is a stain or a blot.

173.   'It may bring us pleasure or pain — our sights are not set on the
       consequence. What is in our destiny, will happen. We leave it to
       God.

174.   'As for us, we know only one thing — to remember your name, all
       the time; to store up your Divine Form in the eyes and to be
       bound to your Word, by day and by night.

175.   'Violence or non-violence, we do not know; for, the Sadguru's
       holy feet are our Saviour. We never think of questioning the
       guru's command. Our duty lies in obeying it.

176.   'Even when the guru's command is clear, the disciple who questions
       the propriety or impropriety, the good or bad of it, has, according
       to me, fallen from his duty.

177.   'Disobedience to the guru's command is in itself the fall from
       Grace of a creature. Obedience to his command is the most vital
       part of conformation to the *Shastras*.

178.   'The mind must always be concentrated at the guru's feet — no
       matter, if life then remains or departs. Guru's command is, to us,
       the only standard of truth. The final effect, the ultimate end, he
       alone knows!

179.   'Our gain or our peril, we know not; nor do we know our own
       benefit or that of others. We only know, to carry out the guru's
       work. And to us, that alone is our spiritual upliftment.

180.   'Before guru's Word, rules and regulations, prohibitions and taboos
       are of no avail. The attention of the disciple must be focussed on
       the duty appointed to him by the guru. The burden of his
       difficulties rest on the guru's head.

181.   'We are slaves to your command and will not question what is
       proper and what is not. We will give our life, if need be, but will
       obey the guru's Word.'

182.   The heart that is naturally compassionate turns to stone and
       Brahmins are ready to do what even the Muslims do not dare.

183. Listeners may find this hard to believe. But this is the mystery that belongs to the Sadguru. Be a slave to the guru's Word once, and you will unravel this mystery instantly!

184. Once the devotee seeks refuge at his feet with utmost faith and beseeches his protection, from then onwards, the guru takes over his burden; he need make no effort, whatsoever.

185. Once he surrenders totally to the guru, there remains no fear for him. For guru alone will give him self-confidence and take him across safely.

186. Disciples are of three types — the best, the mediocre and the inferior or low in their attitude of mind. I shall briefly explain each of these three.

187. Knowing the guru's wish without his having to tell and to begin obeying it as soon as it is understood, without waiting for his actual command, know him to be the 'best' among the disciples.

188. To obey to the very letter, the command when the guru gives it, and to carry it out without any delay — know him to be the 'mediocre' among the disciples.

189. Guru goes on repeating his command and the disciple goes on deferring its execution, thus blundering at every step — know him to be the 'inferior' or 'low' among the disciples.

190. When the mind does not have renunciation in the highest degree and there is no discrimination between the Permanent and the transient, how can such a one enjoy the guru's grace, even if he were to spend a whole lifetime, seeking it?

191. Hence God will fulfil his wish, whose mind is for ever fixed at the guru's feet. God, that Supreme Kinsman, will quickly make him free from all desires and bring him lasting Peace.

192. The power of pure, steadfast faith should be strong, to add to which, there should be a powerful insight. And it should be coupled with a steady, unwavering courage. Spiritual progress then, will be a certainty.

193. Controlling the breath is not needed here. The practices of *Pranayam, Hathayoga, Samadhi* and return to normal physical consciousness from it — these for us are difficult means.

194. When the disciple is well-trained and ready, it does not take him long to receive the fruit from the Sadguru. For the guru is always eager and ready to initiate.

195. Only the true devotees will experience the vision of the manifest Divine Form. Devotion arises in the heart of those who are loving and trusting. To others, it is a heresy.

196. Baba then said to Kaka, "Take this tumbler of water in your hand. I shall now do '*Halal*'[10], most certainly to ensure his onward progress to Heaven."

197. As it was, the he-goat was nearing his end. Fakir Baba had a timely thought. There was a '*takiya*'[11], nearby.

198. So he consulted Baba whether the goat should be killed at that *takiya*. On getting his consent, when the goat was moved from that spot under this pretext, he died a natural death.

199. The death of that goat was inevitable and all of them knew it. But making use of this opportunity, Baba showed his *leela*.

200. Those who surrendered to the Sadguru, became one with him. When salt goes into the sea to bathe, does it ever come back?

201. *Jeevatma* experiences the joys and sorrows of worldly life, while it is God who gives him these experiences. But it is Sadguru alone, who gives him *Moksha*. He is the repository of the Oneness of all souls.

202. When the guru is moved by compassion, he will bestow the Divine Vision, which contains the entire Creation at one and the same time.

203. Hemad has surrendered totally to Sai, offering at his feet his '*Ahamkar*' (ego) and prays to him in his heart to keep him always wakeful and free from ego.

204. Now, in the next two chapters, Sai Maharaj will offer us a feast of humour and jesting. Listen to his marvellous *leela*!

205. It may appear as entertaining humour and jesting, but it is most instructive. The faithful devotee, who studies it carefully, will enjoy great happiness.

Weal be to all! Here ends the twenty-third chapter of
"*Shri Sai Samarth Satcharit*", called
'*Leelas of the Guru and his Devotees*',
as inspired by the saints and the virtuous,
and composed by his devotee, Hemadpant.

Notes

1. A '*yaadgar*' or one who remembers or is mindful of.
2. Allah or God is the Master of all.
3. His name was Ram Baba. This incident took place on 22.2.1914. (Shri Sai Leela, April, 1984, p. 25).
4. This is a Shiva temple. It is believed that if a man bitten by a snake is taken there, he is cured.
5. An exorciser or dispossessor of demons and fiends.
6. Maintenance of a perpetual and sacred fire; an *Agnihotri* is a Brahmin who maintains that perpetual fire.
7. Refer Ch. 8, note no. 10.
8. His name was Bade Baba alias Fakir Baba alias Peer Mohammed Yasin Miyan. Being a *fakir*, he was a wanderer, who first came to Shirdi in 1909 and was asked to put up in the new *Chawadi* and to read the Quran. Later, he shifted to Neemgaon and came to Shirdi in the morning and remained in the mosque till the meal time at noon, in the company of Sai Baba. It is said that baba had instructed him much earlier in Aurangabad and set him up on the spiritual path. He passed away in January 1925, at Nagpur.
9. Refer Ch. 3, note no. 4.
10. To kill according to the forms prescribed by the Muhammadan law.
11. Refer Ch. 5, verse 99.

24

Baba's Splendid Sense of Humour

MY OBEISANCE TO SHRI GANESH, TO SHRI SARASWATI, AND SHRI GURUMAHARAJ! TO THE FAMILY DEITY, TO SHRI SITA-RAMACHANDRA, MY MOST HUMBLE OBEISANCE! I BOW IN REVERENCE TO THE MOST VENERABLE GURU SHRI SAINATH!

1. As promised at the end of the last chapter, I will now narrate how guru Sainath, the Cloud of Compassion, gave instruction even through jesting and humour.

2. Of course, to say that 'I will narrate' is only my ego, while one should always be free from ego, at the guru's feet. Only then will the narration have the power to move the hearts of the listeners. But now, listen respectfully to the tale.

3. The sadhus, the revered and the great are always pure and sinless. They are pure and faultless as the clear, cloudless sky.

4. Singing praises of Sai Maharaj is the means of achieving both material and spiritual welfare. It helps concentrate on the true Self, thereby bringing an inner contentment.

5. He, who is desirous of achieving his spiritual welfare, should listen to the story with reverence. He will enjoy bliss, without an effort and experience fulfilment in life.

6. Those who listen to it will enjoy an inner peace; their baseless fear of worldly life will be dispelled; they will enjoy lasting bliss and emancipation will come to them, readily.

7. With his intuitive powers, Sai Samarth knows full well, the thoughts and feelings of his devotees. He will fulfil his responsibility towards them and redeem his promise.

8. Sai Samarth himself stimulates the mind and it is he, who makes me utter his words. I shall narrate his message in its essence, which is the means of attaining material and spiritual power, to the best of my ability.

9. People are not blind, nor do they suffer from night blindness. Eyes they certainly have, but still they are blind, for they identify themselves with the body and do not understand their own good.

10. Moreover, this body is such that its existence cannot be taken for granted even for a moment. Hence I spread my palms before you to entreat you earnestly, to savour of the sweetness of the tale, for a moment.

11. Everyone likes joking and jesting. But most extraordinary was Baba's way of using such jesting and humour, to impress upon the minds of the devotees, the very essence of his teachings, which was always beneficial to all.

12. Nobody takes a joke seriously; but they took fondly to Baba's jesting, and in fact, waited eagerly for their own turn to come.

13. Usually, people do not like a joke at their cost, but they liked Baba's jokes, immensely. And specially, if it was accompanied by acting and emphatic gestures, the joke achieved its purpose instantaneously.

14. His jokes always had a natural ease and novelty about them. Their spirit heightened by the smiling countenance, the play of the eyes, their charm was simply indescribable.

15. I shall now narrate an experience, a story at once instructive and novel. Listen to those glorious words, through which flowed spiritual instruction, couched in light-hearted jesting.

16. At Shirdi, there is a big weekly bazaar, every Sunday. Pitching tents in the open, buying and selling operations are in full swing.

17. There, on the road itself, fall heaps of vegetables and greens. Numerous traders in oil and betel leaves, areca nuts, tobacco, etc., sit at the cross-roads.

18. One such Sunday, I was with Baba in the afternoon, pressing his feet, when a very strange thing happened!

19. Baba's 'darbar' in the afternoon was always crowded, to add to which, it was a Sunday and the market day. People had flocked to the mosque in large numbers.

20. I sat on Baba's right, facing him and bending my neck, was pressing his feet chanting the *Naam* to myself, ceaselessly.

21. Madhavrao was to Baba's left, Vamanrao, to his right, while Srimant (Gopalrao) Butti sat there, too, waiting his turn to serve.

22. And so was Kaka, sitting there. Suddenly, Madhavrao laughed. 'What, Annasaheb! What are these grains that seem to have stuck here?'

23. So saying, Madhavrao touched the folds of my coat with his finger and lo! there were the grains stuck therein!

24. As I stretched out my left elbow to see what it was, some grains of parched gram were seen rolling down and I saw those around picking them up.

25. When they were carefully picked up and gathered together they came up to about twenty-five grains. That then became the cause for teasing and joking! But how did such a thing happen?

26. Guess followed upon guess; each one was absorbed in his own thought. Those gram-grains coming in contact with the coat was something that puzzled everyone.

27. After all, how many folds could that khaki coat have had? And how would they contain these grains? But to begin with, from where did they come and under what circumstances? No one could understand this with a certainty!

28. While pressing his feet, with my mind engrossed in chanting the *Naam*, how did this tale of the gram suddenly crop up, in the middle of it?

29. Moreover, since so much time had passed while I was serving Baba, pressing his feet, how is it that they did not roll down all this while? That they should have remained stuck there all this time, was something that made everybody wonder.

30. Everybody was thus quite puzzled as to where the grams came from and how the grams settled in the folds of the coat. Listen to what Baba then said.

31. Strange and varied are the different ways of instruction of different people. However, Baba instructed each according to his capacity.

32. Maharaj's ways were most unusual and his manner of instructing was interesting enough to remain in the memory. I have no experience of having seen or heard anything like this, anywhere else.

33. He said, "This one here has a bad habit and is fond of eating things, all by himself. Today, taking advantage of its being a market day he has come here cramming grams into his mouth, without a care in the world.

34. "It is not good to eat (things) all by oneself. But I know his habit and these gram grains are themselves a proof of it. It is not surprising at all!"

35. I then replied, 'To eat without giving it to others, I have never known. Where then is the question of such a bad habit? It will not stick, try as others may.

36. 'Baba, to this moment, I have never seen the Shirdi market and only if I go there can I buy the gram and thereafter, the matter of eating it!

37. 'Those who have such fondness for eating alone, may have it! I for one, do not have this bad habit. Without giving, at least a little of it, to others, I never put anything in my mouth.'

38. But then, just see Baba's ingenuity, how he confirms the faith of the devotee in himself. On hearing my candid words, listen carefully to what he said.

39. "To him, you will give, who is nearby. But if not, what can you also do? And what can I do about it either? Do you remember me?

40. "And am I not near you? But do you offer me even a morsel?" The gram grains were just an excuse to impress the principle firmly on our minds.

41. Great blame attaches to that food, which is taken to nourish your own body, deceiving the gods and goddesses of the sense organs, as also others, the *Panchagni*[1], the *Panchapranas*[2], the *Vaishwadev*[3];

to the exclusion of even the unexpected guest, who arrives at the mealtime.

42. This principle, unimportant as it may appear, is yet, of great significance when applied to the daily life. And what has been said about tasting food with the palate is only a synecdoche (a part for the whole), while it is true of all the five senses.

43. He who has a longing for sensual pleasures can never attain spiritual progress; but he who keeps the senses under control will have it as his slave.

44. Baba was only reiterating firmly through humour and jesting, the *mantra* which the *Shrutis* have proclaimed, viz., 'When all the senses are stilled, when the mind is at rest, when the intellect wavers not — that, say the wise, is the highest state.'[4]

45. And this is true also of the other four, i.e. the word, touch, vision and smell. How instructive, how relevant were Baba's words in the present context!

46. When the mind, intellect and sense-organs are drawn to the enjoyment of sense-objects, think of me, first, and offer them to me, bit by bit.

47. That the senses will remain without being attracted to the sense-objects, is never possible, so long as this world lasts. But if they are offered at the guru's feet, the attachment to them will be naturally weakened.

48. When a desire is roused, let it be only about me. When you are angry, direct that anger towards me. Ego, obstinacy should all be directed similarly, at my feet by the devotees.

49. When lust, anger, ego and other such natural propensities are provoked furiously, make me the target and direct them at me.

50. In this way, Hari will destroy them one by one and the waves of this triple-poison will be calmed by Govinda.

51. Or rather, all these tumultuous passions will merge in my Form or they will become one with me, as they rest at my feet.

52. When such a practice is formed, the passions become feeble on their own, and after a time, are destroyed completely. The mind is then free from passions.

53. Once the mind comes to believe firmly, that the guru is always close by, it will never be plagued in this way.

54. Where this good thought has taken root, there the bondage of worldly life falls off. The guru appears in every sense object; or rather, every sense object is adorned by the guru's form.

55. In ever so slight an enjoyment of a sense object, the thought that Baba is near us, will, at the outset, give rise to the consideration of the worthiness or otherwise, of the enjoyment of that object.

56. That object, which is not suitable or worthy, will be discarded, naturally. The addict thus becomes free of his addiction; the mind becomes disgusted with such undesirable sense objects, once it is turned away from them with constant practice.

57. The devotee then becomes ever watchful and ready to exercise control over sensual desires, the rules for which have come from *Vedas*. He then begins to enjoy the sense objects according to these rules and does not behave wantonly.

58. Once the mind is habituated in this manner, the sense-desires weaken. Instead, there arises a love for *guru-bhajan* and from thence sprouts pure Knowledge.

59. As this pure Knowledge begins to grow, the bondage of bodily awareness snaps, the same intellect now dives deep into the consciousness that 'I am Brahman'. It is then that infinite happiness is experienced.

60. Though the body is transient, it is the only means of achieving the highest goal of human existence, which is higher than *Moksha* itself, because it leads to the *Bhaktiyoga*.

61. Higher than the four *Purushartha*[5] (or the ultimate goals of human life), is this fifth one. Nothing is as great as this, for *Bhaktiyoga* is unique.

62. He who has experienced fulfilment in life by serving the guru, will understand this truth adequately, that his own good lies in attaining *bhakti*, knowledge and renunciation. Only such a one will achieve spiritual progress.

63. He who sees a difference between guru and God, has failed to find that God though he has read the whole *Bhagvat*.

64. It is like reading the whole *Ramayan*, but not knowing at the end of it, how Sita was related to Rama. Give up the thought of duality and know that the guru and God are one and the same.

65. By serving the guru with a pure heart, all desire for sensual pleasures will be uprooted completely. The mind will become pure and unblemished and the self-illumined, real Self will manifest Itself.

66. And so, when Baba willed it strongly, it was as easy for him to produce the gram, as washing his hands! In fact, he showed *leelas* far stranger than these, in no time.

67. An ordinary conjurer waves a charmed bone and produces any substance at will, by his hypnotic powers, just to eke out a living.

68. But Sainath is a conjuror, unique and most remarkable! And oh, how grand was his sport! If he wishes, he will produce innumerable gram-grains, all in a trice!

69. But let us concentrate on the significance of this story, that none of the five senses should enjoy sensual objects, without remembering Baba.

70. Once the mind is taught this lesson, it will be remembered, time and again. The mind will then concentrate on Sai, in every give-and-take of worldly life.

71. The Pure Brahman will most certainly come before the eyes in Its Perfect Form, with all the attributes, giving rise to devotion, liberation and renunciation and leading to the attainment of that highest state.

72. As the eyes gaze upon that comely figure, the consciousness of worldly life, of hunger and thirst, will melt away; the awareness of material pleasures will be lost, too! The mind will then enjoy peace and contentment.

73. The '*ovi*' does not come to mind quickly, try as one may. But grinding the grain at the quern, it comes back, instantaneously. In the same way, describing Baba's *leela* about the gram, I recollect the story of Sudama.[6]

74. Once, while Balaram[7], Shri Krisha and Sudama were staying at Guru Sandipani's ashram, serving him, Krishna and Balaram were sent on the errand to bring wood.

75. Obeying the command of the guru's wife, Krishna and Balaram set out along a forest path. They had hardly left, when Sudama was asked to accompany them, too!

76. He had been given some gram by the guru's wife, who had instructed him that should they feel hungry, while wandering in the forest, the three of them should eat that gram.

77. Later, Sudama met Krishna in the forest, and Krishna said to him, 'Dada, I feel thirsty'. But just listen to what Sudama replied, without a word about the gram that he had with him!

78. 'Never drink water on an empty stomach. Instead, why don't you rest for a while, first?' And even as Krishna rested his head on his lap, he could not bring himself to say, 'Have some of this gram!'

79. Seeing that Krishna had dozed off, Sudama began to eat the gram himself. So Krishna said, 'Dada, what is it you are eating? What is this sound?'

80. 'Oh, Krishna! what is there to eat here? It is this cold that makes my teeth chatter, that is all! See, I cannot even pronounce the *Vishnusahasranaam*, clearly!'

81. Hearing Sudama's reply, that Omniscient Lord Krishna said, 'Oh, really! I too had exactly the same dream!

82. 'When one eats something that belongs to another and, when asked what he is eating, says in annoyance 'Oh, what do I eat — it is only this earth!', pat comes the reply, 'So be it!'

83. 'But of course, this is just a dream, Dada! How will you ever eat anything without me? And even when I asked you what you were eating, I was still dreaming!'

84. Had Sudamji but known in his previous ashram-stage, of Krishna's *leela*, never would he have made such a mistake and suffered its dire consequences!

85. For, were these consequences ordinary? By no means! He had to suffer from extreme poverty! Hence those people, who eat without giving others, should remember this.

86. Although Sudama was a devotee and had Krishna for a friend, yet the moment he swerved, ever so slightly, from the moral path, he had to suffer the blow of misfortune in worldly life.

87. But that same Sudama, when he lovingly offered to Shrikrishna, just a handful of his wife's hard-earned puffed rice, the Lord was pleased and bestowed on him all the prosperity that his heart could desire.

88. But now, here is another instructive tale that I shall narrate; listen to it. It is, at first, full of pleasant enjoyable humour; but ends up in being highly instructive.

89. Some like spiritual instruction; some, logical reasoning and arguments. There are yet others, who are fond of joking and laughter. What everyone seeks is pleasure.

90. This too was a way of joking, when a lady and a gentleman, both were obsinate and in Sai's court, there arose a great dispute, which was settled amicably in the end, without any blame attaching to either.

91. This story is also exceedingly interesting — one to delight the listeners. As the devotees fought with each other, mirth and laughter reached a peak.

92. Damodar Ghanashyam, whose surname was Babare, was a devotee, better known as Anna Chinchanikar. He had a boundless affection for Baba.

93. Hot-tempered, he was given to sharp, cutting words. Without regard or care for others' feelings, or what he said was proper or improper, good or bad, he would speak out openly and bluntly.

94. Though stern, rather fierce by nature, he was equally honest, guileless and *sattvik*. It was as if a loaded revolver was on his head constantly, ready to explode at the pull of the trigger.

95. Everything was done at once, there and then; there was no question of credit dealings. Without deference or consideration for others, all transactions were down-to-earth and prompt.

96. One may be able to hold burning embers in hand; but Anna's temper was more scorching than that. But for all this, he belonged

to a species utterly guileless and straight-forward. That is why Baba loved him.

97. One day, in the afternoon, Baba sat in the mosque, resting his left hand on the railing and surrounded by his darbar.

98. Baba would, at such times, appear to sit quite indifferent and detached; but without anyone realizing it, would spark off quarrels among the devotees, ending in their going off in a huff, sulking. He would then pacify both parties, in the end.

99. Some devotees would be busy pressing the sides of his body, some would be pressing his feet, some others pressed his back and the stomach. They were all eager to serve him in one way or another.

100. Baba was a child-celibate, who lived in perpetual continency and was pure in conduct. He therefore allowed both men and women to serve him.

101. Anna, standing on the outer side, had bent forward and was slowly pressing Baba's left hand. But listen to the position on the right side.

102. There, there was a lady, devoted single-mindedly to Baba, whom he addressed as 'Mother', while all the others called her '*Mavashibai*'[8] (maternal aunt).

103. Though she was, to them, '*Mavashibai*', her real name was Venubai and surname was Kaujalgi. Her faith in Sai was unparalleled.

104. Anna had crossed the fifty-year mark and had lost all his teeth. Mavashi too, was elderly and mature. It was between these two that the dispute arose.

105. Anna was with his wife there, to serve Baba. The matronly Mavashi was a widow. So vigorously did she press Baba's stomach that Mavashi could hardly control her breathing.

106. Pure at heart, Mavashibai put all her strength into serving Baba, as she twisted both her hands to knead his stomach, vehemently.

107. Standing at his back, and taking a firm grip, she began churning his belly by pressing hard, again and again, with both her hands, as if it was buttermilk that she was churning in a vessel.

108. Preoccupied totally in chanting *Sai-naam,* Mavashibai went on pressing and kneading, fearlessly. Baba too, gave no sign of being under any intense, continuing bodily pain — as if it was all conducive to good health!

109. But it was truly a most extraordinary way of massaging, flattening the stomach and back into one! No doubt, it showed her intense love for Baba, but the onlookers were moved to compassion at Baba's suffering.

110. Knowing it to come from pure, sincere love for himself, Sai would of course accept such excellent service from the devotees, so that they may remember him all the time, and thereby achieve their own weal.

111. After all, how much could have been our penance that we should thus have been blessed with the saint's sacred company! Nay, it is truly Sai's mercy in not rejecting his devotees that is responsible for this!

112. Oh, but what skill there was in those undulations of the lady, as she massaged! With her vigorous movements, Baba moved up and down — and so did she! It was an amazing manner of serving somebody.

113. However, Anna on the other side, was quite steady in his movements, as he slightly bent forwards. The lady, who was deeply engrossed in her work, was quite unaware that with her every movement, her face too, went up and down, quite forcefully. Listen to what followed.

114. The lady was quite pleased with herself, as she kneaded Baba's stomach with all her strength, in her sincere desire to serve him. But in so doing, she happened to swing a bit too far to one side; with the result that her face came quite close to Anna's!

115. Mavashibai was very witty and quickly seized this opportunity to say, 'Oh, how wayward is this Anna! He is asking me for a kiss, first!

116. 'Are you not ashamed of your white hair, that you should want to kiss me?' As she said these words, Anna immediately rolled up his sleeves, too!

117. 'Old and haggard that I am', he said, 'am I such a fool, so absolutely crazy? It is you yourself, who have joined the battle here and are all ready to fight with me!'

118. When he saw that a quarrel was flaring up, Baba, who had at heart, a loving concern for both, thought of a clever stratagem to pacify them both.

119. Very affectionately he said, "Anna, why all this unnecessary uproar? And I really do not understand what is so improper about kissing the mother!"

120. In their hearts they both felt ashamed on hearing these words. Words of jesting and teasing remained where they were. Instead, good-humoured laughter filled the air. Everyone enjoyed the joke greatly.

121. The story, as such, seems quite insignificant. But the shrewd listeners will appreciate it for revealing to them as to how one can silence a person in so many different ways.

122. If both of them had had the same affection for each other as between a mother and her child, such a dispute would not have arisen and anger would not have been provoked, either.

123. A person may burst out laughing, while being caned and dissolve into tears when hit by a merest flower! It is the feeling that causes these waves of emotions. Who does not have this experience?

124. Baba's natural ingenuity was truly astonishing! So appropriate were his words to the occasion, that the listeners were not only satisfied fully, but had instantly learned the lesson.

125. On one other similar occasion, when his stomach was being kneaded vigorously, one of his great devotees felt a compassionate concern and anxiety on its being carried too far.

126. 'Lady, have some mercy!' he pleaded, 'Is this any way to press the body? O have some compassion in your heart. Baba's veins will, burst otherwise!'

127. As these words fell on his ears, Baba quickly got up from his seat and taking the baton in hand, struck the ground hard with it.

128. His temper flared up dangerously and the eyes, glowing like burning embers, rotated as he glared all round. At that moment, who would have the courage to stand before him?

129. The eyes shone in the daylight, like those of a cat in darkness. It seemed as though he would burn down the whole creation, there and then, with the fierce flame in his eyes.

130. Holding one end of the baton with both his hands, he thrust it deep into the hollow of his stomach, as he tightly fixed its other end into the pillar, in front, embracing that pillar firmly, so as to exert maximum pressure.

131. The baton, which was in length a full arm and a quarter, seemed to have gone into the stomach, full length, and an explosion of the stomach seemed imminent, putting an end to Baba's life!

132. Firmly rooted as that pillar was, how would it move at all? Baba moved, closer and closer touching that pillar, finally, and clasped it tightly against his stomach. The on-lookers were terror-stricken!

133. Fearing that his stomach would now burst, everyone stood astonished. 'O God! What an unwarranted, shocking situation! What a dreadful calamity!'

134. So the people exclaimed, worried! What is to be done in such a grievous misfortune? And all this calamity just for that Mavashibai? But Baba stood firm on his Promise of championing the cause of the devotee.

135. If anyone were to find fault with, or cricicize the devotee who was serving him, Baba would never tolerate it.

136. Out of his love for Baba, the devotee felt that he should give a hint to Mavashibai, for Baba's comfort. But should it have ended up like this?

137. But God Himself, was moved to compassion! Sai's anger cooled down. Giving up that fearful idea, he came back and sat on his seat.

138. The loving devotee may have been bold and fearless. But seeing Baba's stern nature, he resolved firmly, never to repeat that mistake! He had learnt his lesson only too well.

139. From then onwards, he resolved never to interfere with anyone, but to let each one do what he pleases.

140. Sai Samarth himself was powerful enough and knew well what to permit and what to prevent. Why should one try to judge the merits and faults of those who serve him?

141. For these are only our subjective reactions that 'the service of this one pleases Sai', or 'that of another is painful to him'. We never really know the truth.

142. But now, this was a tale of joking and humour and each one will derive the lesson from the story according to his own capacity. May the devotees savour its sweetness, as a bee from the flower.

143. Hemad humbly bows at Sai's feet. The chapter that follows is even more profound in significance. In it, Sai, the ever-compassionate One, will fulfil the wish of his devotee, Damodar.

144. That too, is a great marvel! Calling Damodar before himself, Damodar, who was harassed and wearied out by the problems in worldly life, Baba gave him relief from his anxieties.

Weal be to all! Here ends the twenty-fourth chapter of
"Shri Sai Samarth Satcharit", called
'*Baba's Splendid Sense of Humour*',
as inspired by the saints and the virtuous,
and composed by his devotee, Hemadpant.

Notes

1. The five mystic fires of the body.
2. Five vital airs, constituting animal life, viz. *Pran, Apan, Saman, Udan* and *Vyan*.
3. A ceremony of the daily course, viz. the casting before beginning the meal, of a little food into the fire, as an offering to Agni.
4. The quotation is from the translation of *Katha- Upanishad*, Ch. II, valli 6, mantra 10, by Swami Prabhavananda and another, *The Upanishads*; Sri Ramakrishna Math, Madras, 1983, p. 37.
5. *Arth, Kaam, Dharma* and *Moksha* are the four goals of human life.
6. The name of an indigent Brahmin, enriched by Krishna.
7. Elder brother of Shrikrishna.
8. Mrs Venubai or Lakshmibai Kaujalgi was the aunt of Radhakrishnabai. Well-informed in *Vedanta*, she used to sing *bhajans* and also attended 'Paramamrut' classes. Sai Baba would show her special favour by letting her worship him. She thought of staying permanently in Shirdi and Baba encourgaed her to do so. He jokingly called her his mother-in-law, which gave the idea to Khaparde that he accepted her as his disciple.

25

Effecting the Devotee's Weal

MY OBEISANCE TO SHRI GANESH, TO SHRI SARASWATI, AND SHRI GURUMAHARAJ! TO THE FAMILY DEITY, TO SHRI SITA-RAMACHANDRA, MY MOST HUMBLE OBEISANCE! I BOW IN REVERENCE TO THE MOST VENERABLE GURU SHRI SAINATH!

1. The Ocean of Kindness, Sai Maharaj is truly an Incarnation of God, Himself! Before this Perfect Brahman, greatest and most excellent among the *yogis*, I prostrate in obeisance.

2. Glory be to this Adornment of the saints, the Abode of all weal, the true Self! O Sai Samarth, who are the repose of the devotees and ever-satiated in all the desires, I bow to you.

3. The narration in the last chapter was about the fond pursuit of humour and jesting as a means to instruct the devotees. And fond as he is of his devotees, this Sai always brings them joy.

4. Sai is the very image of highest Mercy and the one thing needed here is steadfast devotion to him. The devotee should be trusting, should be affectionate. The fulfilment of all his desires will not, then, be wanting.

5. Even Krishna has said to Uddhava that 'the Sadguru is verily in my image'. And such should also be the loving devotion to the Sadguru. This is true, single-minded devotion.

6. A desire arose in my heart to write the life-story of Shri Sai. And Sai relieved my anxiety to do so by getting his marvellous *leelas* written by me, which are so worthy of being listened to.

7. Without my having the authority or the skill that comes of a deep knowledge of the *Shastras*, he has given the inspiration to a lowly creature like me and has got this book written at my hands to bring an awareness to his devotees.

8. When an ignorant person, like me, was commanded to 'keep a record', my dull intellect was enriched with knowledge and confidence, instantly.

9. At once I took courage that this Sai, endowed with most excellent qualities that he is, will get his own records kept, in order to uplift his own devotees.

10. Or else, could I ever have ventured upon this illluminating literary composition, this '*payas-prasad*'[1] of the saint, the nectar of Sai's story?

11. This Life-story of Sai is, to the devotees, is a '*paanpoyi*'[2] of his nectar-sweet stories. With Sai's grace, drink deeply and to your heart's content, to ward off the scorching heat of this conflagration that the worldly life is.

12. This is not just a life -story, but a veritable '*somakant*'[3] from which the nectar of the moon constantly oozes out in the form of Sai's tales. May the devotees, like the thirsty Chakor bird, drink of it to their hearts' content and be satiated.

13. O my loving listener, listen now, with concentration and without any reservations, to this sacred story of Sai, which will destroy the evil propensities and passions of this *Kali-yuga*.

14. Once the devotee begins to cherish a single-minded devotion to Sai, he (Sai) will ward off all his calamities and suffering; he will also grant him all that he desires.

15. A tale, in this context, will bring out Sai's affection for his devotees and when listened to, with respect, will gladden the listeners' hearts.

16. So, with utmost attention, listen to this wonderful story. It will only confirm you in your experience of how the guru, our Mother, is an Ocean of Compassion.

17. Brief as this story is, in significance, it is profound. Attend to it for a moment and all your problems will be solved.

18. Damuanna was a wealthy, comfortably settled devotee from Ahmednagar, belonging to the *Kasar*[4] community. He was greatly attached to Sai.

19. Listening to the story of this great devotee will bring you great joy and will actually demonstrate Sai's ever-readiness to protect his devotees.

20. At the annual *Ram-navami* celebrations, two new large banners are taken out in a procession at Shirdi, as everybody there knows.

21. Of these, one is Nanasaheb Nimonkar's and the other, of this Damuanna. For years now, this practice of theirs, born out of a loving devotion, has continued without a break.

22. Damuanna had two wives, but no son. With Sai's blessings, a son was born to him.

23. By way of thanksgiving, he promised to fly a banner at the *Ram-navami*, taken out ceremoniously in a procession, earlier. From that year began the annual procession, carrying the banner.

24. The preparations for the procession are made in the house of the carpenter, Kondya. From there, the procession, carrying the banners, starts, amidst the clash of musical instruments.

25. The two long banners are then tied to the two ends of the mosque. And that is how the festival is celebrated every year.

26. Similarly, the fakirs who gather there are fed too, till satiated. In this way *Ram-navami* is observed by this Shet (Damuanna).

27. And it is this Damuanna, whose story I shall now narrate to the listeners. When heard attentively, you will experience Baba's prowess.

28. A friend of his from Bombay wrote a letter to Damuanna, saying, 'Let us do business, such as will fetch us a net profit of rupees, two lakhs.

29. 'You and I will become partners and will each earn rupees one lakh. Make haste and send a reply. This transaction is genuine and free from any risk.

30. 'This time we will buy cotton. The prices will soar in no time. However, those who do not secure a good bargain, repent at leisure.

31. 'Let us not lose such an opportunity!' Annas mind was in great
    commotion. He had a firm faith in his friend. Yet, he could not
    make up his mind!

32. 'Shall I enter into this deal or not?' Anna wondered. 'God! What
    will happen? What shall I do?' He was quite perplexed.

33. But Damuanna was also a *guru-putra* (a staunch devotee). He
    wrote a letter to Baba, saying, 'Baba, we have no independent
    mind of our own. You are our Protector, our only Refuge!

34. 'At the first consideration, I feel I should enter into the deal. But
    please tell me whether it will entail profit or loss?'

35. The letter was addressed to Madhavrao, who was requested to
    read it out to Baba and to inform him what Baba's order was,
    though the business proposition appeared to be all right.

36. The letter came to Madhavrao's hand the next day, at about 3-
    3.30 p.m. He brought it to the mosque and placed it at Baba's
    feet.

37. "What Shama! What is all this hustle and bustle about? And
    what is that piece of paper you are placing at my feet?" 'Baba,
    that Damu Shet from Nagar — he wants to ask you something!'

38. "What is it? What does he write? What plans is he making to
    reach out to the sky? He is not content with what God has given
    him!

39. "Read, read that letter of his!" Shama said, 'What you are now
    saying is indeed the very purport of the letter.

40. 'Baba, you sit still, but create a commotion in the minds of the
    devotees. And when they become extremely agitated, you bring
    them to your feet!

41. 'Some of them, you pull to yourself. As for the others, you make
    them write letters and yourself repeat their content beforehand!
    Why then, have them read out at all?'

42. "Oh, Shama! Read it, read it now! Why do you believe what I
    say? Oh, I am just a nobody! I speak whatever comes to my lips!"

43. Madhavrao then read out the letter, to which Baba listened with
    great attention. He then said with genuine concern, "This Sheti
    seems to have gone crazy!

44. "Tell him in reply, what is it that is wanting in his home? Even half a piece of bread is enough for us. Do not be tempted by the lakhs."

45. Damuanna was eagerly awaiting the reply every moment and read the letter the instant it arrived.

46. As he read it, Damu Shet was greatly disappointed. Castles built in the air came tumbling down. The tree of hope crashed down, uprooted.

47. 'Now I will earn a lakh, of which, half a lakh I will lend on interest and will, at once, become a money-lender and will live happily in the town.'

48. Alas! The world of fantasy melted into thin air. Damuanna felt very dejected. Oh, what is this that Baba has done!

49. My writing that letter was itself a blunder! And now, I have harmed my own interests, and kicked out, in no time, the prosperity from my doorstep, and that, by my own deed!

50. However, it was also hinted in that letter to Damuanna that as there can be a slip between the cup and the lip, he should personally come to Shirdi.

51. Such being Madhavrao's suggestion, he thought it best to go personally. Who knows, he thought, it may even prove advantageous! Perhaps, Baba may even give his consent!

52. With this thought in mind, Anna came to Shirdi and prostrating before Baba, came and sat down near him.

53. Slowly he began pressing his feet, but still had not the courage to ask his question! Suddenly, a thought struck his mind that he should offer a share in it to Baba.

54. 'O Sainath,' he said to himself, 'if only you will help me in this transaction, I will offer a part of the profit at your feet.'

55. He bowed at Baba's feet and sat quietly for a moment, his mind crowded with doubts and resolutions, as is characteristic of human mind.

56. Devotees make plans, but they do not know their own benefit. Guru alone knows the devotees' interest, future, past and present.

57. However much one may try to keep to oneself, his secret wishes, Sai Samarth has intuitive knowledge of them all, as he dwells within everyone.

58. When someone relates with love and trust, his innermost wish at Sai's feet and asks his permission, reposing full faith in him, Sai always guides him to the right path.

59. It was his vow and all the devotees knew it, that he, who surrenders to him single-mindedly, will be protected by him from all the calamities.

60. Guru alone, is our mother and father, the Preserver and Protector, from innumerable births. He is Hari (Vishnu) and Har (Shiva) and also, Brahma. He is the doer and also the impelling force behind all action.

61. The child asks for sweets, but the mother gives him a potion of medicinal herbs. It may cry, struggle violently in resistance. But such is the mother's verdict, and all out of a loving concern for its well-being.

62. The bitter potion will be beneficial at the proper time. But what does the child understand of its good properties? Only the mother will know a mother's mark of recognition.

63. Anna may well offer him a share, but was Baba going to be tempted by it? His was a selfless love and an eager readiness for the devotee's welfare.

64. He, to whom wealth, gold, was as dust, of what value was that share to him? These saints incarnate on earth only for the uplift of the meek and the lowly.

65. Only he is a true saint, whose life is enriched by practising *Yama-niyam*[5], *Shama-dama*[6]; who is free from weaknesses such as attachment and envy and whose life is meant only for kindness to others.

66. Damuanna's idea of keeping Baba's share was really a secret of his innermost heart. And now, listen carefully to the reply that Baba gave him, quite openly.

67. Baba knew the secret desires of every living creature. He knew their present, future and past clearly, like a *myrobalan* on one's palm.

68. Baba knew full well the future condition of his devotee. Just listen as to how he alerted him, in clear words and at the right time.

69. Baba warned him affectionately, "Oh, I am not a party to any of this, mind you!" Seeing that Baba had not approved of such a fine business proposition, Anna felt quite abashed!

70. However, on hearing Baba's words, Damuanna got the message. He abandoned the plan in his mind and, with face bent down, sat still, greatly dejected.

71. Again, one other idea came to his mind — shall I trade in cereal grains like rice or wheat? Listen to Baba's reply to this.

72. "You will buy at five seers (a measure of weight) a rupee, but sell at seven seers!" These words made Anna feel heartily ashamed of himself.

73. Nothing ever happens anywhere that Baba does not know! Up and down and everywhere, everything lies open before him.

74. At the other end, his friend was quite puzzled and did not know what to do. From Anna, there was no reply.

75. Meanwhile, that Shet (Damuanna) had already written a letter, communicating all that had taken place, on reading which, the friend was simply amazed! 'Strange are the workings of destiny', he thought.

76. 'What a fine bargain had come our way! Why did he not take a decision, himself? Why should he run after that fakir? In vain he has lost such a profitable deal!

77. 'God gives; and our own *karma* takes it away! For we are prompted to act as is pre-destined. When the deal was so fine, why should the fakir stand in the way?

78. 'Relinquishing all the worldly business, these fakirs wander from door to door, like crazy people, and fill their bellies, asking for morsels! What worldly wisdom can they preach?

79. 'But be it as it may! It was not in his destiny and that is why he had such an impulse! I better look for another partner. What is not destined, will never come about, as the saying goes.'

80. And so! Anna resigned himself to the inevitable! Those who were constrained by their destiny, became partners of that friend, — only to court trouble!

81. They went all out for the speculation, but their luck had run out. By a stroke of misfortune, they suffered a heavy loss. Such is the baton of the fakir!

82. 'Oh, how lucky is Damuanna, how wise! And how true and compassionate is his Sai to the devotees!

83. 'Had he joined me as his friend, in this venture, he would have been greatly deceived. But because he listened to the fakir, he was saved. How steadfast is his faith!

84. 'I laughed at his craziness! But in vain, in vain has been my pride in my own wisdom! Such indeed, has been my experience.

85. 'Instead of reviling that fakir needlessly, if I had followed his advice, he would have given a timely warning to me too, and I would not have been so deceived.'

86. I shall now narrate one more story and wind up Anna's tale! It will give pleasure to the listeners, who will be quite amazed at Baba's *leela*.

87. Once, it so happened that a parcel arrived from Goa, containing the famous Alphonso mangoes and sent by a man called Mamledar Rale.

88. Addressed to Madhavrao, but meant as an offering to Baba, it was received at Kopergaon and from thence had come to Shirdi.

89. When it was opened before Baba, in the mosque, delicious mangoes were found inside. The fruit with its sweet, diffusive fragrance were over three hundred, in all.

90. Baba looked at them and handed over all the fruit to Madhavrao, who put four out of them in the big earthen vessel, carrying home the rest.

91. As the fruit fell in the earthen vessel, Baba said, "This fruit is for Damuanna; let it lie there."

92. Two hours passed after the incident and Damuanna came to the mosque, laden with flowers to perform Baba's *pooja*.

93. He did not know what had passed earlier. But Baba, himself, began saying loudly, "The mangoes are Damya's; they are not ours, though people are eager to pounce on them.

94. Only he should take the mangoes to whom they belong. Why should we want another's things? Only he should eat them to whom they belong — even if he dies eating them!"

95. Anna naturally accepted them, in the faith that they were '*prasad*'. For Anna knew full well that he should not fear any adverse consequences of Baba's words.

96. After finishing his *pooja*, Anna went home, but came back again, to ask, 'I do not know whether I should give this fruit to the elder or younger (of the wives).'

97. "Give them to the younger," Baba said, "she will get eight children. The marvel of these mangoes will bring forth four sons and four daughters."

98. Anna, who had no son, had tried various means. He would worship sadhus and saints to earn their blessings.

99. And hence his earnest pursuit of sadhus and saints! To appease, to propitiate the planets, he undertook a study of astrology, himself becoming an astrologer.

100. And Anna had fully realized by now, that the verdict of astrology was that he was not destined to have any issue. He had thus, given up all hope!

101. But when he heard Baba's Promise, these words coming from a saint like Sai, a new hope sprang up in his heart again, as Sai was pleased with him.

102. And thus, in the course of time, Baba's words came true. His blessings bore fruit and children were born to Damuanna.

103. 'As Baba had said, so it happened. My own prediction was falsified. Sai's words proved unmistakably accurate, and as per his words, children were born.'

104. However, these were the utterances while Baba was still in the physical frame. But later, even after he had given up the body, he had himself assured the devotees of their power.

105. "Even when I am no more, trust my words as the truth. My bones will give you an assurance from my grave.

106. "Not me alone, but even my tomb will speak to you. He who surrenders to it whole-heartedly, with him will it sway.

107. "Do not worry that I will be lost to you. You will hear my bones speaking to you of matters of your own interest.

108. "Only remember me, always, with a heart that is trusting. Worship me selflessly and you will achieve your highest weal."

109. O Samarth Sai, Shri Sadguru, who are the *Kalpataru* to your devotees, may this Hemad never be parted from your holy feet. This is the only favour he entreats of you, earnestly!

110. Come to my rescue, O Guruvara, O Compassionate One! This worldly life allows not a moment's rest. But enough, O enough, of this futile cycle of births and deaths!

111. Restrain us, who run unrestrained after sensual pleasures of this material world and remain engrossed in them. Please turn our minds inward!

112. In this Ocean of worldly life, we are carried away, rudderless, on its tumultuous waves. Give us a hand in the hour of our need and free us from the bondage of worldly life.

113. The senses run amuck and are provoked into sinful behaviour. Build a dam on the wild course of this river, so that the senses may turn back.

114. As long as the senses are not controlled and turned inward, the Self can never be revealed. And without that, how can one enjoy the highest bliss? Life will then have been wasted.

115. Wife, son, a host of friends — but not one of these will be of any use, when the end comes. You, and you alone, are the friend, the companion to the end. Only you can give us happiness and liberation.

116. O Maharaj, by the power of your grace, open up the meshes of *karma-akarma*, to relieve the pain and suffering and to uplift the poor and the meek.

117. By your compassion, O the most holy Sairaya, eradicate the evils of argumentation and disputes. May the tongue get addicted to taking the *naam*, all the time.

118. Inspire such love and affection in my heart that resolves and doubts all vanish and I forget this body, the home and material possessions. Help me conquer my ego.

119. May your *naam* be remembered all the time, so that all else is forgotten; may my mind be calm and steady, shedding its fickleness and caprice.

120. If you take us under your wing, the dark night of ignorance will disappear and we shall abide happily in your Light. What can we, then, want?

121. This nectar of your Story that you have fed us, and awakened us with a pat on the back, is this any common, ordinary merit?

122. The next chapter is sweeter still! It will satisfy the fond wish of the listeners. Their love for Sai will grow and faith in him will be confirmed.

123. A devotee came for Sai's *darshan*, abandoning the holy feet of his own guru. But as he made obeisance at Sai's feet, Sai confirmed his devotion to his own guru.

124. Similarly, one other gentleman, wealthy but in distress, came for Sai's *darshan* with his wife and son.

125. How he fulfilled their wish; how, by his mere *darshan*, he cured the son, suffering from epilepsy, and reminded the gentleman of his earlier experience.

126. Hence, Hemad surrenders to Sai, and respectfully entreats the listeners to have the inclination for Sai's stories, which will bring fulfilment to their ears.

Weal be to all! Here ends the twenty-fifth chapter of
"*Shri Sai Samarth Satcharit*", called
'*Effecting the Devotees' Weal*',
as inspired by the saints and the virtuous,
and composed by his devotee, Hemadpant.

Notes

1. A sweet dish made of milk, sugar and rice.
2. Refer Ch. 10, note 10.
3. Refer Ch. 3, note 5, on '*Chandrakant*', for which '*Somakant*' is another name.
4. A maker of or stringer of glass bangles.
5. Two states of *Ashtanga-yoga* for the control of the mind and the senses.
6. The first two acts of the means for the control of the mind and the senses.

26

Averting Epileptic Fits and Suicide, and Confirmation of Faith in one's own guru

MY OBEISANCE TO SHRI GANESH, TO SHRI SARASWATI, AND SHRI GURUMAHARAJ! TO THE FAMILY DEITY, TO SHRI SITA-RAMACHANDRA, MY MOST HUMBLE OBEISANCE! I BOW IN REVERENCE TO THE MOST VENERABLE GURU SHRI SAINATH!

1. This whole creation, containing within itself, the entire elemental world of animate and inanimate things, and clear as a reflection in a mirror, is really an illusory scene created by *Maya*.

2. In fact, this creation of living and non-living things is not a manifestation, but created only in the mind to which it appears as existing in reality.

3. What it reflects in a mirror is not really present there, just as in our sleep all our desires come true, but are destroyed the moment we wake up.

4. As one wakes up, the dream-world melts away and it is by the Sadguru's explanation of the Vedic aphorisms[1] that the light of blissful non-duality appears.

5. And this revelation will only come when Sadguru, who is God Incarnate and who is the seat of that selfless, creative power of the Universe, is pleased.

6. This is the real Self, self-illumined and eternal, while this created, elemental Universe is the sport or *Maya* of that Creator.

7. From Brahma himself, right down to the tiniest of shrubs, this whole elemental world that stretches out before us, is illusory; it is a spectacle created by *Maya*.

8. Just as a rope, through the ignorance of its real nature, is mistaken for a snake or a garland, or a baton or a stream of water, so is also the case with this vast expanse of the Universe. As such, it has no place in the true Self.

9. This visible world is made up of *Maya* and this *Maya* will be dispelled only with the philosophical knowledge, which is obtained when the guru awakens the disciple by imparting instruction to him.

10. Keeping in mind, the meaning of the third person singular derivative of the Sanskrit root '*gru*', it becomes clear that the guru alone is powerful enough in this world to impart the highest Truth to the disciple.

11. Hence let us pray to Baba that he may create in our minds, a longing to turn inwards, endowing the mind with the power of discriminating between the transient and the permanent, thereby making it ready to renounce sensual pleasures.

12. As for me, I am always thoughtless and foolish, hindered by my ignorance of the occult or mysterious, with a mind ruled by wicked evil thoughts. That is why this puzzles me.

13. Make my mind as clear and pure as a mirror, O Sai, so that I shall repose unwavering faith in the words of the guru and of the *Vedanta*. May the knowledge of the Self be firmly imprinted on it.

14. Above all this, O Sadguru Sai Samarth, let the real significance of this knowledge be understood by me. For, without actual experience, what spiritual progress a mere babble of words can attain?

15. Therefore, Baba, grant me your grace, that by your power, this knowledge may be experienced and thus imbibed by me and thereby I attain to the state of Oneness with the Almighty.

16. Therefore O my God, my Sadguru Sai, I surrender my ego at your feet. Hereafter my responsibility is yours for I have no separate existence.

17. Please take away my ego, for that awareness of pleasure and pain, I do not want. You can then pull the strings as you wish, to restrain my mind.

18. Or, you become my ego, taking to yourself all the experience of pleasure and pain. I do not want the anxiety attendant upon it.

19. Glory to you, O Satiated One! May my love for you grow, day after day. O Abode of all weal, may this fickle mind find rest at your feet.

20. Who else but you can counsel us about our welfare, relieve our pain and suffering and bring peace and contentment to our hearts?

21. Baba, it was great good fortune of Shirdi that you came there and stayed on, even later. Truly, you have given it the sanctity of a place of pilgrimage.

22. Blessed is this Shirdi, that due to its past merit, this all-Merciful Sai has adorned it by his habitation there and thus has bestowed upon it a glorious good fortune.

23. It is you who stimulate and encourage me; you, who stir my speech. Who, then, am I to sing your praises? You alone are the doer and the impeller of all action.

24. Your constant company is, to us, the *Shastras* and the *Vedas*. Listening to your Story every day, is like a perusal of the sacred lore.

25. Chanting your name, without losing a moment, is our *katha-kirtan*; it is our means of communion with you; it is the contentment of our hearts.

26. Such happiness as will turn us away from your *bhajan*, we do not desire. What greater fall than this, from grace or a greater harm to spiritual advancement, can there be?

27. Our tears of joy are the warm water to wash your feet with; pure love is the sandalwood paste that we apply to you, while our good, steadfast faith is the apparel we put on you.

28. With this mental worship rather than with the outward *pooja* rituals, shall we propitiate you and please you.

29. With a perfect, single-minded concentration we will offer at your feet, the pure, eight-petalled lotus of the eight-fold[2] benevolent affections of the body and earn our own reward.

30. On the forehead we shall apply the '*bukka*' (a fragrant dark powder) of simple faith and tie the girdle of steadfast devotion round the waist. In total surrender we shall make an offering, by bowing our neck at the big toes of your feet, thus enjoying the exquisite glorious ceremony.

31. The gem-studded ornamants of our love, we shall use to adorn you and wave round your face the '*Nimblone*'[3] of our very being. Making a '*chamar*'[4] of our '*Panchapran*' (or the vital airs), we shall fan you ceaselessly. Our total absorption in you is the protective umbrella we shall use to shield you from the scorching heat.

32. In this way we shall offer you the '*Ashtang-pooja*'[5], with sandalwood paste, consecrated rice, etc., which is our Self-rejoicing and propitiate you, O Sairaja! for our own good.

33. For the fulfilment of our wishes, we will always chant the *mantra* "*Sai Samarth*", which will also help us in our spiritual advancement and we will experience fulfilment through our staunch faith.

34. In the preceding chapter, it was narrated how Sai Samarth, the Most Compassionate One, would instruct his devotees for their own welfare.

35. Now in this chapter, it will be described how he confirmed the devotees' faith and devotion to their own guru. Listen to this wonderful story about it.

36. Be attentive, O Listeners, in hearing this sweet story of the devotee Pant, so that its lesson is firmly imprinted on the mind;

37. How and what experiences were given to the devotee; how the collyrium of faith was put in his eyes, and how his restless mind was calmed by the reaffirmation of faith in his own guru.

38. Once a devotee called Pant, after many unsuccessful attempts, went at last to Shirdi, with a friend, with a keen desire for Sai's *darshan*.

39. He had already received initiation from his own guru, for whom he had great devotion and hence had a doubt in his mind as to why he should go to Shirdi.

40. And yet, whatever is pre-destined, will, quite unexpectedly, come about. The opportunity for Sai's *darshan* came without any effort and proved beneficial, undoubtedly.

41. Man makes plans, but God wills otherwise! Nothing works against Destiny. Listen at ease, to the experience of this.

42. Planning to go to Shirdi, a group of people set out together from their respective places very happily, boarding a train.

43. As they entered the compartment, suddenly they discovered Pant, sitting inside. Pant then found out that they had planned to go to Shirdi.

44. In the group there were Pant's friends and some close relatives[6], too! With the result, even though Pant had no inclination to join the party, he was persuaded to do so under some pressure.

45. Actually, he had a ticket only up to the destination he had originally intended. But now, he changed his mind.

46. 'Let us all travel together to Shirdi', said the friends and relatives and much against his own inclination, Pant had to acquiesce to their strong persuasion.

47. He then got down at Virar while the others went ahead to Mumbai. Pant borrowed some money towards travelling expenses and joined the others at Mumbai.

48. He had not the heart to disappoint his friends and so got the permission to go to Shirdi from his own guru. Together, they all travelled to Shirdi, merrily.

49. About eleven o'clock in the morning, they went to the mosque and were quite enthused when they saw the devotees crowding together to perform Baba's *pooja*.

50. As they gazed at Baba their hearts were filled with joy. All of a sudden, Pant was seized with a fit and fell down, unconscious.

51. He felt very weak; his body became motionless. His companions were worried and greatly agitated in their minds.

52. But with Baba's grace and the help of the people around, as soon as some water was sprinkled on his head, the swoon disappeared completely.

53. Regaining consciousness, he sat up with a start, as though just waking up from sleep.

54. Through intuition, Baba knew everything. Fully aware of his great devotion to his own guru, Baba assured him protection and confirmed his faith in his guru.

55. "Whatever the situation", he said, "never leave the place of your own guru.[7] Always be steadfast in devotion and recognize the Oneness of all gurus."

56. Pant recognized the mark and thought of his own guru. Of Baba's tender compassion, the memory remained with him, all his life.

57. Similarly, a gentleman from Bombay, named Harishchandra, was in great distress, his son being afflicted with epilepsy.

58. He tried all the remedies, but nothing worked. Seeing that all their efforts had failed, all that now remained was to try saints and sadhus.

59. In the year 1910, Das Ganu was performing *kirtans* and spreading Baba's fame everywhere. With the result, Shirdi was flooded with pilgrims.

60. A small, petty village that Shirdi was, great was its good fortune; it became as holy as Pandharpur. Its importance grew infinitely. The flow of pilgrims knew no bounds.

61. Many had the experience that diseases were cured by Baba's mere *darshan*, or by the touch of his hand or even by his kind compassionate glance.

62. By a whole-hearted surrender to him, devotees attained their highest good. For, knowing their wishes, he satisfied them all.

63. By smearing his *udi*, the evil spirits take to their heels; by his benediction, troubles are averted; by his gracious glance, all harm is prevented. Hence people came running to him.

64. Having heard by the word of mouth, about Baba's great prowess, as described in Das Ganu's *katha kirtan* and his books, he felt a great eagerness for Baba's *darshan*.

65. Taking with him his wife and children and carrying offerings of various fruit, Pitale (Harishchandra Pitale) came to Shirdi, by virtue of his past merit, to have Baba's *darshan*.

66. He laid the afflicted son at Baba's feet and himself, prostrated before Baba, when suddenly something happened, which was quite unpropitious. Pitale was extremely agitated and confused.

67. As the son's eyes met Sai's, the boy became unconscious, rotating his eyeballs, suddenly. The parents were distraught.

68. He fell down, unconscious, to the ground, foaming profusely at the mouth. It caused great anxiety to the father and mother, who blamed it on their fate.

69. Breathing appeared to have stopped; froth flowed freely from the mouth; sweat broke out all over his body. All hope of survival was extinguished.

70. On earlier occasions, the boy was often seized with such fits, but never was their duration as long as the present one.

71. 'Never has been and never will be,' such was the nature of this fit, which brought the boy to a near death condition. The state of the child gave rise to an endless flow of tears from the mother's eyes.

72. Oh, what did we come here for, and now see what has happened! That which was to be a cure has caused the greater harm! Should these feet (Baba's) have become destructive, thus? In vain, in vain has been the whole effort!

73. O, that one should enter a house for the fear of the thief and that the house itself should come crashing down upon oneself! Such indeed, has been our coming here, said the lady.

74. That the cow, fearing the tiger may eat her up, should run away, fearing for her life, only to meet a butcher on the way! This is what has happened to us.

75. That the wayfarer, to escape the burning heat of the sun, should seek rest under the shade of a tree and the tree itself should fall, uprooted! Such was their condition.

76. With full trust in God, one should go inside a temple and the temple itself should collapse on oneself — similar to it was their state.

77. But Baba then assured them, "Have some patience in your heart! Lift him up and carry him away carefully. He will regain consciousness.

78. "Take the boy to your place. After another twenty-four minutes or so, life will return to his body. Do not rush things needlessly."

79. So they did accordingly. Baba's words came true. Pitale and his family were overjoyed. Doubts, misgivings, had all disappeared.

80. On being carried to the *Wada*, the boy at once gained consciousness, bringing great relief to the father and the mother. They were full of joy.

81. Pitale then came with his wife for Baba's *darshan* and prostrated in obeisance before him, with utmost humility.

82. Seeing his son so revived, he sat pressing Baba's feet, with a heart full of gratitude and joy. Baba then asked him with a smile,

83. "Are those ripples of doubts and apprehensions at rest, at least now? He who reposes full trust and keeps his courage and patience high, him will Shrihari protect."

84. Coming from a wealthy, respectable, well-known family, Pitale celebrated the occasion befittingly, by distributing quantities of sweetmeats to all and offering fruit, flowers, etc., at Baba's feet.

85. His wife was a very pious lady, being simple, loving and trusting at heart. She used to sit near the pillar, gazing intently at Baba.

86. And as she gazed, her eyes would suddenly fill with tears. This happened every day. And seeing the marvel of her love, Baba would be greatly enchanted.

87. As with the gods, so it is with the saints! Both are totally bound by the love of the devotees and those who worship them with an unswerving devotion are blessed with their grace.

88. When these people were about to leave Shirdi, they came to the mosque for Baba's *darshan*. They took his leave, received *udi* and were ready to go.

89. Suddenly, Baba took out three rupees from his pocket, calling Pitale to him. Just listen to what he then said.

90. "Bapu[8], I had given you two (rupees) earlier; keep these three along with them and perform their proper *pooja* regularly. It will benefit you greatly."

91. Accepting them happily as *prasad*, Pitale took the rupees in his hand, prostrated at Baba's feet and said, 'Give me your blessings O Maharaj!'

92. However, a thought arose instantly in his mind, 'This is really my first trip here. Then what is this that Baba is saying? I surely, do not understand this.

93. 'I have never seen Baba, before. How did he give me two rupees, earlier? I cannot make anything of this!' Pitale was quite astonished.

94. How can the words be explained? His curiosity grew. But Baba would give no indication and the matter remained undecided.

95. Saints may say something quite casually; yet the words will always come true and Pitale in his heart, knew this. Hence he felt even more puzzled.

96. Later, when he went to Mumbai and went home, there was an old lady in the house who finally, satisfied his curiosity.

97. The old lady, who was Pitale's mother, while she enquired casually about the news from Shirdi, the subject of the three rupees came up, the connection of which with the earlier two could not be established.

98. Pondering over it, suddenly the recollection came back. The old lady said to Pitale, 'Now I really remember! What Baba said is perfectly true.

99. 'Recently, you took your son to Shirdi so that he had Baba's *darshan*. Similarly, in the past, your father too, had taken you to Akkalkot.

100.   'Well-known for his kindness and beneficence, the Maharaj at Akkalkot was a *siddha*. He had intuitive knowledge of everything and was an enlightened yogi. Your father was also pure and sinless in his conduct.

101.   'Pleased with the *pooja* that your father offered, the Yogiraja was pleased and gave two rupees as *prasad* to be worshipped in the daily *pooja*.

102.   'These earlier two rupees too, my child, the Swami had given you as *prasad*, in order to be worshipped.

103.   'The two rupees were placed with the family gods and your father used to perform the *pooja* every day, with great faith.

104.   'I alone know his firm unwavering faith and how this faith guided him in his day to day conduct. But after him, the articles of *pooja* became the playthings for the children.

105.   'The faith in gods began to disappear and performance of *pooja* became a matter of shame. Children were asked to perform it. Who would then bother about the rupees?

106.   'Many years passed in this way. The rupees were utterly neglected. In fact, their memory was completely wiped away and the pair of rupees was thus, lost.

107.   'However, great is your good fortune. for you met Akkalkot Maharaj himself, in the form of Sai, to wipe away the layers of oblivion, and also, to ward off future calamities.

108.   So, at least from now onwards, give up doubts and distrust and remember your ancestors. Give up crooked ways.

109.   'Keep on worshipping these rupees, regularly, and look upon this *prasad* of the saint as an ornament. Sai Samarth has given you the mark to revive your devotion.'

110.   As Pitale heard this story from his mother, his heart was filled with joy. All-pervasiveness of Sai, the significance of his *darshan*, left a deep impress on his mind.

111.   The nectar-sweet words of the mother revived the vanishing faith and the lapse was atoned for by a sincere remorse, paving the way for future good.

112. And so, whatever had to happen, happened. But the saint had awakened him to a sense of his duty, for which he was most grateful and always remained alert to perform his duty in the days to come.

113. I shall now narrate another similar experience. Listen to it at your ease. It will show how Baba restrained the unbridled, wilful tendencies of his devotees.

114. There was an excellent devotee called Gopal Narayan Ambdekar, who lived in Poona. Listen carefully to his story.

115. He had a job in the Excise department under the British government. After completing ten years of service he left the job and sat at home.

116. His fate changed for the worse. All days are not alike. He was caught up in the whirl of adverse planetary situation. Who can give a slip to fate and escape its adverse effects?

117. To begin with, he was posted in the Thane district, but later, he was destined to serve at Jawhar. And there, where he was once an officer, he now became jobless.

118. But a job is like water on a calladium leaf! How will it come back to the former position? He made the utmost effort at the time.

119. But he had no luck! So he resolved to preserve his independence. Trouble followed trouble reaching a peak. He became despondent in every way.

120. Year after year, his financial position was sliding downwards. Calamities followed in quick succession. The domestic scene became unendurable.

121. Seven years passed by thus. Every year he would go to Shirdi, enumerating before Baba all his hardships, prostrating at his feet, day and night.

122. In the year 1916, his distress and disgust for life reached its culmination. And he felt like putting an end to his life in the holy Shirdi itself.

123. At that time, he had been staying in Shirdi, with his family, for two months. Now listen to what happened, one night.

124. As Ambdekar was sitting in a bullock-cart, in front of the Dikshit-wada, wild thoughts raced through his mind.

125. Tired of life itself, he had become disinterested and disheartened. 'Enough', he thought, 'enough of this suffering. I have lost all hope for living.'

126. So thinking, recklessly despondent of his own life, Ambdekar was ready to jump into the well.

127. 'Taking the opportunity, when everything is quiet and no one is nearby, I shall satisfy the desire of my heart and will get freedom from pain and suffering,' so he thought.

128. To take one's own life is really a great sin, yet he made this firm resolve. But Sai Baba, who controls everything, averted this rash action.

129. Just a few steps away from the spot where Ambdekar was sitting, was the house of an eating-house proprietor (Sagun Meru Naik), who was a great devotee of Baba and served him faithfully.

130. Sagun suddenly came up to his doorstep and asked Ambdekar, at that very moment, 'Have you ever read this *pothi* of Akkalkot Maharaj?'

131. 'Let me see, let me see!' said Ambdekar (eagerly), as he took it in his hand and began to glance through its pages, quite casually. He then started reading somewhere in the middle.

132. As luck would have it, the subject that he thus started reading about was most appropriate for his innermost thoughts and made its mark on his mind, at once.

133. I shall now narrate the story that came up for his reading, so very naturally. It will be related briefly and in its essence, so as to avoid making this book bulky.

134. When the great contemplative saint, Akkalkot Maharaj, was at Akkalkot, one of his devotees was undergoing suffering beyond his endurance and was in great distress due to his disease.

135. In order to obtain freedom from his affliction, he served Maharaj for many days. And now, he could bear the pain no more. He was greatly agitated and worried.

136. Determined to put an end to his life, and seeing that it was night, when everything was quiet, he went to a well and jumped into it.

137.   Suddenly, Maharaj came there, took him out with his own hands and said to him, 'Whatever suffering fate has ordained for us, has to be borne.

138.   'Unless we fully suffer the consequences of our previous *karma*, in the form of disease, affliction, leprosy or pain, what can a suicide do?

139.   'Moreover, unless this pain and suffering is undergone fully, another birth has to be taken to complete it. Therefore, bear this suffering a little more. Do not be provoked into destroying your own life.'

140.   On reading this story, so befitting the present occasion, Ambdekar was simply amazed and at once, felt quite ashamed of himself, in the face of such all-pervasiveness of Baba.

141.   In his heart, Ambdekar understood fully well that what is pre-ordained must be endured. This was what was suggested to him at the right moment, and that the hazardous step he had contemplated was not for his good.

142.   This visionary experience was, in effect, as the Voice from Heaven! On seeing Sai's marvellous *leela*, his faith in Sai was strengthened further.

143.   Had the warning from Sai, given so unexpectedly through the book and from Sagun's mouth, been delayed, even slightly, it would have ruined his life.

144.   'I would have lost my life', he thought, 'and brought upon my family great harm, bringing great hardship on my wife. I would thus have lost, materially and spiritually!

145.   'But under the pretext of the *pothi*, it was Baba who induced Sagun to turn my mind back from the thought of ending my life.'

146.   If such a thing had not happened, the poor fellow would have lost his life, in vain. But where there is a Saviour like Sai, how can the killer destroy?

147.   The father of this devotee had great devotion for Akkalkot Swami. Baba merely reiterated through this experience that this worship should be continued in the same way.

148. Thus, everything turned out well, afterwards. Even those days of hardship passed away. He took great trouble to study astrology and soon enjoyed the fruits of his study.

149. By Sai's grace and his *prasad*, he saw better days. He gained proficiency in astrology. The poverty of the earlier days disappeared soon.

150. His loving devotion to the guru grew. Happiness, prosperity followed and he now enjoyed domestic felicity and comfort. In every way, he was now very happy.

151. Innumerable are such miracles, each more interesting than the other, narration of all of which will only increase the volume of the book. Hence only their essence has been narrated.

152. Hemad surrenders humbly at Sai's feet. In the next chapter will follow the interesting narration of how Baba gave the gift of 'Vishnu-sahasranaam' to Shama.

153. In spite of Shama's repeated refusal, out of his boundless affection for Shama, Baba forced the *Sahasranaam* on him, pointing out its great significance to him.

154. So now listen to that story carefully, where Baba will be seen to initiate the disciple at the appropriate time and much against the wishes of the disciple.

155. At the end of the chapter, it will be seen how remarkable is the manner of initiation from the Sadguru. Listen to it, O listeners, with reverence!

156. Beneficence of all beneficence, this Sai is the very treasure of all Excellences! Only the most fortunate get the chance to listen to his sacred, purifying *kirtan* and to the story of his life!

Weal be to all! Here ends the twenty-sixth chapter of
"*Shri Sai Samarth Satcharit*", called
'*Averting Epileptic Fits and Suicide, and
Confirmation of Faith in one's own Guru*',
as inspired by the saints and the virtuous,
and composed by his devotee, Hemadpant.

Notes

1. Refer Ch. 16, note 10.
2. Refer Ch. 6, note 3.
3. Leaves of the bitter Neem tree with salt, mustard, etc., waved around the face of a person to counteract the influence of an evil eye.
4. Refer Ch. 4, note 19.
5. The eight rituals are : *achaman*, *snan*, sandalwood paste, flowers, incense, light, food offering and *pradakshina*. For a detailed explanation of all the sixteen rituals, which include these eight, refer to ch. 13, note 1.
6. These were the parents of his sons-in-law and daughters-in-law.
7. This may also refer to one's internal guru or *Atma-ram*.
8. Baba always addressed an elderly gentleman as "Kaka" "Bapu" or "Bhai" and a grown up lady as "Mother - see chap. 19, V. 41.

27

Bestowal of Grace

MY OBEISANCE TO SHRI GANESH, TO SHRI SARASWATI, AND SHRI GURUMAHARAJ! TO THE FAMILY DEITY, TO SHRI SITA-RAMACHANDRA, MY MOST HUMBLE OBEISANCE! I BOW IN REVERENCE TO THE MOST VENERABLE GURU SHRI SAINATH!

1. When you hold fast to the Sadguru's feet, you are really paying obeisance to the Trimurti, i.e. Brahma, Vishnu and Mahesh; it is an obeisance to the Parabrahman or God Himself, which brings the greatest Self-rejoicing.

2. You take a plunge into the ocean and acquire the merit of having made the pilgrimage to all the holy places. Similarly, you hold firmly to the guru's feet and you will have found all the gods there.

3. Glory to you, O Sadguru Sai, O *Kalpataru* that gives us the *Sayujya-mukti*[1]! Blessed are you, the Ocean of Self-Knowledge! Inspire the listeners' minds with a reverence towards the Story.

4. As the Chatak bird awaits eagerly the raindrops from the cloud, so do the faithful for this nectar-sweet Story. May all your devotees savour this nectar and rejoice, for ever.

5. As they listen to your pure, sacred Story, may drops of perspiration spring up all over their bodies, tears of love gather thickly in the eyes, and the vital airs in their deep attachment, linger at your feet.

6. May the mind be overcome with a powerful love, the hair stand on end, again and again, with excessive joy! May it bring forth sobbing and crying repeatedly, to the listeners and their families.

7. May their resistance to each other, the differences between the great and the small, be shed. For a careful search within will bring the realisation that this is the real awakening to the guru's grace.

8. This perception of the guru's grace cannot be seen by the eyes, for it is beyond all sense organs. And except for the Sadguru, its giver is not to be found elsewhere, search as you may in all the three worlds.

9. Unless there is a deep devotion, unbounded love and an unswerving faith in the guru, the six passions, like lust, anger, etc., will not be abated and the *Ashtabhava*[2] will not arise.

10. The devotee's blissful joy of the Self, brings greatest happiness to the guru. And as the devotee is more firmly set towards the spiritual goal, greater is the guru's fond admiration for him.

11. A total identification with the material — the body, the house, sons and wife as being one's own, is an exercise in futility. For all this is transitory, illusory *Maya*, like the flitting noonday shadows.

12. If one wants to avoid getting entangled in the meshes of this *Maya*, one should surrender with a single-minded devotion to Sai.

13. Trying to unravel the mystery of this *Maya*, the *Veda-Shastras* have accepted defeat. Only he who sees God in all the created things, animate and inanimate, can overcome *Maya*, with certainty.

14. Blessed indeed, was that Patil Chandbhai, who, in the beginning, brought fakir Sai with him to Nevasa, when he left the Nizam's State.

15. There the fakir stayed on for six months or a year. And there it was, that he had for company Kama from Kanad village (in district Rahuri).

16. Later, however, all these people came from there to Shirdi with Baba, Kama and Dagadu Tamboli[3] of the well-known Takli village.

17. Innumerable are the holy places of pilgrimage, spread out in different parts of the country. But to the devotees of Sai, Shirdi alone is the holiest of all.

18. And had not Baba come to Shirdi, by a stroke of fortune, how could we, his humble devotees, have had the good fortune of enjoying his holy company? It was indeed, a great stroke of luck!

19. Whoever among the devotees surrenders to him totally, Sai will guide him properly to the path of righteousness, for his own welfare.

20. Hence, O listeners, read this '*Satcharit*' with concentration, for this sacred Life of Sai is the best means of attaining the guru's grace.

21. In the last chapter it was described how one devotee was confirmed in his faith and devotion to his own guru and how another one was given the mark of Akkalkot Swami, thereby reviving his faith and devotion towards his guru.

22. How yet another devotee was prevented from ending his life and was, by an ingenious plan, saved in a moment, from the brink of death and granted the gift of life, quite unexpectedly.

23. Now in this chapter, it will be narrated how Sai would sometimes be pleased to confer his grace on the devotees, making them happy and content.

24. It was a unique way of granting favour, literally initiation, when, to some, he would bestow it amid humour and laughter! May the listeners listen to this attentively.

25. Many were his ways of conferring grace and instructing, which have been described earlier in this same book. Each devotee was initiated into the spiritual path, according to his capacity.

26. It is the *Vaidya* (doctor) who diagnoses the malady and only he knows the benefits of his medicine. But the patient, who has no knowledge of it, asks first for the sweet jaggery.

27. No doubt the jaggery is sweet, but it is also harmful. The patient, however, is adamant in demanding it, without which he is not ready to take the potion. The jaggery must be placed in his hand, first!

28. Compulsion does not work with the patient. So the *Vaidya* plans his strategy whereby, though the jaggery is given first and then the potion, yet his purpose is accomplished.

29. For the antidote is changed in such a way that the harmful effects of the jaggery are countered and the prescribed medicine remains as effective. Such was also Baba's method.

30. But this was not a rule with him, always. He would suit his manner of initiation to the spiritual capacity, temperament, service and love and devotion of each devotee.

31. Most amazing were Baba's marvellous *leelas*! When he was pleased with anyone, he would give him initiation. Just listen to how and under what conditions!

32. Once it came into his mind to initiate someone, he would bring that devotee a sense of fulfilment of life and that too, quite effortlessly, through fun and laughter — even when such a thought was farthest from the devotee's mind!

33. If a devotee wished to read a particular book, he quite naturally felt that he should first place it in Baba's hands and then receive it back as his '*prasad*'.

34. So that, later when he read the book, he would acquire special merit. And so would the narrator of the holy book and his listeners.

35. Some offered in Baba's hands pictures of the '*Dashavatar*'[4] or the '*Dashavatar*' *stotras*[5]; some brought to him sacred books like '*Pancharatni Gita*', or other holy books, 'Lives', etc.

36. Some offered even Das Ganu's compositions, '*Santa leelamrut*, and '*Bhaktaleelamrut*', while yet others brought '*Viveksindhu*' (of Mukundraj). Baba gave all these to Shama.

37. He would then say, "Shama, let these books be for you. Keep them at home, properly preserved." Shama would obey the command respectfully and keep the books carefully.

38. The devotees used to bring the books from the shops with the intention of placing them in Baba's hands and asking for them, again, as his *prasad*.

39. Generous as was Baba's nature, even to do this needed some courage and hence they used to take Madhavrao with them to convey their wish to Baba.

40. So, it was through him that the books would be placed in Baba's hands at the opportune moment. Baba not only knew the greatness of the books, but also the state of the devotees' mind.

41. Devotees would give the books in Baba's hands; Baba would look through the pages cursorily; the devotees would then put out their hands to receive them back.

42. But Baba would not give them back. Instead, he would hand them over to Madhavrao, saying, "Shama, keep these copies. Let them be with you, just now."

43. Shama would ask very plainly, 'These people who have extended their hands so eagerly — shall I give them back their copies?' But still Baba would say, 'You keep them'.

44. Once, his devotee, Kaka Mahajani, who was very fond of reading the *'Bhagvat'*, came to Shirdi, carrying with him a copy of that book.

45. Madhavrao had come to meet him and casually, picking up the book to read, he carried it in his hand when he went to the mosque. Baba asked him,

46. "Shama, what is this book in your hand?" Shama told him what it was. Baba took it in his hand, looked through it and returned it.

47. It was this book, this same copy of Eknath's *'Bhagvat'*, which Mahajani had received from Baba as *prasad* on an earlier occasion.

48. Madhavrao conveyed to Baba in clear words that the book did not belong to him, but to Kaka Mahajani, and that he had just felt a momentary desire to read it. Hence he had brought it with him.

49. Yet Baba said to him, "Since I have given it to you, you keep it in your collection. It will be useful to you."

50. However, Kaka had again come to Shirdi after a while, and had brought with him another copy of the *'Bhagvat'*, which he placed in Sai's hands.

51. Baba returned it to him as *prasad*, saying, "Keep it with utmost care", assuring him — "it will really be of great use to you."

52. And he added with genuine concern, "It is this that will serve you well, do not give it to anyone else." Very lovingly, Kaka then made obeisance to him.

53. Satiated in all his desires, Baba was absolutely desireless. He whose innate nature it was to worship God, why should he take the trouble of collecting material objects?

54. Who can know Baba's mind? From the practical point of view however, the collection of these books was most beneficial to his devotees as a means of listening to these sacred books.

55. Shirdi has now become a holy place. Baba's devotees from various countries will gather here, time and again, and confer together on matters spiritual.

56. It is then that these books will become useful. We will have gone to our Eternal Abode by then, but Shama will produce these books from his collection and then they will become representations (of the authors thereof).

57. Such are these highly sanctified books. That the devotees may remember these, in Shirdi or elsewhere, must be the purpose in Baba's wishing them to be preserved carefully.

58. Whether it is the *Ramayana* or the *Bhagvat*, or, for that matter, any book on spiritual subjects, while reading the life of Rama or of Krishna or others, one sees only Sai, in front and behind.

59. And one feels that the great personalities of these books are none other than Sai himself, in different garbs, and the narrator and his listeners always see the image of Sai before them.

60. The books are offered to the guru or they are gifted to the Brahmin. That too, is beneficial to the giver. So proclaim the *Shastras*.

61. Baba's command to Shama that "You take these books home and preserve them carefully in your collection", had a most significant purpose behind it!

62. An excellent devotee that Shama was, so was also Baba's boundless love for him. Hence the desire that arose in Sai's mind to impart some discipline to him.

63. And so, just see what he did! Though Shama had not desired it at all, he favoured him with his Grace. And under what conditions, just hear!

64. One day there came to the mosque, a Ramdasi Bua, whose daily practice it was to read the *Ramayana*.

65. Early in the morning, on finishing his morning ablutions, bath, daily worship, smearing of the '*bhasma*', etc., he would don the saffron robe and sit down to the daily ceremonial worship.

66. A recitation of the '*Vishnusahasranaam*' would be followed by reading upon reading, with great faith, of the '*Adhyatma Ramayana*'.

67. After considerable time had passed in following this daily practice, when the opportune moment for Madhavrao had arrived, it came into the mind of Sai Samarth to bless him. Listen to that account, now.

68. Madhavrao's devoted service to Baba had, at last, come to fruition. That Madhavrao should follow a discipline and be inducted into the path of devotion, so that he will enjoy some peace and respite from worldly care —

69. This was the thought that came to Baba's mind. He called that Ramdasi to him and said, "There is a sharp, shooting pain in my stomach, as if the intestines will now break.

70. "This stomach-ache is not going to subside. Go quickly and get some senna powder. Unless I chuck a pinch of it into the mouth, the persistent pain in the stomach will not go."

71. Poor Ramdasi, a trusting soul! He at once put a book-mark in the *pothi*, and ran to the market, obeying Baba's order.

72. No sooner had the Ramdasi climbed down the steps, what Baba here did was, he at once got up from his seat and went near the *pothi*.

73. There, among other books was the '*Vishnusahasranaam*' *pothi*. Picking it up in his hand, Baba returned to his seat.

74. He then said to Shama, "You know Shama, this *pothi* is very, very beneficial. I am therefore giving it to you. You should now read it.

75. "Once I was in great distress, my heart began to palpitate, being restless and agitated. I saw no hope of surviving.

76. "On that occasion, O what shall I tell you, Shama! This *pothi* was so very useful to me, I was saved only because of it!

77. "I laid it on my heart just for a moment and lo! my heart was instantly becalmed. I felt as if God Himself had descended in it! I survived only because of it!

78. "Therefore, Shama, take this for yourself, keep reading it slowly. Even if you try to concentrate on a single letter every day it will bring you immense joy and satisfaction."

79. Shama said, 'Baba, I do not want this *pothi*! That Ramdasi will get furious with me. He will think that it is I who have done this improper deed behind his back.

80. 'He, as it is, is wild by nature, hot-tempered, cross, and loses his head easily. Why provoke a quarrel needlessly? No, no, I do not want all this wrangling!

81. 'Moreover, the *pothi* is composed in Sanskrit, while my speech is uncouth and detestable. The tongue yet falters at a compound letter, making my utterance indistinct.'

82. It appeared as though Baba's whole action was directed towards sparking off a quarrel. And Shama could hardly have imagined the depth of love and concern that Baba felt for him!

83. "Maybe, my Shama is quite crazy! But I have a fond attachment to him. He has inspired a strange affection in my heart, and hence my deep loving concern for him.

84. "With my own hands will I tie this garland of `Vishnusahasranaam` round his neck and it will liberate him from worldly sorrows and cares. I shall create in him a fondness for chanting the *Naam*.

85. "*Naam* can smash mountains of sins; *Naam* can sever the bondage of the physical body; *Naam* can eradicate and destroy crores of evil passions.

86. "*Naam* can break the neck of Death itself; it avoids the pull of the birth-death cycle. Such is the great merit of this `Sahasranaam`, for which Shama should develop a fondness and love.

87. "*Naam*, when chanted with a conscious effort, is indeed excellent. Chanted without a conscious effort, it is not bad either. Even if it comes to the lips unexpectedly, it will reveal its power.

88. "There is no other means easier than the *Naam*, to purify the heart. It is the adornment of the tongue. *Naam* nourishes the spiritual life.

89. "To take the *Naam*, a bath is not necessary; *Naam* has no precepts, no rules, laid down by the *Shastras*. By taking the *Naam* all sins are destroyed. *Naam* is sacred, always.

90. "A ceaseless chanting of my name will also take you across safely. You need practise no other means. For you can attain *Moksha* or liberation with it.

91. "He who repeats my name all the time, will at once have all his sins washed out. He who is murmuring my name, all the time, is to me more meritorious than the most excellent of men."

92. This was the innermost intent of Baba's heart and he acted in accordance with it. Though Shama kept on saying 'no', Baba slipped the *pothi* into his pocket.

93. It is only on the strength of the accumulated merit of the forefathers that this fruit of Sai's grace is obtained. Such is this Self-purifying '*Sahasranaam*' that will remove the restlessness and pain of worldly life.

94. There are elaborate observances and rituals for other religious karmas. But the *Naam* can be chanted ceaselessly and at any time. Interruptions or '*pradosh*'[6] pose no obstruction to it. There is no other form of worship simpler than this.

95. Eknath Maharaj too, had, in a similar manner, forced this '*Sahasranaam*' on one of his neighbours, guiding him thereby to the spiritual path.

96. In Eknath's house, a regular reading and kirtan of the *Puranas* used to take place. However, his neighbour, a Brahmin, neglected even the daily bath and religious observances, being engrossed in sinful behaviour, all the time.

97. He would never listen to the *Puranas*; in fact, the sinner never stepped into Eknath's *wada*. But feeling compassion for him, Nath himself sent for him.

98. Born into a high-caste Brahmin family, he was simply frittering away his life and knowing this secret, Nath was moved to pity, wondering how his sinful behaviour could be stopped.

99. Hence, though the man said 'No', Nath read out and taught him to repeat the '*Sahasranaam*'. And even as he was being taught the verses, one by one, his spiritual upliftment was gradually taking place.

100. The reading or recitation of this '*Sahasranaam*' is an easy, straight-forward way of Self-purification. And this practice or custom has descended to us from our forefathers. Hence, all Baba's strenuous efforts!

101. Meantime, the Ramdasi had returned speedily, bringing the medicine, senna. Anna (Babare), who like Narad[7], delighted in exciting quarrels, stood in readiness and narrated all that had happened, in great detail.

102. The Ramdasi was already impetuous and to add to it, there was the mediation of this Narad (Anna)! Who can adequately describe the uniqueness of that occasion?

103. As it was, that Ramdasi was the very image of doubts and misconceptions! In no time a suspicion arose in his mind about Madhavrao. He said, 'In order to grab my *pothi*, you yourself have made Baba to mediate.'

104. Forgetting all about the senna he had brought, he began a tirade against Madhavrao. His temper flared up, uncontrollably and he showered on him noisy, empty words in abundance.

105. 'The stomach-ache I know was only a pretence, which you, yourself induced Baba to make, because you had an eye on my *pothi*. But I am not going to tolerate this.

106. 'I am, by name, a Ramdasi, bold and fearless. You better return my *pothi*, or else I shall break my head in front of you, in a shower of blood!

107. 'Your eye was on my *pothi*. So you have fabricated the whole thing, laying the blame to Baba's account, remaining aloof yourself.'

108. Madhavrao tried to pacify him in very many ways. But the Ramdasi refused to give in. Listen then, to what Madhavrao said gently,

109. 'Do not blame me needlessly as being deceitful. And what is so great about this *pothi* of yours? It is not even so difficult to get!

110. 'Nor is your *pothi* so precious, as gold or diamonds that you should distrust Baba himself, for it! O shame on you!'

111. Seeing his violent reaction, Baba then said sweetly to the Ramdasi, "And so, what is so very wrong in it, O Ramdasi? Why are you distressing yourself about it needlessly?

112. "After all, Shama too, is our own boy! Why are you straining your every nerve to admonish him? Why be so sad without a reason and make an exhibition of your temper to the whole world?

113. "O how can you be so quarrelsome! Why can you not speak gently, sweetly? You read the *pothis* all the time, and yet your heart is still impure.

114. "Every day you read *Adhyatma Ramayan*, you repeat the 'Sahasranaam'. But you have not given up this wild wilfulness. And yet, you call yourself a 'Ramdasi'!

115. "What kind of Ramdasi are you? You ought to be detached and desireless, in every sense of the word. But here you are, not being able to give up the attachment to that *pothi*! What can one say of this behaviour of yours?

116. "A Ramdasi should have no attachment and treat both the great and the small, alike. And yet you exhibit such hostility towards this boy, clinging to his hand to snatch away the *pothi*!

117. "Go, go back and sit in your place. *Pothis* you can get cheaper by the dozen, but a good person is hard to come by, even to the end of this world.

118. "Whatever may be so great about your *pothi*, this Shamya here, does not know. Moreover, I myself picked it up and it is I who gave it to him.

119. "Besides, you know it by heart. So I thought I should give it to Shamya, who will keep on reading it and it will be highly beneficial to him."

120. How sweet, how compassionate was that speech! And Oh! how cool and refreshing — like the water of the inner Bliss! The words were simply marvellous!

121. In his heart, the Ramdasi had realized full well. Fuming with anger, he said to Madhavrao, 'Look! I am telling you now, that I am going to take from you the *'Pancharatni Gita'* in exchange!'

122. Madhavrao was happy to see that the Ramdasi had cooled down so much. 'Not one', he said, 'but I shall give you ten copies of the Gita in exchange!'

123. Later, the quarrel subsided with the Gita remaining as the surety. But why did he want the Gita when he could not recognize the God of that Gita?

124. He who, sitting near Baba, made reading upon reading of the *Adhyatma Ramayan* — should that same Ramdasi set himself out to quarrel with Sai in this way?

125. And yet, how can I say even this? How can I blame anyone? For if such incidents had not taken place, how would the lesson be impressed upon the others?

126. That (i.e. the *'Sahasranaam'*) which had sparked off such a quarrel; that which had removed Baba's distress and which is also so very beneficial to me, that was really an extraordinary gift of Sai.

127. Had all this effort not been made, Madhavrao would never have been convinced, he would never have learnt it or committed it to memory.

128. Such is this Sainath, so loving and yet so difficult to attain, who engages in the spiritual sport. When and how he will pull the strings, it is difficult to know.

129. Later, as time passed, Shama began to have faith in the *pothi* and Dikshit and Narake, both taught him to recite with correct pronunciation. He learnt to read it, and soon knew it by heart.

130. Thus this debate of Madhavrao's was really an explanation in different words, of Baba's pure instruction. It was undoubtedly, the most delightful sense of humour which brought blissful joy.

131. Similarly, Baba was very fond of those who were studying the *Brahmavidya* and just see how he clearly demonstrated it at the proper time.

132. Once a parcel came by post at the Shirdi post-office, for Jog, and he immediately set out thither to receive it.

133. As he saw the book, it turned out to be '*Gita Rahasya*', a commentary on the *Bhagavad-Gita* by Lokamanya Tilak. Tucking it under his arm, he at once came to the mosque for *darshan*.

134. As he bowed at Baba's feet, the parcel fell at his feet. "What Bapusaheb! What is this?" Baba then asked.

135. The parcel was opened in front of Baba and Jog then told him what it contained. The parcel with the book in it, was then handed over to Baba. Baba looked at it.

136. He took out the book in his hand, glanced through its pages for a moment and taking out a rupee from his pocket, placed it on the book fondly.

137. He then put it into Jog's *uparna* along with that rupee, saying, "Read this from the beginning to the end. It will be beneficial to you."

138. There are innumerable such stories of Baba's favour. If they have been narrated briefly it is only for fear of making the book voluminous.

139. Once it so happened, that Dadasaheb Khaparde came to Shirdi with his family and stayed on, enamoured of Baba's loving company.

140. Khaparde was not an ordinary person. He was a superior personage — very learned. But before Sai, he would stand with folded hands and his head lowered respectfully.

141. Proficient as he was in the English language, he enjoyed the reputation as an effective and impressive speaker in the Legislative Assembly. Yet he would hold his silence in Sai's presence.

142. Baba had innumerable devotees, but except for Khaparde, Butti and Noolkar, no other devotee would hold his silence before Baba.

143. All the others used to speak out; some even argued with Baba, without any reverence, fear or awe. Only these three observed silence in front of him.

144. And this was true not only of speaking, but also of their general manner — they always bowed their head in front of Baba. Their humility and the reverence with which they listened to him, were simply indescribable.

145. That Dadasaheb, from whom it was a privilege to get the *'Panchadashi'* of Vidyaranya explained, even he used to be silent once he came to the mosque.

146. However powerful the brilliance of the *Shabda-Brahma* (i.e. *Vedas*) might be, it dims before the radiance of the Pure Consciousness. Sai who was the Glorious Parabrahma incarnate, would naturally put all learning to shame.

147. For four months Khaparde stayed in Shirdi while his wife was there for seven months. Day after day, they both experienced great joy.

148. His wife had great faith and a loving devotion to Sai and would bring the food-offering to the mosque every day, with her own hands.

149. The lady would not touch food until her offering was accepted by Baba. After Maharaj had eaten, the lady would eat.

150. And so, once the opportune moment arrived. Pleased with the lady's steadfast faith, Baba, ever-compassionate to the devotees, guided her to the best spiritual path.

151. Different people have their own different ways, but Baba's ways were extraordinary. In a playful manner, amid laughter, he would confer grace in such a way that it was firmly imprinted on the mind.

152. Once this lady (Mrs Khaparde) brought a plate full of a variety of delicacies of food to offer to Baba. There were semolina sweets like *'sanja'*[8] and *'sheera'* with fried *puris* (or wheat bread), rice and *daal*, *kheer*[9], *papad*[10], *'sandagaas'*[11], salads, etc.

153. The moment this plate arrived, with great eagerness Baba got up from his seat, rolling up the sleeves of his *kafni*.

154. He went to the dining place, sat down and pulled up a plate in front of himself. He then removed the covering over the plate, all ready to savour the food.

155. Numerous other food offerings would arrive daily, far more delicious than this one, but would lie there for a long time quite neglected. Why then such a strong desire for this one alone?

156. Surely, this was only worldly behaviour! But why should it affect a saint's heart? So Madhavrao at once, said to Sai Samarth, 'Baba, why do you make such differentiation?

157. 'You push aside the offerings of others — sometimes even the silver plates of some, you just fling away! But no sooner this lady's offering comes, you at once get up and start eating. It is really a wonder!

158. 'How only her food is so very delicious, is, O God, a great mystery to us! What is this jugglery of yours? Why do you entertain such likes and dislikes?'

159. Baba said, "O Shama! How can I describe the rarity of this food-offering? In a previous birth, this lady was a well-fed cow of a grocer, yielding abundant milk.

160. "She then disappeared somewhere and took birth in the house of a gardener. Later she was born a *Kshatriya* (the warrior race) and was then married to a grocer.

161. "After that she was born in a Brahmin household. I saw her after a long time. Let me eat in peace and happiness two morsels offered to me with so much love!"

162. So saying, he ate to his heart's content, washed his hands and mouth, expressing his satiety most naturally through belching. Then he came and sat on his seat.

163. The lady then made obeisance and began pressing his feet. Taking this opportunity, Baba spoke to her lovingly of things of her own interest.

164. With his own hands, Baba gently pressed her hands that were pressing his feet. Seeing this mutual loving service of God and his devotee, Shama then began to tease, saying —

165. 'Well, well, Baba! Very fine! What an interesting sight! Seeing this reciprocal feeling we are amazed!'

166. Baba was pleased at heart to see her devoted service and said to her softly, "Keep on saying '*Rajaram*', '*Rajaram*'.

167. "Say this all the time and O Mother! your life will be fulfilled, your mind will be at peace and you will benefit immensely."

168. How wonderful were those words! They smote the heart, at once — as if merely by those words Baba had instantly passed on the divine power to the devotee!

169. So compassionate is this Sainath, the Patron of the humble and the obedient, that he always fulfils the desires of his devotees and ensures their spiritual welfare.

170. I, very lovingly and humbly, wish to make a friendly entreaty to my listeners, in their own interest.

171. Intent on the sweetness of the jaggery, an ant will not let go of it, even if it means breaking her neck. Such should be your absolute surrender to Sai. Then will Sai protect you graciously.

172. The guru and his devotee are not separate. Though they appear to be separate, they are one. He who tries with great effort to separate them, will ultimately, have to give up his conceit.

173. If you find one of them without the other, that guru is imperfect and so too, is his disciple. But he who is trained by a perfect guru, will hold his silence on this matter of duality between them.

174. Those who feel that the guru stays at one place and his disciple, at another (and hence they are separate), know not (the truth).

175. If they are not two at all, then how can they be separate? One just cannot stay without the other. Such is their oneness!

176. There is no separateness betwen the guru and his devotee, too. They are always united (in spirit). The devotee placing his head on the guru's feet, is really a form of worship of the physical body.

177. The devotee worships with the feeling of oneness and the guru also looks upon the devotee as being one with him. Unless there

is such perfect oneness with each other, the whole exercise will be only for name's sake.

178. Do not worry even for a moment how you will get the material necessities of life, like food and clothing. For it comes according to your '*Prarabdha*'[12] and comes without effort.

179. If you make a great effort to acquire these, your exertion will be in vain. Instead, make efforts for your spiritual progress and concentrate on it day and night.

180. 'Arise!' and 'Awake!' Why do you roll, snoring in a deep slumber? So cries Mother *Shruti* at the top of her voice, trying lovingly, to awaken the devotee.

181. Those who are rolling in the slumber of ignorance, which is the seed of all calamities, they should wake up in good time and drink the nectar of the knowledge that the guru gives.

182. And to get it, surrender in all humility at the guru's feet. He alone knows what is proper and what is improper while we are but ignorant children.

183. *Jeeva* is with its ego of scant knowledge and the All-knowing Shiva is ego-less. To realize the oneness between the two, the guru is the only means.

184. To remove the separateness between *Jeeva*, the *atman* limited by ignorance, and Shiva, the *atman* limited by *Maya*, Gururao alone is powerful.

185. Offer at Sai's feet the mind that is governed by resolutions, doubts and misconceptions. So that, Sai himself will be the doer of actions which are inspired thereafter.

186. Similarly, offer at Sai's feet the power of doing all actions. Then act as he commands and in the same manner.

187. Know that Sai is all-powerful. If you act without ego, casting the burden on him, you can attain the *siddhi* altogether.

188. But if you say, 'I will do this', if you have conceit, even in the least degree, you will see its effect at once, without a moment's delay.

189. But as for Hemad, as he turned lazily, from side to side, in the night of ignorance created by *Maya*, he experienced effortlessly, the grace of Hari and Guru.

190. And that too, by his good fortune alone, without study or effort, he enjoyed it. It seems to me as if they (i.e. Hari and Guru) themselves, have glorified me for accomplishing their purpose.

191. Resolving upon writing his own story for the upliftment of his devotees, Sai perforce held his hand and got the book written, in great detail.

192. So let us weave a beautiful garland of multi-coloured flowers of steadfast love, in the thread of ceaseless contemplation and offer it with reverence to Sai.

193. Let us attain to the throne of Self-realization, adorning that glorious seat by our Self-absorption. Let us enjoy that Bliss with happiness in our hearts and without a trace of ego.

194. Such is the unfathomable 'Life' of Sai. The tale that follows is even stranger than this. Be attentive for a moment and your ears will be purified.

195. A series of three chapters will follow hereafter, in which you will see, how, sitting at one place, Baba showed the marvel of his Visions.

196. The first among these chapters, deals with Lala Lakhmichand, who, tied by the string of love, was led to his true Refuge.

197. How he had a very keen desire for her '*Khichadi*'[13], with the result, the lady from Barhanpur became most eager for his *darshan*, thus showing the marvel of his love for the devotee.

198. Later, Megha, another devotee, was given a vision in his dream to draw a '*Trishool*'[14], after which he suddenly received the '*Linga*'[15] of Shiva.

199. Many such stories will follow from now onwards. And if the listeners listen to them with devotion and faith, they will find fulfilment.

200. A lump of salt, when dipped in the ocean, becomes one with it. So does Hemad, who surrenders to Sai and makes obeisance with love and devotion, enjoying with him the oneness of '*Soham*'[16].

201. Moreover, he lovingly entreats that may his mind meditate on Sai, day and night and be always alert, so that none other but Sai enter into it.

202. May the past be erased, the end of the future be pushed further, and what remains betweem the two, i.e. the present, be always spent at the guru's feet.

Weal be to all! Here ends the twenty-seventh chapter of
"*Shri Sai Samarth Satcharit*", called
'*Bestowal of Grace*',
as inspired by the saints and the virtuous,
and composed by his devotee, Hemadpant.

Notes

1. Refer Ch. 11, note 8.
2. Refer Ch. 6, note 3.
3. One who trades in betel-nut leaves or '*paan*', etc.
4. The ten incarnations of Lord Vishnu. They are: *Matsya, Koorma, Varah, Narasimha, Vaman, Parashuram, Ram, Krishna, Buddha* and *Kalaki* (which is yet to come).
5. A hymn or panegyric or praise.
6. A day on which the fourth lunar day, or seventh, or thirteenth occurs in the first part of the night—a season in which the reading of the Vedas is prohibited.
7. Narad, son of Brahma and one of the ten original Munis or Rishis. He delighted in exciting quarrels. Hence an incendiary, embroiler, make-bate.
8. Semolina lightly fried in ghee and cooked in milk or water with sugar and spices.
9. *Kheer* is a dish composed of rice, coconut-scrapings, milk, sugar and spices.
10. A thin, crisp cake made from flour and pulses.
11. This is a savoury preparation, viz. balls of a particular seasoning made from pompion gourd, cucumber, etc., scraped up and blended with other spices, dried and stored, to be fried at the time of use.
12. Refer ch. 3, note 13.
13. A mixture of rice and pulses cooked together with spices.
14. The trident of Shiva.
15. The Phallus or emblematic representation of Shiva.
16. 'He being I and I being He'.

A Narration of Visions

*MY OBEISANCE TO SHRI GANESH, TO SHRI SARASWATI, AND SHRI
GURUMAHARAJ! TO THE FAMILY DEITY, TO SHRI SITA-RAMACHANDRA
MY MOST HUMBLE OBEISANCE! I BOW IN REVERENCE TO THE MOST
VENERABLE GURU SHRI SAINATH!*

1. Sai is not confined to one place; Sai dwells in all things — living
   and non-living. Right from Brahmadev, down to the insects as
   tiny as an ant or a fly, he pervades them all and everywhere.

2. Perfect as he is, in the *Shabda–Brahma* (Vedas), Sai gives the mark
   of the Parabrahma. Being thus perfect in both, he is most
   befittingly, a Sadguru.

3. Though he be possessed of profound knowledge, if he cannot
   instruct the disciple or fix him in his true Self, then such a Sadguru
   is of no use.

4. The mother gives birth to a child's physical body, but this birth is
   followed by death. Far more compassionate is the guru, who
   destroys this birth-death cycle.

5. And now, to pick up on the threads from the previous chapter,
   listen to this chapter about dreams, how Baba appeared in the
   dreams of the devotees, giving them *darshan* in this way.

6. To some, he said, 'Draw a *Trishool*[1] (Trident); from another he
   asked for '*Khichadi*'[2]; to yet another, he appeared as a school-
   master, and, cane in hand, thrashed his back.

7. Going in their dream, he frightened some, just to free them from
   their addiction to alcohol. Saving them, in this way, from many
   calamities, he would create in them a fondness for himself.

8. It has already been described in chapter 13[3], which the listeners know already, how he thrashed the back of someone, cramming his chest with a muller.

9. Most extraordinary is the tale that follows. Blessed will be the listener and also the narrator. Both will sit still, totally engrossed and will experience an everlasting joy.

10. The sins of listening to false, malicious tales or censures, etc., will be washed away. Let us relate, again and again, the ever-sacred purifying stories of the saints.

11. Now O listeners, listen attentively to this story which will reveal Sai's kindness and compassion, at every step.

12. Ralli Brothers was a firm of Greek traders who used to trade all over India and had their offices in various cities, with one such branch also in Bombay.

13. It was here that Lakhmichand was working under their officers, at that time. In his job as a clerk, he was most trustworthy and obedient.

14. In the beginning he was in the Railways; thereafter he worked in the Vyankatesh Printing Press, when he first came to enjoy Sai's company. Listen to how this came about.

15. "My man, even if he be in another country or thousands of miles away, I shall bring him to me, tying a rope to his legs (like the young one of a sparrow)."

16. Many a time had Baba spoken thus and so many people had heard it. It was their experience, too! Let me now narrate this *leela* of Sai.

17. There were many such children, in various countries, whom he had brought to Shirdi and amongst these was Lakhmichand, a simple trusting child of Baba's.

18. It is only when the '*Prarabdha-karma*'[4], accumulated over many births, rises into ascendency, and the darkness of ignorance, born of *Maya*, is dispelled, that one is blessed with the holy company of saints.

19. The fire of the discriminating intellect is enkindled; Renunciation dawns, bringing with it good fortune; the '*Sanchit-karma*'[5] declines, and there is fulfilment of life.

20. Once the vision is filled with Sainath, nothing else can find a place there. And even when the eyes are closed, they only see Sai Baba, who is present all around.

21. Once I met Lalaji (Lakhmichand) and the stories of his own experience which he narrated to me have been stored lovingly in my heart. I am most eager to tell them now to the listeners.

22. Even the call that came to him from Baba was just one of Baba's wonderful *leelas*. May the faithful listeners listen to the story, bringing the heart in the ears.

23. It was during Christmas, in 1910, that Lalaji had this opportunity to go to Shirdi.

24. It was also the first time that he had Baba's *darshan* directly, in person. But he had received an indication of such a visit, a month or two earlier. Listen to how it happened.

25. He was then at Santacruz (now a suburb of Mumbai) and any such thought was farthest from his mind, when he suddenly had a wonderful vision in his dream.

26. He saw an old, bearded man, a *Mahatma*, a *sadhu*, surrounded by devotees, standing before him. With love and reverence, he at once made obeisance to him.

27. A little later, Lakhmichand had once gone to listen to Das Ganu's *kirtan*, at the house of one Dattatreya Manjunath Bijur.

28. It was Das Ganu's regular practice to keep Baba's photograph in front of him during the *kirtan*. As Lakhmichand saw the picture, he at once remembered the figure in his dream.

29. The same age, the same beard, the same limbs and feet — his mind got deeply engrossed as he realized that he was the same *mahatma*.

30. The *kirtan*, as it was, was by Das Ganu; to add to it, the story was of Tukaram, and besides, he had just had the *sadhu's darshan*! Lalaji's mind was totally engrossed.

31. Tender at heart that he was, Lakhmichand's eyes were filled with tears of love and his heart felt a longing as to when he would be able to set his eyes on this loving form.

32. All his attention was fixed only on him whom he had seen in the dream and whose exact replica was now before him in the picture. He would think of nothing else.

33. 'Will I meet a friend who will accompany me to Shirdi? When will I bow my head at the feet of this saint?

34. 'When will I get this *sadhu's darshan*? Will I ever experience the joy of his love?' Such was the constant anxiety in Lakhmichand's mind.

35. 'Moreover, the expenses have to be taken care of. What should be done now? How can I get his *darshan* quickly?' So he began to think of ways and means.

36. But God is forever hungry for the love and faith of the devotee. Just see, what a miracle took place! On that same night, at about 8 o'clock, a friend knocked on his door.

37. As he opened the door to see, it was Shankarrao, his friend, who came to ask Lakhmichand whether he wanted to come to Shirdi.

38. In fact, he (Shankarrao) had wanted to go to Kedgaon for taking the *darshan* of Narayan Maharaj. But he then thought, let me go to Shirdi, first.

39. That for which he wanted to make every effort, came walking at his doorstep! Naturally, Lakhmichand's joy knew no bounds.

40. He borrowed Rs.15/- from his cousin and so did Shankarrao. Thus they were both ready to set out.

41. Packing their bag and baggage, they were ready to leave. They went to the station in good time and bought tickets, thus catching the train comfortably.

42. Shankarrao was fond of *bhajans*. So both started singing *bhajans* in the train. Being curious by nature, Lakhmichand tried to gather some information on the way.

43. If they happened to meet people from Shirdi, they would greet them and ask them for their personal experiences of Sai Baba's great powers, which could bring them conviction.

44. 'Sai Baba is a great saint and is well-known around Ahmednagar', they said. 'Please tell us with certainty, some of your own experiences.'

45. There were four Muslims in the compartment, who came from a place near Shirdi. Talking to these brought them both great satisfaction.

46. Lakhmichand, who was simple and trusting, said very lovingly to them, 'Please tell us if you know anything about Sai Baba'.

47. They replied, 'Sai Baba is a great saint, who has been residing at Shirdi for many years. He is a great '*Avalia*' (saint) and a *Mahant* (a *siddha*)'.

48. Conversing happily in this way, when they both reached Kopargaon, the Sheti, (Lakhmichand) suddenly remembered,

49. 'Sai Baba is very fond of guavas,' said he, 'and Kopargaon produces them in plenty. They are sold on the banks of the river Godavari. We can offer them to Baba.'

50. But when they reached the bank of the Godavari, the beautiful scene elated them so much, that they forgot all about the guavas and the *tonga* had already reached the other bank of the river.

51. From there Shirdi was about four villages away. The *tonga* started running full-speed. Eventually when Lakhmichand did remember, there was not a trace of guavas, anywhere.

52. Suddenly, they saw an old lady with a basket on her head, running after their carriage. They stopped the *tonga* for her, only to find, to their great joy, that the guavas had themselves come after them!

53. Happily, Lakhmichand began selecting the fruit with great care. Of the fruit that remained in the basket, the old lady said, 'Offer these to Baba on my behalf.'

54. Remembering the guavas and then forgetting all about them, the sudden meeting with the old lady and her devotion to Sai, — all this surprised them both, greatly.

55. 'In the beginning the old man appeared in the dream, I saw the same man in the *kirtan*. Could this old lady be related to him also, in some way?' Lalaji suddenly thought.

56. However, the *tonga* then drove on and reached Shirdi in no time.
     The banners flying on the mosque, were spotted from a distance
     and they both joined their hands in obeisance, with great devotion.

57. Immediately on arrival, they went to the mosque, carrying with
     them the *pooja* articles. As they took Sai's *darshan*, their hearts
     were flooded with happiness and contentment.

58. They entered the *Sabhamandap* from the gate of the courtyard
     and as they gazed upon Baba's figure from a distance, thery were
     choked with a powerful emotion.

59. When Lakhmichand had the longed-for *darshan* of Baba, his mind
     was completely engrossed (at Baba's feet). He forgot hunger and
     thirst as he experienced an inner Bliss.

60. Taking some pure, clean water in hand, he washed Baba's feet
     and performed the *pooja* rituals (like *arghya, padya,* etc.), with an
     offering of coconut, bananas, etc.

61. He burned incense, waved lights, offered '*paan*' (betel-nut leaves)
     and *dakshina* and mentally made a '*pradakshina*'[6]. He offered
     flower-garlands and sat down near his feet.

62. Lakhmichand was a loving devotee, who, rejoicing in the guru's
     grace, was absorbed at Sai's feet, as a bee in a lotus.

63. Baba then said, "These wretches! They sing *bhajans* on their way
     and ask questions to other people! What is there to ask others?

64. "They should see everything with their own eyes. Why should
     they ask other people? Can a dream so true, ever be false? Make
     up your mind for yourself!

65. "And where was the need to borrow from a Marwari and come
     for *darshan*? Is your heart's desire fulfilled, at least now?" On
     hearing these words their minds were full of astonishment.

66. 'How did Baba know here, that we had made enquiries on the
     way?' This was a great wonder that Lakhmichand felt at heart.

67. At home, I had a dream; in the train we sang *bhajans*, but how did
     Baba know all this? Oh, what marvellous intuition this is!

68. True, I was most eager for his *darshan* and that I was short of
     money, which I supplemented by borrowing. But just see how he
     knows even this!

69. Lakhmichand was astonished beyond words! All the devotees, who, like the bees to a lotus, are attracted to Sai's lotus-feet, were also greatly surprised. Baba's *leelas* are inconceivable, indeed!

70. To celebrate festivals or to go on pilgrimages with borrowed money, was an indebtedness that Baba did not like. This was the main lesson here.

71. Later, Lakhmichand along with the other devotees, went to *Sathewada* and with a joyful heart, sat down for the meal at noon.

72. Meanwhile, '*sanja*', which some devotee had brought, was being served, a little on each plate as Baba's *prasad* and Lalaji felt satiated and happy, as he ate it.

73. The next day, Lalaji remembered the *sanja* at mealtime, but it was not a daily item. And his desire for it remained unfulfilled.

74. But on the third day, just see the wonder, as to how and by what means, Sai Maharaj compensated for Lalaji's unsatisfied desire.

75. Jog arrived at the mosque for *pooja*, with sandal-paste, consecrated rice, flowers, lamps, bell, etc., and began to ask Baba:

76. 'Baba what should I bring as *naivedya* today?' And Maharaj commanded, "Bring a dishful of *sanja* for me! *Pooja, arati*, etc., can wait, you perform them later."

77. So leaving all the *pooja* ingredients there, Jog at once went back and returned immediately, bringing with him '*sheera*' (or *sanja*), enough for all.

78. Later, the noon *arati* was performed. The devotees had already brought their *naivedya* and now their plates started coming up to Baba. Baba then said to his devotees:

79. "Today is a good day and I feel the *prasad* today, should be of *sanja*. Bring it up here; send for it, quickly! All should eat it to their hearts' content."

80. The devotees went and brought two vessels filled with *sanja*. Lakhmichand was already feeling hungry, though there was some discomfort due to rheumatic pains in his back.

81. The hunger in the stomach, the nagging pains in the back had made Lakhmichand quite restless. But now listen carefully, O listeners, to the words that came from Baba's mouth at that time!

82. "It is good," he said, "that you are feeling hungry. There is pain in the waist, which needs medicine. But now is the time for eating *sanja*. Get ready for *arati*!"

83. Whatever was in Lakhmichand's mind was very clearly expressed in Baba's words — an echo without the utterance! Truly, Maharaj intuitively knew everything!

84. *Arati* was over; *sanja* was served during the meal and Lakhmichand's desire for it was satisfied, making him very happy.

85. From then onwards, love for Baba began to grow. Offering of coconut, incense-sticks, flower-garlands became his regular practice. The practice of performing *pooja* continued, bringing Lakhmichand peace and happiness.

86. The devotion to Sai grew so much, that if he met anyone going to Shirdi, he always sent with him a garland, *dakshina*, camphor or incense-sticks, etc.

87. Whoever might be going to Shirdi, the moment Lakhmichand learnt about it, he would definitely send these three things with *dakshina*, for Baba.

88. It was now during the aforesaid trip, that on the night when Baba went to the *Chavadi*, Lakhmichand went to see the ceremony. Suddenly, Baba had a fit of coughing, which caused him great distress and agitation.

89. Lakhmichand said to himself, 'Oh, how troublesome is this cough! I feel as if it is the evil eye of the people that is giving rise to it!'

90. It was just a thought that rose in Lakhmichand's mind. But when he came to the mosque in the morning, just see the marvel of what Baba said.

91. Madhavrao had come there, too, and Baba said to him, all on his own, "Yesterday I had a severe bout of coughing. Could this be the result of an evil eye?

92. "I really feel that someone has cast an evil eye on me. That is why this cough is troubling me in every way!"

93. In his mind, Lakhmichand was struck with wonder. 'This is just a repetition of my thoughts! But how did Baba know all this? Really, he dwells in the hearts of all.'

94. With folded hands, he prayed to Baba, 'Maharaj, I have been overjoyed by your *darshan*. Please be merciful and protect me, always.

95. 'Except for these holy feet, I now know no other God in this world. May my heart be always engrossed in your worship only,

96. 'I bow at your feet and O Sai Samarth, I now ask your leave to go. Please grant me permission and extend your protection to us, the orphans.

97. 'Have compassion for us, always, so that this worldly life may not torment us. May we increasingly take to chanting your name and experience peace and happinesss, all around us.'

98. With Sai's blessings and *udi* and rejoicing at heart, Lakhmichand returned home with his friend, singing Sai's praises, all the way.

99. Another little sparrow was similarly pulled by the string and brought to Shirdi by Baba, when the right moment had arrived for her to have Baba's *darshan*. Listen to her wonderful tale!

100. This sparrow was a very affectionate lady, whose story is most amazing. At Barhanpur the lady had a Vision, in which she saw Sai.

101. Never had she had actual *darshan* before, but the lady had a dream, in which Baba came to her door and asked her for a meal of '*khichadi*'[8].

102. The lady woke up instantly and looked around, but there was no one there. She hurried to narrate this vison to everyone.

103. Her husband was an officer in the postal department in that same city. Later, when he was transferred to Akola, she immediately made preparations to go to Shirdi.

104. The couple was full of faith and devotion and had a keen desire for Sai's *darshan*. The vision became a matter of fond admiration for them. Sai's *Maya* is really, most remarkable!

105. Choosing a suitable day, they both set out for Shirdi and paying their respects to the sacred Gomati (Godavari) which was on their way, they arrived at Shirdi.

106. Lovingly, they took Baba's *darshan*, offered *pooja* with devotion and stayed on in Shirdi in happiness and contentment, worshipping Baba's feet every day.

107. In this way, the couple stayed happily for two months there. Baba was also pleased with the '*khichadi*', which they offered with so much love and faith.

108. The couple had travelled to Shirdi mainly for offering *khichadi* as *naivedya*. But fourteen days passed and the *khichadi* still remained to be offered.

109. The lady did not like such a long delay in fulfilling her resolve. So on the fifteenth day, as soon as it was noon, she came to the mosque with the *khichadi*.

110. On coming there, the lady learnt that the curtains had already been drawn and that taking his devotees with him, Baba had already sat down to his meal.

111. At such a time, when the meal was in progress, nobody would go behind the curtain. But the lady was too impatient to sit still waiting quietly in the *Sabhamandap* below!

112. She had undertaken the journey all the way from Akola to Shirdi, only out of great eagerness to offer *khichadi* to Baba. How would that extraordinary enthusiasm allow her to sit quietly, waiting below?

113. So, without listening to anyone, she lifted the curtain with her own hands and entered with her offering, thus fulfilling her desire.

114. And Baba also surprised all of them. He showed such a keen desire for her *khichadi*, that he would have it first, before anything else and actually seized the plate in both his hands.

115. Seeing the *khichadi*, he was so enthused that picking up mouthfuls, one upon the other, he eagerly shoved them in his mouth. All watched him fondly, with wonder!

116. This eagerness on Baba's part filled their minds with astonishment. But when they heard the story of that *khichadi*, they realised how extraordinary were Baba's ways.

117. As you listen to the story that follows, your hearts will be overwhelmed with love. It is about a Gujarati Brahmin, who suddenly came to Shirdi to serve Baba.

118. He who had served at Rao Bahadur Sathe's house in the beginning, found refuge at Baba's feet, while still serving Sathe faithfully.

119. That is also an interesting story. Just listen to how Shrihari satisfies the longing of him, whose heart is filled with love and devotion.

120. The name of this Brahmin was Megha. His association with Sai from previous births brought him to Shirdi. But listen attentively now, to his story.

121. Sathe was then an Assistant Collector in the Kheda district and it was there that he met Megha, quite unexpectedly. He took him up in service to perform the daily *pooja* in the Shiva-shrine.

122. Later, this Sathe came to Shirdi and good fortune smiled on him. He enjoyed Sai's holy company and his mind was at once absorbed at Sai's feet.

123. When he saw the rush of pilgrims there, he resolved that he would have his own *wada*, to be able to come and stay there.

124. He met some leading villagers and acquired that piece of land, where, in the beginning, Baba had appeared. The place was fixed for building the *wada*.

125. The importance of this sacred place has already been described in the fourth chapter, repetition of which is not called for here. So let us continue our narration.

126. And so, Megha's accumulated merit being great, he met Rao Bahadur Sathe. For it was by his ardent efforts that Megha was at once guided to the spiritual path.

127. Overwhelmed by circumstances, he had become neglectful of prescribed acts and observances. But Sathe brought him back on the path of righteousness, by initiating him into reciting the *Gayatri Mantra*[9].

128. As Megha began to serve Sathe, their mutual respect grew. So much so, that to Megha, Sathe was his guru, for whom he developed great affection.

129. One day, during a casual conversation, as Sathe was praising his own guru, his heart was overcome with love and he said to Megha,

130. 'I wish with all my heart that I can bathe Baba with the water of the holy Ganga. And it is mainly for this purpose that I am sending you to Shirdi.

131. 'Moreover, when I see your dedicated service to me, I sincerely feel that you should be blessed with the holy company of this Sadguru and develop sincere faith and devotion for him.

132. 'Your physical existence will then be fulfilled and you will have achieved the highest good in this birth. Go, go, worship the Sadguru's feet with mind, speech and action.'

133. Megha then enquired about Baba's caste. Actually, even Sathe did not know it. He said, 'Some call him 'avindha'[10], because he lives in a mosque.'

134. The moment the word 'avindha' fell on his ears, Megha was dejected in his mind. 'There is no creature meaner than a Muslim. Of what worth is he as a guru?'

135. But now if he were to say 'no', Sathe would be angry and if he said 'yes', he would descend into hell. What should he do, he could not think. He was worried and anxious.

136. He was caught between the Devil and the Deep Sea. His mind was wavering and restless. But Sathe, in all earnestness, was urging him to go. So he decided that he would go and have *darshan*.

137. Then Megha came to Shirdi. As he reached the courtyard and began to climb the steps, Baba began his *leela*.

138. He wore a stern, severe look on his face and picked up a stone, saying, "Don't you dare put your foot on the step! This is a place inhabited by a *Yavan* (Muslim).

139. "Oh, you are a high caste Brahmin, and I, the meanest of the mean, a *Yavan*! You will be polluted. Go back, return this minute!"

140. That agitated expression, that flying snappishly at him! It was but another manifestation of Rudra (Shiva) in the '*Pralaya*'[11]. The onlookers trembled and Megha too, began to shake violently with fear.

141. But this anger was only on the surface while the heart within was flooded with a loving compassion. Megha was wonder-struck! 'How did he know my innermost thoughts?

142. 'O, where that far-away Kheda District and where this distant Ahmednagar! Baba's anger is only a reflection of my own mind, so full of doubts!'

143. The more Baba advanced to beat him, the more Megha's courage failed him. And each time he took a step backwards for he dared not come any nearer.

144. In the same situation, he continued in Shirdi for a few days, trying to gauge Baba's mood. He went on serving him in whatever manner he could. But he had no conviction.

145. Later, he went to his own home, where he ran a high temperature and became bed-ridden. A constant longing for Baba grew within him there. So once again, he returned to Shirdi.

146. As he came back, he felt very happy and he stayed on. He developed faith in Sai and became his steadfast devotee. Sai now became his one and only god.

147. Megha was already devoted to Shiva and as his attachment to Sai's feet grew, he saw Shiva in Sainath; Sai alone was his *Umanath* (Shankar).

148. By night and by day, Megha now ceaselessly chanted the name of Sai-Shankar. His mind became one with Sai-Shankar and his heart, cleansed of all blemishes, became pure.

149. Seeing Sai as Shankar, his devotion to Sai became single-minded and with *'Shankar'*, *'Shankar'* on his lips all the time, he refused to accept any other god as his chosen deity.

150. Sai alone now became his daily *pooja* ritual, Sai was his *'Girija-Raman'* (Shankar). With this thought firmly fixed in his mind, Megha was always in a happy mood.

151. Shankar is fond of *'Bel'* leaves[12], but there is no *'Bel'* tree in Shirdi. For its leaves, Megha used to walk two or three miles to satisfy his own desire to offer them to Shankar.

152. What were two or three miles to him! He would even have crossed a mountain just to get the leaves, so that he could satisfy his wish of performing a proper *pooja* and fulfil his heart-felt desire.

153. Going long distances, Megha would bring the '*Bel*' leaves and thus collect all the ingredients for the *pooja* and offer *pooja* to the various village deities in a particular, fixed order, with proper rites and rituals.

154. Immediately on finishing it, he would go to the mosque, lovingly make obeisance to the seat occupied by Baba and after pressing Baba's feet, first drink the '*teertha*' (or the sacred water washed off Baba's feet).

155. There are other stories of Megha too, which will delight listeners and will also show Sai's reverence for the village deities and his all-pervasiveness.

156. So long as Megha was in Shirdi, he regularly performed the noonday *arati*. But he would first offer *pooja* to all the village deities and then go to the mosque.

157. Such was his daily routine, which, one day he missed. In spite of his best effort, Khandoba's[13] *pooja* could not be performed that day.

158. He wanted to offer *pooja*, as usual, but try as he may, the door could not be opened. So leaving the *pooja* unperformed, he came to the mosque with the *arati*.

159. Baba at once, said, "Today there has been a break in your daily *pooja*. All the other gods have been worshipped but one god remains without the daily *pooja*.

160. "Go, perform that and then come back." Megha said, 'Baba, the door was closed and though I tried to open it, it could not be opened. So perforce I had to omit it.'

161. Baba said, "Go and see again. Now the door is open." Without wasting a moment, Megha went back, immediately, and experienced the truth of Baba's words.

162. He then offered *pooja* to Khanderaya. In this way, his own restlessness was also calmed. Baba then allowed Megha to do his *pooja*.

163. With great reverence, Megha offered the *'Ashtopachar' pooja*[14], with sandalwood paste, flowers, etc., and according to his capacity he gave *dakshina*, flower-garlands, and fruit.

164. Once on the *Makar Sankranti* day[15], Megha wished to bring water from the Godavari river, to give Baba a proper bath by applying oil, sandalwood paste mixed with other fragrant ingredients, etc., all over his body.

165. He pestered Baba to obtain his permission and, when ultimately Baba said, 'Do as you please,' Megha picked up the water-vessel and set out to get the water.

166. Before the sunrise, Megha set out, empty vessel in hand, barefooted and without an umbrella, to bring water from the Gomati river.

167. That the distance, both ways, was sixteen miles, and that to traverse it would mean great effort and much trouble, was a thought that never crossed his mind, even in a dream.

168. This was not his worry, at all. On getting the permission he set out, at once. When the resolve is firm, it generates great enthusiasm for the task in hand.

169. The moment it came into his mind to bathe Sai with the Ganga (Godavari) waters, where was the effort; where the exhaustion? Firm faith is the only measure in achieving the purpose.

170. In this way, the water was brought and emptied in the copper vessel. He then kept on pressing Baba to get up and have a bath. But Baba would not listen.

171. The *arati* at noon, was over and people went back to their respective homes. 'Everything is ready for the bath and it is afternoon already', said Megha.

172. Seeing Megha's persistence, Sai, who had incarnated only to show his *leela*, held Megha's hand in his own and said,

173. "Really, Megha! I do not want this bath with the Ganga-water. Oh, how foolish can you be! Why does a fakir like me, want Ganga-water?"

174. But Megha was not prepared to listen to anything. He knew only one thing — that to him Baba was Shankar Himself, and that Shankar is pleased when bathed with Ganga-water.

175. He said, 'Baba, today is the festive occasion of *Makar Sankranti*, when Shankar is pleased with the bath of Ganges-water.'

176. Seeing his overwhelming love, pure heart and firm resolve, Baba said, "All right! Let your wish be satisfied!"

177. So saying, he got up and went and sat on the low stool kept for the bath. He bent his head before Megha and said, "Just put a little water over here.

178. "Of all the parts of the body, head is the chief. Sprinkle a little water on it and it will be equal to a full bath. Listen to me, at least this much!"

179. 'All right', he said and lifting the water-vessel, very lovingly, he poured it over the head. As he emptied it, saying '*Har Gange*', he poured water all over Baba and not only on his head.

180. Megha was very pleased with himself as he thought 'I bathed my Shankar fully, with his garments on.' But lo! As he put down the empty vessel, he stared at Baba in wonder!

181. Although he had poured water all over the body, Baba's head alone was wet while the other parts were dry. On his clothes too, there was not a drop of water!

182. Megha's pride was humbled; and those around gaped in astonishment. Such was Shri Sai's way of indulging his devotees' fancy.

183. 'You wished to bathe me, go ahead and do according to your wishes. But even in that you will get my sign, quite easily.'

184. This is the secret significance of Sai-devotion. You have only to have the good fortune of being in his holy company and then nothing is difficult. By and by, everything becomes easy.

185. Every instant, resting or walking or talking, or taking a round morning and noon, if the devotee kept a steady, immovable faith, he would achieve his desired goal.

186.   But only by giving some such inner sign in the actual practical life and by creating a fondness for the spiritual life, did Sai instruct the devotee, little by little, in that path.

187.   There is another such story of Megha, by listening to which, the listeners will be delighted. Sai's love for his devotees will, surely, gladden their hearts.

188.   There was a large, new picture of Baba, which Nanasaheb Chandorkar had presented to Megha. He used to keep it in the *wada* and worship it with great devotion.

189.   In the mosque was Baba, in person; in the *wada* was his full-length picture, an exact replica. In both these places Megha performed *pooja* and *arati*, day and night.

190.   This daily worship continued and twelve months passed by, easily. Then one day Megha had a vision as he lay awake on his bed at dawn.

191.   While he was in bed, although his eyes were closed, his mind was fully awake, when he clearly saw Baba's figure.

192.   Knowing full well that he was awake, Baba also threw some grains of consecrated rice on his bed and said, "Megha, do draw a *Trishool*," and disappeared that instant.

193.   Hearing Baba's words, Megha opened his eyes at once, but was astonished to see him vanish.

194.   Megha looked all around, only to see the rice all over his bed, even as the doors of the *wada* were fastened as before. He was quite mystified.

195.   He went to the mosque, at once, and after taking Baba's *darshan*, he narrated the incident of the '*Trishool*', asking Baba's permission to draw it.

196.   Megha narrated his vision in detail. Baba then said, "What vision? Did you not hear my words, telling you to draw the '*Trishool*'?

197.   "Calling it a 'Vision', are you trying to evaluate my words? My words have a profound significance. Not even a letter in them is meaningless!"

198. Megha said, 'Even I thought in the beginning that you woke me up. But not a single door was open. So I regarded it as a vision.'

199. Listen to Baba's reply to this, "No door is necessary for my entry. I have neither shape nor size. I am always everywhere.

200. "Casting his burden on me, he who truly becomes one with me, of him I become the controller, regulating bodily functions."

201. But now listen carefully, O listeners, to Baba's wonderful *leela* and you will understand the purpose of the *Trishool*. You will then realize the connection.

202. Here, as Megha returned, he began to draw the *Trishool* on the wall near Baba's picture in the *wada* and it was drawn using the red colour.

203. The very next day, there came to the mosque a Ramdas devotee from Poona. He made obeisance to Baba, very lovingly, and offered him a '*Shiva-linga*'[16].

204. At that moment, Megha also came there and prostrated before Baba in obeisance. Baba said, "See, this Shankar has come for you. Now, you look after him."

205. To get the '*linga*' in this way, quite unexpectedly, and that too, after the Vision of the *Trishool*—Megha stood still, for a moment, looking at the '*linga*'. He was so much overcome with emotion that a lump rose to his throat.

206. The listeners should listen attentively to yet another unique experience of the '*linga*', which Kakasaheb Dikshit had. It will further confirm their faith in Sai.

207. As Megha came out of the mosque, carrying the '*linga*' with him, Dikshit had just finished his bath in the *wada* and was engrossed in chanting the name.

208. A towel on his head, he stood on the stone, drying himself with a clean cloth and remembering Sai.

209. Following his daily practice, he was chanting Sai's name, with his head covered, when he suddenly had the *darshan* of the '*linga*'.

210. 'While chanting the name, why should I get this *linga-darshan* only today?' As Dikshit wondered thus, he saw that Megha was standing near him in a happy mood.

211. Megha said, 'Look, Kaka! See, Baba has given me this *linga*'. Kaka was surprised but pleased to note the special feature of that *linga*.

212. In its form and figure, its shape and special nature, it was the same of which he had *darshan* earlier. Dikshit felt very happy.

213. Later on, the drawing of the *Trishool* was completed at Megha's hand and Sai got him to instal the *linga* near his picture.

214. Megha was fond of performing *Shankar-pooja*. His faith and devotion was confirmed by presenting him with a *Shiva-linga*. Truly Sai's *leela* is inconceivable!

215. Oh, but is there only one such tale? I can narrate innumerable ones like this one but for the fact that the book will increase in bulk. Hence, O listeners, forgive me!

216. And yet, eager as you must be for more, I shall narrate one more in the next chapter and you will hear of even more marvellous deeds of Sai.

217. Seeking refuge at Sai's feet, Hemad makes his audience listen to Sai's Story, which will free them from the fear of worldly life and avert their troubles.

Weal be to all! Here ends the twenty-eighth chapter of
"*Shri Sai Samarth Satcharit*", called
'*A Narration of Visions*',
as inspired by the saints and the virtuous,
and composed by his devotee, Hemadpant.

Notes

1. Refer Ch. 27, note 14.
2. Refer Ch. 27, note 13.
3. In the original Marathi text, Ch. 10 instead of Ch. 13, has been mentioned by mistake.
4. Refer Ch. 5, note 6.
5. Refer Ch. 3, note 17.
6. Circumambulation of an idol or guru or Brahmin, by way of reverence.
7. Refer Ch. 27, note 8.
8. Refer Ch. 27, note 13.
9. A sacred *mantra* from the Vedas, which protects life, when recited. It is supposed to be a very powerful *mantra*.
10. One whose ears are not pierced like a Hindu, hence a Muslim.
11. The period of universal destruction, which takes place at the end of a '*Kalpa*'.
12. *Aegle marmelos* or *Cratoeva religiosa*. A tree sacred to Shiva.
13. An incarnation of Shiva,
14. Refer Ch. 13, note 1.
15. The passage of the sun from Sagittarius into Capricornus.
16. Refer Ch. 27, note 15.

29

A Narration of Stories of Dreams

MY OBEISANCE TO SHRI GANESH, TO SHRI SARASWATI, AND SHRI GURUMAHARAJ! TO THE FAMILY DEITY, TO SHRI SITA-RAMACHANDRA, MY MOST HUMBLE OBEISANCE! I BOW IN REVERENCE TO THE MOST VENERABLE GURU SHRI SAINATH!

1. I shall now narrate in this chapter, Sai Baba's most inconceivable *leela*, which is stranger than the one narrated in the previous chapter, although it is a continuation of the same subject.

2. Having heard of Baba's most wonderful *leela*, a group of devotional singers came to Shirdi in the year 1916, for Baba's *darshan*.

3. They had all been travelling, on pilgrimage to Kashi and having heard of Baba's fame while at Madras, had decided to break their journey at Shirdi.

4. 'Sai Baba is a great saint — resolute, munificent, and self-restrained, who is kind to the pilgrims and distributes money to them.

5. 'One pice, or two annas are as nothing to him; and there is a shower of 4 anna - 8 anna coins! To some he gives ten rupees; to others, twenty and to yet others, fifty!

6. 'And this bounty is not reserved for special or festive occasions, or even for the time of 'Parva'¹. But as mentioned above, such sums he distributes with great pleasure every day.

7. '*Pahuds* and *Bhavayyahs*² come and their men dance; singers sing, the minstrels lavish praises; the entertainers present a salute of honour and respect; the *Haribhaktas* (God's devotees) get totally engrossed as they sing *bhajans*.

8. 'So munificent is Maharaj, so bountiful in his generosity!' This fame reached them by word of mouth and so they wished to have Baba's *darshan*.

9. Baba would also distribute money to the wayfarers, if he felt like it. Compassionate that he was, Sainath would very kindly enquire after and relieve the wants and pain of the poor and the afflicted.

10. This group was of four, comprising a man and three women, i.e. himself, his wife, daughter and his wife's sister. They all had a great desire for the saint's *darshan*.

11. After taking Sai's *darshan*, they all felt satisfied and happy. Every day, they would, very lovingly sing *bhajans* in front of Sai.

12. They belonged to the *Ramdasi panth* (sect). They used to sing the *bhajans* with great enthusiasm and Baba also gave them a rupee or eight annas — whatever came into his mind.

13. Sometimes he would give them some *burfi*[3]; sometimes, nothing! But then, such had always been Baba's ways, nothing was ever certain!

14. That he distributed money, was, however, true! There was nothing untrue about this. But he would not give it to one and all! No one knew what was in his mind.

15. Fakirs, spongers, mendicants — they came to Baba's door, all the time. Kind though he was, Baba did not always give to everyone, in charity.

16. It was only he, whose propitious moment had arrived, who would receive the money sanctified by the saint's touch and would thus get happiness and prosperity.

17. Listeners will be happy to hear a story in this context. Hence I shall first relate it and we will then move on.

18. After the light repast in the morning, as Baba came and sat down near the pillar, which was close to the *dhuni* in the mosque, would then come the little girl, Amani.

19. Timing herself well, the three-year-old naked girl would rush to the mosque, holding a tiny *jintan* box[4] in hand, and accompanied by her mother, Jamali.

20. Amani would go and sit on Baba's lap, giving the little box in his hand and, holding his hand, would clamour, 'Baba, *rupayya, rupayya!*'

21. Baba loved children and this child too, was chubby and pretty. Baba would cuddle her and kiss her, holding her close.

22. But though Baba cuddled and petted her fondly, Amani's heart would be in the rupee. 'Baba, give, O give quickly!' she would say, her mind intent on his pocket.

23. Amani, after all, was just a child! But even the big and the great have the same greed. All run after self-interest. A rare one he is who really believes in spiritual gain.

24. The child would sit on Baba's lap. Standing at some distance, outside the railing, the mother would signal from, far, saying, 'Do not budge until he gives you.'

25. "Do I owe anything to your father, you worthless free-booter, that every now and then you pester me thus?" Baba would say angrily.

26. But this wrath was only superficial and waves of love bounced within the heart. Putting his hand in the pocket, he would then take out a rupee.

27. Putting it in the little box he would close it sharply with a 'pop'! As the box came to hand, she would, in a trice, be on her way home!

28. This happened at breakfast time. Similarly, when he set out to go to the Lendi, he would again scold her lovingly, but give her one more rupee

29. Thus every day, he would give two rupees to her, six rupees to Jamali, five to Dada Kelkar and two each to Bhagya and Sundari.

30. Ten to fifteen rupees would be given regularly, to Tatya, fifteen to fifty would go to Fakirbaba, and eight rupees to the poor and needy.

31. So when those people from Madras heard about such generosity of Baba, they naturally felt a selfish interest in the money they could get and started singing *bhajans* regularly, before Baba.

32.   Outwardly, the *bhajans* were sweet, being full of devotion, but from within, they were motivated by a greed for money and in the hope that he will give them more and more money, the family stayed on in Shirdi.

33.   Three in that group were very greedy and hoped to get plenty of money from Baba. The wife alone had a sincere love and devotion for Sai, while singing the *bhajans*.

34.   As a peacock dances at the sight of the clouds or the Chakor is happy on seeing the moon, so was she in her love and respect for Sai.

35.   Once, while the *arati* at noon, was in progress, Sai, who was kindness incarnate, saw the lady's loving devotion and gave her *darshan* in the form of Shri Ram.

36.   To everyone else he was Sainath, as usual. But to the lady's eyes he appeared as Janakikant (Shri Ram). As the tears overflowed from her eyes, people watched in astonishment.

37.   Clapping with both her hands, she was simultaneously shedding tears. People were puzzled at this strange sight.

38.   At the same time, the spectacle aroused the curiosity of all. Why such a flood of tears? And why should she alone be so overjoyed?

39.   Later in the afternoon (about 4-4:30 p.m.), the lady happily narrated to her husband, of her own free will, Sai's wonderful *leela* in giving her *darshan* as Shri Ram.

40.   'Light-complexioned as the petals of a blue lotus, the wish-fulfilling *Kalpavriksha* to the devotees, this elder brother of Bharat[5] and the joy of Sita's[6] heart — it was this Shri Ram, the son of Dasharath[7] that I saw.

41.   'O, it was that Janakinath, resplendent with the crown and ear-rings, adorned with garlands of wild flowers round the neck, wearing yellow raiment and with four hands whom I saw.

42.   'The Conch, the Disc and the Mace in hands, the mark of Shri Vatsa[8] on his breast and the precious Kaustubh[9] round his neck, it was this most excellent of Men, of a comely face, that I saw.'

43. She said, 'I saw this unique incarnation of Shri Vishnu in human form, captivating the heart, with a bow and arrow in hand, who was the very heart and soul of Sita.

44. 'Outwardly, he may appear to be a fakir; maybe, even asking for alms from door to door; but to me, he appeared as the fascinating figure of Shri Ram, life and soul of Sita, holding a bow and arrow in hand.

45. 'And so, although he is an '*avalia*', to all appearances, and however else he may appear to be, to others, to me he appeared as the heart-winning Lord of Sita, with a bow and arrow.'

46. The lady was simple, trusting and devout, but her husband was very selfish. 'Women are simple and easily trusting. How is it possible that Raghupati (Shri Ram) will appear here, at this place?

47. 'Whatever is in their mind, so it appears to be to the simple, faithful ones! We all saw none other but Sai. How did she alone see Ram?'

48. With numerous such devious thoughts, he derided her. But the lady's spirits were not dampened. For, deluding herself was something she knew not.

49. Earlier, she was well-known for her spiritual authority and had repeatedly experienced the rapture of Shri *Ram-darshan*.

50. But later, there arose in her mind the temptation and greed for money and where there is money, there is no god. *Ram-darshan* also ceased. Such is the natural result of avarice.

51. Baba knew everything and knowing full well that her sinful propensities were completely destroyed, he now gave her *Ram-darshan* and satisfied her wish.

52. But see the marvel of it, on that same night the man (her husband) had a terrible dream, while he was asleep.

53. He dreamt that he was in a city and was arrested by a policeman, who had tied his arms behind and was standing at the back, pulling up tightly the two ends of the rope, with his hands.

54. There, at that same place, was a cell with bars, outside which stood Sai, quietly, without a movement, to see what was happening.

55. When he saw Sai, standing nearby, in a humble supplicant tone, he then said, with folded hands and piteous face,

56. 'Baba, when we have come to your feet on hearing your fame, why then such a calamity, when you are present in person?'

57. Maharaj replied, "We have to suffer for all the *karma* that we have done!" Very humbly the man said, 'But I have done no such *karma*!

58. 'At least in this birth I have not done anything that such a calamity should befall me.' Maharaj then said, "You may have done it in another birth."

59. And the man replied, 'But what do I know of the previous births? And even if I have done something, it should have been burnt to ashes by your very *darshan*.

60. 'How is it then, that as soon as we had your *darshan* that *karma* was not reduced to ashes, as grass before fire, making me free from it?'

61. Maharaj then said to him, "But do you, at least, have that much faith?" When the man said 'Yes', he asked him to close his eyes.

62. Obeying the command, even as he stood, closing his eyes, he suddenly heard a loud thud, as if someone had fallen down.

63. He was quite startled on hearing it and at once opened his eyes, only to find that he was set free from the bondage and instead, the policeman had fallen and was covered with blood.

64. He panicked and began to look at Baba. With a smile, Maharaj said to him, "It is well that you are going to be caught, now!

65. "The police officers will come and on seeing what has happened here, you alone, will be found to be wild and uncontrollable, which will result in your being arrested, once again."

66. In all earnestness, the man replied, 'Baba, what you say is very true. O, please do anything but release me, now! I see no other protector except you.'

67. When he heard this, Sai said to him, "Close your eyes once again!" And when he did so, and opened them again, he saw another marvel!

68. This time, he saw himself out of the cage, with Maharaj Sai near him. He prostrated before Baba in obeisance. Baba asked him,

69. "The salutation that you made just now and the ones that you used to make before, is there any difference between the two? Just think and tell me!"

70. The man replied, 'O, the difference is great — as between heaven and earth! My earlier salutations were purely out of greed for money; but now, it is as to God Himself!

71. 'Earlier, I had no faith. On the contrary, I had a grudge in my mind that yourself being a Muslim, you were polluting us, the Hindus!'

72. So Baba said, "Do you not have devotion in your mind for the deities of the Muslims?" The man said 'No'.

73. Baba then asked him, "Do you not have the '*Panja*'[10] at home and do you not worship it on the day of the '*Taboot*'[11]? Ask yourself!

74. "And you also have '*Kaad Bibi*'[12] in your house and during the wedding celebrations do you not propitiate her, a Muslim deity, by worshipping her with due honours?"

75. The man admitted by saying 'yes' and when asked what other wish he had, he expressed his keen desire for the *darshan* of his own guru, Ramdas.

76. Maharaj then asked him to turn back and see. When he did so, he saw in front of him. Samarth Ramdas, in person.

77. But as he fell at his feet, Samarth disappeared, there and then. The man then began to ask Baba something, out of curiosity.

78. 'Baba you are advanced in years and your body too, looks old. Do you know your life's span?'

79. "What, what do you say? That I look old? Just try running with me!" So saying, Sai began to run and the man ran after him.

80. But Maharaj ran faster and faster, raising a cloud of dust behind him. In that moment, Maharaj vanished and the man woke up.

81. When he was fully awake and began to think of his situation in the dream, at once, his mind was transformed and he began to praise Baba's greatness.

82. Having seen Baba's wonderful *leela*, he developed faith and devotion towards Baba. The earlier state of doubts and misgivings about Baba disappeared altogether.

83. It was really just a dream, but listening to the answers and those questions, the listeners should grasp the deep significance of them.

84. From this dialogue of questions and answers, that gentleman learnt a most valuable lesson. His antagonism towards Sai melted away through humour and laughter.

85. Next day, in the morning, they all came to the mosque for *darshan*. Sainath, in his kindness, gave them '*burfi*' of two rupees.

86. Baba also gave them two rupees from his own pocket and made them stay on for a few days more, which they spent in worshipping him and singing *bhajans*.

87. Some days passed thus. Those people were now ready to leave. Although they did not get much money, they were blessed, amply.

88. "Allah Malik will give you aplenty. Allah will bless you." And it was this that stood them in good stead later, when they were on their way.

89. With Sai's blessings and with Sai's name in their heart and mind, day and night, as they proceeded along their way, they did not encounter any hardships or suffering, even in their dreams!

90. As were Sai's blessings, so did they complete many pilgrimages to their satisfaction, without facing any trouble on the way and returned home safely.

91. Not only did they make all the pilgrimages they had planned, but many more besides. And as they praised the marvel of Sai's words, they were filled with indescribable joy.

92. Moreover, the saint's benediction "Allah will bless you", came true to the letter and all their desires were satisfied.

93. Such were those pilgrims from Madras — righteous and virtuous, devoted to God, whose Redeemer Sai became.

94. I shall tell you another story, which is equally interesting and if the listeners listen with attention, they will be quite amazed.

95. Most compassionate, wish-fulfilling *Kalpavriksha* that Sai is, it will be seen how untiringly he always fulfils the wishes of his loving devotees.

96. Bandra city (now a suburb of Mumbai) is in Thane district. A devotee from there, Raghunathrao Tendulkar by name, was a man of sharp intellect, solemn nature and great learning.

97. Always cheerful and a loving devoteee, he was engrossed at Sai's lotus-feet, ceaselessly chanting Baba's name, hoping to hear Baba's honey-sweet words of instruction.

98. It was he who composed the '*Bhajanmala*', describing Sai's *leelas* in it. He who reads it with love and devotion, will see in it Sai, at every step.

99. Savitri was the name of his wife and Babu was their eldest son. Just listen to their strange experience and Sai's *leela*.

100. Once, this Babu, who had the benefit of Western medical education from a Medical College, was so filled with doubts and misgivings that he would not appear for the examination.

101. He had studied hard, burning the midnight oil, and had casually asked an astrologer whether he would pass the examination.

102. Turning over the pages of the '*Panchang*'[13], the astroger examined the planetary position, counting on his fingers, the stars, the zodiac signs, etc., looking quite grave and concerned.

103. He said, 'You have studied very hard, but this year the planetary position is not favourable. The next year is good and the examination will undoubtedly be passed in that year!'

104. 'What is the use of appearing for the examination, if all the effort is going to be in vain?' thought the startled student, who had taken a dread in his mind.

105. Later, after some time, the mother of the student had gone to Shirdi. She bowed her head at Sai's feet and he enquired after the well-being of all.

106. During the conversation, the topic of the examination came up amid other things, when she said to Baba in a piteous tone, 'Baba, the boy would have appeared for the exam had the stars been favourable.

107. 'The astrologers had seen the horoscope and predicted that there was no chance of success this year. Hence, though well-prepared, the boy is not going for the exam.

108. 'Baba what is this planetary conflagration! Why such disappointment this year? We were all hoping that once and for all, this exam may be passed!'

109. On hearing this Baba said, "Tell him to listen to me! Say that I have said to roll up and keep aside that horoscope and go and appear for the exam, with his mind at rest.

110. "Tell him that do not be taken in by anybody, do not show the horoscope or rely on these palmists and to carry on his studies resolutely.

111. "Tell the boy, 'You will succeed; you should appear for the exam with a relaxed mind and do not get dejected. Have full faith in me!'"

112. Then, taking leave of Baba, the mother returned to her place and conveyed Baba's message to the boy, eagerly assuring him of its absolute truth.

113. Encouraged by Sai's words, the boy appeared for the exam and answered the questions in the written papers, within the stipulated time.

114. The written examination was over; he had answered the questions fully. But then, his self-confidence gave way and the hitherto steady mind began to waver and doubt.

115. He had written the answers well enough to pass the exam. But the boy felt it was not enough and he gave up hope.

116. He began to feel that he had failed, when, in fact, he had passed the written test. He became so dejected that he just would not appear for the oral exam.

117. The oral began. The first day passed in the same dejected state. On the next day, a friend came and saw this boy sitting down to his meal.

118. The friend said, 'O what a wonder of wonders! Do you know, that the examiner himself is anxious for you and has said, 'Go and see why Tendulkar did not come yesterday.'

119. I told him frankly that he had failed in the written exam and is sitting at home, dejected, that why should he take the trouble of appearing for the orals.

120. So the examiner said, 'You go and bring him as he is. Give him the glad news that he has passed in the written exam.'

121. Who can describe the joy that this news produced! Praying to Maharaj Sai for help, he eagerly ran to appear for the orals, without losing a moment.

122. Later, everything turned out well for him. He passed the exam. Thus by satisfying his wish, Sai only confirmed his faith in himself.

123. But as the handle of the quern is to be moved round and round in the hole to fix it tightly, so is also the case with one's faith in the guru. Sai strengthened it by turning it round and round to fix it.

124. Not once did he say anything to anyone, which did not touch their hearts. Such was the usual experience with Baba. That is how he confirmed their faith.

125. Treading on the path suggested by him, everything is pleasurable, to begin with. But later, that path will be so overspread with thorny shrubs, that there will be only thorns on all sides.

126. Faith then begins to waver, the mind is easily swayed by doubts and starts wondering why Sai brings it to this by-path.

127. And it is when you feel thus, that your faith should remain steadfast. These difficulties are the real test and that is how an unshakeable faith is firmly planted.

128. By facing the hardships squarely, with a ceaseless chant of Sai's name, all the calamities will disappear. Such is the tremendous power of *naam*.

129. And this is the main purpose behind these obstacles. For they too, are created by Sai and it is only then that Sai is remembered. The troubles also vanish only then.

130. And it was the father of this same boy, who was a great devotee of Baba — very loving, solemn, generous and righteous. But now his bodily organs had become enfeebled.

131. He had faithfully served in a well-known foreign trading company in Mumbai city.

132.   Later, as he became old, the eyesight became weak and the bodily
        organs became impaired in their functioning. He now began to
        wish for complete rest.

133.   There was no strength left to do any work. So to improve his
        health, Raghunathrao took leave and enjoyed peace and quiet.

134.   The leave came to an end and yet, he did not feel fully rested. So
        he wrote an application, praying for an extension of that leave.

135.   On seeing the application, his immediate boss recommended the
        expected extension of his leave. The chief Officer of the Company
        was very kind and considerate.

136.   When the master is large-hearted, out of consideration for the
        loyal, honest servant, he lovingly offers him half of his salary as
        pension, to provide for his future.

137.   Such is the government practice, which is also followed by the
        best of companies, as an encouragement to their honest servants,
        when the occasion requires it.

138.   But Tendulkar was worried, thinking, 'Will my master give this
        pension when I retire from service?

139.   My salary is only Rs.150/- and the whole burden of sustenance
        will fall on my pension of Rs.75/-.' Such thoughts revolved in
        his mind.

140.   But what came to pass later, was most interesting. Just see Baba's
        leela! Listen to his marvel as he was engaged in a loving dialogue
        with Raghunathrao's wife, about matters of her family interests.

141.   There were still fifteen days for the final order on his pension, to
        be passed, when Baba appeared in her dream and asked her
        opinion.

142.   "It is my wish to give him Rs.100/- (as pension). Will that satisfy
        your wish?" The lady said, 'What is this that you say Baba! Why
        do you ask this? We have full faith in you, and you alone.'

143.   There, a resolution was passed on the application that
        Raghunathrao is a loyal servant, who has served us for a long
        time, to date. Therefore he should be given a pension of half his
        salary.

144.   And although Baba had mentioned a hundred, he added ten rupees more. Such is this kind-hearted Sai Samarth, who has boundless love for his devotees.

145.   Now listen to one more interesting story, which will enhance the devotees' love for Baba and give joy to the listeners.

146.   A doctor, Captain Hate by name, was a faithful devotee of Baba. This is the fascinating story of how Baba appeared to him in a dream he had at dawn.

147.   Hate lived at Gwalior and it is there that he saw Baba in a dream. Just see Baba's skill in asking questions and what Hate said to him in reply.

148.   Baba said, "Have you forgotten me?" Hate, at once, caught his feet, saying, 'If the child forgets his mother, where will he find refuge?'

149.   He hastily got up and went out into the garden from where he plucked some fresh *vaal-papadi*[14]. He also gathered together other uncooked provisions, like rice, pulses, flour, etc., and some cash as *dakshina* and thus prepared a special offering, with great devotion.

150.   On completing the preparation, as Hate was about to offer the scuttle-basket containing all the things, suddenly he opened his eyes and knew that it was just a dream.

151.   He felt that he must get hold of all these things at once and offer them to Baba, personally, going to Shirdi specially for the purpose.

152.   But at that time he was in Gwalior. So he wrote a letter to a friend in Bombay, (Kakasaheb Dikshit) narrating the incident of his dream and requesting him to go to Shirdi, personally.

153.   He wrote that the money would come by post, with which he should buy the proper provisions including the best available variety of the vegetable *vaal-papadi*, which, somehow or other, he should obtain.

154.   The remaining money should be taken to Shirdi to be offered along with the other provisions. After making obeisance the *'prasad'* should be asked for, which then should be forwarded to Gwalior.

155.   As soon as the money arrived, the friend went to Shirdi, bought
       all the ingredients, but had some difficulty in getting *vaal-papadi*.
       Suddenly a basket of the vegetables arrived.

156.   The woman, carrying it on her head, was called, at once. And
       when it was found that the basket contained the very *vaal-papadi*
       wanted, all were greatly astonished.

157.   Then all the ingredients were brought to the mosque and offered
       to Baba. He gave them to Nimonkar, who cooked the food on
       the morrow and offered it as *naivedya*.

158.   Later, Baba sat down for his meal. But he did not even touch the
       rice or *daal*. He only picked up the vegetable, to everybody's
       surprise.

159.   He ate only the vegetable (*vaal-papadi*), it was only the *vaal-
       papadi* that he put in his mouth. When Hate came to know of
       this, he was full of joy.

160.   As the devotion in his mind, so was also Hate's experience. But
       now, listen to the marvel of the story that follows. It will show
       how sweet is the indulgence by Sai.

161.   A desire arose in Hate's mind that he should have in the house, a
       rupee, which is sanctified by the touch of Sai's hand and Sai
       fulfilled his wish.

162.   There are thousands and crores of impulses in the mind. Abandon
       the evil ones and pursue the good. And then see Sai's skill —
       how he stands behind his devotees in full support!

163.   Once a good desire arises, it does not take even a moment for it to
       bear fruit. At that very moment, a friend, desiring Sai's *darshan*,
       was about to set out eagerly for Shirdi.

164.   Of course, the desire should be good and Sai will fulfil it. It is in
       his power to indulge one who is fond of good, righteous thoughts
       and conduct.

165.   Very lovingly, Hate then gave one rupee to that friend, saying,
       'Do not forget, put it in Baba's hands.'

166.   When the friend went to Shirdi, he, at once, took Baba's *darshan*,
       lowered his head on his feet and sat in front of him.

167. When Baba put out his hand for *dakshina*, he first offered his own, which Baba put in his pocket, without a moment's delay. Then he took out Hate's *dakshina*.

168. With folded hands, he put that rupee too, in Baba's hand, saying, 'Doctor Hate has sent this *dakshina* with me.'

169. This Sai, who dwells in the hearts of all, knew Hate's wish, though Hate lived at Gwalior. He sat gazing at the rupee.

170. Overwhelmed with love, Baba held the rupee in front and kept on staring at it. People watched Baba with amazement.

171. With the right thumb, Baba repeatedly tossed the rupee in the air, catching it again in his hand. After playing with it in this manner for a moment, he then returned the rupee.

172. He said, "Give this back to him, to whom it belongs. With it take this *Udi-prasad*. And tell him, we do not want anything of his! Be at ease."

173. After prostrating in obeisance at Baba's feet, he kept the *Udi-prasad* away, safely, and taking Baba's leave, returned home to Gwalior.

174. On reaching Gwalior, he gave the rupee to the doctor and narrated all that had happened. Hate was overcome with love as he heard it.

175. He said, 'What I had wished for, what I had resolved, so did Baba satisfy my wish, knowing well what my heart's desire was.'

176. But although this is what Hate felt, it was only his own notion. For who can understand the plans, the purpose that the saints have?

177. And yet, if we were to say so with any certainty, look at another experience, which is just to the contrary! Ultimately, the saint alone knows his own wishes.

178. To one he gives back his rupee; as for another, he puts his rupee in his own pocket. How can we definitely state any reason for it or what Baba had in mind.

179. Only he knows his own reasons. We can only watch his sport, without losing such a wonderful opportunity. Listen to a story in this context.

180. Once, Vaman Narvekar, whose love for Baba was boundless, brought a beautiful one rupee coin, to offer to Baba with great devotion.

181. On one side of the coin were engraved the figures of Ram, Laxman[15] and Sita and on the other side was a beautiful figure of Maruti[16], with folded hand.

182. The purpose in offering it to Baba was, for the touch of Baba's hand, after which it was expected to be returned, along with *Udiprasad*. Hence it was placed on Baba's hand.

183. Baba, of course, knew what was the wish in everybody's mind. Yet, as the rupee fell on his hand, he immediately put it in his pocket.

184. Madhavrao conveyed to Baba what Vamanrao wished for and urged him sincerely to return the rupee.

185. "Why give it back to him? No, no, it is to be kept for ourselves", said Baba, quite clearly, and in front of Vamanrao.

186. "And yet if he will give Rs.25/- as its price, I will give him this rupee instead," So Baba said.

187. Then, for that one rupee, Vamanrao hastily procured them (Rs.25/-) from different places and gave them to Baba.

188. Those too, were put in his pocket, as before, saying, even if heaps of rupees were brought, they will not weigh as much as this one. Their worth is much less than this.

189. Turning to Shama, he said, "Take this for you, Shama! Let it be in your collection. Keep it in the shrine and worship daily."

190. Now, who had the authority to question, 'Why do you do this?' For Sai knows surely, what is proper and what is not. He alone is the Power that gives us and takes back.

191. And so, as we wind up this tale, let us give some rest to the listeners' minds, whereby they can reflect and contemplate upon the story just heard.

192. Whatever one hears cannot be digested, unless it is reflected on. In addition, if contemplation upon it also does not follow, all that listening becomes purposeless.

193.   Hemad surrenders to Sai and with great reverence, bows his head at Sai's feet, which are the Means of all the means. And the narration to follow, will take its own course.

Weal be to all! Here ends the twenty-ninth chapter of
"Shri Sai Samarth Satcharit", called
'A Narration of the Stories of Dreams',
as inspired by the saints and the virtuous,
and composed by his devotee, Hemadpant.

Notes

1.   Refer Ch. 16, note 4.
2.   Village entertainers or showmen such as buffoons, tumblers, jugglers, exhibitors of snakes, etc.
3.   A snow cake made of sugar, flour and milk.
4.   Tiny black/brown pills, which are popped into the mouth to give taste.
5.   Younger brother of Shri Ram, son of Dasharath and Kaikeyi.
6.   The celebrated Sita, wife of Shri Ram.
7.   The name of the sovereign of Ayodhya, the father of Shri Ram, so named because his conquering chariot overran ten regions.
8.   The mark, a cross-form curl of white hair on the breast of Shri Vishnu (also called the sign of the striking of a kick by Bhrugu Rishi).
9.   One of the fourteen precious things obtained from the ocean, on churning it. It is the jewel of Krishna suspended on his chest.
10.   The iron hand of the Mohammadans representing their five holy personages.
11.   Refer Ch. 7, note 4.
12.   One of the chosen deities of the Muslims.
13.   The Hindu Calendar or Almanac.
14.   A kind of bean.
15.   Younger brother of Shri Ram, son of Dasharath and Sumitra.
16.   Son of the Wind and a dedicated servant of Shri Ram. This is another name for Hanuman, the Monkey God.

30

A Narration of Stories about Vows

MY OBEISANCE TO SHRI GANESH, TO SHRI SARASWATI, AND SHRI GURUMAHARAJ! TO THE FAMILY DEITY, TO SHRI SITA-RAMACHANDRA, MY MOST HUMBLE OBEISANCE! I BOW IN REVERENCE TO THE MOST VENERABLE GURU SHRI SAINATH!

1. O Merciful Sai, always affectionate that you are to the devotees, and the Abode of Kindness, you who dispel the devotees' fear of worldly life by your mere *darshan* and ward off their calamities — to you I bow in obeisance.

2. O Sainath, the most excellent among the saints, in the beginning, you were without form or attributes. But later, being woven by the thread of your devotees' love and devotion, you appeared, endowed with form and attributes.

3. Upliftment of their devotees has always been the inevitable mission of the saints and you are the *Acharya* of all the saints. It is therefore, your inevitable mission too!

4. Those who hold fast to your feet, will have all their sins destroyed; their earlier influences, good and purifying, rise to the surface and their path becomes clear and fearless.

5. Even the Brahmins from the holy places of pilgrimage remember your holy feet and come to recite the *Gayatri mantra*[1], with proper rites and rituals, and to read *pothis* and *Puranas* in your presence.

6. What do we, of little strength and no purifying influences, know of devotion? Yet, even if all others abandon us, Sai will never forsake us.

7. He who receives his grace, will enjoy power, inconceivably great, the treasure of Discriminating Knowledge between the Self and non-Self, and with that will come Enlightenment.

8. The intense desire to hear the words from Sai's lips, makes the devotees go crazy and his every word being firmly imprinted on their minds, with great faith, they seek the experience of the truth of his words.

9. Sainath knows well the wishes of his devotees, and satisfies them, too! The devotees also experience fulfilment through these.

10. O Sainath, come speedily to my rescue! I bow my head in entreaty, at your feet. Forgetting all my faults, do ward off the worries and anxieties of this servant of yours.

11. Thus distressed by the many calamities, the devotee who remembers Sainath, will find in him the one and only solace to his anxious perturbed mind.

12. It was Sai, the Ocean of Kindness, who bestowed favour on me, by virtue of which alone, I have been able to present this most auspicious book to the readers.

13. Or else, what was my authority? And who would have taken upon himself this most difficult task? But when Sai himself takes the responsibility of his own work, what burden can it be to me?

14. When Sai Samarth, the Light of Knowledge and the Destroyer of the Darkness of Ignorance, is there to illumine my speech, why should I have any doubts?

15. With total reliance on that All-merciful God, I did not experience even the slightest fatigue. By his grace, my heart's desire is satisfied.

16. This service to the saint, in the form of this book, is really the accumulated merit of my past birth. And so blessed, so fortunate am I, that you, O God, should have accepted this humble service from me!

17. In the last chapter, you have heard how Sai, the Compassionate One, instructed his devotees by giving them visions of different types.

18. Now, in the present chapter also, listen to the most interesting and joyous tale of a worshipper of the goddess *Saptashrungi* [2].

19. Listen respectfully to this marvel of how gods and goddesses entrust their own devotees to the care of saints.

20. There are numerous stories of Maharaj, one more wonderful than the other. Listen attentively to this story, which is worth listening to.

21. This is not just a story; it is a drink of nectar. It will bring you great satisfaction and will also bring out Sai's greatness and all-pervasiveness.

22. The hyper-critical and the logicians should not go after these stories. What is needed here is not argument and counterargument, but boundless profound love.

23. The listener should be a *Jnani* and yet be devoted, full of faith and utterly trusting, or a servant of the saints. To all others, these stories will appear unreal.

24. This '*Kalpataru*' of Sai's *leelas* is, undoubtedly, one that blossoms into flower and fruit. But only that devotee, who is of a powerful good fortune, will be able to bring those flowers and fruit down from that tree.

25. Listen, O listen, to these most sacred stories which are the chief among all the means, for the spiritual seekers, in the attainment of *Moksha* and most beneficial to all.

26. Drinking the nectar of Sai's stories is an effortless upliftment of the dull-witted creatures; it is the solace of those engaged in the activities of the worldly life, and to the spiritual seekers, it is the means of attaining *Moksha*.

27. While presenting one story here, many others come to mind. Hence, with great humility, Hemad calls upon the listeners to listen to them carefully.

28. Narrating these stories, one after the other, in this manner, their interest and enjoyment in the *leelas* will grow; those suffering in the forest-fire of the worldly life, will get comfort and satisfaction. Such is the great power of Sai.

29. In the village Vani, in the Nasik district, there lived one Kakaji Vaidya, who was the priest in the temple of the goddess, there.

30. The name of the goddess was *Saptashrungi*. This priest had become very restless in his mind, being harassed by the many trials and tribulations of worldly life.

31. When the Wheel of Fortune brings adversity, the mind also begins to spin like the whirlpool; the body runs helter-skelter, allowing not a moment's peace.

32. Owing to this, Kakaji became very sad at heart and going to the temple, began entreating the goddess to have mercy on him and liberate him from worries and anxiety.

33. He prayed for help, with all his heart. The goddess too, was pleased to see his devotion. The same night, he had a vision. Listen, O listeners, to this marvel!

34. Mother *Saptashrungi*, the goddess, appeared in Kakaji's dream, saying, 'Go to Baba and your mind will become calm and steady.'

35. With an eager hope that the goddess will further clarify who this Baba was and where to find him, he waited but, at that moment, he suddenly opened his eyes.

36. His desire to know remained unsatisfied and the dreaming state disappeared at once. Then Kakaji used his own reason as to who this Baba could be, that she had mentioned.

37. 'Maybe, 'Baba' is *Tryambakeshwar*[3], Kakaji resolved in his mind. And he set out at once, and took his *darshan*. Yet the restlessness of his mind would not go.

38. At Tryambakeshwar, Kakaji spent ten days but to the end, he remained sad. His mind could not find peace or happiness.

39. The restlessness would not leave the mind; its agitation would not disappear. Day after day, the disquiet, the anxiety grew. So Kakaji set out on the return journey.

40. Daily, he would bathe at dawn, recite the *Rudra*[4] repeatedly, perform the *Abhishek*[5] on the *Shiva-linga*. But his mind still remined restless.

41. Again, he went at the goddess' door, saying, 'Why did you send me to Tryambakeshwar? Please make my mind steady and peaceful, at least now! O, spare me these journeys to and fro.'

42. In a piteous tone, he thus beseeched the goddess for help. The goddess appeared to him that night, saying in a vision,

43. 'The Baba I mentioned is Sai Samarth of Shirdi. Why did you needlessly go to Tryambakeshwar, I do not understand!'

44. 'Where is this Shirdi and how does one go there? I do not know who this Baba is, nor do I understand how this trip to Shirdi is going to come about!'

45. But he who is absorbed at the saint's feet and has in his heart, a keen desire for his *darshan*, his wish will be fulfilled not only by the saints, but by God Himself.

46. He who is a saint, is also, God Almighty. There is not even the slightest difference between the two. Or rather, to consider them as separate is duality, whereas saints are one with God.

47. 'I will go all by my own efforts, for the saint's *darshan* and thus fulfil my own desire' — to say so is only one's conceit and vaunt. Inconceivable indeed, are the workings of these saints!

48. Without the saints really desiring it, who can go for their *darshan*? It is wonderful how, without their authority, not a leaf on the tree will move!

49. As the eagerness for *darshan*, as his faith and devotion, so is also the intensity of the blissful experience of that excellent devotee.

50. Here, Kakaji was worried as to how he could go for Sai's *darshan*, while there arrived the guest from Shirdi, in search of his address!

51. And was that guest any ordinary person? Oh, no! It was he whom Baba liked better than anybody else; whose love for Baba defied comparison with anyone else's and whose authority too, was very great.

52. His name was Madhavrao; and Deshpande[6], his *vatan*[7]; who alone, and no one else, could coax Baba using fond language.

53. There would, forever, be loving disputes between them and they addressed each other in a familiar way. For Madhavrao, Baba had an extraordinary affection — as if he was his own child. And such was the guest, who had arrived that very moment, at Vani.

54. When her child fell ill, the mother had said to the goddess in supplication, 'I commit this infant to your protection and care. It is now up to you to preserve or destroy.

55. 'When my child recovers, I will most certainly, place him on your feet.' After such a vow was made to the goddess, the child did recover.

56. But, be he the Vaidya, be he God Himself, once the purpose is served, they are forgotten. The vow is remembered only in the time of trouble. And when it thus remains unfulfilled, there is reason to fear.

57. Days, months, years passed by. The vow was completely forgotten. At last, when the mother was nearing her end, she entreated Madhavrao,

58. 'Years ago, I had made this vow, but the delay in its fulfilment has at last, brought us to this day. Such postponement, so much delay is not good. So please go for the *darshan* of the goddess.'

59. There was another vow that the mother had made to the goddess. She was suffering from boils on both her breasts and the pain was just unbearable.

60. 'O Mother, I prostrate before you in entreaty. If you will relieve me from this pain and suffering, I shall offer two silver breasts at your feet, waving them over you.'

61. That vow had still remained unfulfilled, being postponed from time to time. That too, the mother now remembered at the time of her death.

62. So she reminded Babya (Madhavrao) of this too, and taking from him a promise that he would fulfil it, she merged at the feet of Hari, having become desireless.

63. Further postponement followed. Days, months, years passed. Madhavrao had forgotten all about it and the vows remained unfulfilled.

64. After thirty years had passed in this way, it so happened that an astrologer arrived at Shirdi, in the course of his travels.

65. He had a deep knowledge of Astrology and could read the past, future and present. He had satisfied the curiosity of many and had received a wide acclaim.

66. He had, at once, satisfied Shrimant Butti and others, by predicting their future.

67. Bapaji, Madhavrao's younger brother, also asked him to predict his future, when the astrologer told him that the goddess was displeased with him.

68. He said, 'Your mother had asked your elder brother to fulfil her vows, at the time of her death.

69. 'But till today they have not been fulfilled and so the goddess is giving you trouble.' When Madhavrao came home, Bapaji told him the whole story.

70. Madhavrao at once, got the sign. He called the goldsmith and got two silver breasts made from him, which he then took to the mosque.

71. Prostrating before Baba, he placed those two breasts before him, saying, 'Please get the vows fulfilled from me.

72. 'You are our *Saptashrungi*; you are the goddess for us. Please accept this promised gift and be pacified.'

73. Baba replied, "Go to the *Saptashrungi* temple and, with your own hands, offer these finely wrought breasts, which are for her, at her feet."

74. Such being Baba's insistence, and the inclination of Madhavrao's mind also becoming the same, he left home, resolved to go for the *darshan*.

75. He took Baba's *darshan*, praying for his blessings and taking Baba's *Udi-prasad*, set out with his permission.

76. He arrived at *Saptashrungi* and began the search for his family-priest. As luck would have it, it was Kakaji's house that he reached, quite effortlessly.

77. Here was Kakaji, most eager for Baba's *darshan* and just then, this meeting with Madhavrao also came about! Was this any commonplace happening?

78. Kakaji then enquired who he was, from where he had come, etc., and when he learnt that Madhavrao had come from Shirdi itself, his joy knew no bounds. Both jumped at this remarkable coincidence.

79. In this way, pleased at heart, they both completed the ritual for fulfilling the vow, after which, the priest set out for Shirdi.

80. The priest was very happy for this unexpected and distinguished company as that of Madhavrao. His attention was now fully directed to the journey to Shirdi.

81. As they returned after completing the rites and rituals of the vow, they both quickly left for Shirdi, full of love and eagerness for Sai's *darshan*.

82. The earlier state of eagerness and fondness of Kakaji's mind was matched with the haste with which they set out, reaching soon, the banks of the Godavari, from where Shirdi is quite near.

83. The priest made obeisance at Baba's feet, bathing them in the tears that flowed from his eyes. Happiness and peace was restored to his mind by Baba's *darshan*.

84. It was for this purpose that the goddess had appeared in the Vision. The moment Kakaji set his eyes on Sai Samarth, he experienced true joy; his heart's wish was fulfilled.

85. Kakaji was thus filled with happiness on taking Sai's *darshan*; his heart was pleased. As Baba's grace was showered on him, the mind became truly relieved of all the worry.

86. The restless agitation ceased, to his own great astonishment, and he exclaimed to himself, Oh, what extraordinary *leela* is this!

87. 'Not a word has he spoken to me, nor asked me any questions. He did not even pronounce a benediction. It was just his *darshan* that has brought me so much joy!

88. 'My restless doubting mind was calmed merely by his *darshan* and I have attained a unique state of happiness. This is, indeed, the great significance of his *darshan*!'

89. His eyes were rivetted on Baba's feet, holding the words captive. And as the ears listened to Baba's stories, the abounding joy could not be contained within.

90. As the priest humbly surrendered to Baba, with all faith and devotion, he experienced an inner bliss, which made him forget the earlier restless agitation of the mind.

91. In this way, Kakaji stayed on in Shirdi for twelve days and his mind having become steady and peaceful, returned to *Saptashrungi*.

92. Dreams, in order to come true, must come at a particular time - those at daybreak or forty-eight minutes before the breaking of dawn are fruitful — others are in vain.

93. Such is the general belief. But as for the dreams associated with Shirdi, whenever or wherever they come, they always come true. Such is the unfailing experience of the devotees.

94. A short story, in this context, I shall now narrate to the listeners. They will be greatly pleased and enthused to hear more.

95. One day, in the afternoon, Baba said to Dikshit, "Go to Rahata with a tonga and bring back Khushalbhau (a devotee) in it.

96. "So many days have passed and I feel a great desire to meet him. Tell him that 'Baba wants to meet you and has, therefore, called you.'"

97. Bowing respectfully to Baba's command, Dikshit went with a tonga and as soon as he met Khushalbhau, he related the purpose of his visit.

98. On hearing Baba's message, his surprise was great. He said, 'I have just got up from my sleep and in my dream, Baba had given me the same command.

99. 'Just now, as I was resting on my bed after the afternoon meal, as soon as I closed my eyes, Baba told me the same thing in my dream.

100. 'He said to me, 'Come to Shirdi, right now!' I also felt a strong desire to meet him. But what could I do? The horse was not here, with me. So I sent my son to inform him so.

101. 'But hardly had he crossed the village boundary, when your tonga arrived.' Dikshit jokingly remarked, 'Yes, that is why Baba has sent me!'

102. 'Now if you are coming the tonga is ready outside.' Very happily, he came to Shirdi with Dikshit.

103. In short, Khushalbhau came and Baba's wish was satisfied. Seeing Baba's *leela*, Khushalbhau was also overcome with emotion!

104. Once, a Punjabi Brahmin, Ramlal by name, who lived in Mumbai, had Baba's *darshan* in a dream.

105. The knowledge of the outer and inner world, which comes by the power of the elemental deities, such as the sky, wind, sun, water, etc. — this is the waking state.

106. But when all the bodily organs are at rest, the imprints left on the mind during the waking state, come alive and are revived in the form of whatever is worth receiving and one who receives it. This is the characteristic of a dream.

107. Ramlal's dream was extraordinary! He knew nothing of Baba's form or attributes. He had never had his *darshan* before. But Baba said to him, 'Come to visit me'.

108. From his figure, he looked like a great saint, but he did not know where he lived. Ramlal woke up and fell into deep thought.

109. He wanted to go, but knew not his place or his address. But he alone knew his own plan, who had called him for *darshan*.

110. On that same day, in the afternoon, while he was casually walking on the road, he was startled to see a picture in a shop.

111. Ramlal felt it was the same figure that he had seen in the dream. At once, he began to make enquiries with the shop-keeper.

112. He examined the photograph carefully, asking the shop-keeper, 'Who is he? Where does he belong?' And only when Ramlal learnt that this 'Sai is in Shirdi', was he satisfied.

113. Other details he found out later. Ramlal then went to Shirdi and stayed on with Baba till the time of his 'Nirvan'.

114. To fulfil the wishes of his devotees, to bring them for his *darshan* and thus satisfy their worldly and spiritual ends — this and this alone, was Baba's heart-felt desire.

115. Otherwise, he himself was the Satiated One, always free from desire, unselfish, egoless and detached, who had incarnated only to satisfy the wishes of his devotees.

116. He, who was untouched by anger, in whom envy would find no place, who had not a care about filling the belly — know, that he is a real *sadhu*.

117. 'Selfless love for all' is his highest goal in life, and he does not waste his words, even for a moment, except to speak about '*dharma*'.

118. In brief, the real secret here is, that in getting his own 'Life' written by me, by actually holding my hand, Sai only wanted the devotees to be engrossed in remembering him.

119. Therefore, Hemad always entreats his listeners humbly, that they should listen to *Sai Satcharit*, with faith and devotion.

120. It will give them peace of mind; the addicts will lose interest and attraction for their addictions. Instead, devotion for Sai will spring up, which will free them from the bondage of worldly life.

121. Now, the next chapter will contain the story of the Sanyasin Vijayanand, who attained liberation at Sai's feet, while on his way to the *Manas Sarovar*[8].

122. Balaram Mankar, a devotee, also was given eternal rest in the same way and the wishes of Noolkar and Megha were fully satisfied by Sainath.

123. A ferocious animal, like a tiger, was given refuge at his feet. Such are the unfathomable workings of Sai, to listen to which is a rare opportunity for joy and celebration

Weal be to all! Here ends the thirtieth chapter of
"*Shri Sai Samarth Satcharit*", called
'*A Narration of Stories about Vows, etc.*',
as inspired by the saints and the virtuous and
composed by his devotee, Hemadpant.

Notes

1. Refer Ch. 28, note 9.
2. The carved image of this goddess, ten feet high and with eight hands, in a cave at the top of a 3,600ft high mountain, near a place called Vani, in the Nasik district.
3. A famous temple of Shiva near Nasik.
4. A *mantra* from the *Yajurveda*, in praise of Shiva.
5. Dropping of holy water or milk, in a steady stream, on an idol, by way of ceremonial ablutions.
6. A hereditary office of the records-keeper of a *paragana*, i.e. a unit of 20-100 villages.
7. Refer Ch. 12, note 2.
8. Refer Ch. 2, note 5.

31

Importance of Sai-Darshan

MY OBEISANCE TO SHRI GANESH, TO SHRI SARASWATI, AND SHRI GURUMAHARAJ! TO THE FAMILY DEITY, TO SHRI SITA-RAMACHANDRA, MY MOST HUMBLE OBEISANCE! I BOW IN REVERENCE TO THE MOST VENERABLE GURU SHRI SAINATH!

1. In the last chapter I have narrated the story of a devotee of *Saptashrungi* and also, how Sai got Madhavrao's vow fulfilled.
2. How he gave *darshan* to Khushalshet and Ramlal in a dream and how he kept Ramlal with him, till his own *Nirvan*.
3. But this present story is even more unique! May the listeners listen attentively to how a *sanyasin*, who was on his way to Manas Lake, suddenly, attained Liberation;
4. How Baba fulfilled the wishes of Mankar, Noolkar and Megha, too. But these were all men, while Baba gave refuge at his feet to even a most ferocious tiger.
5. The stories are rather long, which will add to the bulk of the book. So I shall briefly narrate only their essence, which will benefit the listeners.
6. As is their thought at the time of death, so is the next birth that comes to the creatures. Out of fear, insects become bees; and out of his love for the young one of the deer, *Jadabharat*[1] was born a deer in the next birth.
7. Whatever the form before the (mental) eye in the moment of death, it is that same form in which the next birth comes. But he who has surrendered humbly at the feet of God, has no rebirth.

8. And it is for this reason that devotees were encouraged to cultivate the habit of ceaselessly chanting the name. So that when the end came, they may not be bewildered, but remember to take the name.

9. Alert all his life, but if a man slumbers in the moment of death, then the ultimate purpose of his keeping the holy company, all his life, is wasted.

10. Hence the simple, the guileless among the devotees entrust themselves in the hands of the saints. For, the saints who know about the rebirth or otherwise, they alone are our companions in the hour of death.

11. As you listen to a sweet tale in this connection, which took place in Sai's presence, you will see, O listeners, Sai's affection for his devotees.

12. O, where Madras, where Shirdi, and where the steep climb of the *Manas Sarovar*! But when the devotees' time was up, how Baba would draw them to himself, bringing them at his feet.

13. Once, a *sanyasin* from Madras, named Vijayanand, set out, very enthusiastically, from Madras to go to *Manas Sarovar*.

14. Having seen a map of the *Manas Sarovar*, which a Japanese traveller had, he firmly resolved in his mind to see the *Manas Sarovar*.

15. He touched Shirdi while on his way, where he heard much about Baba's greatness. So with a keen desire for Baba's *darshan*, he came in search of his dwelling place.

16. When he heard that Sai Maharaj was a great saint, with a world-wide renown, he wished to take his *darshan* and stopped at Shirdi, on his way.

17. At that time, Swami Somadevji of Haridwar was in Shirdi. So they happened to meet each other, in the midst of other devotees.

18. The *sanyasin* then asked him, 'How far is the *Manas Sarovar*?' And the swami said, 'From Gangotri (i.e. the source of the Ganga), it is five hundred miles above.

19. 'There is heavy snowfall there. After every hundred miles, the language changes. The Bhutanese become suspicious, too. Foreign travellers face great difficulties.'

20. On receiving such information from the swami, the *sanyasin* was crest-fallen. His mind became unsettled and he was quite worried.

21. He took Sai Baba's *darshan*, prostrating at his feet and his mind became calm and happy. He sat down in a sitting posture.

22. Suddenly, Baba's anger was provoked. He said to the people around, "Drive this *sanyasin* away! His company is of no avail to us."

23. As it was, the *sanyasin* was new and did not know Baba's nature. Although in his mind he felt quite abashed, he sat on, observing the service that the devotees rendered Baba.

24. It was the morning '*darbar*' (court) and the mosque was packed with people. The *pooja* articles that the devotees had brought and the rituals that were being performed were quite amazing to the *sanyasin*.

25. Some devotees were washing Baba's feet; taking the holy water from Baba's toe — in a spoon, some were drinking it while others applied it to their eyes.

26. Yet others were applying the sandalwood-paste to him while some smeared him with fragrant perfume. They had become quite oblivious of the caste-restrictions between the Brahmins, Shudras and other castes.

27. Although Baba had become angry, the *sanyasin* himself, was overwhelmed with love. He would not move back an inch or get up from where he sat.

28. He had hardly been in Shirdi for two days when he received a letter that his mother was seriously ill at his village. He became very sad.

29. He felt that he should go back to his own place and meet his mother. But he could not leave without Baba's permission.

30. Letter in hand, the *sanyasin* went to the mosque and, describing his mother's condition, began to entreat Baba.

31. 'Maharaj Sai Samarth, there is a longing in the heart for meeting my mother. Please give me permission gladly; take pity on this traveller.'

32. He came running and catching hold of Baba's feet, said 'Will you kindly give me permission? My mother must be lying on the ground, her life in her throat,

33. 'And she must be waiting for me. Let me go and see her, at least, so that the pain will become bearable for her and her end will be peaceful.'

34. Sai Samarth knew intuitively that the *sanyasin's* own life itself, was coming to an end. So listen attentively to what Baba then said to him.

35. "If there was so much attachment to the mother, then why did you accept these robes? Such attachment does not become this attire. You have brought disgrace to the saffron robes.

36. "Go, sit in peace; do not be sad. Let a few days pass and then we shall decide what to do. Have patience and courage.

37. "In the *wada* there are many thieves. Fasten the doors and be alert. For they will rob you of your all and attack you fiercely.

38. "Prosperity is never permanent, and as for this body, it is, forever, transient. Knowing that death is always near, conduct yourself according to *dharma*.

39. "In this world the feeling of 'me' and 'mine', with regard to this body, wife, sons, etc., and the threefold afflictions resultant thereof — these are called the calamities in the worldly life.

40. "The second calamity is other-worldly. The other world or Heaven of which people are desirous after death, even that is an obstacle to the attainment of *Moksha* or Liberation and tends always, to bring about a Fall, back to earth.

41. "No merit can be accumulated in that other world, nor is their attainment free from fear. For there too, the fear of a Fall, once the merit is exhausted, is undoubtedly present.

42. "Hence both, the worldly and other-worldly existences are fraught with calamities. Therefore to renounce them totally, is the cause of origin of pure happiness.

43. "Disgusted with worldly life, those who are absorbed steadfastly at God's feet, will be freed from the bondage of worldly life and the hold of *Maya* or ignorance over them will disappear.

44. "The moment of God's worship, His remembrance, drives away sin, afflictions and distress. When remembered lovingly, He comes to our rescue in the time of trouble.

45. "Great is your accumulated merit that you have come to this place. Now, give attention to my words and find fulfilment in this life.

46. "From tomorrow, begin a real study of *Bhagvat*. Complete three '*saptahas*' of that book, earnestly with your thought, action and speech.

47. "Becoming free from all desires, listen to the reading of that book or yourself read it with full faith, and with a readiness to contemplate upon it deeply, again and again.

48. "God will then be pleased and will put an end to all your sorrows; *Maya*, temptations will be calmed down and you will enjoy true happiness.

49. "After ablutions, with the mind concentrated on Hari, complete this observance fully and you will be free from temptation".

50. When Baba knew that his own life was nearing its end, he followed the same practice and got '*Ram Vijay*' read out to him, by which, Shankar, the Conqueror of Death, is pleased.

51. The next day, in the morning, after his ablutions, he offered flowers to Baba and applied the dust from Baba's feet to his head.

52. Tucking the '*Bhagvat*' under his arm, he selected the quiet and peaceful Lendi, to ensure seclusion needed for reading.

53. Seated in a yogic '*asana*', he then started reading. A *sanyasin*, engaged all the time in God-worship, he easily completed two *saptahas*.

54. As he was about to start the third, suddenly he felt restless; he began to feel a growing weakness. So he left the reading incomplete, where it was.

55. He returned to the *wada* and had hardly passed two days with difficulty when, as the third day dawned, Bua closed his eyes, forever.

56. With his head on Fakir Baba's lap, the *sanyasin* died in peace, freed from the body and all earthly desires.

57. When Baba was told about the *sanyasin's* death, he commanded that the body be preserved for one day.

58. "Do not bury him just yet", he said. So, very hopefully, people guarded his body, thinking that he may be revived into life, again.

59. But once the life is extinguished, is it going to be revived again? And yet, Baba's word was truth. So they preserved the body.

60. And in effect, it did come useful. That unclaimed body was taken care of and the suspicions of the police were allayed. Once dead, what life can there be in the body?

61. And did Baba not know how to restore the dead, to life? (He had that power). But his purpose was that without a proper enquiry the corpse should not be buried under the ground.

62. Whatever is unclaimed belongs to the government and an enquiry is held in cases of sudden death. Baba had put up this pretext, so that the corpse may not be buried without a proper enquiry.

63. And all this came about, later on. The last rites were then performed on the corpse and it was given a burial at the proper place. The saint's purpose was then accomplished.

64. I shall now narrate to the listeners, another tale. Listen to it carefully for a moment and Sai's all-pervasiveness will be revealed to you.

65. Balaram, whose surname was Mankar, was a great devotee of Baba. He was a householder.

66. But later on, his wife died, making it difficult to fulfil the duties of a householder. He lost his peace of mind. But that, in turn, was to bring him the greatest good fortune.

67. By the fruit of his accumulated merit, he came into Sai's holy company and there grew a steadfast devotion to Sai, and full detachment from worldly life.

68. Severing the ties of hopes and desires, of the children and family, this remarkably fortunate Mankar, renounced worldly life.

69. Service of others, which, in worldly life is an ornamental necklace, but in spiritual life an obstacle, Mankar put around his son's neck, thus putting a lock on all his worldly duties.

70. This too, is a kind of *sanyas*. For many are the ways of taking *sanyas*. But that *sanyas* in which efforts made to attain *Brahma-jnana* do not succeed, can create trouble at every step.

71. But, on seeing Mankar's single-minded devotion, Sai, who is Kindness Incarnate, bestowed favour upon him and made him steadfast in his renunciation.

72. The innumerable influences of past births that had enveloped him, would not allow Mankar's wavering mind to steady. Tumultuous waves of heart-felt desires made it difficult for him to be firm in his renunciation.

73. So, to prove it with direct experience that his place is not in Shirdi alone, but he transcends Time and Space, Sai commanded Mankar,

74. "Enough of Shirdi, now! Take these twelve rupees for the travelling expenses and go to Machchindergad (a fort near Satara), for penance. Stay there with a firm resolve to attain happiness."

75. On hearing Sai's words, he respectfully obeyed his command, prostrating at his feet in obeisance.

76. Balaram then said to Sai, with great humility, 'What will I do there — where I cannot even have your *darshan*?

77. 'Here I can take your *darshan*, daily; I can drink the holy water washed off your feet, I can meditate on you effortlessly, day and night. But there, it will be me and me only—a petty, lowly creature.

78. 'Therefore, Baba, I am not able to understand what I can gain without you, there! Why do you send me to that place?'

79. 'But a devotee should not entertain even the slightest doubt about his guru's words', thought Mankar, the very next moment and his mind was cleared of all doubts.

80. And he said, 'Forgive me, Baba! My thoughts were born of a petty, mean mind. I am ashamed of my doubts. Such doubting does not become me.

81. 'I am but your obedient servant. Engaged in chanting your name, all the time, I shall stay happily, even on that '*gad*', only on your strength.

82. 'There too, I shall meditate on you, remember your compassionate face and will contemplate on you and you alone. This will be my constant penance.

83. 'I have surrendered to you single-mindedly and when once I have left the decision of my coming and going in your hands, why should I entertain such a doubt in my mind?

84. 'The power of your command will give me peace of mind even there. When so mighty is your power, why should I worry, needlessly?'

85. Sai Samarth is the Eternal Brahman and his words are the everlasting Truth. He who tries and reposes trust in them, will experience their truth, fully.

86. Baba then said to him, "Listen to my words with an alert mind. Do not be riddled with doubts.

87. "Go to Machchindergad, quickly. Meditate three times, every day. After some time has elapsed you will experience bliss."

88. On getting such an assurance, Mankar was silenced. 'What can I, a poor creature, say?' He was ready to go to the '*gad*'.

89. Once again, he bowed at Sai's feet and after taking *Udi-prasad* and blessings, he then set out, with an easy mind, to go to Machchinder Bhuvan.

90. On reaching there, he was happy to see that beautiful place, with pure, clean water and a softly blowing breeze.

91. Sent by Sai, but still, away from him, Mankar began his penance, as per Baba's instructions and as directed by him.

92. And just see Baba's marvel! While Mankar was engrossed in meditation, Baba actually gave him *darshan* on that '*gad*'. Mankar had this experience, himself.

93. That one should get *darshan* while in the state of *samadhi*, is not surprising. But Mankar saw Shri Samarth while fully awake and sitting in a yogic posture.

94. And not only did he see him with his own eyes, but Balaram actually asked him, 'Baba, why have you sent me here?' What was Baba's reply?

95. "While in Shirdi, many notions, many doubts assailed your mind. Therefore your doubting, hesitant mind was appointed to go to the '*gad*'.

96. "For you I did not exist outside Shirdi and apart from this abode (i.e. body), three-and-a-half cubits in length, which is made up of layer upon layer of a mixture of the five elements, like the earth, water, etc.

97. "But I, whom you see here and now, am the same as the one there. See it for yourself, properly and at your ease. Know, that I sent you away from there, for this same reason."

98. When the intended period was over, Mankar left Machchindergad to return to his own place.

99. He lived at Bandra and felt like going there. So he planned to go from Poona up to Dadar by train.

100. He went to the Poona station and when it was time to buy a ticket, he went up to the ticket window, when a miracle took place!

101. A traveller, who was a stranger to him, and was dressed like a *Kunabi*[2], with a *langoti*[3] round the waist and a coarse blanket on his shoulder, was seen standing near the window.

102. Having bought a ticket for Dadar, the Kunabi turned back and as his eyes met Balaram's, he approached him.

103. 'Where are you going?' he asked and when Balaram said 'To Dadar', he gave the ticket to him, saying, "You take this, now.

104. "I was to go there, too, but have suddenly remembered that I have another important work here. Hence I have cancelled my going."

105. Mankar was only too happy to get the ticket so effortlessly, which even after spending one's money, it was difficult to obtain.

106. So, to pay for the ticket, as Mankar took out the money from his pocket, suddenly, the Kunabi forced his way through the crowd and disappeared. Where he slipped away, Mankar could not make out.

107. Balaram made great efforts to trace that Kunabi, but all in vain. Meanwhile, the train had also arrived.

108. With no shoes, no chappal on the feet, a rag tied around his head, a blanket on his shoulder and a loin-cloth round the waist, who was this Kunabi brother?

109. The fare was, by no means, small. But that too, he paid in cash out of his own pocket. Why, O why, this burden of obligation on me? I cannot solve this puzzle!

110. In outward appearance, a Kunabi, but so generous, so desireless at heart! Who could this Kunabi have been? It was something that remained unresolved to the end, leaving Mankar with many regrets.

111. Full of amazement, and with a hope of meeting the Kunabi, he remained standing near the door till the train was moving out.

112. When the train did finally move out, knowing that all hope of finding him was at an end, he quickly caught the vertical rod of the door and jumped into the compartment.

113. On the '*gad*' there was an actual meeting with Sai and so, was here, but in a different way. The strange garb of the Kunabi created a disquiet in Mankar's mind.

114. Later, this excellent devotee was totally attached to Sai and spent his days in Shirdi in steadfast devotion and faith, thereby experiencing fulfilment in life.

115. Like a buzzing bee that hovers around the pollen on the Lotus-petals, Balaramji was always hovering around Sai, with a murmur of Sai's name on his lips. He thus stayed on in Shirdi.

116. With Baba's permission, he did sometimes, take himself out of Shirdi, in the company of another devotee, Muktaram.

117. But Shirdi always remained the centre to which he returned, time and again. And it was in the sacred Shirdi that he finally gave up his mortal coil.

118. Blessed was he, who met Sai by virtue of his past merit and being engrossed at his feet, had a fearless death.

119. Blessed was Tatyasaheb Noolkar! Blessed too, was Megha, the most excellent among the devotees! Both gave up the body, singing *bhajans*, in Shirdi.

120. Just see Baba's emphasis on the last rites being performed and his friendliness towards his devotees, when Megha died. Megha had already accomplished the purpose of his human birth.

121. When the villagers went to cremate him, accompanied by all the devotees, Baba also went to the cremation grounds, and showered flowers on Megha.

122. After the last rites were performed, there were tears in Baba's eyes too, like an ordinary, sorrowing man, who is caught up in the web of *Maya*.

123. Very lovingly, Baba covered the corpse with flowers by his own hands and turned back, bemoaning the loss in a sorrowful tone.

124. We come across many saints, who uplift the humanity. But oh, how can one describe the greatness of Sai Baba!

125. A ferocious animal like a tiger — is he a *Jnani* like man? But even he surrendered at Baba's feet! Such are the incomprehensible ways of Baba!

126 Now listen attentively to a story in this context, and you will see Baba's all-pervasiveness, his equal concern for all.

127. Once a miracle took place in Shirdi! Just seven days before Baba's *mahasamadhi*, a bullock-cart came to the door.

128. In it at the back was an enomous tiger of a frightful visage, who was tied firmly, with thick iron chains round his neck.

129. He had some ailment, for which the *darveshis*[4] had exhausted all the remedies. In the end, they thought that the best remedy would be a saint's *darshan*.

130. There were three '*darveshis*' and that tiger was their means of livelihood. They would hold shows moving from village to village, and thus eke out a living.

131. While wandering in that region, Baba's wonderful *leelas* came to their ears. So they thought 'let us take his *darshan* and also take the tiger to that place.

132. 'His feet are like *Chintamani*, the boon-granting gem; all the eight *Siddhis*[5] prostrate before him and the nine treasures[6] roll at his feet to take the holy water of his feet.

133. 'So let us bow our heads at his feet and ask his blessings for the tiger. By the saint's benediction we will all prosper.'

134. For this purpose, the *darveshis* took the tiger down from the cart, at the door, holding fast to his chains and stood waiting at the door.

135. The tiger, as it was, was fierce, terrible and wild, to add to which, he was afflicted with some disease. He was, therefore, most restless. All stood watching the spectacle.

136. The *darveshis* then described to Baba, in detail, the condition of the tiger and after first taking his permission, they came back to the door.

137. The chains were then drawn up tightly, so that the tiger might not break loose and escape. And very carefully, they brought him in front of Sai.

138. Nearing the step, the tiger looked at Sai, that blazing Radiance, and God knows why, but he was quite startled, within, and bent down his head in great respect.

139. And oh, what a miracle! As their eyes met, the tiger gazed lovingly at Baba, as he was coming up the step.

140. At once, he puffed up the tuft on his tail, struck the ground thrice with it and surrendering the body at Sai's feet, impaired as he was, he fell down motionless.

141. He gave only one terrifying roar and fell dead, there and then, in that instant. People gaped in wonder at such a death of the tiger.

142. The *darveshis* looked sad; and yet, they were happy too, that the ailing animal, on the point of death, was thus liberated.

143. Great indeed, is the merit for death before the eyes of *sadhus* and saints — then be it a worm, an insect or a tiger. He becomes free, at once, from all his sins.

144. There must have been some debt of the last birth, which the tiger had now repaid thus becoming free from it. At Sai's feet, he gave up the body. The workings of Destiny are truly, inconceivable.

145. The creature, who dies with his head on a saint's feet, is at once, uplifted. This is his real gain in this birth.

146. Unless he was so very fortunate, is it possible that a creature will give up his physical body right in front of a saint's eyes and be liberated instantly?

147. To renounce the body in front of a *sadhu* is as great a happiness as that the poison should be transformed into nectar on drinking it. Of such a death, there is neither joy nor sorrow.

148. Blessed is the body of that creature, who dies at the feet of the saint. For it becomes an offering to Lord Krishna and there is no rebirth thereafter.

149. Death in front of the saints is no death, but the blissful happiness of *Vaikunth*[7]. He has conquered the Kingdom of Death and is free from the sorrows of worldly life.

150. Those who give up the body in front of saints, are not reborn. For that itself is the expiation of all their sins and they attain *Moksha*.

151. Leaving the mortal frame, while gazing at the saint from head to the toe-nails, can this be called death? No, indeed! It is truly, one's upliftment.

152. Considering the event as predestined, maybe he was some meritorious soul, who, in flaunting his knowledge, had insulted a *Haribhakta* (a devotee of God).

153. And as a result of his curse, was born into this cruel genre. But by a mitigation of the curse by the same *Haribhakta*, had come to the feet of a saint. Truly, the doings of these devotees are most remarkable.

154. I feel that because of the mitigation of the curse, he had Sai's *darshan*, which burnt up all his sins, snapped the bondage and put an end to his suffering. As a result, he was automatically uplifted.

155. Without a perfect good fortune, how can death come in front of a saint? As for the tiger, his threefold afflictions, the *triputis* and the *trigunas* were all destroyed and he became one with the Supreme.

156. In this way, by virtue of the previous *karma*, his association with a wicked body was severed; his connection with the iron chains that had bound him, was broken. Such is the Divine Law.

157. Where else can you find the progression to Upliftment, except at the feet of *sadhus* and saints? And when the tiger attained that, the *darveshis* were naturally pleased at heart.

158. That tiger was their means of livelihood; he was their bread and butter. So it was natural that their faces should become sad when the tiger died.

159. They then asked Maharaj, 'What should be done, now? How should he be buried? Please give him, with your own hands, a good passage after death.'

160. Maharaj said, "Do not grieve; his end was to be here. Moreover, he too, was meritorious, that he attained such great happiness.

161. "Beyond the *Takiya*[8], there, there is a Shiva temple! Carry him there and perform his burial rites near the *Nandi*[9].

162. "If you bury him there, he will also have a good passage and, at your hands, he will be freed from his debt and from bondage.

163. "He remained in your bondage until today, only to repay your debt, being your debtor of the last birth."

164. The *darveshis* then lifted him up and went near the temple. He was buried in a ditch, at the back of the *Nandi*.

165. Oh, what a miracle it was to see the tiger dead in an instant! And had the incident ended at this point, it would soon have been forgotten.

166. But exactly on the seventh day from it, Baba too, left his mortal body on the ground. Hence it is, that the memory of the incident surges up in the mind, again and again.

167. The next chapter is even more interesting. Baba describes his guru's fond admiration and affection; how he satisfied the keen desire of Gokhalebai, by bestowing favour upon her.

168. Hemad humbly surrenders to Sainath. Listen to how Baba won his guru's grace by being suspended, upside down, in a well, at the hands of his guru.

Weal be to all! Here ends the thirty-first chapter of
"Shri Sai Samarth Satcharit", called
'*Importance of Sai-darshan*',
as inspired by the saints and the virtuous
and composed by his devotee, Hemadpant.

Notes

1. He was the eldest son of Rishabhdev of Priyamvrat dynasty. He renounced his kingdom and did penance on the banks of the river Gandak during which, because of intense attachment to the young one of a deer, even during contemplation, he was born a deer.
2. An individual of the agricultural order, a cultivator or a peasant.
3. A piece of cloth worn round the loins, covering the privities.
4. A class or an individual of it, of strolling mendicants among Muhammadans. They exhibit wild beasts (like tigers, bears, monkeys), and exact toll from house to house.
5. Refer Ch. 10, note 4.
6. Refer Ch. 10, note 5.
7. The abode of Lord Vishnu.
8. Refer Ch. 5, verse 99.
9. Refer Ch. 11, note 7.

32

The Greatness of the Guru

MY OBEISANCE TO SHRI GANESH, TO SHRI SARASWATI, AND SHRI GURUMAHARAJ! TO THE FAMILY DEITY, TO SHRI SITA-RAMACHANDRA, MY MOST HUMBLE OBEISANCE! I BOW IN REVERENCE TO THE MOST VENERABLE GURU SHRI SAINATH!

1. It was narrated in the last chapter how Vijayanand attained *nirvan*; how Balakram also merged into the Blissful Self at Sai's feet.

2. Similarly, how Tatyasaheb Noolkar and Megha, the devotee most excellent and of the highest degree, gave up the body before Sai's eyes.

3. The listeners, however, have listened in detail, to even a greater marvel than all this — the manner of death of a wild, ferocious animal, like a tiger.

4. Now, in this present chapter, I shall narrate an interesting account, as described in Baba's own words, which will benefit the listeners greatly.

5. Once, while in the forest, Baba had *guru-darshan* quite unexpectedly. Listen, attentively to the marvellous workings of the guru.

6. How can a lowly creature like me, describe adequately the marvel of a tale that brings devotion, faith and liberation and which came straight out of Sai's mouth.

7. Similarly, when a lady wished to have Baba's *darshan*, to stay in Shirdi for three days, with a vow to observe a strict fast —

8. How he contrived a situation whereby he made her break her resolve and got her to prepare '*puran-polis*'[1], most delicious and appetizing.

9. Not only did he get the '*polis*' prepared by her, but made her eat them to her heart's content and impressed upon her mind how the fulfilment in wearing out one's body in the cause of others, is truly great;

10. How there is far greater merit in so doing, rather than in observing fasts. And this was fixed in her mind in such a way that she would never forget it.

11. Similarly, how he who is fond of the spiritual path should do *sadhana* with a firm resolve and venture upon that difficult path to attain the highest and lasting good.

12. A series of stories in this connection, which are sweeter than nectar itself, will generate a loving devotion in the listeners' hearts and will end all their sorrows.

13. From here onwards will follow a sweet tale which will satisfy the fond desire of those who wish to listen; will bring a blissful joy to the narrator and his listeners, and will bring a sense of fulfilment to all those who are listening.

14. Sai will get this extraordinary and loving tale narrated through me, while I, a foolish, lowly creature will experience joy and admiration, at every step, as I write it.

15. As sins by *Ganga-darshan* or suffering by the moon's *darshan* are allayed, so will the words from Sai's mouth destroy all sins and suffering.

16. Now listen respectfully, O listeners, to the description that came from Maharaj Sai's own mouth, as to how he had the *darshan* of his own guru.

17. Even if *Vedas* and *Vedangas* are studied thoroughly and the *Shrutishastra* is read repeatedly, there is no true knowledge without the guru's grace. All other efforts are a futile exertion.

18. This extensively-spread tree of worldly life, first unmanifest, but later manifest and created by the eyes, is both, filled with the pain of birth and death and is destructible.

19. It can be cut down and is destructible. Hence it is called a tree. It is the unmanifest worldly life that assumed a form and became manifest. Therefore it is compared to a tree.

20. This visible, destructible tree of life, which has its roots above and its expanse of innumerable branches is beyond all imagination.

21. From one moment to another, it continues to spread, branching off further and further. From a distance, it looks charming, but once embraced, it reveals nothing but thorns, all over.

22. It is as sapless as a stump of a banana plant; like a mirage or the *Gandharvanagar*[2] that fastens those who resort to it with the water of ardent desires and cravings. Such is this great, outwardly attractive tree.

23. Arising out of the *karma* of wrong, misguided wishes and born from the unmanifest seed, though it is without any real existence, it appears, every moment, to be of a different nature.

24. Disastrous by its very nature, it is born of ignorance and is surrounded by the water of intense desires and cravings that collects around it.

25. This tree of Life which has the retinue of wife, sons, wealth, grain, etc., gains a foothold, because of its identification in men's minds with the material and the physical and it exists only to support this.

26. This tree, whose branches are the numerous creatures of the two sexes and which is restrained by its descending shoots of *karma*, desires, etc., flourishes in its entirety.

27. Covered closely with the leaves of *Shruti, Smriti,* etc., blooming with the newly sprouted, tender leaves of speech, touch, etc., filled with the luxuriant blossoms of the rites and rituals of *yajna, daan,* etc., this tree is endowed with the succulent juices of the pairs of opposites.

28. Unlimited is its fruit and it has become the means of livelihood for one and all. The regions of the earth, that of the '*Antariksha*' or sky, etc. — none of these are without this tree.

29. Sometimes dance and song and instrumental music; sometimes play, laughter, tears — such is this eternal *Peepal*[3] tree, always with its head downwards.

30. Manifest in this illusory universe (of all existence), born of *Maya*, this tree is destroyed by the weapon of detachment or renunciation.

Know its pure origins, i.e. good, virtuous disposition, is in its very nature, Light itself.

31. This Brahman which is Truth, sustains all. The world is as illusory as a dream, which has neither beginning nor end and is without support. How can it sustain itself in such a position?

32. That for which great efforts are made by the detached; to which the saints are always attached, and which the seekers are constantly in search of and the *sadhakas* are most desirous of,

33. When one wishes to attain That, he should surrender to the saints and listen to whatever they say, totally eschewing all doubts and misconceptions.

34. Bundling up all the thoughts in the mind, banishing from it all ingenuity and false wisdom, severing the ties of *Maya* and attachment, he should concentrate on the feet of the guru.

35. Shake off the misleading doubts; or else, they will obstruct your path. Trample under your feet all conceit. Only then will you reach the shore beyond.

36. And now, listen to a sweet tale in this connection which Baba had himself narrated. By so doing you will experience blissful happiness as you drink this nectar of the guru's words.

37. "Once the four of us, having already read the *pothis* and *Puranas* and gained Knowledge, began a debate about Brahman.

38. "Taking up the maxim from the *Gita* that one must uplift himself by his own efforts (*Gita* VI:5), one of us contended that 'it is most improper to depend upon anyone else for it.'

39. "To him, another replied, 'Only he is truly the blessed one, whose mind is fully under his control. Therefore one should always be free from doubts, resolves, etc., knowing that there is nothing in the world except one's own Self.'

40. " 'Everything that is subject to change is transient; what is permanent is that which does not change. Therefore, always think in terms of permanent and transitory,' said the third.

41. "The fourth one did not approve of bookish learning but believed in conducting oneself in conformity with the *Shastras* and offering

oneself totally — body, speech, the five vital airs — at the guru's feet.

42. "A firmly rooted, unwavering faith is necessary to believe that the guru is God Himself, who pervades this entire animate and inanimate Universe, from inside and outside.

43. "Those merely well-versed in the *Shastras*, those who are solely intellectual, or those who are only inquisitive, can never even dream of acquiring true Knowledge. What is needed here is a pure, devout, faithful devotee.

44. "Thus we, the four intelligent men, set out in search of something, intending to make that discovery. That the discovery should be made independently on their own with a mind free of all worry.

45. "Such was the intention in the minds of the three. But while wandering freely in the forest, we met a *Vanjari*[4] on the way, who asked us,

46. " 'The heat of the sun is intense. For what purpose are you going and where?' We replied, 'We are going to search the forest and its interior.'

47. "The *Vanjari* asked us, 'What are you searching for?' We said in reply, 'It is not good to talk about what is a secret.'

48. "But seeing our frantic, hurried running hither and thither, the heart of that *Vanjari* was moved to pity. He said, 'The forest is difficult of access. Unless you know it well, you should not wander in it, at will.

49. " 'To roam such forests you should always have a guide with you. At this high noon, why do you undertake this venture? Why all this arduous effort?

50. " 'Do not tell me your secret mission, if you like, but at least sit down and have a piece of *bhakri* (bread), drink some water and then go. Have some patience in your heart!'

51. "Although he urged us so sincerely, we proceeded on our way without heeding him and scorned at his request. But later, on the way, we found ourselves completely exhausted.

52. " 'Oh, but clever as we all are, we can easily find our way. Where is the need for a guide?' Such was our secret pride!

53. "But the forest was extensive and thickly wooded, with tall enormous trees, where the sun's rays could not penetrate at all. How could one find one's way there?

54. "We lost our bearings completely, wandering here and there fruitlessly. But great was our good fortune that we came back to the same spot from where we had started.

55. "Fate sent us back the way we had come and, once again, we met that same *Vanjari*, 'Looks like you took the wrong path! Sometimes the ingenuity of the mind does not help.

56. " 'The task may be big or small, but someone has to point out the way. And on an empty stomach, nothing is discovered. Even the intellect wanders in bewilderment.

57. " 'Unless it is the plan of the Almighty, you will meet no one on the way. So never turn your back on food offered; never push away a platter of food.

58. " 'When someone offers you a piece of bread, requesting you to eat it, take his words to be a good omen which will remove all obstacles to your work.

59. " 'Now have some repast and keep a little patience in your heart.' But such good counsel did not appeal to the three of them, and once again, they set out without eating anything.

60. "By saying that unless we discover something, we will not eat any food, they became victims of their own obstinacy.

61. "I was hungry, my throat was parched with thirst. Moreover, I was filled with fond admiration for the remarkable love and concern of that *Vanjari*.

62. "We, the learned. the scholarly, knew no kindness nor pity. Being rich (but miserly), nobody bothered to shoo away the crow with the unwashed hand.

63. "But this *Vanjari*, without any learning or authority, of a lower *varna*, and a *Vanjari* by caste — and yet, how much natural affection he had in his heart, that he should say, 'eat some bread and vegetable!'

64. "He who loves in this way, without any expectation, only he is a true *Jnani* and I felt, to show him respect is the most exquisite way of gaining supreme Knowledge.

65. "Therefore with great respect I ate the quarter piece of bread that the *Vanjari* gave me and drank some water. And lo! What a wonderful thing happened!

66. "Quite unexpectedly, Gururaj appeared and said to us, "Why all the arguments and debate?" I then related to him everything, from the beginning to end.

67. " 'Will you come with me? I shall immediately find for you what you are searching. But only he who respects my word will achieve his purpose.'

68. "Others did not agree, but I acquiesced with great respect. All others then went away and Gururaya took me with him.

69. "He took me to a well, tied a rope to both my legs and lowered me in the well in a feet-up head-down position.[5]

70. "Gururaya suspended me in the well in such a way that the hands should not reach the water nor should any water go in my mouth.

71. "There was a tree near the edge of the well to which was tied the other end of the rope. Gururaya then went away, who knows where, with a mind free from doubt or anxiety.

72. "About four to four and a half hours passed by, after which he came back. He then quickly took me out and asked me 'Are you all right?'

73. "I replied, 'I was full of joy. The happiness that I experienced — how can a lowly creature like me describe it?'

74. "Gururaya was very pleased to hear these words. He moved his hand on my back, very affectionately, and made me stay with him.

75. "Even as I am relating this to you, love surges in my heart. The Guru then took me to his school, showing for me the same loving concern as the mother-bird who clasps her young ones under her wings.

76. "And oh, how fascinating was the Guru's school! So much so that I forgot my fond attachment to my parents; the chain of delusion, attachment was broken and I was liberated, quite effortlessly.

77. "Bonds which are undesirable were totally snapped and the bondage that obstructs spiritual inclination was severed. I felt like embracing the Guru, storing up his image in the eyes themselves.

78. "Unless his image lives in the eyes all the time, the eyes will be but two balls of flesh. Or, I would rather be blind without his image. Such was the great importance of the Guru's school to me.

79. "Can there be anyone so unfortunate who, having once stepped into this school, would want to go back! My house, my family, my parents — Gururaya became everything for me.

80. "All my sense-organs, including the mind, had left their places and come to stay in my eyes alone, for the purpose of meditating upon the Guru.

81. "When Guru alone is the object of meditation for the eyes and all else is as Guru himself, so that there is nothing separate from him, then it is called single-minded meditation.

82. "When thus meditating on the form of the Guru, the workings of the intellect cease. Therefore, ultimately, only make an obeisance to him, observing speechless silence.

83. "Or else, one may make a Guru for acquiring true Knowledge, only to discover that as for valuable instruction, there is only a cipher, while good money is lost in giving him *dakshina*. Consequently, one may be left with nothing but regrets.

84. "He, who only babbles about occult knowledge, making a show of honesty and sincerity, but has been nurtured on hypocrisy, what can such a one give to his disciple?

85. "He, who is, to all appearances, pure and holy, but is in reality, immature and is lacking in first-hand experience, the schooling or instruction from such a one is altogether useless.

86. "Where verbal, bookish knowledge abounds, without any real experience of *Brahmajnana*, and where the guru himself glorifies in his own greatness, how can a disciple derive any benefit from him?

87. "He whose word does not touch the heart of the disciple and whose testimony does not bring conviction to his mind, of what avail is his instruction? It is merely an empty, meaningless babble!

88. "In this way he made me do *upasana* and showed me the store of true Knowledge. I did not have to search for it, in the least. Nor did I have to try to understand the deeper significance.

89. "The profound significance dawned on me, all on its own, and the Knowledge was gained, effortlessly. Such is the marvel of the Guru's grace! All search for it ended, there and then!

90. "How I could feel joyous, when Gururaya had suspended me upside down is something that he alone (Gururaya) has the power to understand."

91. The ways of the saints are always contrary to those of the world. This Knowledge is born of experience. Here, faith alone is one's sustenance and the Guru's grace, the only means.

92. To the rigidly ritualistic, there is the binding of injunction and prohibition; to the *Jnani* there is ego in his superior knowledge; and to the yogi the short coming of being a hypocrite. Thus nothing will really work here, except firm faith.

93. The learned pandits are blinded by arrogance. They are the very image of Pride. The *Jnani* runs away at their very sight and does not keep their company.

94. The *Jnani* says can there be any god other than myself? Myself being enriched with true Knowledge, I am myself, the supreme consciousness.

95. By virtue of his own loving devotion, a devotee will never boast of his knowledge. He offers himself, body, mind and wealth, at the swami's feet. He surrenders his all to the swami.

96. He does not swell with the pride, 'This is my achievement; this is the majesty of my power or the grandeur of my powerful intellect'.

97. Whatever happens, happens by God's Will. It is He who raises you up or brings you down. It is He who fights or makes others fight. He alone, is the doer and the impeller of all action.

98. Reposing all the powers of action in the swami's hands, the devotee is humility itself. Devotees are always in the power of God. They have no independent existence of their own.

99. But as for those four learned ones, what they had been searching for, has not been disclosed, so far. So now listen to its clarification.

100. They were all rigidly ritualistic scholars of *Vedas*, and carried a secret conceit about their great learning. While rattling away their bookish knowledge, the subject of God came up.

101. Their intention was to see that, with all their learning, how, in what way, by what means or plan, they could meet God, as quickly as possible.

102. Shri Sai too, was one among these four. When he was Renunciation and Discriminating Knowledge Incarnate, and Parabrahma Himself, why did he assume such lack of discrimination?

103. The listeners may well raise this doubt. But all this was for the instruction and guidance of the people. How can it then, bring any imperfection to Sai Samarth, the Redeemer of the devotees?

104. Himself an *avatar*, he yet gave due respect to the *Vanjari* and with determination, partook of the food, praising its greatness.

105. Similarly, he pointed out how, when one insults proffered food by rejecting it, one suffers a loss and went on to show through the story of the learned pandits that no one can become a *Jnani* without a guru.

106. It is impossible to gain knowledge about the *dharma* without instruction from the father, mother and the *acharya*. And that too, depends upon one's study. It is futile without the proper rites and ceremonies.

107. Their blessings are absolutely necessary. It is a well-known assertion of the *Shrutis*, 'Always worship your mother, father and *acharya*, as if they are gods.'

108. To obey all these three, or to perform *yajna*, recite the *Vedas* and to give in charity — these are the best means to overcome the birth-death cycle.

109. These are all means of purifying the heart. Without them one cannot get the treasure that is, the real Self. A life devoid of these is a life wasted.

110. The profound nature of this Self, which the body, sense-organs, mind and even the intellect cannot comprehend, is revealed to us only by the grace of the guru.

111. Where the testimony of the eyes or the reasoning becomes unacceptable, who else but the guru can reveal it to us, as effortlessly as a *myrobalan* on the palm of one's hand?

112. *Dharma, Arth* and *Kaam*, the three of the four goals of human life, can be attained by making great effort. But all effort to attain the fourth, viz. *Moksha*, the highest goal, is futile without the guru's grace.

113. In the court of this saint of Shirdi, astrologers came too, to salute Baba. They would predict the future of the physical existence, for the great and wealthy.

114. Kings and nobles, rolling in wealth, prosperity and plenty and also the *bairagis*, the *gosavis*, subsisting on alms; the detached and the austere — they were all eager for Baba's *darshan*.

115. Those engrossed in ceaselessly chanting the name and those given to penance and vows; the *sanyasins*, the pilgrims and those residing in holy places of pilgrimage; the singers and dancers with their retinue — they came to Shirdi for *darshan*.

116. The '*Mahars*' too, came to salute in Shri Sai's court, saying, 'He alone is our Protector, who will free us from the futile rounds of birth and rebirth.'

117. He, with a *Shiv-linga* round his neck, *vibhuti* smeared on his forehead, but his eye on the alms of undressed corn, is a *jangam*[6] and the spectacle he presents is worth watching.

118. The wily jugglers came there and so also, the '*Gondhalis*'[7] to perform '*gondhal*'[8], lovingly asking Baba for *jogwa* (alms) in the name of the goddess '*Bhawani*'.

119. The blind, the lame, the '*Kaanphates*[9]'; *jogis*, followers of Nanak[10], minstrels and *divate* or lamp-bearers, — all came running, full of love and devotion for Samarth Sai.

120. *Dugduges* (drummers), *Sarodes*[11], the cripple — even the *Kollhateens*[12] performed there. And there it was that his loving *Vanjari* came too, at the opportune time.

121. Blessed, blessed is Sai's Form, poured in the mould of Renunciation, itself — desireless; alone, without any company, selfless and incomparable in his love for his devotees.

122. But now, in the context of what has gone before, let us pick up the thread of the main story and begin the narration. Please be attentive, O listeners!

123. Baba himself, never remained on an empty stomach, nor did he allow others to do so. One who is fasting can have no peace of mind. How can he then, attain the spiritual end?

124. God can never be attained on an empty stomach. Hence, pacify the *Atman*, first. I shall narrate another story with the same lesson.

125. At the height of noon, when the soil turns upside down, the importance of food becomes clear to the mind.

126. And at such a trying time, if the bodily organs do not receive morsels of food, they become enfeebled and forget to function efficiently.

127. Unless the hunger is appeased with food, how can the eyes find God? How can the tongue sing His praises? And the ears hear them?

128. In short, only when all the bodily organs have the strength can God be worshipped properly. But when they become emaciated for want of food, they cannot progress towards the spiritual goal.

129. But eating in excess is not beneficial, either. Eating in moderation is what benefits, truly. Fasting immoderately always brings on great suffering.

130. A lady once came to Shirdi, with great enthusiasm for Sai's *darshan* and was armed with a letter to Kelkar.

131. The lady had made a firm resolve in her mind to sit at Maharaj's feet, observing a fast for three days. Ultimately, she had to keep her resolve to herself.

132. According to Baba's usual practice, he who wants to tread on the spiritual path, should first make sure of his bread. But the lady's resolve ran to the contrary.

133. He who wishes to meet God should first eat food. For unless the mind is content, how can God be discovered?

134. Never is it possible, even to the end of time, that God can be reached on a hungry stomach. And as for Sai, he would never permit the straits of fast, etc.

135. Maharaj intuitively knew everything already, on the previous day and had said to Dada Kelkar,

136. "Now, on a festive occasion, like this '*Shimaga*' (The 'Holi' festival), will my children go hungry? How will I allow it? Why am I here, then!"

137. No sooner had these words come from Sai's mouth than this lady arrived at Shirdi, the very next day.

138. Her surname was Gokhale and, as mentioned above, she had made a resolve in her mind. She deposited her bundle at Dada's place, having given him the letter she carried.

139. Kashibai Kanitkar, being a relation of Dada, had given the letter, requesting him to arrange for the lady to have Baba's *darshan*.

140. The lady arrived in Shirdi and, at once, went for Baba's *darshan*. Having had the *darshan*, she had hardly rested for a moment, when Baba began instructing her.

141. Whatever the innermost thoughts in anybody's mind, Sainath knows them all. There is nothing on this earth that he does not know.

142. "Food and the one who eats it, are both forms of Lord Vishnu (*Vishnusahasranama stotra*, 205). Fasting and taking '*nirlep*'[13] food, remaining without food and even without water — why all this futile botheration?

143. "And where is the need for us to fast?" So said Baba to this lady, all on his own.

144. "Go to the house of that Dadabhat (Kelkar) and happily make the '*puran-polis*'[14]. Feed them to his children and eat them yourself, to your heart's content."

145. Interestingly, the festival was that of '*Shimaga*' and by a strange coincidence, the lady had arrived on the very day that Dada's wife was unable to touch anything (due to menses).

146. The lady's enthusiasm for fasting melted away. Instead, she had to cook a meal. But she obeyed Baba's command very lovingly.

147. Bowing reverently at Baba's feet, she then went to Dada's house and cooked the feast with '*puran-polis*', which she served everyone and also ate herself.

148. What a fascinating story, indeed! What a summing up of the deep significance it carries! Once you repose such steadfast faith in the guru's word, can your upliftment be far behind?

149. Sai Samarth also remembered another similar story, which he narrated to all his devotees, very lovingly. Listen to it very carefully, O listeners!

150. He who aspires to spiritual progress has to make arduous efforts, be prepared for a deep *sadhana* and also needs a little venture.

151. This nectar of good stories, washed off the saint's feet, should always be taken for one's own good. Once you surrender humbly at the feet of a saint, the heart will become purified.

152. "Once, when I was small, stinting on my own needs, I set out in search of a job for my livelihood.

153. "As I walked on, I came to Beedgaon, where I rested for a while. But my Fakir had a different plan for me, which brought me great happiness.

154. "There I secured a job of doing '*jariwork*'[15]. I worked untiringly and all my toil came to fruition. Such is the power of the Fakir!

155. "There were four other boys, employed before me and much acclaimed for their skill. They too, were working there, and their work was assessed on completion.

156. "One had put in work worth Rs.50/-; another worth Rs.100/- and the third one, worth Rs.150/-. But my work was worth double their amount.

157. "Seeing my skill, my employer was very pleased, and being fond of me, praised me highly.

158. "He presented me with a dress, consisting of a turban over the head and a '*shela*'[16], to take over the body. But the moment it was given, I just tied it in a bundle and put it away.

159. "How can that suffice, which somebody gives you? However much it is, it is always inadequate. But when God gives something, it has no end, even to the end of time.

160. "What my Master gives me is real 'giving'. How can anyone else's compare with it, ever? How can the 'limited' lend distinction to the 'boundless'?

161. "My Master says, 'Take, O take this away!' Everyone says, 'Give, give only to me!' (material things). But no one heeds my words. No one listens to me attentively!

162. "His treasury is overflowing, but no one cares to bring the carts. Nobody will dig, when asked to do so. No one bothers to make the effort.

163. "I say, 'Dig for that wealth and carry it away by the cart-loads. Only he will collect the treasure, who is truly his mother's son.'

164. "And what, after all, is our fate? Dust will return to the dust, and the wind, to the wind. And this opportunity, once lost, will never come back again!

165. "However, the skill of my Fakir, the *leela* of my Bhagavan, the harmonious consistency of my Master is something quite different, quite unique!

166. "I too, go somewhere, sometimes; I just go and sit down at the same place. But the mind is caught in the bewilderment of *Maya* and suffers a dip or plunge (as of a bird or paper-kite).

167. "This *Maya* is very difficult to overcome and has reduced me to a piteous condition. Day and night, I keep thinking of my own people.

168. "As you sow, so you reap. He who will bear in mind the words I have uttered, will enjoy priceless happiness."

169. Hemad surrenders to Sai. The narration of this story has been unique! When Sai himself gets it done, my ego pales before it.

170. It is he who is the narrator of this tale; he is the reader of it and he, the listener. He alone is the writer and the impelling force behind the writing of it. And it is he alone, who explains the significance.

171. Sai is the main character of this story, and he is the sweetness in it. He himself becomes the listener and the speaker. And the enjoyer of the Bliss is also, none other than he.

172. How can the sweetness of such listening ever prove adequate for spiritual progress? Truly fortunate are the devotees who enjoy this happiness.

173. Now, as for the essence of the next chapter, which is the great power of Sai's *Udi*, I entreat my listeners to listen to it respectfully.

174. Hemad humbly says that moved by kindness, Sai Samarth himself has got his own *Satcharit* written through me, the sweetness of which is unique!

Weal be to all! Here ends the thirty-second chapter of
"*Shri Sai Samarth Satcharit*", called
'*The Greatness of the Guru*',
as inspired by the saints and the virtuous
and composed by his devotee, Hemadpant.

Notes

1. A wheat cake with stuffing of Bengal gram cooked in sugar syrup.
2. A city of the Gandharva or celestial chorister, a celestial or enchanted city affirmed to appear and disappear suddenly or in unexpected situations.
3. The holy fig tree, *ficus religiosa*.
4. A caste or class or individual of it. They are carriers of grain, salt, etc., and are Lamanis by caste.
5. About this story, Arthur Osborne writes: 'This is a typical Sai Baba account because the whole story is symbolical. The forest is the jungle of the mind in which the quest for Truth takes place, and the four friends are four modes of approach. The labourer is the Guru and the food he offers is his Grace. 'The Guru appeared' means that after the youth has accepted the food he discovers that the giver of it really is the divine Guru. Therefore he bows reverently, that is, accepts his authority. Tying him head downwards over a well is overturning the ego, binding it and holding it within sight of the cool waters of Peace. (Incidentally, this mode of discipline has been used physically by some Masters). It is because of this that the ordeal is blissful; it is suffering beatified by the end for which it is endured. This absorption in the Guru is the *sadhana* or Path followed and the final 'in silence I bowed down' is the extinction of the ego in Realisation.' (*The Incredible Sai Baba*, by Arthur Osborne; Orient Longman, 1973,. pp. 5-6). However, Dr Marianne Warren observes in *"Allah Malik"* - *Shirdi Sai Baba in the Light of Sufism* that the suspension of an aspirant in an inverted position while performing secluded prayers and meditation is a part of Sufi training, particularly in the Chistiyya Order and is termed as *chilla-i-ma 'kusa*. This practice is said to be very old, having existed among Sufis of eastern Iran before Sufism spread to India.
6. An individual of a particular sect called Lingayat, founded by the religious reformer called Basava in Karnataka. They follow Shiv, and worship the linga.
7. A caste or an individual of it. They are musicians and singers and makers of '*Gondhal*'.
8. A tumultuous festivity in propitiation of the goddess, corresponding somewhat to Wake or Ale.
9. A descriptive term for an order or an individual of it, of mendicants. They wear heavy ear-ornaments and are worshippers of Gorakhnath, etc.
10. Founder of the Sikh sect.
11. Low-caste fortune-tellers, who wander tambourine in hand.
12. A tumbler; a rope-dancer; a mountebank.
13. Food, which on being boiled or being broiled does not become '*kharkata*', i.e. food which is mixed with milk or the juice of any fruit.
14. A wheaten cake with stuffing of coarse sugar, split peas, etc.
15. Embroidering in gold or silver thread.
16. A sort of scarf, a cloth composed of four breadths depending from the shoulders loosely over the body.

33

The Significance of Udi (1)

MY OBEISANCE TO SHRI GANESH, TO SHRI SARASWATI, AND SHRI GURUMAHARAJ! TO THE FAMILY DEITY, TO SHRI SITA-RAMACHANDRA, MY MOST HUMBLE OBEISANCE! I BOW IN REVERENCE TO THE MOST VENERABLE GURU SHRI SAINATH!

1. Now let us bow to the saints, whose glance of Grace will at once burn down mountains of sins and wash away the dirt of evil propensities of this *Kaliyug*.
2. Mountains of their favours, their obligations cannot be repaid — even through innumerable births. Their most casual utterances convey most beneficial advice and bring us great and lasting happiness.
3. Their heart knows no differentiation, that 'this is mine; that, somebody else's. Such thoughts of differentiation that belong to the worldly life, never cross their mind.
4. The last chapter carried, in a very small measure, the description of the guru's greatness. Now in this chapter, listen, O listeners, to the power of the *udi*.
5. Baba would keep on asking for *dakshina*, which he gave away in charity to the meek and the lowly. From the remaining money he used to buy bundles of faggots which would then be piled up.
6. He used to burn this dried up firewood in the *dhuni*, in front of him. And the unlimited quantity of ash thus produced, would be then given to the devotees as *udi*.

7. While returning home from Shirdi, when the devotees came to take leave of Baba, it was Baba's custom to give them *udi* and everyone knew this.

8. Or rather, when he said, "Bring *udi*", they knew that the permission was truly granted and their hearts were gladdened.

9. Similarly, while in Shirdi, whether it was noon, evening or morning, Baba sent everyone home empty-handed, without giving them *udi*.

10. This was the daily practice. But what was the property of this *udi*? Why the perpetually burning *dhuni* in the mosque? And why was this a daily practice?

11. What was the purpose in Baba's mind that this giving of the *udi* suggested? It was this, that this whole visible creation is nothing but ash, and that everyone should know this for certain.

12. Even this body of ours is just a piece of wood, made up of the five elements and remains only for the purpose of experiencing pleasure and pain, after which it will fall motionless and be reduced to ash, without fail.

13. You and I are also in the same position. To remind you of it, and to keep this awareness in my mind, day and night, I give this *vibhuti*.

14. This whole world is a spectacle of *Maya*. Only the Brahman is true, while the Brahmand (or world) is illusory and of this truth, *udi* is the surest mark. Take this as a certainty.

15. Here, nobody belongs to anybody — even wife and sons, uncles and nephews. Naked we come and naked we leave this world. *Udi* is a reminder of this.

16. By smearing this *udi*, mental and bodily sufferings disappear. But the deeper, inner significance of this *udi* is, 'Detachment based on Discriminating Knowledge'.

17. By giving whatever *dakshina* we can, if we can become detached inwardly from worldly life, gradually, the signs of renunciation will become clear to us.

18. But even if renunciation is attained unaccompanied by discriminating knowledge, it will be wasted. Hence accept the *udi* respectfully.

19. Linking together of Discriminating knowledge and Renunciation is the same as that of *vibhuti* and *dakshina*, without which it is difficult to cross over to the yonder bank of the river of worldly life.

20. Great and small, all came for *darshan* and after bowing at Baba's feet, when they returned home Baba gave them *vibhuti*.

21. In the mosque burned the *dhuni*, for ever, day and night. Baba took *udi* by the fistfuls from it and gave them to the devotees when bidding them adieu.

22. The ash was given as *prasad*, smearing it on their forehead with his thumb and at the same time, placing the hand on their head in benediction.

23. 'Raksha' (ash), 'vibhuti' and *udi*, though they are three different words, they have the same meaning. And this was the *prasad* that Baba always distributed unstintingly and in great abundance.

24. 'Worldly life is like this *udi* and a day will come when, like it, we will also become *vibhuti*'. This is the true significance of the *udi*. Keep this in your mind, always.

25. Like water on a lotus leaf, this mortal body will also fall, one day. Hence give up your attachment to it. This is what Baba indicated by giving *udi*.

26. Know for certain, that this whole expanse of the world is like the ash. Think of the illusory nature of this world and trust only in the reality of the *udi*.

27. *Udi* is nothing but dust. All things, whatever they may be, that have a name and a form, will, in the end, go the same way (i.e. reduced to dust). And from the unchanging everlasting property of the dust, we realize the truth that the changes and modifications that things undergo in this world, are only for the name's sake.

28. When in a good mood, Baba himself, has been heard to sing a song. Listen, O listeners, to a pungent piece from it with reference to the *udi*.

29. "Shri Ram has come, O he has come during his wanderings. And he has brought bags full of *udi*," (Refrain). When the fancy took him, he used to sing only this refrain, repeatedly and in a tuneful voice with great joy.

30. In short, Baba's *dhuni* has produced so many bags of *udi* that no one has been able to count them. Such is this most auspicious *udi*.

31. Having understood the deep inner significance in distributing *udi*, as also its spiritual significance, and its implied meaning, the listeners may want to know, with a purely selfish motive, its importance for their day to day well-being in worldly life.

32. Well, *udi* has this beneficial property, too. How else would its importance grow? Sai, an adept of the spiritual path, ensures not only spiritual but worldly welfare too!

33. There are numerous stories of the worldly benefits of this *udi*. But lest it add to the volume of this book, I shall narrate them in brief.

34. Once a (Gujarati) Brahmin of the *Audichya* sub-caste, by the name of Motiram Narayan Jani, lived at Nasik. He was a householder.

35. Ramchandra Vaman Modak was also another of Baba's faithful devotees, in whose service Narayanrao was employed.

36. When Baba was yet in flesh and blood, this Narayanrao, accompanied by his mother, had gone for his *darshan*.

37. At that time itself, Baba had hinted, all on his own that "from now onwards, we will have nothing to do with a job.

38. "Enough of this service now! An independent business would be far better than this." Later on, after a time, God really took pity on him.

39. The job, the dependency, was all over and he began enjoying his independence. He opened a boarding and lodging establishment there, of his very own.

40. He called it '*Anandashram*' and toiled for it sincerely. Day after day, its fame began to spread. This brought him peace and happiness.

41. As he considered how things had happened exactly as Baba had predicted, his faith in Sai grew, developing into a firm, steadfast devotion, as time went by. The experience that followed, left a deep impression on his mind.

42. He experienced the truth of Sai's words and so the listeners now have a story to listen to. His love for Sai went on increasing. Truly, Sai's *leela* is inconceivable!

43. All his utterances were in the first person, but were always about another person. And those who observed him closely, invariably had this experience.

44. Later on, as he had further experiences, his glorious devotion and love grew. Listen to another story of his faith and devotion.

45. Once one of Narayanrao's friends was suddenly bitten by a scorpion, which caused him great pain and suffering.

46. Baba's *udi* was the most useful remedy for applying to the bite. But search as he may, he just could not find it.

47. The friend could bear the pain no longer and yet, the *udi* could not be traced. He took *darshan* of Baba's photograph, praying to him fervently for mercy.

48. At the foot of the photograph he found some ash fallen from the burning incense-stick. And, for the moment, he felt it was *udi* itself.

49. So picking up a pinch from it, he smeared it over the bitten area, simultaneously murmuring Sai's name. As your faith, so your experience!

50. You will be greatly surprised to know that the moment the ash was rubbed on it, with his finger, the pain disappeared altogether, the way it had come. Both were overcome with love.

51. Here, at least, it was *vibhuti* from the incense-stick that was applied to the afflicted. But even the dust on the pathway, when used as *udi*, brings the same experience.

52. And the very touch of this dust benefits not only those who are ill or suffering from a disease, but its application is effective even to others.

53. Once, a father was greatly worried on suddenly receiving news that his daughter, in another village, was suffering from fever caused by eruption of blind tumours (Bubonic plague).

54. The father lived in Bandra while the daughter lived in another village. He did not have any *udi* with him. So he sent a message to Nana (Narayan Govind alias Nanasaheb Chandorkar).

55. He requested Chandorkar to pray to Baba to relieve him of his worry, adding that Chandorkar should send some *udi*, blessed by Baba.

56. The person carrying the message met Nana on the way. At that time, Nana had just set out to go to Kalyan, with his wife.

57. The message was given to him near the Thane station and there was no *udi* at hand. So he picked up some dust on the way.

58. Standing there, on the road, he prayed to Baba in supplication and turning back, applied a pinch of dust to his wife's forehead.

59. Here, that devotee set out from home and reached his daughter's place. The news that awaited him there, made him very happy.

60. For three days the girl had been running a very high temperature and was in great pain. Only on the previous day had she experienced a slight relief.

61. Thinking back, the father realized that it was exactly the same time Nana had made use of the dust as *udi* and prayed to Sai that the girl had begun to feel some relief.

62. However, a detailed account of that illness will be given later, at the appropriate time. This reference was only in the context of the *udi*.

63. This same loving devotee, Nanasaheb Chandorkar, when he was the *mamlatdar* at Jamner, experienced the miracle that Sai, ever-ready for the good of his devotee, performed. Listen to it.

64. Unlimited is the power of this *udi*. Be attentive, O listeners! For I shall now narrate another miracle which will greatly astonish you.

65. Nana's daughter was about to deliver, any moment, and the labour pains were becoming unbearable. At Jamner, Nanasaheb was calling out to Sai Samarth in every possible way.

66. In Shirdi, of course, no one knew about the situation at Jamner. But from the Omniscient, All-pervasive Baba, nothing in this world is hidden.

67. Baba, who is one with the devotees, knew the position in Nana's house. Samarth Sai's heart was moved by compassion and just see what he did!

68. He wished to send some *udi* to Nana. And, all of a sudden, Gosavi Ramgirbua had a strong urge to go to his own village.

69. His village (native place) was in Khandesh. So he made all preparations to go and came to the mosque for Baba's *darshan*.

70. While Baba was still in the physical body, whatever the work, no one ever went without first making obeisance at his feet and taking his permission.

71. For a wedding or a thread-ceremony, an auspicious ceremony with rites and rituals or any other function, or even a mere planning of it, Baba's approval was absolutely necessary.

72. Without his whole-hearted consent, his *udi-prasad* and benediction, the function would never pass off without an obstacle. Such was the firm faith of one and all.

73. So this had become a custom in the village. Accordingly, Ramgir also came, bowed at Baba's feet and asked for permission to go.

74. He said, 'Baba, I want to go to my village in Khandesh. Please give me *udi* with your blessings and permit this servant of yours to go.'

75. To Ramgir, whom Baba affectionately called 'Bapugir', Baba said, "Go, go to your village, by all means. But on the way, take a little rest.

76. "So first go to Jamner and stay there at Nana's house. After enquiring about his well-being you can then proceed further on your way."

77. And he said to Madhavrao Deshpande, "Shama, write down on a piece of paper that '*arati*' composed by Adkar to send to Nana with this *gosavi*."

78. He then gave *udi* to the *gosavi* and tied up a little in a small packet. Giving the packet in his hand, Baba thus sent it to Nana —

79. Saying "Give this packet and this '*arati*' to Nana. Enquire after his well-being and then proceed to your own village."

80. This *arati*, '*Arati Sai Baba*' was just like the one composed by Ramajanardan, '*Arati Jnanaraja*'. Both have the same '*vritta*' or measure of verse.

81. Ramajanardan was a devotee of Janardan Swami[1], while Madhav Adkar was absorbed at Sai's feet. The composition is a truly blessed one. No *bhajan* can be complete without it.

82. And this *arati* was Baba's favourite, too! Listen to it, in full. It was sent along with *udi* by Baba. You will see its fruitfulness, later.

ARATI

I wave lights before you, O Sai Baba, the Giver of Happiness to the creatures,
Give refuge to this servant, to your devotees, in the dust at your feet. [Refrain]

Having burnt down Cupid (i.e. lust), you are always Self-absorbed,
And appear before the very eyes of the seekers, as Shri Krishna, as Shri Krishna. [1]

As is the faith in one's heart, so is the experience you give him, O Compassionate One.
Such is your *Maya*, O such is your *Maya*. [2]

Meditating on your Name, the worldly sorrows vanish. Truly unfathomable is your doing!
You show the way to the friendless, O to the friendless! [3]

Taking '*avatar*' in the *Kaliyuga*, you have incarnated as the true '*Sagun Brahman*',
O Swami *Datta-digambar*, *Datta-digambar*. [4]

Every eight days, on Thursday, the devotees make pilgrimage for
the *darshan* of their God,
Do remove their fear of worldly life, of worldly life. [5]

Service to your holy feet is my treasured wealth, and this is all I
ask for,
O Lord of Lords, O Lord of Lords! [6]

This meek Chatak wishes only for the pure water of Bliss
Give it to this Madhava and keep your Promise,
O keep your Promise! [7]

I wave lights before you, O Sai Baba ...

83. The *gosavi* said to Baba, 'I have with me, only Rs.2/-. With
    these, how will I reach home after visiting Jamner?

84. Baba said, "You go in peace. All your needs will be looked after."
    Keeping full trust in Sai, the *gosavi* quickly set out to go.

85. Obeying Baba's command and after receiving *udi-prasad* from
    him, Bapugir, intent on his mission, set out at once, with Baba's
    permission.

86. There was no railway to Jamner, then as it is now and the journey
    was not easy. The *gosavi* was quite worried.

87. Boarding a train, the travellers had to get down at Jalgaon and go
    the rest of the way on foot.

88. The railway fare came up to one rupee and fourteen annas, leaving
    a balance of two annas only. How was he to travel the rest of the
    way?

89. While the *gosavi* worried thus, as he was at the Jalgaon Station,
    when he came out after surrendering his ticket he saw a *peon* in
    the distance.

90. Already in search, the peon was standing in front of the
    passengers asking, 'Tell me truly, who amongst you is Bapugir
    from Shirdi?'

91. Realising that the inquiry from the *peon* was about him, the gosavi
     came forward and said, 'I am he. What do you want?'

92. He said, 'Chandorkar has sent me for you. Come, sit in the *tonga*,
     quickly. He is eagerly waiting for you.'

93. Bua was very happy. A message must have been sent to Nana
     from Shirdi. That is how the *tonga* has arrived at the right time.
     Indeed, it saves me a great deal of bother!

94. Sporting a beard, moustache and whiskers and clad in a neat
     trouser, the peon appeared to be very clever. The *tonga* looked
     good, too!

95. And as the *tonga* was good, so were also the horses. For they were
     not hired ones, either. They outstripped all the other *tongas*, eager
     to reach their destination.

96. Once the *tonga* set out full speed at about 11 o'clock or so, at
     night, it halted only at dawn, near a stream[2].

97. The *tongawallah* (driver) then let off his horses to drink water,
     saying, 'I will come back in a moment. Then we can have some
     repast, at leisure.

98. 'I will get some water for us; then we can have mangoes and *pedhas*
     and some pieces of '*gur-papadi*'[3]. We can harness the horses
     thereafter and start on our way, again.'

99. On hearing these words, his beard, his Muslim dress, at once
     created doubts in Ramgir's mind as to whether he should partake
     of the snacks or not.

100. So he questioned him about his caste. 'Why do you have doubts?'
     he said, 'I am the son of a Kshatriya Hindu from Garhwal[4] and by
     caste I am a Rajput.

101. 'And these snacks are also sent with me by Nana and for you. So
     have no doubts in your mind. Eat them, at your ease.'

102. When the *gosavi* was convinced thus, they both ate them. The
     horses were, once again, harnessed, their journey coming to an
     end only at sunrise.

103. As the *tonga* entered the town, Nana's office could be seen. The
     horses too, rested awhile. Ramgir was pleased at heart.

104. Bua, who wanted to relieve himself, went on one side of the road. But when he returned to the same spot, a wonder awaited him.

105. No *tonga*, no horses could be seen — even the *tongawallah* had disappeared. At that moment, no one could be seen and the spot was quite deserted.

106. Ramgir wondered as to what this miracle was. 'Having brought me thus far, how could he have gone so far away, in so short a time?'

107. However, in his eagerness to meet Nana, Bua went into his office, only to learn that Nana was at home. So he set out to go thither.

108. Enquiring on the way, he easily found Nana's house. And even as he was just sitting down in the verandah, Nana summoned him inside.

109. They met each other. Bua at once took out the *udi* and *arati* and placed them before Nana, as he narrated all the news to him.

110. But the wonder of it all was, that when this *udi* came, at that same time Nana's daughter was facing some difficulty in her delivery and consequently was in great pain.

111. To overcome that difficulty, '*Havan*'[5] to propitiate the goddess '*Navchandi*'(i.e. Durga) and a recitation of the '*Saptashati Path*'[6] was in progress. The *gosavi* was quite astonished to see all that.

112. A plateful of sweetmeats and delicacies should come unexpectedly before a hungry man, or nectar before a thirsty Chakor — such was Nana's feeling at that moment.

113. He called out to his wife and gave her the *udi* to be given to the daughter to drink, while he himself started to sing the *arati*.

114. Hardly had a moment passed and word came from inside that as soon as the glass of *udi* water was put to her lips, the girl experienced great relief.

115. She was instantly relieved of pain and delivered without any difficulty. Everyone was relieved too, that she had a safe delivery.

116. 'But where is that *tongawallah*?', he asked Nana, 'I do not see him here, too. Where is the *tonga* that you had sent for me?'

117. Nana said, 'What *tonga*? I had not sent it. I know nothing about this. Who knew that you were coming and so why should I send a *tonga*?'

118. Bua then narrated the whole story of the *tonga*, from the beginning and in great detail. Such motherly affection of Baba filled Nana with love and wonder.

119. O, where was the *tonga*; where the *peon*! It is only Mother Sai, who plays these different roles, in different garbs and, out of love for his devotees, comes running to their rescue in the hour of their need.

120. But now, let us continue with the earlier story (of Narayanrao). Later, after some time, Baba also attained '*nirvana*'.

121. In the year 1918, choosing the auspicious day of Dassera, Baba surrendered his mortal body to the earth.

122. Later came the *Samadhi*. But before all that, even while Baba was still in the physical body, Narayanrao had availed of Baba's *darshan* on two occasions.

123. Three years passed after the *Samadhi* was built. But in spite of a very keen desire for *darshan*, he had not been able to find a suitable opportunity. That made him very impatient.

124. A year after the *Samadhi*, Narayanrao began to suffer from ailments. All remedies were tried, but the usual remedies all failed.

125. Though harassed by suffering, he meditated, day and night on Baba. How can Gurumaharaj ever die? Baba gave *darshan* to Narayan.

126. One night, he had a dream. He saw Sai coming out of an underground cellar and standing near Narayanrao. He gave him an assurance.

127. "Have no worry in your mind; from tomorrow, you will get relief. And at the end of one week, you will sit up, on your own."

128. Eight days passed thus and the truth of Baba's words was experienced to the very letter. Once again, Narayanrao was up and about. His joy knew no bounds.

129. After some time, Narayanrao came to Shirdi to have *samadhi-darshan*. It was then that he narrated his experience

130. How can it be said, that Baba was alive only while he was in the physical body and that he is dead because he has taken *samadhi*?

He is in fact, beyond life and death and pervades this creation, animate and inanimate.

131. Just as the fire is always in the wood, but lies latent and is kindled by the process of friction, so is also Sai for his devotees.

132. Once you look to Sai with love and affection, he is in your power, all your life. He wants nothing but single-minded love and devotion and comes running to your help, when you call him.

133. Neither time nor place can then restrain him; he stands behind you firmly, all the time and for ever. How he will press the spring and where we do not know, for all his doings are inconceivable!

134. Such is his planning, that innumerable doubts and misconceptions will arise in the mind. But when we concentrate on his feet at such a time, our power of meditation and contemplation grows.

135. When the mind is concentrated in this manner, meditation on Sai will follow. And this is what Sai gets done. The task is also accomplished without an obstacle.

136. The worldly affairs need not be given up. But the hankering after all things worldly, will automatically cease, once the mind is trained thus and work will get done, effortlessly.

137. Since this body has taken birth in this *Karmabhoomi* (earth), the *Karma* will be performed, undoubtedly. So wife, sons, wealth and house — let all these be collected to the heart's content.

138. Let things happen as they will. But our good lies in meditating on our Sadguru. All doubts, all resolutions will disappear and the predestined calamities will be averted.

139. Seeing the loving devotion of the devotees, this Sai, the Abode of all Virtue, gives them experiences, one after the other, to glorify devotion.

140. Donning any dress that pleases him, he appears wherever he wishes and wanders anywhere just for the welfare of devotees. Only, the devotees should be trusting.

141. Listen attentively, O listeners, to another story in this context, which will show how the saints work untiringly for their devotees, day and night.

142. Throw open the doors of your ears that lead to the temple of your heart, so that this tale may enter it. For it will help overcome the fear of worldly life and calamities.

143. This recent warfare with the Germans (World War I), which has just ended, necessitated the formation of an army to fight the enemy.

144. So the British govertnment was recruiting men for the army everywhere, in all the cities in India.

145. The year was 1917 and the opportune moment had arrived for the devotee, who was then posted in the Thana district. A most amazing incident took place at that time.

146. The name of this devotee was Appasaheb Kulkarni. And by Sai's power, by his inconceivable *leela* it was, that this devotee developed a strong, unwavering faith in Sai.

147. Years ago, Balasaheb Bhate had given him a photograph of Baba, which he had started worshipping.

148. And, with all his heart, action and speech, would he worship it daily, offering whatever flowers were available, sandalwood paste, consecrated rice, etc., and the '*naivedya*' or food offering.

149. 'When will this '*Karmabhog*'[7] be over? When will my heart-felt desire for Sai's actual *darshan*, in person, be fulfilled?' Such was the yearning of his heart.

150. But the *darshan* of Sai Baba's photograph is the same as his *darshan*, in person. But there has to be full, complete trust and you will receive the mark at the right time.

151. And now, listen carefully to the narration of how the *darshan* of his mere photograph is the same as his actual *darshan*.

152. Balabua Sutar, the *kirtankar* from Bombay and known as the 'modern Tukaram', once went to Shirdi for Baba's *darshan*.

153. This was his very first visit. But although he had never met Sai before, as soon as they looked at each other, Sai very clearly said to him.

154. "See, I have known him for the last four years!" Balabua naturally, wondered why he was saying so.

155. 'Baba has not left Shirdi and even I have seen Shirdi for the first time, today. Then how is it that Baba has known me for the last four years?'

156. As he pondered on it, Bua suddenly remembered that four years ago, he had once made obeisance to Baba's photograph.

157. Balabua at once, realized the truth of Baba's words. 'Just see the all-pervasiveness of the saints and their love for the devotees!

158. 'I had made obeisance only to the photograph and set eyes on his form, for the first time, today. But Baba recognized me, though I had forgotten all about it, long ago!' he thought.

159. 'And yet, it is not correct to say 'I forgot'; I did not understand the meaning of Baba's words, immediately. For I had not the power to understand that my obeisance to the photograph was the acquaintance he referred to.

160. 'Baba knew me and I was not even aware of it, in the least! It is only when the saints remind you that everything comes back (to your mind).'

161. Just as we see the reflection of the sun or the moon in clear water or a clear mirror, so is also the photograph a crystal clear reflection, a symbolic representation of the person.

162. Hence the *darshan* of a saint's photograph is the same as his actual *darshan*. This is the teaching of the omniscient saints to all.[8]

163. Now let the listeners be attentive so that they can pick up the threads of the earlier story.

164. Appa resided at Thane and had once to go to Bhiwandi for work. So he left the house saying that he would return after eight days.

165. But hardly had two days passed since he left, when here, at Thane, a most amazing thing happened. A fakir came to the door.

166. As their eyes met, everyone thought that Sai himself had come. For from head to foot, he resembled the photograph, in face and figure.

167. Appa's wife, his children — they all stared at his face in astonishment. They all felt that Baba himself, had come!

168. None of them had had actual *darshan*, before. But from the resemblance to the photograph, they felt sure that he was Baba and hence were most curious.

169. So they asked the fakir, 'Are you that same Sai of Shirdi?' Listen carefully to what that fakir told them.

170. "I am myself, not really Sai, but I am his obedient slave and by his command have I come to enquire after the children and the family."

171. Then he began to ask for *dakshina*. The mother at once gave him one rupee, very respectfully and he too, gave them *udi*.

172. He gave Sai Baba's *udi* to the lady in a packet and said, "Keep this alongside of the photograph. It will bring you great happiness."

173. Having thus accomplished his purpose, he took leave saying, "Sai must be waiting eagerly for me", and went away.

174. As he set out from there, he went the same way as he had come. But what happened at Appa's house was really, Sai's most wonderful *leela*!

175. Appasaheb had no doubt, gone to Bhiwandi but instead of going ahead, he had to turn back as the horses of the tonga took ill. The farther visit had to be cancelled.

176. In the afternoon, he returned to Thane. When he heard what had happened in his absence, Appasaheb had great regrets that he missed the *darshan*.

177. He also felt ashamed that only a rupee was given as *dakshina*. 'Had I been here, I would never have sent him off without offering anything less than Rs.10/- as *dakshina*.'

178. So said Appasaheb to himself. He felt a little sad at heart. Thinking that he may yet find the fakir in the mosque, he set out in search without even taking food.

179. Appa searched for the fakir in all the possible places — mosques, takiyas, wherever the fakirs usually stayed.

180. He was quite exhausted by the search, but the fakir could not be found. Disappointed and hungry, he went home and had food.

181. But what he did not know was that one should never undertake any search on an empty stomach. The *Atman* should first be satisfied and then the search taken up.

182. The truth of this principle is revealed through Baba's story conveying the same significance. But the listeners already know it; then why repeat it?

183. In the previous chapter, a fascinating story called 'the greatness of the Guru' has been narrated, in which Shri Sai, the Compassionate One, has described in his own words the Promise of the Guru.

184. And the truth of these same words was now experienced. After taking his food, Appa set out, once again, for a casual walk, taking with him his friend Chitre.

185. After treading part of the way, he noticed a person who kept on looking at him and walked up hurriedly to where he was, to meet him.

186. When he came and stood near him, Appasaheb took a furtive look at him, thinking in his mind that this must have been he who had come to his house that morning.

187. 'This seems to me to be the fakir for whom I was searching earlier. He resembles the photograph to the very tips of the nails. My mind is quite bewildered on seeing him.'

188. So Appa inferred in his mind when suddenly, the fakir spread out his hand before him, on which Appa placed a rupee at that time.

189. When he asked for more, Appa gave one more and yet, a third one. But the fakir still asked for more. The real wonder was still to follow.

190. Chitre had three rupees with him which Appa took from him and gave them to the fakir. But still, the fakir would not stop asking for more.

191. Appasaheb said to him, 'I can give you more if you come home.' He agreed and the three of them returned to his house.

192. After coming home, he at once took out three more and gave them to him. Now he had given nine rupees, in all. Yet the fakir was not satisfied.

193. When he began asking for more *dakshina*, Appa said, 'Now there remains with me only one ten rupee note.

194. 'All the loose change is finished and nothing else is left.' 'Why not give me that note?" said the fakir. So Appa gave it.

195. As the note came into his hand, the fakir returned the nine rupees. He then went back speedily, the way he had come.

196. The significance of the story is that it is Sai's Promise that he will get fulfilled whatever words a devotee might have uttered.

197. Eager that the listeners are for more, I shall narrate another story with the same purport, which I am reminded of in this context. Listen to it with respect.

198. There was a faithful devotee called Haribhau Karnik. A resident of Dahanu village, he cherished a steadfast devotion to Sai.

199. In the year 1917, on the auspicious day of *Guru Poornima*, he had undertaken a pilgrimage to Shirdi. And that is the tale that I shall now relate.

200. With all the proper ritual, he performed the pooja, making an offering of garments and *dakshina*, and took Baba's leave. As he was coming down the steps, a thought arose in his mind.

201. He felt that he should go up again and offer one more rupee to Baba. But he had to give up the idea and keep back the rupee.

202. The person (Madhavrao Deshpande) who had arranged for the *darshan*, leave taking, etc., earlier, himself signalled to him from above that once he had taken leave, he should now proceed ahead on his way.

203. Implicitly trusting the signal, Karnik walked ahead. On the way home, he and his friend made a halt at Nasik.

204. When Karnik went to have *darshan* at the temple of '*Kala Ram*' at Nasik, unexpectedly, he had the *darshan* of the saint Narsinh Maharaj[9].

205. Although surrounded by a group of devotees, Maharaj suddenly got up and catching Karnik by the wrist, said, 'Give me my rupee!'

206. In his heart, Karnik was quite astonished, but gave the rupee most happily. He felt that Sai himself was accepting the rupee, which he had mentally offered him, earlier.

207. And yet it is not quite correct to say that Sai had accepted it. For when such a thought is farthest from the mind, he just pulls it forcibly from you. And that is exactly what had happened!

208. The mind is always full of resolutions, doubts, etc. Initially, it plans one thing, but when the time comes for executing the plan, wave upon wave of thoughts invade it.

209. But it is only the first thought that arises, provided it is a benign one, which is nourished and this becomes beneficial.

210. On it, the mind should concentrate, study deeply and meditate upon, repeatedly, without allowing it to be forgotten and thus keep one's word, even with a special effort.

211. Appasaheb had uttered the words and would have forgotten, later. So Sai saw to it that they were fulfilled as soon as uttered, thereby revealing to the world the great marvel of Devotion.

212. Why else should the fakir have given back nine rupees when he had with him, full nineteen? Because Appa's unfulfilled desire was to give Rs.10/-, and no less.

213. This necklace of nine golden coins, sanctified by Baba's touch, was really his way of reminding the devotees of the aggregate of the ninefold path of loving devotion.

214. As you will hear the story of Baba's giving up the body, you will see Baba's unique way of giving, when he gave nine rupees to Laxmibai, at that time.

215. Appa's wife had very sincerely and with all her heart, given only one rupee, which he accepted with pleasure. There was no asking for more, then.

216. But Appa considered his wife's *dakshina* as too little, 'I would there and then, have given to that fakir ten times more, had I been there', he thought.

217. Since Appa had actuallay mentioned that he would have given ten rupees, then unless he gave the full amount, how would he keep his word, discharge his debt?

218. This fakir was not like the others. Was he any mendicant to go back, accepting whatever was placed in his hand?

219. The day had not passed when, the same day that the words were uttered, he came back. But it was Appa who had a misconception that he was some other, unknown fakir.

220. When the fakir first asked him for *dakshina*, he had six rupees with him, but he did not give away all of them.

221. And had he not really loved Appa, would Baba have come dressed as a fakir? Moreover, had he not pretended asking for *dakshina*, would this story have been so fascinating?

222. Appasaheb was only an excuse. But the same is true of you and me! We all have good intentions to begin with. But when the time comes, we act quite differently according to the occasion.

223. We are always ready with words and promises. But when it actually comes to giving, doubts cloud our minds and we waver. Rarely is there any resolute action.

224. But rare among us is he, who will speak little and always for the good of others, and will act strictly, according to his word and vindicate it.

225. To a devotee with a single-minded devotion to him, Sai Samarth will grant whatever he desires to have whether it be in this world or the next.

226. Though Appasaheb was clever, proficient in the English education, the government paid him a salary of only Rs.40/-in the beginning.

227. But later, when he got the photograph, his pay increased gradually, to so many times more than Rs.40/-.

228. If you give him one, he gives you ten times more, — ten times more the authority and power. And everyone has had this experience of Baba, from time to time.

229. Moreover, from such steady faith, the spiritual perception begins to grow. Is this any ordinary gain? Baba's skill is really, most remarkable!

230. Later, Appasaheb asked to see the *vibhuti* given by that fakir. It was in a packet, which he opened very lovingly.

231. From the packet came out flowers and consecrated rice, along with *udi*. He put them in an amulet which he tied around his arm, with great respect.

232. Later, when he took Baba's *darshan*, Baba gave him one hair of his, which he, very lovingly, put in the amulet, along with the rest.

233. Oh, what significance Baba's *udi* has! *Udi* also adorns Shankar and he who applies it on his forehead with faith, will have all the impediments in his way, removed instantly!

234. After the morning ablutions, he who applies the *udi* daily and drinks it, along with the holy water washed off Baba's feet, will acquire much merit and be purified.

235. Moreover, another special property of the *udi* is that if taken faithfully, it will bring a long life; all the sins will be destroyed and happiness and contentment will come to stay.

236. In this way, Sai has given a feast of this nectar-sweet story under the pretext of Appa and we have been but uninvited guests, who have feasted at it, to our heart's content.

237. But whether a guest or the host, all have partaken of the same feast, — there is no differentiation as far as sweetness and deliciousness are concerned. Be satiated with this feast of Self-rejoicing.

238. Hemad bows at Sai's feet. What we have listened to, so far, is quite enough. In the next chapter will follow the narration of greater significance of the *udi* —

239. How by smearing of *udi* and Sai's *darshan*, a deep-seated ulcer was totally cured; how the ring-worm and Bubonic plague were cured, too! Listen to it very carefully.

Weal be to all! Here ends the thirty-third chapter of
"Shri Sai Samarth Satcharit", called
'The Significance of Udi (1)',
as inspired by the saints and the virtuous
and composed by his devotee Hemadpant.

Notes

1. Janardan Haripant Deshpande (1504-1575 A.D.), a *vatandar* of Chalisgaon, came to be known as Janardan Swami. He was a disciple of a Sufi *fakir*, Chand Bodhale. He was in the service of Nizam at Devgiri. His devotion to Dattatreya influenced the Muslim ruler and in his time the weekly holiday was observed on Thursday, instead of Friday. He built the *samadhi* of his guru on the Daulatabad fort, while his own *samadhi* is at Kharwandi, Tal. Pathardi, Dist. Ahmednagar.

2. Ramgir Bua describes the experience thus: 'One day, Baba called me to him and gave me a packet of *udi* and a copy of Baba's *arati*. I had to go to Khandesh at the time. Baba directed me to go to Jamnere (sic) (which is 36 miles off by cart route from the station Bhusaval) and told me to deliver the *udi* and *arati* to Nana Saheb Chandorkar, Deputy Collector at Jamnere. I said to Baba that all I had was two rupees and asked how that could take me by train from Kopergaon to Jalgaon and next by cart from Jalgaon to Jamnere. Baba said, "God will give." That was a Friday and I started at once. I reached Mammad at 7:30 p.m. and Jalgaon at 2:45 a.m. . At that station, plague regulations were enforced and I had much trouble. I was to discover what I should do to get to Jamnere. At about 3:00 a.m., a peon in boots, turban, well-equipped with other details of good dress, came to me and took me to a *tonga* and drove me on. I was in terror. On the way at Baghoor, I took refreshments. We reached Jamnere early morning and by the time I attended to my call of nature, the *tonga* and its driver disappeared.' (*Devotees' Experiences of Sri Sai Baba - Part III* by H.H. Narsimhaswamiji, All India Sai Samaj, Madras. 1967, pp. 122-3)

3. A sort of cake made by frying wheat-flour in ghee and adding jaggery to it.

4. A region at the foot of the Himalayas.

5. An oblation by fire to a deity.

6. The seven hundred verses in praise of the goddess in the *Markandaya Puran*.

7. Suffering allotted by destiny.

8. "A thing and its reflection are the same. A picture is but a reflection of the Master. His presence can be felt after repeated prayer. The place becomes holy." - Shri Sarada Devi in 'In the *Company of the Holy Mother*', p. 77.

9. He used to stay at the door of the holy shrine of Kala Ram in Nasik, where his *dhuni* used to burn. He never asked anything from anyone and would distribute to others, whatever he received. He never talked to anyone, would smear *bhasma* all over the body and remained naked.

34

The Significance of Udi (Concluded)

MY OBEISANCE TO SHRI GANESH, TO SHRI SARASWATI, AND SHRI GURUMAHARAJ! TO THE FAMILY DEITY, TO SHRI SITA-RAMACHANDRA, MY MOST HUMBLE OBEISANCE! I BOW IN REVERENCE TO THE MOST VENERABLE GURU SHRI SAINATH!

1   The significance of the *Udi* has been described most truly in the last chapter. In the present chapter too, we shall carry on the same narration, further describing its beneficial properties.

2.   In continuation of the previous chapter, let the listeners listen at their ease and for their own happiness, as to the great power of the *udi*.

3.   In the most painful and hard-to-cure disease, a deep seated ulcer, which could not be cured by any treatment, was cured completely by the smearing of the *udi* at Baba's hands.

4.   Many are such instances about this *udi*, of which I shall relate just one to give the general idea. Being based on a real experience, the listeners will appreciate it greatly as they listen.

5.   At Malegaon in the Nasik district, there was a doctor, a holder of a medical degree. His nephew[1] had some disease which no medicine could cure.

6.   Himself a qualified doctor, he had a friend who was also a doctor. They both tried various remedies. Both were experienced, skilled surgeons. But ultimately, they too, were exhausted and at their wits' end.

7.   The disease was a deep-seated bone ulcer, called in the vernacular as '*Hadyavrana*', often distorted to '*Hadyavarna*'. But it was a

peculiar disease, hard to cure, which would not respond to any medicine.

8. All medicines indigenous and foreign, and whatever remedies occurred to the mind, were all tried out. But everything failed. Even a surgery was performed, but without success.

9. The nephew was young and could not bear the pain. The suffering brought on great agony. And the near and dear ones were distressed to see his pain.

10. Every possible cure was tried, but the disease did not abate in the least. Then the relatives and friends said, 'Propitiate, worship the deities'.

11. Gods, personal gods and family gods — all were propitiated but not one amongst them was of any help. It was then that he came to know that there was a great *avalia*, staying at Shirdi.

12. He was Sai Maharaj, the greatest among the *yogis* and most excellent among the saints, whose mere *darshan* was enough to drive away all the illness. This was really what he heard.

13. So a desire arose for Sai's *darshan*. The father and the mother therefore, decided to at least try the remedy in the name of God.

14. It is said that he is a great *avalia* and if he applies *udi* with his own hands, even the most dreadful diseases are cured. What does one lose in trying out this experience?

15. Come, let us worship his feet; let us try this one last remedy. Oh, let this danger be averted at least by this means! It is our last hope!

16. And so, the parents packed everything and eager for Sai's *darshan*, they at once went to Shirdi.

17. Immediately on arrival they took Baba's *darshan*, prostrated at his feet in obeisance, related to him the suffering of the child, as they stood in front of him.

18. With folded hands and piteous faces, they began entreating Sai in a sorrowful voice.

19. 'This child is in great pain due to his illness', they said, 'We cannot bear to see his suffering and know not what to do next. We see no ray of hope at all!

20. 'Seeing the child suffer thus, O Sai Samarth, we are totally exhausted. Please place your hand of Protection on his head and relieve his suffering.

21. 'Having heard of your great powers, we have come here, all the way. We surrender at your feet with single-minded devotion. Do give us the gift of his life!'

22. Sai, the Compassionate One, then gave them an assurance, saying, "Those who seek refuge in this mosque, will never come to an evil end, even to the end of the world.

23. "Now, have no more worry! Take this *udi* and smear it on that ulcer. In about eight days or so, you will see its good effect. Have faith in God.

24. "This is not just a mosque like any other, it is (Shri Krishna's) Dwaraka. And he who puts his foot into this mosque will at once get back his health and well-being. You will yourself experience it!

25. "That anyone should come here and not experience relief, is a thing that can never happen, either in the past, present or future. Be sure that your object will be accomplished."

26. Then as per Baba's command, the boy was made to sit in front of him and Baba moved his hand over the leg, bestowing on him a glance of Grace.

27. This was, of course, a physical illness. But even when a calamity comes by Destiny or by great mental disturbance, Baba's *darshan* averts it altogether.

28. Gazing upon Sri Sai's face, all the pain and suffering subsided and on hearing his nectar-sweet words the child experienced great relief and happiness.

29. For four days, they stayed there. The illness gradually diminished as the faith in Sai grew.

30. Thereafter, they took Baba's permission and the three of them returned to their place, happy and satisfied.

31. And was this any small miracle? The pain of a deep-seated ulcer disappeared while the only unique remedy was in the *udi* and in Baba's glance of Grace!

32. Such is the importance of a saint's *darshan*. If one is fortunate enough to get his assurance and benediction, the disease is destroyed completely.

33. And so, after a few days, while the *udi* was being applied to the affected part and also given to drink, the wound began to dry up and was healed. The boy regained good health.

34. When his uncle at Malegaon came to know of this, he felt an eager desire for Sai's *darshan* and said to himself that while going to Bombay, he would satisfy his wish.

35. But later, when he set out to go to Bombay, people created doubts in his mind, both at Malegaon and at Manmad. With the result, he abandoned his plan to go to Shirdi.

36. Such is the case with any good resolution. In the beginning, wicked people always create obstacles. Only those who do not give in to what such people say will, in the end, pursue the right path.

37. So, neglecting the saint's *darshan*, he went on straight to Bombay, deciding to spend the remainder of his leave at Alibaug.

38. When he made the resolve thus, he heard a voice in his sleep for three consecutive nights, saying, "Is there disbelief in me, even now?"

39. The doctor was astonished when he heard this ethereal voice, on three consecutive nights. So, trusting the voice to be true, he made up his mind to go to Shirdi.

40. However, he was treating a patient of typhoid at the time. So he decided to go immediately once the patient was better.

41. But he (the patient) was running a high temperature and no medicine was effective. He did not show any improvement. There seemed no chance of his going to Shirdi soon.

42. He then resolved in his mind: 'If this patient improves today, I will go to Shirdi tomorrow itself, without a moment's delay.'

43. Even as he made this firm resolve, within three to seven hours of it, the fever came down. His purpose answered, the doctor at once set out to go to Shirdi.

44. Keeping to this resolve, the doctor thus went to Shirdi, worshipped Baba's feet with all his heart. Baba also confirmed his inner faith and experience and won him over to the guru-service.

45. Placing his hand of benediction on the doctor's head, he gave him *udi-prasad*. Sai's inconceivable power left the doctor wonderstruck.

46. The doctor stayed on for four days and returned home with a joyous heart. Before a fortnight had passed after this, he was sent to Vijapur on promotion.

47. The painful ulcer gave rise to the idea of Sai's *darshan*, which in turn, created a great attachment to the saint, resulting ultimately in a state of everlasting happiness.

48. Similarly, Doctor Pillai was once suffering from the guinea worms and, one after the other, there appeared no less than seven guinea worms. They caused him great pain and suffering.

49. But for Sai Baba he had great love and devotion. Baba too, called him by the nickname '*Bhau*', and would always enquire very lovingly after Bhau's well-being.

50. Morning and evening, Bhau's place was near the hand-railing in the mosque, and for a long time there used to be a mutual exchange of ideas aplenty, with Bhau.

51. While smoking a *chillim*, Bhau had to be there; while smoking a *bidi* too, Bhau's presence was imperative. Bhau was needed while taking decisions in matters. And if Bhau was not present, time would not pass pleasantly.

52 Such was the state of affairs! But when the pain from the affliction became unbearable, Bhau became so weak that he took to his bed. The pain and suffering caused great agitation and despair.

53. Even in that most trying situation, there was a ceaseless chant of Sai's name on his lips. 'Oh, enough of this agony. Even death is preferable to this,' said he, as he totally surrendered to Sai.

54. He sent a message to Baba, 'I am fed up with suffering so much pain. There are so many wounds all over my body! I have not the strength to endure any more!

55. 'When I have been so pure of conduct, why have I to suffer this painful condition? I have always avoided wicked, sinful deeds. Why then the burden of sin on my head?

56. 'The pain of this disease is like that of death. Baba, I really cannot bear it now! It is better that I die. Whatever suffering remains to endure, I shall bear it in the next birth.

57. 'Unless one endures one's full share of suffering, there is no escape, to complete which one may have to take more births. But what is ordained by *prarabdha* can never be avoided. Dull-witted that I am, even I know this.

58. 'I will happily take ten more births to suffer for my *karma*. But give me this one gift that my present birth be terminated.

59. 'Enough, O enough of this life! Release me from this birth. For I can endure this pain no longer. This is my one and only request to you!'

60. Sai, the king among the *Siddhas*, was deeply moved to pity by this prayer. Listen to the nectar-sweet compassion that he showered on Doctor Pillai to console him.

61. And just see the plan that Sai Baba, the wish-fulfilling tree of the devotees, initiated to mitigate the intense suffering of his devotee.

62. The message from Doctor Pillai was brought by Dikshit, on hearing which Baba said, "Go and tell him 'Let your mind be free from fear'"

63. He also sent the message, "Why spread out this suffering over ten births? We can spread it over ten days only by sharing it mutually, and be done with it!

64. "Oh, that you should ask for the calamity of death when I sit here, powerful enough to give you *Moksha*, your material as well as spiritual welfare! Is this all your prowess, your daring?

65. "Let him be lifted up and brought here. Let the suffering be undergone and endured. Let him not be so distracted by fear. Carry him here on your back."

66. And so, in that painful condition the doctor was immediately brought to the mosque. Baba removed the pillow on which he was leaning and gave it to him.

67. It was placed on his right hand — the place where Fakir Baba used to sit. "Lean against this and lie down quietly. Do not worry needlessly," Baba said.

68. "Stretch your leg out, slowly. It will give you some relief. What is preordained will not be over unless it is borne fully. That alone is its remedy.

69. "Good or bad, sorrow or joy, nectar or poison — these pairs of opposites come to us with the current according to our '*Sanchit*'. Therefore, feel neither joy nor sorrow for them.

70. "Endure whatever comes your way. *Allah Malik* is our Protector. Always meditate on Him, for He alone bears the burden of all the cares and anxieties.

71. "With all your heart, wealth, body and speech, surrender humbly at his feet. When you take His Name ceaselessly, you will experience His *leela*."

72. Doctor Pillai then said, 'Nanasaheb Chandorkar had bandaged the wound, but there is no relief.'

73. Baba said, "Nana is crazy! Remove that bandage, or else you will die. A crow will come presently and peck at it and you will be all right."

74. While they were talking thus, Abdul immediately came up to put oil in the earthen lamps. And, quite unexpectedly — what happened next?

75. Narrow as the mosque was, it was already crowded with devotees. To add to it, there was the confusion caused by Pillai's condition. Abdul could hardly move about.

76. Moreover, Abdul was intent on the work in hand, concentrating on the earthen lamps. For a moment he became unmindful of Pillai's presence and then — a most extraordinary thing happened!

77. And what could Abdullah do? What is to happen cannot be avoided. So, by mistake, he stepped on the painful leg which Pillai had stretched out.

78. The leg was already swollen and on that same leg Abdullah's foot came down. O God! the loud piercing cry that Pillai broke into was terrible! He simply writhed in agony.

79. Once, and only once, did he give a shriek in agony, which seemed to penetrate through the head as he entreated Baba piteously with folded hands. Listen to it!

80. The abcesses ruptured and the pus began to flow out of them. With a restless and agitated mind, Pillai, on the one hand, cried out loudly and on the other, began to sing:

    'O *Karim* (Allah)! have pity on my condition,
    For Your name is *Rahiman* (Compassionate) and *Rahim* (Merciful)!
    You alone, are the Emperor of both the worlds, And Your greatness is manifest in the world.
    All the worldly business will become extinct,
    But Your glory is everlasting!
    You are always the Refuge of your devotees.

81. The shooting pain continued to appear every now and again. His mind was greatly agitated and he felt very weak. Everyone realized that all this was Sai Baba's sport.

82. Baba said, "Look, Bhau has started singing!" And Pillai asked him, 'Baba, is that crow still to come and peck at my wounds?'

83. And Baba said, "You go and lie down quietly in the wada. The crow will not come again to peck.

84. "Did he not come just now — he who stepped on your leg? That, that was the crow who pecked at you and then flew away and subdued your painful abscesses."

85. What crow and what pecking! He just brought about what was inevitably going to happen. The crow appeared in the form of Abdullah and Baba proved his words to be true.

86. Baba's words are not just words. They are inerasable as the destiny of Man that Brahmadev writes on his forehead. They can stop effectually the result of a man's *karma*. In a short while, Bhau experienced great relief.

87. Application of the *udi* and drinking it in water had been the only medicine, the only antidote. The disease was totally rooted out as the tenth day dawned.

88. Seven live, thread-like guinea worms came out of the wounds. The severe pain subsided altogether, marking the end of his suffering.

89. Pillai was simply amazed to see this miracle and tears of love streamed down his eyes on seeing Baba's marvellous *leela*.

90. Pillai at once fell at Baba's feet. He was choked with emotion and not a word escaped from his lips.

91. I shall conclude this narration of the great power of the *udi* after relating one more experience. The essence of this gospel is, 'as your faith, so is the experience you get.'

92. Bapaji was the younger brother of Madhavrao, who was the elder of the two. Listen to how he achieved his desired goal by making use of the *udi*, when he was once, in great difficulty.

93. So great is this *udi's* power that I just cannot praise it enough. It is a most remarkable remedy for the Bubonic plague and other diseases. There is none to compare with it.

94. While Bapaji was staying at Saul Vihir (a place near Shirdi), his wife once had high fever and buboes appeared in the region of the groins. In his mind, Bapaji was frightened.

95. In that fearful time of the night, seeing his wife's distress, Bapaji was filled with apprehension and bewilderment. He lost his nerve completely.

96. Trembling with nervousness and fear, night though it was, he went running to Shirdi, immediately, and told his brother, what had happened.

97. 'Two buboes have appeared,', he said, 'and she is burning with fever and is in great distress. Come and see for yourself. This, I think, does not portend any good.'

98. Madhavrao was startled to see Bapaji's piteous face as he spoke. His mind restless and agitated, he too, lost heart.

99. Discriminating though Madhavrao's mind was, he panicked at the mention of buboes. For everyone knows the quick end that follows bubonic plague.

100. Be the occasion a happy or a difficult one, the task auspicious or inauspicious, it was customary in Shirdi to first ask Sai's advice.

101. And then to follow to the last detail, whatever he advises. For he alone wards off the trouble of his devotees. O, how many such experiences one can recount!

102. So, in keeping with this usual practice, Madhavrao also took the decision and prostrating before Baba in obeisance, narrated everything to him, first.

103. He said, 'Glory be to you, O Sainath! Have mercy on us, the helpless ones! O, what is this calamity, now! And what needless worry!

104. 'But then, who else can we entreat but you? Please mitigate the suffering, the pain of that poor girl; extend your benediction to her!

105. 'Please save us from this one calamity. Who else is our saviour except you? Please abate this high fever and keep your Promise!'

106. He asked Baba's leave to accompany his brother back. Baba then said, "Do not go at this odd hour of the night. But send her some *udi*.

107. "What buboes and what fever! Our father is *Allah Malik*. It will be all right, by itself. She will be safe and sound, without a doubt.

108. "But early in the morning, at sunrise, yourself go to Saul Vihir. Do not be in a hurry to go right now! Stay here in peace.

109. "And even tomorrow, when you go, come back soon. Why do you trouble yourself needlessly? Once the *udi* is applied and given to drink, why should we fear?"

110. On hearing this, Bapaji was scared. He was dismayed. For Madhavrao knew herbal remedies. But it was of no use at this time.

111. However, Madhavrao recognized the mark full well, that no medicine would work without Sai's Grace.

112. So he obeyed Baba's command and sent the *udi* with his brother, himself staying back and at ease. Bapaji returned alone, worried and disheartened.

113. Mixing some *udi* with water, he applied it to her body and gave her some to drink. Soon enough, she was drenched with perspiration and fell into a deep sleep.

114. At sunrise his wife felt energetic for there was no trace of either the fever or the poisonous buboes, anywhere. Bapaji was astonished.

115. Here, Madhavrao got up, finished his morning ablutions and came to the mosque for darshan before setting out to go to Saul Vihir.

116. He took Baba's *darshan*, prostrated at his feet and was on his way, as soon as he received *udi* with Baba's blessings.

117. As he was coming down the steps of the mosque, Baba was heard commanding him, "Shama, you must return at once! Delay will not do."

118. On the way, the brother-in-law worried over how the sister-in-law must be suffering, how she would bear the pain of the two burning buboes! oh, how she must be lying in great torment!

119. And yet, Baba must have been hinting at something! Or else, why did he say come back immediately? Shama panicked at the thought and his step quickened as he trod the way.

120. Walking hurriedly, he could hardly wait to reach Saul Vihir. But as he stepped on the threshold, he could hardly believe his eyes!

121. She, who had bubonic plague the previous night, was seen preparing tea as usual. Seeing this sudden change, Madhavrao was astonished in his mind.

122. So he said to Bapaji, 'How is it that she is engaged in the daily chores?' And Bapaji replied, 'All this is most certainly, the marvel of Baba's *udi*!

123. 'As soon as I came home, I gave her *udi* to drink and rubbed some of it all over her body. At once her body was drenched in perspiration and she enjoyed a deep, peaceful slumber.

124. 'Later, as the sun rose, she sat up feeling refreshed and healthy. The buboes and the fever had both disappeared. Truly, this is nothing but Baba's great prowess!'

125. Seeing her present condition, Shama at once remembered Sai's words, 'Come back immediately' and he was quite amazed.

126. Even before he arrived, the purpose had been accomplished. So he drank tea and returned at once. He went straight to the mosque and bowed at Sai's feet.

127. 'What is this sport of yours, O God!' he said, 'It is you who cause agitation of our minds. Sitting in your own place, you generate a whirlwind and you, yourself then restore calm, afterwards!'

128. Baba replied, "Look, this is due to the profound, hidden course of your *karma*. Be sure that I neither do anything nor get anything done. But still, the power of doing it is laid at my door!

129. "I am only a '*sakshi*', a witness, to whatever *karmas* that come about by the force of destiny. God Almighty alone is the Doer and the Impeller of all action. And He alone is the Gracious One.

130. "I am neither God nor the Supreme Being. I am not '*Anal Haq*' (God) either; I am '*Yade Haq*', one who constantly remembers God. I am Allah's most humble slave.

131. "He who extinguishes his ego and with a grateful heart, puts his burden on Him, will surely and safely cross the ocean of worldly life."

132. Now listen to a similar and most significant experience of an Iranian gentleman. whose infant daughter used to lose her speech every hour.

133. For she would be seized by an hourly epileptic fit, her body curving like a bow. She would lie unconscious, as if dead. No remedy seemed to work.

134. Later, a friend of his described to him the great power of the *udi*, saying that 'nowhere else was there such a unique and infallible remedy.

135. 'Go at once to Vile Parle and ask Dikshit for the *udi*. He always has it with him and will give you gladly.

136. 'When you give it to her to drink every day, remembering Sai and keeping full trust in him, these fits will disappear and you all will be happy.'

137. On hearing this, that Parsi gentleman asked Dikshit for *udi* and gave it to the child to drink every day. And she was restored to good health.

138. She, who used to become restless and agitated, every passing hour, obtained relief immediately. The interval between two fits gradually lengthened to seven hours.

139. Thus, the hourly fit that seized her was delayed by seven hours and disappeared altogether after some time.

140. In a village near Harda, there lived an old man who suffered greatly due to a kidney stone. It caused him great pain and distress.

141. Since there was no other remedy for his complaint except surgery, some people advised him to look for an eminent surgeon.

142. The patient was extremely worried and could not make up his mind. His body became emaciated as if on the point of death. The agonizing pain was becoming unbearable.

143. To undergo a surgical operation requires great courage and the patient had no peace of mind. Luckily, his misfortune came to an end. Listen to the marvel!

144. While such was the condition here, news came that the *Inamdar* of the village, who was a great devotee of Sai Baba, had come to the village.

145. Everyone knew that he had always with him Baba's *udi*, to ask for which, relatives and friends of the afflicted came to him.

146. The *Inamdar* gladly gave it and the son gave it mixed in water, to his father to drink. Hardly had five minutes passed when a most astonishing thing happened!

147. As that *udi-prasad* was absorbed in the body, the kidney-stone moved from its place and passed out through the urine. The patient at once, experienced great relief.

148. The wife of a gentleman from Bombay, by caste, a C.K.P. (Chandraseniya Kayastha Prabhu), always became seriously ill when the time for her delivery arrived.

149. However much they might try, not a single remedy seemed to work. The lady used to be in great distress and the poor man would become worried and agitated.

150. There was a Sai devotee, well-known by the name 'Shri Ram Maruti', by whose advice, this gentleman set out to go to Shirdi.

151. When the time for the delivery approached, both used to be in great anxiety. So they made up their mind once for all, to be in Shirdi and get rid of the fear

152. Whatever is to happen, let it happen. But at least, it will happen in front of Baba. Making this firm resolve, they both came and stayed at Shirdi.

153. They stayed on in Shirdi for many months and were happy performing Baba's *pooja* and enjoying his company.

154. After spending some time thus, the time for the delivery approached, causing them great anxiety as to how the calamity could be overcome.

155. Even while they worried, the time, the day of the delivery dawned. The mouth of the womb was blocked and everyone was worried.

156. The lady suffered severe pains and no one knew what to do. A ceaseless prayer to Baba continued. Who else but he would take pity?

157. Ladies from the neighbourhood came running and, petitioning to Baba, one of them took a little water in a glass in which she mixed the *udi* and made her drink it.

158. Within five minutes the lady delivered . The child seemed to be lifeless, having died in the womb.

159. But that was the fate of that foetus! Another child may be conceived later on, but at least the lady was safe and free from fear.

160. She delivered without any pain and was hale and hearty. The moment of grave danger and anxiety had passed and she became indebted to Baba for a lifetime.

161. The following chapter is sweeter than this, listening to which, the fond desire of the listeners will be satisfied. It will cure them

of their bad habit of over-inquisitiveness and instead, increase their devotion.

162. 'We worship only the Formless One and hence we will not offer *dakshina*, nor will we bow our heads before anyone. Only on this condition will we come for *darshan*.'

163. They who had firmly resolved thus, not only prostrated in obeisance, on seeing Sai, but also offered *dakshina*, on their own. Oh, what a miracle, indeed!

164. Also, the most remarkable power of the *udi* and how Nevaskar fed milk to a cobra, with love and devotion, thus observing the duty of a house-holder —

165. These and other such excellent stories will give rise to a loving devotion, when carefully listened to. The sorrows of worldly life will then be mitigated. What greater and lasting happiness can there be?

166. Hence Hemad bows at Sai's feet and prays to him to bestow his compassionate love upon the listeners, so that they may get absorbed in listening to his *Sai Satcharit*.

Weal be to all! Here ends the thirty-fourth chapter of
"*Shri Sai Samarth Satcharit*", called
'*The Significance of Udi (2)*',
as inspired by the saints and the virtuous
and composed by his devotee, Hemadpant.

Notes

1. This incident has been referred to in the statement of Dr D M Mulki, where he states that his nephew suffered from 'Chronic Osteomyelitis'. (*Devotees' Experiences of Shri Sai Baba, Part II*, by H.H. Narasimhaswami, 1966, p. 109.)

35

The Removal of Doubts and Glorification of the Udi

MY OBEISANCE TO SHRI GANESH, TO SHRI SARASWATI, AND SHRI GURUMAHARAJ! TO THE FAMILY DEITY, TO SHRI SITA-RAMACHANDRA, MY MOST HUMBLE OBEISANCE! I BOW IN REVERENCE TO THE MOST VENERABLE GURU SHRI SAINATH!

1. I shall now continue in the present chapter, the narration of the very same stories indicated at the end of the last chapter. Listen to them at your ease.
2. Thinking of one's spiritual progress, there is no greater and more difficult obstacle in one's path than excessive pride in one's own religious sect which obstructs it.
3. 'We are worshippers of the Formless. God with shape and form is the root cause of delusion. After all, saints and *sadhus* are humans. Why then, bow your head before them?
4. 'One should not prostrate before them, or offer them *dakshina*. One should never bow one's head before them, at all. For this is mockery of devotion.'
5. Many said many things about Shirdi, — some this, some that. But not all of them were trustworthy.
6. Some said that when you go there for *darshan*, Sai Baba asks for *dakshina*. But when a *sadhu* begins to pursue wealth, his saintliness is tainted.
7. 'Blind faith is not good. Only when I get personal experience shall I decide in my mind how I should act.

8. 'I will not give *dakshina* for I cannot appreciate the saintliness of one, who has in his mind a desire for wealth. He is not worthy of our respect.

9. 'However, I will go to Shirdi and meet him but will not worship his feet or offer him *dakshina*.'

10. Whoever set out with such a misconception, sticking consciously to his resolve, surrendered to Sai in the end, on taking his *darshan*.

11. Everyone, once he set his eyes on Sai, stood his ground firmly and never once turned back again. He was totally engrossed at Sai's feet.

12. Like one who surrenders in utter penitence, he bowed at Sai's feet, forgetting his resolve altogether.

13. Now, listen respectfully, O listeners, to this chapter, in which false pride in the sect is laid to rest. It brings great happiness to the listeners.

14. Similarly, listen to Bala Nevaskar's experience as to how he treated a cobra with loving respect, regarding him as Sai himself and which also indirectly reiterates the great power of the *udi*.

15. Be gracious to me, O listeners, for I am but a slave to Sai's command and know only to obey the command respectfully. It is from this that the letters and words of this Life Story have taken shape.

16. Concentrating on his feet, I have been busy filling again and again, the ripples of poetry that arise from them, into this pitcher of his Life Story.

17. We are as the little ones of a tortoise, nourished and nurtured on the mother's loving glances only. We are never hungry or thirsty or exhausted but are always satiated.

18. When assured of the comfort and happiness of those glances alone, we need no food or water, for the glances take away all our hunger and thirst. O how then can one praise them enough!

19. Even for us, Sai, the Ocean of Kindness, is the sole object of vision. Here, the object of vision, one who perceives and the act of perceiving — this *triputi* (the aggregate of agent, object and action) vanishes altogether.

20. We similarly see the Light of Sai in both, the skin and the touch. Or, in the nose and the smell too, there is Sai's Presence,

21. Or, as the words fall on the ears, again, Sai's figure appears at once. So that the *triputi*, i.e. the object of hearing, one who hears and the process of hearing — drops off, instantly.

22. Or, when the tongue lingers relishing the taste, Sai becomes one with it. So where is the great wonder of the poor *triputi* — the tongue that savours, the object of the taste and the act of tasting?

23. And it is the same with all the organs of action. If they all render homage only to Sai, then all the *karma* will be destroyed and freedom from the effects of *karma* will be obtained.

24. However, the book is gaining in length and has digressed a good deal, all out of Sai's love! So let us now turn to the earlier context and pick up the threads of our story from there.

25. A non-believer in idol-worship, who was a staunch worshipper of the Formless, once became very eager to go to Shirdi, purely out of inquisitiveness.

26. So he said, 'We will come to Shirdi only to have the *sadhu's darshan*, but will not bow our head before him or give him *dakshina*.

27. 'If these two conditions are accepted, only then shall we come to Shirdi.' When his friend agreed, he set out to go with his friend, with an easy mind.

28. Kaka Mahajani, who cherished a pure love and devotion towards the saint, was his friend. But this gentleman was riddled with doubts and misconceptions.

29. Both of them left Bombay on a Saturday night, arriving in Shirdi on Sunday morning.

30. Both went at once to the mosque to have Sai's *darshan*. Now listen quietly to what happened at that time.

31. Even as Kaka put his foot on the step to come up, seeing his friend in the distance, Baba said in a sweet tone, "Why have you come, please?"

32. Hearing these loving words, the friend at once recognized the mark. The peculiar construction of the sentence, the

manner of pronouncing the words, instantly reminded him of his father.

33. The tone in which Baba pronounced the words, "Why have you come, please?" astonished Kaka's friend greatly.

34. That sweet tone brought to his mind, his late father. The tone, the manner was just like his father's. The imitation, he felt, was exact and perfect.

35. Oh, what charm the style of speech had! Kaka's friend was full of astonishment and said, 'These are indeed, the words of my father! So familiar is the tone!'

36. And as he heard the words as from his father's mouth, the friend's heart was touched. At once he placed his head on Baba's feet, quite oblivious of his earlier resolve.

37. Later on, Baba asked for *dakshina*, but that, only from Kaka, who gave it happily. Both then came back and went to the mosque again, in the afternoon.

38. The friend, of course, was with him, too. They were both to return to Bombay. Kaka asked permission to leave and Baba again asked him for *dakshina*.

39. And that too he only asked from Kaka, saying "Give me seventeen rupees." Of his friend, he asked nothing. In his heart, the friend felt regret and uneasiness.

40. Softly, he said to Kaka, 'Why does he ask only you for *dakshina*? In the morning he asked you for it and even now, he asked only you.

41. 'When I am with you, why does he leave me out for *dakshina*?' Kaka whispered in reply, 'Ask the question to Baba himself!'

42. Suddenly, Baba asked Kaka, "What, what is he saying to you?" The friend then, himself asked Baba, 'Can I give you *dakshina*?'

43. Baba said, "You did not wish to give, so I did not ask you. Now if you wish to give, then give it."

44. When Baba asked and the devotees gave *dakshina*, that friend used to find fault with them. But when he himself asked whether he could give and that too, without being asked, Kaka was full of amazement.

45. As Baba said 'Give if you wish,' the friend could hardly wait and at once offered seventeen rupees at his feet, without being asked.

46. Baba then said to him, "Where is the hurry to go? Wait, sit for a moment." He then gave him advice in sweet words, to dispel his feeling of separateness.

47. "Pull down that wall of the '*teli*'[1], the wall of separateness between you and me. The way will then be wide open for us to meet each other."

48. He then gave permission to go. But seeing the overcast sky, Madhavrao said to Baba that they will be drenched in the rain on the way.

49. Baba replied, "Let them go at ease. They have nothing to fear whatsoever from the rain on the way."

50. So they both bowed at Sai's feet and went and sat in the tonga. Lightning flashed in the sky, the air filled with thick fog, waters of Godavari swelled.

51. The sky resounded with thunder. And they had to ferry across the river. But in Kaka's heart, there was full trust in Baba's assurance.

52. The friend however, was worried, as to how the journey would be safe and comfortable. Considering the trouble they might face on the way, he regretted having come at all.

53. However, they crossed the river in comfort and boarded the train. Only then did the rain begin to pour from the clouds. They reached Bombay safely.

54. When he (the friend) reached home and opened the doors and windows, a sparrow who was confined within, swiftly flew out, while two others lay dead inside.

55. Seeing the sight, he felt very sad that they, poor creatures, had lost their lives without food and water.

56. Had the ventilators been left open before going away to Shirdi, death would not have seized them thus. The poor, hapless creatures have died at my hands.

57. He felt that Baba must have been anxious about the one that flew away and therefore he willingly gave permission to return today.

58. Or else, even she would have died. How could she have survived without food? When life-span is over, this is what happens! At least this one sparrow was saved.

59. There is another experience of his, which is also very interesting and worth listening to. For many months he had been suffering from pain in one heel.

60. Before going to Shirdi, he had endured this pain for many months. But after returning from there, it ceased to cause him any discomfort and in a short while, disappeared altogether.

61. In another similar incident, trying to test the saint's power ended up only in his bowing his head at the saint's feet, much against his own wish. Listen to this story, now!

62. And also, listen to how he was tempted to and did offer *dakshina*, not only against his will, but also in violation of his firm resolve.

63. Dharamsi Jethabhai Thakkar, a solicitor from Bombay, felt a keen desire to meet Sai, purely as a result of his accumulated merit of past births.

64. He was the employer of Kaka Mahajani and both were closely associated with each other. So he felt that he should go straight to Shirdi and meet him in person.

65. Kaka was employed as the managing clerk in Thakkarji's firm and used to avail of all the holidays to go to Shirdi, all the time repeatedly.

66. And once gone, would Kaka ever return on the scheduled time? He would spend eight days on end in Shirdi and would plead that Sai did not give him permission to return. 'Is this any system of working?' the employer thought indignantly.

67. 'And what is this way of these saints! I do not approve of all this fuss about nothing!' So the *Shet* (employer) set out for Shirdi in the '*Shimaga*' (i.e. Holi) holidays to settle this issue about Sai, once and for all.

68. Full of conceit in himself and in the greatness of his wealth, he felt that these saints are, after all, just like other human beings. Why then lower your head before them?

69. Where the great learned *Shastris* and *Pandits* had been brought on their knees before the spiritual and moral authority of Sai, how long was poor Dharamsi's resolve going to last?

70. But then, 'Blind faith is not good', he thought. 'So let me make sure for myself.' Resolving thus in his mind, he made preparations to go to Shirdi.

71. So, like the case of the friend described above, Dharamsi also set out for Shirdi, taking Kaka with him, and said to him,

72. 'You go to Shirdi and always stay on, but it will not do this time. You will have to return with me, know this for sure!'

73. So Kaka said, 'See, this is not in my hands!' Dharamsi then took yet another companion with him.

74. Who knows, in case Kaka just does not come back, it would not do to be without a companion on the way. So he took along a third person and the three of them thus set out for Shirdi.

75. There are types and types of such benevolent devotees, catching hold of whom Baba brings them to himself, to clear them of their doubts and misgivings.

76. And when they return they relate their experience to others or get them written down by someone, just to bring people to the path of righteousness.

77. In short, those who thus went, were satiated with the joy of his *darshan*. And whatever might have been their inclination in the beginning, they experienced Bliss in the end.

78. One might well say that they went of their own accord out of curiosity and inquisitiveness. But the truth was otherwise — they really went only to fulfil Baba's purpose.

79. And it was Baba who gave them that inspiration. Only then could they step out of the house. Thus by activating their natural inclinations, he led them to the spiritual path.

80. Who can understand Baba's plan? For if one tries to comprehend his ways, it will only end in distress. But if you surrender the ego, and roll at his feet in humility, you will come to enjoy great happiness.

81. It is not proper to go empty-handed to the door of God, your Guru or a Brahmin. Therefore, on the way, Kaka bought two seers (i.e. about one kilogram) of grapes.

82. There is a seedless variety of grapes. But only the grapes with seeds were available at the time. So Kaka bought the same.

83. Talking, laughing happily on the way, the threesome reached Shirdi and together, they all went to Baba in the mosque for *darshan*.

84. Another devotee Babasaheb Tarkhad, was also sitting there. Listen to what Shet Dharamsi asked him out of curiosity.

85. 'What do you find here that makes you come over and over again?' 'We come for *darshan*', replied Tarkhad. So the Shet said, 'But I have heard that miracles take place here?'

86. So Tarkhad said, 'This is not my feeling. Whatever may be the keen desire in one's mind, that desire is fulfilled.'

87. Kaka bowed his head on Baba's feet and offered the grapes in his hands. People had already collected and Baba began distributing the grapes to the devotees.

88. Along with others, Baba gave some to Dharamsi, too. But this was the variety he did not like; he liked only the seedless one.

89. He had a distaste for these grapes. A difficulty arose right at the beginning. How to eat them was his problem. Nor could he bring himself to refuse.

90. Moreover, his doctor had forbidden him to eat grapes without first washing them and it would not be proper to wash them oneself. Numerous doubts assailed his mind.

91. But then, come what may, he just popped them in his mouth, carefully putting away the seeds in his pocket. He would not defile the sanctity of a *sadhu's* place by throwing the seeds of chewed grapes.

92. But the Shet said to himself, 'He is a *sadhu* and yet how does he not know that I do not like these grapes? Why does he give them to me compulsively?'

93. Even as this thought crossed his mind, Baba gave him some more. Knowing that they were with seeds, he kept them in his hand instead of putting them in the mouth.

94. True, he did not like the grapes with seeds, but they were given in his hand by Baba. Dharamsi Shet felt most embarrassed and did not know what to do.

95. He did not feel like putting them in the mouth. So he quietly preserved them in his fist. But suddenly Baba said, "O, do eat them up!" Shetji promptly obeyed.

96. Even as Baba said, "Eat them up" and Dharamsi put them in the mouth, they turned out to be all seedless! He was greatly astonished.

97. When he found the grapes to be seedless, Dharamsi was simply amazed and said to himself, 'Truly marvellous is his power! What is impossible for these saints?

98. 'Knowing the wish in my heart, though the grapes were with seeds and unwashed, those that Sai gave me were seedless and beneficial.'

99. He was wonder-struck, quite oblivious of his earlier curiosity and inquisitiveness. His ego was overcome and there arose great love for the saint in his heart.

100. The initial resolve vanished and love for Sai overpowered his heart, justifying all his eagerness and firm resolution to visit Shirdi.

101. Baba Tarkhad was there too, sitting with Sai Baba and had also been given some of the grapes.

102. So Dharamsi asked him, 'How were your grapes?' When Tarkhad replied, 'With seeds', he was quite astonished.

103. But it confirmed his belief that Baba was a *sadhu*. An idea struck his mind to get a further confirmation. 'If you are a real *sadhu*', he said to himself, 'then it will be Kaka's turn next to receive the grapes'.

104. Baba was distributing the grapes to many others. But no sooner had this thought come into Shet's mind than Baba began his next round with Kaka himself. Sheti's wonder grew.

105. These signs of his being a *sadhu*, this power to read another's thoughts was enough for Dharamsi's mind to regard Baba as a *sadhu*.

106. Madhavrao was also present there. As if to explain, he then said to Baba, 'That Shet of Kaka's, you know — this, this is he!'

107. "Who, this? Oh, how can he be Kaka's master? His master is another!" Baba replied at once. Kaka's heart was filled with joy on hearing these words.

108. But the marvel of it all was, that Baba put it on a cook called Appa, who stood just there, near the *dhuni*.

109. He said, "This Shet has come all the way, but he has not taken this trouble for me. He came to Shirdi because he felt a great love for Appa!"

110. Such was the dialogue! Forgetting all about his resolve, Dharamsi, of his own will, prostrated at Baba's feet. Afterwards they both returned to the *wada*.

111. *Arati* took place at noon and they began preparing for the journey home. Time came for obtaining Baba's permission. So they proceeded to the mosque.

112. Dharamsi then said to Kaka, 'I am not going to ask for permission. It is you who need it, so you only should ask for it.' So Madhavrao said,

113. 'There is no saying about Kaka's return. Unless a full week passes by, he may not be permitted to go. It is better that you ask yourself for it!'

114. So when the three of them went to the mosque and sat down, on their behalf Madhavrao asked for permission. But Baba began to tell a story. Listen to it, attentively.

115. "There was once a fickle-minded man, whose house was full of wealth, food grains, etc " Physically, mentally, he had no illness, no afflictions. But he liked to court trouble.

116. "Needlessly, he wandered about, carrying a heavy burden on his head. His mind knew no peace. One moment he would put down the load, only to pick it up the next moment. He could not steady his mind.

117. "Seeing his plight, my heart was moved by compassion and I said to him, 'Steady your mind and fix it on one thing — whatever that may be!'

118. "You wander needlessly. Steadily fix your mind in one place." The words stung Dharamsi to the quick. He thought that it was a warning to himself.

119. With all the prosperity, an abundance of wealth, Dharamsi was, for ever, worried without the slightest reason, causing unnecessary trouble to his own self.

120. Wealth, honour, he enjoyed aplenty but there was no contentment in his mind. He was always engrossed in imagined sorrows and sufferings.

121. When he heard this story coming from Sai's mouth, his surprise was great. This is just the condition of my mind, he thought and with great respect, he listened to it.

122. That Kaka should get permission so quickly, was an impossible thing. But when even that was obtained so effortlessly, Dharamsi was naturally, most pleased.

123. He had wished very much that Kaka should return with him and Baba granted even that wish by giving them consent to go.

124. This was also Shetji's wager. But how did Baba know the mark? This was a most remarkable indication of his being a *sadhu*, which Dharamsi now accepted whole-heartedly.

125. All doubts were resolved. It was clear that Sai was a *sadhu*. As was the feeling in his heart, so was the experience that Baba had given him.

126. Whichever path one wants to follow, he will guide him along that same path. Sai knows the capacity of each and accordingly, they are given spiritual guidance by him.

127. A devotee may be trusting or censorious. But Sai is kind to both, equally. This Compassionate Mother will not neglect one and embrace the other.

128. So as they were ready to leave, Baba asked Kaka for fifteen rupees as *dakshina* and said to him,

129. "He who has given me one rupee as *dakshina*, him will I have to give ten times more in return.

130. "Will I ever take anything free from anyone? I do not ask each and everyone for *dakshina*. The question of *dakshina* comes only for him to whom the Fakir points a finger.

131. "And this Fakir too, will ask only of him to whom he is indebted. When such a giver gives he is only sowing the seeds of which he will reap the harvest later.

132. "Wealth is beneficial to the wealthy only in so far as it is spent on *dharma* and in charity. For, ethical conduct and charity alone make for true knowledge.

133. "But people needlessly treat their hard-earned wealth as being meant for the pleasures they desire and thus neglect to use it for *dharma* and charitable deeds.

134. "But happy is the man, who never spends his tens of crores of rupees, collected so carefully, penny by penny, just for his fondness for sensual pleasures."

135. Everybody knows the Vedic aphorism that 'You never get unless you give'. What was given on an earlier occasion stands clearly before Baba, and therefore he asks for *dakshina*.

136. In his incarnation as Ram, Ramchandra gave away innumerable images of women in gold, and its fruit was enjoyed by Shri Krishna sixteen thousand times, when he incarnated as Krishna.

137. A devotee, totally devoid of devotion, knowledge and renunciation is indeed in a poor, piteous state. He is first fixed in renunciation, and then given knowledge and devotion.

138. His making people offer *dakshina* is really a mark of this renunciation. Later, they are guided to the path of devotion and made proficient in knowledge.

139.　"And what else do we do, but give tenfold of what we receive and gradually lead them to the path of Knowledge?" As he heard this, Dharamsi became greedy.

140.　Of his own will, he placed fifteen rupees in Baba's hand. He forgot his earlier resolve. It was all most strange!

141.　'In vain was my earlier boasting', he felt. 'It is as well that I came personally. I have learnt for myself what *sadhus* are like and have become fond of them through my own experience.

142.　'And so, without proper consideration, I had decided not to come just for making obeisance. In the end, I did that too, and all on my own! Truly, *leelas* of these *sadhus* are incomprehensible!

143.　'And what can be impossible for him, on whose lips is "*Allah Malik*" all the time? But I was eager to see for myself only the miracles that the *sadhus* perform.

144.　'Oh, how vain has been my resolve! I have actually prostrated before a human being and offered him *dakshina* without his asking for it.

145.　'In vain has been my boasting! Of my own will, I lowered my head at Sai's feet in reverence. What greater marvel can there be?

146.　'Oh, how can I describe Sai's skill adequately? Although it is he who is doing all this, outwardly he displays total detachment. Can there be a greater wonder than this?

147.　'You may, or may not salute him; may give or not give any *dakshina*. But this Spring of Joy, this All-Merciful Sai, never scorns anyone.

148.　'For him, there is no joy at being worshipped, regret or pain at being derided. And here where there is no joy, how can there be dejection? This is that very same state that completely transcends the pairs of opposites.'

149.　Whatever might be his intention, once Sai gave *darshan* to anyone, he would win over his love and devotion. Such was Sai's most wonderful *leela*!

150.　And so, after receiving from Sai *udi-prasad* with his blessings, they returned to Bombay, their minds cleared of all doubts. Such was Sai's inconceivable power that,

151.   Before departing from Shirdi, Baba's permission had to be taken and if his command was disregarded, it was an invitation to trouble.

152.   If you returned from there of your own accord, formidable obstacles came on the way which were difficult to overcome, resulting in regret and disgrace.

153.   Such, as is described above, was the position with regard to returning from Shirdi. And so was our condition, too. "Nobody will come if I do not bring him". These were Baba's words.

154.   "Unless I wish it, who can step over his threshold? Who can come to Shirdi of his own will and take *darshan*?"

155.   All our movements are in the power of Sai Samarth, who is Mercy Incarnate. When his heart is moved by compassion, only then can one come for his *darshan*.

156.   This was the condition for coming or going to Shirdi. If Sai's heart was not pleased, no permission would be granted to anyone to go, with his *udi-prasad*.

157.   When one prostrated before him in obeisance and asked permission, his giving the *udi-prasad* with blessings was in itself the permission to go.

158.   Now I shall relate a novel experience about the power of this *udi* and then proceed with the story of the power of Nevaskar's devotion and the favour he received from Sai, the most Excellent One.

159.   A gentleman from Bandra, by caste a C.K.P., was not able to sleep peacefully at night, in spite of all efforts.

160.   The moment he closed his eyes and fell asleep, suddenly his deceased father would appear in his dream and wake him up, every day.

161.   With curses and abuses, he would enumerate the good and bad things of the past, the secret, complex, detestable thoughts and fire at him a volley of stinging, abusive words.

162.   This happened day after day and every night his sleep was ruined. He could not understand it. Nor could he avoid the suffering thus inflicted on him.

163.   The man was tormented on account of this, but could think of no way out. So he asked a Sai devotee what remedy he should try.

164.   'I, for one, know of no other remedy but Sai Maharaj, the Abode of all Excellence. And if you will also keep full faith, his *udi* will manifest its own power.'

165.   Whatever he was told, he followed it precisely. And his experience too, was the same. He never had that nightmare again.

166.   By a wonderful concurrence of Destiny and his good *karma*, his friend happened to be a devotee of Sai Samarth, who praised the remarkable power of the *udi*, offering him a little, at the same time.

167.   And he told him, 'Apply a little to your forehead before going to sleep and keep the rest in a packet near the pillow, remembering Shri Sai in your mind.

168.   'Have faith and devotion in your heart and then see the marvel of this *udi*. It will instantly remove your trouble, for that is its natural property.'

169.   When he followed the instructions, he enjoyed a profound sleep that night, wiping away all traces of that bad dream, to the great joy of that gentleman.

170.   Who can describe that joy! He always kept the packet carefully near his pillow and remembered Sai, constantly.

171.   Later, he brought Baba's photograph and offered it a garland on the Thursday. Placing the photograph on the wall at the head of the bed, he respectfully performed its *pooja*.

172.   He now began taking *darshan* of the photograph and offering it a garland, every Thursday, as he offered *pooja*, mentally. Gradually, all his suffering came to an end.

173.   He kept up the practice faithfully and enjoyed a lasting peace and happiness. He forgot altogether his earlier suffering — the disturbed sleep, the nightmares, etc.

174.   This, however, is just one of the benefits of the *udi*. I shall now narrate another, more marvellous benefit, as to how it fulfils the desired objective when used in the moment of great calamity.

175. There was once a staunch devotee, named Balaji Patil Nevaskar, who had worn out his body in the most extraordinary service to Baba.

176. It was Nevaskar's daily work to sweep the roads of approach to and exit from the village and the road that led to Lendi on which Baba trod.

177. After him, it was Radhakrishnabai's remarkable ability that came useful in continuing the same system of work.

178. The foolish idea never even touched her pure heart as to how to do this mean work when she was born in the revered Brahmin *Varna*.

179. On getting up early in the morning, broom in hand, she would herself sweep all the roads that Baba trod on. Truly blessed was her service!

180. So clean, so quick was her work! Who else could compare with her, in it? After some time, Abdul came forward to take it over.

181. And so, such was that very fortunate Patil, who, though in the worldly life was yet totally detached from it. Listen to that part of his story which describes his great spirit of sacrifice.

182. After the reaping of the harvest from the field was over, he would bring all the grain to the mosque, pile it up in a heap in the courtyard and offer it at Baba's feet.

183. Looking up to Baba as the Master of all that he possessed, he would take home from it only as much as Baba was pleased to give him for the subsistence of himself and his family.

184. The used water that flowed out from the washing place after Baba's bath, and his washing his hands, feet, mouth, etc., was all the water that Bala drank.

185. The practice continued without a break while Nevaskar was alive and his son has carried it forward up till now, though only in part.

186. He too, would always send grain and till his *Nirvana*, Baba used to eat *jowar* bread made out of it, four times a day.

187. Once it so happened that it was Bala's annual 'Shraddha'[2]. Food was cooked and ready and the servers began serving it.

188. According to the estimated number of guests, enough food had been cooked. But as the food was being served, it was noticed that the actual numbers of diners had increased threefold.

189. The hostess grew nervous and began whispering her anxiety to the mother-in-law, 'How can we be saved from this embarrassing situation?'

190. But the mother-in-law had unwavering faith that 'when Sai Samarth stands behind us firmly, why should we worry? Rest assured', she said.

191. Assured thus, the mother-in-law picked up a handful of *udi* and sprinkled a little in each vessel of food, covering it carefully, afterwards.

192. She then said, 'Go and serve without any fear. But remove the covering just enough for the purpose of serving and cover up the vessel, again. This one thing, you must observe without fail.

193. 'This food belongs to Sai, not a particle of it is ours. And he alone will come to our rescue; any shortcomings will be his, not ours!'

194. As the resolve of that mother-in-law, so was her experience, also. Without any obstacle, each and every guest was fed well.

195. All ate and were satisfied. Everything passed off properly and still, the vessels were as full as they had been before.

196. Such is the power of the *udi*. To the saints, all this is easy and natural. As the faith, so is the experience.

197. However, talking about the greatness of the *udi* and the deep devotion of Nevaskar, I am reminded of yet another story about him. Listen to it.

198. I have had a little doubt whether this will be a digression from the main narrative. But now I think, whatever it may be, I must present it to the readers, in the present context.

199. And having made this resolve in my mind, I shall proceed to narrate it to you at this juncture. May the listeners pardon me, if they think it misplaced.

200. Once a resident of Shirdi, Raghu Patil by name, had gone to Nevasa and was staying at his (Bala's) house as his guest.

201. One night, while the cattle were all tied by the rope to the stake, suddenly a cobra entered the cattle-shed making a hissing sound.

202. Caught up in such a perilous situation, everybody was stunned, while the cobra stationed himself there, raising his hood.

203. The cattle moved restlessly, struggling to free themselves. But Nevaskar was convinced that it was Sai himself who had appeared.

204. There was no other way but to let loose the cattle, lest someone stepped unwittingly on the cobra and brought on a disaster.

205. Nevaskar was overjoyed as he saw the cobra from some distance. Hair stood on end all over his body with deep emotion. At once, he prostrated before him in obeisance.

206. 'It is Sai's great favour', he said, 'that he has come to meet us in the form of this cobra.' He brought a '*vati*'[3] filled with milk for the cobra.

207. Truly, what faith and devotion Balaji must have had not to have even a trace of fear. And just listen attentively to what he said to that cobra!

208. 'Baba, why do you make that angry hissing sound? Are you trying to frighten us? Take, take this '*vati*' of milk and drink it at your ease.'

209. But how can a cobra be ever satisfied with just a *vati* of milk? So he brought a vessel-ful of milk and placed it fearlessly, before him. Really, fear is created only by one's mind!

210. Placing the milk near him, Balaji went and sat down at his earlier seat, - neither too far nor too near. His face showed a fond admiration for the cobra.

211. The entrance of the cobra was truly terrifying! And yet, how can everyone's response to the situation be the same? They were all worried and bewildered as to how the calamity could be averted.

212. 'If we go out, there is the fear that the cobra will enter the inner room, from where his coming out will be difficult.' So they sat patiently, keeping a close watch.

213. The cobra here, was satiated and slipped out eluding everybody's notice, no one knew where! All were quite astonished.

214. Then they searched the entire cattle-shed but could not find any trace of him. Most of them were quite relieved. Only Nevaskar had regrets in his heart.

215. The regret was that he did not see him departing as he had seen him entering the cattle-shed, earlier.

216. Bala had two wives and his children were still very young. Sometimes they all came from Nevasa to Shirdi for Baba's *darshan*.

217. For both his wives, Baba used to buy *saris* along with blouse pieces and used to bless them. Such was that great devotee, Balaji.

218. The path of this '*Satcharit*' is simple and straight forward. Wherever it is being read, there is *Dwarakamayee* there, too! And Sai too is present most certainly.

219. And so are there the banks of the Godavari and there, nearby is the holy Shirdi. There, at that very place, is Sai with his *dhuni*, to ward off calamities at the mere remembrance of his name.

220. Where Sai's Life Story is being read, there Sai is present, always. And when it is read with faith, again and again, he is pleased.

221. When Sai, the Abode of Bliss, is remembered, when his name is chanted every day, no other chanting or penance, no arduous effort for meditation and contemplation is needed.

222. Those who smear his *vibhuti* and drink it every day with faith and devotion, will have all the desires of their heart fulfilled.

223. They will attain the four highest goals of human life, like *dharma*, etc., and will find fulfilment. The profound secret significance of both the worldly and spiritual life will be revealed to them.

224. Terrible sins like the '*mahapapas*'[4], as also, all the lesser sins will be destroyed by contact with the *udi* and there will be purification, inwardly and outwardly.

225. The devotees know too well, the great power of the *udi*, when applied. But it is for the benefit of the listeners that the description has been given at length.

226. And yet, it is improper to say that the description is given at length. For I myself, do not know it adequately. But still, I have only briefly narrated it for my listeners' benefit.

227. Hence, I pray to the listeners that after bowing to Sai, they should experience it for themselves. Do listen to my words, this once!

228. Reasoning and arguments are of no avail, here. Only deep reverence is needed. Ingenuity of mind does not help, either. But devotion and faith are required.

229. Those who are intellectual, argumentative, inquisitive but without faith, will never receive the highest knowledge from the saints. It will be received only by him who has a pure faith.

230. Considering the deficiencies in the story to be a part of that inspiration that Sai gave me, overlook these defects as you read this '*Sai Satcharit*'.

231. May this establish Sai's loving, ever-compassionate Image in the hearts of the appreciative readers, as a constant reminder of him to them.

232. Where Gomantak (Goa) and where Shirdi! The fascinating delightful story of a theft there, which Sai narrated quite openly and in detail, will be narrated next.

233. Hence Hemad bows his head at Sai's feet, whole-heartedly and very humbly entreats the listeners to listen to it, respectfully.

Weal be to all! Here ends the thirty-fifth chapter of
"*Shri Sai Samarth Satcharit*", called
'*The Removal of Doubts and Glorification of the Udi*',
as inspired by the saints and the virtuous
and composed by his devotee, Hemadpant.

Notes

1. '*Teli*' is the oilman. Baba often used the words '*teli*' and '*vani*' (grocer) as symbolic of undesirable tendencies. Oil is sticky and soft and is considered to be a symbol of the love of worldly life.

2. A funeral ceremony observed at various fixed periods, consisting of offerings with water and fire to the gods and food to the relatives.

3. A metal bowl.

4. Refer Ch. 3, note 7.

36

Sai's All-Pervasiveness and the fulfilment of His Blessings

MY OBEISANCE TO SHRI GANESH, TO SHRI SARASWATI, AND SHRI GURUMAHARAJ! TO THE FAMILY DEITY, TO SHRI SITA-RAMACHANDRA, MY MOST HUMBLE OBEISANCE! I BOW IN REVERENCE TO THE MOST VENERABLE GURU SHRI SAINATH!

1. To pick up the threads from the previous chapter, a narration of the fascinating tale of a theft will now follow, which I had promised. Listen to it attentively.

2. This is not just a story, but the water of Self-joy which, on drinking, will only increase your thirst for more, to quench which, another story will then be related.

3. So absorbing is this story that the listeners will be delighted, listening to it. It will remove the exhaustion, the sorrows of worldly life and will bring a state of happiness and peace.

4. The fortunate man who really wishes to attain his own good, should always listen respectfully to the narration of Sai's stories.

5. So boundless is the power of saints that no one can truly describe it. What then, of my meagre capacity? And of this, I am fully aware.

6. But even the little ego of the narrator is enough for Sai, who, in his ingenuity, uses anyone to describe his excellent qualities for the benefit of his devotees.

7. He is indeed, that Swan, swimming in the lake that is God; who is not merely absorbed in the state of 'Soham'[1], but is eager to feed on the pearls, that is Brahma, and is very daring;

8. Who, though without a name or place, enjoys unlimited glory and with the power of his one glance can transform a pauper into a wealthy man.

9. He is that *Brahmajnana* Incarnate, who, himself having experienced it, brings people a perception of God in a Vision and brings about various incidents, himself remaining completely out of everything.

10. He plans innumerable marvellous events, and appears in different guises to those on whom he bestows his grace. Listen to his prowess.

11. Those who try to comprehend him by meditating upon him, or sing his praises, are looked after by him completely, all their wants thus removed.

12. He is fond of his own stories. Hence making an excuse of the listeners and the narrator, he fulfils the wishes of his devotees, by reminding me all the time.

13. He who has renounced the worldly life, is constantly and with all his mind and heart engaged in the highest end of man, *viz.* enjoyment of the Divine nature, and has won over Him, who holds the Disc in his hand (i.e. Shri Vishnu), — he has uplifted innumerable creatures.

14. He who is worshipped in and outside of this country, and the banner of whose devotion flies high, he calls to himself the meek and the poor, fulfilling the wishes of all.

15. But now, listen respectfully to this most sacred *Saicharitra*. May the ears of the listeners and the mouth of the speaker be purified.

16. Once two gentlemen from Gomantaka (Goa), came for Sai's *darshan*, and, delighted by the *darshan*, both were engrossed at his feet.

17. Though they both came together, Sai asked only one of them for *dakshina*, saying, "Give me fifteen rupees", which he gave most happily.

18. Though he did not ask the other for anything, he, on his own, offered rupees thirty-five, which Sai promptly refused, to his great astonishment.

19. On that occasion, Madhavrao was present, too, and seeing such differentiation, just listen to what he asked Sai.

20. 'Baba how can you do such a thing? When two friends have come together, you ask for *dakshina* from one and when the other offers you on his own, you return it!

21. 'How can the saints differentiate thus? Of your own will, you ask one for *dakshina*, and return it when somebody gives you voluntarily, much to his disappointment.

22. 'You like to accept the smaller amount, but show detachment towards the larger one. Had I been in your position, I would not have behaved in this way!'

23. "Shamya, you do not understand! I, for one, never take anything from anyone. It is the Presiding Goddesss of this *Mashidmayee* (mosque), who asks for her dues, by paying which the giver is freed of his debt.

24. "Do I have a house or a family that I should require this wealth? I am, in every way, free from all care.

25. "But debt, enmity and murder are such that the doer can never escape them. You make vows before goddesses when in need, but I have to take the trouble to free you from them.

26. "You have not a care in the world about it, afterwards, though at the time of need you beseech abjectly. Truly, I am always pleased with him among my devotees who has no debt to repay!

27. "Initially, this man was poor. He took a vow that if he earned fifteen rupees, he would offer his first salary to God. But later, he forgot all about it.

28. "Fifteen rupees became thirty, thirty became sixty and sixty, hundred. As his salary doubled and increased four times, his forgetfulness also increased.

29. In the course of time he began earning Rs.700/-, when, by a wonderful concurrence (the union of destiny and one's good work),

he has come here, today. And so I asked from him my fifteen rupees under the pretext of *dakshina*."

30. "Now listen to the second story. Once, as I was wandering along the sea-coast, I came across a huge mansion. So I sat down on its veranda.

31. "The master of that mansion was a wealthy Brahmin of eminent descent. He welcomed me cordially, offering me food and drink in plenty.

32. "Thereafter, in that same place, near an in-built cupboard in the wall, he gave me a clean comfortable place to sleep. And I fell asleep.

33. "Seeing that I was fast asleep, he broke open the wall by sliding a stone-slab. And without my knowledge, he cut my pocket depriving me totally of everything.

34. "On waking up, when I realized this, I suddenly burst into tears. For I had lost thirty thousand rupees. My mind was extremely agitated and filled with regrets.

35. "The money was all in bank notes. At the shock of this sudden loss, my heart received a jolt. The Brahmin, on the other hand, began to console me.

36. "I could not relish food or water. For fifteen days, I sat dazed on the veranda, in that same place, in the most pitiable condition.

37. "At the close of the fifteenth day, a fakir, wandering on the road, pronouncing spiritual conundrums aloud, suddenly came there and saw me weeping.

38. "He asked me the reason for my sorrows. I told him everything in detail. He said, 'If you will do as I tell you, all your troubles will end.

39. "I will tell you about a fakir, his place of habitation, etc. You surrender to him whole-heartedly and he will give you back your wealth.

40. "But until you get what you want, you must follow one discipline that I prescribe — give up an item of food that you are very fond of. By doing so, you will accomplish your objective.'

41. "By following his instructions, I met the fakir and I got back my money. I then left that mansion and went along the sea-coast, as before.

42. "Walking along in this manner, eventually I found a boat, but I could not gain entry on it. Suddenly a good-natured *sepoy* found me a place on the boat.

43. "The wind being favourable, the boat reached the other shore in time. I then, sat in a *tonga* and came home, and these eyes saw this *Mashidmayee*."

44. Baba's story ended here. Shama was then commanded to take the guests home and to feed them.

45. Food was served and as they sat down to the meal, Madhavrao's curiosity was aroused. He asked the guests, 'Were you quite convinced of the story Baba related?

46. 'If you consider the facts, Sai Baba has settled down here. He has not known ever, the sea, the boat or the *sepoy*.

47. 'Oh, what Brahmin and what mansion! All his life has been spent at the foot of a tree. From whence came all this wealth that the thief robbed?

48. 'Therefore, this must have been an incident related to you, that took place in the past, which he narrated and he began it as soon as you came, so that you may recognize it.'

49. Choked with emotion, the guests said, 'Sai is all-knowing God Incarnate, who is free from the pairs of duality, is One with God, Indivisible and all-pervasive.

50. 'The story he narrated just now, is our very own story, letter for letter. Come, as soon as this feast is over, we shall tell you everything in detail.

51. 'Whatever Baba said, had all taken place. But how did he know all this, when he does not even know us? Hence all this was very, very strange!'

52. The meal over, while chewing *paan* with Madhavrao, the narration began.

53. One of them said, 'My original place is the *Ghats* (i.e. the mountainous region of the Sahyadris). But there must have been

some connection with the coast-line, as far as my livelihood was concerned.

54.   'And for this reason I went all the way to Gomantak in search of a job. Very respectfully, I had prayed and vowed to Lord Dattatreya for my purpose.

55.   'I had bowed at his feet and prayed, 'O God, a job is a necessity for me to support my family. Please be gracious and give me one.

56.   'If you will keep your promise within a short while from today, I shall offer to you all that I earn in the first month.

57.   'Fortunately, Lord Datta was pleased to grant my wish very shortly thereafter and I started earning fifteen rupees, in the beginning.

58.   'Soon I got promotions, exactly as Sai Baba had described. However, the memory of my vow was completely obliterated from my mind. Hence I was reminded of it in this way.

59.   'Someone may think that he had taken *dakshina* from me. It was not *dakshina* but only a payment of my debt. And under that pretext I was reminded of my very old vow.'

60.   In short Sai does not expect money, nor does he allow his devotees to beg for it. For he always looked upon money as a calamity and saved his devotees from its temptation.

61.   A devotee like Mhalsapati, who was for ever absorbed at his feet, eked out a livelihood with greatest difficulty. But Sai never permitted him to collect wealth, even in the slightest measure.

62.   Often, Sai himself, distributed to the people the money that came to him as *dakshina*. But never once did he give even a pice to Mhalsapati, who was financially in distress.

63.   And Mhalsapati too, was so self-respecting, that in spite of Sai's great generosity, he never spread his palm before Sai, in entreaty.

64.   His financial condition was so low, but his renunciation was of the highest order. Always satisfied with the little that he had, he bore the tribulations of poverty most valiantly.

65.   Once a kind-hearted merchant, Hansraj by name, felt like giving something to Mhalsapati.

66.   On seeing his abject poverty, a kind thought naturally rose in his mind to offer him any help that he could.

67. But though such was his condition, Sainath did not approve of anyone else offering him help, either. He only encouraged in his devotee a disinterest in wealth.

68. So what that merchant did was, in the presence of both Baba and Mhalsapati, he put some money in Mhalsapati's hands, out of compassion, when they were in Baba's '*durbar*'.

69. With great humility, Mhalsapati gave the money back, saying, 'Without Sai's permission I cannot accept it.'

70. Here was a selfless, loving devotee, who hankered not after money, but after spirituality, and who had surrendered his body and soul at Sai's feet.

71. So Hansraj entreated Sai for permission. But Sai would not allow him to touch even a pice and said, "Money will not tempt my devotee. He will never get caught in the splendour of wealth."

72. Now, that second guest began. 'Even I have recognized my mark. Listen and I shall tell you everything. Listening to it, you will derive much pleasure.

73. 'A Brahmin had been in my service for thirty-five years. He was diligent and completely trustworthy. Unfortunately, his good sense betrayed him and he took away my money.

74. 'In the wall of my house, there was an in-built cupboard. He lightly slid the stones and made a hole, without anyone knowing it.

75. 'He made a hole in that same cupboard that Baba mentioned. For that purpose he moved the stones of the wall when everybody was sleeping.

76. 'Then again, Baba mentioned 'My money was stolen', which is also absolutely true. A bundle of notes was robbed.

77. 'And its value was exactly thirty thousand. I do not know how Baba knew all this. But when my hard-earned money was thus gone, I sat weeping, day and night.

78. 'Searching fot it, my mind was totally exhausted, I just did not know what to do. For fifteen days, I sat, caught up in the whirlpool of worry and anxiety, from which I could not extricate myself.

79. 'One day, while I sat in the veranda, saddened at heart, a fakir came walking on the road, putting questions, aloud.

80. 'Seeing my sad face, he asked me the reason for my sadness. When I told him everything, he suggested a remedy for removing it.

81. 'In the Kopergaon taluka, at a village called Shirdi, lives Sai *Aulia*. To him you pray and make a vow.

82. 'You give up eating something that you are very fond of and say to him that, 'I give it up until I get your *darshan*'.

83. 'When the fakir told me this, I gave up food, without a moment's delay saying, 'Baba, when my stolen wealth is regained and I have your *darshan*, only then will I take food.'

84. 'After that, just a fortnight passed. God knows, what the Brahmin thought, but he came to me on his own and gave me back my money.

85. 'My intellect betrayed me', he said, 'and hence such a deed was committed. But now I place my head on your feet. Do say, 'I forgive you'.

86. 'All went well, thereafter. I felt a fond desire for Sai's *darshan* and that wish too, has been fulfilled today. Blessed, blessed is my good fortune!

87. 'But he who came to console me as I sat dejected and in distress in my veranda — him I have not met again!

88. 'He who had such a sincere heart-felt concern for me and told me about Sai, pointing his finger towards Shirdi — him I have not set eyes on, again.

89. 'He whom I met so unexpectedly, as he came pronouncing questions aloud, and who ultimately made me take a vow — him I have not seen, again.

90. 'Truly, Sai, this *aulia* of yours, seems to be that same fakir. He was himself eager to give us *darshan*.

91. 'For the fulfilment of their wishes, people wish for a saint's *darshan*. But I did not even wish for it. However, this fakir himself encouraged me at the outset to have it, so that I may get back my money.

92. 'And it is just not possible, that he, by vowing to whom I regained my wealth so effortlessly, is going to be tempted by my *dakshina* of thirty-five rupees.

93. 'On the contrary, to make us, the ignorant men, eager for spirituality in our own interest, he strives all the time to bring us to the right path under such a pretext.

94. 'Only for this purpose is this '*avatar*'. Or else, how would we, the lowly creatures, without any devotion, be able to get across the ocean of worldly life, safely? Just think of this calmly!

95. 'And so, after regaining the stolen wealth, I was so overjoyed that I consequently, forgot all about my vow. Hard is the temptation of wealth to resist!

96. 'Later on, once while I was at the Colaba side (present Raigad district of Maharashtra), I saw Sai in a dream and I set out to go to Shirdi, at once!

97. 'What Samarth described as his journey — the refusal of permission to enter the boat, and the averting of the difficulty by the *sepoy's* efforts — all that is true.

98. 'These were all my problems. When I reached the spot, where the boat stood, some *sepoy* really pleaded for me.

99. 'Only then did the officer of the boat, who had earlier turned down my request, oblige me by giving me a place.

100. 'That *sepoy* too, was a total stranger, yet he said that he knew me. Therefore no one stopped us and we sat in the boat, quite happily.

101. 'Such is the story of the boat and of the *sepoy*, which, though it had all happened to me, this Sai took it upon himself.

102. 'Thinking of this marvel, my mind is simply non-plussed and I realize that Sai fills this entire Universe.

103. 'Not even a tiny atom of space on this earth is without him. As he gave us the experience, so will he give others, too.

104. 'Who are we and from where have me come! But how great is our good fortune that he has instantly pulled us to himself and brought us to the right path, thereby.

105. 'Oh, that we should have taken a vow, that our wealth should have been stolen! And what a marvel of the manner of the

fulfilment of our vow, too! How effortlessly the wealth was re-gained!

106. 'How great, how inconceivable is our good fortune! Never did we have his *darshan* before, nor meditated on him or had even heard of him. And yet, he remembered us.

107. 'O, how blessed then must be those devotees of God, who had been engrossed in his company for years together and were serving him day and night!

108. 'Rare indeed, is the good fortune of all those with whom Sai sported and laughed and sat, talked and walked, ate, lay down or with whom he got angry!

109. 'Although no service was rendered to him at our hands, yet he was moved with such a deep compassion for us. Then how blessed is your good fortune, who are constantly in his company.

110. 'With all your good, meritorious deeds, you have, I feel, moulded them into a human form and thus, O you highly fortunate ones, have brought this figure to Shirdi.

111. 'It is by virtue of our merit of several past births that we have reached Shirdi. And we feel that for this holy *darshan* of Shri Sai, we should offer him our all.

112. 'This most virtuous Sai is himself an *avatar*, conducting himself as a great Vishnu-devotee. He is truly, the shoot of the Tree of Knowledge, or a veritable Sun in the sky of Knowledge.

113. 'And great indeed, is our merit that we have come across this *Mashidmayee* (mosque), and that he got our vows fulfilled from us, while simultaneously giving us *darshan*.

114. 'To us, this is our Datta and it was he who commanded us to observe the vow. It was again he, who made place for us in that boat and has brought us to Shirdi for his *darshan*.

115. 'In this way Sai has given us an awareness of his all-pervasiveness, his dwelling in the heart of all and his omniscience.

116. 'Looking at his smiling countenance has brought great joy to our hearts. We forgot the woes and cares of worldly life and could not contain our blissful happiness.

117. 'May our mind accept resolutely that whatever is destined, let it happen, but may a loving devotion at Sai's feet remain for ever and may his sacred Form always be before our eyes.

118. 'How unfathomable, how incomprehensible is *Sai-leela* and so boundless his favour! I feel that I should surrender to you this, my body, O Gracious One!'

119. But now, listen to another story attentively, for a moment. The letter that came from Sai's mouth was proven indelible as the writing of *Brahmadev*, himself.

120. Sakharam Aurangabadkar who lived in Solapur city, was eager for a son. So his wife came to Shirdi.

121. Having heard of the wonderful Life Story of the holy saint Sai Baba, she came for his *darshan*, bringing her step-son with her.

122. Twenty-seven years had passed (since her marriage), and yet there was no child born to her. She was tired making vows to various gods and goddesses and was totally dejected at heart.

123. And so this '*suvasini*'² came to Shirdi with the purpose of taking Baba's *darshan*. However, a doubt arose in her mind.

124. 'How will I find Baba alone, since he is always surrounded by the devotees? And how can I convey to him my heart's wish?' She was worried.

125. 'The mosque is open, and so is the courtyard. There are always devotees around Baba. How can I find one private moment to relate to him my eager, heart-felt desire?'

126. She and her step-son Vishwanath by name, stayed in Shirdi for two months, serving Baba faithfully.

127. Once, when Vishwanath or anyone else was not near Baba, listen to the lady's entreaty to Madhavrao.

128. 'Please, at least you convey to Baba my ardent wish, when he is at peace and ease, and at the proper moment.

129. 'And you tell him this only when he is alone and not surrounded by his devotees, in such a manner, as nobody can hear it.'

130. Madhavrao replied, 'Look, this mosque is never empty. Someone or other keeps coming all the time for Baba's *darshan*.

131. 'This *Sai-durbar* is open to all; no one is forbidden to come here. But I will tell you this much, try to understand it!

132. 'To try is my job; the giver of success is God. In the end, only He gives peace and your worries will vanish.

133. 'However, you must sit in the *Sabhamandap* below, on a stone, with a coconut and incense sticks in hand, when Baba sits down to his meal.

134. 'After his meal, when I find him in a pleased, relaxed mood, I will signal to you. Only then should you come up'.

135. By and by, when an opportune moment came, on one occasion, as Sai's meal was over suddenly such an opportunity came.

136. When Sai had washed his hands and Madhavrao was wiping them dry, seeing Baba in a cheerful mood, just see what he did.

137. With a sudden gush of affectionate love, Baba pinched Madhavrao's cheek. Listen to the loving dialogue that followed on the occasion between God and his devotee!

138. Courteous that Madhavrao always was, pretending to be angry, he said to Baba, jokingly, 'Is this really proper?

139. 'We do not want such a mischievous God who squeezes the cheek so hard! Are we, in any way, obligated to you? Is this the fruit of our intimacy with you?

140. "In all these seventy-two generations of our association", said Baba, "have I even touched you with my hand? Just try to remember!"

141. Madhavrao said, 'We want a god who will always give us ever-new sweetmeats to eat, when we are hungry.

142. 'We do not want either your honours or the aeroplane from Heaven. Give me only this one gift that I remain grateful to you, for ever.'

143. Baba said, "It is only for this that I came here and began to feed you all, because of the tender affection I felt for you."

144. After this Baba went and sat on his seat near the railing. Madhavrao gave the signal to the lady, who at once became alert to the accomplishment of her purpose.

145. On receiving the signal, she got up immediately and hastily going up the steps, stood courteously before Baba, with great humility.

146. At once, she offered the coconut and bowed at his feet. Baba banged the coconut against the railing with his own hands.

147. And he said, "Shama, what does this coconut say? The coconut is rattling too much." Shama seized the opportunity instantly, and see what he said to Baba.

148. 'This lady is saying in her heart, may it similarly rumble in my stomach and may it really happen what she is saying. May her heart be attached to your feet, for ever and her puzzle be answered.

149. 'Please look upon her graciously and put that coconut in the lap of her sari. By your blessings, may sons and daughters be born to her.'

150. Then Baba said to her, "What, do coconuts produce children? How do you nurture such superstitions? People seem to have gone crazy!"

151. Shama said, 'Oh, well we know the power, the marvel of your words! So priceless they are that a long train of children will follow, all on its own.

152. 'But just now you are making a differentiation and not giving a genuine blessing. You are arguing needlessly. Give, O give her that coconut as *prasad*!'

153. "All right, break the coconut!" said Baba. 'Oh, give it in her lap', said Shama. And the argument continued for a while in this manner, when, ultimately Baba gave in.

154. "She will get a child. Now, go!" he said. But Shama persisted, 'But when? Please give an answer.' And when Baba said, "After twelve months", he broke open the coconut with a bang.

155. They both shared half of it, returning the remaining half to the lady. Madhavrao said to her, 'See, you are a witness to my words.

156. 'If you do not deliver a child before the twelfth month from today is over, just listen to what I will do!

157. 'If I do not bang the coconut in the same way on his head and send away this god from this mosque, I will give up my name, Madhav!

158. 'I will surely not allow such a god to remain in the mosque and you will get the proof at the right time. Know, that this is my firm resolve!'

159. On getting such an assurance, the lady was very pleased at heart. Prostrating in obeisance before Baba, she then returned to her village with peace of mind.

160. Knowing how deeply attached Shama was to him, Sai, who was tied by bonds of love to his devotees and whose wishes he always fulfilled — he was not angry with Shama, in the least.

161. To prove the words of the devotee, that Compassionate Sai, the only Refuge of all who surrender to him and himself, Kindness Incarnate — he always fulfilled very lovingly, the promise made by his devotee.

162. "Shama is my favourite among my devotees. But he, in his affectionate love, does not know what is proper or improper." But it is the promise of the saints to fulfil the resolve that devotees make.

163. And so, when twelve months were complete, Baba fulfilled his own resolve. When only three months had passed after Baba's blessing, the lady became pregnant.

164. Fortunately for her, she bore a son and when he was five months old, she came with him and her husband, to Shirdi for *darshan*.

165. Her husband also worshipped the feet of Sai Samarth, with great joy and with gratitude in his heart, offered five hundred rupees to Baba.

166. This same money Baba utilized later to build the walls of the place, where his horse Shamakarna is tied, at present.

167. Therefore, contemplate on this Sai, remember him and meditate upon him. To Hemad, he is forever, the Refuge. Do not run around in search, anywhere else.

168. When there is musk in one's own navel, why wander about for it? Hemad is constantly absorbed at Sai's feet and enjoys boundless happiness.

169. The next chapter is even more interesting than this, as to how the loving devotees would joyously bring Baba in procession, from the mosque to the *Chavadi*.

170. Similarly, the story of Baba's '*Handi*'[3], distribution of *prasad* and other humorous stories will come in the next chapter. Listen to them, O listeners, and your eagerness to hear them will increase.

Weal be to all! Here ends the thirty-sixth Chapter of
"*Shri Sai Samarth Satcharit*", called
'*Sai's All-pervasiveness and the Fulfilment of His Blessings*',
as inspired by the saints and the virtuous and
composed by his devotee, Hemadpant.

Notes

1. This means, 'I am That and That I am'.
2. A term of courtesy for a woman whose husband is alive.
3. A vessel with a big mouth, used for cooking rice, etc.

37

The Description of the Chavadi Ceremony

MY OBEISANCE TO SHRI GANESH, TO SHRI SARASWATI, AND SHRI GURUMAHARAJ! TO THE FAMILY DEITY, TO SHRI SITA-RAMACHANDRA, MY MOST HUMBLE OBEISANCE! I BOW IN REVERENCE TO THE MOST VENERABLE GURU SHRI SAINATH!

1. Blessed, blessed is Sai's Story, blessed his daily conduct. His actions too, are incomprehensible, marvellous and impossible to narrate in their proper sequence.

2. Unfathomable indeed, is his true life story; blessed, the account of his Life. Blessed, blessed is his constant, unchanging course of practice, as difficult as walking on a sharp sword-edge and irrevocable.

3. Intoxicated as he would be at times, with Self-rejoicing, at other times he would be content in Self-Knowledge. Sometimes after being the doer of everything, he would yet be totally detached from it. Such was his uncertain state.

4. At times, though not engaged in any activity, he would not be asleep, either. But concentrating on his own good, he would always be Self-aware.

5. Sometimes, happy as the ocean, he would also be, like it, boundless, unfathomable, impenetrable and deep. Who can describe adequately this most incomprehensible figure?

6. Towards men he had a brotherly love, while the ladies were like his mother or sister. He was always well-known to everybody as a celibate, who lived in perpetual continency.

7. May the steadiness and understanding gained in the sacred company of such a one, remain till the time of death.

8. May the desire to serve him ever grow and a single-minded devotion at his feet develop, as also, a love for taking his Name constantly and the ability to see God in all living creatures.

9. Seeing his *leelas*, each more marvellous than the other, those who tried to trace their cause were all at their wits' end and ultimately, had to give up the effort.

10. So many strive for the pleasures of heaven, singing its praises. They look upon this earth with contempt, beseiged with (saying that here there is always a) fear of death.

11. But they themselves have taken shape out of the unmanifest into a state which is called the manifest state. When this manifest state again enters into the unmanifest, it is called 'death'.

12. '*Adharma*', ignorance, anger, envy, etc., are the fetters that take us towards death. Only those who can completely overcome them get an entry into heaven.

13. And after all what more is there in this 'heaven'? The heaven is nothing but the renunciation of desires and cravings, and the exalted experience of the universal Self which is beyond pain and sorrow.

14. Where there is no room for disease, worries, afflictions and pain; where no one suffers from hunger and thirst or from the fear of old age;

15. Where there is no fear of death and no restrictions of what should or should not be done and the creatures move about fearlessly. This is truly, the Divine, heavenly state.

16. The same Principle that completely fills everything, from Brahma to the tiniest material object, both animate and inanimate, is also present in the state that follows death, or here, without any distinction.

17. But to one enveloped in ignorance or *Maya*, even if he has renounced the worldly life, the same Principle appears as not being the Brahman, due to the deceptive forms or properties covering or disguising the Spirit.

18. He who differentiates, saying that the *Parabrahma* is different or separate from me, that I am not That, but I am different — such a one is always overpowered by Death.

19. Death follows birth and after death again comes the rebirth. These revolutions of the birth-death cycle pursue him, for ever.

20. If that heaven, which is attained as a fruit of *yajna*, penance and charity, all so difficult to perform — if that heaven is devoid of the contemplation of Shri Vishnu, of what use is it?

21. We do not want that Heavenly Abode merely as a place of sensual pleasures. Where there is no chanting of God's Name, why do we need it?

22. Whether you go to heaven or hell, there is no difference in the enjoyment of sensual pleasures. Be it Lord Indra, or be it a donkey, the sensual pleasure of both is the same.

23. Indra rolls in the pleasures of Paradise, while the donkey rolls in the rubbish heap. But as for their pleasure, it is the same in comparison, without the slightest difference.

24. Why make efforts to attain that from where there is a Fall when the merit diminishes? Better than such a place is to be born on this earth, whose importance is great.

25. What is so great about that 'Brahmalok', where life exceeds one 'kalpa'[1]? However brief and momentary the lifespan on this earth might be, it is far more important.

26. In this transient earthly life, if you perform a *karma* even for just a moment, provided you offer everything to God, you attain a secure place.

27. What is the use of a place where there are no devotees of God, who do not narrate the stories of God (Hari) and guru, do not sing, dance and worship God?

28. The experience of oneness between God and the Self is the only means of attaining the lasting and highest form of knowledge, which is far more important than heaven itself and this earth is the place for attaining it.

29. With your body, speech and mind, surrender your 'Panchapran' (five vital airs) and also, offer your intellect with humility and determination, at the feet of your guru.

30. Once you surrender to the Sadguru in this way, where is the question of the fear of worldly life? Wherefore then, the worries of daily life when he is there to remove them all?

31. Where *Maya* or ignorance reigns, there are also present the ties of sons, animals, etc., and the worries of worldly life, day and night. There is not a trace of good, nobler thoughts.

32. Ignorance is the root cause of all that creates the illusion of duality between the Creator and His Creation. And it is for this reason that perfect wisdom should be acquired from the *Shastras* in Sanskrit and from the *Acharya* or Spiritual Master.

33. Once ignorance is dispelled, not even a vestige of this feeling of duality remains and then such a one overcomes the birth-death cycle, due to his knowledge of oneness between God and His creatures.

34. But he who holds a sense of separateness, even in the slightest degree, will be caught up in the painful birth-death cycle. Destruction and this created universe will follow him, always.

35. When moral end is the object of knowledge, that knowledge is undoubtedly the true knowledge. When the object is purely a material end, it is called ignorance.

36. The greatest fear in worldly life is that of Death and to be free from this fear, hold tightly to the guru's feet, which will most certainly bring you this knowledge of Oneness.

37. Where the illusory knowledge of duality enters, there also enters this fear. Hence serve those feet which, being without a sense of this differentiation, do not have even a trace of this fear.

38. Apply on his fore-head the sandalwood paste of pure love; dress him in the 'pitambar'[2] of simple, loving faith, so that he will reveal to you, his devotee, the all-pervasive God.

39. When you bathe him in tears of joy, which are replete with the 'ashtabhava'[3], seating him on the throne of an unswerving faith, he will be pleased, instantly.

40. Tying around his waist the '*mekhala*'[4] of devotion, make him your
     very own and making an offering of your all to him with love,
     perform his *arati*.

41. Total destruction of any object or work has for its basis the fact of
     its existence. When an earthen jar hit by a stone is broken, what
     is destroyed is only its shape.

42. But the existence of the jar is not destroyed in the least. For its
     broken pieces yet have the potential of being recreated into a jar.

43. Thus the destruction of an object is always based on the fact of its
     existence. Similarly, the death of anyone does not result in
     nothingness.

44. There is no effect without a cause. Even if the manifest becomes
     unmanifest, it is always related to the truth. And this is experienced
     everywhere.

45. The order of variations in the degree of subtlety also reveals this.
     Even after the destruction of the gross body, its astral body still
     remains.

46. And when even that body is destroyed and what is even more
     subtle, remains, then the power of all the organs of the mind and
     intellect, to enjoy sensual pleasures becomes feeble.

47. In short, where even the intellect is wearied out, there the manifest
     becomes unmanifest. But its existence is not covered up or
     smothered. It shines everywhere by itself.

48. Intellect supports desires. Hence when it is destroyed, the Self
     rises into eminence, instantly, and the Eternal Abode is reached.

49. Ignorance, *Maya*, desires and *karma* are the main qualities of
     Death. When all these are abandoned, the ties of worldly life also
     fall off.

50. And once these ties are severed, the true Self emerges effortlessly,
     as the self-illumined sun shines, once the clouds disappear.

51. 'I am the body; this is my wealth' — this is called the firmly-
     rooted bodily ego and this alone, is the ensnaring cause of
     the bondage of the heart, as also, of the sorrows arising from
     Maya.

52. Even if this body falls and is replaced by another body by virtue of its *karma*, if that man fails to destroy totally the very germ of that *karma*, then rebirth is inevitable for him.

53. The seeds again grow into trees, acquiring new bodies from the seeds of the desires (from previous births). And so the cycle continues ceaselessly, until those desires are becalmed.

54. Once these desires are destroyed totally, the heart is freed from the bondage. Only then does the mortal man become immortal. Even the *Upanishads* give the same message.

55. The state that transcends '*dharma* – *adharma*' is called '*viraja*' or the state of desirelessness, which destroys ignorance and desires and where death has no power, whatsoever.

56. Abandonment of all desires is in itself the means of attaining the highest Bliss, which, though indescribable, is attempted to be put into words and which, though beyond speech, is sought to be rendered into speech.

57. Gaining complete knowledge of the '*Parabrahma*' is itself the end of all that is unpropitious, the fulfilment of all heart-felt desires. And this finds support in the *Shrutis* and *Smritis*, too!

58. 'He who has gained *Brahmajnana* has attained his Eternal Abode', and that alone is the ultimate means of experiencing the bliss of Oneness with the Brahman. What else can be higher than this? 'The Self-realized is the one that goes beyond all sorrows'.

59. This ocean of worldly life, which is the source of the darkness or ignorance (*tamas*), can be crossed over by only one means, which is *Brahmajnana*, the means of attaining everything.

60. "Absolute faith and patience with courage, these are *Uma–Maheshwar* (Shiva and Parvati) and unless their hand of benediction falls on the head, that all-pervading Almighty, who also dwells in our hearts, can never be realized."

61. So said Sainath, the greatest among the gurus, whose words are of unfailing veracity. "Have a little patience, perseverance of a firm faith, and you will acquire the greatest glory."

62. That this whole visible universe is unreal, a dream that we experience actually, and which disappears on our waking up, is something we have to accept.

63. Our intellect can go only so far, no more; and our real awareness of the Self is also, only so far. But where Truth and illusion cannot be known by the intellect, that awareness of the Principle is the true Self.

64. Without the attributes of being real or illusory, differentiation of gender, and without any special qualities — such is the greatness of the all-pervasive *Atman*, which has been described variously.

65. The *Atman* is without any special qualities, beyond old age, birth and death; it is ancient, eternal and always indestructible.

66. It is constant, unborn, old, all-pervasive as the sky, without a beginning, indivisible, not subject to growth and unchanging.

67. Who can describe that which is beyond words, without a form, without beginning or end, immeasurable, indestructible, without fragrance or taste, and unstained?

68. And when such an attributeless *Atman* cannot be known through ignorance, then remove that ignorance with knowledge. But never say that the *Atman* is void.

69. Oh, how glorious was that '*Paramhansa*'[5] state of Shri Sai, that splendid spiritual treasure, all his own! And once Time robs it in a trice, will it ever be seen again?

70. Leave alone the common, average devotee, who is after all attached to wealth, sons, a wife! But even the *yogis*, for all their renunciation, came for his *darshan* and were absorbed at his lotus-feet!

71. Blessed is that devotee in this whole world, who is free from the bondage of desires and *karma*; who has overcome all desires and has detachment towards earthly possessions, like house, his body, etc.

72. When Sai alone is the object for his sight, will he ever see anything else? In this whole visible world, he will not find a place, which is without him.

73. With Shri Sai's name on his lips and Shri Sai's love in his heart, he will enjoy peace and well-being for ever. For Sai himself will protect him.

74. And the same is true of listening. There is no other word for the ear, but Sai; The nose is filled with Sai's fragrance and the sweet name of Sai oozes from the tongue.

75. Oh, how marvellous was Sai's smiling face and the purest of all the pleasures that it brought! Blessed, blessed was the fortunate one, who had actually heard his nectar-sweet words!

76. A store-house of all the weal; the source of joy and peace, with his renunciation and a discriminating knowledge of the real and the unreal, Sai Baba was always wakeful, at heart.

77. Even when satiated with the milk, a calf does not want to leave the mother and has to be tied away from her by a rope. In the same way should this mind be fastened to the guru's feet, drawn away from worldly pleasures.

78. Worship the guru's lotus-feet to win his love and grace and to experience them at every step, make a place in your heart for his beneficial advice and guidance.

79. While enjoying the pleasures of the senses to your satiety, keep Sai's love alive in your heart, constantly. For that alone will be of help in the end, both in the material and the spiritual matters.

80. With the collyrium of a '*mantrik*'[6], who has a command over mystic formulae, spells, etc., a child born with his legs first, can discover a buried treasure. Similarly, the eyes that are covered with the dust from a guru's feet, acquire knowledge of spiritual and material things.

81. Characteristics that distinguish the *Siddhas* are really the means for the seekers, to acquire which, the wise should make a prolonged effort and do *sadhana*.

82. Clarified butter is latent in the milk. But unless it is combined with a sour agent, there will neither be buttermilk nor butter, and that too can be obtained only after it is processed properly.

83. Unless the buttermilk is churned, butter cannot be had and that again has to be heated on fire without which the delicious clarified butter cannot be obtained.

84. What is needed is the strength of the purificatory religious influences since birth and also, a discriminatory intellect cultivated by careful study. Without a deep *sadhana*, the purification of the mind does not come, without which, knowledge is very difficult to gain.

85. Only when the mind is purified can the true Self be realized. Hence the Seeker should never give up devotion to God until he has attained to that state of Self-realization.

86. To raise the temple of Self-knowledge with its shining pinnacle of the four *Muktis*[7], and the banner of Renunciation flying high, the foundation of God-devotion has to be laid firmly, at first.

87. Dogs and pigs roll in the mire, day and night, feeding on the excrement. They also enjoy sensual pleasures. But are these of importance, even on getting a human birth?

88. It is that penance of observance of one's own duty, which purifies the mind and results in the attainment of Brahman, which one has to perform while yet in the human body.

89. The words of the revered old people, that service to the *sadhus* is the abode of emancipation, while excessive enjoyment of women's company (lust) is the gateway to Hell, are always worth pondering over.

90. Blessed is that *sadhu*, who always conducts himself righteously, and, content with food enough to sustain the body, has no desire for a house, family, etc.

91. All those who meditate on Sai constantly (literally, without closing the eyes even for a moment), have marvellous experience which is worth seeing. Grateful to them, Sai himself begins to meditate on them.

92. Great indeed, is the importance of taking the Name. For the guru himself begins to remember his devotees. The meditator thus becomes one with the object of his meditation, both forgetting their own selves completely.

93. "Your own deeds, you know best. But as for me, I ceaselessly think of you, day and night." Such were Baba's loving words, which many will recall.

94. We do not need any tales of wisdom. This *Gatha* or *Pothi* of Sai is enough for us. However numerous the sins on our head might be, he is our only refuge in our troubles.

95. Even if repeated readings are not possible the listeners should regularly listen every day to those chapters dealing with guru-devotion, storing them in the heart as its precious ornaments.

96. He who reads this 'Life' daily, at any time of the day, such a faithful devotee will most certainly be visited by Shri Hari, along with his own *guru-maharaj.*

97. Lakshmi, the goddess of wealth, will always dwell in the house of those who will read it without fail. Or, at least, the poverty of those who complete its reading in a week, will be banished.

98. Do not think that I am saying this. For then your mind will be clouded with doubts. It is Sai who is himself saying this through my mouth. Hence give up all your doubts and misgivings.

99. And it is to the Story of this Sai, who is the mine of all Excellence and the giver of *Moksha* to his devotees, that the listeners should now listen; for his stories wash away the sins of this *Kaliyug.*

100. Oh, how can the poor Heavenly pleasures hold their own against such stories of the saints! And who would even glance at them, ignoring the instantly rewarding narration of these interesting tales?

101. Pleasure and pain are states of mind. And the company of saints always takes us beyond these, making the mind one with the Divine Consciousness, which has no place for joy or sorrow.

102. The joy that a man of detachment derives from solitude, or a devotee from his devotion, is one that even Lord Indra or an emperor can never enjoy to the end of Time.

103. Pleasure and pain resulting from the *prarabdha karma* of the past births, is very powerful and a man is destined to act according to his *karma*. But even these preordained actions can be easily and effortlessly avoided by a devotee.

104. Howsoever arduous, *Bhagirath*[8] effort one might make, the results of previous *karma* cannot be avoided. It is impossible to free oneself from the inevitable.

105. As the sorrows are unasked for, so also are the pleasures unexpected. And the saints already know the course of events resulting from a man's *karma*.

106. Ceaseless repeated chanting of your name is in itself a vow, a penance, a charity for us. A visit to Shirdi from time to time is itself our pilgrimage.

107. Chanting the name 'Sai, Sai', is our *mantra* accompanying religious performances; this is itself our meditation; this, our 'Purascharan'[9]. Therefore, surrender to him, single-mindedly.

108. Try worshipping him with whole-hearted attention and a guileless love and then experience inwardly his marvellous *leela*.

109. But now, enough of this tedious monotonous description, like a cane-crushing machine. We want jaggery instantly. All are eager to listen to the previously mentioned fascinating story.

110. Knowing well this feeling of the audience, I shall now curtail the expanse of this story, to retain their interest and attention in the wonderful tale that I shall now narrate.

111. I, a poor, dull-witted creature do not even have the skill for composing verses. What I write is only what Sai gets written from me, holding my pen in his own hand.

112. Had not Sai given me the intelligence, who was I to write his Story? He is himself the narrator of his own story and he also is getting it written.

113. But now, let us continue with the story about the *Chavadi*, *Handi* and *prasad*, which I had promised to tell. Listen carefully to the narration.

114. And any other stories that come to mind in connection with it, will also be narrated. Listen to them attentively.

115. Blessed is the marvel of Sai's stories! Blessed, blessed is their impact on hearing them! By contemplating on them, our inborn (good) qualities manifest themselves, and our righteous feelings swell at Sai's feet.

116. Now let us first give the *Chavadi* description and sketch a general outline of its ceremonious proceedings. Every other day, Baba regularly slept in the *Chavadi*.

117. One night he slept in the mosque and the second, in the *Chavadi*. Such was Baba's regular routine till his *Samadhi*.

118. Later, from December 10, 1909, Baba's worship, *bhajan* and *pooja*, started in the *Chavadi*.

119. It is this ceremony in the *Chavadi* that we shall now describe to the best of our ability. And by Sai's Grace, which will provide the inspiration, it will be seen through to a proper conclusion.

120. When it was the night for the *Chavadi*, the *bhajan* party would come to the mosque and then the *bhajan* used to be in progress from the afternoon itself, in the *Sabhamandap*.

121. In the rear would be the beautiful, sparkling chariot with the *Tulsi-vrindavan* to its right. Baba would be seated in front, while in the middle would be the devotee-singers of *bhajans*.

122. These devotees, both ladies and gentlemen, with a fondness for *Hari-bhajan* would promply come and take their places in the *Sabhamandap*.

123. Some would take up the '*taal*'[10] in hand; others, the '*chiplis*'[11]; some others would keep time by clapping — some with tabors, yet others with tambourines would join in. And thus the *bhajan* would proceed amidst a great tumult of musical sounds.

124. Sai Samarth, with his magnetic power, would draw to his feet, the devotees as gross iron and without their being quite aware of it.

125. The torch-bearers would then light their torches[12] in the courtyard, where some would busy themselves decorating the palanquin. The staff-bearers standing ready at the gate, would loudly proclaim Glory to Sai.

126. The assembly-place would be gaily decorated with leafy boughs and flower-garlands, banners flying high up in the sky and a dressed-up seat. Adorned with ornaments, little children would flaunt their brand-new clothes.

127. Rows and rows of shining lights would light up the area surrounding the mosque. And Shamkarna, the fine horse, would be standing all ready, at the gate, decorated heavily.

128. Suddenly, Tatya Patil would arrive along with other people and come and sit near Baba, ready to accompany him.

129. Although Baba was ready to leave, he would keep sitting where he was, waiting for Tatya till he came.

130. Only when Tatya Patil put his hand under Baba's armpit to help him get up, would Baba be really ready to go from there to the *Chavadi*.

131. Tatya called Baba '*Mama*[13]'(uncle). Such was their mutual affection that there is no parallel to the feeling of affinity between them.

132. The usual *kafni* covering his body, with the baton tucked under his armpit, and carrying with him the claypipe with tobacco and a piece of cloth flung over the shoulders.

133. When Baba was thus ready, Tatya would cover him with a beautiful *jari*-bordered '*shela*'[14], arranging it properly on his head.

134. At the foot of the wall behind a bundle of faggots would be lying, the tip of which Baba, would slightly push back for a moment, with the big toe of his right foot.

135. At once, he would put out the flame there with his right hand. Only then would he set out to go to the *Chavadi*.

136. As Sai was about to set out, the musical instruments would begin to play and torches and fireworks of various kinds would at once be lighted on all four sides.

137. Some blew horns of different shapes and sizes, some rounded, some bow-shaped; others blew trumpets. Some would keep time by striking the metal plates with sticks and others, on cymbals. And the number of those who clapped their hands would be limitless.

138. With a loving devotion, men and women walked in rows, to the twanging and clanging of the *Veena* and the drums, to the loud proclamations of *Sainaam* and the singing of *bhajans*.

139. Some walked in the procession carefully balancing the banners, others flaunted banners with pictures of the eagle on them. And thus would they proceed, dancing and singing *bhajans* merrily.

140. The procession would set out amid great rejoicing, with flying banners, the loud beating of drums and metal plates, sounding of horns, the noisy, quavering and dancing of the horse, as the loud proclamations of glory to Baba resounded in the air.

141. In such tumult and noise of the musical instruments, Baba would set out from the mosque and as he approached the step, the staff-bearers would loudly proclaim Baba's name.

142. To the accompaniment of '*taals*', tambourines and drums, some played the *Veena*, some kept time with '*chiplis*' while the devotees sang *bhajans* with a sincere love and devotion.

143. As some devotees walked happily carrying flags and banners, others walked on either side of Baba, holding a '*chavari*' over his head and fanning him.

144. Some walked ahead spreading out sheets, some single and some double-folded, on which Baba walked, while others, held his hands and yet others held the '*chavari*' and waved fans.

145. While Tatyasaheb held Baba's left hand, Mhalsapati held the right. Bapusaheb Jog held the large and lofty umbrella over his head. And so proceeded Baba to the *Chavadi*.

146. In front walked the fine, copper-coloured heavily ornamented horse, named *Shamkarna*, the bells on his feet jingling as he walked.

147. The staff-bearers, walking in front, loudly proclaimed Baba's name from time to time. Some carried the large umbrella on his head as others held the '*chavari*'.

148. The musical instruments resounded, the devotees hailed Baba, time and again. And as the devotees walked on, even the staff-bearers joined in with loud proclamations to Baba with loving devotion.

149. And as they repeatedly hailed Baba, there were also proclamations of *Harinaam* from time to time from the throng of devotees who walked keeping time to the beat of the drums, cymbals, etc.

150. As the procession approached the place of assembly, the *bhajan-*
     singers in front who had been shouting Baba's name gleefully,
     would now halt.

151. Then as the '*taals*', the tambourines and the drums all struck
     together and the musical strains of the *bhajan* sung so lovingly,
     swelled into a tumultuous sound of music, the proclamation of
     Sainaam capped it all.

152. Alongside walked men and women, all steeped in the spirit of joy
     and love the *bhajans* generated, and pronounced *Sainaam* loudly
     which seemed to fill the air.

153. As the sky above resounded with the music, the heart of the
     spectators swelled with joy. Such was that glorious, spectacular
     procession to the *Chavadi*, which was worth watching. Its beauty,
     its splendour has no comparison.

154. The radiance emanating from Sai's countenance, as he stood in
     front of the *Chavadi*, was like the brilliant glow of red-hot gold
     — a glow that overspreads the sky at dawn and in the evening.

155. The radiance of his face at that time was like the brilliance of the
     rising sun or like that of the pure fountain of life. Who will ever
     forgo such a gain?

156. Oh, blessed indeed, was the *darshan*, at that time, of that red
     glowing face as he stood facing the north with a single-minded
     concentration, as if beckoning to someone.

157. Amid the twanging and clanging of musical instruments, Maharaj,
     his heart full of joy, would move his right hand up and down,
     repeatedly.

158. With a silver tray full of flowers, in his hand, Dikshit, the most
     excellent devotee, would then shower the flowers all over him,
     again and again.

159. And Kakasaheb would thus, keep on showering roses mixed with
     gulal[15] on his head all the time, with a loving devotion.

160. And as he showered the *gulal*-covered rosebuds, the tambourines,
     '*taals*' and drums would strike in unison in one great tumultuous
     sound.

161. The villagers and Baba's devotees, came lovingly to take his *darshan*. At such time, Baba's face would reflect a reddish glow, quite marvellous and very beautiful.

162. Seeing the play of that radiance on his face, the eyes of the beholders would open wide in awe and wonder and their loving hearts would feel a new eagerness, as if all the sorrows of their worldly life had vanished.

163. Oh, how marvelous, how wonderful was that Divine radiance, as lustrous as the rising sun. In front the drums would beat, loud and for long.

164. For an hour and a half or three-quarters, Baba would stand in that one spot, facing the north and moving his right hand up and down, constantly.

165. Baba's glowing complexion was like the golden yellow of the innermost core of the *Ketaki* flower[16] and with a slight reddish glow on it, the beauty of which the tongue just cannot describe. Eyes alone can relish it.

166. And once Mhalsapati was seized with the frenzy and began dancing, one just marvelled at Baba's unbroken concentration in the face of it.

167. Mhalsapati would stand at his right, holding the end of Baba's *kafni* in his hand. To Baba's left would walk Tatya Kote, holding a lantern in his hand.

168. Oh, how wonderful were all those festivities! That glorification too, of love and devotion! To see its marvel all the great and the wealthy flocked together.

169. Baba's beautiful face with its reddish, fair complexion and a radiance all its own, was beyond description and the eyes of the beholders would be filled with an inner blissful joy as they gazed upon him.

170. Throngs of devotees walked slowly on either side, overcome with a boundless loving devotion and a blissful joy which overpowered their hearts.

171. Now, in the days to come, no one will ever be able to see with their own eyes, such a glorious celebration. Gone are those days,

gone for ever, that time! Memories are the only solace for the mind, now.

172. In this way, amid ceaseless melodious strains from the various musical instruments and loud proclamations of glory to Sai, Baba was led to his seat in the *Chavadi* and offered *pooja* with all the sacred rites and rituals.

173. A white awning would be tied; chandeliers, lamps would be hung, the beauty and brilliance of whose lights would be re-doubled by being reflected in the mirrors that were set up in different places. Such was the sparkle and glitter of that spectacle!

174. All the devotees gathered together and then went to the *Chavadi*. It was Tatyaba who would get Baba's seat ready and then lead him to it by holding his hand.

175. And when that most excellent seat was ready, with a long stuffed bolster at the back to recline on, and once Baba was seated on it, they would put on him the long outer garment.

176. They would dress him up in fine, rich clothes and with joyous hearts, offer him *pooja* with great devotion. Loudly they would sing *arati* and offer him garlands and bouquets.

177. Sandal-wood paste would be applied first, followed by fragrant perfumes being rubbed on his hands. Fine clothes and ornaments would be put on him, ending with the putting of a crown on his head.

178. Sometimes a gold crown, sometimes a fine, rich, gem-studded turban with a plume would be put on, while his throat would be adorned with diamonds and rubies.

179. Necklaces of pure, white pearls round the neck would then follow. Unique was the beauty of that beautiful dress that sparkled in the light of the lamps.

180. Fragrant musk would be used to draw the black vertical line on his forehead, with a black round mark like the Vaishnavites, added to it in the middle.

181. If that rich, heavy purple robe with its intricate *jari*-work in gold, happened to slip from the shoulders, it was safely, delicately held in place from either side, and quite unnoticed by anybody.

182. The crown or the turban had similarly to be held in place, carefully and softly, from the back by the devotees, who took turns.

183. For though their greatest worry and fear was that if it as much as touched his head, he would at once throw it away, yet their eager, loving desire for him to wear it was equally strong.

184. And could Sai, who had intuitive knowledge of everything, not have known this secret of theirs? But seeing their love and eagerness, he would knowingly hold his silence.

185. What adornment would a gold-threaded rich robe be to one who is glorified in his Self-knowledge? What beauty could a crown bestow on one who is adorned by an inner Peace?

186. And yet they adorned Baba with various ornaments of rare beauty and put a mark with saffron, sandalwood paste on his forehead.

187. Some put necklaces of diamonds and pearls around his neck, some drew a mark on his forehead. And Baba indulged his loving devotees by allowing them these little acts of devotion.

188. When all the adornment was complete and the crown put on the head, with pearl necklaces shining around the throat, the splendour, the beauty was unsurpassed.

189. Nanasaheb Nimonkar would hold over Baba's head, a round, white cloth umbrella with a frilled border which, along with the stick to which it was fixed, would rotate, round and round.

190. Very lovingly Bapusaheb would wash his guru's feet and offer oblations, etc., with great devotion. He would then perform Baba's *pooja* properly.

191. Placing a silver dish in front of Baba, he would place Baba's feet in it and wash them very respectfully.

192. Taking a *vati* (metal bowl) of saffron, he would apply the paste to Baba's hands and put a *paan* in his closed fist. During this whole process, Baba's face would wear a very pleasant expression.

193. When Baba was seated in his cushioned seat, Tatyaba and others would be standing there, holding Baba's hand, helping him to be seated. They would then respectfully bow at his feet.

194. Clean and spotless as the floor of the Chavadi always was, it was rubbed and scrubbed hard until it shone like crystal. And there came together all the people, both young and old, who were absorbed in Sai's love.

195. When Baba was thus seated, reclining against the bolster, *chavari*, fans, etc., were waved on him from either side.

196. Madhavrao would then crush the tobacco and prepare the clay pipe, which he handed over to Tatyaba. First Tatyaba would puff at it.

197. When a flame came from the tobacco, Tatyaba would give it to Baba. And after the first puff, Baba would pass it on to Mhalsapati.

198. Then, till the pipe was finished, it made the rounds, from one to another, with Mahalsapati, Shama and Tatya.

199. Blessed indeed, was that pipe! Inanimate though it was, how great was its good fortune! Even we, the living beings, can never equal the true, sincere service it rendered.

200. Most arduous was its penance. In its infancy, it had been trampled upon and crushed under feet, as clay. Then bearing the severe heat it survived the searing heat of the kiln while being baked.

201. With a rare good fortune, it was sanctified by Baba's touch, only to bear again, the ordeal of the scorching heat of the *dhuni*. After being given a coating of the red-chalk dust it was honoured by the kiss of Baba's lips.

202. They would then apply to both his hands, a paste of camphor, sandalwood and saffron, put flower garlands round his neck and give him a bouquet of flowers to smell.

203. He of the ever-smiling countenance, who looked upon all with great love and compassion, what fascination could he have for such bedecking? It was only to honour the wishes of the devotees that he bore it all.

204. He who had the priceless ornament of devotion and was bedecked by Peace, of what value were the material ornaments of gems and necklaces to him?

205. He who was the very image of Renunciation, — why all the necklaces of emeralds to him? But when offered by the devotees, he would wear them around his neck to satisfy the devotees' fond desire for festivities.

206. Beautiful neckalces of gold and emeralds and pearls in eight or sixteen strands, marvellously intermingling with lotus flowers, adorned his neck.

207. Garlands of *Tulsi* (Basil) and fragrant Jasmines lay around his neck reaching down to his feet, and around his neck sparkled pearl ornaments of rare brilliance.

208. And a necklace of emeralds with a shining gold locket lay on his breast, while a black, round mark on his forehead enhanced the beauty of the whole personality.

209. How could he be called a fakir? Indeed, he looked more like a great powerful *Vaishnav* (Vishnu devotee). The umbrella rotated, the fans waved to and fro over his head which was adorned with a gold-borderd *shela*.

210. As the auspicious music played in the background, it was usually Jog, who would perform the *arati* with five lights burning brightly, which would be waved around Baba.

211. After the *pooja* was performed with the customary five *pooja* articles[17], he would carefully pick up the large showy 'Pancharati'with the lights and camphor and wave it around Baba.

212. The *arati* being over, one by one, all the devotees would prostrate before Baba in obeisance and go to their respective homes.

213. After offering Baba the tobacco-filled clay pipe, perfume and rosewater and taking his permission, as Tatyaba prepared to leave for home, Baba would say to him, "Look after me.

214. "Go, but enquire after me from time to time, during the night." 'All right', Tatyaji would assure him and, leaving the *Chavadi*, turn homeward.

215. In this way, when all the people had gone, Baba would open up the bundle with his own hands and spread out, layer upon layer, of folded *dhotis* thus making up his bed with his own hands.

216. About sixty to sixty-five such snow white sheets would be laid,
     one upon the other and then Baba would lay himself down upon
     them.

217. Thus, the story of the *Chavadi* has been narrated, so far, just as it
     took place. Now the remaining story will be related in the next
     chapter.

218. May the listeners forgive me. So unfathomable is the greatness of
     this Sai that though I say I will be brief, no limits can be set and
     it keeps on growing.

219. Now the story of Sai's '*Handi*' and whatever remains of the other
     stories, will be narrated in the following chapter. Please give your
     whole-hearted attention.

220. Ceaseless chanting of his guru's name is to Hemad, the only weal
     — material and spiritual. Bowing his head at the guru's feet, he
     has a sense of fulfilment. For it is only at his feet that the four
     highest goals of human life can be achieved.

Weal be to all! Here ends the thirty-seventh chapter of
"*Shri Sai Samarth Satcharit*", called
'*The Description of the Chavadi Ceremony*',
as inspired by the saints and the virtuous •
and composed by his devotee, Hemadpant.

Notes

1. In terms of human life, 432 *crores*, 20 *lakh* years, which measure up to just one day for *Brahmadev*.
2. A silk *dhoti* with a yellow border — literally a yellow-coloured silk dhoti.
3. Refer Chapter 5, note 3.
4. An ornament of gold or silver, worn round the waist, especially by women.
5. The Perfect Man among the Vedantins is called '*Paramhansa*'.
6. A practitioner of '*mantras*' or spells or mystic formulae addressed to particular deities, command over which is acquired by following a strict code of discipline.
7. Refer Ch. 11, note 8.
8. Refer Ch. 8, note 4.
9. The recitation and other rites prescribed by the *Mantra Shastra*, to be observed by one who would acquire the power of using a *mantra*.
10. A musical instrument of bell-metal, a sort of cymbal, played with a stick.
11. Refer Ch. 15, note 2.
12. These were made of rolls of rags, soaked in oil and tied at the end of a long stick.
13. Maternal uncle.
14. A cloth composed of four breadth, depending from the shoulders, loosely over the body.
15. A red powder, specially used at the festival of *Holi* by the Hindus.
16. A flower tree, *Pandanus odoratissimus*.
17. These are: sandalwood paste, flowers, incense, lights and food-offerings.

38

The Description of the Handi

MY OBEISANCE TO SHRI GANESH, TO SHRI SARASWATI, AND SHRI GURUMAHARAJ! TO THE FAMILY DEITY, TO SHRI SITA-RAMACHANDRA, MY MOST HUMBLE OBEISANCE! I BOW IN REVERENCE TO THE MOST VENERABLE GURU SHRI SAINATH!

1. O *Guruvara*, you who bring joy to the whole world and are eager to help the devotees achieve their desired ends and to remove the threefold afflictions of those who seek refuge at your feet, we make obeisance at your feet.

2. O most Munificent One, Protector of the humble and Deliverer of the devotees that surrender to you, it was for doing good to the people, that you have taken *avatar*.

3. Hail to you, O Destroyer of duality! Glory to you, O Captor of the devotees' hearts and their Liberator from worldly life! O most Compassionate *Gururaya*, we hail thee!

4. What good fortune of ours has come to fruition that we saw your holy feet and experienced the joy of your company! But gone is that time, never to return!

5. The beautiful image that took shape out of the pure molten liquid of the true Self, poured into the mould of Brahman, is this Sai, the greatest among the saints.

6. Sai himself, is *Atmaram* or the Self; he alone is the Abode of Happiness, so perfect, himself satiated in all his desires, he makes his devotees desireless, too!

7. He is described in brief, as one who has the quality of swallowing Death himself, with the unique power of all the Brahmins and Kshatriyas, who are the followers and protectors of *dharma*.

8. He who snaps the bondages of birth and death, etc., before him I, a dull, ignorant one, bow in obeisance.

9. In the last chapter, I described very lovingly, the *Chavadi* ceremony of Sainath. Now, in this chapter, listen to the description of the ever-delightful *Handi*.

10. An infant only knows how to eat but does not know what to eat. And it is the mother who has to care for him by feeding him milk or a morsel of food.

11. So also does my Mother Sai, who makes me hold the pen and out of love for his devotees, has got this composition written effortlessly from me.

12. For every '*yuga*', respectively, the *Dharmashastra* has prescribed proven means to attain *Moksha*, as, for *Krita* or *Satyayuga* — penance, for *Treta* — the attainment of knowledge, for *Dwapar* — *yajna* or sacrifice and for *Kali* — charity.

13. One should keep giving, all the time, in charity, but its main significance lies in the appeasement of hunger. Hence '*annadaan*' or feeding in charity regularly, is the chief among all actions.

14. At the stroke of twelve at noon, one is extremely agitated without food. As with us, so with others. He who realizes this in his heart is indeed, a good man.

15. Among all prescribed rules of conduct, the first and most important is *annadaan*. If you consider carefully, none other is greater than this.

16. Food is just another form of *Parabrahma* and all the living creatures are born out of it. Food alone is the means of sustaining life and after death it is in the food that it merges.

17. When a guest arrives, the householder should satisfy him by offering food, whatever may be the time of the day. Those who turn them away without offering it, invite adversity, unmistakably.

18. When giving clothes, vessels, etc., it is to be considered whether the receiver, is deserving of it or not. But for *annadaan*, no such consideration is needed. Whoever comes to the door and at whatever time, it is not proper to show disrespect to him.

19. Such is the great importance of *annadaan* as described in the *Shrutis (Taittiriya Upanishad* Ch, 3.). Hence Baba also satiated people by offering them food and followed the custom handed down by tradition.

20. Money or anything else given in charity is incomplete without *annadaan*. Is there any splendour to the stars without the moon? Will a necklace have beauty without a locket?

21. As '*varan*'[1] among the '*shad-rasa*'[2] or the six flavours or tastes, so does *annadaan* bring the highest merit among all the meritorious deeds. A spire without a pinnacle, a lake without a lotus will always be wanting in beauty.

22. As *bhajans* without loving devotion, a married woman without *kumkum* or the red mark on the forehead, effort of singing without a sweet voice or buttermilk without a pinch of salt (so is charity without *annadaan*).

23. Even among the receivers of *annadaan*, those who are afflicted, weak, blind, lame, deaf and poor should be given food first; relatives and other people should come after.

24. Now, for the sake of those who are curious, I shall make an attempt to give a general idea of Baba's '*Handi*', to the listeners.

25. In the courtyard of the mosque, a big fireplace[3] would be made up, on which would be placed a broad-mouthed vessel, filled with the required amount of water.

26. Sometimes he would prepare 'sweet rice'; sometimes a '*pulao*' with pieces of meat in it, sometimes lumps of dough squeezed and shaped by the hand would be added to be cooked with the '*varan*'.

27. Along with these, sometimes he would gently slip into the boiling *varan*, lumps of wheat flour dough, patted into '*panagas*'[4] or '*rodagas*'[5].

28. Himself grinding the spices on the stone slab, he would make all the preparation for cooking. He would then pat tiny cakes from the finely ground *Moong-daal*[6] and slip them softly into the *Handi*.

29. In the hope of attaining Heaven, those who perform *yajna* and get the animals killed with rites and rituals, offer them to the

sacrificial fire. Even Brahmins eat the leavings of the meat. This is called 'slaying sanctioned by the *Shastras*'.

30. Baba also sent for the *Mullah* to recite *Fatiah*[7] or *mantras* according to the Islamic scriptures (Quran), and, with proper rites, got the she-goat to be slaughtered.

31. This *Handi* was of two types, sometimes large and sometimes small. Cooking food in it, he used to feed those who wished to partake of it.

32. The one that supplied food for fifty was the smaller of the two, while that which contained food enough for a hundred with some food still remaining, was the larger one.

33. He himself went to the grocer to buy the ingredients and settled the account. Here there was no question of credit; money was paid in cash, by hand.

34. Salt, chillies, condiments like cummin seed, black pepper, vegetables, coconut, coconut kernel — Baba himself purchased it all, considering the requirements, carefully.

35. Sitting in the mosque, Baba would himself set up the quern with his own hands and grind wheat, pulses, *jowar*, etc.

36. All the effort for the *Handi* was made tirelessly by Baba himself. Even the task of grinding spices was undertaken by him with great sincerity.

37. To make the fire in the fireplace burn slow or bright, he himself moved the faggots up and down repeatedly.

38. Having soaked the pulses in water, he would begin grinding them on the stone-slab and prepare a piquant dish, adding to it asafoetida, cummin seed, coriander leaves, etc.

39. Making a coil, about an arm and a quarter in length, of the kneaded dough, he would divide it into balls, rolling each one to make a large '*chapati*', or flat, thin wheat cake.

40. Adding *jowar* flour to an already measured amount of water, he would put some butter-milk in it to make it into '*ambil*', or a thin, sour gruel, in the *Handi*.

41. Then, very lovingly, Baba would serve this '*ambil*' with his own hands, to all, along with other food, with great respect.

42. Thus, making sure that the *Handi* was cooked properly, he would take it off the fire and carry it to the mosque.

43. Then after offering '*Fatiah*' or prayer to that food with proper rites by the *Maulavi*, he would first send the *prasad* to Mhalsapati and Tatya.

44. Then the remaining food Baba would serve with his own hands and would feel great contentment by satisfying the hunger of the poor and the meek.

45. And those desirous of eating would happily partake of the food till quite full, even as Baba pressed them to have more, saying lovingly, "Take, take some more!"

46. Oh, how great must be the merit of those who partook of this most satisfying meal! Blessed, blessed were those to whom Baba served food, himself.

47. Here a doubt may naturally arise, as to why Baba distributed, without any reservations, food with meat in it, to many a devotee.

48. No special effort is needed to clear this doubt. He would serve this food only to those who were habituated to non-vegetarian food.

49. He would not even let them touch meat, who had never eaten it in their lives. He never did anything so thoughtless. Moreover, it was given only to him who had a strong desire for that *prasad*.

50. When the guru himself is giving the *prasad*, if the disciple has doubts as to whether it is proper or improper to eat it, that disciple will head for self-destruction and go to Hell.

51. And Baba would see for himself, through jokes and humour, how far his devotees had become aware of this principle.

52. As I write this, I recollect an anecdote in this context. Listen to it at your ease, O listeners, and for your own benefit.

53. Once, on an *Ekadashi*[8] day, Baba said to Dada (Kelkar), "Will you get for me some mutton from Korhala?"

54. And Sai took out some rupees and counting them, gave them to Dada. "Do go yourself", he commanded, "Only you must do this".

55. Ganesh Damodar, whose surname was Kelkar, was called 'Dada' by all, in deference to his advanced age.

56. He was the father-in-law of Hari Vinayak Sathe. Himself a Brahmin, he was scrupulous in observing religious rites and rituals. He was a man of right-conduct and thought, whose love for Sai was boundless.

57. I know not, how this command did not surprise him, who served his guru, day and night, and yet was not satisfied!

58. Those not feeble of limb, but who have the power and strength born of prolonged *sadhana*, will not have a fickle mind and their intellect is also unwaveringly fixed at the guru's feet.

59. Offerings of wealth, grain, clothes are not the only form of *dakshina*. To obey the guru's command, to propitiate him and thus to please him is also *dakshina*.

60. He who offers all his action, speech, mind, etc., at the guru's feet and in the end wins his Grace, attains true and firm faith.

61. Obeying the command reverently, he quickly dressed and was about to set out to go to that village, when he was called back.

62. "Or else, you may just send someone to make this purchase!" Baba said, "Why needlessly take the trouble of going and coming?"

63. So Dada decided to send Pandu to bring the mutton. But just see what Baba said to Dada at the time.

64. As Pandu set out to go and was already on his way, he said, "Or, let it be, today!" and made him come back.

65. Later, on one occasion, a sudden fancy seized his mind to prepare the *Handi*. Putting the vessel on the fire, he poured the pieces of mutton into it.

66. Then he washed the rice and added it, along with a measured quantity of water, and arranging the firewood in the fireplace, sat blowing it.

67. When the whole village was a slave to his command, anyone would have gladly sat there blowing the fire. But they dared not do so without Baba's command.

68. Even for cooking, for bringing the food, it would have been enough for him just to give the order as his devotees, enslaved by

love, were always so eager. But it was Sai himself, who was not interested!

69. And yet, it is not proper even to say that he was not interested. For, when he had his own gain in view, in preparing the food, why will he trouble others to offer it to strangers?

70. Himself, he asked for '*madhukari*' [9], going from door to door for it, requesting for a quarter piece of *jowar* bread, just enough to sustain him.

71. Such a one will be really satisfied only when he himself toils for the *annadaan* to others. And so he never depended on anyone.

72. He himself carefully selected wheatflour, rice, pulses etc., to cook food for a hundred people paying for the ingredients in cash.

73. And, skuttle-basket in hand, when he himself went to the grocer, it was truly a lesson for people to learn as to how watchful one has to be in one's worldly dealings.

74. Taking a particular ingredient in hand, he would fix the rate only after hard bargaining. No one could cheat him, their pride being completely humbled.

75. He would put up such a pretence of calculating. But while paying promptly in cash, he would give even ten where the shopkeeper asked for only five.

76. He liked to do things himself and would not approve if someone else did the work. Nor did he expect others to do things for him. And yet he was not resentful of people.

77. This was the one principle that was constantly present in Baba's mind, day and night. Hence even in the work for the *Handi*, he never asked for help from anyone.

78. Not only in the matter of the *Handi*, but three-fourths of the eastern wall of the store-room for firewood near the *dhuni* was also constructed by Baba with his own hands.

79. Mahadu would prepare the mortar (a mixture of mud, lime or cowdung and water) and, trowel in hand, Baba would plaster the wall, placing layer upon layer of bricks to erect the walls.

80. Oh, what did Baba not do! He smeared the floor of the mosque with cowdung-wash himself, stitched his *kafni* and *langot* with his own hands without any expectations from anyone.

81. When the steam rose out of the boiling *Handi*, scorching hot, Baba would pull up his sleeves and, thrusting his hand inside, would stir up the contents up and down.

82. Seeing that the vessel was boiling and ready to be stirred, Baba would show his marvellous *leela* at the moment.

83. Oh! where the hand of flesh and blood, and where the vessel scorching hot! But neither any sign of the burns nor a frightened face could be seen!

84. And how could the fire hurt a hand which removed the threefold afflictions of the devotees, the moment it fell on their heads! Did it not know its greatness?

85. The soaked pulses he himself picked, cleaned on the stone-slab and ground them with the stone-roller. With his own hand, he would pat the mixture into small cakes.

86. These were then gently slipped into the *Handi* and stirred, so that they may not stick to the bottom of the vessel. Once ready, he would take the vessel down and distribute the *prasad* to all.

87. 'But why to everyone?' the listeners may ask. 'Sai Baba was a Muslim. Then how could he make them act against their *dharma* in this way?'

88. There is but one answer to this. Sai Baba was constantly aware of what is true *dharma* and *adharma*.

89. And never did Sai insist in the least, that the food cooked in the *Handi* should be eaten by all.

90. But whoever was urged by the good desire that he should get the *prasad*, the desire of such only was satisfied by him fully. He never deceived anyone.

91. Moreover, who knew his caste? Because he lived in the mosque, they all said he was a Muslim. But from his general conduct no one could make out his caste.

92. Does one look for the caste of him, in the dust of whose feet the devotees rolled in their loving devotion, treating him as God? Oh, shame on their spirituality!

93. He, in whom detachment for this world and the next was ingrained and whose wealth consisted in discriminating knowledge and renunciation — should his caste be a consideration, at all? Shame, shame on the spirituality of such!

94. Oh, does one ever think of the caste of him, who is beyond *dharma-adharma*, is pure Bliss? Shame indeed, on the spirituality of such!

95. Such is Baba's Life-Story! I, for one, sing his praises for my own happiness! And it will also satisfy the keen desire of anyone who wants to listen.

96. But we have left far behind the threads of the present story. So now listen attentively to what Baba said to Dada.

97. "Some savoury *Pulao*[10] has been prepared. Have you seen how it has turned out?" 'Oh, yes, yes! It is very good', said Dada, just as a formality.

98. Dada was an old, staunch devotee, who scrupulously observed daily religious rituals such as bath, *sandhya*, etc., and was also particular about conformity or otherwise to the *Shastras*. To him, this did not appear to be the proper thing.

99. So Baba said to Dada, "Never have you set eyes on it before nor has the palate ever tasted it. How can you say it is good?

100. "Just remove the cover of the vessel and put your hand in to see for yourself!" And holding his hand in his own, he just thrust it into the vessel.

101. He then said, "Now take your hand out; take the ladle and serve it in a plate. Do not worry about '*sovala*'[11], do not indulge in such vain talk!"

102. That the saints will ever ask the disciple to do anything to pollute him, is a most improper idea. They are always full of compassion and only they know their own ways.

103. Even a mother, when seized by a sudden surge of affection, pinches the child lovingly. But when the child screams, it is she who will at once hug him.

104. Only when one really wished to taste the forbidden food did Baba satisfy his desire for it. But one who had control over his mind always won Baba's approval.

105. The devotees' firm resolve to obey Baba's command sometimes went to such an extreme that those who had never touched meat in all their lives, also wavered in their belief.

106. But, in fact, Baba himself never induced such devotees to follow what they considered as the wrong path.

107. Thus, before the year 1910, the occasion for the *Handi* used to come very frequently, attended with great enthusiasm.

108. But after that Das Ganu visited Bombay and through his *kirtans*, impressed Baba's greatness upon the minds of all.

109. From then on, the young and the old, they all came to know of Baba's power and innumerable people started visiting Shirdi.

110. Then began Baba's *pooja*, complete with the five *pooja* ingredients and many types of food-offerings — for lunch and snacks at noon and in the afternoon.

111. Rice with *varan*, *seera* with *puris* (or thin puffed wheat cakes), *chapatis*, dressed salads and '*chatani*'[12], varieties of '*Panchamrut*'[13], *kheer* — all such dishes flooded into the mosque.

112. Pilgrims flocked there unlimited in number. Each and everyone would go running for the *darshan* and offered at his feet food-offerings, which naturally went towards satisfying the hungry.

113. Sai Baba began to be treated as a king, the umbrella and the *chamar* being waved over his head amid loud music of '*taals*' and other instruments, as the number of devotees grew.

114. His fame spread far and wide and all began to sing his praises. Later, Shirdi became a holy place of pilgrimage for the pilgrims.

115. Now there remained no reason for *Handi*. So numerous were the food-offerings that much food still remained after satisfying the fakirs, gosavis, etc.

116. Now I shall narrate another story, which you will be happy to hear. Baba was always displeased if disrespect was shown towards one's tutelar deity.

117. Drawing their own inferences, some call Baba a Brahmin, some a Muslim, when in fact, he was without any caste.

118. Without knowing where he belonged, when and in what caste he was born or who his parents were, Muslim or Brahmin.

119. Had he been a Muslim, how would he have allowed fire-worship in the mosque? And, would there have been a *Tulsi-vrindavan*, or, could he have tolerated the sounding of bells?

120. Would he have permitted the blowing of conch or *katha-kirtan* to the accompaniment of musical instruments like *taal, mridanga*, etc., and ceaseless proclamations of *Hari-naam*, in the mosque?

121. If he had been a Muslim, would he have allowed sandalwood-paste being applied to the forehead as he sat in the mosque? And would he eat in mixed company?

122. Had he been a Muslim, would he have had ears that were pricked? And, spending money out of his own pocket, would he have renovated temples that were old and dilapidated?

123. Would he have allowed being dressed in the fine, rich *'pitambar'*[14] after his bath? On the contrary, not for a moment would he brook any disrespect towards any tutelar deity.

124. I remember a very instructive tale in this connection, as I am writing this. I shall very humbly relate it to you. Please listen to it, quietly.

125. Once, it so happened that Baba had just returned from the Lendi and was sitting in the mosque. The devotees had also gathered for his *darshan*.

126. Amongst them was the great devotee, Chandorkar who was so dear to Baba. Eager for Baba's *darshan*, he had come with Biniwale, his brother-in-law (wife's sister's husband).

127. After making obeisance to Sainath, they both sat down in front of him and while enquiries after their well-being, etc., were in progress, Baba suddenly grew angry.

128.   He said, "Nana, how could you forget this? Is this all that you have learnt after spending days with me?

129.   "You who have been in my company, — is this all that it has come to, in the end? Oh, how could your mind be so deluded! Tell me everything carefully."

130.   On hearing this, Nana hung his head and began to look for the reason for this anger. But could not remember any and became very disturbed in his mind.

131.   He could not understand where he had gone wrong, could think of no reason for this anger. But Baba would never hurt anyone's feelings ur'ess something had happened.

132.   So he caught Baba's feet, entreating him in various ways. In the end, he spread his *'uparna'* before him, asking him why he was so angry with him.

133.   "When you have been in my company for years together, why should the state of your mind be still such? What has happened to you?" said Baba to him.

134.   "When did you reach Kopergaon and what happened on the way? Did you get down anywhere or drove the *tonga* straight here?

135.   "Did anything unusual happen on the way? I wish to hear everything in detail. Tell me what happened and where, whether it is trivial or otherwise."

136.   Nana at once understood as he heard this. His face fell. Though in his heart, he was ashamed to tell, yet he narrated everything.

137.   He made up his mind that hide-and-seek will not do here. So he narrated to Baba, in detail, what had happened.

138.   With Sai untruth would never work. Sai's Grace would never be obtained by telling a falsehood. Untruth leads to a Fall and ultimately, to an evil end.

139.   To deceive the guru is a great sin and there is no expiation for it. Knowing this full well, Nana related to Baba what had happened, from beginning to end.

140. He said, 'At first, when we engaged the *tonga*, it was to go straight up to Shirdi. But Biniwale would have missed, thereby, the *darshan* of Shri Datta on the banks of the Godavari.

141. 'Being a Datta-devotee, he naturally wished to get down for the *darshan*, as we were passing by the temple, which was on our way.

142. 'But I was in a mighty hurry and prevented him saying that we could have *darshan* while returning from Shirdi.

143. 'Becoming impatient that it would cause delay in reaching Shirdi, I put it off, thereby disregarding having *Datta-darshan*.

144. 'Later, while bathing in the Godavari, a big thorn got lodged in my foot, causing me great distress and discomfort on the way, until I ultimately pulled it out with some effort.'[15]

145. Baba warned him, "Such haste is not good. This time you have been lightly let off, only with a thorn-prick for disregarding *darshan*.

146. "When a holy tutelar deity like Datta was waiting on the way, to give *darshan*, without an effort, will I ever be pleased with the unfortunate one who disregards his *darshan*!"

147. But now let us talk about the *Handi*. Oh! what sanctity attended that meal with Sai in the afternoon! And what affection Sai had for the devotees!

148. Every day, as the devotees would return after Baba's *pooja* and *arati* at noon, Baba would give *udi* to them all.

149. Baba would come out and stand at the edge of the parapet of the mosque, while the devotees would stand waiting, in the courtyard. Then they would bow at his feet, one by one.

150. And as they stood in front of him, after bowing at his feet, one by one, he would apply the *udi* on the forehead of them all.

151. "Now all of you, young and old, go to your respective homes and have your meal." Obeying Baba's command respectfully, the people would return home.

152. The moment Baba's back was turned, the curtain would be pulled down, as was the daily practice, to the clanging of plates and *vatis* and all the pomp and show of the *prasad* would then begin.

153. Many a devoteee would sit waiting in the courtyard below, desirous of receiving some small portion of the *naivedya*, sanctified by the touch of Sai's hand.

154. Here as Baba sat with his back to the niche in the wall, on either side of him would sit spectacular rows of diners, each one of whom was most happy.

155. Each one would push his own *naivedya* in front of Sai Samarth and he too, would mix all of them together in a large plate with his own hand.

156. Immeasurable good fortune is needed to receive from Baba's hand even a grain of rice which would purify him who eats it, inwardly and outwardly, and bring fulfilment to his life.

157. 'Vadas'[16]; 'anarsas'[17]; 'sanjoris'[18]; puffed fried wheat cakes; sometimes 'shikharan'[19]; 'ghargas'[20]; 'phenias'[21]; a wide variety of vegetables, *kheers* and salads — Baba would mix all these together.

158. He would then offer this food mixed together to God, and Shama and Nana (Nimonkar) would be asked to serve platter after platter filled with it.

159. Then calling the devotees one by one, making them sit near him with great love and joy, he would make them eat till fully satisfied.

160. 'Varan' and 'chapatis'[22] squeezed up together into a mass and making it delicious by the addition of tasty clarified butter would then be served by Baba to all.

161. As one savoured this mixture, prepared so lovingly by Baba — Oh, who can express the blissful joy one experienced! One who tasted it would go, still licking his fingers and being fully satiated.

162. Sometimes 'mandas'[23]; 'puranpolis'[24]; sometimes puffed fried wheatcakes soaked in sugar syrup, sometimes 'basundi'[25]; 'seera'[26] or 'sanjoris'[27], sometimes tasty *chapatis* stuffed with jaggery — such was the varied and delicious fare that Baba served.

163. Sometimes milk-white rice of the fragrant 'Ambemohor' variety with tasty 'varan' and delicious clarified butter on top of it, would be served, surrounded by various types of vegetables.

164. Pickles, *papad*, salad with dressing of curds, types of 'bhajiyas'[28], etc., and, on rare occasions, even sour butter-milk, curds and

'*panchamrit*'[29] were also, there. Blessed are those who could partake of that sanctified food!

165. Where it was Sainath who served it, Oh what to say of the meal! The devotees ate there, till they were full, their satiety being evidenced by belching.

166. Every mouthful brought satisfaction, being pleasurable, nourishing and hunger-appeasing. Such was that tasty, delicious food, sacred and served so lovingly.

167. Taking Sai's name with every morsel, all the diners ate in the spirit of an '*ahuti*' or fire-offering. And yet the vessel did not, in the least become emptied, but remained full, all the time.

168. Whichever delicacy a particular person was fond of, that was served to him very affectionately. Many liked mango juice and very lovingly, it was served to them.

169. Nanasaheb Nimonkar or Madhavrao Deshpande was asked to serve this delicious food, every day.

170. And they too, had made it a daily practice to undertake this work of serving food, very lovingly, although it caused them a good deal of exertion and fatigue.

171. The fragrant '*Jeeresal*' rice, each grain of which was like a jasmine bud; then the golden yellow *varan* of the *toor daal* on it and a spoonful of clarified butter on top of it, was served to all.

172. Its fragrance pervaded the air even as it was being served. The meal would be piquant when served along with different '*chatanis*'[30], and no dish was either half-cooked or tasteless in the least, and everyone ate till they were fully satisfied.

173. The vermicelli on the platter of blissful *Samadhi*, the '*kurdais*'[31] of loving devotion — to feast on these, who will come but one who has experienced Peace and Joy!

174. Where food itself is *Hari*, one who eats it is *Hari* and he who enjoys its taste is also *Hari*, then he who serves this food is truly blessed. Blessed, blessed is he who eats it and he who gives it.

175. And the one genuine source of all this sweetness is one's unswerving faith in the guru. It is not the sugar or the jaggery that is sweet; it is the firmly rooted faith in Sai.

176. Such indeed, was the continual prosperity reigning there. When the '*seera*', '*kheer*', or the mixture of different food items was so plentiful, even a little hesitation or dawdling on the part of the diners would not do, once they sat down to the meal.

177. But the satisfaction of the diners would not be complete, even after such a variety of dishes, without curds and rice. If not so, at least some butter-milk would be asked for.

178. Once, a glass of pure butter-milk, filled by the guru with his own hand, was very lovingly offered to me and when I put it to my lips,

179. Seeing that snow-white butter-milk with my eyes, gave me great pleasure and satisfaction. As I put the glass to my lips, I received the nourishment of Self-rejoicing.

180. 'As it is, my stomach is so full. How will I be able to drink this?' Even as this tortuous doubt crossed my mind, I found the very first draught most delicious.

181. Seeing me feeling so awkward and hesitant, with a sincere entreaty, Baba said, "Oh, do drink it all up!" — as if he felt that such an opportunity was not going to come again!

182. And sure enough, I had that experience soon. For at the end of two months thereafter, Baba gave up the ghost and really attained *Nirvana*.

183. Now there is no other way to quench the thirst for that buttermilk, except by drinking deeply of the nectar of Sai's Story. That is the only way left!

184. Hemad surrenders to Sainath. Whichever story Sai himself reminds me of, that will be narrated next. Let the listeners continue to be attentive.

Weal be to all! Here ends the thirty-eighth chapter of the
"*Shri Sai Samarth Satcharit*", called
'*The Description of the Handi*',
as inspired by the saints and the virtuous
and composed by his devotee, Hemadpant.

Notes

1. A highly tasty dish of pulses.
2. These are: sweet, sour, salty, pungent, astringent and bitter
3. This is a semicircular erection of earth, to contain the fire in its cavity and support the cooking vessel on its rim and is called '*chool ah*'.
4. Dough spread over a leaf and rolled up and thrown into the fire to be baked or steamed.
5. A puffed mass of dough baked on embers.
6. A grain, *Phaseolus Mungo*.
7. This is the first part of the first chapter of the Quran.
8. The eleventh day of the waxing or of the waning moon, when many people observe a fast.
9. Refer Ch. 8, note 10.
10. A variety of rice preparation.
11. Refer Ch. 7, note 6.
12. A paste with seasoning, chillies, coriander leaves, lemon juice, etc.
13. A semi-liquid side-dish prepared with five ingredients, which is a blend of sour, sweet, salty, pungent and astringent tastes.
14. Refer Ch. 37, note 2.
15. What Shri Chandorkar himself once narrated to another Sai-devotee, Shri B V Deo, about this incident, differs in certain details from this account. The real reason for Chandorkar avoiding the *Datta-darshan*, according to his account, was not the fear of delay in reaching Shirdi as stated here, but that he had willy-nilly agreed to pay the *sadhu*, who lived in the Datta-temple, a sum of Rs 300/- towards the construction of a ghat on the banks of the Godarvari. On this particular occasion he did not carry enough money to be able to keep his word. So, to avoid the embarrassment of having to say 'no' to the *sadhu*, he dissuaded his companion, with his concurrence, from alighting there, forgetting for a moment that Baba would always know the truth. His punishment too, was not so slight as a single thorn-prick in his foot, but both he and his companion suffered several painful ones, much to the distress of both. (*Shri Sai Leela*, Vol. 5, issue 11-12, p. 648).
16. Spicy cakes of ground pulses.
17. Sweet cakes of rice flour, crisp, light and rich.
18. Stuffed sweet cakes made from semolina stuffing.
19. A dilute mixture of milk, mashed bananas and sugar.
20. A fried sweet cake or pat of rice or wheat flour mixed with sugar or jaggery and grated pumpkin.
21. A preparation from rice-flour, like a *papad* or wafer cake.
22. Refer verse 39 above.
23. A certain preparation with wheat-flour, considered a great delicacy.
24. Refer Ch. 32, note 1.
25. Milk boiled to slightly thick consistency with sugar and spices.
26. Refer Ch. 27, note 8.
27. Refer note 17, above.
28. Thin slices of vegetables like potatoes, brinjal, onions, etc., dipped in seasoned gram-flour and deep-fried.
29. Refer note 2 above.
30. Refer note 12 above.
31. A preparation of rice-flour resembling vermicelli.

39

The Exposition of a specific verse from the Gita and the creation of the Samadhi Mandir

MY OBEISANCE TO SHRI GANESH, TO SHRI SARASWATI, AND SHRI GURUMAHARAJ! TO THE FAMILY DEITY, TO SHRI SITA-RAMACHANDRA, MY MOST HUMBLE OBEISANCE! I BOW IN REVERENCE TO THE MOST VENERABLE GURU SHRI SAINATH!

1. Blessed, blessed is holy Shirdi; blessed is *Dwarakamayee*, his abode, where the most virtuous and sacred Shri Sai abided till his *Nirvana*.
2. Blessed, blessed indeed, were the people of Shirdi, for whom he came so far, for whatever reason, and has left them indebted to himself.
3. Shirdi, to begin with, was small, but attained greatness by its association with Sai and consequently became a most sacred place of pilgrimage.
4. Blessed are those women of Shirdi, too, blessed their single-minded devotion and faith, that they sang the praises of this unique saint Sai, while grinding or pounding grain or bathing.
5. Blessed, blessed was their love for him that they sang the most excellent songs, which, as one listens to some of the best of them, bring such peace of mind.
6. And, to satisfy the curiosity of the listeners, I shall give some of these becalming songs in the proper context and at the proper time.

7. Shri Sai first appeared under a wayside mango tree in the kingdom of the Nizam and arrived, quite unexpectedly, at Shirdi with a marriage-party from Dhoopkhed village.

8. A most virtuous gentleman from this village, Chand Patil by name, first discovered this treasure and it is because of him that others had Sai's *darshan.*

9. How he lost his mare, how he met Sai who made him have a few puffs of the *chillim* and how he found the Patil's mare for him;

10. How a nephew of Chandbhai's wife had come of a marriageable age and happened to choose a wife from Shirdi and how the marriage-party arrived at Shirdi —

11. A detailed story of all this has already been narrated to the listeners, earlier (in Ch.5). I was only reminded of it in this particular context. But it need not be repeated here.

12. Chand Patil, however, was just a pretext. Most anxious for the upliftment of his devotees, Sai incarnated on this earth and came to Shirdi of his own will.

13. Who but this Sai himself, will uplift the dull-witted, the foolish, the lowly and poor, those without the benefit of the purificatory religious influences since birth, the simple, naive, trusting people?

14. Just eighteen years of age, but from that time, he was accustomed to solitude. At night, he would lay himself down just anywhere, without a trace of fear. For to him, God pervaded everything, everywhere.

15. Where there was a ditch earlier, used by the whole village as a rubbish-heap, there he would lie down at night, after wandering everywhere during the day.

16. Thus passed many years. A more fortunate time had come for that ditch. And a huge *wada* of this compassionate Sai rose all round it.

17. In the end, that same ditch became the *sanctum sanctorum,* a place of repose for Sai's body. There he found his permanent resting place and the present *Samadhi* was built there.

18. And it is this same Sai Samarth, Patron of the poor and humble, who has created this Ark of his own Life Story for the benefit of

the devotees, to enable them to get across this otherwise impassable ocean of worldly life.

19. He did this with an earnest solicitude, thinking 'how will this, my family of blind and lame devotees cross over to the other bank of this river of worldly life, so very difficult to cross?'

20. It is necessary for all to get across this ocean of worldly life. But to do so, our hearts must be purified. Purification of the heart is the chief among all the means for crossing it and its source lies in devotion to God.

21. There is no devotion like listening to the stories of the guru. It inspires love for him, quite effortlessly. The mind becomes cleansed and purified. And from thence, spirituality is born.

22. Innumerable are the stories of Sai. Singing all of them will comprise a big volume. Having resolved to be brief, the expanse still becomes uncontrollable.

23. For as the eagerness of the listener grows, so does the fondness of the narrator to narrate. Let us then satisfy each other's fond wish for them and also attain our spiritual gain.

24. Here Sai himself is the captain of this boat and attentive listening is the fare for this ferry. He who listens to the stories with reverence and faith, will reach, without delay, the shore beyond.

25. In the last chapter, a brief description of the *Handi* was given, as also, the confirmation of faith of a Datta-devotee and the feeding of *naivedya* to the devotees' satiety.

26. Everyone knows that the plan of the chapters, so far, has been, that before ending the previous chapter, an indication was given of the subject of the next.

27. But, while ending the last chapter, I could not remember the story for the subsequent one and thought I would narrate only that subject of which Sai reminds me.

28. And in keeping with what I had so clearly stated, I am narrating here what, by Sai's Grace, I am reminded of.

29. Hence I pray to the listeners that they push aside any impediments and give their full attention, at their ease. It will only make them happy.

30. Once, Chandorkar, a true devotee, was sitting in the mosque, pressing Baba's feet and, at the same time, murmuring verses from the *Bhagavad-Gita*.

31. As his hands pressed Baba's feet, he busied his tongue in murmuring the fourth chapter of *Shri Bhagavad-Gita*. Just see the marvel of what happened then!

32. Sai Samarth who had all the knowledge of the past, present and future, felt that he should explain the meaning of the *Gita* to Nana.

33. So he made an excuse of Nana's indistinct murmur of that chapter dealing with the Yoga of Divine Knowledge (sometimes entitled as Yoga of Knowledge) and (true) Renunciation of Action, to ask him a question.

34. As the thirty-third verse ended with 'All actions in their entirety, O Partha! culminate in wisdom' and Nana went on with the verse, 'Learn that by humble reverence...'etc.

35. At this verse thirty-four, his recitation came to a halt. In his mind, Baba felt like asking a question and to impress his instruction on Nana's mind.

36. "Nana", he said, "What are you murmuring? Do say clearly what you are softly muttering! Allow me to hear what you are murmuring so indistinctly".

37. The moment he was thus commanded, Nana obeyed at once and recited all the four lines of the stanza. Baba then asked him to explain clearly, its significance.

38. With great humility, with folded hands, Nana very happily answered in sweet words and explained the significance of Bhagavan Shri Krishna's intent.

39. Now let us give the original verse, word for word from the *Gita*, so that this dialogue betwen Baba and Nana becomes clear to all.

40. So as to understand the real essence of this question and the way the minds of saints work, I feel I should begin in such a way that the significance will be brought out, without any doubts or difficulties.

41. 'The Sanskrit language is, as it is, difficult to understand. How did it become so easy for Sai?' they all wondered, 'And how did he put so apt a question? Truly, the knowledge that the saints have is inconceivable!

42. 'When did he study Sanskrit? And when did he read the *Gita*, so as to put such a question as befits a learned one who has mastered the very essence of the *Gita*?'

43. To satisfy the listeners and give them an idea of the original verse, I shall repeat, to the letter, the exact words of Shri Bhagvan, which will also be helpful for the discussion.

44. "Learn that by humble reverence, by inquiry (persistent search for the reality by piercing through illusion), and by service; the masters of knowledge who have seen the truth will instruct thee in (that) wisdom."

45. This is that original verse from the *Gita*. Many have been the commentators on this. But they are all unanimous in their exposition of this verse.

46. Nana too, was very well-versed and had made a deep, prolonged study of the commentaries on the *Gita*. He began to explain the significance of the verse word by word.

47. Very courteously, with great humility and in sweet words, Nana was ready to give an exposition, after carefully arranging the words from verse into prose.

48. He said, 'He who prostrates in obeisance at the guru's feet, is ready to give up his life in the guru's service and puts a question to the guru very respectfully, to him the *Jnanis* give knowledge with exposition.

49. 'In brief, what Shri Krishna, Kindness Incarnate, said so lovingly to Arjuna was this, that guru-service and guru-worship alone, are the means of attaining knowledge.

50. 'O Arjuna, if you go along this way, then the Self-realized *Jnanis* will show you the way to Knowledge. Baba, this is the significance that I understand.'

51. Shankaracharya, Anandgiri, Shankaranand, Shridhar, Madhusudan and Neelkantha — they have all described this same

way of Bhagvan Shrikrishna's giving instruction in their commentaries.

52. Sai Samarth accepted the exposition of the first two lines. But as for that of the remaining half of the verse: (i.e. remaining two lines), listen to what Sai said.

53. The other devotees too, sat there open-mouthed, to listen, gazing on Baba's face, like the Chakor bird gazing at the moon to savour the particles of nectar.

54. Baba said, "Nana, try to understand the complete third line, once again. Add the elision mark before the word '*Jnana*' and then see the significance.

55. "Do not think needlessly that I am saying something quite to the contrary, reducing sense to nonsense; how can earlier commentaries be all untrue?

56. "You say that 'the masters of knowledge who have seen the Truth, will instruct thee in that wisdom'. But when you take the word '*Ajnana*' in place of '*Jnana*', you will get the true significance.

57. "*Jnana* is not something that one can talk about. Then how can it be the subject of instruction? So take the opposite of *Jnana* and then experience it.

58. "I have heard your meaning of *Jnana*. But what do you lose by taking the word *Ajnana* in its place? *Ajnana* can become the subject of speech but *Jnana* itself is beyond words.'

59. "The placenta encircles the foetus, dirt covers a mirror and ash, the fire. Similarly *Ajnana* covers *Jnana*.

60. "Bhagvan Shrikrishna has himself said in the *Gita* that *Jnana* is covered by *Ajnana*. Hence once this *Ajnana* or ignorance is removed, *Jnana* shines forth, in virtue of its own nature.

61. "*Jnana* is self-enlightened but is like moss-covered pure water. Only the wise man who removes the moss will get the pure water.

62. "It is like the eclipse of the sun and the moon. They are always illumined. But it is the planets *Rahu* and *Ketu*[1] who come in their way and hinder our sight.

63. "But the sun and moon suffer no harm. The hindrance is to our sight of them. Similarly, *Jnana* is self-illumined and safe in its own place.

64. "What the eye perceives, its power to see, is *Jnana*. The film that grows over it is the *Ajnana* and it is necessary to remove it.

65. "Remove that film or covering with the skill of the hand and dispelling the darkness of *Ajnana*, manifest the power of perceiving.

66. "This whole visible universe is an indescribable spectacle of *Maya*. This is the unmanifest *Maya* or *a-vidya*, which is without a beginning. This, this is the play of *Ajnana*.

67. "*Jnana* is a matter of realization; it is not a subject for instruction. And obeisance to the guru, repeated questions to him and his sincere service, these are the means of winning his Grace.

68. "Reality of this Creation is the greatest illusion. This is the darkness that covers *Jnana*, which has first to be dispelled. Only then will Brahman, which is Absolute Knowledge, manifest itself.

69. "*Ajnana* is the root of all sorrows of worldly life. But when the collyrium of the guru's Grace is put into the eyes, the veil of *Maya* over it, will vanish and what will remain will be *Jnana* which is natural.

70. "*Jnana* is not a thing to be attained; it is already self-enlightened and this is well-known to the *Veda-shastras*. The obstacle in its way is *Ajnana*.

71. "To consider God and devotees as separate, is the greatest *Ajnana*. Once this *Ajnana* is removed, what remains is Perfect *Jnana*.

72. "The illusion of a snake in a rope is *Ajnana* of its true nature. Knowledge of its true nature removes the *Ajnana* and there remains only the true knowledge of the rope.

73. "Gold is within, covered by a layer of dirt. Inside the dirt is its scintillating radiance. But to make it manifest, fire is necessary.

74. "*Maya* is the cause of the birth of this body and the working of the body depends on Destiny. The pairs of opposites too, depend on the preordained. Hence attachment to the body is *Ajnana*.

75. "Hence those who are detached, have no consciousness of joy and sorrow. Only when the stirrings of this attachment die down, will *Ajnana* be dispelled.

76. "Ignorance of the true Self is the source of *Maya*. Once this *Maya* is removed by the guru's grace, the knowledge of the true Self comes naturally.

77. "Why exhaust yourself trying out other means, except the only one of God-devotion? Even *Brahmadev* is governed by *Maya* and the only means of release for him is devotion.

78. "Even after attaining to the *Brahmalok*, there is no liberation without devotion and if God-devotion is missed out even there, man gets caught in the cycle of rebirths.

79. "Hence, to dispel this *Maya* the one and only remedy is God-worship. A devotee of God has no 'Fall', nor does he have the bondage of worldly life.

80. "People say that *Maya* is illusory; but she is a great sorceress and cheats even the *Jnanis*, at every step. But the devotees make her dance at the very snap of their middle finger and thumb.

81. "Where even the great learned ones are deceived, the simple, faithful ones hold their ground, for they have, for ever, surrendered themselves at *Hari's* feet, while the *Jnanis* suffer from the conceit of their knowledge.

82. "Hence to get safely across this *Maya*, hold fast to the Sadguru's feet, surrender to him single-mindedly. And the fear of worldly life will vanish instantly.

83. "When death is inevitable, let it come, but let not *Hari* be forgotten. May the organs function according to the *ashrama* and *varna*, but let the mind meditate on *Hari*.

84. "As the horses are harnessed to the chariot, so are the organs to the body. They are controlled by the intellect with the reins of firm resolution.

85. "The mind is filled with doubts and resolves and tends to run wild as it pleases. And it is the intellect that curbs it with a firm control over the reins.

86. "When the charioteer is so skilled a leader as the intellect, why should the master of the chariot worry? He should carry on the worldly business, with an easy mind.

87. "To see to the proper performance of all the bodily functions is the work of the intellect. Once the mind is habituated to this, all the business turns beneficial.

88. "When the physical organs run after sense-objects, like word, touch, form, etc., there will be a needless waning of strength and also, the fear of fall, at every step.

89. "Whatever pleasure one finds in the five sense-objects, like word, touch, form, etc., ultimately turns into pain. Truly, nothing is so painful as ignorance!

90. "Infatuated by the word, a deer loses its life in the end; an elephant enjoys the touch, but has to bear the irritation of the goad, too!

91. "The form bewitches a moth who finally gets burnt; the fish enjoys the taste but loses its life instantly.

92. "Beguiled by the fragrance, the black bee gets trapped in the lotus. If each one, by itself, leads to such calamities, how disastrous must be all the five together.

93. "After all, these are only animals, birds and aquatic creatures. But even the wise human being, after seeing their sad fate, still runs after the sense objects! Could ignorance be anything different?

94. "When ignorance is removed and sensual pleasures are given up, the agitated mind will be emancipated from the thraldom of Illusion, and the creature will turn towards Self-realization, which will bring him the highest bliss.

95. "In your heart, contemplate on *Hari-guru*; with your ears, listen to his Life Story; let the mind meditate ceaselessly on his form and the tongue chant his name.

96. "Go walking to the place of *Hari-guru*; with the nose inhale the fragrance of his '*nirmalya*'[2]; fold your hands in obeisance to his feet and with the eyes, take his *darshan*.

97. "In this way, when the inclinations of all the sense organs are lovingly directed towards Him, blessed will be the state of the devotees. What else is this but God-devotion!

98. "In short, eradicate ignorance, totally and know that what remains is Perfect Knowledge. Such is the implied significance of this verse which Shrikrishna suggested to Arjuna."

99. As it was, Nana was already full of humility. On hearing this sweet exposition, he prostrated at Baba's feet, making obeisance with both his hands.

100. He then very sincerely and earnestly prayed, 'Baba, please dispel my ignorance and destroy my obstinate ego by educating me properly!

101. 'A fond outward display of rightousness but with a mind full of doubts within and without the capacity to bear insult even for a moment — can ignorance be different from this?

102. 'Inwardly, a keen desire for honour and reputation with an outward show of meditation, while anger, lust smoulder within — what is this but ignorance?

103. 'In reality, full of wicked deeds, without a place for righteous deeds or good thoughts, but flaunting a knowledge of Brahman, outwardly — is this not clearly, ignorance?

104. 'Baba, a Cloud of Compassion that you are, extinguish this fire of ignorance by a shower of your Grace. This and this alone will bless me!

105. 'I do not want a mere talk of knowledge. Please remove this excessive ignorance of mine and bestow your Grace on me. In that itself, lies my happiness and contentment.'

106. Sai is loving and compassionate. Making the pretext of Nana, he gave this exposition of the *Gita* for you and me and for all.

107. *Gita* is the Word of God and therefore, really, a *Shastra*, the truth of which holds in the past, present and future. It should never be slighted.

108. Those who are excessively attached to sensual pleasures and those who are Self-realized, they both have no need of the significance of the *Shastra*. It is created only for the Seeker.

109. To uplift that Seeker who sincerely feels, 'I am so securely tied to the senses, when will I be liberated from them?' — it is for his redemption that these *Shastras* are born.

110.   On seeing such a devotee, the saints are moved by compassion and find some excuse to give him instruction, effortlessly.

111.   Be it God or be it guru; he is absolutely in the power of his devotee. He is anxious for the devotee's weal and takes upon himself all the devotee's difficulties.

112.   Now I shall briefly narrate to you another of Sai's marvellous ways — how he would initiate a piece of work, without anyone being aware of it.

113.   It may be a small task or big, but the real purpose would never be given out, while the work would gradually take shape, without even a mention anywhere.

114.   The project would come up quite casually, and would be initiated without any indication or naming of its real purpose, creating on the contrary, quite an erroneous impression on everybody.

115.   It was, as if Baba was undoubtedly giving the actual experience of the conventional adage, 'What real work will he do who only babbles, and what will it rain that merely thunders?'

116.   Incarnations, like Baba, appear in this world only to do good to others and when their mission is achieved, they merge, in the end, into the unmanifest.

117.   But we do not know the root cause of our existence — from where we have come and where we will proceed or why we were born and what is the purpose of our birth.

118.   We spend our life as we wish. Then comes the time of death. All the bodily organs become feeble and yet, a good thought does not enter the mind.

119.   Although we see the wife, sons, brothers, mother, our chosen friends and kith and kin, dying before our very eyes, yet it does not give rise to any good, wise thoughts in our mind.

120.   But the saints are not like that. They are most alert and having full knowledge of the time of death, they know their own *nirvana*.

121.   While still in the body, they, very lovingly, wear out their body for the devotees and after death, make use of the place of their death for uplifting their devotees.

122. Thus, before giving up the body, some get their *samadhi* built, so that later the body may be laid to rest definitely, at the same spot.

123. And Baba did the same. But nobody realized it earlier. He got his *samadhi-mandir* built. Really his *leela* is marvellous!

124. A very wealthy person from Nagpur, Bapusaheb Butti by name — at his hands Baba had this monument raised.

125. Bapusaheb was a great devotee. Always absorbed at Baba's feet, he came with his family to Shirdi and stayed there to serve Baba.

126. Out of love for Baba, he would always stay there, time and again and later on, felt like staying permanently in Shirdi.

127. And he thought that he should buy some plot of land and construct a small building, so that he could stay there independently.

128. It was here that the seed was sown, initially and the Mandir today, is the tree that grew from it, which is a memorial to Baba's love for the devotees.

129. How it was raised, little by little; in what way it was begun and how it took its present shape — listen to an account of all this, now.

130. Even as the thoughts were passing through his mind, Bapusaheb had an interesting Vision, while he was asleep on the upper storey of *Dikshitwada*.

131. And while Madhavrao too, was sleeping in that same place, even he had the same Vision, to the astonishment of both.

132. Bapusaheb had a dream in which Baba commanded him, "Build your *wada*, most certainly including in it a temple.

133. Immediately on seeing this Vision, Bapusaheb woke up, trying to remember the dream from the beginning, as he lay in his bed.

134. While this was taking place, Madhavrao was suddenly heard weeping and as Butti called out to him to wake up, the dream vanished.

135. When Madhavrao was asked, 'Why were you weeping?' he said, 'I was overcome with love when I heard Shri's loving words.

136. 'My throat was choked with emotion and tears welled up in the eyes. The intense love in my heart that I could not control, burst out in tears.

137. 'Coming close to me, Baba gave a distinct command, "Let the *wada* and temple take a concrete shape. I shall fulfil the wishes of all"'.

138. In his heart, Bapusaheb was quite amazed that both of them should have the same Vision. But this cleared all doubts from his mind and it was resolved to begin the work.

139. Butti himself was born with a silver spoon in his mouth and therefore had the means to build the *wada* and the temple. Madhavrao was just well-to-do. And yet, both had the same Vision.

140. Their dreams tallied with each other's and both were most happy. They fixed the general outline of the project, which was approved by Kaka (Dikshit).

141. So, early next morning, when all the three of them were with Baba, as usual, Baba was scrutinizing Shama's face with great attention and love.

142. Shama said, 'O God, what is this incomprehensible sport of yours? You do not even allow us to sleep peacefully! There too, you make us rave wildly'.

143. On hearing this, Baba at once, put his hands on his ears and said, "Whatever anyone may say, we have been in our own place!"

144. Then the above-mentioned scheme was put before Baba for his consent. Immediately, Baba gave permission to build the house with the temple.

145. Madhavrao was all ready, girding up his loins and at his hands were built the basement and the ground floor. The well was constructed too! And the work progressed thus far.

146. Eagerly, Baba would watch the progress while going to the Lendi or returning from it, as the doors and windows were being fixed.

147. Raising his index finger, he would say, "Put a door here, a window there. Here, to the east, take out a gallery. It will enhance the beauty".

148. Later, according to the law of cause and effect, the work that was to be carried out at the hands of Bapusaheb Jog, was then entrusted to him.

149. And as the work was thus progressing, Butti's mind was inspired by the idea that 'if a *sanctum sanctorum* is also included in this, then an idol of *Muralidhar* (Shri Krishna) can also be installed here.'

150. The idea arose, but without consulting Baba's wishes, and without the guru's express permission, Butti would never begin any piece of work.

151. This had always been the rule with him. Baba's permission was the most important consideration, without which, not a single work would he begin.

152. 'Why do we want a division in the hall? What is its necessity? The wall on either side can be pulled down and the *Muralidhar* installed there.'

153. This was the wish of Bapusaheb, to have a temple in the place of a divided apartment. But Baba's wish must be consulted and if he consents it should be done undoubtedly!

154. Therefore, he said to Madhavrao, 'Let us ask what Baba thinks and then whatever his wish we will chalk out the further plan accordingly'.

155. While on his daily round, as Baba came near the *wada* and reached the door, just see what Shamrao asks.

156. 'O God, Bapusaheb here, says we should pull down both the walls dividing the hall and install there the idol of Shri krishna with the flute.

157. 'Planning in such a way as to have a quadrangle in the centre, we can make a throne there, with *Muralidhar* installed on it, which will add greatly to the beauty.

158. 'So Bapusaheb wants to plan. But your permission is necessary for that. In this way, the temple and the *wada* will both be ready quickly.'

159 On hearing these words of Shama, Baba happily said, "All right. Once the temple is ready, we too, will come there to stay".

160. Gazing at the *wada*, Baba would fondly talk of things, "When the *wada* is complete, it can be used only for us.

161. "For there itself we will move about and talk; there we will all play and embracing each other lovingly enjoy boundless happiness".

162. Then Madhavrao asked Shri Sai, 'If this is the final direction, let us lay the foundation stone on this auspicious day.

163. 'Is this time auspicious, O God? Shall I bring and break the coconut, right away?' As Baba at once said, "Break, break!" he brought a coconut and broke it.

164. Later on, the *sanctum sanctorum* was made, along with the platform for the Lord *Muralidhar*. Even the making of the idol was entrusted to an artisan.

165. But then it so happened that Baba became severely ill and the end came near. All the devotees were greatly agitated in their minds.

166. Bapusaheb, in his mind, grew restless, too, and was very sad as to what the condition of the *wada* would thereafter be?

167. 'Will Baba's feet touch the temple after all? Lakhs of rupees have been spent and now this obstacle has come in the way.

168. 'When Baba gives up his mortal coil, why *Muralidhar* or the house? Wherefore this *wada* or the temple?' Butti's heart was sad and dejected.

169. But later on, by the concurrence of fortune and merit, and by the great good fortune of that *wada*, in the end, everything happened according to the wishes of all and by Baba's own command.

170. In the very last moments, words came from Baba's mouth, "Place me in the *wada*" and everybody's mind was relieved.

171. Then that sacred body of Sai was rested in the *sanctum sanctorum* and the *wada* became the *Samadhi-mandir*. Sai Baba's Life Story is truly inconceivable!

172. Blessed is the good fortune of that Butti, in the *wada* of whose ownership, rests the body of Shri Sai whose very name is so very sacred.

173. Such is this sacred Story, listening to which the listeners will become happy and prosperous. Hemad surrenders to Sainath and does not leave his feet even for a moment.

174. Whatever the experiences may be, good or bad, if you please Sai by conducting yourself according to his instruction and advice, you will, most certainly, attain your weal.

175. When the story, its narrator and the mouth that narrates are themselves Sai Samarth, then who is this Hemad? Just a nickname!

176. Hence you will next hear only that tale, which comes to him by inspiration. Why worry today about that which will be composed only at that time?

Weal be to all! Here ends the thirty-ninth chapter of
"*Shri Sai Samarth Satcharit*", called
'*The Exposition of a specific verse from the
Gita and the Creation of the Samadhi-mandir*',
as inspired by the saints and the virtuous and
composed by his devotee, Hemadpant.

Notes

1   In mythology, they are the demons with the tail of a dragon, whose heads were severed from their bodies by Vishnu. The head and the tail retaining their separate existence, were transferred to the planetary heavens, the first becoming the eighth planet, and the second, the ninth. To them are ascribed the eclipses of the sun and moon.

2.   The stale flowers, offered earlier to God at the time of *pooja*.

40

The Narration of the story of Udyapan

1. Blessed, blessed is Shri Sai Samarth, who has, in the form of this book, brought fulfilment to the devotees and has also accomplished his own purpose by instructing them about the worldly as well as the spiritual matters.

2. He who, in an instant, passes on his own power to the devotees, the moment his hand falls on the devotee's head, thus makes attainable to him the most unattainable of things, removing all separateness between them.

3. When you prostrate before him in obeisance, giving up the feeling of separateness, of 'you' and 'me' and surrender to him single-mindedly, he holds you to his heart in an embrace of love.

4. An ocean and a river are different in name, but in the rainy season, when they become one, their visible form is one and the same, without any differentiation.

5. With that same feeling, when the devotees surrender whole-heartedly to the *Sadgurunath*, seeing their steadfast devotion, he also gives his power to the devotees.

6. Hail to you, O Sainath, who are most loving and merciful to the meek and the poor and, though all-pervading that you are, yet you stay aloof, in Shirdi, for the upliftment of the devotees.

7. A saint that you are, yet when you set up the quern and sit with legs apart to grind the grain, fixing up the handle of the quern, firmly in place to grind the first lot of grain, it caused great astonishment to my mind.

8. And it was the root cause of this book. A powerful desire arose in my mind that by describing all such deeds of yours, the sins can be totally destroyed.

9. Hari himself will be most pleased. For more than his own, He likes the praises of his devotees or their virtues, sung by others.

10. Those listeners who think that statement is without any proof, will naturally have doubts. But they should see the '*Bhavishyottar Purana*', where *Tripurari*[1] himself has said this.

11. And all this was Sai's inspiration, too. But to follow the convention, he gave permission to this composition for the benefit of the devotees.

12. Thereafter the listeners have been lovingly listening to the Story of Sai Samarth, serialized from month to month in the *Sai Leela* magazine.

13. It is the same Sai who has given me permission; it is he who has given me the intelligence; it is again he who originally inspired me and once again, it is he who is himself getting his own story written.

14. Let there be no doubt in your minds that this Hemad is himself composing this according to his own intelligence; and, therefore, I request you that you do not attribute to me either its merit or its faults.

15. Where there is merit, it is Sai's and where there are faults, they too, are his. I am but a puppet in Sai's hand and dance as the strings are pulled.

16. The strings are in the hands of the puppeteer and he will make the characters dance, in a variegated and colourful or strange manner, according to the story.

17. But now, enough of this introduction! The listeners who must be eager to proceed, ask me, 'What is the next marvellous story?'

Let me narrate to them the greatness and glory of the guru and his devotees.

18. Before concluding the last chapter it was decided to start the next with whatever story I am reminded of. So now, listen to this one that comes to my mind.

19. Let the listeners listen attentively to this sweet tale about how highly satisfied Sai is, when the devotee, very lovingly, serves him a meal.

20. Actually, Sai is to his devotee as tender and loving as a mother to her infant and comes running to his aid, wherever he might be. Who can ever repay this great obligation?

21. Physically, he moved about Shirdi and yet was present in all the three worlds. Listen with an easy mind to an interesting account in this context.

22. Balasaheb Deo, a very great devotee, had a firm unwavering faith in Sai. His mother always observed religious vows for the weal of all.

23. Once she had observed many such vows, the '*udyapan*'[2] of which remained to be performed, to conclude them satisfactorily.

24. When the set number of these vows are completed, it is necessary to perform the *udyapan*, or else, no merit is gained through their performance, as they remain incomplete.

25. For the *udyapan* of about twenty-five to thirty such vows, Deo had invited about a hundred or two hundred Brahmins for a meal.

26. He fixed a day for the ceremony and to invite Baba, he wrote to Jog to make the request to him on his behalf, saying,

27. 'Unless you come, the ceremony can never be completed, properly. Hence oblige this humble servant by accepting this prayer.

28. 'I am but a government servant, who has to work for a livelihood and do just a little spiritual *sadhana* that I can manage, of which you know too well in your mind.

29. 'Hence to come personally from Dahanu all the way to Shirdi is not in my power. But I have great hope that you will accept my invitation.'

30. Bapusaheb Jog read out the full letter, to Baba, saying, 'Do help Deo, carry out this *udyapan* satisfactorily'.

31. Baba listened fully to that invitation, sent with such a pure heart, and said, "I always remember him who remembers me.

32. "I need no horses or carriages, no aeroplanes and trains. To him who calls out to me fondly, I appear instantly, without a moment's delay.

33. "You, me and a third one[3], we three shall go together. Send him such a letter. The writer of that letter will be happy."

34. Accordingly, Jog informed Deo what Baba said. Deo was very happy by Baba's words, which were always true.

35. Deo too, had full faith — 'Now Baba will come definitely. But the day I experience this will be a golden day.'

36. But this too, Deo knew that apart from Shirdi, there were only three other places that Baba went to and that too, very rarely. Baba was always in Shirdi.

37. If he felt like it, in six months or so, Baba went to Rahata, sometimes to Rui or to Nimgaon. But otherwise, he stayed in Shirdi, all the time.

38. 'Beyond these three villages, he never goes anywhere. Then how will he come so far to me, at Dahanu?

39. 'But he is a perfect incarnation of Shri Vishnu and can go wherever he pleases. The coming or going is only a worldly convention while he pervades everything, inside out.

40. 'His coming from there to here or going from here to there, are two things, even the sky above will not know, for he fills it completely, from inside and outside.

41. 'Such are Baba's movements, difficult to know. He fills everything totally — animate and inanimate. What then, is coming and going, to him? He appears wherever he pleases.'

42. However, about a month before this invitation, a *sanyasin* had come to the station-master of Dahanu, for his own work.

43. He was a propagator for *Go-shala* and a volunteer of an institution for the cows and had come to collect contributions to improve the financial position of this institution.

44. From the dress, he appeared to be a Bengali. The master told him the trick, 'Go into the town and there you will be well looked after.

45. 'The *Mamledar* is there. Put this scheme before him. The *Shets* and the *Sowcars* (i.e. the wealthy class) you will meet there, who will give you a helping hand.

46. 'Once the *Mamledar* is in your favour, the contributions for the religious cause will come in no time. So go there with an easy mind.'

47. Even as the station-master was saying this inside, the sound of the horse's feet was heard outside. The *Mamledar* himself had come there, had got down and had gone inside the station.

48. As he entered the room to meet the master, the latter said to the *sanyasin*, 'Look! The *Mamledar* has himself come here!

49. 'Now you can tell him whatever you want to say. Luckily, you have met him quite easily.' The *sanyasin* then told him the purpose of his visit.

50. They both came out and sat on a box. The *sanyasin* earnestly entreated Deo, 'This work must be accomplished.

51. 'Cow protection is a religious service. Unless you take it in hand, is it possible in the least that it can be accomplished by an outsider like me?

52. 'You are the officer of this taluka while I am just a beggar, wandering from door to door, to prevent the starvation of the cows.

53. 'If you just put in a word, my work will be speedily done and you will get the blessings of the Mother Cow, since you will undoubtedly succeed in this work.'

54. On hearing this request of the *sanyasin*, Deo said, 'We have just started collecting contributions for some other cause in the town, at present.

55. 'Raosaheb Narrottam Shet, a leading citizen, who is most compassionate to the poor and also, very active, has already started a collection of funds.

56. 'Now you tell me, how will your collection fit in with this? Therefore this time is not favourable for you. But we can see afterwards.

57. 'So you wait for two or four months and then come back to this place. Then later on, we shall see. Today, your work is not feasible.'

58. The *sanyasin* then went away from there. It was about a month later after this that he came back in a *tonga* to Dahanu, once again.

59. Opposite Deo's residence lived one advocate, Paranjpe. It was before his house that Deo saw the *tonga* stop and the *sanyasin* alight from it.

60. Suspicion at once, arose in Deo's mind and he said to his son, 'This is definitely the same *sanyasin* who had come earlier and has now come for the contributions, much before time.

61. 'When hardly a month has gone by, why has he come here? Has he forgotten our earlier conversation?' This was the reason for his doubts.

62. The *sanyasin* let off the *tonga* there itself, where he had got down, lingered there awhile and then came to Deo's house. Listen to what he said.

63. It was just ten o'clock, the time for the preparation of the meal for the Brahmins. Seeing Deo's restlessness, he said, 'I am not impatient for the money.

64. 'I have not come for the money. It is a meal that we want today.' Deo said, 'Come, come! It is a pleasure. Regard this house as your own.

65. Suddenly, the *sanyasin* said, 'I have two boys with me.' 'This is a very good thing', said Deo to him.

66. There was still time for the meal. So Deo asked him, 'Where are you staying? Where can I send someone to call for you?'

67. 'Where is the need for that? When should I come? At what hour should I present myself? Whenever you say, I shall come', the *sanyasin* began to say.

68. 'All right, come at twelve o'clock, bringing the boys, with you, and O saint, take your meal here', said Deo.

69. The *sanyasin* then went away and returned at exactly twelve o'clock. All the three of them sat down to the meal and were fully satiated, having had as much as they wanted.

70. When the food was ready, rows of Brahmins sat down for the meal. The host satisfied all, including the *sanyasin* and the two boys who came with him.

71. Though the *sanyasin* came on his own, bringing two others with him, yet the purpose of the earlier visit had spread a veil of *Maya*.

72. Hence to Deo's mind, it appeared only as if this was some guest, who had come for a meal. The delusion took a firm hold of his mind.

73. In this way, the meal was over. After the meal, '*uttaraposhan*' or '*aachaman*'[4] of clean pure water was offered — the drinking of cool, fragrant water, together with an offering of betel-nut, etc.

74. Deo, with great pleasure and due respect, offered everyone the customary sandalwood paste with flowers, *paan*, rosewater and '*attar*'[5].

75. Thereafter, people went back to their respective homes. The *sanyasin* also returned to his place with the two boys.

76. Though they came quite by chance and uninvited, yet they came at the proper time and had their meal. But to Deo, the *sanyasin* did not appear to be Baba and doubts still lingered in his mind.

77. Although, all this actually happened and the meal was served in front of him to the three uninvited guests, yet in his mind, Deo remained still suspicious. He even asked Jog for some proof of Baba's visit.

78. With the result, when the '*udyapan*' was over, Deo wrote a letter to Jog, 'How is it that Baba has so deceived? Why did he give an assurance about his coming to Dahanu?

79. 'Will it not make me feel that you will accompany him, that his words will not be untrue and that I will get some proof of this?

80. 'And yet, why has such a thing happened? Why was I alone, to be disappointed thus? With great hopes I waited, but had no such experience of the truth.

81. 'So lovingly had I invited Baba and he too, had said to me, this supplicant for his protection, that he would come! But all that was reversed. How, I am just unable to understand!

82. 'Because of my inability to come there personally, due to my dependence on others, I wrote the letter of earnest entreaty and felt truly blessed on hearing that in spite of this fact, you were coming.

83. 'I felt that you would come under any pretext, under any disguise. But how did it not happen, is something that surprises me, particularly.'

84. Jog narrated the full content to Sai. Listen to what Baba, in great astonishment said to him.

85. "When the letter is unfolded in front of me, even before it is read out, all the thoughts of the writer in that letter, stand revealed before me.

86. "He says that after assuring him of the truth of my words, I deceived him. Tell him that if he did not recognize me, why did he invite me?

87. "To all appearances I did not move out of here. Yet, I lunched at the function. I had said I would come, accompanied by two others and so I had gone with the two.

88. "There was still time for the meal. So, walking slowly, I alone went. Do you not remember the *sanyasin's* robes? In this way I first went.

89. "Seeing that I had come unexpectedly, were you not afraid that I would ask for money? And then I cleared your doubts.

90. "Did I not say that I will come only for the meal, bringing two others with me and then came at the proper time with the two and had lunch?

91. "See, just to keep my Word, I will even give up my life! But the words from my mouth will never ever be untrue!"

92. When Sainath said this, Jog's joy knew no bounds. For it was the experience of all that the Promise once given, never remained unfulfilled.

93. Later on, with great happiness Jog conveyed all this to Deo in a detailed letter.

94. When Deo read it, his eyes were flooded with tears of love and joy. 'O shame, shame on me that I blamed Sai!', he thought, inwardly ashamed of himself.

95. 'Blessed is Sai's greatness and shame on my conceit that I know everything! But I do not understand as to how I was to guess that that *sanyasin* was Baba himself?

96. 'Before I invited Baba, the *sanyasin* had already paid his first visit and that too, for his own work of collecting funds.

97. 'I had already given him the time of two or four months for coming again. But when that same *sanyasin* came and asked for a meal, how was I to infer that he is Baba himself?

98. 'But there is only one statement of Baba's, "When I come to have a meal, there will be two others with me", which completely escaped my mind.

99. 'Had I met the *sanyasin* for the first time and that too, only for that meal, after my invitation to Baba, then I would not have been deceived thus.

100. 'But he came in connection with cow-protection and for collecting money to feed the cows. It was after this that I sent this invitation to Sai to come for the *'udyapan'*.

101. 'Hence it was that my mind was deluded due to which, all this took place. Although he had a meal, along with two others, yet I only thought him to be a guest, come to have a meal.

102. 'Had he not been someone I had known before, who had come with any two people, quite unexpectedly at lunchtime, I would definitely have regarded him as Sai'.

103. But such are the ways of these saints, their inconceivable *leelas* and wonderful doings. It is they themselves, who plan these functions at their devotees' houses, much beforehand.

104. When the devotees surrender at his feet, their auspicious functions are performed, quite unexpectedly, in this same way. Truly, incomprehensible are the doings of these saints.

105.   *Chintamani*[6] will give you what you asked for; *Kalpataru* will grant
       the wishes of your heart; *Kamadhenu* produces the thing you desire.
       But it is only Guru, the Mother, who gives you what you had
       never even thought of.

106.   Here of course, Baba was invited and appeared in the garb of a
       sanyasin. But so wonderful is his *leela* that sometimes he came,
       even when uninvited!

107.   Sometimes in the form of a photograph, sometimes in the form
       of a clay idol — there is no limit to his kindness. Sometimes he
       appears, all on his own.

108.   Listeners will be amazed when they hear my experience in this
       context. From this novel, unique tale, they will also come to know
       of the prowess of Sai's *leelas*.

109.   Some may even say of this, 'Is this a true story or some (imaginary)
       tale?' They may say what they please. But you should listen to
       this with respect.

110.   Laziness, sleepiness or exhaustion should be brushed aside. Only
       then will I be satisfied, when you give me the gift of listening
       with full attention.

111.   For a moment, if you drive away all agitation and put your mind
       completely at ease, the listening will be helpful. Reflection,
       constant contemplation will follow.

112.   Thereafter will come direct perception. But the basis for all this
       is listening; it is the essence of these and is certainly the means of
       safely crossing this worldly life.

113.   In the year 1917, on the full-moon day in the month of *Falgun*
       (roughly February-March), as I was asleep in my bed, I had a
       dream in the early hours of the morning.

114.   Just see Sai's doings! He gave me *darshan* in the beautiful dress of
       a *sanyasin* and waking me up in my dream, said, "Today, I am
       coming for a meal."

115.   Waking up in a dream is also a part of that dream. For, on really
       waking up from the sleep, I tried to remember.

116.   As I opened my eyes and looked around there was neither Sai nor anyone else in that place. What I saw a moment ago, was just a dream, without the least degree of wakefulness.

117.   When my mind was resolved thus, I tried to remember the dream and in my mind I recalled each and every letter of what he said, without forgetting in the least.

118.   On hearing Sai's clear words, "Today I am coming for a meal", I felt very happy and told this to my wife.

119.   In the mind, in the heart, there was a constant meditation on Sai alone, and this was a ceaseless practice. Yet in this association of seven years, there was never any idea or expectation of his coming for a meal.

120.   However, I told her (my wife), 'Today is the festival of *Holi*. Remember to cook a quarter seer more of rice.'

121.   On telling her just this much, she began to ask the reason for it. I said, 'Today, on this festive occasion, a guest is coming for lunch.'

122.   So she said, 'Tell me who it is', out of great curiosity. But if I were to tell the real reason, it would only become a matter of ridicule.

123.   This too, I knew full well. And yet, not to tell an untruth, I narrated the truth to her with great faith.

124.   And all this depends on one's faith. As the feeling within, so is the thing true or false. This depends altogether on one's mind.

125.   Try as I would to convince her, her mind would not be convinced. She said, 'Why will Baba come all the distance from Shirdi?

126.   'What meal can we offer him? And what *Holi* festival do we celebrate! Leaving the sweet-meats of Shirdi, will he eat our coarse, unsavoury food here?'

127.   So she said. I replied, 'What big effort do we have to make to cook a quarter seer of extra rice? You are not wanting for a quarter measure of rice!

128.   'Even I do not say that Sai will personally, be this guest. But I undoubtedly feel that somebody or other will come.

129. 'You may then regard him as anyone you like, but to me he will be as Sai. Or rather, I will regard him as none other than Sai and thus my dream will come true.'

130. Such was our dialogue. Then noon-time approached. The *pooja* being offered to the *Holi* (Fire) with the proper rituals, '*patravalis*'[7] were laid out for the meal.

131. For sons, grandsons, daughters, sons-in-law and close friends rows of *patravalis*, *paats* (or wooden seats), etc., were arranged; '*rangolis*'[8] — colourful and variegated, were drawn around the *patravalis*, for the diners.

132. Amidst all these, in the main row, a *paat* was put in the centre with a plate for Sai and food was served on it, along with that for the others.

133. A colourful, bright *rangoli* was drawn round this plate. For each diner a metal drinking vessel for water, a little, tall, cylindrical metal glass and a tiny ladle was laid out. It was the same for all.

134. *Papads*[9], *sandagas*, salads, tasty pickles, along with a variety of vegetable, *kheers*, etc., were served. Almost all the preparation was over.

135. Seeing that it was twelve o'clock, the diners wore the '*sovala*'[10] or silken *dhotis*, and one by one, came and sat on the *paat*. Still, no guest turned up.

136. All the places were occupied. Rice, *varan*, *chapati* were served and nothing was wanting in that place except the guest in the vacant seat in the centre.

137. They all waited for some guest to come. Even I became doubtful in my mind. How long should one wait?

138. So the door was bolted; '*anna-shuddhi*' (or putting clarified butter on the rice as purifying of the food) was quickly served; *naivedya* was offered and it was time for offering of various types of food as *Vaishwadev*.

139. The diners were about to take '*Pranahuti*' (Offering food to the five vital airs) when suddenly, footsteps were heard on the staircase, as someone asked, 'Where is Raosaheb?' The diners sat still in their places for a moment.

140. So I went to the door, as I was thinking in my mind that somebody had come. As I slowly unbolted the door, I saw two persons on the stairs.

141. One of them was Alli Mohamed and the other, a disciple of Saint Maulana, Ismu Mujawar by name. Both were very happy.

142. They saw that everything was in readiness for a meal and that the people were waiting, the food being already served on their plates. On seeing all this, Alli requested, 'Pardon me for the trouble I have given.

143. 'It appears that you have rushed from your meal for my sake and for you, the others too, are kept waiting.

144. 'So just take this thing, which is yours. I shall meet you later, when I have some time and will tell you in detail, the marvellous wonder about this.'

145. So saying, Alli took out a parcel from under his arm and placing it on the table in front, began to undo the knot.

146. As he removed the newspaper wrapping, in that instant was seen a bas-relief of Sai. He said, 'You keep this thing, accepting my request."

147. On seeing Sai's bas-relief the hair on my body stood on end, from deep emotion. My heart was overpowered by love and joy and at once, I placed my head on Sai's feet.

148. When I saw this wonderful *leela* of Sai, I thought it to be a great marvel and I felt that he had blessed me by showing his great prowess in this way.

149. Out of great curiosity, I asked him from where he got it. He said, 'I have bought it at one of the shops'.

150. Then, without waiting for another moment they both said, 'We are both going away, now. You can have your meal peacefully.

151. 'If I begin to explain the reason just now, the people will unnecessarily be kept waiting for their meal. So I shall tell you all that afterwards, at leisure.'

152. I also thought it to be proper. Moreover, I was deeply engrossed in my own joy at the arrival of that bas-relief, in the nick of time. So, thanking him, I said,

153. 'All right, you may go', and I shall also narrate the reason for the arrival of that bas-relief here later on. What is the need to narrate it, today itself?

154. And so, when they were gone, the bas-relief was placed on the *paat* in the centre, as already decided.

155. All were very happy in their minds. Truly, incomprehensible is Sai's *leela*. Under this guise he came and proved his words in my dream.

156. They, who had expected that, in case a guest arrived at that time, he would come and sit there in a row of diners, — Oh, what a surprise it was to them!

157. Everyone was delighted to see the beautiful image in that bas-relief. They all wondered how this came about in such an unexpected manner.

158. Thus when the bas-relief was installed, *pooja* was performed with all the proper rites and rituals like *arghya, padya,* etc. After the *naivedya* was offered with love and devotion everyone began the meal.

159. From then onwards till now, on every *Holi* festival, this bas-relief gets the *pooja* performed with the proper procedure and all the 'ashtopachar'[11].

160. Along with the other gods in the *pooja*, it is also worshipped in the shrine. Such is the unique *leela* that Sai shows to the devotees, at every step.

161. And so, the two men kept putting off their visit to explain, for nine whole years and I did not see them during all that time.

162. By a concurrence of Destiny and *karma*, at last I casually met Alli Mohamed this year, as I was walking on the road.

163. On meeting him, I was most eager to ask him about the marvel of that bas-relief and said, 'Why have you been silent for so many years?

164. 'Today, as before, we have met unexpectedly and as this opportunity has come our way easily, tell me that interesting account.

165. 'I know well, that you are also a devotee of Sai. But how did you find it appropriate to come unexpectedly, on that particular day only?'

166. Then Alli narrated the whole story, saying, 'Listen, I shall tell you, in detail and see Sai's marvellous *leela*, which is full of wonder.

167. 'What is the significance of this *leela*, what is his purpose and what is its essence for the devotees — Sai alone, knows this properly!

168. 'As for us, we should only listen to these *leelas* from each other or sing them with our mouths, they being most beneficial for us.'

169. Now, the account that follows will be fully narrated in the next chapter. It will gladden the listeners. Sai's Story is unfailingly beneficial to all.

170. Sai, the Cloud of Joy and without hatred for anyone, should be worshipped ceaselessly and constantly and you will enjoy happiness and contentment. Your mind too, will become free from desires.

171. The Chatak bird, for his selfish purpose, entreats the cloud, but the cloud satiates the whole Creation. Balasaheb invited Baba, but Baba then called his devotees, too!

172. The listeners are also included among the devotees, who have listened to the story of '*udyapan*', so lovingly and thereby experienced the joy of Sai's company, indicating their satiety by belching.

173. How he came uninvited, how he appears in physical form, how he fills his devotees with a sense of obligation and how he gives them awareness at every step!

174. And so, Hemad surrenders himself to Sai. He will get the presentation of the next chapter arranged as he wishes. For the next chapter will follow the same pattern as the last.

175. He affords protection to those who seek refuge. And it is for this Promise of his that Hemad embraces his feet and he also does not push Hemad away.

Weal be to all! Here ends the fortieth chapter of
"Sri Sai Samarth Satcharit", called
'The Narration of the Story of Udyapan',
as inspired by the saints and the virtuous and
composed by his devotee, Hemadpant.

Notes

1. Lord Shiva, who killed the demon, Tripur.
2. The ceremony closing and concluding any religious observance.
3. One of them was Bapusaheb Jog and the other was Swami Sai Sharan Anand (Vaman Prangovind Patel before his *Sannyasa*).
4. Both these terms mean sipping of water from the palm of the hand, after a meal.
5. The perfume of roses or other fragrances.
6. Refer Ch. 16, note 2.
7. A trencher or plate, formed of leaves, tacked together.
8. Powder made by pounding particular soft stones and used in drawing lines and figures before an idol or on the floor, where a meal or other entertainment is to be given.
9. Refer Ch. 27, notes 9, 10 and 11.
10. Refer Ch. 7, note 6.
11. Refer Ch. 13, note 1.

41

Sai's Kindness and Conferring of Grace

MY OBEISANCE TO SHRI GANESH, TO SHRI SARASWATI, AND SHRI GURUMAHARAJ! TO THE FAMILY DEITY, TO SHRI SITA-RAMACHANDRA, MY MOST HUMBLE OBEISANCE! I BOW IN REVERENCE TO THE MOST VENERABLE GURU SHRI SAINATH!

1. Such is the greatness of Sai's Story that however much you listen to it, it needs no encouragement for listening further and in fact, it is the listeners who themselves keep the earlier context in mind and are most attentive in listening.

2. When the listeners themselves are so attentive in listening to the story and already have such concentration, why then, need one request their attention?

3. Singing or listening to the greatness of one's guru, the mind will become purified and if his name is chanted, meditating on him steadily, then his form, which brings the highest joy, will appear to you.

4. In the last chapter it was narrated how the '*udyapan*' of a vow was completed satisfactorily, giving the sign of the reality of the dream.

5. Similarly, now listen to the story about how a clay bas-relief of Sai arrived in time and quite unexpectedly, to satisfy the wish of the devotee.

6. Once, on the day of the *Holi* festival, Sai came in the dream to say, "I shall come for a meal today", and fulfilled a heart-felt wish.

7. This story has already been narrated in detail; but today, listen respectfully to the miracle as to how that bas-relief came at the right time.

8. Alli Mohamed narrated the story, which I felt was most astonishing. But after all, was it not also one of the most amusing of Baba's *leelas*?

9. It was this same Alli Mohamed who had brought the bas-relief at the right moment at noon, on that *Holi* day, when we were about to sit for a meal and had delighted me.

10. This is the earlier context of the story. Now O listeners, be attentive and listen to the narration, further. Sai's Life Story is most purifying.

11. This is that fascinating story! The listeners are already attentive; the narrator is engrossed at Sai's feet and Sai's Life is unfathomable!

12. The very image of beneficence that Sai was, he wore out his body for the good of others and always in a state of being without enmity, had dedicated himself to the performance of good deeds.

13. Whether in a good state or bad, the body is never free from its *karma*. So direct your mind to the guru's feet, with love.

14. And then see from your most excellent experience and with love for the guru in your heart, how the guru provides effortlessly, subsistence and protection to his devotee.

15. This is a state not to be attained, even on asking. But it can be attained only by singing the praises of the guru. What cannot be had even with the greatest effort, comes to you on its own by the power of the guru's grace.

16. Those who came with conceit to observe him critically, returned with vanquished pride, happy in the great pleasure of his *darshan*.

17. Success, Wealth, Generosity, Knowledge, Peace and Detachment, with these six virtues was Shri Sai fully adorned, as Shri Vishnu Himself.

18. How great is our good fortune, by virtue of which, Sai, the Cloud of Universal Consciousness, gives us *darshan*, without our worshipping or offering him *pooja*!

19. It is said, where there is devotion, there is God. And with us, devotion is wanting. But great indeed, is this Sai, who feels compassion for the poor and the meek.

20. But now, O listeners, listen to the detailed account that Alli Mohamed narrated and you will know how incomprehensible is Sai's *leela* and how great, his power.

21. 'One day, in the city of Bombay, as I was walking on the road, I saw a Trader selling beautiful pictures and bas-relief.

22. Looking at those fine picture of saints, *mahantas*[1], *avalias*, etc., I felt like finding out whose pictures they were.

23. So, as I began to see them, one by one, it was the beauty of this bas-relief that appealed most to my heart. Moreover, it was my chosen deity, too!

24. Already there was a fondness for Sai in my heart and then, when I saw his image in front of me, I was impatient to purchase it. At once I paid its price in cash.

25. I brought the bas-relief home and hung it on the wall. Happily, I used to take its *darshan* every day, for I had great affection for Baba.

26. Three months before I gave it to you, I was not in good health and stayed at the house of my brother-in-law, in his company.

27. Noormohamed Peerbhoy was my brother-in-law. My leg was swollen and was operated upon.

28. Being thus unwell, I stayed there for three months, and there was no one staying in my house during those three months.

29. However, the famous Baba Abdul Raheman[2], Maulana Saab[3], Mohamed Hussain[4], Sai Baba and Baba Tajuddin[5] — they did not leave my house.

30. Beautiful pictures of all these and others like them, were on the wall in my house. But even they were not free from the Wheel of Fortune!

31. Such was my distressing condition here, but why this 'saadesati'[6] for these pictures? I feel, once a thing is created, its destruction too, is inevitable.

32.   However, when such was the state of affairs, how Sai alone, was exempt from it? This is something which nobody has been able to tell me, till today.

33.   You hear the story about this from the beginning and you will be simply amazed! You will also realize Sai's oneness with all things — animate and inanimate — and his ingenuity which is inconceivable!

34.   A small picture of the saint Baba Adbul Raheman was in the possession of Mohamed Hussein, known by the nickname Tharia.

35.   Many years ago, he had given me a copy of it, which I had given to my brother-in-law, who was his disciple.

36.   Even with him, it was lying in the drawer of his table for full eight years. Once he came across it casually and quite unexpectedly. So he took it to the shop of a photographer in Bombay.

37.   He got a fine picture made from it, of the great Baba Abdul himself, in order to take it to him as a present, expecting him to be pleased and be overcome with love, on seeing it.

38.   He got copies made from it and gave them to all the relatives and close friends. One of thses copies was given to me, too! And I had put it up on the wall.

39.   When the *darbar* of Abdul Raheman was assembled, Noormohamed was all set to present that most exquisite picture to the saint.

40.   On seeing the picture and realizing his intention, Abdul Raheman became very angry and got up to beat him.

41.   Treating him with indignity, he drove him away. Due to this, his face became very sad and he became greatly worried.

42.   Being humbled and pitiful, he became agitated in his mind and dejected. 'Not only has money been spent, but an obstacle has come in the way of the guru's grace.

43.   'Today, I who was blesssed with the guru's grace, have become the cause of his displeasure'. So saying, with a mind filled with doubts, he began immersing them in water.

44. He said, 'These pictures of the saints should never be kept in the house. Because of them, I have lost my guru's love. Why then, this ungainful effort?

45. 'This picture, due to which my guru was displeased with me, will, sometime or other, harm me. It is of no use to me.

46. 'That too, was a way of worshipping the idol, which if my guru does not like, then causing his displeasure, what is its use to me?

47. 'Even though much money has been spent to collect these pictures, there is no other way now, but to immerse them in water.'

48. So, taking that photograph with him, my brother-in-law went to the wharf to immerse it in water and would not have given it to anyone, even if asked for.

49. He went straight to the Apollo Bunder, hired a boat and sailing as far into the water as he could, ultimately consigned it to the waters.

50. And, he did not stop at that, but started the same procedure at Bandra, after collecting all the photographs by entreating the relatives and friends to whom he had given them.

51. He said to them, 'Baba Abdul was very angry. So whoever has the photographs should return them to me, for they must be immersed'. Thus he requested them all.

52. From me too, he took the copy he had given and so also, from my brother and my sister. Thus he got hold of all the six copies.

53. Then, taking all the copies and filled with anger, he reached the sea at Bandra, where the stretch of land ends and water begins.

54. Calling a fisherman to him, he entrusted all these pictures to him, and got them immersed in the waters of the sea.

55. I too, was ill at the time and staying with him. So he advised me similarly, saying that, 'these pictures bring calamities.

56. 'Hence when you collect all of them and immerse them in the sea, only then will you get rid of your illness. Know this for sure'.

57. So I also called my *Mehta* (assistant) and, giving him the keys, asked him to bring all the photographs of the saints from my house, which I then entrusted to my brother-in-law to be disposed of.

58. At once, he sent for his gardener and got them immersed at his hands in the sea-waters near the Chimbai temple.

59. After two months had passed and I felt better, as I went back to my house, I was most astonished.

60. On seeing the bas-relief which I gave you, still on the wall facing the door as before, I was greatly surprised.

61. The *Mehta* had brought all the pictures. Then how did he miss only this bas-relief? So I took it down, at once and hid it in a cupboard.

62. If my brother-in-law were to see it, he will immediately take it away from me to immerse it in water, so I felt in my heart.

63. It was no use keeping it in my house, for the moment my brother-in-law would see it, he would immerse it. But I could not give it away, with any certainty, to someone who was not a devotee.

64. If I was to give it to someone without due consideration and it was not looked after properly, there would always be a restlessness in my mind. This was my constant worry for a long time.

65. Hence I must find a proper place. He who will keep it safe and look after it well, only to such a person should it be entrusted.

66. When my mind was in such a dilemma, Sai himself, inspired a good idea in my mind that I should go to the *darbar* of Maulana and narrate the whole account to Ismu.

67. At once, I went to the *darbar* of Peer Maulana and in private, narrated the whole story very respectfully to Mujawar Ismu.

68. We both decided it would remain safe with you. So we both made such a resolve on that same day —

69. That this bas-relief of Samarth Sai should be kept at your house and that we should present it to you ourselves, so that it will remain at the proper place.

70. As per that firm resolve, we presented it to you and seeing that your meal was all ready, I came back, immediately.

71. You did not then have the time to listen to this long story. So, thinking that I would tell that to you leisurely, sooner or later, I came back.

72. Postponing it from day to day, nine whole years passed by, when today, quite unexpectedly, we have met each other.

73. So I remembered this old story and you also told me of the marvel of your dream, which has a most remarkable connection with my story. Is this not a wonderful *leela?*'

74. Now, O listeners, listen to another story with full attention, as to how very affectionately Sai treated his loving devotees

75. Those who were truly fond of the spiritual path were very dear to Sai. Removing all their difficulties, he helped them attain a state of Self-rejoicing.

76. In this connection, there is a fascinating experience where, fulfilling the fond wish of Balasaheb Deo, Baba helped him carry out his resolve and also inspired devotion in him, along with it.

77. Deo had no other means of earning a livelihood, but by serving in a job during the day. But then, why should obstacles come in the way of his spiritual *sadhana* at night?

78. For a long time, he had wished to read *Jnaneshvari* regularly, every day. But due to some obstacle or the other, he could not fulfil his wish.

79. But unlike the one chapter of *Bhagavad-Gita*, which he read every day, his resolve to read one chapter of *Jnaneshvari* could not be carried out without some obstacle arising.

80. Other books, when taken in hand, were read with regularity, but with *Jnaneshvari* for reading which he had such a keen desire, the resolve would not be carried through.

81. Once Deo went on three months' leave and went to Shirdi. From there, he proceeded to his home at Pound, to enjoy some rest and leisure.

82. There too, all other work was complete; the *pothi* that he used to read daily, was read regularly. But the fond desire for *Jnaneshvari* remained unfulfilled, its turn never came!

83. Whenever he took up *Jnaneshvari* to read, some doubts and misapprehensions would arise in the mind, which led only to a superficial reading, without inspiring any genuine love for it.

84. And the resolve made with such a heart-felt longing, was not carried out successfully. In fact, even five verses could not be read, every day, regularly.

85. 'I made such an earnest resolve to read at least five verses daily. But even these were not being read by me regularly with any enthusiasm.

86. 'So I then decided that when Sai himself will inspire me with love and tell me to read, only then will I make a beginning, without any doubts in my mind.

87. 'When Sai gives the command, only then, will I read *Jnaneshvari*, reposing full faith in Sai's feet. Such was the firm resolve that I made'.

88. When the '*Mahodaya Parva*'⁷ came, Deo went to Shirdi with his mother, sister, etc., to see the glorious spectacle of *Guru-pooja*.

89. There Jog asked Deo, 'Why do you not read *Jnaneshvari* regularly, these days?' Listen to the reply that he gave.

90. 'I have a keen desire for reading *Jnaneshvari*. But I am not able to fulfil it successfully. Now, when Baba himself asks me to read, only then will I read it.'

91. So Jog told him a trick, 'Bring a *pothi* of *Jnaneshvari* and give it in the hands of Sai Baba. When he gives it back to you, then you should start reading it.'

92. 'I need no such tricks. Baba knows my mind. Then why does he not fulfil the desire of my heart and say clearly, "Read"?'

93. Then when he took *darshan* of Samarth, he offered one rupee at his feet. "Why only one? Bring twenty", said Baba to him.

94. So he brought twenty rupees and gave them to him. At night, Deo met Balakram. So he asked him about an earlier incident as to how he won Baba's grace.

95. 'I will tell you everything tomorrow, after the *arati*', Balakram assured him. 'All right', said Deo to him.

96. The next day, when Deo went to the mosque for *darshan*, Baba again asked him for twenty rupees, which Deo gave very gladly.

97. Seeing the place so crowded, Deo stood aside. Baba asked, "Where, where is he hidden in some awkward place, in all this crowd?"

98. Deo replied, 'Here, here I am, Baba'. So Baba then asked him, "Why did you give me only seven?"

99. Deo said, 'I gave twenty'. "Whose is the money?" asked Baba. 'Baba, it is yours', he said. "Then why are you running away?

100. "Come, come here and sit near me, with your mind at ease". Deo faithfully obeyed as commanded.

101. The *arati* took place, as usual, and people went back to their respective homes. Deo met Balakram and began to ask the same question as before.

102. He asked him for an account of what had happened earlier. Balakram also told him everything, from beginning to end. Deo then said to him, 'How did he guide you to the *upasana*?

103. 'Did he tell you how to meditate on the Brahman? Do satisfy my desire for knowledge!' Deo requested.

104. And as Balakram also began to answer him, to satisfy his desire, Baba himself sent for Deo.

105. How affectionate is Sai! He sent Chandru to call Deo. Without a moment's delay, Deo came to meet Shri Sai.

106. It was four o'clock in the afternoon and he saw Shri Sai before him, leaning both his hands on the parapet of the mosque.

107. On reaching there, Deo at once made obeisance. Baba then asked him a question, "Where and with whom were you conversing?"

108. Deo replied, 'I was listening to your own glory, from Balakram, on the upper floor in Kaka's *wada*.'

109. "Bring twenty-five rupees", Baba commanded Deo. Immediately, he brought the rupees and offered them to Baba.

110. "How many have you brought?" asked Baba. 'Twenty-five', said Deo. "Come, come and sit with me." So he went to the mosque with Baba.

111. Baba sat near the pillar. There was no one else in the mosque. He said, "You have stolen my piece of rag, without my knowledge."

112. 'I do not know of any rag', Deo assured him. So Sai said to him, "Then it must be somewhere here only".

113. 'Where is any rag here?' said Deo at the time. Baba got up saying, "You search for it. This tendency of yours is evil.

114. "Maybe some mischievous child has taken it! See, see, it must be here, somewhere." Hearing this, Deo began searching further, but could not find it.

115. Wrinkling his eyebrows, looking around here and there, Sai glared at Deo, as he roared at him,

116. Saying, "You are yourself a cheat. Who else except you will come at this time to steal a piece of rag? I regard you, and you alone, as the thief.

117. "Here that you come like this, is it to steal? Grey as your hair has turned from black, not in the least have you got rid of your bad habit!

118. "I will strike you with an axe; I will cut you up; I will kill you! Where can you escape from my hands? Wherever you go, there I will kill you.

119. "To Shirdi you come all the way from home, is it to steal? Take back your money, and bring me my piece of rag."

120. Sai turned red in the face with anger[8], indulging in abuses in the wildest terms. Abuses and curses rained in a torrent. He seemed to be burning with fury.

121. Deo looked on with affectionate awe and admiration as Sainath was filled with rage. He stood speechless with an astonished mind.

122. Deo was all alone with him and it looked as though he was in for a good beating or, maybe, Baba was revealing the Wondrous Vision of the Cosmic Form (*Vishwaroopdarshan*) and the thought filled his heart with joy.

123. 'Will he now pick up the baton and strike vehemently? I am trapped in his hands, being all alone! But let him do what he wants!

124. 'And yet, what is this puzzle about the rag?' It was something that Deo just could not solve. At the same time, when Baba said, "Go, get out of here!" he then moved towards the steps.

125. I am powerless to know the secret meaning of this 'piece of rag'. But by Sai's grace, when I know it, I shall narrate it for the listeners.

126. After about twelve minutes, Deo again came before Baba. The shower of abuses still continued. "Why have you come up?" Baba said.

127. "Go away; be gone to the *wada*!" On hearing this, Deo obeyed the command respectfully and making obeisance at his feet, returned to the *wada*.

128. He then narrated from the beginning and in detail, to Jog and Balakram, all that had happened, as it took place.

129. Then, for about 24 minutes or so, the volley of abuses and curses was being fired. After four or five hours had elapsed, Baba himself began to call people to him.

130. Deo also went there and sat among others. Shri Sai said, "The old man must have felt hurt.

131. "After all, of what importance is a mere piece of rag? Yet I wounded his feelings with a torrent of abuses. But he had stolen it. Then what could be done? I could not help saying it!

132. "But Allah will see everything. He too will bless him." Then that ever-forgiving Shri Sai asked, "Bhau, will you give *dakshina*?"

133. 'How much shall I bring?' asked Deo. "Bring twelve, quickly." But when Deo looked into the pocket, there was only a note, for which he could not get the change.

134. Deo said so to Baba. "Let it be, I do not want", Baba said. "In the morning, you gave me twice. I did not remember it."

135. Yet Deo obtained the required amount and gave it to Baba, making obeisance at his feet. Listen to the words that came from Baba.

136. "What do you do these days?" 'Nothing much', said Deo. So he commanded Deo, "Go on reading the *pothi*, regularly.

137. "You should go and sit in the *wada* and read the *pothi* regularly, every day. And while reading, keep on giving exposition faithfully, to all.

138. "When I sit here ready to give you a whole '*shela*', resplendent with *jari*-work, why do you go to steal pieces of rags? Why do you indulge in this habit of stealing?"

139. 'Thus, the words from Sai's mouth, "Do the reading of *pothi*" gave me my inner mark and I became very happy.

140. 'Obeying that command respectfully, I then began reading of *Jnaneshvari* from that day, regularly, and also began giving an exposition, while reading.

141. 'I got the command that I wished for and the anxiety of my heart that was under a vow was laid to rest. From hence, I shall now be able to read *Jnaneshvari*, with regularity.

142. 'Now I am under the command from the guru and Jnaneshvar himself will be pleased with me. Whatever has happened so far is now left behind. But hereafter, I must read regularly.

143. 'My own mind is my witness. In addition, Sai's command is the only measure of Truth for me. On the strength of his command, the repeated readings of the *pothi* will take place, without any difficulty.

144. 'Baba, I prostrate in obeisance and surrender to you single-mindedly. Take this child under your wing and get the reading done by me.

145. 'Now I realize what that piece of rag meant. It was really what I had asked Balakram. And this it was that Sai did not like and which filled him with rage.

146. 'Baba did not like that I asked Balakram as to how he was guided to the proper *Upasana*, to the meditating on the Brahman.

147. 'When there he was, all too ready to answer any questions, why should I enquire about these matters independently from Balakram? Hence the great harassment!

148. 'But to say 'harassed' is in itself a daring statement. He who is overflowing with love for the devotees and will not even dream of harassing them, for him, 'harasses' is certainly the most inappropriate verb.

149. 'He did not harass but taught me that 'whatever wish arises in your mind, it is I myself, who will fulfil it. What is stolen can never be of any use.'

150. 'Although outwardly, Sai appeared to be angry, in his heart he was always filled with joy. He looked infuriated with rage from outside, but inwardly, he was happy and content.

151. 'The customary pettiness of anger from outside, while the glory of blissful joy within, such was Sai, to sing the magnificence of whose *leelas*, great good fortune is necesary.

152. 'He, in whose heart there is keen desire to achieve his own good, will regard the abuses and curses as a shower of flowers, being quick to see his own benefit in it.'

153. Listening to the harsh, vulgar words, did not swerve Deo's mind. His heart overcome with a deep love, he felt them as a battering with flowers.

154. From the milk-filled teats of the cow, only the fortunate one will get the milk. But the leech that clings to the teat will have nothing but impure blood as its lot.

155. The frog has lotus-roots for a neighbour. But whereas the black bee with its boundless good fortune drinks freely the nectar of the lotus, to the luckless frog, the feast is of mud and mire.

156. So are you the fortunate ones! We have met each other. Ask what you want and get your doubts resolved, so said Sai.

157. 'Just see, how my obstinate insistence that I will not open the *Jnaneshvari*, until Baba says 'Read', was readily complied with, by Baba.

158. 'This is the story of the sweet experience of how a mother indulges her child by fulfilling his fond wishes and it confirms one in one's devotion.

159. 'Nor did Baba stop at telling me to read', said Deo, 'but hardly had the year ended when he gave *darshan* appearing in my dream and enquired after me. Listen to this.

160. 'It was a Thursday, the second of April in the year 1914, when I received his Grace in a dream, at dawn.

161. 'Sai Samarth came in my dream. He was sitting on the upper storey of the *wada*. He asked me, "Do you understand the *pothi*?" I replied in the negative.

162. 'Then came the next question, "When is it going to be understood?" Tears welled up in my eyes and what did I say in reply?

163. 'Unless I receive your Grace, reading the *pothi* is a futile exercise. It is even more difficult to understand it. This much, Baba, I tell you quite frankly.'

164. 'Baba said, "While reading the *pothi*, you do so very hastily. Now sit near me and read it in front of me!"

165. 'What shall I read?' asked Deo, and Baba commanded him to red the chapter on spiritual matters (i.e. Ch.9). I got up to bring the *pothi* and my eyes opened immediately.'

166. Deo was wide awake. Listeners can imagine what he must have thought as he remembered his dreaming state!

167. After waiting for a year, who will worry as to whether Bal obeys the command properly, whether or not he reads the *pothi*, daily —

168. Whether he follows the discipline and the practice regularly or does he make a mistake, due to some reason or the other — who will observe this all the time?

169. Who else but Mother Sai herself, will personally prove how careful a reader has to be, where he should pay special attention, and so on?

170. Such is the *leela* of Sai Samarth, such the celebration of Self-rejoicing, which I have seen innumerable devotees enjoying, with my own eyes.

171. Now let all of us, listeners, surrender humbly at the guru's lotus-feet and listen later, to the novelty of the next chapter, at the proper time.

172. Remembering Shri Samarth, Hemad prostrates in obeisance at his feet with pure feelings and surrenders with faith and devotion, for that alone will remove all the sorrows of worldly life.

173. Sai alone is all his material striving; Sai, who brings the highest Bliss, his only spiritual striving; for Sai alone will bring him fulfilment. Such is his firm faith.

Weal be to all! Here ends the forty-first chapter of
"Shri Sai Samarth Satcharit", called
'*Sai's Kindness and Conferring of Grace*',
as inspired by the saints and the virtuous and
composed by his devotee, Hemadpant.

Notes

1. The chief or head of an order of *Gosavis, Byragis*, etc., a religious superior.
2. Baba Abdul Raheman, after whom a road opposite Crawford Market, Bombay, has been named, passed away on February 13, 1918, at the age of over 100 years. Earlier, he used to wander about in Bombay, but when a bullock injured him, his Mohamedan devotees rented a house and maintained him in a good state. He was unapproachable except from a distance. He had many supernatural powers. It is said that Satam Maharaj of Sawantwadi, who ran a liquor den, was converted into a *sadhu* by a movement of his fist in his direction.
3. Maulana Saab: Peer Maulana, for whose *darshan* Dabholkar refused to accompany Yunus Mujawar (Ch. 21, v. 7-10), was a *Siddha*, who passed away on February 7, 1909. He lived in the masjid on the S. V. Road, Bandra, Bombay and his *darga* is at the end of the lane called Maulana Lane. An annual festival is held at Bandra in his honour. It is said that a Gaud Saraswat doctor once called on him. He was commanded by Peer Maulana to take a seat. The doctor did his bidding and strangely, did not move from there for five years, as a total change came over him, finally passing away in the same place.
4. Muhamed Hussain: He passed away on October 6, 1921, at the age of about 80 years. His darga is next to that of Maulana Saab at Bandra.
5. Tajuddin Baba: He was living in a village called Waki, near Nagpur and was spotted by Shrimant Raghujirao Bhonsle, who installed him near his house, making arrangements for him. He was the patron saint of Justice M. Hidaytulla, former Chief Justice and Vice-President of India. Baba passed away on August 17, 1925. His *darga* is at Tajabad Sharif in nagpur.
6. This is an expression used for a period of grievous calamity or distress. Because Saturn, a planet of inauspicious influences, abides seven years and a half in or in the neighbourhood of one's '*Janma-nakshatra*' (or the planet under which you were born), viz. two and a half years in the *Janma-nakshatra*, two and a half years in the '*rashi* ' (or the sign of the zodiac) preceding it and two and a half years in that following it.
7. A certain festival, a day of synchronism of the day, i.e. Sunday, the '*Nakshatra*', the '*tithi* ', the change of the moon, in February, which yields great merit to one who performs any meritorious deed.
8. In the text, the reference is to 'abusing his mother, sisters, etc.'; which is not to be taken literally. Baba's words, according to Swami Sai Sharan Anand, referred usually to the activity of the subtle or astral body and not to the activity on the gross level. When he abused anyone's mother, the abuse referred not to him, but to the mother, symbolising lack of knowledge (*avidya*) and ignorance about the Divine mystery. Sometimes, Baba's abuses were not addressed to anyone specifically, but were general. Swami Sai Sharan Anand says with clear conviction, born out of his experience, that in such cases, they were addressed to the entity (demon or fiend) intent on harming the *bhakta* whose presence was not visible to the naked eyes of an ordinary human being, but clearly perceptible to the *yogis*.

42

Shri Sainath's Niryan

MY OBEISANCE TO SHRI GANESH, TO SHRI SARASWATI, AND SHRI
GURUMAHARAJ! TO THE FAMILY DEITY, TO SHRI SITA-RAMACHANDRA,
MY MOST HUMBLE OBEISANCE! I BOW IN REVERENCE TO THE MOST
VENERABLE GURU SHRI SAINATH!

1. Obeisance to you, O most generous Sadguru! O greatest among the saints, who wanders along the banks of the Godavari, clad in a *langoti*, and are the *Parabrahman* Incarnate, to you I bow!

2. It is this Sai in his *avatar* as a saint, a veritable *Kalpataru* in the cause of his devotees, who shows how to cross the river of worldly life and gives refuge at his feet, to the meek and the lowly.

3. In the last chapter, the fascinating tale of Sai's marvellous *leela*, as to how his bas-relief was protected from being immersed in water has been narrated.

4. As also, how a devotee's wish was fulfilled by Sai, who appeared in his dream and gave a clear command, therby helping him to get on with his reading of *Jnaneshvari*.

5. In short, in the fortunate moment of the guru's grace, the riddle of fear of worldly life is solved; the door opens up for the attainment of *Moksha* and all the sorrow and suffering is transformed into happiness.

6. When the Sadguru is remembered all the time, the obstruction caused by impediments vanishes; Death itself dies and worldly sorrows are forgotten.

7. Hence the listeners should listen to the Story of Sai Samarth for their own benefit, which will truly bring them the highest purification.

8. Now in this chapter, let us describe the nature of Sai — whether he was harsh and rough, or mild and gentle.

9. You have listened with concentration so far, to Baba's way of conducting himself. Similarly, listen attentively now, to the story of his giving up the body.

10. Blessed, blessed are the people of Shirdi, who enjoyed the rare happiness of Baba's company for more than half a century.

11. In 1918, in the first month of '*Dakshinayan*'[1] (or the southerly declination of the sun), on the *Vijayadashmi* day (i.e. the *Dassera* festival), in the bright half of the moon, Baba gave up the ghost during the daytime.

12. In the Muslim month of *Muharram*, it was the ninth day and that night was 'the night of slaughter'[2]. On that day, around 2:35 pm Sainath made preparations for his '*niryan*'.

13. As the birthdate of Gautama Buddha is celebrated, so is also celebrated the date of '*niryan*' of Sai. The birthdates of gods and goddesses are as much a cause for celebration as the death-anniversaries of the saints.

14. The clock struck the hour of 12:30 in the afternoon; the tenth day of the lunar month was over and '*ekadashi*', or the eleventh day began. So Baba's *niryan* was really on the '*ekadashi*' day.

15. But since it was *dashmi* (or tenth day) at sun-rise on that day, *Vijayadashmi* is regarded as the day of Baba's *niryan* and celebrations take place accordingly on that day.

16. That Tuesday was the night of slaughter, a most famous day. Hence on that day, the great Sai merged the flame of his life into the Eternal Flame.

17. In Bengal, it is the well-known *Durga Pooja* Festival, which ends on this day and even in north India, it is a day of celebration, for all.

18. It was on this day of *Vijayadashmi*, in the year 1916, that in the evening, Baba gave a hint of the events to come.

19. I shall narrate the wonderful *leela* as to how he did it. The listeners will be quite astonished. But everyone will then know of Samarth Sai's skilful and most inconceivable planning.

20. In the year 1916, at the time of '*Shilangan*'³ on the *Dassera* day, a marvellous *leela* was manifested by Baba, after returning in the evening from his usual round.

21. Like the clouds that thunder in the sky, quite unexpectedly, with the sudden loud crackling of lightning, so Baba appeared as *Jamdagni*⁴, himself.

22. He took off the piece of cloth around his head. In a jiffy, he removed the *kafni* and the *langot* round his waist. And as he put them all in the fire of the *dhuni*, it flared up, instantly.

23. Already, the fire was burning brightly. And to it was now added this offering of abundant fuel. With the result, the flames rose high in a tumult, much to the agitation of the devotees around.

24. All this happened quite suddenly and no one knew what was in Baba's mind. But in that moment of *Shilangan*, his countenance was most frightening.

25. The fire spread around its own powerful brilliance. But far greater was the brilliance with which Baba's face shone. Dazzled, the eyes of the onlookers closed involuntarily, as they turned their faces away.

26. *Agninarayan* (the Fire God) was pleased on consuming the offering at the saint's hands, while he, who was like *Parsuram*, the son of *Jamdagni*, became naked. Blessed indeed, were the eyes of all those who looked on!

27. His eyes glowed with anger. In a fit of rage and with glaring eyes, he said, "Now, decide, decide for yourselves whether I am a Muslim or a Hindu!

28. "Today, see clearly, whether I am a Hindu or a Muslim!", roared Baba. "Decide in your minds, till you are satisfied and have all your doubts removed!"

29. Seeing this spectacle, people trembled with fear and kept on worrying as to how he could be pacified.

30. Sorely afflicted as Bhagoji Shinde was, yet he was a great devotee of Baba. Taking up courage, he came near Baba and put a *langot* round him.

31. 'What is all this, Baba?' he said, 'Today is *Shilangan*, the festival of *Dassera!*' Baba said, "This is in itself my *Shilangan*", as he went on striking hard with his baton.

32. In this way, Baba stood, all naked, near the *dhuni*. It was the day of *Chavadi* and people began to be anxious as to how the *Chavadi* ceremonies could be performed.

33. Nine o'clock was the time for *Chavadi* procession and it was already ten o'clock. Baba had not yet calmed down. People stood still as they were, in different places and stared wide-eyed, in silence.

34. Gradually Baba's temper cooled down. It was eleven o'clock. Baba then wore a *kafni* and a brand new *langot*.

35. The bell rang for *Chavadi*. People, who had been sitting in silence now decorated the palanquin with flowers and with Baba's permission, brought it to the courtyard.

36. The procession then set out for the *Chavadi*, as on every alternate day and was with adornments befitting that of a king, replete with the silver staff, banners, *chavari*, the regal umbrella, flags, etc.

37. And as it started, there was one loud clang of musical instruments. Who can describe the loud acclamations of glory to Sainath that accompanied it! There was an overflow of joy everywhere.

38. He then picked up a piece of cloth, clean and snow white, which he tied round his head and took up the clay pipe, tobacco, baton, etc., in hand as if signalling that this was the most auspicious moment to set out for the *Chavadi*.

39. Some held up the umbrella, some, the *chavari*; still others, the bunch of beautiful peacock feathers. Some took up the flags bearing a picture of an eagle, others took the ornamental umbrella and yet others, took in their own hands, the staff of the *chopdar* (or mace-bearer).

40. In this way, Baba hinted, under the pretext of *Shilangan*, that to cross over the border of the ocean of worldly life, *Dassera* is the only auspicious time.

41. Thereafter, Baba remained with the people of Shirdi for only one more *Dassera* and regarding the very next *Dassera* to be the best and most auspicious day, surrendered his mortal coil to the earth.

42. And not only did he just suggest this, but demonstrated it himself, giving them the actual experience, by offering a pure, white piece of cloth (i.e. his body) to the fire of *Yoga*, on the same day.

43. He truly made the *Dassera* festival of the year 1918, a most auspicious day and merged his own form into that of the Brahman.

44. As I write this, another such experience of Baba, comes to my mind, to prove that this same day of *Vijayadashmi* had already been fixed by him for his *niryan*.

45. Once Ramchandra Patil (Kote) of Shirdi became very ill and was unable to bear the distress of the life-threatening ailment. Such was his great suffering.

46. No cure remained to be tried and yet, when the ailment could not be controlled, he became tired of life itself. Patil was greatly harassed.

47. While in this state of mind, one day, Baba suddenly appeared at his bedside, at midnight.

48. Patil at once, clasped his feet and said to him in great dejection, 'Baba, tell me only this once! When will death come definitely?

49. 'I am now tired of life and death is to me, no great calamity. I am only waiting for death to come to me!'

50. Then Baba, who was Compassion Incarnate, said to him, "Do not worry. The imminent danger from your dreaded sickness is already overcome. Why do you unnecessarily, worry?

51. "For you there is absolutely no fear. Your '*hundi*'[5] has returned fully. But O Ramchandra, I see no hope for Tatya (Patil).

52. "In the year 1918, in the month of *Ashwin* (October) during the sun's southerly passage, on the *Vijayadashmi* day, in the bright half of the moon, Tatya will go to his Eternal Abode.

53. "But do not tell him about this, or else he will take a dread in his heart and pine away, by day and by night. Nobody likes the prospect of death".

54. Only two more years remained. The time for Tatya came near. Ramchandra was worried, for Baba's words were like a '*vajralep*'[6].

55. He kept it a secret from Tatya, but disclosed it to Bala Shimpi (i.e. the tailor), entreating him not to tell anyone else. Both of them grew worried.

56. And, Ramchandra Patil really got well. From then onwards, his illness left him, completely. The days passed quickly, after that, without his even realizing it.

57. Just see the precision of Baba's words! The month of *Bhadrapad* (August-September) of 1918 had just passed and *Ashwin* began, when Tatyaba took to his bed.

58. There, Tatya suffered from high fever, but here, Baba began to shiver with cold. Tatya's full reliance was on Baba, but Baba's protector was *Shri Hari*, Himself!

59. Tatya could not even get up from his bed and hence was not able to come for Baba's *darshan*. So greatly did the body suffer that he could bear it no longer.

60. For one thing, he was distressed by his own illness, and yet, his heart was with Baba. He was unable to walk or move about. The illness was taking a turn for the worse.

61. Here, Baba's moaning and groaning increased doubly, day by day. And in no time, his ailment too, became uncontrollable.

62. The day predicted by Baba drew near, all too soon. With fear and apprehension, Bala Shimpi broke into cold sweat. And so did Ramchandra Patil.

63. 'Baba's words really seem to be coming true', they said. 'The omen does not appear to be good and the illness is becoming critical'.

64. Then came *dashmi* (tenth day) in the bright half of the moon; the pulse grew feeble as Tatya lay dying. His relatives were frightened.

65. But what happened later was a real marvel! The danger to Tatya's life was averted. Tatya remained while Baba it was, who passed away, as if in exchange for Tatya!

66. And see the marvel of Baba's words! He took Tatya's name, but was really making ready for his own *niryan*, without missing the exact time, even by a second.

67. And yet he had given the warning, bringing to the notice of all, the future event. But until it happened actually, no one had realised it.

68. People say, Baba averted Tatya's death by giving his own body in exchange. Baba alone would know his own *leela*!

69. On the day after Baba gave up the ghost, in the early morning, at sunrise, Baba appeared in a vision in Das Ganu's dream at Pandharpur.

70. "The mosque has tumbled down. All the grocers and oil-merchants of Shirdi have harassed me. So I am now going away from there.

71. "Hence I have come up to here. Cover me up in an abundance of flowers. O, do fulfil this wish of mine! Come! Come immediately to Shirdi!"

72. Meanwhile, as the letter was despatched from Shirdi, he came to know of Baba's *Mahasamadhi*. As he heard it, Das Ganu set out for Shirdi, without losing a moment.

73. With the group of disciples that accompanied him, he stood before the *samadhi* and began singing *bhajans* and *kirtan*, day and night, with loud proclamations of *Naam* by the devotees, from time to time.

74. Himself, he wove a most beautiful flower-garland of *Hari-naam* and lovingly offered it at the *samadhi*, along with 'anna-daan'.

75. The loud ceaseless chant of *Hari-naam* made Shirdi appear to be a veritable *Vaikunth* (the abode of Shri Vishnu) on this earth. It was indeed, as a market of loud proclamations of *Naam*, which Ganu Das was pouring out, lavishly.

76. But why was Baba so fond of *Dassera*, in particular? Because out of the three and a half most auspicious days in the year[7], that day is considered to be specially auspicious for going anywhere. This is well-known to everyone.

77. And yet, this is not really correct either. How can there be '*niryan*' to one who is beyond all coming and going? And for such a one, where is the need for an auspicious day?

78. He who is above the bondage of *dharma-adharma* and has shed all such bondages, he whose life had no departure, — what *niryan* can there be for him?

79. There is no coming or going to Sai Maharaj, whose state is such that 'having become one with Brahman he goes to Brahman'[8]. Then how can he be in a state of '*niryan*'?

80. Be it the northerly or southerly revolution of the sun, what is it to him, who does not have to depart but whose life merges with the Brahman, in its own place, like the extinction of light in a lamp?

81. This body is, after all, only a borrowed one and it is the five elements who lend it. Once our purpose is served, it is to be returned to them, to whom it belongs.

82. Baba gave a warning of things to come, much in advance, causing surprise to people. That priceless moment (of his *niryana*) has passed away, leaving its glory behind, forever.

83. A running fever was the apparent cause and following the ways of the world, Baba would sometimes groan, sometimes moan, but was Self-aware, for ever,

84. In the day, when it was about 9:30 or 10 o'clock and the time was approaching for the *niryan*, Baba sat up, without anybody's help and with a perfectly composed and undisturbed mind.

85. Looking upon Baba's face at the time, a sea of hope surged in the hearts of the devotees as they all felt that the terrible, inauspicious moment was averted.

86. And, as they all sat there, sad and worried, Baba's end drew near. Listen to what happened then.

87. When there was hardly a moment left for life to depart, one knows not what came in his mind. But realizing that it was the time to give in charity, he put his hand in the pocket of his *kafni*.

88. The virtuous Laxmi, whose conduct justified her name and who was always absorbed at Baba's feet, was with him at that time.

89. Fully aware that in a moment he was going to give up his mortal coil, it was to her that Baba gave some money in charity, very carefully.

90. This was that Laxmibai Shinde, who used to serve faithfully in the mosque, observing all the rules and regulations about work.

91. It was a regular practice that during the day Baba's *darbar* was open to all and for the most part, nobody was prohibited. But during the night, the restrictions were severe.

92. Once he returned from the evening round and the people went back to their respective homes, they came to the mosque only after dawn, the next day.

93. But knowing the devotion of Bhagat Mhalsapati, Dada and Laxmi, Baba did not prohibit them from coming, even at night.

94. And again, it was this Laxmi, who sent Baba, very lovingly, *jowar bhakri* (bread) and vegetables every day, at the appointed time. Who can describe her sincere service, adequately?

95. And when the story of the '*bhakri*' is heard, you will realize Baba's affection and compassion and the listeners will be amazed at Baba's oneness with dogs and pigs.

96. Once, as Baba sat in the evening, leaning his breast against the wall and conversed affectionately, Laxmi came there.

97. Tatya Patil was nearby and some others were present there, too! Laxmi made obeisance to Baba. Then Baba said to her,

98. "Laxmi, I am feeling hungry". 'Baba, I will go this instant and get some *bhakri* for you'.

99. So saying, she went away and returned without delay, bringing with her freshly baked *bhakri* with some vegetables, etc., and placed the snack before Baba.

100.   Baba picked up the plate and placed it before a dog. Laxmi asked, at once, 'Baba, what is this you have done?

101.   'So hastily that I went and prepared the *bhakri* in minutes, — and is this all its fruit? It is to the dog that you gave all the true enjoyment.

102.   'You were feeling hungry, but is this any way to appease that hunger? Not a morsel did you put in your mouth and here am I, fretting in vain!'

103.   Then Baba said to her, "Why do you feel sad, needlessly? Know that the satiety of this dog is my own satiety.

104.   "Does this dog not have life? All living creatures experience the same hunger. Though he is dumb and I am vocal, is there any difference in the hunger?

105.   "Know that those who give food to one suffering the pangs of hunger are really putting it in my mouth. And this is true everywhere."

106.   It was a simple incident of daily life, but its lesson was a spiritual one. Such were Sai's words of instruction, a fruit perfectly ripe and mellow with love and affection.

107.   Speaking a simple language of daily life, he would sketch the outline of spiritual matters. Without putting his finger on anybody's faults or secrets, he would please his devotees.

108.   Thence began Laxmi's daily *bhakri*, as per Baba's instruction. She would crush it in milk and offer it lovingly to Baba, every day.

109.   Baba also began eating it regularly with love. And if on occasion, it was delayed, he would miss it so much that he would not relish the meal.

110.   If Laxmi's *bhakri* was late in arriving, even if the meal was all served and the usual mealtime had passed, he would not put even a morsel of food in his mouth.

111.   The food might grow cold on the plates; the hungry diners might be kept waiting, but until Laxmi's *bhakri* arrived the meal would not be touched.

112. Later on, for some time, Baba would daily ask at about 3-3:30 pm
      for vermicelli at Laxmi's hand and, sitting near her, he would eat
      it.

113. Baba would of course eat only a limited quantity thereof and the
      remainder would be sent to Radhakrishnabai at the hands of this
      same Laxmi. For she (Radhakrishna) was fond of eating the left-
      overs from Baba's meal.

114. But O listeners, say not as to why this idle, irrelevant talk about
      bhakri, right in the middle of the description of Baba's *niryan*.
      For it is indicative of Sai's all-pervasiveness.

115. This most exalted Sai, fills completely and for ever, that which is
      beyond this visible world of things, animate and inanimate. He
      who is unborn and immortal, he is this Sai.

116. And the essence of the story lies in this one Truth. I really think
      that the sweet tale of Laxmi that I remembered so casually, was
      really for the listener's benefit, alone!

117. So great was Laxmi's service! How would Sai forget it, ever?
      Listen with reverence to an account of the marvel of Sai's
      remembering it.

118. Although life rose into the throat in extreme distress; though the
      body was exhausted and there was no strength left, yet Baba gave
      in charity with his own hands, to Laxmi in that moment of life
      ebbing away from the body.

119. He took out from his pocket first, Rs.5 and then again Rs.4 and
      placed them on her hands. And this was Baba's end.

120. Was this the sign that Baba gave, of the nine-fold path of devotion,
      or of the *pooja* of Ambika (goddess Durga) at the end of the
      'Navaratri'[9] festival, and that it was the *dakshina* of 'Shilangan' or
      crossing of the border?

121. Or was he giving a reminder of the nine qualities of a disciple,
      which Shri krishna told Uddhav in *Shrimad Bhagvat*?

122. And just see the marvel of the sixth stanza of the tenth chapter in
      the eleventh *canto* of the *Bhagvat*! In that stanza, it is narrated
      how a disciple should benefit from a guru, and how he should
      conduct himself in order to get that.

123. There, in its first half, five qualities have been described, while in the later half, only four have been described. Baba also followed the same order, methinks, with the same purpose in mind.

124. The disciple should remain indifferent to honours, insults, fame, etc.; be alert to his own spiritual weal; be without jealousy; detached and dedicated to the guru's service; ever intent on Knowledge of the Brahman and firm and steady within.

125. He should be one who knows not what is envy and does not indulge in vain, senseless talk. These are the qualities with which he should strive to gratify his guru.

126. This must have been the purpose of Sainath too, which he expressed in this form. Saints are always gracious and kind, for the benefit of their own devotees.

127. Laxmi was well-to-do. Of what significance were nine rupees to her? She could have easily given away the same amount in charity. But this was a unique gift to her.

128. And this great good fortune of hers was rare too. That is why she received the nine gems, all in a row, from Sai's own hands, which were symbolic of Sai's grace.

129. Many a time such a sum of nine rupees must have been given away by her and will do so in the future. But this gift was most unique, for it will be, to her, a reminder of Sai, to the end of her life.

130. Death was drawing near. Yet Baba remembered to keep his memory alive, till her death, by giving her Rs.5 and 4, in that order.

131. Showing an alertness of mind, he sent away those who were near him, to have their meal. But two or three villagers wanted to stay.

132. Seeing how critical the time was, some of the loving devotees insisted that they be not asked to go away from Baba.

133. But, as if afraid that in the moment of death he may get entangled in *Maya*, Baba hurriedly sent everyone away.

134. Realizing that '*niryan*' was at hand, Baba said to Butti, Kaka and others, "Go, go to the *wada* and come after your meal".

135. Anxiety and worry on the faces of those around, made Baba's own mind falter and hence he ordered them all, "Go, go and have your meal and then come back".

136. It was thus that those constant companions, close friends as they were, by day and by night, got up to go by his command, though uneasy in mind.

137. They would not disobey his order. And yet, they could not leave his company, either. But they would not incur his displeasure and hence went away to the *wada* for meals.

138. His illness had taken a serious turn. What meal and what food! Their minds, their hearts were all with Baba and not even for a moment could they bear the thought of separation.

139. All the same, they went and sat down to the meal. Suddenly, they were all called away urgently. Without finishing the meal, they all rushed. But still, they missed the last meeting.

140. The oil of life was exhausted, the flame grew dimmer. And there, on the lap of Bayaji Kote lay the body in eternal rest!

141. Not lying down or sleeping, but sitting upon the mattress, calmly and after giving away in charity with his own hands, did Baba give up his mortal coil.

142. Without anyone knowing his heart's secret, he gave up the body effortlessly and merged with the Brahman.

143. Saints appear in this world, assuming a body through the power of *Maya*. When their work of upliftment is over, they immediately merge into the unmanifest.

144. An actor appears disguised in different costumes, but knows full well his real identity. Then what danger of death can there be to one who has taken an 'avatar', of his own free will?

145. He who had incarnated to guide the people, ended his 'avatar', when his mission was over. How can he be tied to birth and death? For he has taken on a body, of his own free will.

146. What possibility of death is there for him, whose glory is *Parabrahman*, Itself? How can creation and destruction harm him, who experiences detachment, all the time?

147. Though he appeared to be performing *karma*, not in the least did he really perform any. Being absolutely without ego, he always performed *karma* without considering himself to be the doer of it.

148. 'Without working out the *(prarabdha) karma*, that *karma* is never, destroyed. This secret about the *karma* has been revealed in the *Smritis*. And he who has realized the Brahman, has no doubts about it. For he sees Brahman in all things.

149. All the fruits of *karma* result from the *karma* performed. This differentiating quality of the *karma* is well-known. But even that is regarded as the Brahman by the *Brahma-jnanis*, like seeing silver on the oyster-shell.

150. A Compassionate Mother, like Baba — how did she fall in the jaws of death? This happening was verily like the dark night swallowing the day.

151. Now let us end this chapter here, observing the limit (of the number of verses) for each month.[10] If the chapter is extended any further, it will make the listeners restless.

152. The remaining story of the *niryan* can be heard later, in its proper order. Hemad surrenders to Sainath. For, his Grace has brought him fulfilment.

Weal be to all! Here ends the forty-second chapter of
"*Shri Sai Samarth Satcharit*", called
'*Niryan of Shri Sainath*',
as inspired by the saints and the virtuous and
composed by his devotee, Hemadpant.

Notes

1. This is the month of *Ashwin* according to the Marathi calendar, corresponding to September-October.
2. This is so-called because on that night Imam Hussain, the second son of the Prophet's daughter, Fatima and Hajarat-Ali, was slaughtered at Karabala, along with other youths in 680 AD by the army of Yajidbin Muaviya.
3. The passing of the border in pompous procession on the festival of *Dassera*.
4. The name of a sage. Applied to an irascible or passionate person.
5. An indigenous form of a Bill of Exchange.
6. A coating or plaster of very hard mortar, used figuratively to express the durability, immutability of promises, determinations, etc.
7. Three ausipicious seasons or periods and a half season; *viz. Dassera*, the new moon during *Diwali* festival and *Gudhi Padva* or the New Year of the people of Maharashtra, Karnataka and Andhra Pradesh, over whom Shalivahan kings once ruled.
8. This is an extract from the *Brihadaranyaka Upanishad* (Ch. 4, Brahmin 4, *mantra*) which says, 'One who has no desires, or whose desires have left him, or whose desires are satiated, he whose desires are centred in the *Atman* alone, the life in him does not depart. Becoming one with Brahman, he goes to Brahman.
9. The festival celebrated in the month of *Ashwin* for a space of nine days and nights, which ends on the tenth day, that is *Dassera*.
10. *Shri Sai-Satcharita* was first serialized in "*Shri Sai Leela*", the monthly magazine published by the Shirdi Sansthan of Shri Sai Baba.

43

'Niryan' of Shri Sainath (Contd...)

*MY OBEISANCE TO SHRI GANESH, TO SHRI SARASWATI, AND SHRI
GURUMAHARAJ! TO THE FAMILY DEITY, TO SHRI SITA-RAMACHANDRA,
MY MOST HUMBLE OBEISANCE! I BOW IN REVERENCE TO THE MOST
VENERABLE GURU SHRI SAINATH!*

1. In the last chapter, the *niryan* of saint Sai Samarth has been described. Whatever remains incomplete from that account will now be completed in this chapter.
2. Sai Samarth himself inspires the marvellous love for him and Hemad, who is totally absorbed at his feet, is writing this, his Story.
3. Sai himself, gives this loving devotion and he alone, adds to the greatness of this Life Story, because of which, there is all the glory in worshipping him and which gives rise to a detachment from worldly life.
4. Hence I make a thousand obeisances to him, with all my heart, speech and action. His greatness cannot be fully realized by merely contemplating on him, but only by surrendering to him whole-heartedly and single-mindedly.
5. To wash away the dirt of all the sins that have accumulated, and to purify the heart, all other means are futile.
6. Even if you search, there is no other means to purify the heart, which is simpler and easier than to remember the glory of God's devotees and to sing their praises in *bhajan* or *kirtan*.
7. So let us now gather the threads of the previous story, contemplate on it briefly and proceed with our account of Sai, the Abode of Self-rejoicing.

8. Earlier, it has already been narrated in detail, why his *niryan* was on the *Vijayadashmi* only and how, under the pretext of Tatyaba, the future events had already been foretold.

9. And later, how he gave in charity to Laxmi, thus remaining alert about *dharma* at the time of giving up the body. All this has been described.

10. Now in this chapter, it will be narrated how Baba listened to the *Ramayan* for his own good, and read by a Brahmin, when his end came near;

11. How the place for the *samadhi* was planned; how his favourite brick slipped from the hand, quite unexpectedly — listen to all this attentively.

12. Similarly, listen to how on one occasion, as Baba went into (*nirvikalpa*) *samadhi* for three days, people were convinced that it was not *samadhi* but his *niryan*;

13. How they made preparations for the last rites and, when Baba suddenly regained normal consciousness, how people were startled in their minds.

14. But this is the story of *niryan*, which no one really likes to hear and the listeners will tire of listening even to this account of *niryan*.

15. This, however, is the *niryan* of saints and *sadhus*, which will purify the listeners and the narrator. Hence, for fear of its becoming too lengthy, listen to it in parts, till you are satisfied.

16. By casting off the physical body, Baba attained to that Eternal state of Self-rejoicing, which is free from rebirth, though difficult to attain.

17. While in the physical body, he was manifest; by abandoning it, he became Unmanifest. His incarnation at one specific place, for one particular purpose ended, revealing his all-pervasiveness.

18. His belonging to one place was over and he became omnipresent. Merging with his real Self, he became eternal, completely.

19. Sai was the centre of everybody's life; nay, he was the very life of them all. Without Sai, the villagers of Shirdi became piteous and meek.

20. As the body grew cold and insensitive, a loud wail arose. Young and old, all worried excessively — as if it was the end of their own life.

21. Physical ailments like fever, etc., afflict only those in worldly life. They never cross their limit to trouble the *yogis*.

22. By kindling their own light, the saints burn their own bodies in it. Baba did the same with his own hands.

23. What should not have happened at all, had already come to pass. Maharaj merged with the Brahman. Their spirits dampened, people sobbed their hearts out.

24. 'Oh, how much better it would have been, had I not gone away from him! I missed the last meeting, thus. Maybe, I could have been of some service. How, O how could my mind have been so befogged at such a critical moment!'

25. Such were the different thoughts that saddened each one at heart. Yet, who can know what was passing in Baba's mind.

26. No rattling in the throat, no gasping for breath, no cough, no violent agitation — Baba went away, happy and peaceful.

27. Where O where Sai's *darshan*, now? Where, that pressing of his feet? How can Sai's feet be washed any more, or partaking of his *teerth*?

28. Seeing that his end was approaching, why did he send away those loving devotees around him, causing them so much heart-ache and repining?

29. Perhaps, seeing all those dearly loved devotees around at the time of *niryan*, Baba's love for them would have upsurged in that moment!

30. And these bonds of love come in the way of the attainment of *Moksha*. If these are not snapped in time, how can the mind become free from desires?

31. So that, when the body is cast off without this happening, and the spirit rises, a new involvement with worldly life begins in that very instant, bringing with it a tumult of new hopes and aspirations.

32. Saints and *sadhus* are, for ever, quick to avoid this and Baba too, was firmly resolute in his mind, to perpetuate this custom of the people.

33. And this is an awareness one must keep in the last moments of life — to be alone, with a mind perfectly peaceful and free from doubts and apprehensions, so that the mind can dwell on one's chosen deity.

34. Everyone knows the famous words, 'As the thoughts at the time of death, so the next birth one gets.' Therefore the devotees of God themselves, put this in practice. This is their way of continuing the prevalent custom.

35. Only fourteen days remained, Baba's end came near. So Baba appointed Vaze to read *Ram-Vijay* to him.

36. Vaze sat down in the mosque. The repeated readings of the *pothi* began and Baba began listening to the *pothi*. Eight days passed by.

37. Later, Baba commanded, "Let the reading of the *pothi* proceed, clear and uninterrupted". Vaze went on reading for the next three days and nights.

38. Altogether, he read for full eleven days. By then he was exhausted, due to weakness. As he kept reading, he became tired. Three days passed in this way.

39. Then what Baba did was, he stopped the reading altogether and sent Vaze away, himself remaining calm and peaceful.

40. Listeners may say, 'Tell us the reason for sending Vaze away'. So I shall narrate it as best as I can. Listen attentively.

41. As the end approaches, saints, *sadhus* and the virtuous, have *pothi-puranas* read out to them and listen to them attentively.

42. Shukacharya[1] read *Mahabhagavat* ceaselessly for seven days to King Parikshit[2], listening to which the king was satisfied and died peacefully.

43. He who leaves this world listening to God's *leelas*, seeing God before his eyes, all the time, truly achieves his weal.

44. Such is the inclination of people's minds and such is always the practice of the saints. They never deviate from the path of guiding the people. Or rather, they incarnate only for that purpose.

45. It is only natural that they who are indifferent towards their elemental body, should not be agitated by sorrow or pain at leaving that body.

46. But here, the listeners may have a doubt. Is it appropriate to say about those who are already enjoying eternal bliss, that they are affected by *Maya* or delusions?

47. How can the nearness of the devotees be an obstacle to him who is constantly absorbed in the Self and contemplates ceaselessly on '*Allah Malik*'?

48. For him, the worldly life had already ended and the spiritual life had stood still; the feeling of duality was totally rooted out and he had merged into his true Self.

49. All this is true, to the letter; there is not an atom of untruth about this. But the saints fulfil themselves only by accomplishing the purpose of their incarnation, which is to guide people to the path of righteousness.

50. Saints are free from the six passions[3]. Always in an unmanifest state, they appear only for uplifting their devotees. Then how can they have death?

51. Coming together of the body and the bodily organs is birth; their separation is death. To be caught up in the worldly life and to become free from it is called birth and death, respectively.

52. With birth comes death, inevitably. They cannot be separated from each other. Death is the natural state of the Being, while life of the *Jeeva* is unnatural to it.

53. But what do they care about the span of their life, who slay Death itself, hold sway over it and incarnate of their own will?

54. They who take different *avatars* with the one desire of uplifting their devotees, can they be bonded by births and deaths? Both these notions, in themselves, are false.

55. He who has reduced his body to ashes, even before it finally falls, what fear has he of death? He has burnt down Death itself!

56. Death is the natural state of the body; it is its pleasurable state. It is life that is the unnatural state of the body. So say the thoughtful.

57. Sai Samarth, the Cloud of Joy, to whom the birth of the body was never known, how can his body then have death? He was not even aware of the existence of his physical body.

58. Sai was the Perfect *Parabrahman*. How can he have birth and death? To him, the Brahman alone is real, while the whole world is illusory. To such a one, how can there be any awareness of the body?

59. His being in the body or abandoning it, his wandering everywhere without being seen by anyone — these are all *leelas* born of his *yogic* powers, and that, only for the upliftment of the devotees.

60. People say that the sun is eclipsed; that it has become invisible. But this is merely the fault of vision. The same is true of the death of saints.

61. To them, the physical body is merely an exterior obstruction. What then are its physical or mental afflictions to them? If there are any such afflictions brought on by 'prarabdha', they are not even conscious of these.

62. He whose incarnation was the result of the accumulated merit of previous births, of the devotees, and was filled with their devotion in the unmanifest state, has incarnated for their cause, when he was seen in Shirdi.

63. Now that the cause of the devotees is accomplished, therefore, it is said, he has abandoned the body. But who will believe these words? Does a *yogi* have *niryan* and rebirth?

64. Empowered with the ability of death-at-will that Sai Samarth was, he burned down his body in the *yogic* fire and, himself merging into the Unmanifest, he yet dwells in the hearts of his devotees.

65. He, remembering whose name, the very thought of birth and death vanishes, how can he be in the state of death? He only returns to the earlier Unmanifest state.

66. Going beyond the gross state, Baba merged into the Unmanifest. Even there, he remains Self-absorbed and always alerts his devotees.

67. The form that throbbed with the divine Life-force, is firmly imprinted on the hearts of the devotees. Can that body be said to be dead? Such words the mind refuses to accept.

68. Hence this Sai, without a beginning and an end, will be alive even to the end of the world and will never be caught up in the birth-death calamity.

69. Did Jnaneshvar Maharaj really die? He gave *darshan* once again, after three centuries! Eknath Maharaj actually met him and the world remains indebted to him.

70. As that gracious Eknath Maharaj was the bright flame in Paithan, so was Tukaram Maharaj in Dehu and Narsimha Saraswati in Alandi.

71. In Parali, it was Samarth Ramdas; in Akkalkot, Akkalkot Maharaj; in Humanabad, Prabhu Manik and so was this Sai in Shirdi.

72. As the faith in each one's heart, so is his experience, even today. He whose power is thus proved by actual experience, how can he be in the state of death?

73. Such was this Champion of the cause of his devotees, who, though he abandoned his mortal coil in Shirdi, pervades the whole animate and inanimate creation in his spirit, and has the power to incarnate at will.

74. Do not entertain such doubts that 'Now that Samarth has merged in the Brahman, what is left in Shirdi?' For Shri Sai is beyond Death.

75. Saints manifest themselves for the good of others and without the help of the womb. They are highly meritorious souls who are Brahman incarnate.

76. To these *avatars*, the states of birth and death never come. Their mission fulfilled, they become one with their real Self and merge in the Unmanifest.

77. And is Baba contained only in this body of just three and a half cubits? It is not right to say that he is of a particular colour or form.

78. The power of one who has acquired the eight *siddhis*, like *Anima, Garima,* etc., is not increased or decreased by the coming and going of people. For the perpetual grandeur is all his own. Such is his fame.

79. The sole purpose of the birth of such *mahatmas* is the weal of the people. And that which arises into being has also continuity in being and cessation. The saints are always ready to guide the people.

80. For the conditions around them are full of misconceptions about birth and death and the permanent state of oneness with the spirit is, to these people, like the happinesss experienced in a dream.

81. Even otherwise, he who was a mine of Knowledge and was always Self-absorbed, to him the nurturing of the body or its fall is all the same.

82. And so, Baba's lifeless body fell, crushing them all under a mountain of sorrow. Laments and wails arose everywhere in Shirdi, vehement and wild.

83. As they heard the news of Baba's *niryan*, it was as though an arrow had pierced through and through. The daily routine was interrupted. In utter confusion, people scattered everywhere.

84. As the inauspicious news got around, it was like a thunderbolt for all. The thoughtful sat silent; others gave vent to loud lamentations.

85. Their throats choked with overwhelming love and from the eyes streamed tears of sorrow, as in their distress, they uttered 'Shiva, Shiva, Hare'.

86. Chaos reigned supreme in every household, accompanied by scenes of uproar. With their hearts beating fast, people ran quickly.

87. Maharaj had passed away. The villagers felt it like a peril threatening their own lives. 'O God! How terrible is this moment! How heart-rending!' They exclaimed.

88. One and all, they started running to the mosque, so that its *sabhamandap* was packed, totally. Seeing the heart-rending situation there, throats choked with grief.

89. Gone, gone is that splendour of Shirdi! All its happiness, its good fortune is forever, lost! The eyes of all filled with tears and courage failed them.

90. How glorious was that mosque, which was reckoned one among the '*Saptapuris*'[4] and to which Baba always referred most resolutely, as '*Dwarkamayee*'.

91. Be it '*niryan*'[5], '*nirvan*' or '*nidhan*', Dwarkamayee is the place of '*Sayujyamukti*' for all. And he who meditates on God ceaselessly, finds a place there.

92. Such was this *Gururaj Sairaya*, the Compassionate Father and Mother to the devotees and their place of Repose. He is remembered, always.

93. Shirdi was desolate without Baba; all the ten directions seemed forlorn. Shirdi was like the body from which life has departed.

94. As, when the water in a pond dries up, the fish toss and turn in extreme distress, so the people of Shirdi wilted with sorrow.

95. A lake without a lotus, a home without a son, a temple without a lamp, so were the surroundings of the mosque, vacant.

96. As a household without its master or a city without a king or a treasury without money, so was Shirdi reduced to a forest, without Baba.

97. As a mother to a child, or the water from the cloud to the Chatak, so also was Baba's love to the people of Shirdi and to all his devotees.

98. Shirdi became lustreless, as if dead, piteous and sorrowful. As a fish without water, so the people tossed and turned in agony.

99. Like a wife who abandons her husband, or a mother, her infant, as a calf of a cow that has lost its way, so were they all, both old and young.

100. To the people of Shirdi, the grief became uncontrollable, as they ran helter-skelter in all the four directions, scattering in lanes and by-lanes.

101. Because of Sai and Sai alone, that Shirdi had sanctity; because of him, Shirdi had a character of its own. It was because of Sai alone, that it became a place of pilgrimage. It was Sai alone, who was the shelter for all.

102. Some cried out loudly; some rolled on the ground in their grief, others fainted — all were stricken with sorrow.

103. As tears of sorrow rolled down their eyes, men and women were in great distress. They were incapable of touching either food or water; their faces had become piteous.

104. When the villagers saw Baba in that state, their grief reached the point of culmination. All the devotees, young and old, were filled with great disquietitude.

105. Where there were once sweet, fascinating tales, where there was joy, in various ways, where it was not possible to gain entry quickly — that same mosque, today, looked like a wilderness.

106. The constant prosperity and sanctity that was in Shirdi earlier, was entirely due to Baba. And hence the villagers were naturally filled with regrets.

107. O Sainath, the root of all Happiness and Joy incarnate that you are, you took on a body for the cause of the devotees and having fulfilled your mission, alas, you cast off that body in this Shirdi.

108. Bewildered that we were, you so sincerely instructed and guided us for our own good, day and night, throughout the eight watches and without weariness.

109. But all that advice and instruction was wasted as water poured on an upturned vessel. Not a drop of it has remained.

110. At every step, you would tell us that "When you speak slightingly to someone, I instantly feel the pain." But we never heeded your words.

111. Never having listened to your beneficial advice, we are really your great offenders. Is that why you made us atone for that sin of disobedience to your command, in this manner?

112. Baba, is this the full measure of all our sins? But what is the use of repenting, now? All the suffering for it must be endured willingly!

113. And, is that why you grew tired of us and have gone behind the curtain? O, how could Death strike us such a hard blow!

114. You seem to have become weary of dinning into our heads, till your throat parched and our showing complete disinterest in what you said.

115. Being thus offended with us, you forgot all your earlier love for us. Or, maybe, our association from previous births has come to an end, today. Or, perhaps, the milk of your divine love has dried up!

116. Had it been known that you would go away so quickly, it would have been so much better! At least, the people would have remained more alert, from the start.

117. But we were all indolent. Filled with sloth and languor, we sat idle. With the result, we got cheated in the end. Our being there or not being there, was all the same.

118. We became disloyal to the guru and did nothing in time. Had we even sat still, it would have been something. But we did not do even that!

119. We would travel long distances to go to Shirdi, only to engage in idle, empty talk. Totally forgetting that we were at a holy place, we would behave, even there, just as we pleased.

120. There were devotees of different types — some *Jnani*, some egoistic, some simple and faithful, while some others, inquisitive. But looking to their real Self, Baba treated them all as same. For, to differentiate between more or less, he knew not.

121. He saw only God and nothing else in the world. Such being his outlook, he did not consider himself as separate or different.

122. The devotees themselves are God and the guru is not different from them, either. It is when they both forget the true Self that both consider each other as being separate.

123. In fact, we ourselves are God. But when the true Self is forgotten, it forms the main characteristic of this separateness and this itself is the Fall.

124. The sovereign dreams that he is begging for alms from door to door. But when he wakes up to reality, he sees himself in the same position as before.

125. Whatever one is doing in the waking state ceases to be as one enters the dreaming state. But the real awakening comes with one's own experience of merging totally into the Brahman and his Creation.

126. Baba dearly loved all who sought refuge at his feet, whether *Jnani* or ignorant. To him, they were nearer than even his own self and he made not the slightest difference between them.

127. He was God in human form and although he had given them personal experience of this, the devotees were completely taken in by his tender affection for them.

128. To some, he gave wealth; to some, children and a happy family life. But they were deluded by all these and thus lost the chance of attaining Knowledge.

129. When he sometimes laughed and joked with someone, that person would swell with pride that he alone enjoyed Baba's unique love, which Baba never displayed towards others.

130. But when he spoke to someone angrily, they said, 'Baba does not like him and has respect only for us, which he does not give to others.'

131. Even as we vied with each other thus, regarding his favour, which Baba never even dreamt of, in vain were we cheated out of our own weal and forgot our duty.

132. When by our great good fortune, the very *Parabrahman* stood at our bedside, in a human form, we forgot his real mission and grew fond of his jesting and joking, instead.

133. As soon as we arrived, we would take Baba's *darshan*, offering him fruit and flower, but when he asked for *dakshina*, we would falter and would not stay there any longer.

134. You talked to us about things that were beneficial for us. But on seeing our mean, petty attitude, methinks, you became sad and quickly went away to your Eternal Abode.

135. But now, can these eyes ever see you again in that wonderful Self-absorbed state? Gone indeed is that Joy incarnate — lost to us for ever, having disappeared for our several births!

136. Alas for our terrible *karma*! We have lost our truest friend Sai, so near at hand that he had been! A selfless, compassionate One like him, has today become a stranger to us!

137. "It is not good to harass anyone. It makes me ill." But we never heeded these words of Baba and went on quarrelling, just as we pleased.

138. We troubled the devotees and the non-devotees, too. And in the bargain, we have now lost Sainath! O, how we regret it now, as we remember his words!

139. Maharaj had told the devotees that "I will manifest myself, among the people, as a child of eight years."

140. These are the words of a saint and no one should regard them as futile. Shri Vishnu had done the same, when he took the *avatar* as Shrikrishna.

141. The radiant eight-year-old figure of Krishna, with weapons in his four hands, had appeared before mother Devaki in the prison.

142. There, the purpose was to ease the burden of sinners on this earth; here it is to uplift the poor, meek devotees. So why should we entertain doubts in our mind? For the *leelas* of saints are inconceivable.

143. And is this the resolution of just one birth? No, indeed, it is the close association of the devotees for seventy-two generations. So Baba said in the course of conversation.

144. And the devotees felt sure in their minds that tying the bonds of love in this way, Baba has just gone on a journey and will come back again.

145. Many had actual *darshan*, though to most he appeared in a Vision. Quite a few were secretly given supernatural experiences.

146. To those without faith he is invisible. To the faithful devotees, he appears wherever they may be. As their natural inclination, so is their actual experience.

147. In the *Chavadi*, his presence is invisible; in the mosque, it is in the form of Brahman; in the *Samadhi Mandir*, in a state of *samadhi*, while everywhere else, it is as Joy incarnate.

148. But at present, the devotees should keep a firm faith in their hearts that there is no impediment to the presence of Sai Samarth and that he dwells here, for ever, without destruction.

149. The gods go to their own abodes, but the saints attain the Brahman, here itself. They know no going or coming as they are merged into Eternal Bliss!

150. Hence, bowing respectfully, I make this one humble request to all, old and young alike, to which please listen with reverence.

151. May we always have the company of those who enjoy an excellent reputation and feel a selfless love towards the guru; may we cherish a keen desire to describe the virtues of our guru and thus nurture a pure, loving devotion towards him.

152. May we develop for him a lasting devotion and may the bond of our friendship never be snapped, so that the devotees enjoy peace and happiness, day and night, at the guru's feet.

153. And so, later, Baba's disciples and all the people of the village began to consider as to what should be befittingly done with his body.

154. Shrimant Butti was a very devout soul, who, as if as a memorial to this future event, had already built a most spacious, beautiful *wada*.

155. Then, for the next thirty-six hours, they debated as to where that corpse should be placed, though that which was destined to happen, came to pass, in the end.

156. One said, the Hindus should not be allowed even to touch the corpse; let us take it ceremoniously to the Mohammedan cemetery.

157. Another said, that 'the corpse should be kept in the open; let us build a beautiful tomb, where it should remain, for ever'.

158. Even Khushalchand and Amir Shakkar thought the same. But, 'let this body rest in the *wada*', were Baba's words.

159. Patil Ramchandra was, however, very resolute. He was also one of the village officers and Baba's loving devotee. He said to the villagers,

160. 'Whatever may be your thoughts, they are not acceptable to us, at all. Sai should not be kept, even for a moment, outside the *wada* or anywhere else'.

161. The Hindus according to their religion, and the Muslims according to theirs, debated the whole night as to what would be proper and what not.

162. Here, in his house, as Laxmanmama lay asleep, in the early hours of the morning, Baba appeared in his dream and, holding his hand, said, "Come, come! Get up quickly!

163. "Bapusaheb will not come, today. For he thinks I am dead. So, at least, you perform my early morning *pooja* and *arati*".

164. Getting up at once, Laxmanmama arrived at the appropriate time, carrying *pooja* articles, as was his daily practice, thus presenting himself for performing the *pooja*.

165. He was the '*gram-joshi*'[6] of Shirdi and maternal uncle to Madhavrao, who performed Baba's *pooja* every day in the morning.

166. Mama was scrupulously exact in the discharge of all religiously enjoined acts, and words. After taking a bath in the morning and putting on clean, washed clothes, he would take Baba's *darshan*.

167. He would then wash Baba's feet, apply sandalwood paste and consecrated rice, offer Tulsi leaves, flowers, etc., and after waving lights, burning incense and offering *naivedya*, he would offer *dakshina* in the end.

168. Then, prostrating in obeisance with prayers, he would take Baba's blessings and thereafter, offer *prasad*, and apply sandalwood paste on the foreheads of all. He would then go away.

169. Thence he would go to offer *pooja* to Ganesh, Shanidev, Shankar, Maruti, who was the son of Anjani.

170. Thus, this *gram-joshi* performed the *pooja* of all the village deities, every day. Now, very lovingly, he offered *pooja* with all proper rites to that corpse.

171. Mama was already a devout soul and to add to it, he had had a vision. So he came with ingredients for the *kakad arati* (*arati* at dawn) in hand and prostrated before it in obeisance.

172. Removing the covering on the face, he gazed at it affectionately. Then washing the feet and hands and giving him 'achaman' (water for sipping), he performed all the ritual of *pooja*.

173. The Maulavi and other Muslims objected to his touching the body. But without paying attention to them, Mama applied the sandalwood paste and performed the entire *pooja*.

174. The corpse was that of Shri Samarth, his chosen deity — not even in dream would Mama ever think whether it was the corpse of a Hindu or a Muslim.

175. When that most revered form was alive, so grand was the *pooja* ceremony. And even when the same had become a corpse, the *pooja* ceremony would not become a mere formality.

176. Moreover seeing Baba in that state, Mama was already filled with grief and had come to perform the *pooja* for the last time, as his *darshan* would no longer be possible any more.

177. His eyes filled with tears and he could not even bear to look at him, the hands and legs trembled and his mind became sad and dejected.

178. However, opening his tightly-closed fist, Mama put in it, *paan* and *dakshina* and covering up the corpse as before, Mama then went away.

179. Later on, Bapusaheb Jog performed the noon *arati* of Sai in the mosque, as usual, along with others.

180. And now, the description of what happened after this, will be given in the next chapter — how the funeral rites, according to Hindu religion, were performed on Baba's body in a very spacious place;

181. How the breaking of his favourite brick, his companion of many years, foretold the inauspicious event of his *niryan*;

182. How it would have been a great calamity, had, what happened now, had happened thirty-two years ago, when he went into *nirvikalpa samadhi*;

183. How, at that time, the devotee Mhalsapati guarded Baba, day and night, and how, when everybody had given up hope, Baba revived quite unexpectedly.

184. Such a *Yogacharya*, who practiced celibacy till death and was the greatest among the *Jnanis*, who can describe his glory?

185. He, whose greatness is such, let us bow to him with good thoughts and feelings. This poor Hemad surrenders to him with a single-minded devotion.

Weal be to all! Here ends the forty-third chapter of
"*Shri Sai Samarth Satcharit*", called
'*Niryan of Shri Sainath (Cont...)*',
as inspired by the saints and the virtuous
and composed by his devotee, Hemadpant.

Notes

1. Son of the sage Vyas, and a sage, himself.
2. Grandson of the Pandavas and son of Abhimanyu, who succeeded them to the throne of Hastinapur.
3. These are: lust, anger, greed, temptation, conceit and envy.
4. These are the seven sacred cities, which are : Ayodhya, Mathura, Maya (Haridwar), Kashi, Kanchi, Avantika (Ujjain) and Dwarawati (Dwaraka).
5. '*Niryan*' is leaving this world, '*Nirvan*' is Eternal Peace or to be one with the Brahman and '*nidhan*' is death.
6. The village astronomer. He frames almanacs, casts nativities, announces lucky seasons, etc.

'Niryan' of Shri Sainath (Concluded)

MY OBEISANCE TO SHRI GANESH, TO SHRI SARASWATI, AND SHRI GURUMAHARAJ! TO THE FAMILY DEITY, TO SHRI SITA-RAMACHANDRA, MY MOST HUMBLE OBEISANCE! I BOW IN REVERENCE TO THE MOST VENERABLE GURU SHRI SAINATH!

1. Om Shri Sai, obeisance to you, who are filled to the brim with the Universal Divine Consciousness; who are the Abode of Happiness and a Treasure-house of Prosperity and by whose grace poverty vanishes.

2. Bowing at your feet, even casually, all the sins are washed away. Then, he who worships you and sings your praises, with faith and devotion — oh, how blessed he must become!

3. As one gazes into your smiling countenance, all the sorrows of worldly life are forgotten and hunger and thirst satisfied, there and then! So marvellous is your *darshan*!

4. He who ceaselessly meditates on '*Allah Malik*' and is free from desires and the ego; whose mind is without any greed, any cravings — how can I describe the greatness of such a one?

5. He whose peaceful nature is such that he always does good even to those who do harm, no one should forget him ever, even for a moment, but should give him a place in their heart.

6. Rama and Shri Krishna have beautiful, lotus-like eyes; saints have only one eye or are sometimes, without eyes. Gods are comely, beautiful in appearance, while the saints are always the very Joy Incarnate.

7. Gods look upon us with grace only when we call out to them; but as for saints, there is no end to their bestowal of grace on us.

Gods say, 'As men approach me so do I accept them'; but the saints are moved by compassion, even for those who revile them.

8. There is no difference between the three — Ram, Krishna and Sai. They are different only in name and are all one and the same.

9. To say that this thing has a state of mortality, is altogether false. How can he be troubled by death, when he has complete power over it?

10. I do not understand about *Prarabdha, Sanchit* and *Kriyaman*[1]. But I know that Sai is compassionate and I beseech his mercy.

11. As the waves of numerous desires surge upwards, the mind has no peace and unless you bestow grace on this creature, his mind will have no stability.

12. I was not able to fulfil the promise, which I gave at the beginning of the last chapter and the narration was not complete. Hence listen to it now, from beginning to end.

13. Knowing that the end was near, Baba listened attentively, day and night, to the *Ramayan*, read to him by a Brahmin.

14. When two weeks passed in this way, listening to the *Ramayan* and as the day of *Vijayadashmi* arrived, Baba gave up his body.

15. It has been narrated in the last chapter that when Baba passed away, Laxmanmama performed the *pooja* and Jog performed the *arati*, lighting the 'niranjan' (a metal lamp dish).

16. After that, it took thirty-six hours for the Hindus and the Muslims to deliberate on how the corpse could be placed at the best and most appropriate place.

17. How the place for the *samadhi* was aleady planned, how the falling of the brick ocurred quite unexpectedly; how once, Baba went into *nirvikalpa samadhi* for three days;

18. How everyone had doubts whether it was *samadhi* or death, when on seeing his breathing had stopped, his revival seemed impossible;

19. And when three days had passed thus, how they were convinced of his death, and everybody naturally began thinking of the funeral rites;

20. But how, even at that time, Baba, who was constantly alert within, unexpectedly regained normal consciousness, relieving people of their worry, etc.;

21. Listen lovingly, O listeners! to all these stories for they will gladden your hearts and your throats will be choked with emotion, as you listen.

22. These are not just stories, but a box that contains within, the most precious gem, Sai. Open it lovingly and look inside, to experience the joy of his *darshan*.

23. In all these chapters, you will find Sainath filled to the brim within, and by listening to them, the desires of your heart will be satisfied. By remembering him, you will have a Protector.

24. This is the Story of Sai, whose conduct was most generous. Be ready to listen to it with love and concentration.

25. As they listen to this most purifying story, the hearts of the devotees are never satiated. For they are filled with a blissful joy and exhausted as they are, by the toil of worldly life, they enjoy peace.

26. The joy of a gladdened heart, the Self-rejoicing appears before them. Such being this Life of Sai, it is the purest of all happiness.

27. However often one listens to it, there is always something novel. And this, this is the characteristic of true beauty and charm. Hence, listen to this sacred story of the saint with undivided attention.

28. And so, they were all exhausted debating as to what would be the best place for the corpse to be placed in. But just see what their actual experience was, in the end.

29. The part of the large room in Butti's *wada*, where it was planned to have a *sanctum sanctorum* for installing the *Muralidhar* (Shri Krishna) idol, was decided upon as the place for Baba.

30. Earlier, when the foundation was being dug, as Baba was going to the Lendi, Baba had nodded his head in approval, to Madhavrao's request.

31. As the *sanctum sanctorum* for *Muralidhar* was being dug, giving a coconut into Baba's hand, Madhavrao had entreated him to bestow his glance of grace on it.

32. And, seeing the moment to be auspicious, Baba had said, "Break the coconut. We, all the children, will pass our time here, itself.

33. "And as we move about here, we will also converse about our joys and sorrows. Here itself, all the children will find peace of mind."

34. Initially, everyone thought that Baba said this just for the sake of saying something. But later, they realized the significance, when they got the actual experience.

35. As Baba passed away, the installation of Muralidhar remained unperformed. Instead it was considered to be the best place for preserving the treasure, that was Sai.

36. Baba's last words, "Let this body rest in the *wada*", became the final decision and Baba himself, became *Muralidhar.*

37. Shrimant Butti and all the people, Hindus and Muslims, agreed to this plan and the *wada* was thus utilized for a good purpose.

38. And had Baba's body lain just anywhere, when such a precious *wada* was available, that *wada* too, would have appeared to be empty and desolate.

39. The *pooja* and *bhajan*, *Katha-kirtan*, reading of *Puranas* and 'anna-daan' to the visiting guests that goes on there, today, is entirely due to Shri Sai.

40. Today, the satiety through partaking of a meal, performance of 'Laghu-rudra'[2], 'Maha-rudra', by people of different countries, that is seen, is due to Shri Sai, alone.

41. So, the words of a saint should be carefully stored in the ears, word for word. Never dishonour or reject them, as if the saints are saying just anything.

42. In the beginning, however nonsensical or obscure they may appear to be, their significance is understood as time goes by.

43. Earlier, when there was yet time for Baba's *niryan*, there occurred in the mosque at Shirdi some bad omens about things to come.

44. Of these, I shall now narrate just one to the listeners. For, if all of them are narrated, the book will become too lengthy.

45. For years together, there used to be an old brick of Baba's, on which he rested his head, while sitting in *yogasan*.

46. Every night, taking support of that brick, Baba used to sit in the mosque, in solitude, very peacefully, in a *yogic asana*.

47. This practice had continued, unhindered, for years, without a break. But regularity of a practice does not help when things are pre-ordained and the rule is broken, quite suddenly.

48. Once, when Baba was not in the mosque, a young boy was sweeping it. He lifted the brick just a little to sweep underneath.

49. The brick, which was destined to break, slipped from the boy's hand and fell down with a crash, instantly breaking into two.

50. When Baba heard this, he said, "It is not the brick, but fortune that is broken". He was filled with regrets and his eyes filled with tears of sorrow.

51. When the brick which Baba took for support as he sat in the *yogasan*, daily, broke in this way, his heart was torn with grief and his throat choked with emotion.

52. Seeing that old brick of so many years, the main support of his *yogasan*, broken suddenly, in such a way, the mosque itself, looked forlorn to him.

53. That brick was, to Baba, dearer than life and seeing it in such a condition, Baba was greatly distressed in his mind.

54. It was this same brick, resting his elbow on which, Baba would spend hour after hour, sitting in *yogasan*, all ready for *Yoga*. He naturally had great love for it.

55. "The brick, in the company of which, I go into a state of Self-absorption, and which was dearer to me as life itself — that companion of mine is broken and I too, cannot remain without it.

56. "That brick, my companion of a lifetime, has gone, leaving me behind". Remembering its many qualities in this manner, Baba started crying.

57. A doubt may naturally arise here — is not that brick just as transient? Then why lament for it thus? What will people say?

58.   Such a doubt may arise in the beginning, in anybody's mind. So, to satisfy it, I shall explain, after first bowing to Sai.

59.   The saints incarnate only for the upliftment of the world and for taking safely across the ocean of worldly life, those who are poor and lowly. They have no other purpose.

60.   Laughing, crying and all other forms of appearances are only to follow the conventional ways. This is the essence, here. And as the great conduct themselves, so becomes the convention among the people.

61.   Although the saints are perfect *Jnanis* and all their desires in this world are satiated, yet they are induced to do *karma* for uplifting the people.

62.   However, thirty-two years before this *niryan*, Baba's *samadhi* would have come about. But Mhalsapati's alert mind really prevented this inauspicious event.

63.   Had this evil happening not been prevented, how could the people have enjoyed Sai's beneficial company? Such was that inauspicious conjunction of forces that he would have parted from us forty-three years earlier.

64.   It was the full moon in the brighter half of the month of *Margashirsha* (December), when Baba became restless with an attack of Asthma and in order to be able to bear the physical affliction, he went into *nirvikalpa samadhi*.

65.   And Baba had already told everyone, "For three days from now onwards, I shall go into *samadhi*. Do not try to rouse me".

66.   That corner of the *Sabha-mandap* that you see, that was the place to which Baba had pointed his finger and said, "Dig the *samadhi* there and place me at that spot".

67.   Addressing Mhalsapati, Baba had himself said, most positively, "Do not abandon me with unconcern, the next three days.

68.   "And put up two flags at that place as a sign indicative of the spot". So saying, he went into *nirvikalpa samadhi*.

69.   And, as in a sudden fainting fit, his body fell down, motionless. Mhalsapati took his head on his lap; but the others gave up all hope.

70. It was night time; the clock had struck ten, when this incident took place. People fell silent, thinking , 'Alas! what a sudden calamity!'

71. No breathing, no pulse — life seemed to have abandoned the body. To the people, it appeared a terrible state; but to Sai, it was a state of greatest happiness

72. Thereafter, Mhalsapati, who was always alert in his mind, kept guard over Baba, day and night, sitting up wide awake, all the time.

73. Although it was a command from Sai's own mouth, to dig his *samadhi*, yet no one had the heart to do so.

74. The whole village gathered there to see Baba in the state of *samadhi* and people stared at him in utter astonishment. Bhagat, however, would not put down Baba's head from his lap.

75. 'So that it may not be a sudden shock to the people to see that life had departed from his body, Baba had asked them to guard him for three days. Really, Sai had deceived them', thought the people.

76. His breathing ceased; all the bodily organs became still, without any trace of activity and the glow of life over it dimmed, too!

77. Consciousness of the outside world was lost; speech fell silent. Everyone was deeply worried as to how he would regain consciousness.

78. The body would not gain consciousness. Two days passed in this way. *Mulla, Maulavi, fakir* — all came and began discussing what was to be done next.

79. Appa Kulkarni, Kashiram came, and took a firm decision that Baba had attained his Eternal Abode. So his body should be laid to rest.

80. Some said, 'Wait a moment; such haste is not good. Baba is not like others. His words are always true'.

81. At once, the others replied, 'From where will life come into a body that is already cold? How thoughtless all these people are!

82. 'Dig the grave at the spot indicated. Oh, do call all the people and give a timely burial! Get everything ready for it'.

83. And even as the debate continued, the period of three days passed. Then, early morning, at three o'clock, they saw signs of life returning.

84. Gradually, consciousness returned; the twisting and turning of the body began; breathing too, resumed and the stomach could be seen heaving up and down.

85. The face began to look pleased and happy, the eyes opened. The motionless state had disappeared and signs of life, of waking up, appeared.

86. It was as if the bodily consciousness which was forgotten so far, was remembered again, or the treasure that was lost, was found again, and the treasurehouse was opened up.

87. Everyone was pleased to see that Sai had regained consciousness. By God's Grace, a great calamity was averted. But still, the devotees were filled with amazement.

88. Bhagat gazed into his face with fond admiration and Sai too, nodded silently. The *Maulavi* and *fakir* turned pale in the face. Thus a terrible situation was prevented.

89. Had Bhagat failed to obey Baba's command; on seeing the obstinate insistence of *Maulavi*, had his resolution wavered ever so slightly, then indeed, the situation would have been terrible.

90. The *samadhi* would have come forty-three years earlier. Where then, would be his conversation; where, his enchanting, joyous *darshan*?

91. In the cause of people's welfare, Sai came out of the *samadhi* and revived to life, to the great satisfaction of the devotees.

92. He who was exhausted, working for the benefit of the devotees and had gone into *samadhi*, how could he have been revived any earlier? Truly inconceivable is his *leela*!

93. Seeing that Baba had regained normal consciousness, all the devotees rejoiced. Each one rushed for his *darshan*. Thus Baba's revival from the state of *samadhi* was a matter of great joy for all.

94. So, the uncompleted story of Baba's *niryan* has now been narrated fully, as I remember it today.

95. Hence, all you listeners, ask yourselves for a moment as to why we should rejoice or grieve? Are both these not equally indiscriminate?

96. This large vehicle of three and a half cubits, which is the framework of this body with all its organs, is this really all that our Sai is? Give up this delusion, totally.

97. If 'Sai' is only this body, then there is no term for the incorporeal Spirit; nor has it any form. But Shri Sai is beyond form.

98. The body is destructible; but the Spirit is free and indestructible. The body is in the five elements; but the Spirit is without a beginning and an end.

99. And it is the pure *Sattvic* Life-force in it, that is Brahman Itself which controls the gross physical organs, that is called Sai.

100. And that, of course, is beyond the bodily organs. The gross physical organs cannot know It. It is this that induces the organs to function and stirs the vital airs.

101. This power is called Sai. There is no place which is without It and all the ten directions are empty in its absence. It pervades the whole animate and inanimate creation.

102. And Sai's incarnation is also this same state. What was unmanifest earlier, has now manifested itself, bearing a form and a name and, having completed the mission, has now merged with the Unmanifest again.

103. Like all the incarnations that enter into their Eternal Abode, after completing their mission and giving up the body, Sai's doing too has been the same.

104. Just as, when once it came into his mind to disappear, Shri Narsimhasaraswati suddenly went away from Gangapur, saying that he was going on a pilgrimage to the Mountain;

105. And as the devotees tried to obstruct, satisfied them by saying that 'This going of mine is only conventional; I am not leaving Gangapur.

106. 'Bathe on the banks of Krishna, in the morning; do '*anusthan*'[3] at the Bindukshetra and worship my *padukas* in the Math, as my Presence will be there, eternally';

107. So too, was Sai Baba's way! His *niryan* was only conventional. If you see, his Presence is there in all the animate and inanimate things and in the hearts of all.

108. As is one's devotion, so is the constant experience one gets. Have no doubt in your minds. For Sai is beyond death.

109. Sai fills the entire Creation, animate and inanimate; Sai dwells in all — inside and outside; Sai dwells for ever, in you and in me.

110. Sai Samarth is compassionate to the poor and the meek and is the Protector of his simple, faithful devotees. He is hungry for the deep sincere love and has great affection for all.

111. Though not visible to the ocular perception, yet he is everywhere. Himself hiding in the Subtle Principle, he yet bewitches us.

112. His *niryan* is only a pretence, a disguise to deceive us. Faultless as he is, he enacts different roles. Thus, though destroyed in the body, he has become immortal.

113. Let us hold fast to the love that is in his heart and try to understand him thus; thereby achieving our purpose.

114. By worshipping sincerely and remembering him with faith and devotion, all the devotees will get the experience. And they will realize his all-pervasiveness.

115. Creation, Preservation and Destruction do not threaten the Self. It is forever, filled with Pure Consciousness and has no place for the passions.

116. It is like gold, which always remains gold, even when not moulded into ornaments. Though various adornments are made from it, it does not lose its quality as gold.

117. The different ornaments are destructible and can be melted to pure gold, which is unchangeable and has neither shape nor name.

118. May this Hemadpant merge into this gold, absolutely and completely, and dwell at the feet of this Sai, who is adorned with all the virtues, to the end of this world.

119. Later, the thirteenth day (after Baba's *niryan*) was observed. Balasaheb (Bhate), a gem among the devotees, collected Brahmins from the village and began the funeral rites.

120. After a bath, with his clothes on, *'Tilanjali', 'Tiltarpan'* and *'Pindapradan'*⁴ was done at the hands of Balasaheb.

121. All the *'Uttarkriya', 'Sapindi'*⁵, etc., were performed at the proper time, every month, according to the *Shastras*.

122. Upasani, the great devotee, went to the banks of the holy Bhagirathi, along with Jog and performed the *'Hom-havan'*⁶.

123. And after feeding the Brahmins, giving *'anna-daan'* to the poor and after offering *dakshina*, as prescribed by the *Shastras*, they then returned.

124. Though now, there was no Baba any more, no more dialogue with him, yet on seeing the mosque, all the joyous conversations of the past came back to the mind.

125. And to experience, once again, the pleasure of seeing Baba, sitting in his usual *yogasan*, the very best among his portraits has been installed, very lovingly, in the mosque.

126. Although Baba's form is no longer before the eyes, it is seen again by the *darshan* of his portrait. And, to his faithful, loving devotees, Sai Baba himself appears to have come back in person.

127. Shamrao, whose surname was Jayakar, has drawn this beautiful portrait. Such is this wonderful portrait which always reminds us of Baba.

128. A great painter that Shamrao was, he was also a great devotee of Baba, who, after careful thought, acted according to Baba's order.

129. He was asked to paint many other beautiful portraits, which are installed in the homes of devotees, for them to meditate upon.

130. Saints never die. This has already been explained many times earlier, if you remember, and needs no further clarification.

131. Today, Baba is no longer in the body. Yet he looks after the welfare of those who remember him, as if in body, as before.

132. He may have told someone something, which has not yet been experienced as true. But do not consider the words in vain, just because he has given up the body.

133. For Baba's words are as the writing of *Brahmadev*. Have faith and await experience. Though it may not come soon, it will most certainly come after some time.

134. However, with the mention of the name 'Jog', I am reminded of a brief story while narrating the main story. Listen to it and you will see its uniqueness, as also Sai's love and affection.

135. Though the dialogue is rather brief, it is very instructive to the guru-devotees. He is really very fortunate, who already has an awareness of renunciation and detachment, while unfortunate is he, who is in the bondage of worldly life.

136. Once Jog asked Baba, 'Why am I still in such a state? Why is my fate so strange? When will I experience a better condition?

137. 'For many years, I have had the opportunity, O God, to serve you single-mindedly. And yet, this fickle mind of mine has no rest, no peace. Why is this so?

138. 'Oh, how could I be so unfortunate! Is this all my gain in the company of a saint? When, on what occasion, will I enjoy the good results of keeping the company of the saintly and virtuous?'

139. Listen calmly to the reply that Sai Samarth so lovingly gave, on hearing this prayer of the devotee.

140. "I will consider you of great good fortune, only when all your sins are burnt down, reducing sins and merit to ashes and when I see a 'jholi' (symbolic of a fakir) under your arm.

141. "I will regard you as truly fortunate, when all the delusions created by *Maya* are given up and a fond attachment is developed for God's worship always, resulting ultimately in the snapping of all the ties of hopes and desires.

142. "When excessive attachment to the sense objects is considered worth abandoning and the differentiation between oneself and others as altogether improper; when you become fit and deserving by conquering the palate and the reproductive organs, then will I think of you as fortunate."

143. And so, some time after this, Baba's words came true. By Sadguru's grace, Jog attained that detachment, which Baba had spoken about.

144. Free as he was, of the ties of sons, children, he saw also his wife attain a good passage after death. He renounced everything before leaving the body and thus detachment came to him easily, naturally.

145. But this Jog too, was fortunate! Sai's words came true. Becoming a *sanyasin*, he merged with the Brahman, in the end.

146. And as Sai had said, so his condition changed in the same manner. Sai's utterance came true. Jog was most fortunate, indeed!

147. In brief, Baba, ever compassionate to the poor and the meek and deeply concerned with the good of the devotees that he was, offered in abundance, the nectar of instruction and advice, while in Shirdi, at morning, noon and evening. Listen to it, now!

148. "I am always in the eyes of him who is most fond of me. To him, the whole Creation is empty without me and in his mouth, there are tales of me and me alone.

149. "He meditates on me, ceaselessly. And his tongue repeats but my name. Coming or going anywhere, he sings only my praises.

150. "And when he becomes one with me thus, he forgets both action and inaction. Where there is such eagerness and reverence to serve me, only there I wait, all the time.

151. "Surrendering to me single-mindedly, he who remembers me, ceaselessly, his debt is on my head, which I shall repay by uplifting him.

152. "I act according to the wishes of him, who intently meditates on me and does not eat or drink anything without first offering it to me.

153. "He who hungers and thirsts after me alone, and to whom no one else is like me, I also, think of him alone, and act according to his wish.

154. "He who has turned back from father and mother, relatives and friends, wife and son, such a one is lovingly attached to my feet.

155., "In the rainy season, as the different rivers, overflowing their banks, meet the ocean, they forget their identity as rivers and become the one great ocean, itself.

156. "Their form is lost; their name is gone; only, their water merges with the ocean. The river and the ocean are wedded. Their duality is lost in oneness.

157. "Having merged completely — the name, form, everything — the mind will be forgotten and will automatically see me by its natural disposition. It will have no other place, except me.

158. "Those proficient in book-learning and engaged in meaningless babble, brought iron bars to prove to the people that I am no 'Parees' (the Philosopher's stone), but only an ordinary stone.

159. "When I was struck with the bars, they turned, on the contrary, into gold, thereby disproving my being a stone and were astonished by this experience.

160. "Without even an atom of ego, you should surrender to me, who dwell in your heart. Instantly, your ignorance or *Maya* will be dispelled and no cause will remain for listening to a discourse on knowledge.

161. "From *a-vidya* or ignorance comes the identification with the body and from such identification arise mental and physical afflictions. It is this identification with the body that pushes man towards the rules of what is proper and what is improper, which are obstacles to Self-realization.

162. "You may ask as to where I am now, or how I will meet you. But I dwell very near you, in your own hearts and can meet you without any effort.

163. "You will then say 'Who and how is this dweller in the heart? What are his characteristics and what is his mark by which we can recognize him?'

164. "So, be attentive and listen now, to the clear description as to who this dweller in your heart is, to whom you should surrender.

165. "This Creation is full of numerous forms with varied names, which no one can count. All these are different forms of *Maya*.

166. "Similarly, the desire of the Spirit, which goes beyond the *Trigunas* — *Sattva*, *Rajas* and *Tamas* — that is the manifestation of the Dweller in the heart.

167. "Apart from the name and the form, the 'You' that remains behind, that is the mark of God. Know this and surrender to Him.

168. "When you see yourself as me and when this attitude is extended further, then all the creatures are one with your guru and there is not a place which is without me.

169. "And as your *sadhana* progresses in this way, you will experience my all-pervasiveness. Then you will become one with me and enjoy the state of complete Oneness.

170. "You will concentrate on the Universal Consciousness and will become pure of heart. You will bathe thus in the holy Ganges, without being touched by her waters.

171. "Conceit about the natural *karmas* brings a firm bondage. Hence the wise are forever, alert in their minds, not to let it cling to them.

172. "He who is firmly fixed in the Self and will not swerve, even an atom, such a one has no need, either for going into *samadhi* or revival from it."

173. Therefore, O listeners! I bow my head at your feet and lovingly entreat you to have devotion and love for all — Gods, saints and the devotees.

174. So often had Baba said that if anyone speaks cuttingly to another, it is me whom he hurts and pierces to the heart.

175. When a person rails and rattles at another using bad language, it makes me ill, at once. But he who bears it patiently, gives me satisfaction for a long time.

176. Thus Sai fills all living creatures — from inside and outside. And but for love, he is fond of nothing else.

177. Such was the most beneficial and excellent nectar which always flowed from Sai's mouth. It was as if the deep love for the devotees was thus flowing out. Is there any fortunate one who does not know of this?

178. Those who had the privilege of his company at meals, those with whom he laughed and played, those who were left with a longing for his return — O, what must they all feel!

179. And at the meal for such venerable souls, I claim only the left-overs, which I have gathered together, grain by grain, and am now distributing the pleasure to all.

180.   And, what does Hemadpant really know of the stories narrated
       so far! Sai Samarth is their real narrator and he alone, writes
       them and gets them written.

181.   Such is this Story of Sai Samarth, narrating which I still have no
       satiety. There dwells a constant fond desire for more, in my mind
       and the listeners too, are happy as they listen to them.

182.   Moreover, those who sing the praises of Sai, as also, those who
       listen with good feelings, they both become one with Sai. Bear
       this firmly in mind.

183.   As this chapter is concluded, Hemad lovingly clasps Sai's feet as
       he offers it to him. Further narration will take its own course.

Weal be to all! Here ends the forty-fourth chapter of
"*Shri Sai Samarth Satcharit*", called
'*Niryan of Shri Sainath*' (*Concluded*),
as inspired by the saints and the virtuous
and composed by his devotee, Hemadpant.

Notes

1.   Refer Ch. 3, note 16.
2.   Singing praises of Shankar in a chant to be recited 122 times and 1331 times, respectively.
3.   Performance of certain ceremonies and works in propitiation of a god.
4.   '*Tilanjali*' and '*Tiltarpan*' are a part of funeral rites carried out for the dead person for
     ten days after death, in which sesamum seeds, put in water, are offered, accompanied
     by recitation of mantras. '*Pindapradan*' means offering of the *Pinda* (a ball of rice) to
     the manes of ancestors.
5.   '*Sapindi*' is the offering a ball of rice, etc., to the manes of a deceased relative, on the
     twelfth day after his decease. '*Uttarkriya*' are the funeral rites performed every month,
     for one year.
6.   The several acts and points appertaining to oblation by fire.

45

Greatness of the Guru's feet

MY OBEISANCE TO SHRI GANESH, TO SHRI SARASWATI, AND SHRI GURUMAHARAJ! TO THE FAMILY DEITY, TO SHRI SITA-RAMACHANDRA, MY MOST HUMBLE OBEISANCE! I BOW IN REVERENCE TO THE MOST VENERABLE GURU SHRI SAINATH!

1. He who prompted the writing of his own Lifestory, as he, quite casually, set up the quern to grind corn, thereby guiding his devotees on the path of righteousness, O how remarkable is his skill!

2. The guru is even more powerful than *Moksha*, which is the greatest of the four ultimate goals of human life and when the holy water (*teerth*) of the feet of such a guru is taken, *Moksha* comes home, quite imperceptibly.

3. Only when the guru bestows favour will the worldly life be happy. Things will happen which would never have happened, normally, and in half a second, he will take you to the Shore Beyond.

4. Though so much of this *pothi* has been narrated, yet the story has only been told in a condensed form. Oh, how much of Sai's unfathomable glory can I narrate!

5. That divine figure of Sai is lost, whose *darshan* always brought great satisfaction, whose company meant the enjoyment of greatest happiness as he liberated us from the fear of worldly life.

6. Gone is that radiant form of Sai, that induced us to follow the spiritual path, who turned us back from *Maya* and delusions and brought us our greatest welfare and security.

7. Lost indeed, is that figure of Sai, because of whom there was no fear of worldly life, but an awareness of a spiritual way of life prevailed and we developed a fortitude in the face of trouble.

8. Leaving behind his own figure in our memory to meditate upon, Sai has gone to his Eternal Abode, ending his *avatar* on this earth. Truly, inconceivable is his state of *Yoga*.

9. No sooner was the mission of his incarnation fulfilled, than his mortal coil has disappeared from our sight. Yet his memory will be revived at every step by this book, which is a literary embodiment of Baba.

10. Besides, the concentration that the mind gains on listening to his stories, the peace born thereof, is simply indescribable in words.

11. All you listeners, you are wise; and before you, I am of slight knowledge. But this is a sacrifial offering of speech to Sai. Hence revere it gratefully.

12. This sacrificial offering of words is beneficial and Sai, who knows his mission, is getting it done through me. The all-knowing listeners know this well.

13. After making obeisance at Sai's feet, first, he who listens to these auspicious and purifying tales with a concentrated mind;

14. The devotee, who being most eager to attain his own weal, listens to these nectar-sweet tales with devotion and single-minded concentration;

15. His cherished ends will be accomplished by Sai; his worldly and spiritual ends will be fulfilled. In the end, he will thus get fulfilment. His service will never go waste.

16. At the end of forty-four chapters, when the story of Sai's *niryan* has also been listened to, towards the end, yet the progress of this *pothi* still continues. This is a mystery one fails to understand!

17. In the previous chapter, the account of Sai's *niryan* has been completed, in its proper order. Still, Sai's *leela* knows no rest, even for a moment, like the insect '*Kateen*'[1].

18. And if you go to see, this is not really surprising. For the *niryan* is only for the body, while this Sai is beyond birth and death and continues to dwell in the Unmanifest, as before.

19. The body has gone and so has the form; but he still remains in the Unmanifest, just as he was. Everyone knows of his *leelas*, which continue even after his abandoning the body.

20. And as for narrating them, these are also unlimited in number. But to avoid lengthening this book, we will just take from them their essence and present it to the listeners.

21. Blessed is our good fortune that, at the same time that Sai incarnated, we too, had his holy company, easily and repeatedly.

22. But in spite of this, if we did not renounce the worldly life, if we did not nurture a love for God, can there be a greater Fall?

23. To have all the bodily organs filled with Sai-devotion is the true Sai-worship. Or else, the eyes may be gazing at Sai's form, but the speech fails as the mouth will not open;

24. The ears may be listening to *Sai-kirtan*, but the tongue is busy savouring the sweet mango-juice, and the hands may be touching Sai's sacred feet but they may be finding the touch of the soft mattress just irresistible!

25. Can he become a true Sai devotee, who can bear to be away from Sai, even for a moment? Can he be considered as attached to Sai's feet, who is not detached from the worldly life?

26. A woman will bow respectfully to anyone else, coming her way, other than her husband, looking upon him as her father-in-law or brother-in-law or a brother.

27. Such is the unswerving mind of a chaste, dutiful wife, who never abandons her home, but has boundless love for her husband, who is her one refuge in her lifetime.

28. Such a chaste, virtuous, saintly wife never imagines anyone else as her husband or thinks of taking his *darshan*.

29. To her, her own husnband is the one and only one with whom no one else can ever be compared. For him alone, is her steadfast love. And so also, is the love a disciple feels for his guru.

30. A disciple's love for his guru is compared to the steadfast love of a chaste wife for her husband. But the disciple's love towards the guru has no limit. Only the true disciple knows its greatness.

31. And then, those who are of no help even in the worldly life, of what help can they be in the spiritual life? Be it the father-in-law of a son or a daughter, or a son-in-law, or even one's own wife, you can be sure of none.

32. Mother, father, will shower love and affection; one's own son will have an eye on the wealth; the wife will shed tears for the husband's long life. But there is no companion in spiritual life.

33. If one concludes on careful thought, as to who then remains who can help attain spiritual progress, the answer that remains in the end is you, yourself!

34. Blessed is he, who, discriminating between the transient and the eternal, gives up the desire for the fruit, in this world and the next and, practising the six basic disciplines of *Shama, dama*, etc., finally attains *Moksha*.

35. Giving up dependence on another, he who keeps a firm confidence in himself and girds himself for the effort, he alone, will attain *Moksha*.

36. Brahman is Eternal, the world is transient. Guru is the only true Brahman. Abandon the transient, for guru alone is worthy of being meditated upon. Such a constant feeling is the only means of spiritual progress.

37. By abandoning the transient, detachment is generated. The universal consciousness of the Brahman fills the Sadguru and the presence of God is felt in all the living creatures. This is called the worship of Non-duality.

38. Know that whether out of fear or love, whoever meditates constantly upon whatever object, that meditator will become one with that object — as happened in the cases of '*Kamsa*'[2], Ravan and the insect (who became Krishna, Ram and the black bee, respectively).

39. There should be single-mindedness in the meditation. Then there is no other means like meditation. He who does this *sadhana*, on his own, will uplift himself at once.

40. Then how can there be birth-death here? The consciousness of the body is completely forgotten, the awareness of the worldly life disappears and only the bliss of Self-absorption is experienced.

41. Hence go on repeating the name of your guru. From it is born the highest bliss and God is seen in all the living beings. What can be the great significance of *Naam* other than this?

42. My sincere obeisance to him whose name has such greatness and power. I surrender to him single-mindedly with my heart, speech and action.

43. I shall now narrate to the listeners a relevant story in this context. So, for your own benefit, listen to it with concentration.

44. Everyone knows that the late Kaka Dikshit used to read *Eknathi Bhagvat* (a Commentary on the eleventh Canto of the *Bhagvat*) every day, by the command of Sai Samarth.

45. One day, after the meal was over, Dikshit read the *pothi*. as was his daily pratice, at Kaka Mahajani's residence at Chowpatty in Bombay.

46. As the listeners heard that most remarkable and interesting second chapter of the *Eknathi Bhagvat*, their hearts were filled with peace and happiness.

47. Kaka Mahajani, along with Baba's devotee Madhavrao, sat listening with great concentration.

48. Fortunately, the story too, turned out to be fine and very sweet, so as to satisfy the fond desire of the listeners and create in them a love for God-worship.

49. And the sweet tale, which has come up for narration, is also the pleasing and instructive one of the nine illustrious brothers - Hari, Antariksha, etc.[3] — who have enhanced the glory of the Rishabh family.

50. All the nine of them were manifestations of God, who had in them, boundless peace and forgiveness. Listening to the power

and glory of *Bhagvat-dharma*, King Janak became silent with wonderment.

51. What is one's greatest weal? What is the highest devotion to God? How can Hari's *Maya* be crossed over easily? It is the guru's feet, which are most beneficial.

52. The essence of action, inaction and wrong action is only one — that the guru is a manifestation of God and the worship of the guru is *Bhagvat-dharma*.

53. Drumilnath has narrated the Life of Shri Vishnu, describing the special qualities of each of his incarnations. He has also narrated how to recognize the '*Purushavatar*', describing the incarnation as Narayan.

54. Later, Chamasnath described for Janak, the plight of those who do not worship, showing how destruction follows those who fail to perform the *karmas* prescribed by the *Vedas*.

55. God dwells in the hearts of all. Hence one should not hate anyone, but should see God in everybody. For not an inch of space is without Him.

56. In the end, Karabhajan, the ninth brother, concluded by saying which idols should be worshipped and meditated upon in each *yuga*, like *Krita, Treta*, etc.

57. In the *Kaliyug*, the only means is to remember Hari and guru. That alone, will destroy the fear of worldly life. The feet of Hari and guru are the only refuge to protect the supplicants seeking protection.

58. When the *pothi* had proceeded so far, Kakasaheb exclaimed, 'How wonderful are the doings of these *Navanath* (the nine brothers)! Their attitude of mind is really inconceivable!'

59. He then said fondly, to Madhavrao, 'Really, how very difficult is such devotion! Fools that we are, Oh, how shall we ever have such power? This will not come about during all our several births!

60. 'O, where these most powerful *Naths* and where we, the born sinners! Is such devotion at all easy? Blessed are they indeed, who are Truth and Knowledge incarnate!

61. 'Will such devotion ever be ours? And by what means can it be achieved? I, for one, am in total despair. I have no hope! In vain has been this birth!'

62. Kakasaheb was a loving devotee. Why should he have such regrets? Why should the steadfastness of his mind thus give way to restlessness and doubt? Shama's mind was agitated and disturbed on hearing this.

63. Shama was the name of Madhavrao, who had a friendly feeling for Kaka. And he did not like Kaka's attitude of mind and his being overpowered by such a feeling of wretchedness and lowliness.

64. He said, 'He who has been fortunate enough to have an adornment like Baba — why should he make such a piteous face? Vain, vain indeed, is his being alive!

65. 'When there is such steadfast devotion and faith at Baba's feet, why then this agitation of the mind? And even if the devotion of the Nath brothers is powerful, is not ours too, a loving devotion?

66. 'It had been his most categorical command to you to read every day the eleventh canto of *Bhagvat* with commentary by Eknath, and the *Bhavarth Ramayan*, as well.

67. 'So also, was it Baba's teaching to chant the name of Hari and guru, which will take you safely across the ocean of worldly life. Then what is the reason for you to worry?'

68. Still, it was Kaka's constant worry as to whether it will ever be possible for him to follow, even in the slightest degree, the conduct of those nine *yogis* and to practise their observances and vows, which were as hard as walking on the sword's edge.

69. It became a great earnest longing in his heart that only the devotion of the nine *yogis* was the highest and the best and by what means will that be revealed to him. Only then will God be truly near.

70. And so, such was the uneasy hankering in his mind. Sitting, sleeping, the same thought occupied him. The next day, a miracle took place. Listen to it in detail, O listeners!

71. Just see the marvel of that experience. Early in the morning, Anandrao, whose surname was 'Pakhade', came to look for Madhavrao.

72. And that too, he came in the morning, at the time when Dikshit read *Bhagvat*. Anandrao sat near Madhavrao, narrating to him the novelty of his dream.

73. Here, on the one hand, the reading of the *pothi* was in progress, while there, they both kept whispering to each other. As a result, the concentration of both, the reader and his listeners was disturbed.

74. Anandrao was, by nature, fickle-minded. He began narrating his dream to Madhavrao. Talking, listening in this way, they both continued whispering and the *pothi* remained aside for a moment.

75. So Kakasaheb then, asked them, 'What is such a wonderful thing that has happened? But only you two are in such a happy mood. Do let us know also what it is!'

76. Then Madhavrao said, 'Only yesterday you had a doubt! And here is its solution, in an instant! Just see the characteristic of that devotion which takes you safely beyond this worldly life.

77. 'Listen to Pakhade's dream and how Baba gave him *darshan*. Your doubts will be resolved and you will also know that the devotion with which you worship the guru's feet, is enough.'

78. Now, everyone was most curious to listen to that dream. Especially so was Kakasaheb. And initially, it was his doubt, too.

79. Seeing everybody's eagerness, Anandrao narrated his dream. The listeners, who were well-disposed and had faith, were also astonished.

80. 'In an ocean, I stood in waist-deep water. Suddenly, Sainath came there before my eyes.

81. 'On a bejewelled throne sat Sai, whose feet were under the water. Such was the figure I saw.

82. 'Looking upon that radiant form, contentment flooded my heart. Who remembered then, that it was but a dream? The heart was overjoyed with that *darshan*.

83. 'And what a coincidence, that there itself, stood Madhavrao, who said to me, with some feeling, 'Bow at his feet, Anandrao!'

84. 'So I replied to him, 'Oh, I too, have a keen desire to do so. But his feet are under the water. How will they come into my hands?

85. 'When the feet are in the water, how can I place my head on the feet? What should I do now? O, I really do not understand anything!'

86. 'On hearing this, listen to what Madhavrao said to Baba. 'O God, do take your feet out, which are under the water.'

87. 'And the moment he said this, Baba took his feet out of the water. At once, I caught them and made obeisance.

88. 'When I thus held fast to his feet, Baba pronounced a blessing, "All will go well with you. There is no reason for you to fear".

89. 'Baba said further, "Give a *dhoti* with a silk border to my Shamya. And you will enjoy peace and happiness".

90. 'Hence obeying his order with reverence, I have brought a silk-bordered *dhoti*, which, Kakasaheb, please make Madhavrao accept at your own hands.

91. 'Do please agree to my request and make Madhavrao wear it, which will make me happy and I will be extremely grateful to you.'

92. Madhavrao had himself heard this request of Anandrao. But when Kakasaheb began giving it to him, he would not accept the *dhoti*.

93. He thought in his mind that, 'This is merely a dream. I must get a sign to convince me. Unless I have a Vision, I should not accept it.'

94. Kakasaheb then said, 'Now, let us experience for ourselves. the truth of Baba's words. Whether it would be proper to accept it or not, will be indicated through chits.

95. 'Whichever chit Baba gives us, will be regarded by us as his command.' So they cast the chits at his feet, resolving to follow Baba's command.

96. Kakasaheb's reliance was wholly on Baba, that he should first be consulted and then to proceed further in any matter.

97. And this was so, even during Baba's lifetime. After his *niryan*, his permission would similarly be obtained first, but by putting chits and Dikshit would act accordingly, with a firm determination.

98. Be the work big or small, without taking permission through chits, he would do nothing, even at peril to his life. Baba's permission was always the ultimate authority.

99. When even the body which is offered at Sai's feet is no longer one's own, then what right has that man over its movements?

100. Just consider how he spurned an earning of lakhs of rupees on this faith! And he remained firm in his resolve to the very end of his life.

101. "Your faith and loyalty will bear fruit. I will send you an aeroplane and take you away on it. Have not a care in your mind!"

102. Baba's words of benediction came true to the letter. The readers of '*Sai Leela*' magazine already know the unique manner in which Kakasaheb passed away.

103. When those conditions are called to the mind, Oh, how can going away in an aeroplane be any different? What a happy death it was amid ceaseless chanting of the *guru-naam*!

104. So, Dikshit was thus of a resolute mind and his heart was always engrossed at Sai's feet. Giving the same advice to friends and acquaintences, he, at last, merged at the guru's feet.

105. Now, to proceed with the tale, both of them accepted this stratagem of chits, for they were both fond of Kaka. Then, without further delay, the chits were written out.

106. In one chit, it was written, 'The *dhoti* should be accepted', and in the other, that, 'It should be refused'. Then they were cast at his feet below his portrait.

107. When a child, who was there, was asked to pick up one of these, the command came for Madhavrao to accept it.

108. As was the dream, so too, was the chit. Everybody was delighted. Then the silk-bordered *dhoti* was put in Shama's hands.

109. When Anandrao's dream and Madhavrao's chit concurred mutually, the joy could hardly be contained! It brought happiness and satisfaction to both.

110. Madhavrao was pleased at heart; Anandrao was happy, too. Sai-devotion was enhanced and Kaka's doubts were also resolved.

111. However, the essence of this whole story is that each one should think for himself that once you bow at the guru's feet, the words that come from the guru's mouth should be carefully attended to.

112. Our condition, our role, our thoughts and attitude, only the guru knows, totally, and better than ourselves. So also, does he know the way to our upliftment.

113. As is the malady, so is the diagnosis; and so also, is the medicine or the antidote that the Sadguru administers to the disciple, for curing the disease, that is the worldly life.

114. The way in which the guru conducts himself, should not be imitated. But follow respectfully, what comes from the guru's mouth.

115. Concentrate the mind only on those words and contemplate on them alone, all the time. For that itself will be the cause of your upliftment. Always remember this.

116. Whatever the guru tells you is the *Pothi-puran*; it is also, its own clarification. But our attention must be on the main instruction. For, to us, that is the *Vedas*.

117. Never show disrespect to the words of any saint. But, who else will look after us as our own mother?

118. Her tender affection and love for the child is genuine. But the child does not know her pleasure in what she does for him. Whatever his fond desire, she always indulges him.

119. There are innumerable saints in the world. But the moving, earnest words from Sai's mouth that, "Our father (i.e. guru) is, ultimately, our father (guru)", should be engraved on our hearts.

120. Hence keep your attention fixed on the words from Sai's mouth. For he, who is the store-house of compassion, he alone, will remove the threefold afflictions.

121. Only he knows his own ways! We should just watch with fond admiration how wonderful are his *leelas* and how effortlessly they come about.

122. Whatever another man may say, we should just listen to it all. But our aim should not be lost sight of, and the words of our own guru should never be forgotten.

123. It is here and here alone, that our highest good lies. In this itself, is our overcoming the fear of worldly life. All our *Pothi-Puran*, our *japa*, penance, religious observances — all are in this and this alone.

124. In short, love your guru; with single-minded devotion, make obeisance to him. How can there be darkness before the sun? Similarly, the ocean of worldly life does not exist for such a one.

125. Be anywhere in this world — near or afar, even beyond the seven seas. But the guru's love for his devotees has no bounds.

126. And so, as I write all this, another tale comes to my mind, as to how he brings trouble upon himself, who does something, on seeing somebody else do it.

127. Once, when Baba was in the mosque with Mhalsapati, he suddenly remembered his earlier bed of the wooden plank.

128. In breadth, only one and a quarter '*veet*'[4], with pieces of rags tied at both its ends, the plank was suspended from the roof of the mosque, like a swing.

129. One should not sleep in the dark. So Baba used to sleep on the plank, at night, with earthen lamps burning at the head and foot of his bed.

130. A detailed description of this plank has already been given in an earlier chapter (Ch.10). So now, listen to its significance.

131. Once, as Baba was earnestly describing the importance of this plank, listen to the thought that arose in the mind of Kakasaheb Dikshit.

132. And he said to Baba, 'If you are so fond of sleeping on the plank, I shall very lovingly, suspend it from the roof. Then you can comfortably lie down on it.'

133. Baba said to him, "Leaving Mhalsapati below, how can I sleep up, alone? I am all right below, as I am".

134. So Kaka, very lovingly, said further, 'I will suspend another plank. You can sleep on one, and Mhalsapati, on the other.'

135. Just listen to Baba's reply to this. "Can he sleep on the plank, indeed? Only he can sleep on the plank who is an aggregate of virtues.

136. "Sleeping on the plank is not easy. Who can sleep on it, except me? Such sleeping is possible only for him, who can drive away sleep and keep his eyes open.

137. "When I go to sleep, I command him (Mhalsapati) 'Put your hand on my heart and keep sitting near me'.

138. "But even this work he cannot do. He keeps nodding drowsily, where he is sitting. To him, this plank is of no use. This plank is my bed only.

139. "In my heart the chanting of the Name goes on, ceaselessly. See for yourself, by keeping your hand there and if I happen to fall asleep, wake me up." When such is my instruction, to him,

140. "When he himself falls asleep instead, his hand becomes heavy as a stone. On my calling out '*Bhagat*', the sleep disappears from his eyes, causing him confusion and fright.

141. "One who cannot sit steadily on the ground, whose seat is not firm, the man who is a slave of sleep, i.e. *tamas*, how can he sleep on a height?"

142. Thus Baba pointed out, at the appropriate time, and out of affection for the devotees, "Do the duty ordained by your own nature and do not imitate the law of another".

143. The *leelas* of Sainath are inscrutable! Hence, Hemad is absorbed at his feet and Sai too, remembers him, having blessed him with his grace.

Weal be to all! Here ends the forty-fifth chapter of
"*Shri Sai Samarth Satcharit*", called
'*Greatness of the Guru's Feet*',
as inspired by the saints and the virtuous
and composed by his devotee, Hemadpant.

Notes

1. This is an insect of the spider tribe, that makes a hard and bright-shining cocoon and not a web, to catch flies. It has long legs and a little black body.
2. The uncle of Krishna and also the latter's enemy.
3. Refer Ch. 1, note 4.
4. A '*veet*' is the measure of the thumb and the little finger extended. In Ch. 10, v. 15, however, the breadth of the plank is given as only one '*veet*'.

46

Journey to Kashi–Gaya and
The story of the goats' past birth

MY OBEISANCE TO SHRI GANESH, TO SHRI SARASWATI, AND SHRI GURUMAHARAJ! TO THE FAMILY DEITY, TO SHRI SITA-RAMACHANDRA, MY MOST HUMBLE OBEISANCE! I BOW IN REVERENCE TO THE MOST VENERABLE GURU SHRI SAINATH!

1. Blessed are your feet, Shri Sai; blessed, O Sai, is your remembrance, and blessed, blessed is your *darshan*, all of which liberate us from the bondage of *karma!*

2. Though invisible in form, now, yet when faith and devotion are reposed in you, your spirit in the *samadhi* is awakened. And the devotees experience this, even today.

3. Such is the fine string that you hold, that, try as we may, you do not make it visible to us. All the same, you pull your devotees to yourself with it, whether they be in this country or in any other.

4. And as you bring them to your feet, you embrace them, lovingly. As a mother, her own children, so you nurture them, easily and effortlessly.

5. And such is the manner of your pulling the strings, that nobody knows where you are. But the results make us believe that you stand behind your devotees, at all times.

6. The learned pandits, the clever and comely get stuck in the mire of the worldly life, due to their conceit. But with your own power, you sport with the simple and trusting, the ignorant and unknowing.

7. Inwardly, you play all games and strategems, yet pretend to be aloof, detached. After doing everything, you yet call yourself a non-doer. Really, nobody can understand your ways.

8. Therefore, let us offer at your feet our action, speech and mind and have on our lips a ceaseless chant of your name. Only then will our sins be washed away.

9. You satisfy the desires of those who have desires; to the desireless, you give them the Abode of Eternal Bliss. Such is your sweet, pleasurable name, which is the easiest means for the devotees.

10. By repeating it, sins are destroyed; *Rajas* and *Tamas* disappear, without a doubt; and *Sattva* accumulates, gradually, which results in a store of moral and religious merit.

11. When God-devotion and moral consciousness is awakened in this way, renunciation follows speedily; sensual desires are totally annihilated and Self-realization appears, instantaneously.

12. When knowledge is gained through a discriminating intelligence, the whole concentration is on Self-absorption, which, in itself, means abiding humbly at the guru's feet. This is called a complete surrender to the guru.

13. There is only one sign of the mind having totally surrendered at Sai's feet — the seeker's inclination towards peace and then his devotion is totally exulted.

14. A loving devotion to the guru is called '*dharma*'. 'Everything is I', is the essence of knowledge. Distaste for sensual pleasures is the greatest detachment and there follows a cessation of worldly life.

15. Blessed is the greatness of such devotion, which, when practised single-mindedly, brings peace, renunciation and fame, which three are always in its power.

16. How can he be wanting in anything, who has such guru-devotion? Whatever he wishes for in his mind, will all come to him, quite effortlessly.

17. And such devotion has '*Brahma-sthiti*' (the state of Oneness with the Brahman) for a slave, being presented as '*Andan*'[1]. There nobody gives importance to *Moksha* and the holy places of pilgrimage roll at the feet.

18. In the last chapter, the narration was about Dikshit's *Bhagvat*-reading, a description of the devotion of the nine *yogis* and about the *darshan* of Sai's feet.

19. I also narrated the marvel of the dream of Anandrao, whose surname was Pakhade, and the glory of Sai-devotion.

20. He, whom Sai takes under his wing, whether he is at home or on an island, near him is Shri Sai, most certainly, by day and by night.

21. Wherever the devotee goes, and to whichever place, there he goes before him and gives him *darshan*, quite unexpectedly.

22. I shall now narrate to the listeners a novel story, with the same significance, listening to which, they will be quite astonished and glad at heart.

23. To the trusting devotee, who listens here with faith to the words from Sai's mouth, even the joy of *samadhi* will not be equal in comparison with it, as he will swell with Self-rejoicing.

24. This sweet tale in which there is a miracle at every step, will make the listener oblivious of himself and his heart will be overcome with a powerful emotion.

25. It was decided to celebrate the thread ceremony of Babu, the eldest son of Kakasaheb Dikshit, at Nagpur.

26. Similarly, the wedding of Nanasaheb Chandorkar's eldest son was also, to be celebrated, for which it would be necessary to go to the Gwalior city.

27. Nana felt that after the thread ceremony, going to Gwalior for the wedding may cause some delay to Kaka, on its account.

28. To avoid this, he fixed a '*muhurt*' (auspicious day and time) which was mutually convenient, so that Kaka could comfortably come to Gwalior from Nagpur.

29. After that, that exalted devotee Nanasaheb came enthusiastically to Shirdi for Sai's *darshan* and also, to invite him personally to the wedding.

30. Kakasaheb was already there. Nana went to the mosque and with folded hands, extended to Baba an invitation for the wedding.

31. Baba then said, "All right", and added, "Take Shamya with you".
    Two days later, Kaka also asked, inviting Baba for the thread
    ceremony.

32. To him too, Baba said the same, "Take Shamya with you".
    Kakasaheb pressed Baba to be present himself.

33. To that also, the instant reply was, "After visiting Kashi-Prayag
    quickly, I will arrive even before Shama. What can delay my
    coming there!"

34. Now the listener should note these words carefully and understand
    their significance, so as to be able to experience their truth and
    Baba's all-pervasiveness.

35. And so, after the meal was over, Madhavrao thought to himself,
    'Once I go to Gwalior, how far is Kashi from there!'

36. He borrowed a hundred rupees from Nandaram for his expenses
    and went to take Baba's permission. Most respectfully, he asked,

37. 'Now that I am going up to Gwalior for the wedding and thread
    ceremonies, I think it only proper that Kashi-Gaya should also
    be visited, suiting the occasion.

38. 'Hence O God, I bow at your feet and pray, shall I visit Kashi-
    Gaya, also?' Baba then gave Madhavrao permission to go, with
    pleasure.

39. He further said to him, "What is improper in what you ask?
    Whatever comes about easily, effortlessly, should most certainly
    and without a mistake, be availed of".

40. Such was the command. Madhavrao hired a bullock-cart and
    proceeded to Kopergaon, when he met Appa (Kote) on the way.

41. Appa was going to Chandwad to bring back his grand-daughter.
    When he heard about the pilgrimage to Kashi, he just jumped
    out of his *tonga*.

42. Although he had no money for the journey to Kashi, he could
    not give up such company as Madhavrao's.

43. And when Madhavrao reassured him, Appa Kote was only too
    ready. Happily he sat in the bullock-cart, quickly, to avail of such
    an opportunity.

44. Appa Kote Patil was wealthy. But, being in transit, he had no means of getting any money and on that account, he might miss going to Kashi. This was his greatest worry.

45. Why not avail of the opportunity, knocking at the door, and that too, in company like Madhavrao's? Such was the innermost wish in Appa's mind.

46. So, knowing his difficulty and giving him a timely reassurance, Madhavrao took Appa with him, so that he might get the merit of a pilgrimage to Kashi.

47. Then they went to Nagpur for the thread-ceremony, when Kakasaheb gave two hundred rupees to Madhavrao for his expenses.

48. From there they went to Gwalior for the marriage ceremony there. At the time, Nanasaheb gave a hundred rupees to Madhavrao.

49. Shrimant Jathar, the bride's father, also gave him a hundred rupees. In this way, Nana's *guru-bandhu* had quite a collection, given to him very lovingly.

50. On the *Mangalghat* at Kashi, there is a Laxmi-Narayan temple, beautifully carved and with '*Jadav*' work[2], of which this Jathar was the owner.

51. Jathar owned a beautiful temple of Shri Ram in Ayodhya, too. At both these holy places, attentions and courtesies to these guests were entrusted by Jathar to his *munim*.

52. From Gwalior, they went to Mathura. They were accompanied by Ozay, Biniwale and Pendharkar, also. But the three last-mentioned, returned home thereafter.

53. Madhavrao and Kote, however, went to Prayag from there and entered Ayodhya in time for the *Ram-navami* celebrations.

54. They spent twenty-one days there and two months at Kashi. The sun and moon eclipses over, they both set out for Gaya.

55. In Gaya, the epidemic of plague had broken out. In lanes and by-lanes, people stood, anxious and worried. This was the news they both heard while still in the train.

56. The train puffed into the station at night. So they both rested in a nearby '*Dharmashala*'[3], for the night.

57. In the morning, a Gayaval[4] came to meet them, saying, 'Come on, hurry up! The whole crowd of pilgrims has set out to go'.

58. Disturbed and frightened in his mind, Madhavrao asked him, in a low tone, 'We will come, but is there an epidemic in your locality, too?'

59. So he replied to him, 'Oh, do come there and see for yourself. There is no such thing there. Come with me, without a doubt.'

60. So they both then went to the Gayaval's place and were pleased at heart, to see his spacious house.

61. Another reason for their happiness was, that even as they sat down there, on seeing Baba's picture right in front of him, Madhavrao was overcome with powerful emotion.

62. Never had it entered their minds or thought that at a distant place like Gaya, their eyes will alight on Sai's picture. Amazement filled the hearts of both.

63. Madhavrao was overwhelmed with love, as tears of joy welled up in the eyes. So the Gayaval asked, 'Why are you crying?'

64. On seeing Madhavrao cry, without any reason, the Gayaval grew suspicious and anguished.

65. Gayaval was greatly worried, thinking that since there was plague in Gaya, Madhavrao must have been anxious as to how his pilgrimage would be completed, as per plan.

66. 'I have already told you that here there is no plague and yet you worry. I am really surprised!

67. 'If you have no faith in me, then do please ask everyone, here! You need not fear for even a single hair on your head, here. Then why do you shed tears?'

68. 'Having taken a dread of the epidemic of plague and having lost his nerve, this pilgrim weeps unnecessarily, like this, all the time.'

69. So thinking, the Gayaval tried to explain and to pacify. But in Madhavrao's mind, the thought was 'How has my Mother (Sai) come here before me today?'

70. Earlier, Baba's words had been, "Visiting Kashi-Prayag, quickly, I will arrive even before Shama", and here was the direct experience of their truth.

71. On entering the house, when Baba's picture stood before the eyes, this quite unexpected experience caused them great wonder.

72. The throat choked with love; a flood of joyous tears poured from the eyes, and the hair stood upon end as beads of perspiration sprang up all over the body.

73. Such was Madhavrao's condition, while the thought uppermost in Gayaval's mind was quite different and he really thought that Madhavrao was crying because he was afraid of the plague.

74. Being most curious, it was Shama himself, who later asked Gayaval, 'How did you get this (picture)? Tell us everything in detail.'

75. Gayaval then began to narrate the detailed account to Madhavrao about the marvel that had happened twelve years ago. Listen to it.

76. Gayaval had two to three hundred people on his payroll, who used to maintain a detailed register about the pilgrims at Manmad and Puntambe.

77. It was the regular business of the Gayaval to make the necessary arrangements for the pilgrims. While his work was going on thus, Gayaval went to Shirdi.

78. He had heard that Sai Samarth was a great saint. So he wished that he should be blessed by taking his *darshan*.

79. He took Sai's *darshan*, made obeisance at his feet and then he felt a keen desire to obtain Sai's picture.

80. Madhavrao had a picture hanging on the wall, which Gayaval asked for. And with Baba's permission, Madhavrao gave it to him.

81. 'This is that same picture which belonged to me, and this was that same Gayaval', then Madhavrao remembered. 'And how did Baba send me to the same place? And oh, how he has brought about this meeting after such a long time!

82. 'In fact, who and why will anyone remember a thing that happened twelve years ago? It had never come to my mind, at all.'

83. But Baba's ways are inscrutable! He sent Shama to that same place and there itself, he gave him *darshan*. Gayaval too, was greatly pleased.

84. 'It was this same (picture) that I had given after taking Sai Baba's permission, and that, to this same Gayaval', Shama now remembered.

85. 'It was at his place that I had stayed earlier, after coming to Shirdi and it was he, who had arranged for me to have Baba's *darshan*', remembered Gayaval, too.

86. Because of the favour done earlier to each other, their joy knew no bounds. He made excellent arrangements for Shama in Gaya.

87. So great was his wealth, that elephants waited at the Gayaval's door. Himself, he sat in the palanquin and made Shama ride on the elephant.

88. Happily, they went to the '*Vishnupad*', with articles of *pooja* and after performing *pooja* with '*abhishek*'[5] to the god, they also, offered '*pinda-daan*'[6] to the manes.

89. Then the Brahmins were satiated with a meal and *dakshina*, after first making '*naivedya*' to the gods. Thus the pilgrimage was completed satsifactorily, or rather, Baba got it completed by them.

90. The essence of this whole story however, is, words from Baba's mouth always come true; each and every letter is proved by actual experience. His love for the devotees is also, boundless.

91. But this is only, so far as his love for the devotees is concerned. In fact, he looked upon other creatures as equal, too! Not only was he exceedingly fond of them, but was one with them, at heart.

92. Returning to the mosque from the Lendi, while walking casually on the way, if he sometimes met a herd of goats, Baba would feel most happy.

93. He would then cast his nectar-like glance over them all, sometimes selecting a goat or two out of it.

94. Whatever price the owner asked, Baba would pay him at once and keep the animals with Kondaji. Such was Baba's usual practice.

95. One day, Baba bought two goats, paying Rs.32 for them. Everyone was surprised.

96. As he saw the two goats, he suddenly took a liking to them and going near, patted them on their backs.

97. On seeing them born as animals, Sai Samarth felt compassion for them and was moved by their condition. He was overcome by a profusion of love.

98. Drawing them close to himself, Sai lovingly passed his hand over them. The devotees were astonished by Baba's strange behaviour.

99. Sai remembered his great affection for them in their previous birth and was overcome with love. On seeing them born as goats, he was deeply moved by pity.

100. For a goat that cost two or three or four rupees, Baba had actually paid sixteen. Tatyaba was simply amazed to see this strange doing.

101. When they saw with their own eyes this buying of a thing by paying whatever price the trader had asked, Madhavrao, as well as Tatya, indignantly protested against Baba's action.

102. Why did he pay sixteen rupees for a thing worth two rupees? Did Baba have no value for money and hence was doing things just as he pleased? But even this argument was not satisfactory.

103. Both chafed and fumed within. Why did Baba make such a bargain? Is this any way to bargain? Both blamed Baba.

104. How could Baba be so deceived! All the people gathered there to see this. Baba was calm and composed in his mind — as if nothing in the least, was lost!

105. Although the two of them were thus angry and began blaming Baba, Baba himself was not in the least perturbed. He remained perfectly at peace and was quite happy.

106. Humbly, they both asked Baba, 'What is this strange way of your generosity! Are not thirty-two rupees lost?'

107. On hearing this question of mere money, with a smile, Baba said to himself, "Truly crazy are these people! Oh, how will I make them understand?"

108. But Baba's peace and calm was most remarkable! The steadfastness of his mind was not at all disturbed. This is the characteristic of true everlasting Peace. Everyone was most surprised.

109. He who knows no anger, but experiences a lasting peace and sees God in all the creatures, how can indiscretion ever touch him?

110. Those who have the power of discriminating knowledge, will never allow anger to be aroused. And if such an occasion unexpectedly arises, a treasury of Peace will be thrown open.

111. He who meditates ceaselessly, on '*Allah Malik*', how can his greatness be described? His life is incomprehensible and profou i, most sacred and highly beneficial.

112. He, of a compassionate mind, who is knowledge personified, a store of Renunciation and the Ocean of Peace — listen to what he really said.

113. On seeing the insistence of both, Baba also made up his mind. He said, "I, who have no place even to sit and no home, why should I want possessions?

114. "Go to the shop, first, and buy a *seer* (a measure) of pulse. Feed them to their heart's content. And then, return them to the shepherd."

115. Obeying the command, the goats were fed the pulse, immediately. Then, without losing any time, they were sent back to the herd.

116. Benevolence personified that he was, Sai was truly an *avatar*! What good, kind thoughts Tatya, Shama or anyone else, can inspire in such a one?

117. Feeding them the pulse, most lovingly, and seeing that the goats were fully satisfied, he then said, "Give them back to their owner. May they rest with their herd."

118. In this way, the rupees were gone, and so were the goats! Then Baba narrated the whole amazing story of their past birth.

119. As was Tatya, so was Shama, to Baba. He loved them both equally. To appease their anger, Baba narrated this delightful tale.

120. Sai, on his own, narrated to them both the story of the goats' past birth. Listeners may also listen to it.

121. "In their last birth, the goats were fortunate. Both of them were then human beings and they stayed with me. But they too have to suffer for their *karma*.

122. "These goats that you see, were brothers in the last birth. Quarrelling with each other to the extreme, they died and this has been the result.

123. "In the beginning, great affection subsisted between them. The brothers would eat, sleep, together, regularly and always wished each other well. Thus there was great unity between them.

124. "But though they were real brothers, through an unfortunate concurrence of destiny and merit, a terrible greed for money gave rise to a great enmity between them.

125. "The elder brother was very lazy, while the younger one was industrious and worked hard, day and night. As a result, the latter collected heaps of money, of which the elder brother became envious.

126. "'Better to remove this thorn in the flesh. Then there will be no dearth of money.' With this thought and overpowered by greed for money, the elder preferred to follow evil ways.

127. "Such greed for wealth obstructs vision. So, although with eyes, he became blind and forgot the loving brotherly relationship. He was all set to destroy the younger brother.

128. "Suffering brought on by one's *'prarabdha'* is very hard, indeed. It gave rise to needless enmity. The treacherous secret scheming and plotting came to light and the fit of avarice was uncontrollable.

129. "Their life-span was really over. So that they forgot the brotherly affection, completely, and were roused to anger by their ego. They fought each other as sworn enemies.

130. "Hitting hard on the head with a baton, one felled the other to the ground, while the other suddenly struck down the first one with an axe, thus killing his own brother.

131. "Both fell down unconscious, shattered and covered with blood. In a short while, life departed from the bodies of both and thus they both died.

132. "When they died in this manner, they entered this genus. Such is their account, which I remembered in detail, when I saw them.

133. "To work out their *karma*, they were born as goats and on seeing them suddenly, in the herd, I was overcome with love.

134. "Hence, spending money out of my pocket, I thought I should give them some respite. But, in your form, their *karma* stood in the way.

135. "I felt compassion for the goats, but on your insistence, I too gave in, in the end and returned them to the shepherd."

136. And so, the story ends here. Do forgive me, O listeners. When, later on, you listen to the next chapter, your hearts will be gladdened.

137. And the next chapter too, is filled with love; that too, is the nectar from Sai's mouth. Bowing humbly at Sai's feet, Hemad entreats the listeners.

Weal be to all! Here ends the forty-sixth chapter of
"*Shri Sai Samarth Satcharit*", called
'*Journey to Kashi-Gaya and the Story of the Goats' Past Birth*',
as inspired by the saints and the virtuous
and composed by his devotee, Hemadpant.

Notes

1. '*Andan*' means presents (of land, animals, slaves, etc.) additional to the customary and necessary presents (of money, trinkets, and articles of apparel) made at marriages, by the bride's father to his daughter or to his son-in-law.
2. This means setting, inlaying, infixing gems in gold or silver.
3. A building erected for the accommadation of travellers.
4. A Brahmin subsisting upon the offerings made by pilgrims at Gaya, serving them by uttering for them '*sankalpa*' or a solemn and formal enunciation of purpose as preparatory to important religious rites or works.
5. Dropping, drop by drop, holy water, milk, etc. over an idol, king, officating priest, etc.
6. Refer Ch. 44, note 4.

47

The Tale of Veerabhadrappa
and Chanabasappa

MY OBEISANCE TO SHRI GANESH, TO SHRI SARASWATI, AND SHRI GURUMAHARAJ! TO THE FAMILY DEITY, TO SHRI SITA-RAMACHANDRA, MY MOST HUMBLE OBEISANCE! I BOW IN REVERENCE TO THE MOST VENERABLE GURU SHRI SAINATH!

1. His face, looking upon which, even for a moment, the pain and sorrow of innumerable births is destroyed and which is the source of highest Bliss, blessed, blessed is that holy countenance of Shri Sai!

2. Sai's grace liberates one from the bondage of *karma*, instantly, and his devotees enjoy the blissful joy, without a moment's delay.

3. He, before whose glance of grace the knots of *karma* and non-*karma* open up; in the light of the sun of his grace, the fire-fly of worldly life fades away and is completely lost.

4. *Bhagirathi* (Ganges) washes away the sins of the world, which makes her muddy. To cleanse the dirt so collected, she longs for the dust of the *sadhus*' feet.

5. 'O, when will the *sadhus*' feet touch my banks? When will they come to bathe in my waters?' For, she knows for certain that without this, her sins will never be cleansed.

6. O, faithful, righteous listeners, listen with respect to this most purifying tale, knowing full well that these words are of Sai Samarth, the gem in the crown among such *sadhus*.

7. The wonderful significance of this story is this: be the listeners knowledgeable or ignorant, when listening to this, the bondage of their *karma* will be snapped. Such is this sacred tale!

8. Sai, who is the vision of all the eyes, the audition of all the ears, he has himself entered my heart and narrated this story.

9. Sai is a great saint, himself. As the listeners listen to the marvel of this story, they will forget their bodily consciousness and their hearts will be overcome with the '*ashtabhava*'[1] of love.

10. This is a tale, straight from Sai's mouth. When its essence is carefully grasped, with an eye on its moral lesson, the listeners will get satisfaction.

11. Hence, O listeners, listen to my prayer. I am, no doubt, the narrator of this tale. But if I do not concentrate on its essence, I will remain as empty as you are.

12. As one recalls his love for the devotees, the mind forgets its tendency to worry, and those wearied by worldly life enjoy peace of mind. What higher gain than this can there be?

13. Now listen, O listeners, attentively to its connection with the previous story. You will feel satisfied when you listen to the story without any impediments.

14. At the end of the last chapter, the listeners heard the story of the goats, Baba's love for them and his recollection of their past life.

15. Similarly, listen attentively to this story, which is also about how the excessive greed for money can lead to a man's fall.

16. It is Sai himself, who very kindly suggests these stories, one after the other, and thus prevents any break in the listeners' listening, thereby adding to their pleasure and satisfaction.

17. When the story, the narrator and the narration, all these are Sai Samarth himself, then who and what for is this Hemad, except as just a nickname?

18. Sitting as we are, on the shores of this ocean of Sai's tales, why should we make any laborious effort for the stories? At the foot of the *Kalpataru*, no sooner does a wish arise, than it is fulfilled.

19. Does one worry about a lamp in the house of the sun? He who drinks, for ever, of the nectar, why should he fancy the poison?

20. When we have a Protector like Sai, all the time, what dearth can there be of nectar-sweet tales? Happily savour them to your heart's content.

21. Thr law of *karma* is difficult to understand and cannot be comprehended by anyone. Even the *Jnanis* are deceived, while the simple, ignorant ones are saved.

22. Similarly, the Divine Law is hard to violate. Who can transgress it? Hence, always do your duty according to convention, performing the necessary *karma*.

23. Or else, one's conduct will not conform to the Moral Law and after death, the next birth will be according to his *karma*.

24. As one's *karma*, one's knowledge, accordingly, he mingles with the male sperm and entering the female womb, takes birth in the movable genre, while another is born in the immovable one.

25. Who does not know the meaning of the *Shruti*, 'As one's thoughts, so is his next birth'? And if one must be born again, it should be a birth one likes.

26. Foolish, ignorant people, who are eager to enter into another body, should know that as their merit or otherwise, so will be the body they will get.

27. Hence, he who does not waste the precious opportunity to gain knowledge of the Self in the human birth, before the body falls, he is truly a wise man.

28. He alone, will be free from the bondage of worldly life. All others are caught on the wheel of worldly life and can never avoid entering another body, thus never missing the pain and suffering of another birth.

29. Now the marvel of this story is that the memory of the evil thought that 'I am the body' will be wiped out, and the *Sattvic ashtabhav* will be roused.

30. One who is a miser by nature, despite his unlimited wealth, shame, shame be on such a life! He will experience only weariness till his death.

31. Moreover, even a trace of enmity is not good. Restrain your mind from it, or else it will destroy your life.

32. The result of mutual enmity is that though born in a good genus now, one gets birth in a lower genus. The result of debt, enmity and murder is such that until you suffer for the sins fully, the cycle of birth-death pursues you.

33. I shall respectfully present to the listeners the nectar-sweet and most purifying words from Sai's mouth, with this significance. Be attentive while listening to it.

34. And that story too has remained in my memory, just as I had heard it. In the same words that Mother Sai uttered, I shall now narrate it.

35. Sai is himself the author of his story and gets the account of the Story written, while Hemad is only an instrument. It is he himself, who is the puller of the strings.

36. "One day, in the morning, at about eight o'clock, after finishing my usual repast, I went out for a walk.

37. As I walked on the way, I felt tired. So when I reached the bank of a river, I washed my feet and took a bath, which gave me great satisfaction.

38. And the river too, was as large as the one at Rahata, with the water flooding both its banks, which were overgrown with a rush-like grass called '*lavala*'.

39. There was a rough footpath there, as also a clearly marked track made by bullock-carts. Trees grew dense on the banks, which extended excellent cool shade.

40. A soft breeze blew, pleasant and refreshing. Seeing that cluster of numerous trees, I sat down leisurely, in their shade.

41. In order to fill the clay-pipe, as I went to wet the piece of rag to wrap around the pipe, I heard a croaking sound which, I thought, was that of a frog.

42. And what was so surprising in that? For where there is water, a frog will naturally be there! After wetting the piece of rag, I came back and took the flint in hand.

43. As the flint gave out a spark, the clay-pipe was lighted, ready for smoking. Suddenly, there appeared a wayfarer who came and, making obeisance, sat near me.

44. With great humility, he took the pipe from my hand into his own and said respectfully, 'You have come very far!

45. 'The mosque is quite far away from here, and it will be very hot by the time you go back there. My house is just yonder. Let us go there, after smoking the pipe.

46. 'You can eat a piece of *bhakri*, there itself, and rest for a while. Then when the sun goes down, you may comfortably go back.

47. 'I shall also accompany you'. After saying so, the wayfarer lighted the pipe and very respectfully, gave it to me to smoke.

48. There, the frog began crying aloud, piteously. So the wayfarer enqired, 'Who is this crying aloud?'

49. So I said, 'A frog is in trouble, near the riverbank. His *karma* is pursuing him. Listen to the story that I shall narrate to you.'

50. Whatever you have done in the past birth, you have to pay for it in this birth. And one should be prepared to suffer for one's *karma*. Why cry now?

51. On hearing this, the wayfarer gave the pipe in my hand and walked away from there, saying, 'I will go and see,

52. 'Whether it is really a frog or some other creature. Let the mind be clear of doubt as to what trouble he is in'.

53. Such being his wish, I said, 'Go and see for yourself how the frog, fallen in the jaws of a big snake, is crying out.

54. 'Both, in fact, are wicked; the deeds of both were satanic and terribly sinful, in the past birth, to pay for which they have got these different bodies.'

55. While such thoughts were passing through the mind, the wayfarer went to that place and came back after seeing what was happening. He said, 'What you say is true.

56. 'That snake has a monstrous jaw, like Death itself. And the frog too, is frightening. But for the snake, the frog has become his food.

57. 'He is as a sacrificial offering in the snake's mouth and will last only for half an hour or one! How strange are the ways of Destiny! He will be laid to rest, in just a moment!'

58. So I then said to him, 'Oh, how can he put that frog to rest! Am I, his Father (Protector) not sitting here? What am I needed for?

59. 'Now that I have come, leaving my own place and am sitting here — will I allow that frog to be swallowed? Just watch how I release him!

60. 'Now, when I have separated them, we will go to our respective houses. Go, go, fill up the pipe once again. Let us see what the snake does next!'

61. The traveller at once filled the pipe and, lighting it himself, puffed at it once and then presented it to me. I then took it in my hand to smoke.

62. I puffed at it once, twice, and then taking with me that wayfarer, made my way through the grass, till I reached that particular spot.

63. On seeing that snake again, the wayfarer was terrified. 'Oh, what a monstrous creature', he said and, out of fear, tried to restrain me from going forward.

64. 'Oh, please do not advance', he said, 'That snake will move towards us and the place is too narrow and awkward for us, even to escape. Please do not go forward!'

65. When he saw the whole scene, the wayfarer feared for his very life. Listen to the account of the mutual enmity of both that I then narrated.

66. 'O Veerabhadrappa, has not this Basappa, your enemy, yet repented, even after being born a frog?

67. 'And you too, are born a snake. Yet such mortal enmity? O, have some shame, at least, now! Give up the enmity and be at peace!'

68. No sooner were these words out of my mouth than the snake let go of the frog and glided away so fast that, quickly entering the deep waters, he disappeared from sight.

69. Swiftly, the frog leapt off from the jaws of death and quickly hid in the vegetation. The wayfarer was filled with amazement.

70. He said, 'I do not understand this, at all! O, what with the words coming from your mouth and how the snake let go of the frog, instantly! And how the snake himself disappeared, too!

71. 'But of these, who is Veerabhadrappa? And, similarly, who is Basappa?' He also asked me for the reason for their enmity, saying, 'O, please tell me all!'

72. 'All right. But first, we will go and sit under the tree and smoke the pipe. Then I shall satisfy your curiosity. Afterwards, I shall return to my place.'

73. We both came to the tree where there was deep shade. A gentle, cool breeze was blowing. Once more, the pipe was lighted.

74. The wayfarer smoked it first, after which he gave it in my hand and while I smoked it, I narrated the fascinating story to him.

75. Just about four or six miles from my place, there was an old, famous holy place.

76. There, there was an ancient, dilapidated temple of Mahadev (Shiva), which all the people there thought of renovating.

77. They collected a big subscription for it. A large amount was collected. Arrangements were made for the daily *pooja*, etc., and a complete outline was drawn up.

78. A wealthy man from that place was appointed the administrator. The amount was handed over to him, with the complete decision-making powers.

79. He was to keep separate accounts and add to the funds his subscription amount in cash. This work he was expected to do honestly and without error.

80. But, by nature, he was a miser and would carry on the work in a manner, without a dent to his own pocket. As a result, the work was not getting completed.

81. The whole amount got spent, but the work remained half-finished. He just would not spend anything from his own pocket. Not a pice would he part with.

82. Though a big money-lender, he was avarice personified. He would talk sweetly, all the time, yet the work would not take shape.

83. Later on, those people who had collected subscriptions gathered at his house, saying, 'Of what use is this, your money-lending business?

84. 'Unless you help, we don't know how the renovation of this Mahadev temple will be completed. O, just consider this a little!

85. 'Once again, we will persuade the people and collect subscriptions. And that amount too, we will pass on to you. But do please get this work completed!'

86. Thus more money was collected and it came to hand in an excellent manner. But it was of no avail. The wealthy man did nothing further.

87. However, after a few days God Himself felt like doing something, and it was at that time that the wife of the miser had a Vision.

88. "You, at least, wake up and go build a dome to the temple. Neelakanth (Shankar) will give you a hundredfold of what you spend."

89. Next day, she narrated her Vision, in detail, to her husband. But he, to whom spending even a pice was like death, found this Vision most disturbing.

90. He, whose mind knew no other preoccupation except collecting money, day and night, how will he ever accept the message of the dream, to spend the money?

91. He told his wife, 'I do not believe in this Vision. I have absolutely no faith in it'. And he began ridiculing her.

92. As is the inclination of the mind, so appears the condition of the world. If himself a rogue by nature, others also appear to be the same.

93. 'Had God wanted to take money only from me, was I so very far away from you? Why did he appear in your dream only, and not mine?

94. 'Why only you had the Vision? Why did not God appear to me? Therefore I am not convinced. Nor do I understand the significance.

95. 'Either the dream is false, or it may be a Divine effort to cause a rift between husband and wife. This is the sign I read.

96. 'In the work of renovation, is my help any the less? Month after month, the purse we filled is being emptied.

97. 'Outwardly, people appear to bring such a large amount. But in truth, this commercial system of accounts is a great loss to me.

98. 'Yet, how will you understand what even the people fail to see? So this Vision of yours simply cannot be regarded as true.

99. 'If it is taken as true, we will be completely deceived. Can anyone regard as true the Vision that is the result of a disturbed sleep?' Such was the conclusion that the wealthy miser arrived at.

100. On hearing this, the wife fell silent. She was at a loss for an answer before the husband. Though people were collecting money, it was rarely given happily and willingly.

101. God does not like what is given without love, but out of being urged to give on the ground of respect for Him or out of embarrassment. But when it is given lovingly, however little it may be it is very precious to Him.

102. When the money was collected, the work would proceed; when it stopped coming, the work would stop, too! Thus it went on being delayed.

103. When the wealthy man like a miser refused to spend even a single paise from his purse, listen to how his wife had another Vision.

104. "Do not press your husband to give money to the temple. Your faith and devotion is enough for God. Give whatever you wish to give.

105. "Even one paisa of your own, when given sincerely is like a lakh rupees. Offer it to God, after consulting your husband.

106. "Do not tire yourself out. One should give only what one feels like giving, and which belongs to oneself, however little it may be. Offer it.

107. "Here it is only devotion and faith that matters. And as God knows that you have it, He is repeatedly urging you to give.

108. "Hence, whatever little money you have, give it and let your mind be at peace. Giving without love is most improper and God does not like it in the least.

109. "He who gives without a loving faith, his offering will have no value and will be absolutely fruitless, in the end. He will experience this, without delay."

110. So, on hearing the words of the Vision, she resolved in her mind to sell the ornaments given by her father, to fulfil this demand.

111. She then told her husband of her resolve. He listened to it and was greatly agitated in his mind.

112. How can there be any reason where there is greed? And that too, of giving in charity in the name of God? In his mind he thought, 'Oh, how thoughtless of her! She has really become deluded!

113. 'I think all her ornaments should be valued and their value being fixed at one thousand rupees, a piece of land should be transferred to her name.'

114. So he bought her ornaments himself and in lieu of money, gave his wife a piece of reclaimed land of his ownership, which had been mortgaged to him by somebody.

115. That too, was waste land. Nothing grew on it even during the rainy season. So he said to his wife, 'Offer this to Lord Shankar.

116. 'When you offer this to God, as was your Vision, this piece of land worth a thousand rupees, He will be pleased and you too, will have discharged your debt.'

117. So, obeying her husband's word, the wife of this miser, lovingly offered the land to please Lord Shankar.

118. In fact, the land belonged to one Dubaki, who had mortgaged it to this money-lender against a debt of two hundred rupees.

119. Dubaki was a poor woman, who owned this land. But even that land she had to mortgage for want of money.

120. But that money-lender was most avaricious and was not afraid of deceiving even God Shankar. He pocketed his wife's 'streedhan'[2] too, and was happy in gain, even though it be through deceit.

121. This hankering after sensual pleasures is very bad and destroys him who longs for them. If one wants to live well, one should never get entangled in the meshes of sensual pleasures.

122. The strong desire to hear the sound destroys the deer; the beautiful gem destroys the cobra whose forehead it adorns, and the attraction of the light burns the moth to death. Such is the destructive nature of sensual pleasures.

123. Moreover, to enjoy such sensual pleasures, wealth is needed and when strenuous effort is made to acquire it, the thirst for more, also grows with it, which becomes uncontrollable.

124. To begin with, the land was reclaimed and even with great effort, could produce not a grain. That was the land he asked her to offer to God. What is the merit in such an offering?

125. What is offered to God without a trace of expectation, such an offering is called free from desire, and not such an offering as this, which will only be sinful and will bring sorrow, in the end.

126. Here, the poor Brahmin, who used to perform the *pooja* of God was very happy, when the land was acquired for God.

127. However, after some time, a strange thing happened. During the '*Krittika nakshatra*'[3], there was a storm accompanied by a downpour, which caused great destruction everywhere.

128. Suddenly, the lightning struck, pulling the whole building to the ground. Only the land without its rightful owner, remained safe. The rest was all burnt down.

129. Ruin came upon the wealthy man too! He, along with his wife, died. And so did Dubaki. The lives of all the three came to an end.

130. Later the wealthy man was born to a poor Brahmin in Mathura, while his devout wife was born to a priest.

131. She was named Gauri. Dubaki had a different fate. She was born as a male child, to a '*gurav*'[4].

132. At the naming ceremony of this boy, he was given the name Chanabasappa. Thus all the three underwent a transformation, the result of the *karma* of each.

133. After his rebirth, the wealthy man was named Veerabhadra. Such is the essence of one's *Prarabdha karma*, that it ends only after it is worked out fully.

134. I was very fond of that priest of Lord Shiva, who used to come to our house every day and smoke the pipe with me.

135. Then we would converse happily, the whole night. Gauri grew up and became of a marriageable age. The priest used to bring her also, with him.

136. And even she used to worship me. One day, the priest asked, 'I have been looking out for a good match for Gauri. But nowhere have I succeeded.

137. 'Baba, I am exhausted searching for a suitable match; all my efforts have failed and I am at my wits' end.' I said, "Why do you worry? The groom is already on his way.

138. "Your daughter is very fortunate and will become very wealthy. It is in search of her that her groom is coming to her, of his own accord.

139. "He will come to your house, shortly, and fulfil your wish. He will accept her hand in marriage as per your words."

140. Here, due to abject poverty, Veerabhadra set out leaving his home, after reassuring his parents.

141. From village to village, he roamed begging for alms, or sometimes earning by manual labour and being content with eating whatever he got.

142. In the course of his wanderings, as luck would have it, he came to the house of this priest. Everyone liked him. Truly inconceivable is *Allahmiyan's leela*.

143. Gradually, he won the priest's affection. So that the priest felt that he should offer Gauri to him in marriage. The horoscopes matched and the priest was very happy.

144. One day the priest came, bringing Veerabhadra with him. Seeing them both together at that time, suddenly an idea struck me.

145. And the idea immediately found expression in words, 'If an auspicious day is available currently for wedding, give Gauri to him and be free of the responsibility.'

146. He took his wife's consent and Veerabhadra was fixed as the groom. An auspicious day was chosen and the marriage was performed, most befittingly.

147. Ceremonies over, the couple came for my *darshan* and blessings for a happy, fruitful married life.

148. Happily, I gave them my benediction. Assured of two square meals, Veerabhadra's face glowed with thoughts of comforts and happiness.

149. And he too, began to worship me. Shortly, they set up their home. But is there a man so fortunate who is not wearied out for want of money?

150. This money is such a snare that even the great and the wealthy cannot escape its harassment. From time to time, Veerabhadra too, began to feel the pinch. Such is the trick that money plays!

151. 'Baba, these fetters of marriage are very hard. And for want of money, I am completely exhausted. Please show me some way out, whereby I will be able to cope with these family responsibilities.

152. 'I fall at your feet in supplication. Such deception is not good. Please remove my difficulties. For you alone, are responsible for the marriage!'

153. I also, used to advise him repeatedly and bless him with affection, saying, "Only *Allah Malik* knows this and He alone, will resolve your difficulty."

154. Knowing the wishes of Veerabhadra's heart and so that they may be fulfilled, I used to reassure him and tell him not to be unhappy, at all.

155. "Your prosperous period is at hand; do not get agitated needlessly. Wealth will be, to you, a facility like washing your hand and you will have it in abundance."

156. 'Wealth scorns me! And my wife's demands for this and that, have no end. Enough, O enough of this ignominy! I do not want this greatness of married status.'

157. But later, a marvellous thing happened! Just see the wonder of Gauri's planetary position, that the piece of reclaimed land shot up in value. Truly God's *leela* is inscrutable.

158. A buyer approached with an offer of one lakh rupees. Half the amount he paid in cash on the spot and the remaining half he agreed to pay in instalments.

159. It was decided that he should pay instalments of two thousand per year, with interest, thus paying the entire remaining amount over the next twenty-five years. In this way, Gauri would collect quite a large amount.

160. Everyone approved of this decision. But the gurav Chanabasappa, stood up, saying, 'The gurav is the first owner of the money that is offered to Shiva.

161. He said, 'Half the yearly interest is for me, as my share, without which I will not be satisfied.'

162. Veerabhadrappa would not part with anything and Chanabasappa would not keep quiet. Both of them engaged in a heated argument and then they both came to me.

163. I told them both that Shankar was the absolute master of that land, which would not be of any use to anyone else, and so not to get entangled in greed.

164. "The price is most certainly, of the land offered to Lord Shankar and anyone, except Gauri, who desires it will starve to death.

165. Whoever touches this money without God's permission will bring upon himself God's wrath. For this wealth belongs, totally, to God."

166. This land, of which the priest was the owner and over which Gauri's claim was by way of inheritance, how could an outsider do anything about it? This wealth was entirely Gauri's own.

167. So I told them both, 'You will have fulfilled your duty only if you act with Gauri's consent, treating it as belonging to her.

168. 'But if you act against her wishes, God will not be pleased. Veerabhadra has no right to act independently, on his own.'

169. Although I voiced my true opinion in this way, Veerabhadra got very angry with me and showered abuses on me.

170. He said, 'Baba, in your mind, the idea must be to establish my wife's ownership and then of swallowing the whole amount yourself, just to gain your own benefit!'

171. On hearing these words from him, I became speechless with amazement. But inconceivable are the ways of *Allahmiyan*! Why should I have any regrets?

172. Veerabhadrappa said this to me; but at home, he stormed and fumed in rage against his wife. So in the afternoon, she came for *darshan* and began entreating me.

173. 'Baba, by listening to the words of anybody else, please do not be displeased with me, I pray earnestly. Have a kind thought for me, your daughter!'

174. On hearing her words, I reassured her fully, saying, 'Oh, I shall, with my grace present you, even the seven seas (i.e. cross the seven seas to protect you). Do not be sad.

175. On that same night, while asleep, Gauribai had a Vision, when Shiva appeared in her dream. And listen to what he said.

176. "All this money is yours. Do not give anything to anyone. And you manage it in the way I tell you, on a permanent basis.

177. "The money for the temple should be expended as Chanabasappa tells you, for I trust him. Make this a rule.

178. "If the money is to be spent on other works, to prevent it being mismanaged, no arrangements should be made without first consulting the Baba in the mosque."

179. Gauribai narrated her Vision to me, in detail. I also, gave her the right adviee to trust in her Vision.

180. 'You take your capital amount and give half the interest to Chanabasappa. Follow this practice, regularly. Veerabhadra is, in no way, concerned in this.'

181. While we were talking thus, both of them came there, quarrelling with each other. I made every attempt to calm them down.

182. I narrated to them, in detail, the Vision of Lord Shankar, which Gauri had. On hearing it Veerabhadra became wild with rage.

183. Veerabhadra freely showered abuses on his opponent and began speaking preposterously, which made the other bewildered and frightened.

184. Veerabhadra grew delirious, as he rattled away, senselessly, saying, 'Wherever I catch you, I will destroy you!'

185. In his wild delirium, Veerabhadra said, referring to Chanabasappa, 'I will cut you up into pieces and then swallow them all up!'

186. The terrified Chanabasappa held tightly on to my feet, saying, 'Please free me from this calamity.' I then promised him protection.

187. At that time, I reassured poor Chanabasappa and said, 'I will not let you die at the hands of Veerabhadra."

188. Later on, Veerabhadrappa who had gone into delirium, died and was reborn as a snake. He was thus transformed with another body.

189. Chanabasappa took a mortal dread, which brought on his end and he was born a frog. Such is his story.

190. Due to the enmity from previous birth, Veerabhadra had the next birth as a snake and so he pursued the frog, Basappa, whom at last, he caught.

191. Poor Basappa, in the form of a frog, fell into the jaws of Bhadrappa, the snake. On hearing his piteous cry, my heart was moved to compassion.

192. Remembering my promise given earlier, I kept my word by liberating Chanabasappa from the snake's mouth.

193. Allah rushes to the rescue in the hour of his devotee's difficulty and He Himself, sent me here, thus protecting his devotee.

194. This has actually, been the experience, here. Veerabhadra was turned away and Chanabasappa was saved from the calamity. All this is God's *leela*.

195. But now, do fill the pipe. After smoking it, I will return to my home. You too, go back to your village. But keep your mind concentrated on my name!

196. After so saying, we both smoked the pipe and I had the happiness of saintly company. Thereafter, rambling along the road, I came back. In my heart, I felt great contentment.

Weal be to all! Here ends the forty-seventh chapter of
"*Shri Sai Samarth Satcharit*", called
'*The Narration of the Story Heard from Shri Sai's Mouth*',
as inspired by the saints and the virtuous
and composed by his devotee, Hemadpant.

Notes

1. Refer Ch. 6, note 3.
2. '*Streedhan*' is property altogether at the disposal of the wife and given to her by her father at the time of marriage.
3. '*Nakshatra*' is a lunar mansion and '*Krittika*' is the third of twenty-seven such '*nakshatras*', which is the same as '*Pleiades*'.
4. A caste, individuals of which are employed in the service of the temple and are worshippers of Shiva.

48

The Bestowal of Grace upon a Doubting Devotee

MY OBEISANCE TO SHRI GANESH, TO SHRI SARASWATI, AND SHRI GURUMAHARAJ! TO THE FAMILY DEITY, TO SHRI SITA-RAMACHANDRA, MY MOST HUMBLE OBEISANCE! I BOW IN REVERENCE TO THE MOST VENERABLE GURU SHRI SAINATH!

1. As this chapter was started, a listener who was listening with great reverence, asked, 'Is Shri Sai a guru or a Sadguru?'
2. To satisfy him, let us briefly state the qualities of a Sadguru, so that we can identify those marks of a Sadguru in Shri Sai Samarth.
3. The knowledgeable do not call him a Sadguru, from whom the *Vedas* are studied or a knowledge of the six *Shastras* is gained or by whom an exposition of *Vedanta* is given.
4. Some hold up their breath in *Pranayam*, wear on their bodies marks made by red-hot metal coins or amuse their listeners by lecturing on *Vedanta*. But the knowledgeable do not call these Sadguru.
5. In conformation with the *Shastras*, they also give the *mantra* to their disciples with proper rites and rituals and command them to do '*japa*'. But no one is really sure as to when this will bear fruit.
6. That discourse on the Brahman, which is highly interesting and rhetorical, but sadly lacking in Self-experience, such knowledge is hollow and literal.
7. When listened to, attentively, it may create a disgust for the worldly and other-worldly enjoyments, but he alone, who has experienced

it himself, can convey the sweetness of the actual experience (of Oneness with the Brahman).

8. Only he has the authority to instruct the disciple, who has a complete knowledge of the *Vedas*, and has also a full experience of giving his disciple the actual experience of it. And only such a one can be called a Sadguru.

9. But he who has no experience himself, what can he give to his disciple? He, without such actual experience, should never be called a Sadguru.

10. He who does not even dream of taking any service from his disciple, but, on the other hand, wishes to wear out his body for the disciple's cause, know that he is a Sadguru.

11. That Sadguru alone, is beneficial, who does not have the conceit that the disciple is insignificant, while the guru is the greatest among the great.

12. The disciple is looked upon as Brahman Itself and is loved as a son, without expecting from him any support for a livelihood, such a Sadguru is the greatest in the world.

13. Know him to be a Sadguru who is an abode of Peace, has no conceit for his learning and knowledge and to whom, small or great, all are equal.

14. Such generally, are the qualities of a Sadguru, in brief, which I, the humble one, have narrated to the listeners, having put them all together.

15. To those fortunate ones, whose eyes are already satiated with Sai's *darshan*, what more can I say about the qualities of the Sadguru?

16. It is only because the merit of innumerable births had accumulated in abundance, that we came to the feet of Sadguru Sai.

17. Even in the very prime of his youth, he had no possessions; he was without any support, without a home and a hearth. All that he possessed was tobacco and a pipe and great self-restraint.

18. Since the age of eighteen years, he had absolute self-conquest. Always, he would sit in solitude, self-absorbed and fearless.

19. When he saw the pure loving devotion of the devotees, to prove to them that it was his Promise that 'he was a slave of his devotees',

he would always be present wherever there was such loving devotion.

20. Hail, O Eternal *Parabrahman*, You who uplift the poor and the meek and have always a pleased countenance; who are filled with the universal consciousness and are entirely in the power of your devotees! Please give *darshan* to the devotees.

21. You, who are beyond the pairs of dualities; are both *sagun* and *nirgun*, omniscient and beyond everything, glory be to you! You are incomprehensible to those who do not worship you.

22. All hail, O *Sadgururaya*, You who remove the pain and sorrow of this worldly life and destroy the elephant that the worldly life is; who love all those who take refuge at your feet and protect them in their difficulties.

23. When you merged with the Unmanifest, your form became formless. But even after leaving the body, your work of uplifting the devotees has not come to an end.

24. All that you did while in the body, still continues, even after merging with the Unmanifest and those who worship you have the same experiences even today.

25. Making me, a lowly creature, your instrument, you have brought out the sun of your Life Story, which is powerful enough to uplift your devotees by dispelling the darkness of their ignorance.

26. The belief in the existence of God, the faith and devotion for Him, is itself the earthen lamp that is the devotee's heart and when the wick burns bright with the oil of love, the flame of knowledge appears.

27. Without love, knowledge is dry. Of what use is it to anyone? Without love, there is no satisfaction. But that love should be undivided.

28. O, how can the power and greatness of love be described? Everything is insignificant before it. And unless one has deep love in the heart, all the listening and reading is fruitless.

29. In love resides true devotion. In it lies all the peace and renunciation, and *mukti*, with all its wealth, stands behind it, too!

30. But love does not arise without faith and know that where there is faith, there is God. From faith is born absolute, profound love. Ultimately, to cross the ocean of worldly life safely, faith alone, is the means.

31. Great is the sweetness of *Sai Satcharit*, which is as pure as the Ganges-water. Sai has himself, adorned its verse; Hemad is but his instrument.

32. Listening to *Sai Satcharit*, listeners and the speaker are both purified, for ever, and sins and merits are all washed away, as they are both liberated, once for all.

33. Extraordinarily fortunate are the ears that listen to this Story; most remarkable is the tongue that narrates it. Blessed, blessed is the *Shri Sai-Stotra*, which is so very sacred to his devotees.

34. Those who listen to this Story with a pure mind and good thoughts will have all their wishes fulfilled and their life will always be fruitful.

35. Those who listen to this *Satcharit* respectfully and with great faith, will automatically develop devotion to the Self, without any delay.

36. When Sai is served with faith and devotion and is remembered all the time, the bodily organs do not get out of control and the ocean of worldly life is quickly and easily crossed.

37. Like water to a Chatak bird, this narration of *Sai Satcharit* is life itself to the devotees. The listeners should contemplate on it after listening, and be blessed by God's grace.

38. If the listeners listen to this, under all conditions, with attention, they will easily cross the ocean of worldly life, as the bonds of their *karma* will be snapped.

39. But now the listeners will say to themselves, 'When is the story going to begin?" So I shall remove their uneasiness by beginning the prelude.

40. In the last chapter, it was narrated that to clear away the sins of enmity, murder and debt, one is reborn to work out one's *karma*.

41. They may not remember their past, but the saints never forget it and ward off the difficulties of their devotees, wherever the devotees may take birth.

42. A similar story will now be related, about how the devotees attain success when they keep full trust in the saints, at every step and in everything.

43. At the commencement of every piece of work, if God is remembered, He will Himself rid the devotees of their worries, provided of course that the devotees themselves are careful in their work.

44. He who makes a firm resolve that 'the *karma* alone is mine, while the fruit is given by *Hari-Guru*, who is all-powerful', the work of such a one will be accomplished successfully.

45. Saints appear to be stern, to begin with. Yet they have an unselfish love. Only, one should have patience and courage in one's heart and they will work for your weal, in the end.

46. When in saintly company, suffering resulting from another's curse or one's own misfortune, and similarly, attachment and affections based in self-interest — they all disappear, instantly. Hence one should bow humbly at their feet.

47. With humility and without conceit, one should surrender to the saints and tell them, with a prayer, one's innermost secret wish. And they will bring to the mind great satisfaction.

48. Those who doubt the words of saints, being misled by their ego, born of scant knowledge, they may first suffer loss but once they keep full trust they benefit in the end.

49. Whether with a pure heart or with deceit, he who follows a true saint will be liberated, in the end. Such is the inconceivable power of the saints!

50. Listen attentively, now, to an instructive story in this context. The listeners will be filled with joy and even the narrator will be enthused in the narration of the tale.

51. Listen to the experiences of a lawyer from Akkalkot, whose name was Sapatnekar it will please your heart.

52. When he was studying hard, day and night, for law, he met another student Shevade, and they began exchanging notes about each other's studies.

53. Some others, studying with them, came there too, and they all sat together in that same room and began asking questions to each other, to test how much they had studied.

54. It was to see who makes a mistake and where, whose answer comes correct, etc., so as to clear any doubts and gain some peace of mind.

55. Shevade's answers came all wrong. In the end, all the students said, 'How will he pass the examination? All his study is incomplete.'

56. Though they derided him thus, Shevade had full faith that 'Whether the study was complete or incomplete, when the time comes I will pass.

57. 'Even if I have not studied, my Sai Baba is there to pass me. Then why should I worry?'

58. On hearing these words, Sapatnekar was surprised and taking Shevade aside, he began asking him,

59. 'Who is this Sai Baba, whose virtues you praise so much? And whom you trust so completely? And where does he live?'

60. In reply, Shevade then described the greatness of Sai Baba and quite frankly told of the state of his absolute faith in him.

61. 'In Shirdi village, in the well-known Nagar district, a fakir lives in a mosque, who is a very famous and virtuous man.

62. 'There are many saints in different places, but unless you have accumulated abundant merit, the good fortune of meeting them will not befall, however hard you try.

63. 'I have complete faith in him. What he says, that alone will come about; only what he utters will take place, and nothing can ever prevent it.

64. 'However great my efforts this year, I am going to fail in the examination. But next year, I will most certainly pass, effortlessly.

65. 'This is his assurance to me and I have full trust in him. His words will never be untrue. This I have firmly resolved.

66. 'It will be no wonder at all, when I pass not only this examination, but even the examination after this.' Sapatnekar had no doubt that these words were vain and ridiculous.

67. His mind was filled with doubts. How then would he believe such an utterance? However, Shevade then went away from there. But listen to what happened thereafter.

68. When some time had passed, Shevade's words came true, as proved by experience. To the great astonishment of Sapatnekar, Shevade passed both the exams.

69. Ten years passed after this. And misfortune befell Sapatnekar, suddenly, causing him great distress and agitation. He became sad, dispirited.

70. His one and only son died of diptheria, in the year 1913. He became absolutely disgusted with worldly life.

71. So he set out on a pilgrimage to all the holy places, like Pandharpur, Gangapur and the like. But peace of mind eluded him. He then began reading *Vedanta*.

72. Some time passed in this way. As he hopefully waited to gain some peace of mind, he suddenly remembered Shevade's account.

73. He recalled Shevade's determination and his faith in Sai Baba. He now felt that he should also go for Baba's *darshan*.

74. He wished for that Saint's *darshan*. In the year 1913, he decided to go to Shirdi and set out to go with his brother.

75. Really, it was Sai himself who had called him to himself, to worship his feet, recollection of Shevade's story being just an excuse. Listen to this, attentively.

76. Taking his younger brother, Panditrao, with him, Sapatnekar set out with his family to go to Shirdi for the saint's *darshan*.

77. They both came there and went for Shree's *darshan* at once. They had *darshan* from a distance, but felt satisfied in their hearts.

78. As their eyes met Baba's from a distance, they quickly approached him and with folded hands, both stood waiting, in front of Baba.

79. Both prostrated before Baba, with great humility, and with a pure, loving heart, offered a coconut at Sai's feet.

80. As Sapatnekar offered the coconut at the feet of Samarth, Baba turned him away, scornfully, with the words, "Get out!"

81. Sapatnekar got worried as to why Baba got so angry, and said to himself, 'I must ask the meaning of this to someone who knows Baba well'.

82. He who should have been delighted with the *darshan* moved backwards, with a start, at these words and sat down, sad and worried with eyes downcast.

83. 'Whom should one approach, now? To which devotee should I ask as to the significance in Baba's words? Whom should I ask what is in Baba's mind?'

84. On learning of this wish of his, someone suggested the name of Bala Shimpi (tailor), for the satisfaction of his query. So he searched for Bala's place.

85. Sapatnekar told him all that had taken place and said, 'Baba turned me away with very harsh words.

86. 'At least, if you come with me, I may get his *darshan* in peace and he may bestow his grace on us, without getting angry.'

87. Bala agreed to this and Sapetnekar was relieved of his anxiety. He got Baba's photo purchased and set out to have Baba's *darshan*.

88. Bala Shimpi accompanied him. Taking the photo in his own hand, Bala gave it to Baba and prayed,

89. 'What is this picture, O God?" Baba looked at it and replied, "This is a photo of his friend", pointing his finger at Sapatnekar.

90. So saying, Baba smiled. Others smiled, too! 'Baba, what is the meaning of this?' Bala asked Baba.

91. At once, Bala said to Sapatnekar, 'Take *darshan*, be quick!' But as he made obeisance, he heard the words, "Get out!"

92. 'Oh, that same old "Get out!" pursues me, still! Now, what other way should I follow?' This was Sapatnekar's great puzzle.

93. And as they both stood waiting before Baba, with folded hands, at last, Baba commanded them, "Go away from here, at once!"

94. 'O Swami Samarth, your command can never ever be disobeyed by anyone. Then what to say of us, the poor lowly creatures? Now, this instant, we go away!

95. 'Having heard that you are most generous, we came to have *darshan*. But we were welcomed only with the words 'Get out!' What this mystery is, we know not.

96. 'But do look upon us kindly and give us your blessings, that we may have your *darshan* soon, again.' Such was the assurance they asked for.

97. Is there such a *Jnani*, who will know what is in Baba's mind? But they obeyed the command and returned to their own place.

98. Such was their first *darshan* of Baba, which made them both very sad. They went back to their village, without the least delay.

99. One more year passed by. And yet, his mind had not steadied. Again, he went to Gangapur. But the agitation in his mind grew.

100. Sapatnekar then went to Madhegaon, for rest. At last, he decided to go to holy Kashi.

101. When only two days remained to leave for Kashi, his wife had a Vision and the journey to Kashi was stayed.

102. I will relate the novel way in which this miracle of the Vision took place. Be attentive as you listen to these *leelas* of Sai.

103. While his wife was asleep on the bed, in her dream she saw herself going to the well of Lakkadsha, with a pitcher.

104. 'There, at the foot of a Neem tree, a fakir, who had a piece of cloth wrapped round his head, came near me', she said.

105. 'In a tender voice the fakir said, "Why do you toil so, needlessly, my child? I will fill up your pitcher fully, with pure, clean water."

106. 'I was frightened of the fakir and taking up the empty pitcher, made my way back homewards, with the fakir following behind me.

107. 'As I saw this dream, I woke up and opened my eyes'. When Sapatnekar heard the dream that his wife narrated, he decided to go to Shirdi.

108. Immediately, they both set out, reaching Shirdi the next day. On arriving, they at once went to the mosque. Baba had gone to the Lendi at that time.

109. So they both sat there, waiting for Baba, till his return. Soon Baba came back.

110. The lady was astonished to find the same figure from head to foot, which she had seen in the Vision and went on observing closely.

111. After Baba's feet were washed, the lady went to take *darshan* and making obeisance at his feet, went on gazing at him, as she sat.

112. Sainath was delighted to see her devout attitude. In a soft, low voice, Baba began a tale about removing her affliction.

113. And, as usual, Baba began to tell, in detail, about his own affliction, very lovingly, to a third person who was present there.

114. In truth, it was the story of the lady, which should have been narrated to her. But when he began relating it to a third person, in her presence, that lady heard it with rapt attention.

115. "My hands, stomach, waist, all have been aching severely for many days. I am tired, trying out medicines. The ailment just does not go.

116. I am really exhausted taking so many medicines, but none has been effective. And I am surprised that now, it has suddenly disappeared."

117. Such was her story, told to a third person, without even mentioning the lady's name. It was all her own story and that was her connection with it.

118. Later on, at the end of a month ot two, when the affliction that Baba had described as his own, was cured, her experience convinced her of its truth.

119. The lady's wish was fulfilled. But then, when Sapatnekar took his *darshan*, Baba treated him, once again, to the earlier "Get out!"

120. 'I do not know what my fault is, that Baba scorns me so unerringly! As I make obeisance, his reply to me is one and one only!

121. 'What is my sin of the past birth that he is angry only with me, while in my presence, he is so very loving towards others?

122. 'If you go to see, morning and evening, all the people always enjoy with Baba, the happiness of a festivity. Why only I am destined to hear "Get out!"?

123. 'Has my *karma* been so wicked, so as to lead me to '*adharma*' and an accumulation of innumerable sins, that Baba is so displeased with me?

124. 'In the beginning, I entertained doubts and misconceptions about Baba and therefore, I feel, Baba is himself, drawing me closer to him in this way.'

125. Therefore, Sapatnekar decided to remain in Shirdi itself, with a mind steadily concentrated on Baba, till Baba bestowed grace on him.

126. Is there anyone, who, when afflicted by the threefold afflictions and yet thirsting for *Sai-darshan*, has gone away dejected and without any satisfaction in his heart?

127. That day, feeling very sad, he did not relish any food or drink, nor coming or going anywhere. Sleepless he lay on the bed, with eyes wide-open.

128. 'Making sure that nobody else is nearby, and that Baba is alone on his seat, I will seize such an opportunity to hold fast to Baba's feet'.

129. Thus resolved Sapatnekar and his resolve bore fruit, as, overcome with deep emotion, he caught Baba's feet.

130. As he bowed his head on his feet, Baba placed his hand on it. Sapatnekar then began to press Baba's feet, when a shepherdess came there.

131. As soon as she came, she began massaging Baba's waist, vigorously, and, as usual, Baba began talking to her.

132. The marvel of that talk was, that as Sapatnekar listened to it very carefully, he found all of it to be his own story, letter for letter.

133. Though the shepherdess signified her attentiveness from time to time, vocally, yet Sapatnekar was filled with astonishment as he listened to his own tale. He was simply amazed!

134.   It was the story of a grocer, but in fact, it was his own story. In the course of it, a mention of the death of his late son came up.

135.   It was narrated in full detail, from birth to death, as if a very close relative was giving the account.

136.   The story was being narrated to the woman, who, in fact, had no connection with it. It was the story about a father and a son. The subject was only of the two of them.

137.   And so, as he listened to the story from Sai's mouth thus, Sapatnekar was greatly surprised in his mind. His reverence for Sai was confirmed.

138.   He was full of admiration as to how Baba knew it all, like a myrobalan on the palm of his hand.

139.   To him who is one with the Brahman, the whole world is his own family, or rather, he is himself the whole Creation. And that is the mark of Sai.

140.   Sai Baba's *avatar* is the actual manifestation of his Oneness. How will he then, differentiate between 'mine' and 'yours'? He is himself present in the form of this Universe.

141.   He who is absorbed in God Almighty, how will he speak the language of duality? The difference between the Perceiver, Perception and the object of Perception does not exist for him, like the sky that cannot be coated with anything.

142.   Baba's intuitive knowledge was great. Even as this thought crossed his mind, listen, O virtuous listeners, to what Baba said to him.

143.   Pointing his finger to Sapatnekar, Baba exclaimed in great surprise, "I have killed his child, he says. He has made this accusation against me.

144.   "If I kill people's children, then why does he come to the mosque and weep? All right, I will now do this. I will bring his child back as his son.

145.   "Just as I gave that lady back her dead son, Ramdas, so will I bring back his son to him, once again"

146.   On hearing this, Sapatnekar sat there waiting, his eyes fixed expectantly, on Baba's face. Placing his hand on his head, Baba reassured him.

147. He said, "These feet are very ancient. All your care is removed. Have full faith in me. Soon, you will be fulfilled."

148. While pressing Baba's feet, when Sapatnekar heard Baba's sweet words, his eyes filled with tears and he bowed at His feet in obeisance.

149. The '*ashtabhav*' choked him and tears of joy sprang up in the eyes, with which he washed Baba's feet, as he was overcome with love.

150. Once again, Baba placed his hand on his head and said, "Be at peace". Then Sapatnekar returned to his place with a joyous heart.

151. *Naivedya* was prepared, which he gave in the hands of his wife and after the *pooja* and *arati* were over, he placed the plate in front of Baba.

152. Then sprinkling water around the food-plate and touching the eyes according to the ritual, he offered it to Baba, after first offering it to the five vital airs.

153. Then, in keeping with the usual practice, as soon as Baba's hand touched it, to indicate that he had accepted it, Sapatnekar felt very happy.

154. Then Sapatnekar pushed his way into the crowd of other devotees present there, who were bowing at Baba's feet and quickly made obeisance, once again.

155. And so, in that great rush, when Baba saw head banging against head, he calmly said to Sapatnekar,

156. "Oh, why this salute upon salute, repeatedly? Done with reverence only once, is quite enough!"

157. That was the night for *Chavadi*. With great love and fondness, Sapatnekar walked happily, in front of the procession, staff in hand.

158. But the listeners already know about this *Chavadi* procession. Hence its repetition has been avoided for fear of lengthening the book.

159. And just see Baba's *leela* that night! Gazing at Baba, Sapatnekar felt that he was actually looking at Pandurang of Pandharpur!

160. Later, when Sapatnekar asked Baba's leave to go, he was asked to have his meal first, and then go. Without disobeying Baba, in the least, he then went for *darshan* just before leaving.

161. Suddenly a thought crossed his mind, 'If Baba were to ask for *dakshina*, how can I comply with his wish?'

162. The money that he had with him was over, except for an amount enough to cover the fare. So, if Baba were to say "Give me *dakshina*", he made up his mind what to say.

163. 'Even before he asks, I will place a rupee in his hand. If he asks again, I will offer one more. Thereafter I will say to him that I do not have any more.

164. 'I will say to Baba quite frankly, that I have kept only what is necessary for the railway fare.' With this resolve, he went to meet Baba.

165. As per his resolve made earlier, when he placed one rupee on his hand, Baba asked for only one more and when given, Baba said quite clearly,

166. "Take this coconut and put it in your wife's lap. Then you may leave peacefully, and forget all your restless agitation".

167. After twelve months had passed, a son was born to the couple. They then came back for *darshan*, with their eight-month-old child.

168. They placed the boy on Baba's feet. Oh, how wonderful is the *leela* of these saints! Listen to this prayer, with folded hands.

169. 'Oh, Sainath, how to repay your generosity, we know not. But we bow humbly at your feet.

170. 'We poor creatures, are mean and lowly. But please have mercy on us, the helpless ones, and may we always find refuge at your feet, from now onwards.

171. 'Awake or dreaming, numerous waves of thought arise in the mind, giving us no respite, during the day or night. Therefore, draw us to you in worship'.

172. Later on, as the birth of that boy, Murlidhar, was followed by that of two more, Bhaskar and Dinkar, Sapatnekar was greatly pleased at heart.

173. And so, when he bowed to that most compassionate Sai, and having steadied his mind and accomplished his purpose, Sapatnekar returned home with his wife.

174. In the beginning, the intention in my mind was to narrate the story in brief. But it is Sainath who makes me narrate and so it is, that this book has become lengthy.

175. Surrendering to him totally, Hemad now indicates to the listeners the connection and essence of the next story.

176. And that story is far more fascinating than this, as to how the incomparable Sai satisfied the fond desire of a devotee, who liked miracles.

177. People extol Sai's virtues, but he who always likes to find fault will see only faults in him. Himself being interested in neither material nor spiritual desires, the sole object in his mind is to find fault.

178. 'Sai Baba may be a saint. But I will not believe in him, unless I have personal experience and he gives it to me'.

179. He who goes only to test, finds his desires fulfilled too! This is the story in the next chapter. May the good listeners listen to it carefully.

Weal be to all! Here ends the forty-eighth chapter of
"Shri Sai Samarth Satcharit", called
'The Bestowal of Grace Upon a Doubting Devotee',
as inspired by the saints and the virtuous and
composed by his devotee, Hemadpant.

Testing the Saint and Control of the Mind

MY OBEISANCE TO SHRI GANESH, TO SHRI SARASWATI, AND SHRI GURUMAHARAJ! TO THE FAMILY DEITY, TO SHRI SITA-RAMACHANDRA, MY MOST HUMBLE OBEISANCE! I BOW IN REVERENCE TO THE MOST VENERABLE GURU SHRI SAINATH!

1. Where the *Vedas* and *Puranas* are exhausted, praising the Sadguru in all his aspects, it is better that an ignorant one like me, who does not understand anything, should remain silent.

2. In fact, to remain silent is to praise the Sadguru, most truly. But Sai's virtues, one after the other, make me forget to keep silent.

3. Blessed is Sai's incomprehensible *leela*, on seeing which, I just cannot remain silent. And as the palate savours sweetmeats, I also remembered the listeners.

4. So I took it into my head that I should include them in this feast, too, which will double the pleasure of its sweetness. That is why this feast has become truly interesting and enjoyable.

5. However delicious the sweet be in itself, but if the company of good, virtuous friends is not there, it will not be relished, all by oneself and its sweetness also fades.

6. Fully satiated as Sai is, in all his desires, he is the adornment of all the saints. Sai is, to all his devotees, the Abode of Peace and Rest, who dispels the most difficult of delusions about the worldly life.

7. His *leela* is beyond all utterance, which my speech is unable to describe. How can I comprehend the incomprehensible skill and ingenuity of one who is himself inconceivable?

8. Sai, the weal of all weal, reminds me very kindly of his Story, and thus brings this book to completion.

9. As one tries to sing of his greatness, who is powerful enough to be able to narrate it? And, where *'Para'*[1] herself turns back in her inability, what to say of *'Pashyanti'* and *'Madhyama'*?

10. And where all these three do not open their mouths, then what to say of *'Vaikhari'*? But though I know this full well, yet my mind will not rest.

11. Unless absorbed totally at Sadguru's feet, his true form is not comprehended. Hence one should pray for the bountiful Grace of the saints, who are themselves Shri Hari (God) incarnate.

12. To be fondly attached to the guru's feet is our highest gain. May we develop a fondness for the company of saints and for their love in many forms.

13. The attribute 'devotee' does not become him, who is filled with egoism (attached to the body). Only he is a true devotee who is completely free from ego.

14. Wherein lies the prestige of him, who is stiff with pride at being a *Jnani*, has a false conceit of his greatness and is a home of hypocrisy?

15. Those unfortunate ones who do not sing the glory of their own guru, do not listen to it though able to hear, they are foolishness personified, indeed!

16. Penance is higher than pilgrimages, vows, sacrifices or charity; but worship of Hari (God) is even higher, while meditating on one's guru is the highest of all.

17. Sai alone is the meditation of his devotees; he alone is their *pooja* of gods and goddesses; he is their secret treasure, too, which they have to guard carefully, but not like a miser.

18. Once in a while I might feel lazy; but Sai, the dweller of my heart, knows no laziness. If I forget about the story, he reminds me at the right time.

19. Were I to say that I will rest for a moment, yet my writ does not run here. For suddenly such a story is inspired from within that I am compelled to take up the pen in hand.

20. To narrate to his devotees so many of his marvellous stories and also, for my own good, he has induced me to write this *Satcharit*.

21. As it is, the stories of a saint are composed and written by himself alone. For unless inspired by him, they become dull and uninteresting, at every step.

22. However, most compassionate that Sainath is, he has entered my heart and has got his book written, fulfilling also my innermost wishes.

23. When the tongue ceaselessly repeats *Shri Sai-naam*, the *chitta* (mind) contemplates on his words and the *manas* (heart) meditates on his divine form, it brings me complete satisfaction.

24. He on whose lips Shri Sai's name is present, all the time, and in whose heart dwells a deep love for Shri Sai and the *karma* that he performs is only for Sai, to such a one Sai is greatly indebted.

25. There is no other means than this to snap the ties of worldly life. Sai's Story is most purifying. Reading it or listening to it, always brings great satisfaction.

26. Make a '*pradakshina*'[2] round him on your own feet; listen to the narration of his *Satcharit*; embrace him with love and have his *darshan* with your eyes.

27. Prostrate before him in obeisance; lower your head on his feet; let the tongue repeat his name and the nose inhale the fragrance of his '*nirmalya*'[3].

28. Now, to pick up the threads from the previous story, a promise had been made to the listeners in the last chapter, that I will narrate the story of a devotee who was fond of miracles.

29. Himself not being interested for any material or spiritual desires and having no awareness of the saints' spiritual powers, he distrusts their description given by anyone else.

30. When friends related stories of Sai, he listened but with a view to find fault. Unless supported by direct self-experience, he would not accept anything in the world.

31. His name was Hari Kanhoba. He set out on the journey from Bombay, with friends, in order to test Sai for himself.

32. But Sai, who illumines the hearts of all — can the skill and uniqueness of his art be understood with certainty, by anyone?

33. As Haribhau set out for Shirdi, Sai Samarth knew the reason, that he had a fondness only for miracles and that, that was all his worth.

34. So he was given a taste of only that and was won over, heart and soul. Thus his effort, too, was made fruitful. Truly, how skilled contrivers are these saints!

35. Haribhau sat in a *tonga* at Kopargaon, along with his friend and, after taking a bath in the Godavari, started for Shirdi at once.

36. On arriving from Kopargaon, Haribhau washed his hands and feet and immediately set out to see the saint.

37. Feet shod in brand new foot-wear and a *jari*-embroidered turban on the head, Haribhau eagerly came to take Sai Baba's *darshan*.

38. Then as they approached the mosque, seeing Sai from a distance, he felt like going nearer and prostrating before him in obeisance.

39. But the new foot-wear posed a problem, for there was no safe place to keep it. Finally, finding a corner there, he just shoved them in.

40. Then he went up for *darshan*. He made obeisance at Sai's feet, very lovingly, and came back on receiving *udi-prasad*, to return to the *wada*.

41. But as he looked about for his foot-wear, he just could not find it, search as he may. With a sad face, he returned bare-foot, having abandoned all hope.

42. For too many people were coming and going there, all the time. Whom could he ask? He just could not think.

43. His mind grew restless and agitated. The lost foot-wear kept coming before the eyes and the mind was continually plagued by the thought of that foot-wear. All the concentration focussed on that one object.

44. 'Oh, how fondly, with what eagerness it was bought! Gone, gone indeed, is that foot-wear, completely lost! No doubt, some thief has stolen it!' he felt certain.

45. However, he then took a bath and after the *pooja, naivedya,* etc., he sat down, along with the others, for a meal. But in the mind, there was no feeling of satisfaction.

46. '*Sabha-mandap* is Sai's place. Who could have taken away my foot-wear, escaping Sai's notice so completely? Is this any small wonder?'

47. Uneasiness, regrets filled his mind; he had no relish for food or drink. He came out with others to wash his hands.

48. Suddenly, a Maratha boy appeared there quite unexpectedly, holding aloft a stick at the end of which, like a flag, was the lost foot-wear.

49. Having finished the meal, people were just washing their hands, when the boy came searching and said, 'Baba has sent me giving this stick in my hand —

50. 'And saying, "My child, go crying aloud '*Hari Ka beta, jari ka pheta*' (Hari, son of Kanhoba, with a gold-embroidered turban), and to him, who will cling to you eagerly saying that, 'These are my very own', you give these to him.

51. "But first, it must be ensured that he is '*Hari Ka beta*' and has a *jari-turban*, and only then you should give it, in the end, without making much noise about it, earlier."'

52. On hearing this cry and after recognizing the foot-wear by looking at it, Haribhau rushed forward, much astonished in his mind.

53. Tears of joy sprang up in his eyes. Haribhau's throat choked with emotion. On seeing the lost foot-wear, he was simply amazed!

54. He said to the boy, 'Come, O come here! Let me see, bring those sandals to me!' Having carefully examined them, he said, 'Where did you find these? Tell me quickly and quite frankly!'

55. The boy said, 'That, I do not know. I have to obey Baba's command. He who is *Hari Ka beta* (son) has to show me his '*jari-turban*'.

56. 'Only to him will I give the sandals. I do not recognize anyone else. But he who convinces me about the marks indicated by Baba, he alone will take these sandals.'

57. Haribhau said, 'My child, they are but mine!' But the boy would not give. So he convinced the boy of all the marks indicated by Baba.

58. And he said, 'O child, I am Hari, the son of Kanhoba, and the words are absolutely true, which apply to me perfectly.

59. 'Now, look at my *jari-turban* and the doubts in your mind will be resolved and it will be proved that the sandals belong to me. No one else will then have any claim on them.'

60. Ultimately, the boy was convinced and gave the sandals to Haribhau. His wish was fulfilled and he experienced for himself, that Sai was a saint.

61. 'That my turban has *jari* embroidery on it, is no great secret. For it is on my head, visible to all.

62. 'But when I was in a totally different place and this is my very first trip to Shirdi, how did Sai Baba know my name to be Hari?

63. 'Kanhoba, my father, has not even been seen by anyone here. But when he was referred to by the letter '*Ka*', I am greatly surprised.

64. 'Earlier, when my friends told me of the greatness of the saint Sai, I disregarded their words. But now I sincerely regret it.

65. 'And now, when I have the experience myself, I know the power of Sai Baba. There is no room for any doubt that Shri Sai is a great *mahatma*.'

66. As the faith in his heart, so was Haribhau's experience. To test the saints was his keen, fond desire and he had no desire for spiritual gains.

67. Friends and relatives had narrated their experiences as to how Sai Samarth was a great *mahatma*, and to see the wonder, to experience it himself, was the reason for his going to Shirdi.

68. 'To surrender yourself, heart and soul, at the saint's feet and thus to reach God' had never been the keen desire in his mind, in the least. How far can the reach of a chameleon go?

69. When he wanted to go to a saint's door only to see miracles, the lost pair of his brand new sandals came back, delivered at home.
70. Or else, by losing a trivial thing like a pair of sandals, what great loss could have been incurred? But since his mind became restless and wearied for them, it could not be calmed down until they were found.
71. There are two ways of gaining the favour of saints, one is devotion and the other, *jnana*. But the efforts of *Jnana-marga* are arduous, while the means of devotion are easy.
72. But then, if devotion is so easily attainable, why do not all follow that path? Because even there, one needs the wealth of the greatest good fortune. Only then can it be attained.
73. Only when the merit of *crores* of births is accumulated, will one meet the saints and it is only then that one enjoys the happiness of the company of saints, which fosters devotion.
74. We know only the worldly life; there alone is our attachment and we know not how to liberate ourselves from it. Where such is the inclination of the mind, can it be called devotion?
75. As is our devotion, so is our gain. And this is sure to happen, at any time. Here, there is not the slightest doubt.
76. For the enjoyment of sensual pleasures, by day and by night, we have gathered near Sai and so for us, the gift is also, of the same kind. But to the spiritual seekers, the gain is also spiritual.
77. And now, about one more swami called Somdev, who came personally to Shirdi, to put Sai to test.
78. In the year 1906, this man who was staying at a *dharmashala* in Uttar Kashi, met Bhaiji.
79. This famous Bhaiji was the brother of the well-known, late Shri Dikshit. He met Swamiji on the way, while on a pilgrimage to Badrikedar.
80. Badrikedar was left behind, when Bhaiji got down. On the way, as he wandered from place to place, he came across resting places, where he found some travellers sitting.

81.   One man among these, later became famous as the Swami from Haradwar and he came under the influence of Baba.

82.   This is a most instructive story about him, which will clarify Baba's nature, give pleasure to the listeners and happiness to all.

83.   As Bhaiji was going for his morning ablutions, he met this Swamiji on the way and, casually conversing with each other, both felt a certain mutual affinity.

84.   This region of their meeting, is below Gangotri. There, while Swamiji was at a place called Uttar Kashi, which is a hundred and forty miles from Dehra Doon, this meeting took place.

85.   A metal water-pot in hand, Bua had set out in the morning to go for toilet, in the open. Bhaiji too, was going to the same place, for the same purpose.

86.   First, they just looked at each other. Later, as they met again, on the way, they happily conversed about each other's well-being, etc.

87.   And as they went on talking, a certain friendship sprang up between them, leading to their enquiries about their respective places of residence.

88.   'You live at Haradwar; we, at Nagpur. If, at any time, you happen to come that side, do visit us.

89.   'When you are on a pilgrimage, please sanctify our home by giving *darshan*, once again, and allow us to serve you, a little.

90.   'Do remember us. Our only prayer is, that your feet may purify our house by their touch.' 'May Narayan satisfy this wish of yours!' said Swamiji.

91.   Such was the conversation that took place between them in the year 1906, below Uttar Kashi.

92.   Both asked each other's address and having now come to the open ground, both parted from each other.

93.   Five years passed by. As the appointed time for Swamiji's meeting with Sai approached, Swami felt a strong urge to meet Bhaiji.

94.   So, in the year 1911, Swamiji came to Nagpur and on hearing the sacred Story of Shri Sainath, felt very happy.

95. After Bhaiji had given a letter of introduction and made arrangements for his reaching the holy Shirdi comfortably, Swami left Nagpur.

96. When he got down at Manmad, the train for Kopargaon was already there. On getting into a *tonga* there, he happily set out for Sai Baba's *darshan*.

97. Wherever you may go, the *sadhus* are always different, one from another, in their conduct or way of life. Nowhere is it the same.

98. The conduct and behaviour of one saint is never the standard for another saint. And this is no means of surmising about what is proper and what is not.

99. And, first of all, why should a person going for *darshan*, bother about this at all? If he were to sit in judgement over their conduct, he would only get cheated out of his own weal.

100. But Swamiji's nature was such that his mind was always clouded with doubts and misconceptions. On seeing the flags at Shirdi from a distance, Swami's mind was assailed with doubts.

101. People who were with him, lovingly made obeisance, as soon as the flag on the spire came in sight.

102. Although the heart was eager for Sai's *darshan*, that would come later. But he could not bear to disregard the flag that he saw.

103. That the sight of the flag stirs a great love from within, is the experience everywhere, for it is the sign of a loving devotion. There is nothing unusual about it.

104. But in the Swami's vile mind, doubt after doubt arose, on seeing the flag from a distance. Strange indeed, was the make-up of his mind!

105. Oh! Is this any sign of being a *sadhu* that there should be such fondness for banners? That the flag has to be put up on a temple, is really a blot on saintliness!

106. For a *sadhu* to ask for respect in this way, is really indicative of his hankering after honour and fame. The saintliness of such has no appeal to the mind! Actually, this is their deficiency.

107. In short, as one's natural inclination of the mind, so also, is his insistence in judging a *sadhu*. Swami's mind was quite made up! 'I do not want Sai's Grace.

108. 'In vain have I come up to here!' Swami felt a great disresepct towards Baba and at once, he made a firm resolve to go back from there.

109. 'This is nothing but false pride in the desire for fame and honour! Why does a *sadhu* need honours? On seeing this flag, I for one, can imagine no other reason.

110. 'This *sadhu* simply flaunts his greatness by flying the flag and this itself is a grave deficiency in his saintliness. Why should I go for the *darshan* of such a *sadhu*?

111. 'How can the mind find any peace by taking such a *darshan*? Oh, flying the flag is but an exhibition of hypocrisy! There is no satisfaction in this.'

112. So he said to himself, 'It is better that I return home the way I came. The idea of taking his *darshan* does not appear to be good. Oh, how I feel absolutely tricked!'

113. His companions then said to him, 'Why have you come so far, at all? Why do mere flags and banners agitate your mind so?

114. 'We have now come quite close to Shirdi. And when you see the chariot, palanquin, horse and all the other paraphernalia, how much more agitation they will cause!'

115. On hearing this, the Swami felt even more annoyed. Those *sadhus* with airs and affectations, who want drums, palanquins, horses — O, have I not seen enough of them!'

116. Such thoughts assailing his mind, Somdevji turned to go back, thinking, 'The idea of going to Shirdi is by no means a good one. Better to take the road back to the river!'

117. But his travelling companions then began to press him, 'You have come all the way up to here. Please do not, now, turn back!

118. 'Having come thus far, come a little further. Do not entertain irrational doubts! This flag on the mosque has nothing to do with the *sadhu*.

119. 'For, this *sadhu* needs no flag, nor does he want fame or honour. It is the villagers, who like this kind of adornment, purely out of devotion.

120. 'And then, do not look at the flag. Merely go and have *darshan*. You need not wait even a moment longer, but return immediately.'

121. In the meantime, Shirdi had come near. So, on hearing that sincere, straightforward advice, he thought, 'Why not do away with the restlessness of the mind, once and for all? At least, there will be no regrets!'

122. By the *darshan* of Shri Samarth, Bua's heart simply melted. Love flooded in the eyes; the throat choked with powerful emotion.

123. His heart was filled with joy and the eyes, with pleasure. He could hardly wait to be bathed in the dust under Baba's feet.

124. On seeing that beautiful face, the eyes and the heart were rivetted on it, as he kept gazing at him, held captive by a profusion of love.

125. All the doubts in the mind were resolved and the heart melted with joy of his *darshan*. The 'sagun' form was deeply impressed on the eyes and Bua was totally absorbed in the blissful experience.

126. Seeing the *Mahatma* with his own eyes, Somdev experienced great joy and he felt so completely at peace with himself that he felt like staying there for ever.

127. The mere *darshan* dispelled all his doubts; the mind was stilled; the feeling of separateness faded away and there was Onenesss from within and without.

128. Speech fell silent as words failed to articulate; the eyes forgot to blink; Universal Consciousness flooded him from within and without and the mind in total absorption, experienced a rare contentment.

129. At first, on seeing the flag, he had turned back. But later, the eyes filled with tears of profound love. The *sattvic* 'ashtabhav' burst forth and love for Baba engulfed him.

130. He then remembered his guru's words that 'Where the mind is totally engrossed, that is one's own place' and Bua was overwhelmed with love.

131. As Bua slowly moved forward, Maharaj's anger too, rose, gradually. And as abuses were showered on him freely, Bua's love for Baba also redoubled.

132. How extraordinary are the doings of Samarth Sai! The most remarkable *Narasimha avatar* that Baba assumed was exact and complete.

133. "Let our hypocrisy be with us! Get out and be gone!" he said, "And don't you dare approach my mosque, again!

134. "Why take the *darshan* of one who puts up flags on the mosque? Is this any sign of a saint? Not even a moment should be wasted here!"

135. Later, his mind filled with fear and doubts, Swami entered the *sabha-mandap*. Looking at Sai's form from a distance, Swami could not sit still.

136. And when an echo of his own thoughts, word for word, dashed on his ears, Bua felt abashed, where he sat and said to himself, 'Truly, Maharaj has an intuitive knowledge of everything!

137. 'Oh, how foolish I am and how perfect in knowledge is Maharaj! How very contrary were my notions and how pure his heart!

138. 'Sai embraces some, others he touches with his hand. To some, he gives an assurance while on others he bestows his glance of Grace.

139. 'He looks at some with a smile while he soothes and comforts others in their sorrow. Yet others are given *udi-prasad*. Thus he satisfies one and all.

140. 'When such is the case, I feel that his anger against me must be due to my earlier behaviour. This is not anger, but a lesson to me, which will eventually make me happy.

141. And what happened later on was the same! Swami was so much engrossed at Baba's feet that by Sai's Grace he became purified and stayed at his feet, for ever.

142. May the power, the greatness of Sai-devotion drive away evil desires and envy and give rise to Peace, Prosperity and Courage and thus bring fulfillment to his devotees.

143. This entire Creation is filled with Gandharvas[4], Yakshas[5], and gods and demons. And although the all-pervading God always fills this entire Universe —

144. Yet if he had not taken on a form, but had remained form-less, it would not have benefitted us, the human beings, who are with a form.

145. In short, had Sai, with his *leela*, not taken on a body and guided people to the right path or had not put up resistance to the wicked ways and opinions of the sinners, how would he have been able to show kindness and mercy to his devotees?

146. As this chapter comes almost to its close, I am reminded of an account which is an example of Sai's instructive teaching. He who will believe in it, will benefit from it.

147. The acccount is very short. But he who will always keep it in mind, will ensure his own weal. Hence I entreat the listeners to give me their attention for a moment.

148. Once, a great devotee Mhalsapati, along with Nanasaheb, was sitting in the mosque. Listen to the marvel that took place, then.

149. A wealthy gentleman from Vaijapur, who was eager for the *darshan* of Sai Samarth, arrived there, with his family.

150. On seeing the ladies wearing a '*burkha*'[6], Nana felt awkward and felt that to put them at ease, he should move aside to make room for them.

151. So he got up to move aside, when Baba stopped him, saying, "Those who want to come will come up! Be at ease and sit where you are."

152. 'They are also here for *darshan*. You may come up, there is no objection', somebody suggested to that gentleman. So they all came up and made obeisance to Sai.

153. While doing so, one lady amongst them, slightly moved her '*burkha*' aside. Seeing her face adorned with great beauty, Nana was quite bewitched.

154. But he felt awkward to stare at her in the presence of other people and yet he could not restrain himself from looking at her. What should he do? The temptation was irresistible.

155. He was feeling shy from within, in Baba's presence and could hardly lift his head. But hesitantly, the eyes kept turning in that direction. Nana was caught in a dilemma.

156. This was Nana's state of mind, which Baba, the dweller of the hearts of all, knew only too well. How can others experience it? They will only struggle with the meaning of the words.

157. Baba, who knew in his heart, Nana's bewildered state, in order to bring his mind back to normalcy, gave him advice. Listen to it.

158. "Nana, why do you get so disturbed in mind? That which follows quietly its natural propensity, should never be hindered by anyone. For there is no loss in that.

159. "When *Brahmadev* has created this Universe, if we do not appreciate it, his ingenuity and skill will be in vain. 'By and by, everything will fall into place'.

160. "When the front door stands open, why go to the back door? Where the mind is pure, there is no difficulty.

161. "He who has no evil thought in his mind, why should he fear anyone? Eyes do their work of seeing. Then why be embarrassed?"

162. Madhavrao who was inquisitive by nature, was present there at the time and to satisfy his own curiosity, asked Nana the meaning of those words.

163. When Madhavrao asked this, Nana said, 'Oh, please wait just now! When we are on our way to the *wada*, I will tell you the purport of Baba's words'.

164. After the usual enquiries about the well-being, etc., were over, when Nana had made obeisance to Sai Samarth and was returning to his place, Madhavrao accompanied him, too!

165. At once, he asked Nana. 'Nana will you tell me clearly, the significance of Baba's words, such as 'By and by everything will fall into place', etc.?

166. Nana could not bring himself to tell the meaning and gave many evasive replies. Madhavrao grew even more suspicious and his mind would not keep quiet.

167. Then, on Madhavrao's persuasion, Nana opened out his heart and told him everything that had happened there. Madhavrao's puzzle was solved.

168. Truly how alert Baba was! Wherever anyone's mind may wander, to him who was Omniscient, it was like the actual happening before the eyes.

169. Listeners will be surprised to hear this brief but amazing tale. But if its essence be considered, it results in gaining the most precious steadiness and peace of mind.

170. Mind, by nature, is fickle and should not be allowed to become unbridled. The organs[7] may run riot, but the body should not become impatient.

171. The organs cannot be trusted; hence one should not hanker after sensual pleasures. Gradually, by constant study, the fickleness of the mind will go.

172. Never be in the power of the senses. Even they cannot be suppressed, always. But they should be regulated at the proper time and with a proper plan.

173. Looks are the subject for the eyes. One should admire the beauty of a thing, fearlessly. What is the reason for being ashamed, here? But give no place to evil thoughts.

174. Observe God's creation, with a mind free from desires. It will regulate the senses easily and naturally, and enjoyment of sensual pleasures will be forgotten.

175. As the charioteer is the main cause for taking the chariot to the right place, similarly, intellect, our benefactor, is always alert to control the senses.

176. The charioteer controls the chariot. By regulating the senses, the intellect controls the body from being unbridled and the mind from being uncontrollably fickle.

177. The Jeevatma, who is made up of body, senses and the mind, when he finishes experiencing the pleasure and pain preordained for him, he attains the state of Oneness with God. Such is the power of the intellect.

178. Among the senses, organs like the eyes, should be regarded as various horses, while all the objects of sensual pleasure, like looks, palate, etc., are the ways leading to Hell.

179. Even the slightest greed for sensual enjoyment will ruin spiritual happinesss. Hence abandon these completely. Only then will you attain *Moksha*.

180. Even if outwardly, the organs are detached, if the mind longs for these, there is no end to births and deaths. Thus the senses are most dangerous.

181. If you get a charioteer with a discriminating mind, he will hold the reins in hand with discrimination and then, the horses, that is, the senses, will not go astray in the least, even in a dream.

182. If you are fortunate enough to get such a satisfactory, determined, alert, skilful and ingenious charioteer, then how far is *Vishnupad* (state of Oneness with God)?

183. That state itself, is the all-pervasive Parabrahman, the God Almighty. Vasudev is just another name of Him. And that is the most excellent, everlasting and highest place, that is Moksha.

184. And so, this chapter is completed. The next one is even more fascinating and will engross the hearts of the good devotees. Listen to it as it comes in its due order.

185. In the end, Hemad bows his head gratefully at the feet of the Sadguru, who runs this Creation and inspires the intellect.

Weal be to all! Here ends the forty-ninth chapter of
"*Shri Sai Samarth Satcharit*", called
'*Testing the Saint and Control of the Mind*',
inspired by the saints and the virtuous
and composed by his devotee, Hemadpant.

Notes

1. Speech in the first of its four stages: - the first stirring of the breath is '*Para*'; '*Pashyanti*' is the second of its four stages, from the first stirring of the air or breath to the articulate utterance; it is the faint whispering at the breast. '*Madhyama*' is the third stage, preceding articulate utterance in the fourth stage which is '*Vaikhari*'.
2. Circumambulation of an idol or saint by way of reverence, keeping the right side towards him.
3. Flowers and other offerings of *pooja*, which have now become stale.
4. Celestial choristers.
5. A class of demigods or minor deities or an individual of it.
6. A cloth drawn or prepared for being drawn over the face or head as a veil.
7. Kabir, the great saint, has also said, '*Mana gaya to jane de, mata jane de Shareer / Na kheche kamaan, phir kahan lagega teer?*' (If the mind strays, let it be, but control your body. If you do not stretch the bow, how will the arrow hit the target?)

50

Detailed Exposition of Bhagvad Gita, Chap. IV., V. 34

MY OBEISANCE TO SHRI GANESH, TO SHRI SARASWATI, AND SHRI GURUMAHARAJ! TO THE FAMILY DEITY, TO SHRI SITA-RAMACHANDRA, MY MOST HUMBLE OBEISANCE! I BOW IN REVERENCE TO THE MOST VENERABLE GURU SHRI SAINATH!

1. There is no limit to the obligations of my mother and father who gave birth to me as they have given me a human body. I was fortunate not to be born an intestinal round worm!

2. Nor was I born to cause pain to my mother's womb, by being born blind, lame, squint-eyed, a stammerer, or even deaf and dumb; but was born with a healthy body.

3. And by God's Grace, I was born in that most excellent Brahmin *varna*, at whose feet even the gods bow. Thus I am most fortunate, indeed!

4. When we are born *crores* of times, in every birth we have a father and a mother. But very rarely does one get parents who can prevent our birth-death cycle.

5. He who gives birth is a father; but so is he who performs the (sacred) thread-ceremony. And he who nurtures us by feeding, etc., is the third father, while the fourth is one who releases us from fear and difficulties.

6. All these are equally important in this world. But there is no true father other than the compassionate Sadguru. Just see his marvellous *leela*!

7. He is the father only in the biological sense who, by depositing the sperm in the mother's womb, gives birth through the female genitals. But the Sadguru is a unique father.

8. Without even the tiniest particle of the sperm and without making use of the vagina, he gives birth to his son and bestows Grace upon him.

9. To that all-pervading, most compassionate *Guruvarya*, who releases us from the birth-death cycle, gives us the Light of Knowledge and explains the mysterious, profound truth of the *Vedas* — to him I bow in reverence.

10. I make obeisance to the *Guruvarya*, who is the sun in the darkness of worldly life, is most excellent among the self-realized saints, is the moon to the devotees who are the Chakor birds and is also our *Kalpataru*.

11. The greatness of the *Gururaya* is boundless, describing which, speech sheds its pride and it is better that lowering one's head at the guru's feet, one holds one's silence like a mute.

12. Unless great penance has been performed in the previous birth, one does not get the *darshan* of a saint, which destroys the three-fold afflictions.

13. He who wants to make spiritual progress, attain *Moksha* or achieve his own weal, should surrender to a saint. He will not want anything at all.

14. Blessed, blessed is the company of saints. Who can describe its great importance! It brings to the virtuous devotees, discriminative knowledge, renunciation and peace.

15. Sai is the very image of Universal Consciousness. From the Unmanifest he came to the Manifest state. Who can, with certainty, describe that totally detached state of his?

16. For the faithful devotees and loving listeners, he, the ever-compassionate One, very affectionately narrates his own fascinating Life Story, which, to them is like a holy temple.

17. He, whose hand, the moment it falls on the head, crushes the ego completely, the chanting of the *mantra*, 'That I am', begins in the mind and there is joy everywhere.

18. How can a mean, lowly creature like me, have the power to sing his glory? It is he himself who has very graciously brought out this *pothi*, out of love for the devotees.

19. I prostrate in obeisance before the feet of that Sai and salute my listeners. I bow to the *sadhus* and saints and the virtuous; I lovingly embrace them all.

20. Sai would talk about things casually, playfully; but they had perfect rules of ethical conduct implicit in them. He who was adorned with everlasting Peace, was meditated upon by the most righteous and virtuous of men.

21. He cannot be compared to the sun, who sets in the evening. And if he be compared to the moon, the moon is subject to waning, whereas Sai is always whole.

22. At his feet Hemad bows humbly and lovingly entreats the listeners to listen to this story fondly, with faith and devotion and with full attention.

23. The land has been properly ploughed and the seed has been sown. But unless you, O Gracious Clouds, bring the rain, will the crop be ever produced?

24. When the saints' stories fall on the ears, no sins can remain, but as you listen to these stories merit is born. Reap, O reap the benefit of this '*Parvani*' (plenitude).

25. We do not have any keen desire for the four '*muktis*'[1], like *Salokya*, etc. May our steadfast devotion be to Sai; that is our highest gain.

26. We are not in bondage at all. How then are we concerned with liberation? Let there be an awakening in the heart, of devotion to the saints. That itself will purify the heart.

27. We should develop that single-minded devotion and attain to '*sahaj-sthiti*' or the natural state of perpetual consciousness, without the stirring of the feeling of duality or the feeling of 'you' and 'I' as being separate. This is all that we ask of Sai.

28. And so this is the request to the listeners, that they should see the oneness between the subject of reading, the act of reading and the reader, when they take this volume in hand to read.

29. Leave Hemadpant out of consideration, for he is not the creator
     of this *Satcharit*. He is merely an instrument used for the benefit
     of the devotees.

30. Those who abandon the oyster-shell that they have luckily found,
     lose also the pearl along with it. What have we to do with the
     origin of the *Peepul* or the holy fig tree? (i.e. the tree of worldly
     life with its roots above and branches below) A man should never
     be indifferent to his own weal.

31. Here there is no one but Sai Baba to add the '*matra*'² to the word.
     He alone is the subject of listening, the listener and the process of
     listening. Let not this oneness between the three be forgotten.

32. Or else it is not reading at all, where the ears are not respectfully
     alert and where the mind is not concentrated. Who will then
     take cognizance of the meaning of the words?

33. Listening to these stories, there should be no conceit, and even
     the listeners should appear to the mind as Sai himself. Only then
     will that listening be worthwhile. Thus keep a ceaseless awareness
     of non-duality.

34. Only then will all the inclinations of the physical organs merge,
     most certainly, into Sai and these tendencies will become one
     with him, as the waves with the water on which they rise.

35. Only then will the *Jnanis* receive spiritual instruction; the humour-
     loving, the joy and mirth born of humour; and the connoisseurs
     of poetry, the pleasure of metrical composition, from this book.

36. And so, earlier in this *Satcharit*, in the thirty-ninth chapter, the
     instruction that Shri Sai Samarth imparted to one of his excellent
     devotees —

37. While that devotee was, at the time, reciting from the beginning,
     the fourth chapter of *Bhagvad-Gita* to Baba (was narrated).

38. On the one hand, he was pressing Baba's feet and murmuring
     softly; on the other, as the thirty-third stanza ended, he began
     reciting the thirty-fourth.

39. He was muttering it to himself, with a mind fully concentrated
     and completely absorbed. But since what he was muttering was
     inaudible, others did not know the source-book of the recitation.

40. As he began the thirty-fourth stanza, Baba felt in his heart that he should bestow grace on this excellent devotee and show him the right path.

41. The name of that devotee was Nana. So Baba said to him. "Nana, what is it that you are muttering to yourself? Why do you not say it distinctly?

42. "For so long have I been watching that some muttering is going on. But the sound of words does not come out distinctly. What, what is this secret?"

43. Nana then said very clearly. 'I am reciting the *Gita* and, so as not to be a nuisance to others, I am murmuring it softly.'

44. "All right, this is for the people. But speak distinctly, at least for me! Let me see if you have yourself understood properly what you are reciting!" said Shri.

45. Bowing in obeisance, first, Nana then recited, loud and clear, the stanza beginning 'Learn that by humble reverence... etc.' On hearing it Baba was satisfied.

46. Then, when asked the meaning of this stanza, Nana narrated in detail, the significance, as given by the early commentators, to which also Baba nodded his head in approval.

47. Again he asked Nana the question, "Nana, just look at this third line, 'The masters of knowledge... will instruct thee in (that) wisdom', and reflect upon it.

48. "Just consider, if by adding an elision mark before the word *Jnana* and taking it as *Ajnana*, if the meaning is reversed.

49. "The exposition that commentators like Shankaranand, Jnaneshvar, Anandgiri, Shridhar, Madhusudan and others give, pertaining to the word *Jnana* —

50. "And which is acceptable to all, is also known to me. But why unnecessarily miss the marvel arising out of the addition of that elision mark?"

51. So saying, the particles of nectar-sweet instruction which Sai, the Cloud of Compassion, showered for the Chakor and Chatak birds or his devotees, have already been related earlier (in Chapter 39).

52. But it is surprising that not all the readers of the *Sai Leela* magazine appreciated that meaning and some remained doubtful!

53. Hence I shall make yet another small attempt to justify, with some proof, the word *Ajnana*, in order to satisfy them.

54. Some may even doubt as to how Baba could have had any knowledge of Sanskrit. But know, that to the saints nothing is unknown and the real reason for their doubt must lie elsewhere.

55. O listeners, who does not accept the words of the *Shruti* that 'Having known the One, all else is known'? Sai Baba had the same direct, intuitive knowledge of all things.

56. Saints who see the whole universe like a *myrobalan* on the palm of their hand and because of whom the sun shines, what do they not know?

57. They who have this knowledge, how can ignorance remain with them? They are in possession of all the *vidyas*. Of what consequence, then, is Sanskrit?

58. However, some readers of the *Sai Leela* say, 'Nana is unreliable and the addition of the elision mark which is unnecessary and indicative of ignorance, is all a figment of his own imagination.

59. 'He has himself made up this fabrication of the chapter of *ajnana* with the elision mark, to raise a meaningless controversy to parade his own knowledge, all the time.

60. 'Inserting an unwarranted elision mark, he has put *ajnana* in the place of *jnana* and has given a contrary interpretation of the *Gita*.'

61. But if you consider the facts and think carefully in your mind, you will find no inconsistency in the story in the thirty-ninth chapter, given in *Sai Leela*.

62. Whoever may have whatever notions about Nana being honest or unreliable, we should not regard his narrative as futile, meaningless babble.

63. Leaving their aversion for Nana aside, and without being carried away by their own emotions, if the readers will remove the defects of their views, they will see everything in the proper perspective.

64. It will not be possible to progress easily and smoothly through this chapter without first reading that most excellent thirty-ninth chapter in *Sai Leela* magazine.

65. In the thirty-fourth stanza of the fourth chapter of the *Bhagvad-Gita* called *Jnanayajna*, which came out from the mouth of Shri Krishna, appeared this discourse on the subject of *a-jnana*.

66. "Learn that by humble reverence, by inquiry (persistent search for the reality by piercing through illusions) and by service, the masters of knowledge who have seen the truth will instruct thee in (that) wisdom."

67. This is that original stanza from the *Gita*. In the third line of this stanza, if you put an elision mark before the word *jnana*, it makes the word *ajnana*.

68. If the elision mark is not brought to the mind, then, undoubtedly, the word *jnana* remains. And no one has any obstinate insistence against this, for that meaning is acceptable to all.

69. It is a universallay accepted aphorism of the *Shruti* that '*Moksha* is attained only by knowledge'. Yet it does not necessarily follow that it is a subject of instruction by the masters of knowledge.

70. I, the *Atman*, am just the Eternal *Sakshi* (witness), am unblemished and pure, omniscient and ever free. I am the Pure Consciousness present in all the creatures. Being unwavering and secure, I am filled with the joy of Oneness or non-duality.

71. But I am not *Ajnana*, nor is the work of *Ajnana* mine. Know that I am that *Atman* in the *Mahavakya* of *Atharvaveda*, which says, 'This *Atman* is Brahman'[3]. And I am also the repository of the *Mahavakya* of the *Rigveda* that '(Absolute) Knowledge itself is bliss'.

72. Know that a constant awareness of the *Mahavakya* of the *Yajurveda* that 'I am Brahman' is itself pure *vidya* or knowledge, while the generation of the feeling that I am a sinner, unfortunate and luckless, is *a-vidya* or ignorance.

73. Both these are ancient, beginningless powers of *Maya*. One (*a-vidya*) leads a creature to bondage, while the other (*vidya*), to liberation from bondage.

74. All this illusion of name, form, etc., is but the confusion or bewilderment caused by *Maya* and even more difficult to cross.

75. Every stirring of imagination is the abode of *Maya* and the ideas of bondage and liberation are born, most certainly, from the imagination.

76. The aphorism of the *Shruti* that 'Moksha is attained only by Knowledge' is undoubtedly true. But unless the sinful *karma* is destroyed, the realization of knowledge is impossible.

77. Know that he who has imbibed pure knowledge will be abandoned by desires, resolutions, etc. He has no bondage of *Maya* and has no place for passions and emotions.

78. Even a great *Jnani* like Shukadev[4] had to suffer harm because of his suspicions. From suspicion originated ignorance, which cannot be removed except by the guru.

79. When suspicion and doubt enter *Jnana*, even the *Jnani* becomes conceited, as milk in a vessel curdles by even a drop of sour gruel, which spoils the whole milk.

80. Hence first, recognize ignorance, for by dispelling it the heart is purified and only then will perfect *Jnana* appear and uninterrupted *samadhi* will be attained.

81. He who thinks all the time of wealth and prosperity, is insatiated with enjoyment of sensual pleasures and dwells constantly on his wife and children, the *Jnana* of such a one is nothing but ignorance.

82. When such is the infatuation with wealth, sons, wife, etc., though he be a *Jnani*, he does not know his own good. Hence, so long as he is without devotion, his *Jnana* is covered up by ignorance.

83. This whole multitude of living beings is full of ignorance. To be liberated from this ignorance and become *Jnani* and go beyond *Jnana'* is, most certainly, to be one with Brahman.

84. When ignorance is removed, *Jnana* appears. He who can readily forgive is a *Jnani* . But so long as the ego is not shed, he is under the power of *Maya*.

85. This *Maya*, who bewitched all the others, was but a slave to the command of incarnations like Ram, Krishna, etc., and the great *Jnanis*, like Sanak, Sanat, etc.

86. Although God dwells in the heart of all the creatures, nobody is aware of this, their own state. Such is the inconceivable and great power of illusion of this *Maya*.

87. Hence, without giving up the false ego that 'I am the doer of action, I alone, am the enjoyer', and without surrendering to Him who dwells within, we cannot be liberated.

88. Discriminate between the Eternal and the transient; listen, reflect and contemplate deeply on it and attain the six *sadhanas*[5] or means, like *shama, dama*, etc. Only then will ignorance be destroyed.

89. 'The world is separate from me, while I am limited, differentiated'; the awareness that 'This body itself is me' — this is ignorance, pure and unalloyed.

90. In the *Vedanta-shastra* which propounds *Jnana*, the most compassionate commentators have described in detail, the '*Anubandha-chatushtaya*'[6].

91. Three of them are '*Adhikari*', '*Vishaya*' and '*Sambandha*' and the fourth '*Anubandha*' is the '*Prayojan*'.

92. The Oneness between the Being and the Brahman is the main subject of this *Vedanta* and the removal of ignorance about this proposition of Oneness, is the '*Prayojan*' or object.

93. The dispelling of this basic ignorance is in itself the realization of the true Self. Hence by some ingenious device or other, it is necessary to destroy ignorance.

94. So long as the idea of separateness between them is not removed, no one can be called a *Jnani*. The *Jnana* of the egoist can only be called total ignorance.

95. Himself, he parades as a *Jnani*, but his conduct is improper, his awareness is accursed. He is as soundly asleep as Kumbhakarna[7].

96. He who does not act in conformation with the *Vedas*, nor observes the rules of *Varna* and *Ashram*, for such a one, the only means of purifying his heart is the removal of ignorance or *a-vidya*.

97. Even Brahmadev and others have been cheated by the *trigunas*, like *Sattva*, etc., by different passions of sense-objects, like word, etc., by the reproductive organs and by the tongue.

98. All the animate beings in the world are enveloped by the beginningless *a-vidya* and *Maya*. Attracted by anger, envy, and other passions, these are all engulfed by ignorance.

99. The being is bound by ignorance. He must sever all connection with the bonds of ignorance, desire and *karma* for the pure Self to manifest.

100. Leeches cling tightly to the teats which are swollen and oozing with milk. But their real fondness is for the impure (blood). What do they care for the milk?

101. Look at the frog and the black bee! The beautiful lotus is the abode of both. But the bee flits amid the fragrant pollen, while the frog feasts on the mire.

102. In front of him, he sees a store of knowledge, yet the fool is drawn towards ignorance. To the fool, ignorance itself appears as knowledge. What will an elaborate discourse on *Jnana* be to him?

103. When ignorance is eradicated, *Brahmajnana* will appear on its own. Hence know, that it is necessary to establish first, what ignorance is.

104. Nothing is as sacred as *Brahmajnana* in all the three worlds and it is to the instruction in it that the greatest importance attaches. Without it life is futile.

105. Had Brahman been the subject of intellectual exercise, at least one of the various organs would have indicated or proved its existence.

106. Though the *Smriti* proclaims that 'the principle of Brahman, though beyond the comprehension of the organs, is comprehensible to the intellect', yet it is not acceptable to the *Shruti*.

107. If intellect, etc., cease to exist, then the very object of comprehending also ceases and there remains no room for accepting the existence of Brahman.

108. It is well-known everywhere, that whatever can be known by the organs, exists. But if it be so, then the Brahman should never exist at all.

109. Such will be the interpretation. But this is meaningless. According to the traditional interpretation, based on profound, careful thought, the intellect also has a perpetual, ceaseless existence.

110. It may disappear, but even there, it is present by the experience of its existence. The Atman is undoubtedly, the origin of the Universe. Hence even when anything appears to be extinct, its existence always continues.

111. When a stone is thrown at an earthen jar, the shape is destroyed, leaving only the pieces. Though the shape of the jar disappears, the pieces indicate the existence of the jar.

112. Though the purpose of the jar is destroyed, there is no end to the existence of the jar. The pieces of the jar are the evidence of its existence and the essence of the existence of its purpose remains in them.

113. The end of any work is never in a void. Its end always implies its existence and its proof is that good conscience is implicit in the experience of Truth.

114. Places of pilgrimage, religious vows are all sacred, but the holiest of holy is *Jnana*; *Bhajan, pooja,* etc., are meaningless without *Brahmajnana.*

115. The mind is polluted by ignorance; but the cleansing of that mind is not possible without devotion of God. Without devotion *Jnana* does not sprout.

116. Hence first recognize ignorance. Clearly understand its nature and description, so that release can be obtained from its bondage. Devotion alone, is the means of knowing this.

117. As the child born with his legs first, will see the buried treasure, the moment collyrium is put in its eyes, similarly, once refuge is taken in devotion, ignorance is dispelled and knowledge arises.

118. Knowledge itself is Self-realization and its basis is dispelling of ignorance. But unless devotion to God comes, the power of *Maya* cannot be overcome.

119. Knowledge and ignorance are all mixed up together, from which, ignorance must be picked out, carefully. Leave out the stones and take only the rice to cook in the boiling water.

120. Seeing God everywhere, in all beings, he who performs various forms of worship such as *Jnana, Yajna,* etc., and thus sees the all-pervading Shrikrishna, he burns all ignorance for the sake of knowledge.

121. Now see the nature of this *Jnana-yajna,* where the aphorism, 'I am Brahman' is the pillar (to tie the sacrificial animals); the five gross elements are the canopy for the *Yajna* and the separateness between God and his creatures is the sacrificial animal.

122. The five sense organs, the five vital airs are the ingredients for the rites and rituals and in the '*Kunda*'[8] which is the mind and the intellect, the fire, i.e. Knowledge, is kindled.

123. Man is the master here, who is performing the *Yajna* and who offers ignorance as the clarified butter, to this fire. His being absorbed in Self-rejoicing is the '*Avabhruthsnan*'[9] that the man receives.

124. In short, without the clarified butter of ignorance, the fire of Knowledge can never be kindled, in which is burnt the separateness or duality between God and the Being, to bring out the true knowledge of oneness between them.

125. As a crystal-clear mirror covered with dirt or the glow of fire dimmed by smoke, so is Knowledge which is overpowered by passions, like lust and anger, covered up in ignorance.

126. *Rahu*[10] swallows up the moon or the moss covers clear water, so does this *Maya* cover Knowledge which is itself, self-illumined.

127. Even the minds of great *Jnanis* are bewildered and they have a fall. After knowing the remedy too, they are not saved and behave as they like.

128. They are blinded despite of having eyes. Giving up good company, they take to loose, shameless behaviour and are perforce, ruined by the bad company they keep and begin to behave as they please.

129. Having once taken up '*Vanaprasthashram*'[11], they turn again to '*Grihasthashram*'[11], doing, without fail, that which they should not do. They accept as a cherished thing, what they were earlier disgusted with.

130. Those who had exerted themselves to avoid sins are, by their destiny, induced to commit them. What can one say of such a state of things! Is this to be regarded as a class of *Jnanis*?

131. Though a great *Jnani*, who wants to avoid even the shadow of a sin, yet as a moth attracted to the lamp, he forgets to discriminate between good and bad.

132. Knowing full well that to commit a sin is ignorance, strongly induced by desire, he simply does not care for that anymore.

133. This whole class of actions is the work of desire. Desire is the root of all disaster and it comes out in the form of anger.

134. When fulfillment of a desire is thwarted, the same desire flares up in anger. And it is this that comes in the way of *Moksha*, at every step. This is the tendency that is obstructive to Knowledge.

135. As it is, this creature is harassed by desires and anger. These passions are always hovering around Brahman, quite in a line with the *Jnana*.

136. Without water, they drown you; without fire, they burn you; without weapon, they kill you and without rope, they bind you.

137. Even a *Jnani* does not last before them. They defeat a *Jnani* on a wager and have the power to bring about *Mahapralaya* (or total destruction of the Universe), and swallow up a creature, quite without his knowledge.

138. Just like the coils of the *Kalasarpa* or Death at the root of the sandalwood tree, similarly, the placenta of desires and anger lies, coiled up, surrounding the foetus, i.e. knowledge.

139. Organs, intellect and the mind are the seats of desire. Through them, she (*Maya*) acts to cover up Knowledge and tempts that creature.

140. If you want the sandalwood, then destroy that serpent. By removing the veil of desires and anger, gain that treasure of Knowledge.

141. Can anyone get the sandalwood without destroying the serpent? Without killing that wicked serpent, can anyone reach the buried treasure?

142. Similarly, to have Self-realization and to reach God, removing the veil of *Maya* is the only means.

143. Hence first, the organs must be subdued, which will destroy passions like lust and anger. The being is over-powered by desires and passions, and ignorance completely covers up Knowledge.

144. Senses are more subtle than the body, but the mind is even more subtle. Subtler than the mind is the intellect, while more subtle even than the intellect, is God.

145. Beyond the customs and conventions of worldly life, is this highest, eternal truth, which itself, is that most beneficent God and is also the nectar-sweet real Self.

146. Pure, Enlightened, Eternal and Ever-free, is the same Principle, which remains undifferentiated. It is that same Principle in the highest Bliss, which is the Pure Consciousness within.

147. What is called '*Panchikaran*'[12], is the manifestation of the form of *Maya* and to understand it, the only means is '*Adhyarope*' and '*Apavad*'[13].

148. The five elements, when not combined and gross or '*a-panchikrit*' are called '*Panchatanmatra*'[14]. Their function is to bring to the *Pran*, mind and intellect, the astral body of the *Atman*.

149. See the five elements that have undergone '*Panchikaran*', from there is born '*Virat*', that being the name by which the *Jnanis* call the physical manifestation (gross body) of that Universal *Atman*.

150. It is only ignorance of the real Self, which is the efficient Cause of the gross body (*sthool-deha*) and of the astral body (*sookshma* or *linga deha*). Know that it is apparently substantial but unreal and unmanifest and is the efficient Cause of the *Atman*.

151. This, well-known as '*Karan-shareer*' (or *Karan-deha*)[15], which is the reflection of the Pure Consciousness and is also called illusory and unmanifest, is created only out of ignorance.

152. Ignorance of the *Atman* is the cause of this, which is neither with bodily organs, nor without them, nor is it both. This body is destroyed only with the knowledge of Oneness between the Brahman and the *Atman*.

153. To be Self-absorbed is itself called *Moksha*; there is no *Moksha* other than this. To be fixed in the true Self is *Moksha*.

154. Only by the Knowledge of Oneness between the Brahman and the *Atman*, will ignorance be dispelled. Hence it is necessary to describe what is ignorance in order to understand it.

155. Because of ignorance or *a-vidya*, it became '*shabal*'[16]. It brought differentiation or '*shabalatva*' to the Brahman. It was given the name '*Sat*' and in this way it became a subject of speech.

156. Although originally it is beyond the comprehension of the sense-organs, speech made it comprehensible to the intellect. Only then did it enter the mind and find expression in '*Omkar*'.

157. He who leaves this body, meditating on this '*Omkar*' and chanting God's name, will find fulfilment of his life.

158. Through this expressible form of Brahman, i.e. '*Omkar*', the unmanifest manifests itself. From the Unmanifest comes the '*Mahat-tatva*'[17], which gives rise to the ego.

159. In the ego are the '*Panchtanmatra*', from which come the five elements. Ultimately, it is from the five elements that this world is created.

160. The manifestation of this *a-vidya*, *Maya*, is itself the form and attributes of this world. To destroy this *a-vidya*, it is necessary to describe ignorance.

161. The most holy, clean, Pure Consciousness and '*shabal*', which is different from it, cannot be mixed up.

162. Know that the (directly) perceived Brahman is different; it is very much different from the describable Brahman. Hence these veils of ignorance should be removed by the power of instruction.

163. When one dreams in the sleep, though the eyes are closed, the seeing mind itself sees all the three worlds. And it is *a-vidya* which is the cause of this.

164. In reality, the object is one thing, but it appears to be quite another. A rope appears to be a snake or an oyster-shell seems to contain silver within.

165. These are just the sun-rays, and yet people call them a mirage. This is only a sport of *Maya*, before whom even the *Jnanis* are powerless.

166. Taking in hand a lighted firebrand, when someone turns it round and round quickly, an (illusory) ring of fire is produced and we realize how inconceivable are the doings of this *Maya*.

167. Really, it is only fire and there is no place for a ring of fire. Similarly, all this business and fuss of *Maya* and temptations has needlessly created this worldly life.

168. With such a firm resolve of the mind, when delusion goes away, this worldly life too, fades away in an instant, and, 'I am this body' and, 'my home, my wife', all this is reduced to a futile exercise.

169. Totally ensnared by the bonds of desire, such as sons, livestock, and so on, even those who call themselves *Pandits* and *Jnanis* can enjoy not an atom of happiness.

170. In their minds they have a great conceit that they are proficient in the *Shastras* and very wise; that there is no one like them, and therefore they are always discontented.

171. This is *Maya* or ignorance or *a-vidya-Prakritipradhan*[18]. It is this that the *Jnanis* dispel at the beginning, so that *Jnana* or Knowledge manifests itself.

172. *Jnana* is self-enlightened and it does not need to be taught or instructed about. Once ignorance is removed, the brilliance of Knowledge will appear on its own.

173. When a scintillating gem gets buried in dirt and debris and years have passed by, its memory too, is extinguished.

174. When by a wonderful concurrence of destiny and one's merit, it comes to hand at some future date, it appears to have lost all its original radiance, being buried under mud and stone.

175. But once it is scrubbed clean and the covering of dirt removed, it regains its original brilliance. Same is the state of Knowledge.

176. The dirt and mud is ignorance. It is this ignorance that covers Knowledge. Once the dirt is removed, the gem will naturally scintillate.

177.   Discriminating Knowledge about things transient and permanent, destroys sinful deeds and brings purification and virtue. It is this that gives rise to Knowledge.

178.   This world is a market place of *Maya*, full of variegated things, real and fake. Many are the customers here, who buy the fake, mistaking them for the real.

179.   And even the great and the wise are at their wits' end, separating the fake from the real. One must understand those qualities which are deceptive.

180.   Hence one must have with him a knowledgeable man or an expert. He (here Sadguru) will at once show why a fake thing looks like the real one and ignorance will then disappear, at last.

181.   When ignorance is removed, only Knowledge will remain and *Maya* will be easily dispelled. Know that what remains is the Truth. What is real needs no proof.

182.   Although the mind's eye is bright and clear, it is enveloped by the darkness of imagined notions. That darkness is dispelled by instruction. All that then remains is *Jnana*.

183.   Really, it is just a garland that one sees on the way, but seen in the fading light of the evening, it appears to be a snake, the reason for the illusion being the veil of ignorance.

184.   When the torch hidden in the pocket is lit, the ignorance disappears and the real form manifests itself. The illusion of the snake is automatically dispelled.

185.   Hence to remove the harm caused by ignorance, instruction is the only means, for which the *Jnanis* wear out their bodies in explaining what ignorance is.

186.   It must, first of all, be recognized that whatever one is destined to endure, good or bad,while in this worldly life is due to the past *karma* performed out of ignorance.

187.   *Jnana* is the only Truth and Brahman is eternal, while *Maya*, *a-vidya* are all illusions. When these illusions are removed, only then will the confusion about *Jnana* be removed.

188. Who will call him a *Jnani* whose ego is not subdued? The seat of ego is called ignorance incarnate.

189. This visible, bewitching worldly life, which is called a deluge of *Maya* and in which this world is totally engrossed, has for its basis, ignorance.

190. It is created from ignorance and its splendour is also born of ignorance. The feeling of plurality where there is oneness, has its seat in ignorance.

191. At a time when the light is dim with a shade of lingering darkness, the rope on the way appears to be a serpent, though in reality it is a rope and this creates intense fear.

192. The illusion of a snake is nothing but ignorance, which has covered up Knowledge and unless this ignorance is removed, the mind will not become fearless.

193. To some, it is a flower-garland; to the eyes of some others, it is a stick. In short, it is all a delusion, boundless tricks of misconceptions.

194. Conforming to the aphorisms of *Veda-Shastras*, the Theist who believes in God, he alone is deserving of *Brahmajnana*. An Atheist will never gain it for birth after birth.

195. Those who look upon this world from a contrary viewpoint see it as it appears (as opposed to the world as a manifestation of God). But this is their misconception. They have no release from the birth-death cycle. The *Brahma-tatva*, which is so very inaccessible to them is very easy of attainment to the spiritually deserving.

196. Here, a mere discourse is of no avail, nor any authoritative knowledge of the *Vedas*, or the intellect to comprehend many learned volumes or having read and being proficient in them.

197. Words will give only literal knowledge. How can they convey the true perception of the Brahman? The intellect has all the power of discriminating knowledge, but the real thing, i.e. Brahman is beyond its power.

198. The *Shrutis* had great and earnest desire for it, but had to turn back, not having found the Brahman. Such is the magnificence of this real Truth. The intellect can go no further.

199. The '*shat-darshanas*' are exhausted and kept on arguing and debating about it, while the real thing remained where it was as the words could never comprehend it.

200. Even the great scholars were before it as glow-worms before the sun. For once the Brahman is attained the web of empty words fades away.

201. Just see, in this world, at night, all the activities are carried on in the light of the lamp, but when the sun rises in the morning, the lamp is disregarded completely.

202. Hence, how can that be instructed, which is not the subject of speech at all? So while narrating an allegorical tale, the aim of the speaker should be the removal of ignorance.

203. When *upasana* is carried out with the belief in the existence of the *Atman*, the *Atman* is pleased and reveals his real nature, thus becoming accessible to his worshipper.

204. The *Atman* favours those who worship him, when they meditate on him as God Himself and regards them both as one and the same.

205. For it, there is no other means. The *Atman* must show favour. Seeing that the Seeker is inclined towards himself, the *Atman*, on his own, bestows Grace on him.

206. At the conclusion of the subject of a book, the speakers always entreat the listeners to pardon them for the exertion of listening that they have been subjected to. This is the customary manner of the wise and the learned, everywhere.

207. But this is not so about this *Satcharit*. The skill of writing it is not mine. Sai himself, has got his own story written, giving the pen in my hand.

208. Hence I am not the author and no one here, is wearied out on my account. If I say to the listeners, 'forgive me', then the merit of writing it falls on my head.

209. But no credit is mine here, nor does any blame attach to me. Where Sai himself is the doer, it is only by his Grace that the subject is brought to a conclusion.

210. Taking Sai's permission, I have written it as he related to me, the narration about ignorance, for everyone to listen to.

211. To display his own glory, his prowess, his consequence, Gurudev entered my mind to narrate the significance of the subject.

212. Those who find fault with this book or those who consider it as an adornment to me, they are both equally worthy of respect and are Shri Narayan, incarnate.

213. For the greatest benefit of the devotees, Shri Sai himself created this, his own Life story and holding his hand in his own, got Hemad to write out the story.

214. His incarnating in a human body was solely for instructing the people graciously; for destroying evil thoughts and obstinate resistance and for leading the people on the right path.

215. Hence Hemad prostrates in obeisance, single-mindedly, at his feet. May the listeners listen with full concentration to the fascinating stories that follow.

Weal be to all! Here ends the fiftieth chapter of
"Shri Sai Samarth Satcharit" called
'Dispelling of Ignorance',
as inspired by the saints and the virtuous
and composed by his devotee Hemadpant.

Notes

1. Refer Ch. 11, note 8.
2. The oblique line raised upon the horizontal limb of the Nagari character, conveying the power of the vowels, like 'a' and 'o'.
3. The four great aphoristic dicta, which reveal the Supreme Truth.
4. He was the son of Krishnadwaipayan Vyas. He was a born yogi. His book of discourse of King Parikshita is known as *Bhagavata* and is one of the 18 *Puranas*.
5. Refer Ch. 17, note 3.
6. The four *Anubandha* or correlations of a treatise or discourse, viz. *Vishaya* or the subject matter; *Prayojana* or the use, purpose or object; *Sambandha* or the congruity, consistency or coherence (as of style or diction or manner of treatment with the subject matter, or object); and *Adhikari* or the person for whose use it is designed or to whom it is addressed or is appropriate.
7. The name of a drowsy demon brother of Ravana.
8. An enclosed space on the surface of a metal, square-mouthed vessel for receiving and preserving consecrated fire.
9. *Avabruth* is a ceremony at the conclusion of a sacrifice, and *snan* is ablutions. Hence the formal ablutions after the performance of *Avabruth*.
10. Refer Ch. 39, note 1.
11. This is the third of the four stages or *ashrams* in life where, renouncing the second *Grihasthashram* (Householder's-stage), they return to it once again.
12. Combining amicably together of the five elementary substances (earth, water, air, fire and ether), as in the formation of worlds.
13. *Adhyarope* is superimposition and *Apavad* is exception.
14. The five principles, essences or subtle rudiments respectively of the five elementary substances.
15. As *sthool deha* and *linga deha* are the product of ignorance, the *karan deha*, after all its causation and production, falls resolved into ignorance or *a-vidya*.
16. To become differentiated because of *Maya*.
17. Pure Knowledge.
18. It is also called *Pradhan-tatva*.

51

A Narration of the Accounts
of three Devotees

MY OBEISANCE TO SHRI GANESH, TO SHRI SARASWATI, AND SHRI GURUMAHARAJ! TO THE FAMILY DEITY, TO SHRI SITA-RAMACHANDRA, MY MOST HUMBLE OBEISANCE! I BOW IN REVERENCE TO THE MOST VENERABLE GURU SHRI SAINATH!

1. Glory to you, O Sai! The Mainstay of the devotees and greatest among the gurus that you are, who explains the significance of the *Geeta* and gives all the *siddhis* to the devotees, bestow favour on me.

2. To cool the heat, there grows sandalwood on the *Malaygiri*[1], or, to comfort people in the world rains the cloud on this earth.

3. Or, the flowers bloom in Spring, so that the gods may be worshipped. Or again, a series of tales, fables and parables come into existence to bring contentment to the listeners.

4. The listeners who listen and the narrator who narrates are both sacred. The ears of one who listens, become purified and so does the speech of one who narrates.

5. In the last chapter, an exposition of the stanza 'Learn that by humble reverence...etc.' was given to point out how Knowledge appears when ignorance is dispelled.

6. At the end of the *Bhagavad Geeta*, in stanza seventy-two, at the end of the eighteenth chapter, Shrikrishna asks Arjun.

7. "Has the exposition that has been given so far, dispelled thy distraction (of thought), caused by ignorance?" Such was the clear question. He did not ask, "Have you gained Knowledge?"

8. And similar had been the acknowledgement given by Partha (Arjun), who said, 'Destroyed is my delusion and recognition has been gained by me through Thy Grace.' He did not say that 'Knowledge has been gained', but only that *Maya* has been destroyed.

9. And *Maya* itself, is ignorance. Those who have understood the significance of the *Geeta*, already know that they only appear as two words, while there is no difference in their meaning.

10. And Arjun has also said the same to Shrikrishna at the beginning of the eleventh chapter that 'The Supreme Mystery[2] — the discourse concerning the Self, which thou hast given, out of Grace for me — by this, my bewilderment is gone from me'.

11. Now in this present, new chapter, let us relate the amazing account about how Baba firmly established Kakasaheb (Dikshit) in Shirdi, in the beginning.

12. Listen to it all from the beginning, as to how his preordained link (*rinanubandha*) with Shirdi and his close and steadfast connection with Sai, was responsible for this event.

13. Young and old, already know many stories of Kakasaheb. But everyone does not know how he initially came to Shirdi.

14. Grace of God is a matter of previously accumulated merit and it leads to the meeting with the Sadguru, which, in turn, brings the disciple a blissful joy of Self-rejoicing.

15. It is in this context that this chapter will describe to the listeners, three tales about the rare good fortune of three devotees, listening to which, the hearts of the listeners will be filled with joy.

16. *Crores* of other means for attaining spiritual progress, will not help, unless the Sadguru bestows his grace.

17. Listen to a sweet tale with the same purport. It will satisfy the fond desire of the listeners and in their minds will develop a strong wish for attaining their own weal.

18. May the listeners listen attentively to this most purifying and beneficial chapter, which brings great satisfaction to the guru-devotees.

19. Hari Sitaram Dikshit, remembered with love and respect by all Sai devotees, was well-known by the name Kakasaheb.

20. And it is his past account, which is so delightful to the well-informed connoisseurs, that I shall present respectfully, to the eager and faithful devotees, for their pleasure.

21. He who had not even known the name 'Sai', till the year 1909, became a great, well-known devotee of Sai, later on.

22. Many years had passed after the completion of his University education, when Nanasaheb Chandorkar once visited him at Lonavala.

23. Dikshit was his old friend and as they were meeting after many years, they also talked about each other's joys and sorrows.

24. In the city of London, as Dikshit was getting into a public transport vehicle, his foot slipped and the injury caused to the leg could not be set right, even by a hundred different remedies that he had tried.

25. The topic of that ailment casually cropped up, during conversation, when Nana suddenly recollected Shri Sai Baba's powers in that context.

26. 'Do you sincerely feel that the lameness of that leg should go completely? Then come for my guru's *darshan*', said Nana to him, at that time.

27. Nana then most gladly narrated to Dikshit, as a thing of great marvel, everything about Sai and about the great power of that greatest of saints.

28. "My man, however far away he may be from me — even beyond the seven seas, I will at once, draw him to me, as a sparrow is pulled with a string tied to her."

29. Such were always Baba's words and to explain further, Nana added, 'Unless you belong to Baba, you will never be attracted to him.

30. 'You will never have his *darshan*, if you are not his own. And this itself, is Baba's surest mark. You can never go there, all of your own will!'

31. So, on hearing Sai's description, Dikshit felt great satisfaction in his mind. He said to Nana, 'I will take Baba's *darshan*.

32. 'Oh, what is the importance of this leg of mine? After all, this whole body is destructible. May the deformity of the leg remain for any length of time! I am not worried about it.

33. 'If I go for your guru's *darshan*, it is to attain the blissful *Moksha*. I do not desire these trivial pleasures and I do not entreat them.

34. 'There is no happiness other than the Brahman. That is the one and only invaluable pleasure and for this one priceless pleasure, I will become your guru's servant.

35. 'Let the lameness of the leg remain. About that I am not bothered. But 'bring this lame, weak mind of mine to its proper state'. This is my prayer.

36. 'Doing '*upasana*', I am wearied out, and yet, my mind does not remain firm and steady. With great effort, I try to keep it under control, but it slips away, unknown to me.

37. 'Firmly resolving in my mind, however alert I may keep, there is no saying when it will give me the slip. Such is the puzzle of this mind!

38. 'And hence, Nana, I will take your guru's *darshan* with all my heart and will entreat him to remove the lameness of my mind'.

39. Sai has the greatest pleasure and enthusiasm for the spiritual welfare of him, who, being disinterested in the pleasures of this mortal body, has great fondness for the highest Bliss.

40. Those days, the only subject everywhere was the forthcoming election to the Legislative Council and many people were engaged in this work at different places.

41. Kakasaheb too, was meeting friends to gather public support for his candidature. And in connection with this work, quite unexpectedly he came to Ahmednagar.

42.   There was one *sardar* there, called Kakasaheb Mirikar, with whom Dikshit was on friendly and cordial terms, so he stayed at his place.

43.   At that same time, an exhibition of horses was held at Ahmednagar, for which various people were engaged in work.

44.   Balasaheb Mirikar, the *mamledar* of Kopergaon, had also come to Ahmednagar for it.

45.   The work for which Dikshit had come, was finished and he began to think, 'How can my visit to Shirdi be arranged? Who will take me up to there?' and so on.

46.   As soon as his work there was over, his thoughts turned to Shirdi and the only preoccupation of his mind now, was to have the opportunity of Baba's *darshan*.

47.   Dikshit was very much worried as to 'who will come with me and take me forward to present me at Baba's feet?'

48.   As soon as the election work was over, Dikshit began to worry about going to Shirdi and began asking Mirikar very eagerly, regarding this.

49.   Balasaheb was the son of Kakasaheb Mirikar. So they both began to deliberate as to who should accompany Dikshit.

50.   For, if one of them were to go, no other companion would be needed. So they began to think who between them should definitely go with him.

51.   The plans a man makes have human limitations, while God's plans are altogether different. For Dikshit's visit to Shirdi, an unexpected thing happened.

52.   Here, Dikshit had a restless agitation of mind, but there, at another place, there was a different kind of movement. Seeing such a keen desire of the devotee for his *darshan*, Samarth himself was moved by compassion.

53.   Worried and thoughtful as Dikshit sat, Madhavrao himself arrived at Ahmednagar, to the astonishment of all.

54.   Madhavrao's father-in-law wired him from Ahmednagar that his mother-in-law was very serious and that he should come with his family to meet her.

55. On receiving the telegram, he at once prepared to leave and on obtaining Baba's permission too, both he and his wife went to the Chithali station.

56. They caught the three o'clock train and both went to Ahmednagar. The *tonga* stopped at the door and both got down.

57. Meanwhile, Nanasaheb Panse and Appasaheb Gadre happened to pass that way, at that very moment, on their way to the exhibition.

58. Quite unexpectedly, they saw Madhavrao alighting and were both very much surprised. But they could hardly contain their joy.

59. They said, 'Just see what a stroke of luck that Madhavrao, the '*badva*'[3] of Shirdi should be here! Who could be a better person than him to take Dikshit to Shirdi?'

60. Then calling out to him, they said, 'Dikshitkaka has come to Mirikar's house. Go and see for yourself Baba's marvellous *leela*!

61. 'Dikshit is a remarkable friend of ours. You will also, be introduced to him and since he is very eager to go to Shirdi, he will be very happy by your coming here.'

62. So saying to him, they also gave the news to Dikshit, on hearing which, his worry was removed and he felt very happy.

63. And as he went to his father-in-law's house, he found that his mother-in-law was well. Madhavrao rested a little, when Mirikar sent for him.

64. In deference to the invitation, as the sun went down a little, Madhavrao went to meet Dikshit.

65. That was their first meeting. Balasaheb introduced them to each other and they both made a firm plan of going to Shirdi by the train at ten o'clock at night.

66. Having decided thus, just see the wonder, thereafter. Balasaheb moved aside the curtain on Baba's picture.

67. This was Baba's photograph, which Megha, Baba's steadfast devotee, used to worship with a loving devotion, regarding him to be the god Shankar of the three eyes.

68. And because its glass had broken, it had initially been taken from Shirdi for Ahmednagar with Balasaheb, to be repaired.

69. This was that same photograph, which being now repaired seemed to have been waiting only for Dikshit, as it was kept in Mirikar's drawing room, covered with a piece of cloth.

70. There was still some time before Balasaheb could return after the horses' exhibition was over and hence it was entrusted to Madhavrao, to be taken to Shirdi.

71. After removing the covering, it was left open and entrusted to Madhavrao, when Mirikar said, 'Go happily to Shirdi in Baba's company'.

72. As that most marvellous photograph came before his eyes, for the first time, Kakasaheb was filled with joy, and having made obeisance, kept gazing at it.

73. On seeing such a strange event, as also, the beautiful sacred picture of Sai Samarth so unexpectedly, Dikshit's eyes were bewitched.

74. That on the way itself, the very figure of him, whose *darshan* was desired so keenly, should come before the eyes, was something that gave him great pleasure.

75. And then again, that it should have come from Shirdi to Kakasaheb Mirikar's house, when Dikshit too, happened to be there, was a coincidence most strange!

76. As if Sainath had himself come under this pretext to the house of his devotee Mirikar, to satisfy the wish in Dikshit's mind!

77. The meeting with Nanasaheb at Lonavala and the conversation with him there, was itself the beginning of Baba's magnetism, when the seeds of the meeting with him were sown.

78. Why else, should this photo from Shirdi come here at this very time and remain covered for so long at this place?

79. However, having planned thus, taking the photograph with them, Madhavrao and Dikshit set out for Shirdi very happily.

80. That same night after dinner, both went to the station and purchased second-class tickets, which they took with them.

81. The rattling of the train was heard at the stroke of ten and they saw that the second class compartment was packed to capacity.

82. In the face of this difficulty, both grew very worried. Moreover, very little time was left for the departure of the train. What arrangement could now be done?

83. And so, on perceiving the crowds, both decided to go back to their respective places and go to Shirdi the next day.

84. Suddenly, Dikshit found, quite unexpectedly, that he knew the guard of that train, who made arrangements for them to sit in the first-class compartment, quite comfortably.

85. Later on, after boarding the train, stories of Baba flowed freely and to their hearts' content. Madhavrao narrated the nectar-sweet stories and Dikshit was overcome with joy, as he listened.

86. In this way, time passed quickly during the journey, being occupied with varied pleasures. The train reached Kopergaon, where they both got down very happily.

87. At that time Dikshit was most happy to see Nanasaheb at the station. Both were meeting each other, most unexpectedly.

88. As it happened, he was also going to Shirdi to take Baba's *darshan* and all the three were quite astonished at this unexpected conjunction of circumstances.

89. The three of them, then hired a *tonga* and set out, conversing with each other. On the way, they bathed in the Godavari and thus arrived in holy Shirdi.

90. Later, on taking Sai's *darshan*, Dikshit's heart melted with love; the eyes filled with tears and the water of Self-rejoicing flowed freely and profusely.

91. Sai then said very clearly to him, "I too, waited for you and then sent Shamya straight to Nagar to meet you".

92. With powerful emotion the hair on Dikshit's body stood on end, the throat choked with a flood of tears; the heart became elated as perspiration broke out all over the body.

93. The body quivered imperceptibly; the mind became Self-absorbed and the eyes half-opened with the profusion of joy that crowded in them.

94. 'Today my eyes are fulfilled', so saying he embraced Baba's feet. His heart felt blessed and the entire creation could not contain his joy.

95. Many years passed, thereafter. Full faith was reposed in Sai's feet. He attained Sai's Grace totally and he offered his body in Sai's service.

96. He also built a house, to be able to serve Baba properly. For many years he stayed in Shirdi and spread Sai's greatness.

97. In short, one who desires his *darshan* will certainly have his wish fulfilled. Sai is the Abode of Peace and Rest to his devotees and brings them greatest happiness.

98. There are many Chakor birds longing for the moon, but there is only one moon to them all. Similarly, though a mother may have many sons, there is only one mother to all of them.

99. To the sun there are many lotuses, but to the lotuses there is only one sun. To your devotees there is no limit, but you are their only father and *Guruvar.*

100. Numerous Chatak birds long for the Cloud, but there is only one Cloud to these Chatakas. Similarly, he has many devotees, but he is their only father and mother.

101. All those who easily surrender with good feelings, he not only protects their honour, but lovingly, takes their work to successful completion. This can be seen even today, after his *niryan.*

102. In this world, death puts an end to the life of every living creature. But to Dikshit, Sai made a promise: "I will take you away in an aeroplane."

103. And as were Sai's words, so was Dikshit's end, even as he was singing Sai's praises. This, I have seen with my own eyes.

104. While we were both sitting on a berth in a train engrossed in stories of Sai Samarth, he seemed to have been quickly lifted up in an aeroplane.

105. See how he suddenly availed of the right moment and resting his neck on my shoulder, unexpectedly, got into the plane and attained the boundless, lasting happiness.

106. There was no turning and twisting of the body, no rattling in the throat, no pain. While walking and talking normally, the body just became still and lifeless, in front of everyone.

107. In this way, he let go of the human body, and merged the flame of his life with that of the Self in an instant.

108. At the end, since his mind was absorbed at Sai's feet, his bodily ego was completely shed; his mind was an absolute offering to God.

109. It was on the *Ekadashi* day in the dark fortnight of the lunar month in the month *Jyeshtha* (May-June), in the year 1926, that Dikshit attained to *Brahmapad*, abandoning this earth.

110. You may call it death or that an aeroplane came for him, but he merged at Sai's feet. And this will be accepted by anyone.

111. He who feels that he can repay the debt of this kind should really be regarded as one without faith and devotion. For, this debt cannot be repaid, even in a dream, by giving anything that is visible in the world.

112. If you try to give the '*Chintamani*', you will only add, forever, to the worries, and if you think that by giving it you will have repaid him who gives the inconceivable, your reasoning is childish.

113. And even if you offer the *Kalpataru* to the guru, the guru is himself skilled in giving a thing, which is unchangeable or unparalleled. How can that be repaid?

114. Now, over and above all these, if you give the '*parees*' to the guru, that *parees* will only transform into scintillating gold, whereas the guru will give you the bliss of the Brahman to drink.

115. If you offer *Kamdhenu* to the guru and feel that you have repaid his debt, you will only increase toil. The guru, who is himself free from desire, gives that which involves no toil or trouble.

116. Those who wish to repay the guru's beneficence, by offering him all the wealth in the world and thus offer what is *Mayik* or illusory to him who gives what is not illusory but real, can they ever repay him by doing so?

117. Even if this body be given in offering, to the guru, the body too is but mortal and even if the *Jeeva* be surrendered to him, it is, in itself, illusory.

118. Sadguru is the giver of the true, the real thing. By offering the Sadguru illusory things how can that giver repay him? It is just impossible.

119. Hence, with single-minded devotion and faith, prostrating in obeisance, worship the Sadguru's feet by bowing your head on them, and remembering with gratitude his beneficence.

120. To remember the debt of the guru constantly, is truly an ornament to the disciple; while those disciples who try to repay it will only lose their own happiness.

121. Having heard the story so far, the listeners are now thirsting for more and, seeing their eager curiosity, I shall narrate one more story.

122. Like the worldly people, the saints also show their brotherly love, or rather convey in essence, how they are prompt in guiding the people.

123. Or, maybe, Sai instructs in spiritual matters, for the benefit of his devotees, by himself taking on different roles.

124. A brief story with this significance will now be narrated. Listen to it respectfully, O listeners, so that you will come to know how the saints recognize the mark of other saints, without being told.

125. Once, Sri Vasudevananda of the order of *sannyasins* called 'Saraswati' came to the famous Rajmahendra city, on the bank of Shri Godavari.

126. He had great intuitive knowledge and was a staunch advocate of *Karma marg* (Path of Action), the sacred Ganges of whose fame, still echoes on the surface of this earth.

127. On hearing such fame that travelled from ear to ear, faithful devotees from Nanded, like the noted lawyer Pundalikrao and others, made a firm resolve to take his *darshan*.

128. And so, these people set out and arrived at the Rajmahendra city. In the morning they went to the banks of Goda for the Swami's *darshan*.

129. In the auspicious time of the morning, all those people from Nanded set out to bathe in the Ganga (i.e. Godavari), singing *stotras*.

130. Seeing the Swami standing there, they prostrated in obeisance, with good feelings. As questions of well-being, etc., were mutually being exchanged, the topic of Shirdi came up, quite casually.

131. And as Sai's name came to his ear, Swami folded his own hands in obeisance and said, 'He is our brother and is completely free from desires. We have great love for him.'

132. Picking up a coconut from there and giving it to Pundalikrao, he said, 'Offer this at the lotus feet of our brother with folded hands, when you go to Shirdi.

133. 'Convey my obeisance and tell him from me that, 'May your Grace be upon this poor creature that I may never forget him. Let my love for him keep on growing, for ever.'

134. 'When you go to the Shirdi village again, remember to offer this to my brother with my regards.

135. 'Although we, the Swamis, have the restriction that we should not bow to anyone, yet on certain occasions it is beneficial to violate that rule.

136. 'Hence, when taking *Sai-darshan*, let not this thing be forgotten and remember to offer this coconut at Sai's feet.'

137. On hearing his words, Pundalikrao bowed at his feet and said, 'As is Swami's command, so will it be obeyed.

138. 'With great respect, I will obey the command. For I consider myself blessed, on account of this.' In this way, surrendering to the Swami with a single-minded devotion, Pundalikrao went away from there.

139. When the Swami called Baba his brother, was it meaningless? Baba always acted according to the *Shruti* which says, 'Till you are alive, always follow the vow of *Agnihotra* (i.e. keeping the fire, morning and evening, after offering the fire a handful of rice).'

140. What people called the '*dhuni*', would always be in front of Baba, burning day and night. It was Baba's vow to keep it so.

141. The well-recognized means like *Agnihotra*, for purifying the heart, which lead to attainment of Brahman, Baba practised in order to guide the people to the right path.

142. Shri Vasudevananda Saraswati was also a *yati* (*sannyasin*) as well as an observer of vows. Was it then meaningless that he called Baba his brother?

143. Then, before a month was over, Pundalikrao had an opportunity to go to Sai's *darshan*, with four friends.

144. They took with them their luggage, some fruits and also, without forgetting, the coconut. Their minds happy and at peace, they set out for Sai's *darshan*.

145. Then, they got down at Manmad and feeling thirsty they went to the stream, as there was still some time for the train to leave for Kopargaon.

146. As drinking water on an empty stomach is harmful to health, somebody who had brought a packet of '*Chivada*'[4], took it out.

147. A pinch of it in the mouth and it was found to be too hot. All their effort, they felt, was in vain as it would not be eatable without some fresh coconut.

148. So one of them said to the others, 'I think of a way out. Let us break a coconut and mix it in the *Chivada* and then just see the marvel of the taste!'

149. No sooner was the word 'coconut' pronounced than lo! here was a coconut, all ready! Where was the delay in breaking it open? Once mixed with it, the *Chivada* was simply delicious! After eating, they all drank water.

150. The moment the word 'coconut' was uttered, there appeared the coconut! No one asked whose it was. Such was the intensity of hunger, that it made them oblivious of everything else.

151. Later, after returning to the station and boarding the train to Kopargoan, Pundalikrao suddenly remembered the coconut, on the way.

152. Seeing that Shirdi had come near, Pundalikrao became very restless and agitated, that it was the coconut given by Vasudevananda, which was mixed in the *Chivada*, by mistake.

153. On realizing that the coconut had been broken, Pundalikrao was filled with fear and his whole body began to tremble. An offence had been committed against a saint.

154   He felt very sad, thinking, 'O, how grave a sin have I committed! Now the Swami's curse will come upon me. All that I prattled away there, has been in vain!'

155. On seeing such a fate of that coconut, Pundalikrao was stunned with amazement at his own deception.

156. 'Now, what can I offer to Baba? How can I explain to him? Oh, how can I show my face, now that I have lost the coconut!'

157. Pundalikrao was very sad in his mind on seeing that, that which was to be offered at Sai's feet, had already been eaten up. He thought to himself that it was indeed an insult to the saints!

158. 'Now, when Baba asks for the coconut, all will put their faces down in shame. Because in everyone's mind will be the guilt that it had been their snack at Manmad.

159. 'Today, the coconut is not with me, anymore. To tell him the truth, I feel ashamed; but it will not do to tell a lie, for Sai Maharaj is omniscient.'

160. However, when they took Sai's *darshan*, they were all very happy. With tears of joy springing in their eyes, all their faces were most cheerful.

161. At present, we send messages, day and night, on the wireless and flaunt our achievement, being filled with pride.

162. For this, we have to set up wireless stations, for which unlimited money is spent. But the saints do not require such means; they send messages through their minds.

163. At the time, when the Swami gave the coconut to Pundalikrao, he had already sent a wireless message to Sainath.

164. When Pundalikrao was taking *darshan*, Sai Baba said, all on his own, "Bring my thing which you have brought from my brother."

165. Greatly saddened, Pundalikrao said, holding fast to Sai's feet, 'There is no other way for me, but to beg your forgiveness. What can I say?

166. 'I had remembered about the coconut, but hungry as we were, when we went to the stream, all of us forgot, completely.

167. 'And as we ate the *Chivada*, this very same coconut was broken and mixed with it. But I will bring another coconut. Please accept it, without any anger.'

168. So saying, as Pundalikrao began to get up to bring the fruit, Sai Maharaj was seen stopping him, by holding his hand.

169. 'Unknowingly, I have betrayed the trust. But merciful as you are, please take me under your wing. I beg your forgiveness. Be merciful to me, for I am your great offender.

170   'A great, virtuous *sadhu*, like Swami, but even his word have I disregarded and that fruit which should have been offered to you, I have eaten it up.

171. 'This is to trangress the limit set by the saints. O, what a great sinner I am! Is there any way to atone for this sin? How, O how, could I have become so shameless!'

172. After listening to what had happened, Shri Sainath said, with a smile, "Why should one take the coconut in hand, at all, if it could not be safeguarded properly?

173. "Feeling certain that you will give me my thing, my brother placed full trust in your words.

174. "But should it result in this? Is this all your trustworthiness? My brother's wish was not fulfilled. Is this the way you work?"

175. He said, "The value of that fruit can never be equalled, even if you bring many others. But now, what had to happen, has happened. Why feel sad for it, needlessly?

176. "When Swami gave you that coconut, it was by my wish and it is only by my wish that the fruit was broken. Then why regard yourself as the doer unnecessarily?

177. "You harbour an egoistic attitude and hence regard yourself as an offender. But just adopt this attitude of being a non-doer and all your troubles can be avoided.

178. "Why do people own their meritorious deeds alone, and not their sins? After all, the power of both is the same. So, act without ego.

179. "That coconut fell in the hollow of your palms, only because I wished that you should come to meet me. This is the whole Truth.

180. "You are also my children. The fruit that fell in your mouth, has itself been offered to me. Regard it as having reached me, most certainly!"

181. Only when thus persuaded, did Pundalikrao's mind calm down by Baba's words and slowly, his sadness disappeared.

182. Loss of the coconut was just an excuse. By Baba's instruction his sadness of mind melted away. In this way, they who were enveloped by a false ego, became free from conceit and faultless.

183. This is the whole essence of this story, that as the mind becomes free from ego, so also does it become more deserving of spiritual welfare and will cross over this worldly life, effortlessly.

184. Now, listen to the unique and charming experience of a third devotee, and you will gradually see Baba's incomparable glory and the grandeur of his power.

185. In the northern part of Bandra *taluka*, near the suburb of Bandra, at a place called Santacruz, lived one 'Dhurandhar' family, who were Hari devotees.

186. All the brothers were fond of saints and had a steadfast devotion to Shri Ram, with a single-minded faith in *Ram-naam*. They did not like to interfere with other people's business.

187. Their way of life was very simple and so was the life-style of their children. The ladies of the house were also faultless in their behaviour. And hence *Chakrapani* (Shri Vishnu) was indebted to them.

188. Balaram was one of them, who was renowned for his meritorious deeds and whose standing with the rulers was very high. He was a devotee of Shri Vitthal. Everybody liked him.

189. This gem, born to a Ram devotee, appeared on this earth on 19th February, in the year 1878.

190. This adornment of the Pathare Prabhu community[5], was born in Bombay, in a well-known respectable family in the year 1878.

191. He was proficient in western education, had been enrolled as an advocate, was well-versed in philosophy and famous everywhere as a learned man.

192. He had a loving devotion to the god Panduranga and was fond of spiritual pursuits. Whereas the father's chosen deity was Ram, the son's devotion was to Vitthal.

193. All the brothers were degree-holders, with a religious bent of mind. On Balaram, however, the purifying, sanctifying influences of the pure seed (his father) were most remarkable.

194. An attractive, beautiful presentation of arguments; pure, straightforward thinking, a sharp intellect and righteous conduct, these were his virtues, worth emulating.

195. He had done a good deal of social service and had himself written an account of his community. When this self-imposed responsibility was discharged, he set out on the spiritual path to attain his spiritual weal.

196. There too, he made good progress and becoming proficient in the *Bhagvad Gita* and *Jnaneshvari*, which he studied carefully, he became renowned for his knowledge in spiritual subjects.

197. He was a great devotee of Sai. He died at a young age, in the year 1925. Listen to his brief life-story.

198. On 9th June, in the year 1925, he ended his earthly journey and merged with Shri Vitthal.

199. The Dhurandhar brothers had an opportunity to go to Sai's court for the saint's *darshan*, on an auspicious day, in the year 1912.

200. Six months earlier, the eldest brother Babulji, along with Vamanrao, had returned happily from Shirdi after taking *darshan*.

201. To experience for themselves this sweet experience and to get the benefit of that unique *darshan*, Balaram and others went to Shirdi.

202. Even before they arrived, Baba said in front of everybody, "Today, many people from my *darbar* are coming here."

203. On hearing of these loving words, the Dhurandhar brothers were much astonished. How did Baba get this news, when nobody had been informed about it?

204. Then, on seeing Sai with their own eyes, they rushed forward and embraced his feet. In soft tones, the conversation proceeded, to the joy and satisfaction of all.

205. Moreover, seeing these people arrive, Baba's words at once came forth, "See, these people of my *darbar* have come — the same that I had said, are coming."

206. And listen to Baba's words that followed, word for word, "You and I are known to each other earlier, from sixty generations."

207. Balaram and all the brothers were full of modesty and stood with folded hands in front of Baba, gazing at Shri's feet.

208. After taking Shri Sai's *darshan*, Balaram and others experienced a state of loving joy and felt their visit to Shirdi to be worthwhile.

209. The eyes filled with tears; the throat was choked with tears; the hair on the body stood on end and their hearts were crowded with the 'ashtabhav'.

210. Seeing Balaram's condition, Sai Samarth felt very happy and started talking to all of them, instructing and advising them, lovingly.

211. "He who worships me increasingly, like the waxing moon in the brighter half of the lunar month and who has surrendered to me totally, all the feelings and inclinations of his heart, he is truly the blessed one.

212. "With a steadfast faith in his mind, he who is engaged in guru-worship, to him God is altogether indebted and no one can cast an evil eye upon him.

213. "He who is fond of *guru-bhajan* and does not waste even half a minute, to him the guru will give boundless happiness and take him safely beyond this worldly life."

214. On hearing these words, the eyes of all filled with water; their minds were full of joy and their hearts swelled with emotion.

215. Then, making obeisance, they all wore round their necks the flower garlands of Sai's utterances. Overwhelmed as they were with a loving devotion, his words made them very happy.

216. And so, they later on came back to the *wada* and rested awhile,
      after the meal. In the afternoon, at about four to four-thirty, they
      went to the mosque again and prostrated in obeisance before Baba.

217. Balaram, with great humility, began pressing his feet. Baba put
      forward his clay pipe and signalled to him to smoke it.

218. Though not used to it at all, yet as *prasad*, he smoked it with a
      painful effort and returning it to Baba's hand, bowed with good
      feelings.

219. It was a day of great good fortune to Balaram. For, from thence,
      his asthma completely disappeared and he felt greatly relieved.

220. This asthma had not been of a short duration of a day or two.
      The affliction was from full six years. The clay pipe was so
      powerful, as if a *mantra* had been whispered in his ear by someone.

221. Puffing at the pipe once, he returned it, bowing his head with
      great humility. From then onwards, the asthma disappeared and
      never afflicted him again.

222. However, only on one day, in between, Balaram had a coughing
      fit. Everyone was surprised. No one could understand the cause
      of it.

223. On making enquiries afterwards, they all knew that it was on that
      day that Baba gave up the body, thus giving a sign to the devotees.

224. The day on which Balaram was coughing, was the same day that
      Baba gave up the body to the earth, and this was the mark he gave
      them.

225. But from then onwards, never again did he have a bout of
      coughing, till the day he died. Can anyone ever forget this
      experience of the clay pipe?

226. So, that day (of their visit) being a Thursday, was also the day of
      the *Chavadi* procession. Their joy was doubled and it became a
      truly memorable day for them.

227. From eight o'clock to nine, the most melodious and absorbing
      bhajans would be sung to the accompaniment of 'taal' and
      '*mridanga*', in front of Baba in the courtyard.

228. Singing 'abhanga' on one side, they used to decorate the palanquin on the other, and after the palanquin was ready, Baba used to set out to go to the *Chavadi*.

229. Earlier, in the thirty-seventh chapter, the marvel of the *Chavadi* has already been described in detail, and it will only be a repetition in this place.

230. It was Baba's regular routine to spend one night in the mosque and the next in the *Chavadi*, which he observed without a break, till his *samadhi*.

231. Loving Balaram had an eager enthusiasm to watch the pomp and show of the *Chavadi*. Hence the Dhurandhar brothers returned at the time of the *Chavadi*, to see it.

232. Men and women of that holy Shirdi set out with Baba to go to the *Chavadi*, joyously proclaiming glory to Baba.

233. The horse '*Shamsunder*', who was covered with a cloth richly embroidered in *jari* and was adorned with beautiful ornaments, was in front of the procession, quivering and dancing noisily.

234. Horns, trumpets of all descriptions, were sounded and Sai walked ceremoniously, with the royal umbrella on his head, with the palanquin and the much-decorated Shamkarna, surrounded by devotees.

235. Flags and banners in hand, the devotees would hold the regal umbrella on Shri's head and gently wave the *chavaris*, holding torches on all the four sides.

236. The throng of devotees would walk on both sides of Baba and sing *bhajans*, taking with them sweet melodious instruments like '*taal*', '*dhol*', '*mridanga*', etc.

237. And so, as that grand procession reached in front of the *Chavadi*, Baba would stop and facing the north, would make some gestures with his hands, with the proper rituals.

238. To his right would be Baba's '*Bhagat*' (Mhalsapati) who held the end of the cloth on Baba's shoulder, with his own hands, while on the left would walk Tatya Patil, lantern in hand.

239. As it was, Baba's face was fair and of a a yellowish complexion and when the light of the lamp blended with it, his face would appear yellowish gold with a tinge of copper-red, resembling the glow of the rising sun.

240. Blessed was that sacred *darshan* of that time! Facing the north with a concentrated mind, he seemed to be calling someone, half raising his right hand.

241. From there, Baba was taken inside the *Chavadi* and respectfully made to sit. Precious ornaments and rich clothes were offered and sandalwood paste was applied over the body.

242. Sometimes a fine, rich, gem-studded turban with a plume, sometimes a gold crown or sometimes a dark-coloured turban would be put on his head, with a beautiful dress, heavily embroidered in *jari*.

243. Necklaces of diamonds, pearls and emeralds were lovingly put round Baba's neck. Some would apply to his forehead a round mark of the fragrant musk.

244. Some would wash his feet and perform *pooja*, offering oblation and worshipping his feet. Some would apply the saffron paste to his body and put '*paan*' in his mouth.

245. Taking the *arati* with five lamps and '*niranjan*' with camphor, when they waved the *arati* round Baba, the glorious spectacle was just incomparable.

246. The Dhurandhars were surprised to see the same divine glow on Sai's face, which beautified the face of the idol of Panduranga.

247. As the flash of lightning in the sky people on earth are unable to look at, the same scintillating light on Sai's face now dazzled their eyes.

248. At dawn, there was *kakad-arati*. The Dhurandhar brothers went for it, too. And even there, they saw that same bright glow on Baba's face.

249. From then on, till the end of his days, Balaram's faith and devotion to Baba was so steadfast that it never wavered, in the least.

250.   Hemad surrenders at Sai's feet. In the next chapter the book will be complete and there will be a pause and review of the previous chapters. Give me your attention this one last time!

Weal be to all! Here ends the fifty-first chapter of
"Shri Sai Samarth Satcharit", called
'A Narration of the Accounts of Three Devotees',
as inspired by the saints and the virtuous
and composed by his devotee, Hemadpant.

Notes

1. A mountainous range along the west of the peninsula of India, the Malabar Ghats.
2. 'That means the illusion that the things of the world exist in themselves and maintain themselves, that they live and move apart from God, has disappeared'. (S. Radhakrishnan.)
3. One of an establishment of Brahmins, entertained at the temple of Pandharpur, for the service of the idol. The word means one who beats or bruises. They are so called because they pommel and cudgel the people that crowd around the idol.
4. A medley of various parched grain, like puffed rice, ground nuts, gram, etc., fried together and seasoned with salt, red pepper, chillies and spices.
5. A caste or an individual of it, of Hindus.

52

Epilogue

MY OBEISANCE TO SHRI GANESH, TO SHRI SARASWATI, AND SHRI GURUMAHARAJ! TO THE FAMILY DEITY, TO SHRI SITA-RAMACHANDRA, MY MOST HUMBLE OBEISANCE! I BOW IN REVERENCE TO THE MOST VENERABLE GURU SHRI SAINATH!

1. Now we will take a look backwards to review the foregoing chapters, after which we shall complete this book by giving the summary of the chapters in an epitome[1].

2. To remind his devotees of the experiences, which he gave them from time to time, while yet in the body, he got them written in a book which is serialized in the '*Shri Sai Leela*' magazine.

3. '*Shri Sai Leela*' is a most sacred magazine. In it, a series of tales of Shri Sai, which make up the Life story of our guru and which are instructive about this world and the next, can be read by all.

4. Sai Baba got his own '*Satcharit*' written by holding the hand of Hemadpant, who had a collection of innumerable stories. but who is without any learning or knowledge of the *Shastras*.

5. Some gurus make their disciples listen to their own account, by narrating it themselves. And it is from this that inspiration for writing their Life story is derived, after their *niryan*.

6. When Sai narrated various stories with profound significance, the listeners used to be totally engrossed, forgetting even hunger and thirst.

7. All those who had Sai's *darshan* became free from the threefold afflictions. How can the impact of such tremendous power be described adequately?

8. And it was for the upliftment of all those who worshipped Sai, so renowned for his benevolence, that he wrote down his own Life story.

9. After first bathing in the sacred Godavari and taking the *darshan* of his *samadhi*, this '*Satcharit*' should then be listened to, so that the threefold afflictions will be removed.

10. Even when his stories are narrated quite casually, one gets spiritual benefit, without realizing it. Therefore look into this book lovingly and *crores* and *crores* of sins will be destroyed.

11. Those who sincerely wish to escape the pain and suffering of births and deaths, should cultivate a ceaseless devotion to the guru's feet and to the chanting of his name.

12. Error through heedlessness is the cause of ignorance and hence, of not realizing the true Self. From this arises the birth-death cycle, which is the root of all evil.

13. *Maya* is illusory knowledge. Identification of the body with the real Self and attachment to it, is called 'death', by the wise and the learned.

14. Churning the ocean of Sai's stories, the stories that have a sweetness that is ever new, and which have been narrated so far, will prevent the listeners' Fall.

15. If Sai's manifest form, with all its attributes, be constantly meditated upon, the manifest form will disappear and the subtle, true Self will appear.

16. Unless one enters through the manifest form, it is not possible to know the true Self and it becomes difficult to know the formless *Parabrahman*, completely.

17. You, who lovingly drew your faithful devotees to your feet and, although still in the body, made them forget their bodies, thereby leading them, unknowingly, to the spiritual path.

18. You remove totally the sense of duality, once the devotee surrenders to you, like the river that forgets her separate identity, on embracing the ocean.

19. Two lights become one when they embrace each other, instantly losing their dual existence and shine brightly as one light.

20. Can the fragrance of the camphor ever exist apart from it, or the sunlight from the sun, or its shining brightness from the gold?

21. Just as the river, on entering the ocean, becomes the ocean itself, or the salt falling into the ocean at once, becomes one with it —

22. Similarly, once the devotees surrender at Sai's feet, there remains no duality, as they beome one with Sai, abandoning their separate identity.

23. Once the mind is completely filled with Sai, whether in the waking or dreaming or sleeping state, what else is that state but of the renunciation of the worldly life?

24. But now, prostrating in obeisance, I entreat only this one thing of you, that let not my desire wander anywhere else, away from you.

25. He who, like the sky, fills this whole creation, from inside and outside, right from the Brahman to the tiniest bush, the earthen vessels and the homes, and who makes no differentiation —

26. To whom all the devotees are equal; who knows no respect or disrespect; whose mind has no likes and dislikes and who shows not the slightest inequality in his treatment of others -

27. To that Sai Samarth, let us surrender whole-heartedly; He who satisfies all our desires, merely by our remembering him, at his feet let us bow our heads, finding fulfilment, thereby.

28. And now my righteous listeners and great devotees, I make obeisance to you all. And to you, my friends, I make just one request. Please listen to it.

29. Till now, you have spared some time, month after month, to listen to the stories of one, whom now you should not forget even for a moment.

30. And the more you listen eagerly, with a loving heart to the stories of Sai, the more pleasure will Sai give me, the speaker.

31. Similarly, when the listeners are not attentive, the speaker will never be happy and without such mutual pleasure, all this effort of listening (and speaking) is in vain.

32. Very difficult is this ocean of worldly life, to cross. The surging waves of *Maya* are uncontrollable, which dash against the shores of thoughtlessness, felling the majestic trees of courage.

33. The wind of ego roars, stirring up the depths of the ocean, where the fierce crocodiles of anger, envy, etc., find a fearless home.

34. The crocodiles of 'I' and 'mine', the innumerable whirlpools of desires and doubts and the countless aquatic creatures of censure, jealousy, scorn, etc., are afloat on it.

35. Terrifying as this ocean is, our *guruvara*, in the form of Agasti, drinks it all up and those who are slaves at the feet of the Sadguru have not the least cause to fear it.

36. Therefore Sadguru Sai Samarth has become the ark on the ocean of worldly life and will take us, who take refuge in him, safely to the shore beyond.

37. The ocean of worldly life is very difficult to cross. Make a boat of Sai's feet and he will show you the other shore, without any fear. Such is the marvel of unswerving faith.

38. If you observe this vow, you will not feel the intensity of the sorrows and pain in this world. There can be no other gain comparable to this. And this alone, is the strength that stands us in good stead.

39. With hearts filled with intense devotion to Sai, may his form fill the eyes and his Presence be seen in all living creatures. May all his devotees attain such a state of mind.

40. Behaving at my own sweet will and pleasure, resulted in a fall in my last birth. May I have the strength at least now, to renounce the sensual pleasures so that I may get a good passage.

41. 'When Shri Samarth stands behind you, no one can touch you'. Those Sai devotees who rest asssured in this faith, are truly blessed.

42. However, a thought comes to my mind, that holding Baba's feet, I should make him one request, for the sake of all the devotees.

43. That may this book find a place in the homes of all, for their daily reading. For it will ward off all the difficulties of him who reads it daily, with love.

44. After his bath he who finishes reading it with faith and love, in seven days, will have all his adversities overcome.

45. This book has been woven with the threads of spirituality; is filled with stories of Shrikrishna and the Brahman; has become succulent with the sweetness of non-duality between the *Atman* and the

Brahman and is steeped, as never before, in the principle of *Advait* (or non-duality).

46. In this '*Nandanvan*'[2] of saint Eknath's poetic composition, in this '*Vrindavan*'[3] of thirty-two chapters, both the *Jnani* and the ignorant are absorbed in the enjoyment of the sweet, delicious milk.

47. If this '*Satcharit*' is listened to or read repeatedly, every day, then Sai Samarth will avert their difficulties, at once.

48. Those desiring wealth will get wealth and success in their pure, straightforward day-to-day dealings. They will get the fruit according to their faith. For unless there is faith and devotion, there is no actual experience.

49. When this book is read with reverence, Sai Samarth is pleased and destroys the poverty of ignorance, giving the reader wealth and prosperity of knowledge.

50. The plan for the composition of this book was Sai's, and such was also his secret wish. Blessed is the life of that devotee who is firmly attached to his feet.

51. With full concentration of the mind and as a strictly observed rule, at least one chapter of this book *Satcharit* should be read, daily. It will bring the reader unlimited happiness.

52. He who has any thought for his own good, should read this book, sincerely. And birth after birth, he will happily remember Sai's beneficence.

53. On Sri Sai's festive occasions, such as *Gurupoornima*, *Gokulashtami*, the anniversary of his *Mahasamadhi* and *Ramnavami*, this book should be read in the house, as a rule.

54. As is the wish in the mind, so is the birth one gets. Even the *Shastras* say that, 'As the thoughts at the time of death, so is the next birth'.

55. Shri Sai is the Protector of the devotees. Without him the impediments will not be removed. After all, what is so surprising that the mother should feel such a compassionate love for her child?

56. More than this, what can I say? Where words themselves come to a stop, there I feel, I should remain silent. For that alone, would be the most befitting praise.

57. Hence, with an intense desire for *Moksha* in the mind, by always doing auspicious *karmas* and by following the path of the nine-fold devotion, like listening, etc., the heart will be purified.

58. But this will not come about without the Sadguru's grace. Without him, there can be no knowledge of the Parabrahman, nor the constant remembrance that 'I myself, am Brahman'. Nor will he be induced to repose full faith in the guru.

59. In saying that the relationship between the guru and his disciple is like that between the father and the son, the comparison to the father is but for name's sake. The father makes his son worthy of worldly pleasures, while the guru gives his disciple the joys, not only of this world, but even the next.

60. The father will give wealth which is transient, but the wealth that the guru gives, has no end. Not only does he give the experience of what is eternal, but will give it directly, in hand.

61. The mother nurtures the child in the womb for nine months, but brings him out into the world, in the moment of birth. With the guru-mother, it is exactly the reverse; he takes in the disciple who is outside.

62. When the disciple chants '*Guru, guru*' in the end, he attains to the highest stage of *Moksha* (Oneness with the Brahman). When the guru himself beats the disciple, the latter becomes completely one with the Brahman.

63. A blow from the guru's hand will end the birth-death cycle. Who then, can be more fortunate than him, whose life has been brought to an end by the guru himself?

64. The guru will have to take in hand a sword, a club, an axe, a spear, etc. And as he strikes the blow, the disciple will have a true awakening and will then see the form of his Sadguru.

65. However much one may shield the body, it is going to fall, some day or other. Then if it be destroyed at the guru's hand, it will, at least, prevent rebirth.

66. Do beat me up, O Sadguru, till I am dead; destroy my ego, completely. Give me such a severe beating that I will not have a rebirth.

67. Burn down my *karma* and *a-karma* (inaction); ward off my qualities, good and bad and dispel my pleasureable delusions, born of *Maya*.

68. Clear my mind of resolves and doubts, making me steadfast and firm of purpose. I do not want merit, nor do I want sin. In truth, I do not want this meaningless, laborious exertion of being born.

69. When I try to surrender at your feet, you stand on all my four sides, to the east, west and in all directions, as also, down and up, in the sky and in the netherworld.

70. Your Presence fills all the places and you dwell in me, too! Or rather, the idea of separateness between 'you' and 'I' is a painful effort for me.

71. Hence Hemad surrenders to the Sadguru single-mindedly, holding fast to his feet and escaping the cycle of death-rebirth, attains his own upliftment.

72. And, is this *leela* any less marvellous, that making an instrument of Hemad, he should create his own Life story, for the upliftment of his countless devotees?

73. That this '*Shri Sai Samarth Charit*' should be written at my hand, is in itself, a great wonder. Or else it would have been impossible to do so, for a lowly creature like me, without Sai's Grace.

74. Mine was not an association of many days, nor had I the capacity to recognize a saint. I had not the intrepidity of a penetrating, discerning eye, but had rather a doubting, unbelieving mind.

75. Never have I done '*upasana*' with a steadfast mind; never have I sung *bhajans*, even for a moment! And yet, it was at such hands that he got his Life story written, to show the world.

76. To accomplish his own purpose, Sai himself, reminded me of this book and fulfilled his own object. Hemad is just for the name's sake.

77. Can a fly ever lift the Meru mountain? Or a lapwing suck the ocean? But when the Sadguru stands behind you, he makes marvellous things happen.

78. And so, my listeners, I now make obeisance to you. This book is complete and Sai's book is offered at Sai's feet.

79. One by one, before all the listeners, both great and small, I prostrate in obeisance. I have completed this series of stories from *Sai Charitra*, in your righteous company.

80. And yet, who am I to complete? This is only my vain conceit! Where Sai is the puller of the strings, who am I to say this?

81. Hence, abandoning the ego, which is the root cause of all evil, sing the praises of your guru, again and again. I now end this sacrificial offering of words, which captivates the heart and instructs the mind.

82. Here the book ends. My wish is satisfied and Sai's work is accomplished. I feel fulfilled, too.

83. Such a book, when studied fully, thoroughly, will satisfy one's desires. When Sadguru's feet are clasped to the heart, the ocean of worldly life will be crossed over, safely.

84. Those afflicted with disease, will regain health; the poor will become wealthy; doubts and misconceptions will give way to stability and peace and even the poor and the abject will become generous.

85. By reading the book repeatedly, those suffering from demoniac possession or fits of epilepsy, will become free of them. Even to the dumb, the disabled, the lame and the deaf, by listening to this will bring happiness.

86. Even those who, engulfed by ignorance, have forgotten God Almighty Himself, will be uplifted.

87. Those who waste their bodies by behaving like demons, although born as human beings, and regard this worldly life as the storehouse of happiness and peace, even they will be uplifted.

88. Incomprehensible are the doings of Sainath. He has firmly and totally absorbed this Hemad at his feet and making him serve himself, Sai has got this work completed through him.

89   In the end, I offer my pen and my head, without any reservation,
      at the feet of Sadguru, who controls and sustains the whole world
      and inspires the mind.[4]

Notes

1. The epitome was not given in the manuscript, although in the very first verse it is said
   a summary would be given.
2. Lord Indra's pleasure-ground, Elysium.
3. Refer Ch. 18, verse 85 and note 5.
4. Unlike in the chapters so far, there is no concluding verse in the manuscript of this
   chapter.

53

Epitome

MY OBEISANCE TO SHRI GANESH, TO SHRI SARASWATI, AND SHRI GURUMAHARAJ! TO THE FAMILY DEITY, TO SHRI SITA-RAMACHANDRA, MY MOST HUMBLE OBEISANCE! I BOW IN REVERENCE TO THE MOST VENERABLE GURU SHRI SAINATH!

1. Shri Sai is Brahman incarnate, an Emperor Paramount among the saints and is renowned throughout the world as a Samarth Sadguru, who inspires the mind.

2. Surrendering to him single-mindedly, let us now worship his holy feet, so that he who averts birth-death will remove our fear of worldly life.

3. In the last chapter, it was promised that 'After first reviewing all the chapters, I will complete this book by writing an 'epitome' (Summary)'.

4. Though Hemadpant said this, it did not come about so. Whether he wrote a summary of the book, or whether it was left out through forgetfulness, one does not know.

5. But it is the rule everywhere that he who begins writing a book, should himself complete it by giving an epitome.

6. However, there are exceptions to a rule and this is our experience here, too. Nothing happens according to our wishes, it is Baba's wish which overpowers all.

7. Hemadpant suddenly passed away, making everyone most sorrowful. No one could think of anything, nor could the epitome be traced.

8. It was difficult to find Annasaheb's (Dabholkar) writings. With great effort, his son Shri Gajanan searched for them and gave me whatever material was necessary.

9. Thrifty in his habits as Annasaheb was, he would not waste any scrap of paper, but work, using them neatly and ingeniously. Such was his temperament.

10. He would write a chapter on slips of paper and give the same to the printers. Unnecessary expense always pricked his conscience. Truly, nobody can compare with him!

11. Moved by compassion, Hemad probably thought, 'Poor lifeless bits of paper! How will these be uplifted unless used in the service of the great saint Shri Sai Baba.'

12. Such seem to have been the thoughts of Hemad, so that he collected the slips together and made them serve Baba. This appears to have been his noble purpose.

13. Even the last chapter was written in the same way, on slips of paper. But even after much thought, the epitome could not be traced amongst them.

14. The matter was related to Gajananrao and others, as also, to Babasaheb Tarkhad (the then treasurer of Shirdi Sansthan and editor of the *'Shri Sai Leela'* magazine). They all opined that an epitome must be there.

15. Babasaheb published this in *'Shri Sai Leela'*, setting a time limit for its writing. The limit expired but the epitome did not appear.

16. Hemad, i.e. Govindrao, was a mine of virtues and was steeped in Vedanta. His language and expression in the book is truly, blessed. The doings of the Sadguru's Grace are simply marvellous.

17. Many are the devotees of Shri Sai Sadguru. Among them, Hemadpant is a gem of a poet. Only he, who is a wise *mahant* (a great man) like him, can write this epitome.

18. And yet, the epitome would not appear from anywhere. This saddened my heart, greatly. I prayed to Shri Sai Baba, who is Dattaguru Himself, and entreated His mercy.

19. 'I am a lowly slow-witted creature, without even a trace of learning. How will I, who knows nothing of writing verse, write this verse-composition?

20. 'And yet, for this there is only one support. When Shri Dattaguru is favourably disposed, he can make even a fly lift the Meru mountain. Such is his great authority and power.'

21. Once again I prayed to Sai-Narayan, who is Lord Shankar Himself, to have mercy on me and inspire my mind quickly, to write the epitome.

22. I do not have that power to write verse. But Shri Gururaya knows the dullness of my mind. Therefore, making obeisance at his feet, I now proceed to write this epitome.

23. This epitome, which is a part of this book, will be completed by Shri Sai, who is Gajanan Himself. Magnificent, most marvellous is his grandeur, while I am but his instrument.

24. The first chapter contains the invocation of the Divine and obeisance to Shri Gajanan, the remover of all impediments, the material cause of the world and the ornament round the neck of Shankar-Parvati.

25. The powerful goddess of Speech, with a great ingenuity of mind, who charms the world and grants all desires — to that Shri Saraswati, an obeisance was made.

26. To the family-guru, relatives and other gurus, to the saints and the virtuous who are incarnations of God Almighty, and to Sadguru *Sai-Bhagvan*, who is worthy of being surrendered to, being the secret treasure of *Moksha* — to all these obeisance was made.

27. Thereafter, narrating the story of how the epidemic of cholera was totally eradicated by Baba, by grinding wheat, the glorious power of Sai was described.

28. Chapter two states the purpose of the present work and describes the naming of Dabholkar as Hemadpant, confuting of the argument that guru is not necessary and how Hemad had *Sai-darshan*.

29. How the command came from Sai's mouth for the writing of this book and a full account of the Rohilla forms the content of the third chapter.

30. There follows a detailed narration in the fourth chapter, as to the reason for the appearance on this earth, of sadhus and saints, who are an adornment to God, the Controller of the Universe.

31. This chapter also has a description, at length, of how Sai, a *Datta-avatar* and a veritable *Kalpataru*, first came to the holy Shirdi.

32. The fifth chapter deals with how Baba disappeared from the holy Shirdi, only to reappear in the company of the wealthy Patil, to the astonishment of all;

33. How he moved about with Gangagir and other saints and how he created a garden, himself carrying water for it, on his head.

34. There is an interesting narration in the sixth chapter, of the great festival of *Ramnavami*, about Balabua Kirtankar and of the renovation of the mosque.

35. In the seventh chapter comes the narration of Baba's *Samadhi* and *Khanda-yog*, *dhoti-poti*, his pretence about being a Hindu or a Muslim, as also the incomprehensible mind of the saints.

36. This chapter also describes Baba's dress, his conduct, his giving medicines to the suffering, his clay pipe, his caste, the *dhuni*, lighting up of the mosque and the temples, Baba's illness and his service by the devotees, which was an amazing spectacle.

37. The leprosy of Bhagoji Shinde, the treating of Khaparde's son, suffering from plague; Nanasaheb Chandorkar's wish of visiting Pandharpur — all these are narrated by the learned Hemadpant in this same chapter.

38. The eighth chapter has a happy narration of the unique importance of the human birth, a description of Baba's manner of collecting alms, Bayajabai's service to the saint, Baba's extraordinary way of taking meals —

39. And also, how Baba, Tatya, Mhalsapati, all three slept in the mosque at night and Baba's remarkable love, which was equal for both:

40. The mutual and loving relationship betwen Khushalchand of Rahata village and Baba, who was a mine of Peace and Knowledge — all this is in this same chapter.

41. The ninth chapter gives an account of the great repentance on disobeying Baba's orders, on the part of devotee Tatya Patil and a great Englishman.

42. It also narrates very cleverly, how Baba used to eat the food given in alms, after first getting the '*Panch-mahayajna*' performed, along with Baba's authority for collecting alms,

43. And the excellent story of how Babasaheb Tarkhad, a staunch follower of the *Prarthana Samaj*, became Baba's steadfast devotee.

44. Chapter ten narrates about the greatest of yogis, i.e. Baba, sleeping on a wooden plank suspended from the roof, which was about four-arms in length and the measure of the thumb and the little finger extended, in width;

45. As also, a moving account as to when Baba first put his foot in Shirdi, how many years he stayed there, when he gave up the body;

46. And about the steadfast constant attitude of *Gururaya* in guiding the people to the right path and showing ghoulish tendencies outwardly, while perfectly at peace and totally desireless within.

47. This chapter also includes a description of the most remarkable skill of the Sadguru in explaining the characteristics of '*dharma*' as explained in the *Vedas* and *Shastras*, his skill in imparting worldly and spiritual instruction and in testing the minds of both devotees and non-devotees;

48. Baba's seat, his knowledge, his personality, his authority as a guru, his power and greatness — all this makes up chapter ten.

49. Chapter eleven dwells on Baba's world-wide fame of being in a state of *Sat-chit-anand*, the loving devotion of Dr Pandit, a description of Siddique Phalake's reverence for Baba,

50. Baba's control over the menacing rainclouds and over the whirlwind, his protection to the devotees from the roaring fire, etc.

51. It is in chapter twelve that a charming description of the various incidents relating to Kaka (Mahajani), Dhumal, Nimonkar, a *mamledar* and his friend, a doctor, occurs.

52. Agnihotri Mule of Nasik, a man of doubting nature, and a devotee of Gholapswami, as also the marvel of his *Sai-darshan* — this account also is given in this chapter.

53. How Bala Shimpi's malaria was cured by feeding rice and curd to a black dog and Bapusaheb's cholera, by giving him walnuts and pistachio, is narrated in chapter thirteen.

54. This chapter also deals with many stories such as the cure of the ear-ache of the swami from Alandi by a mere blessing; that of the diarrhoea of Kaka Mahajani, by giving him peanuts;

55. The stomach-ache of the devotee Dattopant from Harda by blessing him in front of all;

56. The consumption of Bhimaji Patil by applying *udi* — these are all given in this same chapter.

57. Chapter fourteen gives us the story of the famous merchant from Nanded, Shet Ratanji Parsi, who was sad at heart for want of a son and was made most happy by a gift of a son;

58. As also, the wonderful story of how everyone recognized saint Maulisaheb, who was working as a coolie, by the sign given by Sai.

59. Chapter fifteen describes how Baba explained to Das Ganu, the style of *kirtan* by Narad; how he made Cholkar drink tea with sugar, in fulfilment of his vow; as also,

60. How Baba narrated the story of the lizard that came from Aurangabad to meet her sister in the mosque, merely from their chirping.

61. The interesting story in chapter sixteen is about how a gentleman, with wealth, children, etc., on hearing Baba's fame, came to Shirdi to get *Brahma-jnana*;

62. And was told that, 'He who desires *Brahma-jnana* has first to renounce worldly life, giving up completely the hankering after wealth;

63. And how, though the man had bundles of notes in his pocket, would not lend even five rupees to Sai, yet expecting to get the Brahman;

64. This story in the fascinating style of Sai's instruction joined with the blessed language of Hemad, in this chapter sixteen, is like adding sugar to milk.

65. The same story continues in chapter seventeen which is an interesting narration, at length, about *Brahma-jnana* and the giving up of greed for wealth, altogether.

66. Chapter eighteen has a skilful narration by Hemadpant, of the story of Sathe's reading of '*Guru-Charitra*', the advice and instruction to Radhabai Deshmukh and Baba's '*anugraha*' to Hemadpant.

67. Chapter nineteen tells us in greater detail, the story of this '*anugraha*' and the deep thought and reflection on the instruction given by Shri Sai.

68. Then follows the story in chapter twenty, as to how Das Ganu started writing '*Ishavasya-Bhavarth-Bodhini*' and asked Baba the doubts that arose in his mind while writing;

69. And how Baba told him that his doubts will be resolved by Kaka's (Dikshit) maid-servant. Such is the sweet narration of the Sadguru's unique power described here.

70. The twenty-first chapter narrates the story of the bestowal of Grace upon a righteous deputy collector, on another learned man called Patankar and a third individual, a lawyer.

71. The twenty-second chapter describes how, when Baba said to all the people that the '*Mashidmayee*' took us safely across the worldly life, that she was herself *Dwaravati* and *Dwaraka*, not one of them understood the real significance of his words.

72. How Baba extolled the virtues of this *Mashidmayee*, and averted the calamity of a snake-bite to Mirikar and Butti, cured Amir Shakkar's rheumatism, averting the danger of a snake-bite to him, too;

73. And how Baba averted the danger of a scorpion bite to Hemadpant and of snake-bite to others, thereby warding off the calamity of a premature death.

74. Chapter twenty-three describes how the doubts of a student of *Yoga* were resolved and Madhavrao's snake-bite cured, describing beautifully, Baba's *dhuni*, the fuel for it and the story of the killing of a goat.

75. As also, Baba's respectful treatment of Bade Baba, but the latter's lack of faith in the guru's command and the greed of his discontented nature, for more, however much he might get;

76. The steadfast faith of the great devotee Kakasaheb (Dikshit) in his guru's command and the marvellous *leela* of the Sadguru.

77. Chapter twenty-four contains an account of how Baba made an excuse of the parched gram to teach Hemadpant that without remembering the Sadguru, one should not enjoy any sensual pleasures,

78. And of how Sai sparked off a quarrel between Anna Babre and Mavashibai, as the poet brings out the novelty of jokes and humour in these situations.

79. In the twenty-fifth chapter comes the story of Damuanna Kasar from Ahmednagar, who wished to trade in cotton and rice on a large scale,

80. And how Sai, the sun of knowledge, told him that he will incur a loss in such a trade, but that he will get a child, if his wife eats a mango.

81. The twenty-sixth chapter tells about a devotee called 'Pant' who had taken '*anugraha*' from another saint, and was quickly given a mark of this, by Baba, to his great delight.

82. In this same chapter is included the story of the devotee Harischandra Pitale, whose epileptic son was cured of the disease, merely by a glance of Grace;

83. That Pitale was given three rupees by Baba, who said that two rupees had been already given earlier, and was told to keep them in the *pooja*.

84. Chapter twenty-seven tells the story of Kaka (Mahajani), who gave *Bhagvat pothi* in Baba's hand, with a desire to get it back as *prasad*, but instead, Sai gave it to Madhavrao,

85. And the story of how the '*Vishnusahasranaam*' which was among the *pothis* of a Ramdasi, was given by Baba to Shamrao, without the knowledge of the Ramdasi,

86. And by giving the '*Vishnusahasranaam*', how that compassionate Sai bestowed Grace on Shamrao.

87. Chapter twenty-eight dwells on how devotee Lakhmichand Munshi, Chidibai from Barhanpur and the meritorious Brahmin Megha, came to Baba's feet.

88. How by appearing in a Vision in their dream, Baba gave them the experience of its truth in a waking state, thus describing the incomprehensible *leela* of Sadguru, the Mother.

89. In chapter twenty-nine appear the stories of the *bhajan*-singing group from Madras, who had gathered at the sacred Shirdi to witness the grand spectacle of the munificence of Baba, who was the simple, guileless Lord Shankar;

90. The astonishing manner in which Raghunath Tendulkar's son passed the examination, Baba's marvellous *leela* in removing Tendulkar's worry about his pension,

91. How devotee Doctor Hate, who was Baba's loving devotee, was given *darshan* in a dream at dawn, in an interesting account of these.

92. The thirtieth chapter contains the stories of one Kakaji Vaidya, a devotee of the goddess Saptashringi, the vision that the goddess gave him, saying, he should see Sai, the chief among the saints.

93. And how Shamrao, who had made a vow to that same goddess, went to Vani after thirty years, to fulfil that vow;

94. And also, the stories of Sheth Khushalchand of Rahata, and Ramlal, the Punjabi Brahmin, in whose dreams Shri Sai went, to say, "Come to Shirdi".

95. In chapter thirty-one, we are told how the *sannyasi* Vijayanand, set out from Madras to go to Manas Sarovar, but was made to stay back by Shri Sai, who is Shrikrishna Himself;

96. How the great devotee Mankar, who was like the black bee in the lotus feet of Sai, and also the fierce, cruel tiger were both uplifted.

97. Chapter thirty-two quotes Sai's words that, "We four virtuous people wandered around in the forest in search of God and when I had given up my ego completely, *Gururaya* gave me *darshan*."

98. This story, along with another, narrated by Sai, and the story of Gokhalebai, who went on a fast, are narrated in this chapter by Hemad, who sings about their novelty.

99. Chapter thirty-three comprises the stories of a friend of Narayan Jani, who was suddenly bitten by a scorpion; of the daughter of another devotee, who was plagued by fever;

100. About the daughter of Chandorkar, harassed by labour-pains, who, when no one could think of anything to relieve her pains, became very sad at heart;

101. About the great devotee Kulkarnisaheb and Balabua, the *bhajan*-singer; all of whom realized the great impact of Baba's *udi*;

102. And lastly, the charming and instructive tale of the *dakshina* given by the devotee Haribhau Karnik, who was very devout and trusting.

103. The thirty-fourth chapter narrates the stories of the nephew of a doctor from Malegaon, who was suffering from a bone-tumor; of the staunch devotee Doctor Pillai, who was severely afflicted by the guinea-worms;

104. The story of Bapaji of Shirdi, whose wife suffered the pain of bubonic plague; of a small Irani child suffering from fits;

105. A gentleman from Harda, seriously ill with kidney-stones and the wife of a Kayastha Prabhu gentleman from Bombay, who was troubled by a difficult delivery.

106. In all the above-mentioned stories of chapter thirty-four, it has been narrated in an interesting manner, how these afflictions were instantly and totally removed, merely by the touch of Baba's *udi*.

107. In chapter thirty-five follows an account of how a friend of Mahajani, who believed in worshipping the Formless, turned an idol-worshipper, on taking Baba's *darshan*;

108. How a solicitor from Bombay, Dharamsi Jethabhai Thakkar, was given by the Guruvar, grapes transformed from the seeded to the seedless variety;

109. A Kayastha gentleman from Bandra, who could not sleep peacefully and Bala Patil of Nevasa — how they both experienced the curative effect of the *udi*.

110. The thirty-sixth chapter is about the two gentlemen from Gomantaka, who had made vows separately — one, for a job; the other, for tracing a robbery;

111. How they both forgot about their vows and were reminded of them by Sai Samarth, who knows past, present and future, pervades the Brahmand and whose greatness is indescribable;

112. And the story of Sakharam Aurangabadkar's wife, who rushed to Sai's feet to pray for a son and how Sai gave her a coconut and her wish was fulfilled.

113. The thirty-seventh chapter charmingly describes the spectacle of the *Chavadi* ceremony, which is rarely to be seen anywhere, but which Hemad had seen with his own eyes.

114. This is followed by chapter thirty-eight, which contains a most interesting account of how the different dishes were cooked together in the Handi, to prepare various sweet dishes that were served by Baba to all, as *prasad*.

115. In chapter thirty-nine comes the exposition of the stanza from the *Geeta*, beginning, 'Learn that by humble reverence... etc', that Baba gave to Chandorkar, to remove his conceit about his knowledge of the Sanskrit language,

116. And the Vision in which Sai, the King among the saints, appeared to Bapusaheb Butti, commanding him to build the temple.

117. Chapter forty narrates the story of how Deo wrote to Baba, to invite him for the '*udyapan*' of his mother's vows, when he was going to feed the Brahmins;

118. How three honourable individuals, dressed as *sannyasins*, came on that day and went away after having their meal with the Brahmins and yet Deo did not recognize the guru's *leela* in this;

119. And also, the story of how, after appearing in a Vision to Hemad, Baba came to a meal as promised, but in the form of a bas-relief.

120. Continuing the same story of the bas-relief in chapter forty-one, the poet describes at length to the devotees, in his charming style, the incomprehensible power of the Sadguru,

121. And also, how Sai appeared like Rudra, when he became red as the glowing embers, with anger and showered abuses on Deo;

122. How Sai, Shri Hari also, told him in a dream to read *Shri Jnaneshvari*, every day, as a rule, explaining the proper method of reading it.

123. Chapter forty-two, tells us about the prior hint given by Sai, about his *nidhan*; how the death of Ramachandra and of Tatya was averted;

124. Then, the sacred account of Sai Sadguru's '*niryan*' which makes the listeners sad and agitates Hemad's mind.

125. In the next two chapters — forty three and forty-four, Hemadpant completes without a doubt, the account of Baba's '*niryan*', which had remained incomplete in the previous chapter.

126. In chapter forty-five, we have an account of how Kakashaeb Dikshit, when he was once reading *Nath-Bhagvat*, with Kaka Mahajani and Madhavrao, was assailed with doubts;

127. And Madhavrao's explanation did not satisfy Dikshit's mind, but Anandrao Pakhade resolved his doubt by narrating his dream;

128. And also, how Sai Samarth answered the question as to why Mhalsapati could not sleep on the plank suspended from the roof — all this has been told in a skilful narration.

129. Chapter forty-six describes Baba's marvellous *leelas* of wandering freely everywhere, though seated in his own place; his going to Kashi-Gaya in an unusual manner, to show a miracle to the people;

130. How Baba, a gem among the saints, permitted Shama to attend the marriage of Chandorkar's son and at Gaya, Baba's photograph suddenly, came before his eyes;

131. And how Sai, the veritable Lord Shankar of the three eyes, narrated the story of the previous birth of the two goats, such are the interesting, sweet and profound stories in this chapter.

132. Similarly, in chapter forty-seven, Sai who was Brahma-Vishnu - Mahesh incarnate, narrates the past history of a frog and a snake, — or rather, of a greedy money-lender and his debtor,

133. To show through this nectar-sweet story, how one has to take a rebirth to atone for the sins of enmity, murder and debt. Hemad has beautifully described this, here.

134. Chapter forty-eight deals with the stories of the staunch devotee Shevade's law examination, and the grace bestowed on Sapatnekar, who had no faith.

135. Chapter forty-nine narrates the stories of Hari Kanhoba from Bombay and the malicious-minded Swami Somdev, who came to Shirdi, with conceited minds to test the saint.

136. And how, on their taking *darshan*, Sai, at once, pronounced their inward thoughts, to their instant, inward abashment, drawing them to his feet and cleansing their sins of many births;

137. Similarly, how Chandorkar, who was sitting near Baba, was stirred by emotion, on seeing the beauty of a lady.

138. In chapter fifty, Dabholkar has given, at length, the significance of the same stanza from the *Geeta*, which begins with, 'Learn that by humble reverence.... etc.", supporting the exposition given by Baba.

139. Chapter fifty-one describes how Hari Sitaram Dikshit, devotee Balaram Dhurandhar and the lawyer from Nanded, called Pundalik, first came to Shirdi,

140. And the extraordinary story of each of them, which will astonish the listeners and make the ocean of love in their hearts, upsurge.

141. In chapter fifty-two, reviewing the fore-going chapters of the book, Hemadpant asks for a '*pasayadaan*'[1], that may Baba destroy the wickedness of the wicked and protect the righteous;

142. And bowing at the Sadguru's feet with humility, offering his head and pen at his feet, Hemad completes the book, feeling fulfilled in the writing of it.

143. In this way, Govindraya completes the chapters of '*Shri Sai Satcharit*'. Bowing lovingly at his feet, I make obeisance to the Sadguru, the Mother of the Universe.

144. The narration, chapter by chapter, of the summary of a book is called the 'Epitome', which becomes a true highway to *Moksha*, for those Seekers, who desire *Moksha*.

145. This epitome may be slighted as being a torn rag used for an ornamental border and end of a beautiful, rich '*shela*'. But the intelligent listeners should listen to the request of this servant, just once.

146. This book is not a '*shela*', but rather, a sweet, plump child, to whom this Bal has boldly applied the black mark in the form of this epitome, so that he may not suffer from an evil eye cast on him.

147. The book is like delicious food, replete with the six juices or flavours, and the epitome is like a glass of butter-milk, to help the digestion of the various dishes, i.e. the chapters.

148. This book is the wish-fulfilling cow *Kamdhenu*, with the chapters as her beautiful, well-proportioned parts. And this epitome is the necklace of black beads put round her neck to protect her from the influence of a malignant eye.

149. And so, I shall now narrate, according to my understanding, the arrangement of chapters as followed by Pant Hemad. May the listeners listen to it with respect.

150. In the beginning come the praises of the Sadguru. Then follows a narration of Vedanta and Sai's *Brahma-swaroop*. After that there is a narration of the devotees' experiences.

151. Hemadpant was, to begin with, proficient in the *Shastras* and in literature. To add to this, Sadguru Sai was pleased with him, so that, in an instant, he illumined his intellect to create the sweet-meat, that is this book.

152. Those who will experience the sweetness of this book, will end the revolutions of the birth-death cycle and attain the everlasting wealth of *Moksha*.

153. Hemadpant's language, which is sweet and succulent, has gained much by Sai's Grace. And as such is the delectable combination, comparable to that of milk and sugar-cane juice; who can describe the grandeur of the book?

154. There are many writers of books, but the authority of a blessed tongue will never come to them, until they get a real Sadguru, who is Shri Vishnu incarnate and sustainer of this world.

155. You may have studied the *Shastras*, but still without the Sadguru's grace, such a book can never be written. This is absolutely true.

156. Who can praise '*Shri Sai Satcharit*' adequately? How incomparable is the value of this book! And it is a great good fortune of the seekers, that the book has an author like Hemadpant.

157. As long as this book remains on this earth, so long will his fame remain in the world, for Govindraya has provided a timely feast for the Seekers.

158. Blessed is this book, born out of the Sadguru's Grace. The Seekers will accept this book, which will remove poverty of thought.

159. It was due to the accumulated merit of many births that Govindrao was able to serve Sai and he enjoyed its delicious fruit in writing this book.

160. Hemadpant was a steadfast devotee, a poet, fond of *Vedantic* learning, and absorbed at Sadguru Sai's feet, day and night.

161. *Vedanta* is a profound and difficult subject. And without guru's Grace, it is difficult to write a book on *Vedanta*, which also has renunciation, devotion and knowledge.

162. These are not chapters, but are as gold-sockets and in them are set by Govindraya with great effort, the precious gems of the stories, emanating the brilliance of their significance.

163. These various chapters are the fragrant flower-garlands, offered round Sadguru's neck by his loving child, Govind, with pure devotion.

164. These chapters are pitchers of gold in which this son of Raghunath (i.e. Govind) has filled the sacred Ganges water, to destroy the ego of the Seekers.

165. In this book, which is the sky of a battlefield, the sword of the intellect of this son of Raghunath, has slain the demons of pride, conceit and hypocrisy, to raise the victory-pillars, that are the chapters.

166. The book is an *arati* of five lights, the significance of the stories in the chapters, shining out as the light of the wicks and Peace and Renunciation come to wave this *arati* around this King among the saints.

167. This book is *Maya*, the bewitcher of this world, whose body is adorned by ornaments, i.e. the meaning of the chapters, like armlets, etc., and who comes with her arms, i.e. the chapters, raised high, ready to embrace Sai, who is Brahman incarnate.

168. *Sai Satcharit* is the emperor among books, with its chapters as the ingenious bards or minstrels, who praise the boundless splendour of his glorious faith, knowledge and *Vedanta*.

169. *Sai Satcharit* is the market of spirituality, with each chapter as a trading place. In this, the articles of trade, i.e. the stories and experiences, have been carefully set out by the poet.

170. This book is as the expansive bed of the river Ganga; the arrangement of the chapters is like the neat *ghats* on the banks. The power of the guru's grace being great, the stream of the nectar-sweet stories flows with tremendous force through it.

171. This is not a book, but a *Kalpavriksha*, which appears to be dry to the worldly people, but to the Seekers, it is *Moksha*, itself. Experience it for yourself.

172. This itself, is a true memorial, which destroys ignorance and sorrow of worldly life; saves us from the hell of *Maya*, delusion, etc., and gives us lasting peace.

173. Govindrao, the author, had become a black bee, hovering round the lotus feet of Sadguru Sai, to taste the ever-new, sweet nectar.

174. Govindrao's surname was Dabholkar. He had learning, modesty and good conduct and was an ever-alert officer in the service of the British rulers.

175. His wife, Rukhmabai, was of a good disposition, pious, a mine of virtue, a dutiful wife and modest of speech, who had a firm faith in Sai.

176. Originally, the ancestors of the poet belonged to 'Dabholi' near Vengurla, but later shifted to the 'Kelwa' village.

177. In the year 1859², on the fifth day of the brighter half of the lunar month of *Margashirsh*, this meritorious Govind was born to Laxmi, the wife of Raghunath.

178. Born in the Gaud Saraswat Brahmin community, with Bharadwaj gotra, he died in the year 1929, on the ninth day of the brighter half of the lunar month of *Ashadh*.

179. He began writing the book in 1922, in the month of *Chaitra* (March-April) and completed the fifty-second chapter in the month of *Jyeshtha* (May-June), in the year 1929.

180. Govindrao had only one son and five daughters, of whom four are married. The son is also married and is studying medicine. The unmarrried daughter is studying medicine, too.

181. Now I shall describe the method of '*Parayan*' and the easy way of doing a '*saptah*' (reading the book in seven days), which is given in the '*Gurucharitra*' and other books. Listeners may please attend carefully.

182. Making your heart pure, start the '*parayan*', with faith and devotion, completing the reading in one, two or three days, which will please Sai-Narayan.

183. Or, start a '*saptah*' and you will acquire the wealth of accumulated merit; Sai will fulfil your heart's fond desire and the fear of worldly life will be destroyed.

184. Begin reading on a Thursday. After taking a bath at dawn, sit on your seat, after quickly finishing your daily rituals (like *Sandhya*, etc.)

185. Have a large, beautiful '*mandap*' covered with banana leaves, canna leaves, cloth, etc., to decorate it.

186. Place a stool in it and draw around it a colourful variety of designs, with coloured powders (*rangoli*), that will please the eye.

187. On the stool, carefully place an idol or a photograph of Sai Sadguru, bowing to him in a loving obeisance.

188. Wrapping the book in a silk cloth and placing it in front of the Sadguru, offer *pooja* to both, using the five *pooja* articles and then begin reading the book.

189. For the next eight days, strictly observe the prescribed rules of conduct, taking only milk, or fruit, or roasted grain, or, eating nothing during the day except once, either at night or sometime during the day.

190. Facing the east and remembering the Sadguru's form in the mind, continue reading the book happily and with a peaceful mind.

191. Eight, eight and seven, eight, six, eight and seven, with such a division of chapters, in that order, read, for seven days, leaving only the 'epitome' for the eighth day.

192. On the eighth day, after completing the vow, offer *naivedya* to Sai-Narayan and then serve a meal to the Brahmins, relatives and friends, giving appropriate *dakshina* to the Brahmins.

193. Inviting the *Vaidic* Brahmins at night, get the *Vedas* recited loudly by them, satisfying them by offering sweetened milk to drink.

194. In the end, making obeisance at the Sadguru's feet, the guru should be given proper *dakshina*, which should be sent to the treasurer of Shirdi Sansthan, to add to the collection of the Sansthan.

195. By doing so, Sai Bhagvan will be pleased and will give '*pasayadaan*' to the devotees, destroy the snake of the fear of worldly life and reveal the secret treasure of *Moksha*.

196. O listeners, you are saints, the Retreat of Peace and Happiness. This slave prays at your feet that if this epitome is forgotten, be it so. But keep your concentration on the significance of this book.

197. O listeners, righteous as you are, you are the destroyer of Death himself. This Baba's Bal bows at your feet and entreats you to have mercy on this slave, always.

198. Whatever is lacking in this epitome, is entirely mine. Give it to me, taking only the essence, O listeners, and feeling happy.

199. Obeisance to Sai-Shri Ganesh (son of Shiva); to Sai-Brahmadev and to Sai-Shri Vishnu! O Sai-Shankar, I bow to you humbly.

200. Obeisance to you, O Sai-Dattatreya; to Sai Indra and to Sai, the Moon! To Sai-Agninarayana, I make obeisance!

201. Obeisance to Sai-Shri Vitthal; to Sai, the Sun; to Sai, the Ocean of Knowledge! O Sai-Shri Jnaneshvar, I bow in obeisance!

202. This epitome is a handful of flowers, i.e. words, as also are the series of obeisance made above, which I offer at the lotus-feet of the guru, with a prayer that may Mother-Sai be pleased with me.

Inspired by Shri Sai Sadguru and composed by
Baba's slave Bal, the fifty-third chapter of
"*Shri Sai Samarth Satcharit*" called
'*The Epitome*', is complete here.

Notes

1. This is a prayer for the Grace of God for universal happiness and peace and occurs in *Jnaneshvari*, Ch. 18, vs. 1793-1801.
2. Though the year of his birth is given here as 1859, the year mentioned in the sketch at the beginning of the *Shri Sai Satcharit* is 1856.

Dr. Indira Kher is a retired Professor of English. A graduate of Nagpur University, she had the distinction of topping the list of successful candidates at the Intermediate Arts Examination in 1949 and of winning the Radhabai Paonaskar Silver Medal and the Hari Pandit Prize.

After a break of twelve years, she pursued her post-graduate studies in English Literature at Bombay University, securing the second place in the American Literature Paper at the M.A. Examination and winning a prize from the U.S.I.S., Bombay. A U.G.C. Junior Research Fellow, she was awarded a Ph.D. in 1970 for her thesis, *"Lewis Carroll, Man and Writer"*.

Dr Indira Kher started her career in 1972 and taught at various Bombay colleges. She had a brief stint as a lecturer at the State Institute for Administrative Careers, Bombay. She retired as the Head of the English Department from one of the local colleges.

She was the Editor of *Sri Sai Leela* magazine, Shirdi, English Edn., for two and a half years from July 1985. She is also the author of *Avadhuta Yogi Pant Maharaj of Balekundri*, published by Bharatiya Vidya Bhavan, Bombay.